HOW TO MAKE $100,000 EVERY SUCCESSFUL CONSULTANT IN YOUR OWN FIELD

The Complete Guide to Succeeding In the Advice Business

Dr. Jeffrey Lant

Published by JLA Publications
A Division of Jeffrey Lant Associates, Inc.
50 Follen Street, Suite 507
Cambridge, Massachusetts 02138
Tel: (617) 547-6372

HOW TO MAKE *AT LEAST* $100,000 EVERY YEAR AS A SUCCESSFUL CONSULTANT IN YOUR OWN FIELD

The Complete Guide to Succeeding In The Advice Business

Dedication: For my mother, Shirley, popularly known as POM. Coming late to ventures entrepreneurial, she has nonetheless amptly demonstrated that age is no bar to success. Yes, this one's just for you!

Acknowledgements: For every book I write, people are generous with their time and knowledge. This book has been no exception. The "Rogues' Gallery of Absolutely Must-Use Experts" at the conclusion of this book demonstrates the extent to which you, the reader—as well as I—have benefited from the advice of experts. A few people, however, have gone beyond the call of duty and deserve special recognition. I am delighted to be able to thank Jackie Masloff, ever my computer guru; Gary Lowenstein, CPA, my accountant, for tax & financial planning information; Alan Oxman, prompt and efficient, a mighty resource of insurance intelligence; Kathy Ackerman, who took time from a very busy schedule to revise her section; Jeff Clark, for helping ensure that all the data in this book is correct and up-to-date, and John Hamwey who has again, as he has for so many years, provided his printing and lay-out savvy. Thank you all!

TABLE OF CONTENTS

SPECIAL PREFACE FOR SECOND EDITION

Since you're reading this book, you probably already possess specialized problem-solving information and skills and want to profit from them to the greatest extent possible.

I'm glad to say you're in the right place. Using your problem-solving skills and the tested techniques in this book, you'll soon have what you need to make a very handsome annual income. Yes, at least $100,000 every year... and a whole lot more if you follow the specific techniques in this book and the accompanying 6 volumes in the series.

How can I be so sure? Because for the last 12 years, I've not only been a successful marketing consultant in my own right but, through my books, audio cassettes, workshops and direct one-on-one consulting, I've helped tens of thousands of people just like you turn their specific problem-solving skills into a certain money-making process; a process that'll give you more prospects faster, produce bigger project and retainer contracts, and enable you, if you're truly dedicated, to create your own multi-million dollar information empire with products that'll bring you handsome sums every single day.

None of this is pie-in-sky. It's all possible. If you can really solve people's problems and you're really ready, willing and able to do what it takes to bring these people success and then market these successes to the others who want them, you, too, can join the ranks not only of the six-figure income consultants but those who have a net worth of well over a million dollars.

So, pay close attention to what follows. Yes, it's rigorous. Yes, it's demanding. No, you're not going to be able to breeze through this book in a single evening... or get everything out of it in a single reading. But, after conscientious study and application, you'll find your consulting practice — and income — growing nicely.

As that happens, let me know. Over the years, I've heard from hundreds and hundreds of my readers who have been happy to share the gratifying tales of their progress and enrichment. I want to hear yours, too, especially if you've improved on the methods you've found here and are willing to share what you've learned!

Turn the page, then, and begin. What you'll find in the pages ahead can change your life. This information can make you richer, can make you a more proficient problem-solver and, perhaps most importantly, it can give you a desirable autonomy that most people never achieve.

I'm looking forward to hearing from you — soon!

Your personal enrichment consultant,

Jeffrey

Cambridge, MA
September, 1991

PREFACE

Why I Wrote This Book

We are now well into the Great Age of Information. It is indeed truly said that information is power. But more than some Machiavellian pursuit, the information you have at your disposal is powerful because it:

- helps other people solve their problems
- provides you with an excellent means of gaining control over your time and indeed your life, and
- gives you a superb means of making money — lots of money!

That's why you've come to this book: To see whether it can help you achieve these three critical objectives. Let me tell you something: you've come to the right place.

HOW TO MAKE AT LEAST $100,000 EVERY YEAR AS A SUCCESSFUL CONSULTANT IN YOUR OWN FIELD is the fourth volume of my "Get Ahead" Series and the tenth book I've written in as many years. It is a natural extension of the first volume in this series. Entitled **THE CONSULTANT'S KIT**, this well-known book has now helped well over 25,000 people establish part-time or full-time consulting practices in hundreds of different fields.

THE CONSULTANT'S KIT was always designed to be a good introductory book to the very alluring subject of consulting. I wrote it because there wasn't anything good on the market on this subject and because people with information and useful problem solving techniques at their disposal needed to learn how to profit from what they knew and could do. Since then, of course, many, many other books on consulting have been written. But the need for **THE CONSULTANT'S KIT** has not diminished: it remains (in my humble opinion) the best short work introducing the subject of consulting in a precise, thorough, non-threatening, and unpretentious way.

But frankly, that book was never meant to be definitive. It's to give people a start into a very desirable field, to help them get launched with good, solid, basic information. I was under no illusions that all anyone would ever need to succeed in the advice business was contained in that single guide. To succeed in the advice business, to succeed in *any* small business, you have to know more, often much, much more. And so my "Get Ahead" Series was born.

Almost every year since the initial appearance of **THE CONSULTANT'S KIT**, I've published another volume in this series. If you've been in business for any length of time you probably know that your greatest problem is marketing yourself. And unless you have an independent source of income you probably don't have a lot of money to buy paid advertising and hire promotional and marketing assistance. I know I didn't! I had to do what most of you have to do: outdo the experts with my brains, not my checkbook. The result was my book **THE UNABASHED SELF-PROMOTER'S GUIDE**. Subtitled **"What Every Man, Woman, Child And Organization In America Needs To Know About Getting Ahead By Exploiting The Media,"** this book is designed for people who need to get their message across to the maximum number of client prospects at absolute minimum cost. It's packed with marketing and promotional suggestions which I myself use daily.

Once that was published, I went on to write **MONEY TALKS**. I've been getting clients, exposure, and much-needed cash from the talk circuit for many years now. I do over 100 programs annually across the nation and regularly get clients from them. I've often wondered how any advisor could succeed without doing such programs, and it's no surprise to me to see the lecture circuit these days made up of information experts, much more so than celebrities. **MONEY TALKS** tells you how to succeed similarly, cut your marketing expenses to next to nothing, and turn every marketing appearance you make into a significant profit center.

After **MONEY TALKS** was out I turned my attention to helping my readers sell their products and services as fast as possible. The result was my two marketing books, **MONEY MAKING MARKETING: FINDING THE PEOPLE WHO NEED WHAT YOU'RE SELLING AND MAKING SURE THEY BUY IT** and **CASH COPY: HOW TO OFFER YOUR PRODUCTS AND SERVICES SO YOUR PROSPECTS BUY THEM... NOW!** The first of these tells you how to create a cost-effective, targeted marketing plan and process that produces prospects and buyers expeditiously for the least possible expense. The second takes up the important matter of how to create marketing communications — ads, buyers, brochures, letters, proposals, flyers, etc — that get your prospects to buy fast... and your buyers to buy again soon.

Having outlined the procedures on how to create a profitable consulting business, how to market it for the least expense and how to create profitable talk programs, I then took up the question of how to use your detailed technical information to create a multi-million dollar Info-Empire. This book, all 552 pages of it, is called **HOW TO MAKE A WHOLE LOT MORE THAN $1,000,000 WRITING, COMMISSIONING, PUBLISHING AND SELLING 'HOW-TO' INFORMATION.** It was — and remains — the most detailed resource ever written on how to take your problem-solving information and turn it into continuing revenue from Special Reports, audio cassettes, booklets and books. You're sure to want it.

I then turned to revising all my books and this year-long project has produced up-to-date information on how you can make money from your technical information in the 'nineties. This is one of the books I've reviewed — and in this case retitled. Previously called TRICKS OF THE TRADE, I wrote it because of my vast disappointment and dissatisfaction with other books on the subject. Too often these books suggest the advisor is an arcane, disembodied intelligence who deals magically and magisterially with, what?, certainly not real people and the way real people react to change. Too many of the books are written, too, in turgid, impenetrable academese which, to me, is valueless.

There are two key problems in the advising business: how to get the client in the first place and how to work with the client to do what's good for him. Virtually all the academic books entirely ignore the first problem, no doubt feeling that the mechanics of the marketplace are beneath the god-like advisor. Nothing, of course, could be further from the truth. I don't care how bright you are. If you cannot market your practice, you'll never get the chance to display what you know, and your intelligence, for all its sublimity, will be practically useless.

By the same token, too many of the books written by advisors themselves seem to ignore the change process in favor of concentrating on often very elementary marketing techniques. These writers seem to suggest that if you can satisfactorily handle marketing, you don't have to worry about the actual work you do with the client. This, of course, is ridiculous. Marketing must always be a significant part of the life of the advisor; face it, however: you're going to have to know what to do once you get the client. To my complete dismay, I've found that all too many advisors, having won the battle to get the client, lose the war to convince him to follow their good suggestions, thus insuring client unhappiness and a growing feeling of powerlessness and dissatisfaction on the part of the advisor who finds himself heard, perhaps, but not heeded.

HOW TO MAKE AT LEAST $100,000 EVERY YEAR AS A SUCCESSFUL CONSULTANT IN YOUR OWN FIELD addresses both these issues in very practical detail. But it goes one step further than any other book on this subject.

Virtually every book on advising as a profession makes the assumption (often thoughtlessly) that an expert can make sufficient income merely from the sale of time, of hours, weeks and months. This is true, of course, if you have fairly modest income objectives. I don't. My income expectations, like most of my generation, are very, very high. Unfortunately there are only so many hours in the day, and you'll find that you'll reach a peak where you're working the maximum number you can and where you cannot push up your hourly rate very much higher without sacrificing badly-needed business. You are, in short, stuck in an income groove. But there's absolutely no reason for this to be the case.

One of the very important ways **HOW TO MAKE AT LEAST $100,000 EVERY YEAR AS A SUCCESSFUL CONSULTANT IN YOUR OWN FIELD** varies from any other book on this subject is that it provides unique information on how you can build a national advising practice by creating a series of problem solving products and services under the umbrella of what I call the Mobile Mini-Conglomerate, a 10-part wealth producing machine based on the information and problem solving processes you have at your disposal. With the Mobile Mini-Conglomerate progressively in place (for, like Rome, it cannot be built in a day) you will free yourself, forever, from the time trap and make yourself recession proof as well, thereby eliminating one of the greatest anxieties of the advisor who otherwise rightly worries about an overgreat reliance on too few problem solving services.

What I am trying to tell you, then, is that **HOW TO MAKE AT LEAST $100,000 EVERY YEAR AS A SUCCESSFUL CONSULTANT IN YOUR OWN FIELD** is a unique book which goes way beyond the usual run of consulting and advising books. But that doesn't mean it's an easy or even an effortless book. It's not.

As Juliet Brudney, careers columnist for the *Boston Globe*, wrote of **THE UNABASHED SELF-PROMOTER'S GUIDE** when it was first published, this isn't a book for a light read or to daydream over. Like all my books, **HOW TO MAKE AT LEAST $100,000 EVERY YEAR AS A SUCCESSFUL CONSULTANT IN YOUR OWN FIELD** is a book to be lived with, referred to, studied, pondered, made part and parcel of your life! This isn't necessarily the message you wanted to hear when you picked it up. But if you're sorry, I can't help it! There are many prerequisites to achieving success in this world. This book deals with those which are absolutely necessary to succeeding as an advisor. I have a lofty, perhaps an unattainable objective in life, which this book moves me a little bit closer to realizing. I want to change people's habits, your habits, improve your business techniques, and help to make you as successful as possible. I want you to understand what you must understand to succeed: that success means constant, unremitting, continuing and continual effort and a resolute commitment to achieving that success.

I daresay you, like some of the people who have come in contact with me, don't particularly want to hear this. We Americans have a national penchant for the easy, the effortless, the undemanding. We reject as tiresome, or worse, that which demands our persistent effort. This often makes us 'fun' to be around, no doubt, but such traits have taken their toll on our well being. In this book I fight against them and invite you to join me not merely in succeeding in the Great Age of Information but in the concommitant reformation of mores and morals which must accompany your own transformation into a comfortable mogul.

About Your Guide Jeffrey Lant

As you will already have noticed, I have a number of reasons for having written **HOW TO MAKE AT LEAST $100,000 EVERY YEAR AS A SUCCESSFUL CONSULTANT IN YOUR OWN FIELD** and as you may perhaps have detected I am a man of strong opinions and often deflating candor. You won't always like it, but I beg you to consider that I am candid as much for your sake as for mine. Throughout this book you are my client and I am your advisor. Like all advisors I am powerless to influence your behavior beyond the terms of my commission, in this case the pages of this book. You will make the final decision about what you will do, just as the client always does. What you need from me is just what your clients need from you: the most hard-hitting, precise, informative, unabashedly candid advice possible. You clients won't want you to mince words about what you think is in their interest and how to help them realize their objectives, and I don't intend to mince words with you either. I call a spade a spade, and I apologize in advance for any ruffling of feathers which may take place. Remember, as the mother said while spanking the child who wouldn't eat his lima beans, "It's all for your own good!"

I ought to fess up here, too, to some other particulars which, together, are both responsible for and compose my point of view. Each author, of course, has a point of view. All too often, however, they are not candid in sharing it with their readers. I think an author has an obligation to do so. This viewpoint should approach truth, to be sure, but I would not have you believe that I think mine anything more than a subjective reality. That's why I feel it necessary to stud this book with the names and addresses of other experts in many other fields who will not only provide you with other critical information you need but will right the balance. Still, here's something you need to know about me before we begin our journey together.

JLA: My Advice Conglomerate

Jeffrey Lant Associates, Inc. is a Mobile Mini-Conglomerate which exists to solve people's problems through a wide variety of problem solving products and services. It has, as you'll see, many divisions, including publishing (for my books, special reports and audio cassettes); direct mail marketing (my catalog and card-deck), syndicating (my column), workshop and seminar and, yes, consulting. It is based in my international headquarters, as the space inside my Cambridge, Massachusetts condominium is grandiloquently called, hard by Harvard University and the heartbeat of Harvard Square.

Operating Method

I am a one-man band. By this I mean that in most cases I work alone. Where other specialized skills are needed, I subcontract or manage a team of experts which are either contracted to my clients under the name of my firm or independently, as the case warrants. This is done through what I call my Supergroup of Independent Contractors, a concept you will learn about later in this book.

I have no staff beyond a part-time go-fer, delivery boy cum housecleaner (a necessary luxury). If you call me, I answer the telephone. And I type the answer to any letter you send me. I am a stickler for prompt response, too!

This is the way I work. I am not going to be proselytizing you to adopt a similar working method, but I will urge you strenuously to find out what vocational mode and style truly suits your lifestyle — and then to construct it using the techniques in this book. The real message of **HOW TO MAKE AT LEAST $100,000 EVERY YEAR AS A SUCCESSFUL CONSULTANT IN YOUR OWN FIELD** is to find the way that suits you — or make it. Which is, of course, the true problem of all human life.

What You'll Find In This Book

Of course, I've already given you a hint about the contents of **HOW TO MAKE AT LEAST $100,000 EVERY YEAR AS A SUCCESSFUL CONSULTANT IN YOUR OWN FIELD**, but before I conclude this preface let me tell you how the book is arranged. **HOW TO MAKE AT LEAST $100,000 EVERY YEAR AS A SUCCESSFUL CONSULTANT IN YOUR OWN FIELD** contains 14 chapters, some very lengthy indeed. It also contains a Samples Section and concludes with an extensive catalog of resources which you'll want to use to supplement this book.

The first four chapters deal with your necessary preparation for succeeding as an advisor, for preparation is at the root of all success. Chapter 1 deals with adopting the right mental attitude, some definitions of advising, what kinds of people succeed as advisors, and why people buy and use advisors. Chapter 2 provides three sets of prerequisites you need to be successful in your advising career: the prerequisites you need to succeed as a sales person (a very necessary aspect of advising success), those you must have to be successful working with clients (which will be stressed again and expanded upon in a later chapter), and the ones you need to run a demanding small business. Chapter 3 deals with positioning and marketing basics. Chapter 4 provides information on the Problem Solving Process, the backbone of any advisor's practice.

Since failure to understand and utilize low-cost, continuing marketing techniques is one of the leading reasons why so many advising practices fail, Chapters 5, 6 and 7 contain critical marketing information of an often very advanced kind. It is clear to me that mastery of the many superb low-cost marketing and promotional techniques which are available could save many, many advising practices. Chapter 5 sets forth crucial information about necessary and inexpensive marketing documents including the Précis, the Success Letter and several others. Chapter 6 includes detailed information on networking, telemarketing, and workshops and seminars as client recruitment, profit and publicity centers. Chapter 7 provides information on bringing your advising practice to the attention of client prospects through the free media.

Chapter 8 begins with a section on working with clients. This chapter specifically deals with the precontract stage of your relationship. Chapter 9 deals with contractual matters. Chapter 10 tells you precisely what to do with your client on the job, providing you with very necessary information on how to manage the change process to your and your client's advantage.

Chapter 11 provides absolutely essential information on how you can benefit from what you know when you are not physically present. This chapter provides information on the Mobile Mini-Conglomerate, which will lift you beyond the constraints of the time trap and provide you with a continuing income from what you know through a variety of information-based products such as booklets, books, cassette tapes, and catalog deals.

In Chapter 12 I take up the matter of how to run your demanding small business. Here you will find information on establishing your Mandarin Network, running a home-based business and such critical matters as disability insurance and financial planning, both essential to your peace of mind and ultimate autonomy.

Chapter 13 takes up the (to many) vexing question of computers and your advising practice. My computer advisor Jackie Masloff has helped me supply detailed information on computer selection techniques and how to use modern telecomputing technology to your advantage.

Finally, in Chapter 14, the final chapter, I take up the question of "The Life Of The Advisor," providing you with useful information on stress and time management and smart traveling. Too many advisors burn out with the fast-paced, demanding lifestyle. Now you don't have to be a casualty of your own success.

Following Chapter 14, as in all my books, you'll find a Samples Section packed with helpful documents and formats. And then a bountiful catalog of other resources provided by many of America's top advisors and business experts. All provide valuable information to ensure the success of your advising practice.

As you can see, we have much to do together. To begin, I ask this single thing of you. Try to get into the spirit of this book. Do not block what I'm saying. Don't tell me you cannot do some of these things I recommend. Try to incorporate them into your behavior and profit from them — just as thousands of my workshop participants nationwide have already done.

If you're like most people, you will find the rat-tat-tat style of this book occasionally wearing. You'll wonder where you'll get the enthusiasm, the energy, the time, the stamina to do all that needs to be done. If you feel worn down, don't despair. In Chapter 14, I've got information for you on how to avoid energy drain! Put down this book, relax a moment, return refreshed and ready to continue. Remember: I've been at work on these techniques, day in, day out, for 12 years now. And I'm still learning how to do things more creatively, more intelligently, more profitably all the time.

With this caveat, we are now ready to begin. Ready to begin a journey which will at its conclusion help provide you with three of the most meaningful conditions of life:

- A means of helping others
- A way to control your own life, and
- A process for producing very, very substantial profit for yourself.

After you finish this book, I hope you'll write and tell me how you liked it, or go farther and share with me your own **WAYS TO MAKE AT LEAST $100,000 EVERY YEAR AS A SUCCESSFUL CONSULTANT IN YOUR OWN FIELD**, for I, too, am always at work to become a more complete master of my art. And don't forget: I have become friends with many of the people who have read my books and taken my workshops across the country, and I hope that you and I will connect too, colleagues in one of America's most satisfying careers, fellow adventurers in one of the great ages of the world, the Great Age of Information, confreres who have found through the advising profession a satisfying means of realizing three of the great conditions of a life well spent and infinitely productive. I mean it!

CHAPTER 1

Beginning At The Beginning

What is an advisor? Generally speaking, an advisor is an individual who recommends a course of action to someone who needs (but may not realize he must have) help. All of us have found ourselves in this (occasionally unpleasant) position from time to time. Indeed, there is probably no person in recorded history who has not given someone a piece of advice, often heatedly! Most people, of course, don't get paid for doing so, except in psychic satisfaction and a pronounced smugness as to their own value and worth (which are, of course, very real currencies in our imperfect world.) Or they get paid far less than the advice is really worth: a very real problem.

You want to be different, of course, and so you shall be. By the time you've finished mastering this book, finished implementing its many suggestions and recommendations, and altered your behavior to benefit from what follows, you will be among the fortunate people who not only are regularly remunerated for what they say (and can do) but build an independent and lucrative practice by doing so. For here is where this book makes its significant departure. While virtually everyone in the world gives advice, this book has as its purpose the goal of providing you with the information you need to build a profitable part-time or full-time career doing so.

Advisor: A Better Definition

For our purposes, we need another, clearer definition of the advisor and what he does. In my definition, an advisor is the individual who has at his disposal problem solving processes and information which he persuades the client effectively to utilize and so produces in the process a disproportionate benefit compared to fee. More simply, the advisor is the individual who knows what he's doing, persuades the client to use his recommendations and use them fully, and produces as a result a condition which is significantly more valuable to the client than the money it costs him to bring it about. This is the definition I shall use throughout this book.

You Want To Be An Independent Advisor But May Be Hesitating

Chances are you may already be in the advice business — and benefitting someone else. Thus one of the reasons why you are reading this book is because you have already discovered you are producing not only a significantly disproportionate benefit for the people you work with but for the people you work for — your employer. This is the sad condition of most advisors: bit by bit it dawns on them that what they know is terribly significant, most valuable not only to the people they work with on a regular basis but to the employer who is nicely remunerated for what they do. This suggests that an independent course of action would make a lot of sense. But you may feel inhibited about going out on your own:

- People are dependent on you and what you earn and you feel you cannot take the risk.
- You get a good salary now and are not overtaxed in what you do.
- You hate marketing and feel unsure of your ability to do what it takes to bring a business to the attention of those who could profit from what you know.
- You have limited start-up capital and restricted assets to use as collateral to get more.
- You know little or nothing about the ins and outs of the small business you'd necessarily find yourself operating.

Fortunately each of these problems can be dealt with and many are — right here in this book! Remember: to profit as an independent advisor you do not have to sacrifice at a single stroke your present situation. Using this book you can move deliberately to achieve your objective. The important thing to remember is that if you are now feeling the urge to become more independent, this expresses an important aspect of your personality and your self image and to stifle this may lead to significant later unhappiness and the permanent taint of regret.

Why You Want To Be An Independent Advisor

There are both shrewd business reasons and profound psychological motivations which propel people into a career as an independent advisor.

- You want to derive the full benefit from what you know and can do. This will always be a significant reason why people who have had specialized training and have at their disposal information, techniques, processes and procedures set out on their own. I am a firm believer that the individual who can produce a benefit should derive a significant profit from what he knows and can do. But so long as you work for someone else this will rarely be possible. Over 95% of the millionaires in this nation wor'ι for themselves, and it will be ever thus. The fact that you know you are not going to get the full benefit from what you know and can do psychologically represses your creativity, intelligence and zest for your job — and hence for life itself. One reason people have to change jobs more and more often is to rekindle some semblance of the creativity and intelligence they originally had upon entering the labor market. When you become an independent advisor this creativity, this intelligence and this zest come as standard equipment. So does the enhanced profit which comes from operating on your own.

- You need autonomy. Freedom is not merely some abstract concept. It is something each human being deeply wants and needs. But the person who sets out to create an independent advising business arguably has a greater need for autonomy than most people. For some advisors, their need to do their own thing in their own way actually outweighs their desire to get the utmost financial benefit from what they know. If you are such a person and are still working for someone else, you are probably a disputatious and often ornery employee. If you find yourself nagging others at work, resisting your employer (whose limitations you not so secretly abhor), picking fights, being surly, or just plain dreaming the day away, you may well have a pronounced need for the kind of autonomy which independent advisors characteristically have.

- You want to help others. Often times the standard work setting inhibits people not only from getting the true benefit from what they know and can do, but actually impedes them from being helpful. All of us have examples of people who have been worn down by the traditional workplace, having begun as bright, cheerful, and creative individuals and left the merest husks of humanity, bereft of the vital traits we were so drawn to and which under other circumstances could have provided them with a significant life capital. You may find yourself in an office where the following statements constrain your ability to be the helpful person you really are:

  — "We don't do things like that around here!"
  — "You don't have the right degree to do that!"
  — "You can't make that decision yourself!"
  — "That isn't part of your job!"
  — "You shouldn't have done that without telling me!"
  — "If I let you do that, then everyone will want to do it!"
  — "Not now!"

These debilitating statements heard often enough (and they are said millions of times daily) destroy the initiative, creativity and sheer humanity of even the most resilient.

Independent advisors are characteristically among the most helpful people in the world. We get a thrill knowing that through our daily worklife and customary activities (for which we are handsomely paid!) we regularly secure a satisfying answer to why we are on this earth. Good advisors don't suffer from malaise or ennui. We know why we're here. We know the good we're doing. And we take comfort, as well as substantial financial benefit, from doing manifestly evident good.

- You need to be honest. As I've often said, the traditional workplace does not value honesty or candor. It values, instead, the ability to be a team player, which, it seems to me, is merely another way for playing, at one time or another, the roles of the monkeys who neither see, hear, or speak evil. Being in the regular workplace means to make a daily compromise with candor, honesty, and, ultimately, with integrity in order to be perceived as the "good guy," the "team player." The independent advisor has an acute need to call things as he sees them: he is instinctively honest and blanches at the thought of being anything other than honorable, direct and straightforward. Such directness, of course, can be very, very unsettling to the customary procedures of the usual hidebound, muddling-through office. Ironically, however, and delightfully, this trait of candor, so disapproved and unappreciated in the standard office from the standard employee, is exactly what makes an independent advisor so valuable and indeed mandatory to use. For this candor which is inadvisable — even unnerving — coming from an employee is yet required by the organization and, hence, we independent advisors become the more needed by the fact that the traits we possess in such abundance are so thoroughly snuffed out in the officeplace.

Yes, there are very good reasons for becoming an independent advisor, the better state of your financial health being matched *pari passu* by your improved psychological and physical state. All this would count for nothing, of course, if people didn't care to buy what we have to sell. But, hallelujah!, they do. Each year billions and billions of dollars are spent by people who need advice, securing the assistance of people like us who can provide them with it. And each year the amount spent on buying advisors grows substantially and will continue to do so as the ramifications of our information-based society make themselves more and more deeply felt. But why, really why, do people buy advisors?

Why People Buy Advisors

People buy advisors for reasons both self evident and those which usually go unstated. They include the following:

- An advisor's knowledge on a given subject is more complete than the client's.

Advisors are retained because an individual does not possess, or an organization does not have, technical and informational competence in a given area. Thus, the best advisors begin by mastering a core of useful information which is not otherwise easily available to a significant group of people who must have this information (technology, technique, process or procedure), to reach objectives which are important, if not pivotal, to them. Good advisors, particularly at the genesis of their independent careers, are not generalists; they are always particularists possessing a body of valuable, often arcane, highly technical information. We can do for others what they cannot do for themselves.

- Advisors train clients in their techniques.

Most advisors not only solve problems themselves using their information and technical specialities. They train others in how to do what they do. Thus most advisors early on in their independent careers become trainers, if they were not already training beforehand. The client always wants to believe that he can master what we already know and can do and thus obviate the need to work with such expensive talent as we are. For most clients, this wish is simply that: more often than not, the client cannot adequately grasp in the short time he wishes to spend what has taken us years and singular application to master. But his hope to be able to do so provides (in his mind) a compelling reason to hire us.

- Advisors remove the perceived responsibility for a controversial decision from the person actually making the order.

We live in an age where more and more people want less and less to be identified with the decisions they make. Ours is an age where the lust for power is no less pronounced than in any other (and arguably is much more virulent), but where decision makers long to be removed from perceived responsibility for the decisions they make. Advisors are, therefore, often brought in after a decision has already been made, after the client already knows what he's going to do, to make recommendations for public consumption and to take the heat for what has in fact already been decided. Many advisors find this political aspect to the advising profession particularly burdensome, even horrifying, but it is one of the very real reasons why we get purchased. Advisors are in the business of being particularly public, highly visible, eminently sacrificial (though nicely compensated) scapegoats.

- Advisors provide their clients with perspective.

It is now a cliché of our times that we live in an age of galloping segmentation where the general is forever breaking down into the particular, the parochial, the isolated and the precise. In such circumstances it is easy for our clients to lose sight of what is happening in the world, even in that part of the world which most affects their interests. Advisors always necessarily have a world view, a broad perspective. In part this is because, unlike most people, we deal with different ramifications of the same cluster of problems as seen around the nation if not around the world. We are thus in a position to see (and to solve) many aspects of the same problem. Advisors cannot afford to become parochial. If we do, we lose one major source of value to our clients. We provide these clients with the information that allows them — like us — to see the forest instead of merely the trees. And, of course, to profit accordingly.

- Advisors foster a climate of beneficial change.

The good advisor is necessarily always on the side of progressive change. We are always the enemy of the standpat, the unblinking response, the stogey standard.

Good advisors are always in the vanguard of progressive change. But we are never in favor of change for the sake of change. We are only in favor of change to effect the beneficial result desired equally by our client and by ourselves. More often than not, we advisors desire this change more wholeheartedly than our clients. Remember: in this nation most people speak an overheated change language. We advisors, however, earnestly desire change and have the means at our disposal, more so than our clients, to bring it about. Thus, for them, the goddess of change is most often appeased through supercharged talk, nothing more; for us, on the other hand, she can only be conciliated through substantial action towards a beneficial end. Therefore, when a decision maker is ready for change, really ready, it is inevitable that such a decision maker turns to us, the independent advisor, to help him bring it about.

- Advisors provide the illusion of change without the reality.

The flip side of the previous point, of course, is that a decision maker can retain an independent advisor when he wishes to provide the appearance of change without the reality. Bringing in an outside advisor can well be used to appease individuals who really want to provoke change when the decision maker himself is actually resolutely opposed to it. Remember: there are legions of individuals in this country who are perfectly happy with the status quo, for whom change is anathema and deeply threatening. But these people, like the rest of us, live in a society whose chief diety is change. They, like the rest of us, must learn the language of change and be regularly seen doing obeisance to the demanding change goddess despite the fact they are uncompromisingly devoted to obstruction. For such people the advent of the perceivedly catalytic advisor is a godsend to be recompensed handsomely for diverting the winds of change until such time as they are blown inconsequential.

- Advisors provide honest, hard-hitting, candid advice.

Decision makers are in need of a colleague knowledgeable about their professional problems and their business in general and its climate and opportunities, a colleague who will not pull any punches with them but give plain, unvarnished, disinterested, independent truth. Most executives sadly lack this necessary friend, which is why even the most powerful of people often make such (to me happily) dramatic mistakes. A smart executive retains an independent advisor to listen to without getting angry or irritated, as he might well do with a similarly knowledgeable (but lower status) employee whom he could shut up with no more than a gesture. Advisors are meant to provide honest, often unpalatable, absolutely mandatory information and home truths. The higher an individual rises within the standard organization, the more apparently successful he becomes, the more difficult it is for him to get this absolutely essential advice and information, the more his usual associates shield him, becoming in the process the emasculated "yes men," who constitute a debilitating nexus of corporate drones. Hence there is always room at the top for advisors, even if that advisor does no more than remind the ascendent executive that he, too, is no more than human and hence subject to error. Should the executive hear no more than this, the advisor has earned his fee. Remember: just because your advice is not new, not revolutionary, does not make it any the less valuable to your client.

- Advisors provide the client with structure.

Not only do senior executives need a candid friend. They also need good old-fashioned structure. The higher any executive moves in any organization, the less structure there is and the greater opportunity to get lost and fail to achieve further success. Thus the need for an independent, goals-oriented advisor.

The best advisors are firm task masters working with their clients to determine reasonable objectives, a calendar for reaching them, and implementing task action procedures for reaching the new goals. Executives who feel uncertain or even merely sluggish (and study after study shows that these are the prevailing characteristics of senior American management) need an independent advisor. Constructive discipline, clear tasks clearly stated and assiduously pursued, these are at the root of success. The executive probably got ahead in the first place by working this way. An independent advisor can help him continue his success by working with him to recapture the traits and techniques which helped him advance in the first place.

These are the major reasons why people buy advisors. Let me say as strongly as I can: people want and need to buy your technical skills. The following pages provide you with the information you need to make sure your buyers know who you are and what you can do for them, the information, in short, that ensures they will buy you and buy you often. But before we go into these necessary matters, I want to make sure you do not defeat yourself, that you make it as easy as possible for those who have need for your information and problem solving skills to benefit from them without having to deal with the burdensome obstruction of your self-destructive behavior.

Crafting The Right Mental Attitude For Advising Success

I have now dealt with thousands and thousands of people across the nation who tell me, often with great enthusiasm, they want to achieve success as an independent advisor. But many of them fail ignominiously. And it is their own fault. Some, of course, have insufficient technical skills. They really don't know what they are doing. Some fail to master the marketing and promotional strategies of this book. Others have poor personal and professional habits which, in short order, sabotage their ability to be successful. Sadly, however, many others, perhaps the majority, fail even before they begin, because of their own lack of self confidence and lack of commitment to themselves and their own success.

I wish I could say that this is an infrequent or occasional problem. It is not. I must stress again: without the proper mental attitude, your pursuit of success as an independent advisor will be a long, tormented, unsatisfactory process. With this commitment, of course, the regular problems of business will still recur; you will be better situated, however, to dispatch them without anxiety and confusion.

Here are some steps to help you achieve the proper state of mind to achieve the success you wish to have:

- Each morning when I wake up I look in the mirror (at the often frightening face staring back) and remind myself that billions and billions of dollars will be spent this very day. That people are spending money this very minute to achieve their deeply-desired objectives, that they are buying advisors to help them do so. My goal, every day, every minute, is to achieve my rightful portion of this money being spent.

To know just how much this is, just contemplate the Gross National Product on any given day and ask yourself, "Am I getting my share?" Then tell yourself that by helping others achieve their objectives through the use of your information and problem solving abilities you will. This cheers me up no end, and you should find the exercise similarly salubrious.

4

- Consider, too, that whatever shape you are in, no matter how sagging you feel, there are those near at hand and around the nation and the world who need you, you!, just as you are. They need the abilities and expertise you have *now*! They need the degree of problem solving sophistication you have achieved *today*! They can benefit from the knowledge you have at your disposal *this minute*! I am continually asked by people about the level of professional and technical achievement they must have to begin their advising businesses, and my answer is invariably: you are ready to begin when you have identified a group of individuals which has a need for the level of expertise you have attained this minute, and which can compensate you satisfactorily so that you are better off as an independent than as an employee. It is not merely a question of what you know, but what you know that others can benefit from now, that really matters.

On the days when I am feeling less than boyishly alert and magnetic, this thought lifts my spirits and ensures that the day will be productive. Too many bright, useful, competent, attractive people don't do this — and consign the prospects of their independent advising businesses to perdition. In this regard I think of two people who contacted me just as I was writing this chapter: their problem was not technical competence but mental commitment and well being. One was a West Virginia nurse with the experience of over twenty years of technical skills at her disposal. She sat in my living room one afternoon, having come by to pick up some books, and I could see from her body language alone, much less her admission of uncertainty and insecurity, that the problem was not technical competence: it was mental preparedness. The same thing happened a few days later when I received a letter from an advisor who had just finished a book on a health-related subject. Despite his evident knowledgeability, he admitted to a pronounced lack of confidence which preyed on his ability to be successful.

These stories grip at my heart; they make me angry and outraged. The definitive book has yet to be written about why such bright, productive, entirely beneficial people, multiplied by their tens of thousands, have been reduced to this state of unconfidence and what destructive agent in our society so undermines their ability to achieve. But I know this: they cannot achieve success, cannot fully realize their potential for themselves and for others, until they overcome it. Neither can you. That's why you must:

- Expect success. Each day, and I mean *each* day, I expect to be productive, successful, rewarded. I am prepared to do my part to make sure this happens. If you do not expect success, you cannot have success. It's as simple as that.

- Be precise about the success you desire. Success, of course, is a relative and an abstract term. To achieve success, you must be precise about the kind of success you want: for this day, this week, this month, this year of your professional (or indeed your personal) life. Over and over again I am told by people that they want to achieve success, and yet they cannot tell me, not by a country mile, what this means to them. And I know, with a sinking feeling I have too often experienced with others, that for them success will never be anything more than a word on a page. Write down precisely, specifically, and in detail what it is that you want to achieve and when you want to achieve it.

- Visualize this success. We know that pictures better capture a person's imagination than simple words. Harness this psychological truth to your success machine. Don't merely write down what you want to achieve, picture yourself having it. And, since your ability to conjure up such satisfying scenes may have atrophied from years of under-use, clip pictures of them from publications and pin them up where you can constantly see them. Bit by bit your ability to see, taste, smell and experience the precise success you desire will grow. Being able to experience it in advance contains its own kind of pleasure; moreover, if what you want truly suits you, this kind of mental experience should confirm the desirability of the course of action you want to pursue, thereby strengthening your wish to succeed in it.

- Reward yourself for achieving success. Whether you are hesitant about committing yourself or without reserve in doing so, reward yourself when you achieve something meaningful towards the realization of one of the professional objectives you set for yourself. This reward need not be something elaborate, but the more difficult the task was for you to achieve, the more valuable the reward you should give yourself.

As you are no doubt well aware, very few people achieve the rewards in life to which they feel they are entitled. Sadly, they wait and wait for others to provide them with recognition and reaffirmation. Don't be daft! Do it yourself. You know (if you're honest) the degree of difficulty of the objective you set for yourself. You know the pangs and anxieties with which you faced it. How can you possibly expect others either to know or to empathize when in virtually every case they are deeply sunk in their own (often anxious) affairs? Thus, give yourself the recognition and rewarding you desire and make it commensurate not merely with the achievement itself but with the obstacles which threatened that achievement. In my own case, as a collector of eighteenth and nineteenth century portraits, I often give myself another painting for my collection. Snicker's bars just won't do.

You know, as I know, that your ability to command your own mind is a necessary precondition of success. It is, of course, also an insufficient one. You must have the technical skills and business procedures at your disposal, too. **HOW TO MAKE AT LEAST $100,000 EVERY YEAR AS A SUCCESSFUL CONSULTANT IN YOUR OWN FIELD** gives you an abundance of these. Nonetheless without the right mental conditioning, the technical skills are also insufficient to enable you to attain your objective.

This chapter has been short, the shortest in this lengthy book. But it contains an important message that belies its limited extent. This message is clear: success in the advising business is yours to have. I know. When I began twelve years ago now, I began with pitiably little money and along the way towards establishing my practice made an abundance of mistakes, none catastrophic, all wounding to my pride or pocketbook. But the one thing I had, and still have, which always stood me in good stead and which you, too, must share was an invariable belief that because people needed the knowledge and skills I had, neither they nor I could afford the luxury of my failure. Both of us had a significant stake in my forging ahead until such time as I actually connected with them and set to work helping them solve their pressing problems. Any lack of confidence you may feel, any weakening of your will, you must recognize as an expression of selfishness, of egotism, which undermines not merely your own prospects for success but equally those of the clients who so need the problem solving information at your disposal.

Therefore I regard, and I ask you similarly to regard, your commitment to your own success as a peculiarly moral statement, something you may not have previously considered. Any falling away from this commitment into despair, lethargy, passivity and anxiety are conditions which threaten not only your own betterment but that of your clients and prospects as well. For they need you. They need to benefit from what you know and can do. Thus to give way to any unhappy, ill disposed state of mind or any disharmony in the operation of your advising practice must be resolutely opposed by you. For you are a moral as well as a technical agent with much to accomplish and little enough time to do so without the drawbacks of any debilitating, destructive influence. If you find, then, that you cannot quite manage to achieve on your own account the degree of mental steadfastness you need, still push yourself to reach it — for the benefit of those who need you.

Resource

For further assistance in the matter of preparing your mind to be receptive to success and improving your chances to succeed read my friend Russ von Hoelscher's book *How To Achieve Total Success: The Revolutionary Mind-Science Manual*. Available from Profit Ideas, 254 East Grand Ave., Escondido, CA 92025.

CHAPTER 2

Technical Prerequisites For Advising Success

In Chapter 1 I discussed the kind of mental attitude you need to ensure success as an advisor, the extent of commitment you need to make to yourself, the betterment of your client prospects and to your success in general. This kind of commitment is, however, a necessary but not a sufficient precondition for your success as an independent advisor. You must also have certain necessary success prerequisites. These generally fall into five areas:

- Your informational and problem solving skills
- Your presentation skills
- Your sales and marketing skills
- Your on the job/working with the client skills
- Your small business management skills.

Of these I propose to say the least about the first of the categories: your information and problem solving skills. This is not a book about how to get to be an expert in your field. It's a book about how to survive and prosper as an independent advisor once you have amassed a body of problem solving information of interest to a defined client body. How you become an expert in financial planning, architecture, engineering or whatever, you'll have to look elsewhere to find out. But what you do to achieve independent advising success once you've mastered your individual problem solving skills, you will find right here.

Hence this chapter really begins with information on the presentation skills you need, the first prerequisite of advising success. Remember: it is almost never enough merely to have mastered your individual problem solving skills and technical information to be assured of success. Unless you have a field both arcane and essential to your buyers that they can afford to — and indeed must — overlook glaring deficiencies of yours in these areas, you must know that simply being technically competent will never be enough to ensure your success. Always remember that your clients are not buying only your technical competence but you, the person, too. If they dislike or mistrust you as an individual, unless your skills are irreplaceable and nonduplicatable (a dubious proposition for most people) you'll lose the contract. Hence the need to master the following areas which are touched on in this book rather than taught. Indeed, there is scarcely one among them which has not in its own right been the subject of a considerable body of its own literature.

Prerequisite I: Presentation Skills

To be successful as an independent advisor means to master a series of necessary presentation skills, those skills, that is to say, which allow you to communicate crucial ideas to the would-be client about who you are, what you can do, and what your understanding of his problem really is. These skills include:

- Good writing skills
- Good speaking skills
- Good telephone communication skills
- Good personal image creation skills
- Good organizational skills.

Each of these factors is critical. Failure to master any one (much less more than one!) can result in rejection by a client prospect even before the question of your technical competence has even arisen!

• Good Writing Skills

Whatever your field, you cannot succeed as an independent advisor unless and until you have secured good writing skills; the ability, that is, to write clean, crisp prose which clearly sets forth who you are, what you can do for the client, and why he needs it. This sounds easy, but it isn't. Most adults (much less their children!) are verbose, meandering, nonspecific, pompous writers. Yet the best business writing is lean, direct, specific, and natural — like this book!

Take my word for it: you're going to be doing a lot of this writing no matter how technical your field is. Independent advisors produce proposals, contracts, marketing documents, brochures, précis, memoranda, letters, reports, success letters, media kits, and training guides, to name but a few of the formats which are our stock in trade. Failure not only to master the necessary formats but to master the necessary details of content ensures problems for you and your business.

I can say unequivocally from dealing with so many advisors nationwide that one of the chief problems they have is being unable to set down in a precise, meaningful, directed way the specifics of what they do, for whom they do it, and why it's necessary in ways that can beneficially attract the notice of would-be clients.

Thus: if you now have a problem in writing, you must deal with it. Keep close at hand a book like Diane Booher's HOW TO WRITE YOUR WAY TO SUCCESS IN BUSINESS. (Harper & Row, 10 E. 53rd St., New York, NY 10022.) Take a course at a local college, a basic writing course which forces you to do the only thing that really can produce a good, clear writer: writing itself. Computerized or not, other things being equal, the individual with writing talent will find success easier to achieve than the one without it.

• Good Speaking Skills

Poll after poll shows that Americans fear public speaking more than anything. Yet speaking publicly and to strangers is a part of the job of any independent advisor. You must:

- satisfactorily handle face-to-face meetings with client prospects
- learn the essentials of negotiation and persuasion including how to influence people who are not well disposed to the matter at hand
- master summarizing and presentation of large amounts of data, often when you have had very little time to familiarize yourself with it
- become skillful at running goal oriented, directed meetings
- perfect the ability to defend your point of view without offending others who dispute it
- gain the ability to criticize inadequate performance in front of others without creating an inveterate opponent
- learn how to compliment and praise
- master the essentials of motivational and exhortatory speech.

Yes, the advisor must become adept at succeeding in both small and large group presentations. Here as with the writing skills you need, you must have the ability to speak precisely, directly to the point at issue without obfuscating with jargon or other inappropriate or imprecise language. The best advisors are those who can state the issue in a sentence or two, marshall their data plainly and sequentially, and summarize clearly. My object, then, is not to turn you into a charismatic evangelical speaker but to enable you to make your presence felt (and to achieve your objectives) in meetings of every kind through appropriate speaking skills.

Resources

The literature on making successful presentations is immense. My own book **MONEY TALKS** will be of the utmost assistance if your advising practice can benefit from a talk-for-profit/training/instructional component. Or check out a solid book like *How To Prepare, Stage And Deliver Winning Presentations* by Thomas Leech. (American Management Association Publishers.)

• Good Telephone Skills

Most people misuse the telephone, badly. I recall during the writing of this book my receiving a call from an independent advisor attempting to sell me a service. Unlike many professionals, I take my (particularly long distance) calls as they come, not least because I am a frugal Scotsman who dislikes having to pay to place them at a later time, and because I often use these prosaic quotidian examples in books and articles I'm working on and like them to occur without being changed in any way by me. So it is with this case.

As it happened, this man made very bad use of the telephone. In fact, he utterly wasted his money, the cardinal sin to a parsimonious Scot. He didn't ask whether he had called at a good time *for me*. He had no way of dealing with the points I raised (since, it soon became clear, he was following a script and not dealing spontaneously and directly with the actual client prospect). And he didn't take into account the ways I indicated I could use his service (for I presented a quite clear way of mutual benefit) and how I'd like the follow-up handled. All this went in one of his ears and out the other. Yet, in the end, when I did not buy his service he was disappointed and not a little angry!

This poor fellow had made the chief error of telemarketing and telephone use, for while there are in fact five key points (listed below), one of these is crucial: being client centered.

To utilize effectively the telephone means to:

- alert the would-be buyer in advance to your intentions for him (through a letter usually)
- use your voice evenly and modulate it regularly for maximum effectiveness
- select appropriate language for the client
- utilize client centered (marketing) behavior
- follow up by doing what you say you're going to do and so establish credibility for yourself.

All this looks simple, doesn't it? Yet I can guarantee you that four out of five people calling me to attempt to gain my patronage fail to follow at least one of these five steps and hence generally fail to make the sale which they purportedly believe would actually benefit me. I shall have more to say on effective utilization of the telephone and telemarketing later, but for now suffice it to say that these are the critical five steps you must master to make the best use of the telephone.

Resources

Art Sobczak is the best known authority on correct telephone usage and successful telemarketing. For a free copy of his *Telephone Selling Report* newsletter, contact Art at Business By Phone, Inc., 5301 S. 144th St., Omaha, NE 68137 (402) 895-9399; Free Telephone Tips Line (402) 896-TIPS.

- ## Good Personal Image Creation Skills

Much drivel has been written on the whole question of personal image creation. The debate so far has centered on the kinds of dress appropriate for success in Fortune 500 companies. But as I pointed out in **THE UNABASHED SELF-PROMOTER'S GUIDE** to treat this important matter as if the entire world centered on these companies is a great mistake. In considering the question of image the following points are the important ones:

- Will what you wear and how you look (including such matters as clothes, hair style and general grooming) be thought odd, unfamiliar or inappropriate for the people you will be dealing with? If so, to gain the support of the client prospect you need to change your image for this occasion. And by image, I mean aspect, demeanor, mien and presentation.
- Will what you wear and how you look draw attention to yourself and away from the client prospect? If so, your image is wrong for this occasion.
- Will what you wear and how you look create tension in the people you will be dealing with? If so, your image must be altered for this occasion.

As it is clear from these three questions, image has more to do with others than with you. In considering your image you need to do what is necessary to put the people you are dealing with at ease, to make you seem one of them, to sell them, in short, on you by emphasizing your similarity to them. Only the insensitive, those without competition or the blithely unconcerned can afford to ignore the question of image and go "as they are." The rest of us must make sometimes major, sometimes subtle modifications in our basic style in order to minimize the barriers which are always present between people, ready to be raised or lowered as circumstances dictate.

As will become clear as you read this book, mine is very much a client centered approach to success. The more you are able not merely to identify with the client and understand his needs but to be perceived to have this identification, the more successful you'll be. Remember: a client buys not only your problem solving skills but you the person. If you fail to persuade the client that you are yourself likeable, worth knowing, interesting to deal with, or, worse, if you seem simply unable to fit into the client's milieu, unless you have an absolutely must have, available-no-where-else service, your chances of being bought are negligible. That's why you need to ask yourself a series of questions before you meet with anyone from whom you want something:

- Who am I meeting with?
- What kind of person is this?
- What are his tastes and predilections likely to be?
- What does this person want me to be like?
- What does this suggest about my dress, grooming, demeanor in general?

Then having considered these points, ask yourself:

- Can I make these changes in my style?
- Having made these changes will I feel comfortable, or will I, in turn, by making these changes feel awkward?

Remember both you and the client prospect must feel at ease. It does no good to make alterations in your style and image if, as a result, you come across as plastic or unnatural. That, too, will handicap your cause. Face it: in the final analysis your style must be one which both makes clients feel at ease and which is both natural and genuine to you. The trick, of course, is to accentuate with different people different aspects of your personality so that the greatest number will feel you are truly genuine and hence deserving of their patronage.

Resources

One way or another the question of image will arise in several places in this book. For further information see my discussion of creating a Quintessential American Success Image in **THE UNABASHED SELF-PROMOTER'S GUIDE.** Women may also find the discussion of image and dress helpful which appears in *The Working Woman Report: Succeeding In Business In The 80's*. It's written by the Editors of *Working Woman* magazine, with Gay Bryant and is published by Simon and Schuster.

- **Good Organizational Skills**

Advisors are their own worst enemies for getting their practices to succeed. Let me give you one example of what I mean. Several years ago I wrote an article for *The Financial Services Times*, a newspaper devoted to the interests of financial planners. This article concerned my dealings with a number of financial planners whom I'd sought out to buy a tax shelter. Despite their ostensible interest in helping me (and profiting themselves), in this article I demonstrated in detail how 4 out of the 5 firms profiled destroyed their chances of getting my business chiefly through disorganization, poor and nonexistent follow-up, etc. Four out of five!

As a result of this article, you might have thought financial planners around the country would have been up in arms protesting that such numbers were subjective, inaccurate, or unrepresentative. Not a bit of it! Of the many letters I received from readers, not one took this tact. Rather, there seemed to be a collective admission that, yes, this situation was representative, albeit reprehensible.

Don't let this happen to you!

Your success as an advisor is largely predicated upon having and using good, solid organization skills:

- Doing what you say you're going to do when you say you're going to do it.
- Being organized for business.
- Following through on contacts once begun.
- Being consistent, predictable, and thorough.

Particularly new advisors may feel that the success of their practice involves finding something new and original, something creative, something daring, perhaps. Nothing could be further from the truth.

It is nice, of course, if you can be innovative. But not for the sake of innovation. It is wonderful if you can add something new and different to the sum total of human understanding. But you don't need to seek for something wonderful when the admittedly prosaic will do. Therefore remember this: most of your clients' problems will have similar elements. Many of the situations you confront will be common and ordinary, even mundane. You will solve them through the consistent application of your problem solving information and by being precise, well ordered and unremittingly rational and well organized. This may not be romantic. But it does ensure success for both you and your client.

Prerequisite II: Sales and Marketing Skills

About marketing I shall have more than enough to say in the next several chapters. Let me therefore concentrate on absolutely necessary sales skills here. Many people, of course, use the words "sales" and "marketing" interchangeably. This is, however, quite wrong. Generally speaking, marketing involves strategic considerations: the identification of a need, the people with the need, the numbers of these people, the available ways of reaching them, and the necessary positioning that must take place so that the people with the need will know that you can satisfy it. Sales, by contrast, is the tactical element: it is the actual act of selling, the more direct steps of the individual offering the service to the one in need which culminates in an exchange between the two. Logically, marketing precedes sales and the exchange between those involved in the sale is the final step in the marketing process; thereafter the cycle begins again, for once a prospect has been sold your service, the first step of the next marketing cycle is to determine how he can be sold something else.

Here, then, are the skills, beyond those already stated, which are necessary to the successful sales person:

- Target those who can buy your service.
- Learn as much about them as you know about yourself.
- Master access techniques which ensure your ability to bring you face-to-face with your prospects.
- Clearly outline the benefit to them of what you are selling.
- Perfect the ability to close the sale.
- Develop "selective hearing".
- Learn to be persistent.

Target Those Who Can Buy Your Service

One of the key rules for succeeding in sales is to make sure the person you are dealing with can actually buy your service. If he cannot, then don't waste your time making a full-fledged presentation or in any way trying to persuade him about the benefit of what you are selling. Instead, ask this individual to provide you with the name of the actual decision maker and to do what is necessary (such as making a telephone call, sending an intra-office memo, actually scheduling your visit) to provide you with the access you need to the person who can actually make the decision.

One of the greatest problems in selling advisor services is that the would-be advisor is often uncertain about precisely who he should be talking to, about precisely who buys the kind of service he is selling. In my workshops, I often ask participants to write down the advising service they are selling (you could do this now, too, of course). Having done so, write down the specific title(s) of the individual(s) who can buy this service. Right now. You'd be amazed at how few people can do this. To sell my fund raising advising service, for instance, I first need to be in contact with executive directors of nonprofit organizations. Individual board members and chairmen of boards can be helpful, too, but without the crucial support of the executive director it is unlikely I'd be retained.

Your job selling services will be infinitely easier and more productive if you make it a point to spend your time targeting those individuals who can buy what you are selling and to use others who have connections to these individuals as a means of networking you into access with the decision makers.

Learn As Much About Them As You Know About Yourself

All too often the sales people I encounter are woefully unprepared to deal with me. Instead of learning about me, my problems, objectives and aspirations, they have concentrated instead merely on learning about their own products and services. Such knowledge, of course, is necessary for sales success. It is, however, insufficient. Understand that what you are selling is only of interest to the buyer insofar as it meets his objectives and serves his need. You cannot expect this buyer to match your enthusiasm for its particular characteristics, nor should you do so. He doesn't care whether what you've got is new, unusual, innovative, creative, or startling. All he wants to know is: how can this service (or this problem solving product) help me meet my objectives? To be able to respond to this supremely valid point, you've got to know what this person's objectives are. That's why from now on, whenever you meet someone who seems to you to be a client prospect, as well as those you are actually trying to sell, question that individual to get the following kinds of information:

- What is your objective?
- When do you want to achieve it?
- What are you doing to achieve it?
- What are the obstacles to your achieving it?
- Would you like (or do you need) help to achieve it?
- Why do you want to achieve it (if not self evident)?

Like most people, I cannot resist talking about myself and my projects. If, say, a marketing advisor wrote (or even called) me and asked these kinds of questions, I'd be very likely to answer them. And I'd surely be much more interested in answering them than I would be about hearing of his product and service. Yet, most sales people thrust their product or service at me without troubling about the necessary advance work. Remember: that product, that service *per se* are of no interest to the prospect. Only his problems and their solution are of concern.

By providing this kind of information to the advisor, however, I've also provided him with not only what he needs about me to make a contact mutually profitable but an outright invitation ("Would you like help to achieve it?") to return. It is perhaps because I am at root a shy person that I have spent much time perfecting those ways which help motivate other people to *invite* me to sell them my problem solving products and services. The way to do this, of course, is no mystery: find out, first, what they want to accomplish and then propose a way of helping them do so which is very much to their benefit, and — though you won't say so of course — to yours.

Master Access Techniques Which Ensure Your Ability To Bring You Face-To-Face With Your Prospects

My workshop participants are perpetually quizzing me about how to get access to decision makers. They complain about feeling shut off, unable to permeate the inter sancta of people who could buy their services. This is preposterous! If you have the perceived ability to help someone solve their problems they will be anxious to see you and be cordial to you. This book is full of access techniques to decision makers. Here is just a sampling of how to get access to people you need to see:

- Network through your current clients and professional associates.
- Write problem solving process articles on topics of interest to client prospects.
- Make problem solving presentations at professional meetings.
- Send success letters to client prospects highlighting objectives reached with previous clients and designed to excite envy and the wish to replicate these results.
- Create problem solving products containing an invitation for those with such a problem to get in touch with you.
- Make problem solving appearances on the electronic media to showcase you and your ability to help would-be clients.

Take my word for it: once you master these, and the many other access techniques discussed in this book, you will find that a large percentage of your clients seek you out. The most productive access techniques are those which are so designed that the prospect's natural reserve and suspicion are overcome by the prospect himself rather than by you directly. If you properly master the essentials of access techniques, you will find yourself welcomed in the offices of your client prospects and the discussion quickly focusing not on your qualifications to do the job but on the prospect's needs and what you can do to meet them.

Clearly Outlining The Benefit To The Client Prospect Of What You Are Selling

No sales conversation should ever deviate too far from the only essential point of the discussion: what you, the advisor, can do for the prospect. If you want to succeed at sales keep the advantage to the prospect clearly in mind at all times and continue to hammer it home, one way and another, in any sales meeting you have.

In advance of this meeting:

- Write down the specific, precise, actual, tangible dollar (or other ultimate) advantage to be gained by the prospect. Know how well the prospect can do with your service before you are actually in any meeting with him.

During the meeting:

- In any meeting (and this, of course, necessarily involves telephone meetings, too) begin the encounter by telling the prospect that you are here to help him reach his objective. Be specific! Tell him precisely what objective you are there to help him realize. You must always keep this tangible objective clearly before both you and the prospect. The extent to which you keep this benefit clearly before the prospect will be the extent to which you will be successful. Make sure you use the meeting to gain a clearer understanding of precisely what objective the client is trying to reach and that you sharpen your own results-oriented presentation accordingly.

At the conclusion of the meeting:

- Ask the prospect whether he is convinced that what your are offering can help him reach his objective. If the prospect is uncertain (or even negative!) take this opportunity to answer each and every one of his objections. Let the prospect know that his objections are reasonable (even if they're not!) and that you can and will answer them all.

As follow-up to the meeting:

- When you return to your office and write the prospect a follow-up letter about the meeting, reiterate what benefit he will have by using your service or problem solving product. Don't be shy about this. Do not concentrate on the service or the product itself, of course. Concentrate on the benefit and only subsidiarily how the product or service will help the prospect get it.

Perfect The Ability To Close The Sale

Whatever you've done to understand your prospect, his problem and objections will go for naught unless you can actually close the sale. Many advisors make the profound error of assuming that the client prospect will close the sale himself, leaping up like a crazed salmon to grab your tantalizing lure. Don't count on it. Here's what you have to do:

- Always expect to ask for the sale. *N.B.* This asking need not necessary take place at the end of the sales meeting. Having begun such a meeting by informing the prospect what benefit he can expect to derive from using your service or problem solving product, you can then say, "I'm here to ask you to try it." Don't be shy! Remember: if your product or service really does what you say it does, then you have a moral obligation to get the prospect to use it. If you leave the prospect's office without having made the sale, not only will you be out of luck, but so will the prospect. Many professionals suffer from the foolish delusion that their prospects should be grateful to them for their (the professional's) sales visit. That they, the prospect, should cajole, beg and plead for the privilege of working with the professional. Don't be ridiculous! You should be grateful for the opportunity not merely to help yourself but also to help the prospect reach his objective.

- If the prospect asks for more time, ask why. Don't just accept the fact that the prospect automatically needs more time to make up his mind. Perhaps he really doesn't. Perhaps he could make the decision right now if he had more precise information of the kind you should have readily available about the benefit to him using your product and service. Find out.

- If the prospect raises a point which you cannot answer right then, however, don't worry. Say so. Yes, it would be better if you had all the information you need at your fingertips, but it occasionally will happen that you don't. Don't panic. Tell the prospect exactly when you can have the information needed and then make sure you get it to him. Remember: the savvy prospect may actually understand he needs a problem solving process like yours but may feel uncertain about your ability to deliver. This could be his way of checking you out. If you fail to follow through, of course, his need for the problem solving service has not diminished but his need for you has — perhaps forever!

- If the prospect seems uncertain about using your service or product, say so. There's no crime in this. Yes, it is possible that the prospect may reject you. It's not the end of the world! Moreover, you may learn you are being rejected for very good reasons. Perhaps your presentation isn't up to the level of others he's seen; perhaps you have not yet perfected your problem solving process techniques. Perhaps you are overpriced. It's very helpful to you to know this. On the other hand, if the prospect is operating under a misapprehension, you ought to have the opportunity to say so, clear up the matter, and move towards the close.

- If the prospect says, "No!", find out why. "No" in Lant language is only a deferred yes. I reckon that if I have done my homework properly, if I have indeed identified someone who has a problem I can solve, then in a worst case scenario this "No!" only means "No, not now!"; I need to find out when I can return and try again.

Resource

As long as you're selling advising services, you will have to be concerned with the matter of perfecting your sales close. In this connection, see *Secrets Of Closing Sales* by Charles B. Roth and Roy Alexander (Prentice Hall). It'll help.

Develop Selective Hearing

Properly understood, the development of what I call selective hearing is really an aspect of mastering effective closing techniques. Because of its importance, however, I wish to treat it separately.

You will find in selling your services and problem solving products that many, even most, discussions will meander. Such meandering, however, is done for a variety of reasons. True, many people cannot stay on the point of a discussion, even when the topic under consideration is their own welfare. But it is also true that such meandering is actually a way of ascertaining what kind of person you are and whether the prospect can work with and trust you. In any event, you need to keep the advantage to the client in mind before, during and after any meeting you have with him. Know what you want, know why it is in the prospect's interest to have it happen, and attempt to keep the meeting moving forward to a mutually beneficial close by screening out those things said by the prospect which do not bear on closing a deal.

This means that you'll have to ignore much that may arise in any conversation. Some people will enjoy flexing their macho muscles at you to demonstrate their power. Learn to cut through what they are saying and to keep the meeting on track. Others, a growing group nowadays, will try to persuade you that they are powerless to make a decision when in fact the reverse is true. Ignore what they are saying: keep the objective in mind and move towards a close. Some will attack you or your problem solving service. Others will compliment both. Some will simply be quiet, difficult to reach and let you do all the talking. These are my particular aversion. Your object remains the same: to move the meeting towards a successful close.

You may find this difficult to do at first. It is easy to rise to the bait when you feel you are being attacked and to attack back. Don't. It is easier still to feel that any compliments you may be getting will lead on ineluctably to a sale. Don't be so sure: compliments are a very good way of getting rid of people without hurting their feelings. (Remember: we Americans have a popularity fetish and like to let people down kindly.) Your job either way is clear: to keep the beneficial objective you can render the prospect in mind (and your own, of course!) and to keep working to achieve it.

One thing that happened to me last year perfectly exemplifies the point. A man who owed me a considerable sum of money decided not to pay it. After an exchange of letters which grew ever more heated and belligerent, I referred the matter to my attorney who said I would have to work towards a settlement since the amount at issue, while large, was not sufficiently so to warrant action in a federal court, which must have occurred since the debtor resided in another state. This was, then, a perfect sales situation: I had to sell this irksome individual on the benefits of a settlement, when he seemed utterly unwilling to resolve things. This was the objective, the closing, if you will, which I worked towards.

In the course of moving towards it, the debtor used every sort of foul language against me, accused me of every natural and a good many creatively unnatural crimes as well. I screened all that out using selective hearing and selective reading. Finally, a bit of information fell into my hands. In response to one of my letters, his wife (and partner) responded by informing me that he was in the hospital, ill. It was just what I needed to know. I immediately wrote back to his wife indicating that I hoped our difficulties (then going on for 11 months) could be immediately resolved so that they would not trouble his convalescence. I named settlement terms which were less than either of us had demanded and hoped they could be adopted now to clear the matter up promptly. Within a week I had a check in my hands for the amount named and a letter of agreement, too.

What this story indicates is clear:

- Do not interpret the concept of sales too narrowly. All selling is simply convincing someone to exchange benefits with you. That's precisely what happened here.
- You must keep your objective in mind at all times and learn to ignore that which is said and done that obscures the real objective. Much had to be ignored in this case. It was not easy; it was, however, essential.
- Despite much that at the time seems detrimental to your interests and may immediately suggest that no closing is possible, if what you are proposing is truly in mutual interest of the parties, ordinarily a beneficial conclusion can and will be reached. Selective hearing is one key attribute to bringing it about. The other is persistence.

Learn To Be Persistent

The longer I am in business, the more clear I am that it is not ruled by reason, by rationality, or even by logic. Thus you must learn that people will not move speedily in pursuit of their own best interests even when these interests can be made patently apparent to them and when the effects of their lack of action are also apparent. Expect this. It's irritating, irksome, frustrating, but it is a fact of business. Thus you must learn to be persistent as you approach the selling of your services and products. You must realize that:

- prospects will act more slowly in pursuit of their interests than you will be able to identify those interests and the means of best realizing them.

- prospects often obstruct the realization of their interests by ignoring those matters of greatest concern in favor of lesser items.
- prospects generally approach the matter of making a decision, any decision, with great caution. Many people find it most difficult to make any decision at all about their own interests, despite the fact that a failure to take action is itself a decision of the most pronounced kind.
- prospects are often cushioned from the ill-effects of their sluggishness about making necessary decisions by being part of organizations which, despite their negligence, yet move slowly ahead because of general inertia. There is thus no compelling reason to take action now.
- prospects often do not plan; they react. If circumstances are not sufficiently bad to warrant immediate action, the decision maker may postpone the decision until a later time, when matters have reached crisis point.

None of this, of course, is good. But it does at least account (if unhappily so) for the fact that many decision makers, when confronted with the prospect of buying your sensible problem solving service, fail to do so, preferring to put the matter off, hoping, indeed, that both you and the need which occasions your presence will go away. Unless the latter does, you shouldn't either.

You must, therefore, be prepared to return and return again to this (often infuriating, self-destructive) prospect until such time as he does, indeed, decide to take the beneficial action you first recommended. Each time you return you need to place before him, as forthrightly as ever, the benefits he will secure with your problem solving service and why now is the time to take advantage of it.

Over time this decision maker will become used to you, will come to like you, and will find, through renewed proximity, that he does, at last, see the benefit of what you are offering. Remember: many people fail to take action which is directly beneficial to them because they do not sufficiently know or trust you, who are offering them the benefit. They fear that you merely talk a good line, and that you will be unable to deliver on your promises. Once this problem has been dealt with they are often ready to proceed.

This is what happened with one of my best clients who, despite every well-reasoned suggestion on my part that they should take action in pursuit of their objectives, waited over a year to sign up for one of my advising services. Having done so, they were more than happy with the result and renewed the service for another year. Only then did they acknowledge that they would have indeed been better off had they started earlier — just as I said they would! But by then, of course, the reasons which had blocked an earlier decision had been satisfactorily dealt with.

Prerequisite III: Your On-The-Job/Working-With-The-Client Skills

The skills that are necessary to work successfully with clients get short shrift in most books on advising. This is very unfortunate. Using the techniques in this book, you will get the job. You will, in fact, get as many jobs as you can handle. Yet to truly be an independent advising success, you are going to need success on the job working with your clients, too. For with these successes you can leverage other, even better clients. Fortunately this book contains just the kind of information you need to make sure your relations with clients will be mutually profitable.

Generally speaking, the kinds of technical skills you need for working successfully with clients break down into five areas:
- setting objectives
- preparing to realize these objectives
- working towards the objectives
- reporting on the objectives
- utilizing successful objectives.

Setting Objectives

At whatever stage you are in working with your clients, you need clear, written, mutually agreed upon objectives. These objectives may be changed, of course, as your degree of knowledge about the client expands as you see how the client goes about working with you to realize the objectives he says he wishes to attain. But right from the start, when your information about the client is necessarily limited, you should at least have a draft set of objectives to be realized during the course of your advising relationship. These objectives should involve:
- what you wish to accomplish
- your understanding of what the client has agreed to accomplish
- a detailed list of the kinds of resources and assistance you need from the client, including personnel and supplies, to accomplish the objective(s)
- a calendar of objectives and deadlines for achieving them
- a precise indication of when meetings will take place, who is responsible for calling them, who will participate, and how they will be followed up.

As you know your advising business better and better, you'll find you are able to go into even introductory client prospect meetings with at least general answers to these points. You can use that introductory meeting (and, of course, later meetings, too) to gather still more detailed answers and to make necessary modifications in your plan. But the fact that the plan can be made more precise later does not negate the need for it from the first moments of your contact with a client prospect.

Preparing To Realize Objectives

You need the following technical skills to be adequately prepared to work with your clients to realize their objectives:

- ability to identify the skills needed by part-time and full-time staff so as to make the most of what you can offer
- ability to recruit and train such staff
- ability to handle research and data collection
- ability to build problem solving teams
- ability to develop necessary documents
- ability to ascertain what the decision maker really wants to achieve and what resources he will really put towards solving the problem you are there to deal with.

• Ability To Identify The Skills Needed By Part-Time And Full-Time Staff So As To Make The Most Of What You Can Offer

As an advisor, you will generally be working through other people who will actually implement many of your recommendations. Thus you must have a precise understanding of the skills needed by those on the staff who will actually carry out your suggestions. We advisors are, by our very nature, expert at the business not only of knowing what needs to be done to achieve a client's objectives but the precise skills and technologies which people need to have to be able to carry out our suggestions. One of the crucial mistakes particularly new advisors make is to assume that once they have made their suggestions, they have finished with the job. Nothing could be further from the truth. You must think through everything. I recall in this regard a very minor example of what I mean: I was putting on a program one day where the secretary had to write down credit card numbers on a form. She did that difficult task well enough but as no one had bothered to tell her she needed to record card expiration dates as well, she didn't. And we had to take time from the program to get the information she might so easily have gotten from the start — had I not made the assumption that she knew what she was doing.

Thus as an advisor you must be prepared to:

- work with the client on a mutually agreed upon set of objectives
- gather the information you need to make sure these objectives are sensible
- make recommendations on how to reach these objectives
- identify the staff needed to reach them, and
- both recruit and train the staff needed to implement these suggestions.

• Ability To Recruit And Train Staff

Since recruitment of new staff and the training of both existing and new staff is so important to your success as an advisor, you need to familiarize yourself with both personnel recruitment and training techniques. If you do not, you may find yourself in the uncomfortable situation of having to wait for the client to recruit necessary personnel and train them before being able to utilize your services. It is very easy, things being as they are, for the client's immediate enthusiasm for your project to wane during the time it takes to gear up to use you. If you can be a part of the recruitment and training processes, however, you will at least have the opportunity to protect your interests, try to keep the client on track, and gather a staff both sympathetic to you and trained by you to reach the mutually beneficial objectives.

Resource

The best place to look for information on training techniques and the training profession in general is *Training Magazine: The Magazine Of Human Resources Development*. It's published monthly by Lakewood Publications, 50 South Ninth St., Minneapolis, MN 55402. Lakewood also publishes many books and newsletters helpful to those in the training profession. You can request a free copy of their Lakewood Books & Newsletter Catalog by calling 1-800-328-4329.

• Ability To Handle Research And Data Collection

Advisors must become expert at knowing how to find the information they need and how to use it. That's why so many advisors have academic and research backgrounds. Living as we do in the Great Age of Information there is a distinct premium on what I call secondary research skills: the ability, that is, to find information that other people, the primary researchers, have actually gathered together. They create information. We advisors have to be adept at finding what they have produced and at using it.

Resource

The best short guide to finding the information you need quickly is unquestionably Alden Todd's superb little book *Finding Facts Fast: How To Find Out What You Want And Need To Know* published by Ten Speed Press.

• Ability To Build Problem Solving Teams

Advisors, as should now be clear, rarely work alone. We are, instead, responsible for creating a series of problem solving teams which ordinarily change with each assignment. These teams may be both internal and external, drawing on the existing (and recruited) staff resources of the client and utilizing experts whom we ourselves make available as independent contractors either under our own business entity or through direct contact with the client. These are, however, mere details. What is important is knowing:

- who is necessary to solve any given problem
- how to find them
- how to structure an appropriate agreement with them
- how to work with them for maximum effectiveness
- what can be expected of them
- how effectively to motivate, chide, goad and manage them to achieve the objective.

The answers to these questions, of course, vary somewhat depending on whether the team we are working with is external to the client or internal staff. But the fact remains: if we fail to learn how to build and manage teams, we will fail as advisors.

• Ability To Develop Necessary Documents

Document development is an essential part of becoming a successful advisor. While there are also many marketing documents to develop, here are the necessary on-the-job formats to master:

- objectives memoranda
- task action minutes of meetings
- narrative minutes of meetings
- success reports
- confidential memoranda to decision makers
- training guidelines
- proposals for future projects.

All too often advisors are rightly criticized for reckoning an assignment to be a success if they have produced a ton of verbose, meandering verbiage studded with technical jargon. I disagree strongly with this kind of shoddy, unprofessional behavior. Advisor reports should be sleek, objective, action oriented, relevant data elegantly arranged and concluded with the advisor's recommendations and reasons for suggestions made. Indeed, each document you produce, each of the documents above, can and should be a model of its kind, for the objective of all documents is clear: to state clearly the objective to be reached with the document, to arrange to best effect data under consideration, and to move towards a firm conclusion in the most expeditious way. Writing such documents, of course, is a decided skill, but it is a skill you can master — and must for the success of your practice.

• Ability to Ascertain What The Decision Maker Really Wants To Achieve

As you already know, most people in this nation are imbued with a progressive oriented success tradition. But many people do not actually live by this tradition. With them, it's all lip service. You will find that some of your most frustrating assignments will involve a client who speaks the last word in goals oriented success language but who works assiduously to undermine the realization of what he continually says he wants to achieve.

I recall in this connection one of my earliest advising assignments, when I was still young and gung-ho. The client said he wanted to reach a particular objective; the overall decision maker in the organization confirmed this objective. But secretly the final decision maker was working to oust the junior decision maker (my actual client) from the organization, and this man in turn only wanted to hang on long enough to get his pension. He had no interest in reaching the objective, whatever he said to the contrary, but every interest in making it appear that he did. In reality, his object was having pleasant lunches, talking about reaching the objective, and doing nothing at all — except wasting time, his prime object. He was willing to have the organization pay me a very nice monthly honorarium for over a year until such time as he had reached his goal and the pretense of sustained action no longer had to be maintained.

Remember: to succeed as an advisor, you must become adept at distinguishing between people's ostensible motives and their actual ones. Must be able to differentiate between the rhetoric they give you about wanting to reach the objective and the actual commitment they make to you to do so. This becomes more and more easy to do, of course, the longer you are in the advising business. Now deeply experienced, I can often tell in a short telephone call whether the client prospect is serious or not. In the beginning of your career, however, you will perhaps naively believe that people really want to reach the objectives they say they want to reach. You may be inclined to believe their overheated oratory on the subject of their desire to be successful through the utilization of your talents and the following of your noted regimen.

But oratory isn't enough. As will become clear throughout this book, your commitment, as an advisor, to the client's success will often be greater than his is. That is because the client is often protected from failure through the inertia of his organization. You are not. You must bring about success with your clients in order to leverage new and better clients, to build a practice. Therefore when you get into a situation where the client is not living up to your expectations, say so. Or make a calculated decision, as I finally did in the example above, to let this particular assignment run its course while understanding that, as a result of its probable lack of success, you will be able to derive no further benefit from it beyond your immediate paycheck. The decision, however, is yours.

Working Towards The Objectives

To achieve success while actually working with the client towards realizing his objectives, you need the following sets of skills:

- ability to speak up if client deviates from agreed objectives and working conditions
- ability to recognize and cope with staff resentment
- ability to face senior management as peers
- ability to deliver appropriate problem solving solutions
- ability to generate appropriate alternate courses of action for the client
- ability to cope with your own frustration when the client does not heed your suggestions
- ability to accept the fact your client will test you
- ability to motivate and exhort your client, reminding him of his dreams and objectives.

• Ability To Speak Up If Client Deviates From Agreed Objectives And Working Conditions

Many of the problems that undermine advisor-client relationships could be avoided if, upon first being noted by either party, they were brought up and dealt with. Now, my purpose here is not to advise clients how to deal with your less-than-perfect behavior; it is rather to suggest how you deal with that of the client.

Thus, when crucial aspects of your problem solving process are not adhered to, when you are not given the support of staff, the resources you need, the attention of management, &c., don't be quiet feeling that you will lose your position if you speak up or that things will probably get better. They probably won't. Bad habits are notoriously difficult to break. Bring these matters up promptly, professionally. If you are disappointed in the way the client is handling your working relationship, say so. If the failure of the client to live up to your agreement imperils your ability to bring about success, say so. One of the things advisors need to learn is genuine behavior. There is no point in pretending things will always go smoothly with every client. They won't. But you can remain true to yourself and true to the mutually-agreed upon objectives by giving vent to your appropriate, genuine human feelings and emotions.

Resource

In this connection I find Peter Block's book *Flawless Consulting: A Guide To Getting Your Expertise Used* very helpful indeed. It's published by Learning Concepts and distributed by University Associates.

• Ability To Recognize And Cope With Staff Resentment

Face it: staff people understand not only that advisors are better treated than they are but that the advent of advisors ordinarily means change, often substantial change, not excluding the loss of their jobs. You cannot expect the staff, therefore, necessarily to greet you with open arms and hosannas with palm leaves. And if they do, remember the historical sequel to the most well known occasion when such behavior did take place: crucifixion. No, it's far more realistic for you to expect not merely resentment but outright or, worse, subtle obstruction. Your ability to cope successfully with this situation depends on your ability to:

- keep the full support of those who will be implementing your suggestions. If they waver, then your credibility and ability to function effectively will be undermined.
- identify those individuals in the organization who will benefit from any possible changes and gain their adherence to the new order.

- use language which minimizes the extent of change while proceeding on course with what needs to be done to realize the agreed-upon objectives.
- gain a complete understanding of what opponents to change can actually do to obstruct it and be prepared to recommend necessary (and already considered) counter measures as these obstructive signs develop.

It is important for you to keep in mind that while your commitment really is to change, most other people feel deeply threatened by it — not entirely without reason, either. Thus you must expect and anticipate obstructive behavior, learn to identify it, and be prepared to deal with it.

Advisors, after all, change people's lives. There is no way around this. Many people do not want their lives changed and will fight against any such change rigorously. As they see that the change will come notwithstanding their pronounced opposition to it, they will become belligerent, even offensive. That's unfortunate. But with your now developed skill of selective hearing you should be able to screen out the rude cacophony of the malcontents. In any event, if you wish to achieve the objectives you set out to achieve, you must learn to ignore it. You are being paid, after all, to render catalytic recommendations which may not be popular. As a result you will often be a scapegoat, rarely a hero. This comes, however, with the territory.

• Ability To Face Senior Management As Your Peers

Our society is infinitely more hierarchical and class conscious than at first appears to be the case. Advisors, however, necessarily deal with decision makers, senior management, boards of trustees and directors. Whatever your age, you must be prepared to deal with these people as peers, for if your problem solving abilities can help them reach one of their desired objectives then you are, indeed, a valued colleague.

Advisors do not fit neatly into an organizational hierarchy. This is happily very much to our advantage. Rather, we are free to move in and about and through an organization to gather the information and assemble the internal teams we need to help reach the objective; while doing so we operate in the reflected status of the decision maker retaining us.

Because, however, we have no actual power to order decisions, we have to be very careful about how we are perceived both by those our recommendations may influence and by the management which actually orders change. Hence, we must be perceived as peers by those who retain us. It is difficult for many to carry this peer relationship off unless they are at a similar (or older) age to the individual retaining them. But I wish to point out that what gives you your standing is not your age but the ability of your information base to bring about the desired solution to the client's problem. There is absolutely no reason why a young person, even a very young person, could not carry off a collegial relationship so long as the information at his disposal was crucial to the client. Whatever your age, however, you must be prepared to deal as a peer with the individual retaining you. Otherwise, you will be treated as an employee and, suffer the consequences, for no employee can ever rise to the eminence that virtually every advisor begins by having.

• Ability To Deliver An Appropriate Problem Solving Solution

Clients rightly complain that advisors make recommendations which are not appropriate for their circumstances. It is your job as an advisor, and it takes great skillfulness, not only to understand in the abstract what solutions will work for the client, but, given the client's circumstances, which are appropriate and acceptable for the client now.

I recall in this connection one of my clients which had collective rather than individual leadership. My fundraising model is very much geared to the traditional nonprofit organization having a board of directors, executive director, and the usual senior management. This organization, by contrast, had radically departed from the customary structure. In such a situation your job is to:

- point out the very best courses of action and make your initial recommendations.

If the client rejects your suggestions not because the recommendations *per se* are not useful, but because in the client's situation they are not appropriate, then you must work to create other, more tailored recommendations, syncretized with the client's situation.

• Ability To Generate Appropriate Alternate Courses Of Action For The Client

Whether you like it or not, either because the client doesn't like or approve your initial recommendations, because they feel they are inappropriate to their situation and values, or because they do not have the resources to carry out your recommendations, you will find your suggestions modified, if not rejected outright. The *leitmotif* of the successful advisor, fortunately, is flexibility. Yes, it would be nice, wonderful in fact, if clients simply, humbly, promptly accepted your good ideas and considered recommendations. But they rarely do.

Advisors are always in a recommending position. We are always in the position of putting proposals before decisions maker, and occasionally a good decision will be rejected merely because the decision maker wants, just then, to flex his muscles and show who's boss. A good idea is no proof against rejection, as I know for a certain and unhappy fact.

This doesn't mean, of course, that some aspect of the original idea cannot be maintained. It doesn't even mean that, in due course, the good idea cannot be resurrected in its entirety. But the good advisor knows that there are many ways to skin a cat, that all roads lead to Rome: the important thing may not be that a given recommendation is adopted in its entirety (or even that it is entirely rejected) but that the momentum of a project be maintained through any kind of decision which keeps the client moving towards the desired objective.

Resolve right now that movement towards the objective you and your client have agreed upon is more important than any particular recommendation of how to achieve that objective. It'll save you much grief later.

• Ability To Cope With Your Own Frustration When The Client Does Not Heed Your Suggestions

I hear from distressed advisors over and over again, a kind of problem solving Greek chorus, about how their clients are ignoring, not hearing, overriding, or just plain mutilating their recommendations. This, as this book makes perfectly plain, is the right of the client. It is unfortunate, of course, that:

- your client isn't as smart as you are
- he wants to do things on his own way rather than yours
- the persuasiveness of your arguments, the full weight of your logic, and the complete measure of your rationality have had no impact on him.

But that's the way it often is. Prepare yourself for it. In this business, where each of us advisors is nothing more than a recommending machine, we must be prepared for this development — and not be frustrated, much less tormented, by it.

This is a skill which parents often master (by the time of their second or third child!) by watching the apple of their eyes do awkwardly what the parents themselves could do in an efficient instant. But the wise parent, understanding the need of the child for self expression and growth, forbears to intervene and grits his teeth — often to the accompaniment of shattered glass or some other music of catastrophe. So must you. In the advising business, you can plan on being ignored, unheard, and unheeded. Matters only become truly serious, however, when you are unpaid.

• Ability To Accept The Fact That Your Client Will Test You

One of the most infuriating aspects of the advising business is the fact that clients will test you, will acknowledge the wisdom of your advice, but, despite your best efforts and strong condemnation, do what they want to do, perhaps to see whether your predictions turn out properly.

There is scarcely a client born who will not, in this way, give you an ironic means of proving just how valuable and correct your advice really is. Expect it. I have often thought about this peculiarity of the advising business and have come to the conclusion that this test is the client's way of finding out whether we are, as we appear to be, a different, more knowledgeable species of human, or the same garden variety prophet so often discredited and discarded in the past. If you know what you are doing, can predict with relative accuracy what will happen when the client fails to follow your suggestions, and, indeed, does the exact reverse of what you've suggested, and (a particularly valuable skill) if you can pick up the pieces left by the client's demonstrated wilfullness, you will actually come out of this testing process immeasurably better off, more influential.

I think, for instance, of a passage from *The Siege Of Krishnapur* by J.G. Farrell. In that fictionalized account of one of the sieges of the Indian Mutiny of 1857 two doctors duel about their different approaches to curing cholera. The one believes the disease airborne; the other asserts equally vehemently it is carried by water fouled by those already ill with the disease. To prove his point, the first doctor drinks some of the diseased water, while the other urges him to resist. In this instance, the death of the first doctor through his own stupidity does not, I'm afraid, allow him to benefit from the lesson he might have learned by testing the real expert. But at least the second doctor comes out well from the ordeal: he inherits the first doctor's entire practice! Let this be a lesson to you during the inevitable time when your client will test your skills and problem solving techniques. If you know what you're about, that invariable variable, you will shortly be better off.

• Ability To Motivate And Exhort Your Client, Reminding Him Of His Dreams And Objectives

The good advisor provides his client with technical expertise, reasonable objectives to be reached in rational fashion, and a continuing supply of oversight, good humor, exhortation and motivation. You must be the master of each of these skills.

Generally when an advisor is introduced to an organization at least the individual retaining him is enthusiastic about the prospects of the project. Others, of course, whose jobs and comfortable operating patterns may be threatened by the impending change, can be expected to be less enthusiastic; still, the decision maker will often be noticeably aroused by the prospects for beneficial change that seem to arise with the advisor. This honeymoon period, of course, doesn't last very long. Very soon the new advisor, from whom so much was expected, becomes in turn an old face in his own right, now perhaps part of the problem as he had once been the harbinger of a solution. This is a very dangerous period for both advisor and client, and you must develop your skills to bring both of you from it in good order and so carry on towards the agreed-upon objective. How can you do this?

- As you see spirits flagging, make sure you take the necessary time to remind the client of the end towards which you are working. It is terribly easy in the daily press of human existence to lose track of the desired objective in the morass of petty, draining details. It is your task to remind the client of how desirable the end result is.

- It is your job, too, to remind the client of how far you have come from the beginning of the project. Yes, there was more enthusiasm about the journey down the yellow brick road in Munchkinland, but Dorothy and her attendants were far closer to the Emerald City when they reached the unnerving recesses of the haunted forest. Your job is to remind the client, whose memory for such details may be short and befogged by all that now needs to be done, of the progress that has in fact already been made.

Be assured that progress is only in retrospect a glorious, enthralling thing. At the time it is being made it is generally prosaic, mundane, confused, disorienting and very much at cross purposes, the good and the bad coexisting in the greatest possible disorder. You know this. The client may forget. And when he does, it is your job to recall the benefits towards which you and the client are striving and to renew the dream which far transcends in importance those picayune details which at any moment threaten to sap the vitality of even the most remarkable project. To the advisor, with your long view of things, falls the necessary task of remembering from whence the enterprise now in hand has come and whither it goes. This, as much as the continuing oversight you provide and your technical skills, is at the heart of why you are so valuable to the client and your presence so very necessary.

Reporting On Objectives

It is not enough to be able to achieve success. You must become adept, too, at reporting on success and, when it comes, on failure as well. You need to learn how to:

- develop a success report. This report should summarize precisely what was done in the reporting period, to what extent it was done, who was responsible for the work, what difference the success makes, and how this success compares to what was predicted for the period. It should provide perspective for those who may not have a detailed knowledge about the project and what it is intended to accomplish.

- report on failure. A mere recitation that during a certain period you failed to reach any given objective may do you and your client an injustice. All reports should, first, be rendered so that it is clear what did in fact happen. Even during a period of failure it is quite likely that some success resulted. If so, say so. As above, first consider what was done, who was responsible for whatever did work, what difference even the marginal success being reported makes, and how this success compares to what was predicted would happen. Any failure report should be sure to deal with unusual circumstances arising during the report period, particularly those circumstances which are not expected to recur in the next reporting period to block future progress.

As with all documents, those dealing with success (or partial success) should be action oriented, sleek, marshalling their information in the most persuasive way and pointing to objectives realized rather than merely presenting undigested information which the client will have to consider (perhaps inadequately) on his own.

Utilizing Successful Objectives

Once you have achieved success working with a client, you need to learn how to leverage this success to achieve the following:

- better cooperation from the client on other aspects of the project on which you are working
- future advising assignments from the client which your enhanced prestige and credibility now make possible
- new advising assignments from client prospects who should now be interested in having you replicate your success for them.

As I have said before, until such time as you have the trust and confidence of the client you cannot attain the best working relationship and hence the best results. This trust, this confidence are ordinarily slow to build. Whatever your reputation, a client will generally maintain (sometimes substantial) reserve about your ability to help solve his problem. Not until such time as you have in fact helped bring about some (perhaps introductory) success working with the client will this reserve be (perhaps only minimally) diminished.

Prepare for this. Your first objective in working with a new client should be to achieve some introductory success at the earliest possible moment. This success will solidify your position and, by diminishing the client's reserve and increasing his confidence in you, will make it possible for you to push ahead on other aspects of the project.

As soon as you have this success, you need to see the client-decision maker and press your immediate advantage. Make it clear, firmly but professionally, just what needs to be done now. Go into this meeting with a precise idea of where you intend to spend the currency of your newly enhanced standing. Clients, remember, no less than others, have very short memories. If you wait too long to use this currency it will depreciate in value, and you'll have to wait until you have another success with which to bargain.

At this time, and as your short-term successes on the road to the longer-term objective pile up, don't forget to lay the groundwork for future assignments with this client. One of the skills you need in establishing a successful advising practice is to develop a feeling for when to broach the subject of the future objective you hope to reach while working with the client. The moment to deal with this topic is, of course, when you have already achieved some success, for that is the time when your credibility is at its highest.

By the same token, as you wrack up successes with any given client you must keep an eye cocked in the direction of other would-be clients who might well like you to duplicate for them the success you have now helped your original client achieve. Another section of this book will tell you in greater detail how to leverage your advising successes and so achieve new business. Suffice it to say here, however, that you need not wait until the end of an advising assignment to begin to reap the benefits from it in terms of new business. As soon as you have helped create a success, *any* success, which may be meaningful to another organization similarly situated, that is the moment to begin your marketing effort to bring it to their attention.

Prerequisite IV: Your Small Business Management Skills

Your advising business should fulfill 5 distinct objectives. It should:

- solve your client's problems
- provide money for your current operating expenses
- create a profit at year's end
- provide you with adequate provision for your old age through pension and financial planning vehicles
- develop a practice for you, not just episodic dealings with *ad hoc* problems thrown your way.

The first of these has already been discussed. Now it is time to deal with the remaining four in terms of the skills you must have to successfully manage your business and reach these key objectives.

The First Great Skill: Determining What Kind Of Lifestyle You Want

Advisors, as much as any professionals in the nation, can not only determine what they want to do but how they wish to do it. You can:

- operate your business from home
- operate it from a standard office setting
- work 16 hours a day, 365 days a year
- keep very part-time hours
- do no traveling
- do extensive traveling
- have one information-based problem solving skill and service
- develop a cluster of information-based problem solving products and services
- make just enough money to get by
- go for really substantial profit and wealth.

The choice is yours. Now that I've come in contact with so many thousands of advisors and would-be advisors, principally through my books, workshops and media appearances, I know that these are the truly difficult decisions for people. By comparison the matter of how to become technically proficient at what you do is a relatively easy question to deal with.

Thus the first thing you must do to achieve a successful advising business, the first skill you need, is the ability to make choices for yourself and to live with the decisions you make without anxiety or regret. Too many people I have met have hamstrung themselves by failing to make any decision at all feeling that to make a decision is to lose something; usually they call this "something" their freedom to be whatever they want to be. This is true, of course. One cannot make the decision, say, to do no traveling and to do extensive traveling simultaneously. But the failure to make any decision at all means that you will be at the mercy of events, the individual with the least freedom of any of us, with a loss which compounds as your life continues.

General Small Business Management Skills

Having once come to grips with the need to make a decision about lifestyle and understanding that this decision will have a substantial impact on the kind of advising business you create, you will yet need three very critical, general skills for business success:

- deliberation
- determination
- the ability to place failure in perspective.

Deliberation

Those who succeed in the advising business are not impulsive, spontaneous, or impetuous people. Instead they plan, mull, consider, and deliberate over a course of action before moving ahead with it fully. Such people I call plodders — and I venerate them as the salt of the earth.

Such people are generally not the first to be seen in a given place, not the first to say something new, not the first to try an innovative approach. But they are the ones who ultimately win the race from having considered the value and utility of what is available and how it may be used for their benefit and that of their clients. More facile creatures are prone to criticize the plodders as being unimaginative, slow, and unglamorous. That's true. Plodders win, however. While considering this question I began studying the men who created the first of America's great fortunes: Vanderbilt, Astor, Carnegie, Rockefeller, and Morgan, all men of mind-boggling wealth and success. In researching their careers (through books like Matthew Josephson's *The Robber Barons,* for instance) I was pleased to discover that each was a decided plodder, rarely the first to seize upon something new but always decidedly thorough once a course had in fact been determined to be advantageous. It is such people who achieve business success, not the glib and superficial. These flitting personalities cannot select a reasoned course of action and abide with it, building a staggering success from a series of small, often miniscule victories.

Determination

When I began my advising business, I did so with very little money, pitiably little in fact, but I did have one very valuable item in my kit bag: unrelenting determination to succeed. So determined was I to succeed, both on my own behalf and on that of the clients whom I firmly expected to serve, that I never considered failure. Failure was a luxury I could not afford. And so I have continued to believe even unto this day.

Each day, therefore, I am determined to have a success; each week a series of successes; each year a wide ranging set of successes. I am determined that it shall be so and despite the (yearly diminishing) doubts of some, the days which don't quite work, the projects which sometimes do not quite succeed, the moments when doubt does appear, it is generally so. Perhaps I should say more and still more generally so as time goes by. So must it be with you. To achieve this necessary condition you must resolve today, this minute!, that:

- your advising business will be a success
- you will do whatever is necessary to make it a success
- you will not sleep on any given day until you have reached a success
- you will not be satisfied until you have brought this success to the attention of others who can benefit from the processes which brought it about
- you will not blame others for any lack of success but blame yourself
- you will find in any failure some kernel of success, some benefit of experience which you can profit from another time
- you will consider each great success, which you set down in writing, attainable by achieving a continuing number of small, easier to reach successes
- you will never give way to sustained doubt and despair
- but that if you do you will return to these pages and begin working again using these techniques until such time as you have again achieved a success. At that moment, write to me and tell me how you have succeeded, for you are the kind of person, determined, unshakably resolved to succeed, that I want to know. Yes, you are my kind of person and you will, by not giving in, create an advising business which will help not only you but all those who can benefit from the skills you have mastered. This, in the final analysis, is the real value of the determination you must never cease to foster in yourself.

The Ability To Place Failure In Perspective

I tell you right now in your advising business you will sometimes fail.
- The good advice you give will not always be followed, will often in fact be ignored.
- The advice you give will not always be accurate.
- You will predict too much and help deliver too little.
- The client will not always (or even usually) give you credit for what you have helped to do.
- Those whose lives you change, even when they are better off as a result, may abuse you.
- Those whose lives you cannot change, though their worst fears go unrealized, will criticize you.

All this is part of the life of the advisor.

Time after time over the last several years, I have had telephone calls and visits from advisors who were crushed by one or more of these matters. My advice to them is the advice my wise father gave me at some now unremembered crisis of my youth. "This too," he soothed, "will pass."

In the advising business, as in life itself, you will discover that only rarely does the best that can be occur and equally rarely does the worst take place. The exalted aspiration you have for yourself may prove just tantalizingly beyond your grasp. But then so is the imminence of the hell you fear. Instead of giving way, then, to despair, do this:
- Write down every bad thing that could occur as a result of the failure you are now contemplating. Every one of them.

- Put the list away.
- Wait.
- Wait as long as you can. Then take the list out of the drawer where you put it and review. What in fact has already happened to confirm your worst fears? How really little has occurred?

Now see, after considering the circumstances as they appear to you, whether you cannot benefit from the failure:

- Write down what you have learned from it.
- Note how you can improve the relationship with your current client as a result and how, knowing what you know now, you can enhance the likelihood of a success after all.

Failure will accompany you all the way to your grandest successes. And the greater any success, the more likely it will be that you will experience equally grand failures, too. Savor them. Out of savor comes knowledge. And out of knowledge, you, advisor, should know better than anyone else, will come further success, more masterfully accomplished. I promise you.

Specific Skills For Small Business Management Success

• Providing Money For Your Current Operating Expenses

Your first need is to provide for your current operating expenses. This is best done by honing your ability to discover the value to the client of the disproportionate benefit you help produce for him. The more important the benefit to the client, the more you can charge, the greater your current operating revenues and ultimate profit will be. Success in the advising business is not necessarily a question of hours worked. It is, instead, a question of perceived benefits to the client which you have helped deliver. Throughout this book the message is clear: do not so much concentrate on what you can do as what value the client realizes from your skills. Insofar as you can learn to quantify this benefit and to express it in terms which can excite other, would-be clients to want to have it, too, you will get the clients you need at a price which provides not only your operating expenses but also a substantial profit.

• Creating A Profit At Year's End

In addition to your skill at discovering the disproportionate benefit gained by your clients through your technical skills, two other critical skills can help you make a profit at year's end:

- an ability to cut overhead and expenses
- good record keeping.

I shall have more to say about both these matters later. For now, however, I shall simply point out that an advisor is almost uniquely situated to benefit from both. To begin with, you can start and maintain an advising business with very limited direct expense. Unlike most other businesses, your initial investment in an advising business can be very low indeed. Thus a very large percentage of monies coming to the firm will actually be profit. Remember: people are buying you for your ability to solve their problems, not for your surroundings and expensive overhead. Thus until such time as you have money to burn, there is no need to place an extensive amount in items which will not in themselves produce more clients and an expanded profit.

As far as record keeping is concerned, no good business can succeed without benefit of proper records. By keeping proper records and utilizing every available tax benefit, however, you'll find yourself retaining a substantial amount of the money you make. Chapter 12 provides additional, detailed information on this matter.

• Providing Yourself With Adequate Provision For Your Old Age

The successful advisor functions effectively and simultaneously in the past, present and future. From the past he gleens what he can from previous successes and from failures which may provide useful experience to help fashion both present and future successes. Working in the present, the successful advisor helps to bring about successes while working with current clients. And while doing so, he considers how monies now being raised can best be put to work to guarantee future comfort while diminishing impending taxes. Sadly, too few advisors give a thought to anything beyond the immediate needs of their existing clients. This is a great mistake. At the very least you must give consideration to maintaining your marketing and so maintaining a steady stream of clients. Beyond that, however, you must also learn how to manipulate your money so that, using both business deductions and the wonders of compound interest, you provide for the future. Sadly, I see too few advisors with any idea that they will in due course decay. Too few believe that at some point, not so many years ahead either, they will be unable to ply their trade. More than that, sickness or some dread disability may inhibit them long before they plan to retire. Such is man's lot. No one, therefore, should undertake to establish a small business of any kind, much less an advising business which so often is dependent upon the skills and well being of a single person, who is not prepared to spend the time it takes and set up the processes needed to ensure his own health and general financial well being.

- **Developing A Practice**

The matter of making your advising business a practice where people return to you regularly for benefit of what you know and can do is really a marketing question and as such will be addressed in full detail in later chapters. Here it will suffice to point out that you must develop the habit of thinking sequentially, connectedly, not episodically, of perceiving each individual client contact as a means of getting both more business from this individual and of leveraging the successes which come about through this relationship to get other, even better clients.

Too many advisors approach each client, each problem they are solving, as somehow distinct and autonomous from every other client and problem. Nothing could be further from the truth. Each client, properly handled, will return to you to let you deal with both similar and other problems which are connected to the first you settled. Each client, properly leveraged, can get you new and better business. These necessary developments can only happen, however, if you perceive the connection of any individual event to where it may lead, both with an individual client and with other organizations (would-be clients) who are similarly situated. Of all the many skills I have mentioned in this chapter, this ability to extrapolate beyond the individual situation and think in terms of the future usefulness of your present work is among the most valuable and should be cultivated assiduously.

- **Two Significant Final Points**

Conscientiously followed, the skills addressed in this chapter, taken along with the necessary mental attitude previously discussed, will stand you in good stead and move you towards the creation of your successful advising business. This chapter, however, would rest incomplete without a mention of two more essential skills: your ability to be candid about your own weak points and their need for correction and your ability to remain resolutely client-centered in all your dealings.

1. On The Need For Continuing Advisor Education

Every small business is demanding, but an advising practice, in which you offer your problem solving information through a variety of products and services, surely stands at the top of the list. You must master such diverse and demanding matters as:

- the intricacies of your information base
- its continuing developments
- marketing and promotion
- a wide variety of written documents
- the writing and production of booklets, books and audio cassettes
- procedures on the talk circuit
- small business management and development
- taxes
- pensions and financial planning.

These are only some of what you must know! No successful advisor can ever afford to stop learning, stop renewing what he knows and discovering how to bring his problem solving processes to the attention of the largest number of people who can benefit from them. We are the change agents, but we lose our place on the cutting edge if we ourselves stop changing.

2. On The Need To Remain Client Centered

All the other skills in this chapter are necessary. Be assured of that. They are, however, insufficient to ensure success. This last one is the keystone of the arch: the skill of focusing on your client and running a client centered business.

I hear a lot about client centered marketing these days; it's a faddish phrase. But I do not see a lot of client centered marketing practiced. This is one of the chief reasons why so many businesses of all kinds, advising businesses in particular which are without retail outlets and catalog distribution, have such abbreviated lifespans.

To succeed as an advisor, to reach your objectives, you must see the client's situation simultaneously in two ways: as a detached, objective observer and from the client's own quite subjective vantage point. They rarely yield the same result. Of course so seeing these realities is not easy. Ours is an egocentric culture where we have been taught to focus on ourselves first, last and always. Now I am telling you that to succeed in the advising business you must not only focus on the client but be continually perceived to be focusing on him and his problems.

This book, fortunately, describes in detail how to accomplish this necessary feat, how to ensure that all you do is client centered. The extent to which you succeed in so being is the extent to which you will, in turn, reach your own considerable objectives.

Now we are ready to go on to the difficult, unending, absolutely critical task of marketing, which is neither more nor less than a client prospect (seen or not yet known to you) coming to understand that you, above all others, understand his problem and can offer appropriate solutions to reach his objectives. Before you turn the page, however, let me conclude by saying that if in the future you find yourself reaching your objectives too slowly, or falling short of them altogether, I invite you to return here, to this critical chapter on the skills needed by the successful advisor. Go through them carefully and ask yourself if you really have the ones you need to succeed. If you do not, work to remedy the deficiency. For, change agent, I say this to you: if you cannot accept the need for change in yourself, and will not work to achieve this change, how do you dare offer it as a prescription to others?

CHAPTER 3

Introduction To Successfully Marketing Your Advising Practice

There is nothing mysterious about marketing. Marketing is the art of targeting the right buyers of your problem solving product and service and continually bringing to their attention in a variety of ways the benefits they will derive from using what you are offering. Marketing is a skill for letting the right people know there is a coincidence between the would-be buyer's need and your service. Marketing is not so much persuasive as it is a clear statement that you have readily available something which the buyer already knows he needs and wants. You are merely indicating how he can go about meeting his need in the easiest fashion.

Having said this, and as should be perfectly clear by now, I don't think most advisors market very well or very thoroughly. As for myself, I spend a very considerable portion of my time marketing:

- I market when I need new clients.
- I market when I have clients and want to secure my future income through new clients.
- I market while I'm with a client (by learning more about his needs) so as to be able to sell more problem solving products and services, both my own and other people's.

Marketing is a key part of my day; like brushing my teeth, it is something I do every day. It is one of the three significant activities that advisors must do every day, for we must:

- work directly with our current clients to help solve their problems
- develop new problem solving process products and services, and
- market to gain new clients.

Many of my colleagues don't do this and wonder why, as a direct consequence, their businesses don't grow. Let us first explore the reasons professionals glibly provide for not marketing.

- *"Marketing is unprofessional."*

Look no further than the last Chief Justice of the United States, Warren Burger. Chief Justice Burger had a bee in his bonnet for years about marketing legal services. He believes that it is unethical and unprofessional for lawyers (who are, of course, advisors) to advertise and promote their services. His argument is a variant on the old refrain, "If you're good, people will find their way to you." (Though, I suspect, he has nothing against the good old fashioned kind of marketing that goes on in clubs and golf courses across the land.)

This argument is, of course, nonsense and is being hotly disputed by many lawyers nationally. Characteristically I am on the side of the insurgents, but not just because I am a natural anarchist and like to tilt against the windmills of obstinate authority. No, properly understood marketing (and its constituent parts, advertising and promotion) are consummately professional.

The truth of the matter is that when most people go to look for a professional service of the kind advisors provide, they have a very limited notion of how to go about doing so. When a professional markets a service it is to the benefit of the individual needing that service, because now he has a place to begin to solve his problems.

Those who oppose this kind of marketing say things like, "Well, sure, the person marketing his service is good at marketing, but he may be lousy at the law." This, of course, is true. But the person who doesn't promote may also be lousy at the law — and also lousy at marketing. The principle of *caveat emptor*, let the buyer beware, holds true whether the professional markets or not.

Instead, what the professional usually means when he says "marketing is unprofessional," is "marketing is beneath me." There's a curious and pervasive myth that suffuses every professional community that once someone has achieved the necessary mastery of one's field, as evidenced by securing licenses, diplomas, degrees, certificates and professional expertise, one is somehow beyond such mundane activities as those which are essential for small business success, including promotion, advertising, marketing and all the other client outreach activities. This form of snobbery, for it is nothing less, is extremely pervasive and is most detrimental to your success.

I know what I'm talking about on this point. I hold two Harvard degrees and while I was at Harvard (between 1969 and 1975) the notion was extremely prevalent that it was beneath us to consider promoting ourselves in any way. If we were good, the "right people" would find out, and we'd find ourselves almost mystically raised to greatness. Not surprisingly given the environment, most of us believed this hokum. I felt prey to it until I awoke one day in 1975 to discover there were no jobs in my field in college teaching and that Harvard's snobbery had been preparing me for a kind of life which no longer existed. I was predictably upset, but it was my own fault I had taken the so-called experts at their word and not applied my own intelligence. I definitely felt like the Sleeping Beauty — only I awoke to find myself being kissed by the toad.

Let me say this as strongly as I can: successful marketing is a necessary precondition for success as an advisor. It is as important as knowing your technical field backwards and forwards and as significant as diversifying your business so that you derive maximum benefit from what you know and become recession proof, too. Is this strong enough? If not, I'll say it again and again, until you wake up in the middle of the night saying it by rote.

Professionals raise other objections to marketing:

- *"It's too expensive".*

I'll tell you this: any marketing that doesn't work is too expensive. I'm a New England Yankee, and I hate spending money. I don't spend money wantonly, and I'm not going to advise you to do so either. I have a quintessentially American respect for the good old yankee dollar, and I advise you to have it, too.

Having said this, you cannot afford not to market yourself. You have, after all, already spent tens of thousands of dollars on your education and on keeping yourself up to the pitch of professional perfection. But the information you have available is aging rapidly, ever more rapidly in fact as time goes by. Thus you have readily at hand investment material — information — which must be used — now! — to secure maximum benefit. Whatever you now invest in your marketing effort will be considerably less costly than the funds and time (for you devoted your salad days, didn't you, to getting ahead?) you have already invested. And if you wait, the investment you have already made becomes less useful as the information you have at your disposal ages.

No, marketing is not expensive. Rather, it is the refraining from marketing which is expensive — and downright suicidal.

The objective of this chapter, and indeed of this entire book, is to show you how to go about handling your marketing in a thoughtful, considered, conservative and inexpensive fashion so that you reach the maximum number of suitable buyers (that is buyers whose problems will be solved by your products and services) for the least possible cost.

- *"I don't know how it works."*

Neither is marketing taught in our professional schools nor is any advisor required to have a basic familiarity with the elements of marketing. It is quite possible to become an expert in any field (except marketing itself, of course!) without having the faintest idea of how to handle the necessary success prerequisite of knowing how to bring this information to the attention of those who need and can use it. This is a crime and an outrage, and when you have the opportunity to talk to curriculum planners in any field you should protest this mindless insularity and academic provincialism. No expert should be released into the world without an understanding of what marketing is, what it does and how it works. Quote me.

Having said this, I firmly believe that each advising professional, you!, can learn what you need to know about marketing and positioning (for that is really what marketing is all about) and so maximize the value of what you know and can do.

You already know I have no staff: no clerical, no secretarial, certainly no marketing staff, just a necessary go-fer. Yet I tell you this most pointedly: if I can handle my own marketing as effectively and inexpensively as I do without ever having had a marketing course but solely through the application of the principles and processes found in this and my other books, so can you!

It is to the advantage of marketing experts to make other people believe what they do is arcane, difficult, and demanding. But for us advising experts selling products and services, this is simply not true. What marketing demands is a clear understanding of:

- who you are selling to
- the problems these future clients/buyers have
- the various means of connecting our problem solving processes with their problems
- how to write the various marketing documents that we need in ways which increase the likelihood our future clients will respond to this information promptly
- the need for grit and determination so that we build a long-term marketing plan and not expect instantaneous results.

Can you do these things? You bet your life! You can and you will when you've finished this book.

- *"It takes too much time."*

I hear this objection all the time from advisors, and I've frankly never understood it. As I've said before — and will say again until I feel the utmost assurance you've internalized this absolutely critical message — marketing is something that must be done daily. Daily! Daily!

The important thing to remember is that done daily, for perhaps an hour or so, done conscientiously, you'll build up a tremendous array of contracts and potential opportunities. The activities which must take place are:

- identification of those people and organizations who need your service. Be specific! This is the key to marketing in the Great Age of Information.
- listing all the means of reaching these people

- developing the appropriate documents to do so

- following up your initial approaches with telephone calls, meetings, and further mailings.

Very few of your days need ever be devoted entirely to marketing. Instead, set aside a portion of each day to do what needs to be done. Begin the day, as I do, "warming up" by writing to:

- individuals and organization with whom you'd like to work

- following up on previous correspondence to same

- contacting appropriate media sources, those, that is, who can most easily connect you to individuals and organizations who have the kinds of problems you solve

- following up on those who haven't yet responded to previous contacts.

Then place your telephone calls. And again at the end of the day place telephone calls (if you're in the East) to other time zones and make your final efforts to connect with those who can buy you.

Understand that in marketing a single letter, a single telephone call, a single contact of any kind is usually insufficient to induce the desired action. Will this discourage you? I have spent up to a year and longer without a response carefully tracking individuals and organizations I knew from the first day had need of me, my products and my services. Sure I get discouraged when this happens. I get discouraged at the general level of idiocy of most people who can't quite visualize and understand their needs as clearly as I do. But that's the fate of bright people like us: we see longer and clearer, and we suffer more poignantly. At least, however, we have the satisfaction of knowing that through this frustrating process we are ennobling our souls. Besides which, the persistence pays off. We get the clients. Consider this: the Great Boz, Charles Dickens, referred to himself as "The Inimitable." Because of my incessant, never ending, never-say-die marketing which gets the client in the end, as sure as the man in the white hat gets the girl at the conclusion of any western, I refer to myself as "The Inevitable." If you have a problem I can solve, at one time or another, and usually at many times, you will hear about me — and at last take utilitarian action to solve the problem. This is probably the sequence of events that resulted in your purchasing this book. So believe!

You will use your evenings and week-ends where necessary; (it will be necessary, too, — in the beginning because you are not yet known and must work overtime to become so. Later, because you are so well known you'll need the extra time to accommodate the new demands upon you). During these evenings, these week-ends, use the time to continue to refine your sense of who you are marketing to, being as specific as you can possibly be, and to craft the necessary documents for reaching them and to master the means of doing so. In other words, all the advance work should (if possible) be handled when you cannot accomplish the necessary task of connecting with client prospects, in other words when they are not physically available. The fact that other people are slothful and are not easy to reach for extensive periods of time should not preclude your making use of that most valuable commodity: time.

It is, then, not that marketing takes too long to do but that it takes a routine, a set of procedures, some of which can only be accomplished by connecting with others during regular hours, some of which can advantageously be accomplished on your so-called "downtime" (which is, of course, something of a joke to an accomplished advisor!)

Marketing, then, is a necessary procedure which must effectively be integrated into the life, not just the professional life either, of the advisor and independent professional. This is because marketing can go on at all hours of the day and night, which will become patently apparent as this book rolls along.

While in the process of writing this book, for instance, one morning (it was about 1 a.m.) the telephone next to my bed rang — not once but in a sixty minute period over 30 times with people leaving messages for me to send them information (read marketing) packets on promoting their products, services, and businesses. This is not exceptional in itself. What was different, however, is that I had no prior knowledge that T.V. 38 (a Storer Broadcasting channel which syndicates programming throughout New England) was re-broadcasting a previous show that I'd been on. Since I always include a means for people to get in contact with me, I was thereby put in a situation, despite the fact that I was sleeping and it was the middle of the night!, of making money by having a media source pull qualified prospects for me — at no cost. Remember: you need not be present to handle your marketing effectively.

In short, marketing for the advisor is an activity which never stops and which, properly handled, is never seen as intrusive and vulgar, a great fear of most professionals, but rather as an action which is to the benefit of the individual or organization you are dealing with. Marketing is the ultimate service to a buyer prospect, because it enables him to see, clearly, quickly, easily, that someone else has the solution he needs to his problem. And if this isn't service, what is?

- *"It takes too long for results to show."*

This is a statement I hear a lot. Many advisors use it as a justification for sloth, rather than action. Most marketing activities are slower moving than any of us would like. Even done perfectly and with the utmost care and consideration, marketing can take a substantial period of time to achieve results. What does "substantial" mean, though? The definition of this word is dependent upon what you are offering and how great the perceived need for it is. And, of course, "perceived need" is in itself a function of successful marketing.

Each day individuals and organizations are assaulted by a barrage of offerings most of which, even the most desirable and needed, do not produce results. This isn't because the individuals contacted are not interested but rather because they are easily distracted by the current demands of their positions and the fact that your message can be easily pushed aside by the next one coming in. Never believe for an instant that you are doing your marketing in a vacuum in which you have the undivided attention of your audience. Even when you are face to face with a client prospect, you are competing with his memories, fears, irritations, aggravations, frustrations, hopes for the future and other persistent, if unremarked, interruptions. No, we very rarely have the *undivided* attention of our prospects. Knowing this should prepare you for the long haul.

- People generally do not take action the first time they hear about a product, service, or message — even if it can clearly benefit them. Accustomed as we are to advertising campaigns, they usually figure that if what's being pitched at them is any good, they have plenty of time to act.

- People are lazy. Thomas Jefferson had it absolutely right in the Declaration of Independence when he wrote, "all experience hath shown that mankind are more disposed to suffer, while evils are sufferable, than to right themselves by abolishing the forms to which they are accustomed." Even when people are in a state of discomfort, they are unlikely to make the necessary exertion to change their state. People are, of course, fearful of change, even change which is to their benefit. Thus they need to be convinced, as good Americans, that the change will not be too difficult, too dislocating, or too demanding of them. You and I know differently, of course, but it does not do to discourage the client prospect.

- People get distracted. Even when they want to take action, if they don't follow through on all the necessary steps to reach the result, then it is quite likely something else will occur to them and so distract them.

- People have very short attention spans.

- You have competition. Consciously or subconsciously, people wonder whether you or your competitor offers the best service. Because they are afraid of taking the wrong step (either because they mistrust their own judgement or because they have made mistakes in the past), they fail to take any action at all. The reality of competition is not only that people might select another service or product but that because of competition they are so immobilized they take no action whatsover, thus depriving both you and your competitor of the business — and themselves, of course, of the solution they need.

- People don't need the service right now. Yours may be an advising service or product people only need occasionally, like my capital campaign fund raising advising. If this is the case, you may be pitching your service to an audience which will have the need but doesn't have it just now. Hence the need for patience.

- People forget. The sad fact about marketing in the world in which we live is that marketing is not forever. Marketing is a very ephemeral activity. The best success I've ever had with a marketing device (in this case an article in the *Boston Globe* about one of my advising services) is one that drew clients for me over a year. This I regard as exceptional.

Discouraging though it may seem to you, your marketing activities must be carried on in season and out, carefully, conscientiously, persistently — even when you have the exact knowledge that what you are selling, the service you are offering, is needed NOW by people you're approaching.

- One more thing. F. Scott Fitzgerald noted that "the rich are different." This is true in marketing, too. The richer a client prospect is the slower he often is to act. This is because he is relatively comfortable today and will be relatively comfortable tomorrow. There is thus no acute need for him to act NOW. Thus, as will become more and more clear, you must impart into all your marketing an element of tension, of drama, of urgency, of the need to act NOW so as to induce people to do what you always knew was in their best interests.

- *"Someone else should do it for me."*

All professionals, all advisors, suffer from the Panjandrum Syndrome: the acute desire tc have others do things for them. Having suffered, so they seem to reason, to achieve their present place in the sun, it is now time to be waited on for the remainder of their lives. Nurses, of course, bitterly complain about hospital physicians as particularly exemplifying this kind of behavior but in fact it is a behavior which, without straining oneself, one can find in all the professions. I have to tell you that I regard it as foolish and detrimental to your own interests. I am the great advocate, of course, not so much of doing things yourself (for there are things that I want and need others to do) as understanding how things are done — which often means having done them yourself so as to gain an at least introductory under-standing of how they work. It is my firm belief that only after you know how things are done, in this case things relating to marketing, can you afford to delegate them to someone else. For only at that time will you know whether or not the service you are buying is really a service, or just an unfortunate expense.

Thus, make up your mind right now, that at least at the beginning of your business, you'll do all the marketing yourself and not think too longingly of the day when you can delegate it to someone else. As you handle the marketing, you'll be in a position to ascertain whether you really understand the problems of your buyers (not just the reasons why they could use your product or service but the reasons why they don't act punctually to buy them). You know whether your documents adequately represent you and your products and services. You'll get a chance to understand which of the paid marketing avenues is really effective and why and how to make your unpaid marketing (that is, your promotion and public relations) truly effective. These things you can only effectively learn by doing. Thus, don't fall too easily into the Delegation Trap until you know the basics. With such knowledge, if the day does dawn when you want to work with and through others, you'll know how to evaluate what they are doing for you.

- *"So many people can use my product/service that I don't want to target (don't feel the need to target). I like the shotgun approach."*

This comment is utterly prevasive among those needing to market. The truth is, we live in the age of vertical marketing, which means highly selected, targeted marketing. Only those companies with large markets, numbering in the millions, can afford the luxury of even relatively undifferentiated marketing. And even these, soft drinks and soap companies, are not so undifferentiated if you look carefully at what they are doing.

Recently I addressed a conference of agricultural public relations directors, that is public relations practitioners for large agri- and chemical businesses. Some of the questions at this meeting concerned me in that they basically indicated a lack of knowledge about vertical marketing and differentiation. One professional told me his company wanted to get out the message to Americans to buy more food and employ more farmers. This message is so hopelessly amorphous as to be unsalable. Instead, the benefits of each kind of food product needs to be considered and targeted to that part of the market needing the benefits of the individual item. This is far easier than you might think.

Thus in my advising business, while there are in fact about one million voluntary agencies needing fund raising assistance, the kinds of marketing I do are very specifically geared to certain sectors of the market: nonprofit organizations, principally in health and human service fields, which previously relied upon government sources of revenue and now must fund raise independently, &c.

The shotgun approach to marketing simply doesn't work and it will involve you in great expense. Throughout this book the message will be very clear: know your market. Know precisely who you are marketing to. Know as much about them as you know about yourself. Understand how they spend their money. What their hopes and aspirations are. Get a bead on their anxieties and be able to say succinctly, cogently how your product and service can relieve them.

The more targeted and precise your marketing is, the less demanding and more profitable your marketing efforts will be. Let me give you a single example which I'll reinforce later in the chapter dealing with Success Letters. During the writing of this book, I was the featured luncheon speaker for the New England Society of Association Executives, a relatively small (at about 150 members) regional trade association. Following my customary practice, which I'll explain, once this engagement successfully took place, I mailed a follow up letter to all NESAE members indicating that my books were available and appropriate for them and that I was ready, willing and able to give talks to their members, enter into book distribution agreements, advise their members, etc. The letters went out on a Wednesday. Within 24 hours I had been retained by one of the members to give a program at their annual meeting. Moreover, after this meeting took place, I contacted the comparable state associations of the other 49 states and leveraged my success to get additional gigs from organizations composed of the same kind of people who wanted to achieve the same successful results.

The total cost of this mailing was about $40. My engagement with the member alone brought in more than $1000, not a bad return on investment.

The lesson here is very, very clear.

- Draft a narrative description of who you are marketing to. Clearly state what problem(s) they have. Reduce these problems to single lines if possible. Indicate how you know that these are problems. If a source within the industry has told you, note that. If the information has appeared in a trade publication, note that. Be prepared to quote these sources. The more substantial the problem seems, the more you have sources, reputable, significant sources, available to prove the need to be acute, the better for you. When you are targeting a problem within a precise market, you need to be as specific as possible.

- By the same token, you need to be specific about the products and services you are offering and why they can solve the client prospect's problem. Too often advisors are so enamored of their services, their gleaming, much-considered services or products, so happy to tell you all about them, how much they cost, their history, &c. that they forget the buyer cannot reasonably be expected to be as interested in these (actually quite mundane) details as they themselves are. That's all right and not a sign of downright sedition! Their problem — and getting a solution to it — is what interests the buyer. There is no reason for interest in any product or service, none whatsoever, unless it clearly solves a targeted buyer's problem.

Targeting, as with the above-mentioned example with the small list of NESAE members demonstrates, works. Why then don't more people do it? (Gratefully so, I must say, as regards my own competitors!) I'll tell you why. Because most people who have a problem solving service or product to sell are afraid that "out there" in that elusive country, just over the next hilltop, there is another buyer for what they are offering, and they don't want to miss him! They are, of course, probably right. They are right that in any vast multitude of people there may well be another buyer for what they are offering. But they need to stop and consider the cost, financial, psychic and emotional, about getting to that particular buyer and whether what they are doing will actually pay off.

When I approached the small NESAE list, I knew that a 1.5% (standard) response on my books alone would cause the mailing to break even and that if even one association purchased a problem solving workshop or advice service, my highest priced items, it would be very profitable, indeed. Marketing is the art of taking your product to just the right buyer prospects, the most likely, the highest motivated, those with the greatest anxiety (and hence, the most need for action) with a product or service that can produce dramatic results for them, results which can be with some confidence predicted in advance.

This, of course, means targeting. All others stay clear!

- *"I feel sheepish saying good things about what I can do."*

Are you laughing and doubting that this is often thought and said? Then think again! In a recent issue of a publication for computer users entitled *Northern Bytes* the following appears in a review of my book the **THE UNABASHED SELF-PROMOTER'S GUIDE:** "If you follow the advice in Dr. Lant's book, your name will be constantly appearing in newspapers and magazines and your voice and face will be familiar to radio and television audiences. *Many of us wouldn't be comfortable with that kind of exposure."* (My emphasis added.) This comment, in this review, is regarded as unfavorable, and it decidedly suggests that getting your message out through the media is demeaning.

Laugh though you will, this is a familiar attitude, and I bet you suffer from it, too. But this review, like the attitude in general, disastrously misses the point.

If you are marketing properly, you are not so much saying good things directly about yourself (certainly not in the spirit of adolescent braggadocio) but rather indicating strongly that what you have and are doing meets a felt need of people who are anxious and uncertain. Your service, however, can save them. If you feel diffident bringing to the attention of others in the same situation the necessity of following your advice, using your service or product and so saving themselves, you shouldn't be in business at all but in some mountaintop religious retreat, since you are evidently too good for this world!

I fail to see, and I shall come back to this point again and again, how notifying those in need (as your client prospects certainly are, whether they know it or not) that you have a beneficial product or service can somehow be construed as degrading or bragging. Yet it continually is. Let's face it, however; not only is there a large element of idiocy in this point of view, but a dollop of jealousy, too.

The truth is, you should feel you are performing nobly by bringing what you have and can do to the attention of those in need. Following the methods of this book, moreover, you need never be seen in any other light than a flattering one, as an indispensable part of what keeps your clients healthy and profitable. Surely you can stand this kind of image, no?

- *"Can't I just do some marketing once and have done with it?"*

This attitude is downright silly; yet it exists. Marketing is not like a smallpox vaccination. As previously pointed out, people are continually assaulted by a wide variety of marketing images and offers regularly. Nowhere is it more true to say than here that "out of sight is indeed out of mind." So long as you are in business, you are in the marketing business. There's nothing disheartening or discouraging about this either.

Too many Americans nowadays have a disposability complex: we want quick fixes to everything. Something has to be new to be good. Of course this is ridiculous. When you go into business, you are necessarily in for the long haul. If you know this you won't get (as) discouraged by all you need to do to make your advising practice the success that it will become. Marketing, as must now be clear, is a daily activity. Properly designed, properly handled, you will be seen as The Inevitable in your clients' lives: just as you want to be. And if you stop marketing, you are, sooner or later, out of business. Keep this in mind on days when you want the money from your business but don't feel like putting in the marketing effort.

Having said so much, I feel sure you suffer from at least one of the destructive attitudes I've written about above. I know it because I encounter these unhelpful states of mind daily in my professional practice and with my adult workshop participants. Overcoming these attitudes takes time and work. It doesn't happen overnight. Having written so much, however, let's go further into the business of successful marketing.

What You Are Really Selling

As I said above, you may think you are selling a product or a service. Don't believe it for a minute. Only you are interested in the product or service *per se*. The client rarely, if ever, really is, unless for quite personal reasons he is interested in who you are and what you are doing technically. Otherwise he is simply interested in the results. It is therefore the results you should concentrate on.

But what kinds of results are you, as an advisor, really selling? The longer I am in business, the more I am convinced that people buy my professional services and products because they help them reach ultimate objectives, not immediate ones. By the same token, the more such people I can assist the greater my likelihood of reaching my own ultimate objectives.

What are the objectives? They are now what they have always been in terms of selling. We advisors are selling:

- money
- sex
- personal freedom

- financial independence
- attractiveness
- health

- autonomy
- salvation
- social popularity and status

And other similar ultimates. Our job is to show a client, who has the right to be somewhat dubious about our claims, how we can help him reach objectives which are as simple as they are cosmic. For make no mistake about it: if you had been writing a marketing book for the ancient Romans, you'd be writing about the same ultimate objectives that people want today. In this sense, people's desires have remained constant over time. The means of reaching them, of course, have varied dramatically, but these are only the means. The ends, the real reasons people buy, have remained the same.

Getting back to this kind of simplicity is, however, difficult to modern day professionals who have been taught to think about complexity and not about simplicity. Ronald Reagan and his often superb ability to communicate have buffaloed many of these people who have found it difficult and indeed troubling that statements which are often factually wrong, syntactically garbled and rich with other errors still manage to convince people in overwhelming numbers. But the essence of good marketing is always the utmost simplicity.

It took me a while to be aware of this to the extent necessary to secure substantial profit. When I became aware of it, I began to understand that in part of my advising practice I really am an unusual kind of banker. When I offer my advising techniques of raising money for nonprofit organizations, I am saying, quite directly, "Buy me. Have the money you need."

My pitch to those who buy my other books and take my workshops on, say, successfully establishing a consulting business is a little different. "Buy me," I say in effect, "and have not only money but personal autonomy, too. Freedom over your own life." This double whammy is extremely effective for those who not only want to achieve wealth but want to have personal freedom and autonomy, too, in a world that is continually undercutting an individual's independence.

Your first and arguably hardest task as an advisor aiming to sell yourself is to begin to think simply and concretely about what you are doing and which ultimate(s) you have at your disposal.

Recently, for instance, a client came to me who is involved with an agency of the mainland Chinese government. He is attempting to popularize in the West certain folk medicine practices of the Chinese at the instigation of their ministry of health. Having looked through all the marketing materials he gave me, I caught an incredible sense of defensiveness in what I was shown. A lot of technical terminology. A lot of numbers. A lot of grandiose back up materials, all operating, I'm afraid, to put the reader off.

I looked at this mass of indigestible material. Then I asked him what he was selling. He told me the name of the medical technique. "No," I told him, "you are selling health. And nowhere in your material do you talk about the two things that will effectively sell your procedures. Namely that they bring about health and that they work!" So simple — unless you are an expert in the field.

We live in a world where simplicity is no longer valued. However, as I well know, you cannot market successfully unless you reduce whatever you have to a clear problem needing a solution and an equally clear indication that what you have solves that problem. Never forget this and work to refine what you're doing so that it is always clear: Problem. Solution.

Sadly, intelligent and creative people like to show off. I know. I am one myself and for a long time I battled the urge to show off rather than solve problems. I hope I needn't say this is counterproductive. Think about it. Are you really more interested in solving the problems of your buyers or do you want to impress them with how bright and clever you are? So long as there is the slightest suspicion of the latter, then you will never successfully solve your marketing problems — which is, quite simply, to get people to spend their money on your offering.

Many professionals (particularly those around my neighborhood in Harvard Square) have never learned this message. Many seeming hay seeds from the boondocks have. That's why the "hay seeds" are millionaires and many elaborately trained professionals continue to wait tables while spewing their vague criticisms against a system which doesn't value them. I've never bought that argument. It's the height of unholy hubris not to bend to others, not to try and understand what their problem is and not to try and apply any solution techniques in ways which are most widely understandable.

A Difficult Advisor Marketing Problem

One of the difficulties advisors face in launching their businesses is that they do so under rather adverse circumstances.

On the one hand, they are themselves their most expensive product. Their own billable time is and will be for most advisors the most expensive thing they have to sell. The problem, however, is that when you enter the market you are often least well situated to persuade people with problems that buying you makes the most sense.

This is the case for a couple of reasons:

- You may not yet have a reputation in your industry to draw upon and sustain your marketing.
- You are often not yet at the right status level for your buyers.

Remember this sad fact of advising: you are often bought for other reasons than you can solve the client's problem economically and expeditiously. If we lived in a perfect world, this wouldn't be the case. But we most decidedly don't live in any kind of halcyon paradise.

People buy less good advisors over good advisors. People buy more expensive advisors over less expensive advisors. And in both cases, they may well know what they are doing.

One of the reasons why people buy advisors is that they reflect the perceived status levels of their buyers. That is, wealthier, better placed clients tend to select wealthier, better placed advisors, despite the fact they may work less hard and charge more money. This discourages many new advisors. You shouldn't get discouraged, however. You should instead adapt yourself to this situation and act accordingly. Here are three suggestions:

- Know the client as well as you know yourself.
- Understand that studying and understanding your market is a constant, not intermittent, task.
- Discover what the client wants to buy and then sell it (which is not, of course, necessarily what you first thought you'd be selling at all!).

One of the problems advisors have is that we have all been elaborately trained in our disciplines. By this I don't necessarily mean we've taken a degree course in the service we're offering, for some of us have learned what we do by doing it and are in fields where there is little, if any, formal academic preparation — like my fund raising service, for instance. Having learned this material, we either consciously or unconsciously make the decision that others are going to benefit from what we know. We thus set up a business in which we intend to use our knowledge whether we know or not that anyone really wants to use it, whether they are ready to use it, or whether there are a host of well-placed competitors.

I know what I'm talking about! Each year in my advising workshops I confront hundreds of individuals who have all made an at least tentative decision to launch a practice. You should see some of the specialities in which they feel sure they are about to find fame and fortune! All too often such people will have had a hankering after independence, a desire to cut loose from another, more stifling career, and a long latent desire to begin a particular kind of business. They start this business without knowing enough about it and without having a clear idea of whether people will actually buy what they've got to sell.

This situation gets even worse, of course, if the individual has worked for many years towards a particular degree or credential and at the very least wishes to get his money back — and more — to compensate him for all his trouble.

When you approach establishing an advising business, or any small business for that matter, you cannot afford the luxury of these inimical instructions. Setting up a small business of any kind, but particularly an advising business, should not be an emotional decision. It should be as brisk and bracing as a dip in a mountain stream at sunrise — which one surely contemplates with deliberation before attempting.

I write with passion about this issue from sad experience. In 1975, I finished a doctorate at Harvard dealing with the pomp and pageantry of the nineteenth century British monarchy. During my stay in graduate school, however, the national job market worsened, particularly as regards people schooled in the humanities. As England sunk into continuing insignificance, my academic field — modern British history — dropped in attractiveness. For a time I was in shock. Then I shook the dust off my feet and made the best of a bad situation. I still like English history. I still enjoy reading, and even occasionally writing, about the monarchies of the world — but as an avocation. Learn, reader, learn from my experience! I was elaborately trained for a field of study which ceased to exist in 1901 (that I knew when I entered) but which grew progressively less attractive to contemporary sensibilities. (Of course, you really can't beat it as a hobby! Unless, however, you have a substantial trust fund, you can't live off the odd check from your avocational activities. Hence, the need for the following check list which will allow you to select a remunerative field.)

Towards Selecting Your Advising Niche

Follow this list religiously. Each time you launch, a new product, a new problem solving service, enter into a new marketing territory, refer back to these points. If you do, you'll save yourself a lot of grief and aggravation. Don't be one of the unfortunate high flyers I so often encounter who believes the system doesn't apply to you, that you'll somehow get by on your native ingenuity and insight. Damn the torpedoes, says he. Full speed ahead.

Don't you believe it! Use the list instead.

Advisors succeed in the beginning because, á la Darwin, they find an ecological niche and adapt themselves to it. This means that at the beginning of your practice, it pays to be specific, as specific as you can be practicing your technical knowledge around the nation or world. Many people in my workshops ask me whether you can begin by being a generalist, a jack of all trades. And, invariably, my answer is "No!"

The trick to building a practice in its early stages is to find a specific service which produces for the client a disproportionate benefit compared to your fee and to leverage each individual success (in ways I'll discuss later) to get further clients. Doing things this way will ensure that you'll make a comfortable, if not spectacular, living. I know. This is what I did in the first year of my advising business while I was puzzling how to break out of the Time Trap.

This trap is, of course, a very significant problem for advisors. Logistically you can only handle a finite number of clients on a one-to-one basis because there are only so many working hours a week. The rest of the time you'll be working on your marketing and promotion, on keeping up to date in your field, on running your small business (see Chapter 12), &c.

As the direct, one-on-one client advising portion of your business begins to succeed, you have an important decision to reach which will, of course, affect your marketing. What are your business and personal objectives? If you are happy doing what you are doing (and many people, of course, are), you don't need to worry about diversifying, only ensuring that the income you need to maintain your lifestyle is constant. If, however, you want the truly spectacular success that many of the top advisors have, you'll have again to go through the following steps.

Step 1: Make a Tentative Selection of Field.

We don't live (thank God!) in a socialist paradise and even if we did, we'd find more often than not that the state had assigned us to the wrong position. Thus in this country many of us select jobs and even careers which, for a multitude of reasons, are quite ludicrous. You know you are supposed to approach the solution of a client's problem with the utmost objectivity and detachment. Do the same with your own business, too, when you are, in effect, acting as your own business consultant.

When you select a field in which to practice, do so tentatively until you absolutely know, not by intuition but by deduction, that it can sustain your business and personal objectives. If you find when you have finished the following exercise that it can't, change your field. There's nothing wrong with that. Accepting reality is something all of us advisors are very good at telling our clients to do and is part of our necessarily candid operating procedure, but you must also learn to follow your own advice. You can, after all, keep your initial interest as an avocation, as I did, while following the trail which leads you to a comfortable lifestyle and the successful realization of your other ultimate objectives.

Step 2: Determine Your Marketing Area.

Where do you intend to practice? Most people live and work within a very small area. But should you as an advisor do so?

The top advisors, those who make incomes approaching a million dollars and more a year, practice nationally or internationally. While they may have begun as a local expert practising their trade, they soon see the benefits to helping people solve the problems of their expertise wherever they arise. Hence a dramatic marketing territory. *N.B.* A marketing territory is, quite simply, that area from which you intend to draw clients, can draw clients, and will promote yourself and your services to draw clients.

I'm quite convinced that unless you have special constraints that make it impossible for you to ply your trade in the largest possible area, you should make the decision to cast your net as widely as possible. So long as the disproportionate benefit that you are assisting others to achieve is large enough to justify the extra expense of your travel, then you owe it to yourself to practice nationally. Moreover, with the advent of a large number of discount airfares nationally, this statement is truer than ever!

In fact, however, people do have many constraints that practically limit their ability to have a national practice. One radio talk show host began an interview with me by saying, "Is it true, Jeffrey, that all advisors are single, divorced, or incapable of a sustained relationship?"

Building a national practice is demanding, often grueling. Make no mistake about it. For years, I've spent most Friday evenings in an airplane, most Saturday evenings in an airplane and many other days of the week on the road. It has affected my social life!

If you have young children, a new marriage, elderly parents who need your attention, you may have to make the decision to rein in your practice. Part of what this book is all about is helping you decide what you want to achieve with your advising practice and with your life.

If you keep your practice local, you can achieve a quite comfortable living, but again the truly spectacular success of the best known advisors and independent professionals will elude you. If this is going to bother you and eat away (as it does with some people), then you have two basic choices: change the way you live or change the dimension of your objectives.

Step 3: Take A Census.

Part of determining your marketing territory will be the decision about whether there are a sufficient number of available client prospects (as compared to existing competitors) within your designated marketing area to sustain your income objectives. There is no hard and fast formula for determining this outcome. You'll learn your individual formula only through experience.

First things first, however. To do proper marketing means taking a proper census of the individuals and organizations available to buy your offering and which can do so; (these are, of course, two very different things).

Finding Out Who Exists

Here are a few key resources:

- *Census Catalog And Guide* (1990 most recent edition). Published annually by the Bureau of the Census, this publication is a bibliographic listing of all resources produced by this branch of the government. The Commerce Department does much more than just issue the national census. Here you'll get a good sense of a wide range of developments and client possibilities. Stock # 003-024-07169-0 available from the Superintendent of Documents, U.S. Government Printing Office, Washington, D.C. 20402-9325. MasterCard and Visa orders through 202-783-3238. $14.

N.B. There is no cumulative guide to federal government publications, but you can request from the U.S. Government Printing Office Bookstore in your area a free subject bibliography index which lists the areas in which information is published. You can follow up accordingly in your particular area.

- *Cumulative List of Organizations.* IRS Publication 78 is useful for people like me who practice in the nonprofit world. It lists the names of virtually all 501(c) 3 tax exempt organizations but not their complete addresses. For these you must refer to a local telephone directory or specialized directory. Still this is a useful publication. Stock # 948-010-00000-3 ($41 annual subscription) available from the Superintendent of Documents, above.

- *Directory of Directories* (8th Edition, 1990). Published by Gale Research Co., 835 Penobscot Building, Detroit, MI 48226, this pivotal directory is a superb annotated guide to business and industrial directories, professional and scientific rosters, directory data bases and other lists. Since Gale is a major compiler of useful research information for advisors (including a directory of consulting organizations), it is advisable to be on its mailing list.

- *Directory of Postsecondary Institutions 1989–90.* 2 Volumes. Vol. 1 is two- and four-year institutions. Order both from Supt. of Documents, Stock # 065-000-00428-3. Vol. 2 is less than two-year institutions. Stock # 0765-000-00429-1.

- *Encyclopedia of Associations.* Three critical volumes published by Gale Research Company indexing approximately 20,000 national organizations of the United States. A very good place to look for leads about your particular field.

- *National Trade & Professional Associations Of The United States.* Published by Columbia Books, Inc., 1212 New York Ave., NW, Suite 330, Washington, DC 20005, this directory lists many organizations that Gale does not, although it indexes many fewer overall than Gale.

- *(Johnson's) World Wide Chamber Of Commerce Directory.* A complete list of Chambers of Commerce in the United States and around the world including manager or president of the chamber, the address, zip code, area code and telephone number. Published annually in July by the Johnson Publishing Co., 1880 S. 57 Court, Boulder, CO 80301.

These kinds of resources will provide you with leads. To be sure, in some fields it is easier than others to get the names of individuals and organizations which can make use of your services. For instance, I enjoy working as a fund raising and development advisor to visiting nurses associations, home health care agencies, community health organizations, and related health and welfare associations. Each of these organizations is usually part of a state and national association. Many of these associations are quite protective (for reasons which are very obscure to me) about making a list of their members available. Personally, I don't feel that any association office should act to censor information or make it difficult for those of us who have something beneficial for their members to get access to them.

In this connection, since getting these lists is of the utmost importance for marketing purposes, you must work hard to lay your hands on such membership lists. Ordinarily the best way to get them is to have a client or friend who is a member lend you their list. Don't wait until they offer it either; as soon as you've achieved an initial success with a client, ask for it. When we come to the Success Letter, you'll see why you need it! Presume, then. After all, presumption is at the root of success.

Step 4: Open A Competition File.

It goes without saying that all these organizations are not going to be able to hire you — right away, anyway! For one thing, you have competitors.

As long as you're in business, you've always got to keep an eye peeled on what your competitors are doing, just as they're going to be interested in what you're about, so long as they think you are really serious about what you're doing.

There's a lot of nonsense written about competition, how to regard it, and how to learn about your competitors. Here's what I've decided is important:

- Open a Competition File and keep it open on your direct competitors so long as you're in business.
- This file need not be elaborate. I use cardboard boxes into which I throw all the materials about my competitors which from time to time I consult.

- What you want to know about your competitors is this:
  — the name of the principal(s)
  — their address
  — telephone number
  — marketing territory
  — principal services
  — preferred client profile
  — growth, expansion and diversification plans.

Some of this information is easy to get. Some isn't. All is helpful.

The first five items should be self-explanatory. The sixth probably isn't. All advising firms prosper by finding a niche and holding it. Within this niche, each firm has a preferred client group to which it markets. It is your task to find out if your competitors are marketing to the same kinds of client prospects as you are considering. You will need to know this to determine whether to go head to head with them (will the market bear such competition?), or whether to diversify or slant your service in such a way that you are not seen as being directly in competition.

Your competition, of course, will be producing a preferred client profile on their targeted clients. But you, too, should draft one concerning the firms you think are your most likely competitors. Such a profile is a report in about 250 to 500 words of who they are marketing to, why they have selected them, the problems these client prospects have, the services your competitors are offering them, as well as any demographic information you can discover about their numbers in your marketing territory and growth prospects.

Now how do you get this information? Some of it, of course, comes right out of your competitors' brochures and marketing documents. In this connection, see whether you can get a mail box at your clients' offices into which all the direct mail offerings sent to them will be placed for your benefit. I have such a box at many of my clients or an arrangement whereby we swap information. In this way, many of my clients are responsible for bringing to my attention offerings of my competitors and so keeping me abreast of what they're doing.

It is important that you have this information and have some general familiarity with what your competitors are doing so that when client prospects ask you how you differ in services from other firms you can give them some indication. *N.B.* Given the opportunity, do not attack or otherwise denigrate a competitor. Such opposition doesn't do much to harm a competitor and makes you look small minded; it lowers your professional standing.

There are other ways to get information about your competitors, too:

- subscribe to their newsletters
- read their books and other publications (I know my competitors read mine!)
- ask people who have worked with them what the experience was like. (In this case it's perfectly acceptable to find out where your competitors fell down on the job so that even without mentioning them in future interviews you can stress those aspects of your own services which are stronger and which, no surprise!, directly correlate to the weakness of your competitors.)
- at trade shows, hit their booths.

To find out the expansion plans of your competitors it usually takes meeting them. But why should any competitor want to talk to you?

In practice, I have found my competitors to be reasonably open about their plans and practices. This doesn't mean we are necessarily bosom buddies and pals. We seldom are. There is always a necessary wariness in dealing with a competitor. That's not necessarily bad, either. It keeps you on your toes! Advisors and other information brokers approach their competitors in different ways depending on how many products and services they are offering.

If you are offering merely a single service, you are probably not going to need to keep in as close touch with your competitors as if you are offering all those pertaining to a Mobile Mini-Conglomerate. And if you are operating a Mobile Mini-Conglomerate, you are not necessarily going to be in direct competition with your so-called competitors at all times and in all situations. Here's what I mean.

Step 5: Make Deals With Your "Competitors".

When I began years ago my first advising service was to help a certain kind of nonprofit organization raise necessary capital, project, and operating funds through corporation and foundation grants. It was a very precise service offered (as it still is) to a very precise kind of client.

I offered that service mainly in and around metropolitan Boston. Thus, I had only to worry about my competitors within this area. Given that I had only a single service at the beginning there wasn't much possibility for collaborating except with those who were offering other services to nonprofit organizations and could attempt to create a Supergroup of Independent Contractors by adding my service to their offerings. Obviously this couldn't happen with my direct competitors.

This situation began to change dramatically as I began to implement the different stages of the Mobile Mini Conglomerate. Then I was not offering a single service but a cluster of related (and very different) products and services. In such a situation, it did become possible to make constructive deals with former "competitors."

Here's what I mean. Based on my inauguration of a successful fund raising practice, I wrote a book entitled **DEVELOPMENT TODAY: A GUIDE FOR NONPROFIT ORGANIZATIONS.** Once the book was available it was possible (as it still is) to enter into constructive marketing and distribution agreements with former competitors who having no book would nonetheless like to sell mine to their clients as an instructional aid.

This process becomes infinitely more complicated (and rewarding, of course) the more products and service you are able to develop. And make no mistake about it, in most cases (for there are always exceptions) substantial financial success as an advisor is contingent upon your developing this wide array of products and services.

But as you begin to do so you need to rethink the entire matter of competition and what it means to you and your business. I like (in this connection) to consider the oligopolies and cartels of the nineteenth century. These were of course largely based on products: Carnegie with steel, Rockefeller and oil, later, Ford and cars.

Today's situation involves knowledge products.

The problem we are dealing with as regards competitors is a complicated one. How to enter into constructive engagements while not threatening our basic livelihood and how, simultaneously, to break out of the Time Trap and reap the truly impressive returns on what we know.

Step 6: Write a narrative description of your own Preferred Client.

You need to develop, as should by now be clear, a profile of your own preferred client. Just as you need to be aware of who your competitors are marketing to, so you need to develop a written narrative profile of who you are marketing to.

Step 7: Determine what are they buying today.

People and organizations are ALWAYS spending money no matter how bad the economy gets. This has always cheered me right up. To know that on any given day billions and billions of dollars are being spent sends a chill of excitement right through me. My task, and yours, is simply to figure out how to get my share of these unbounded riches.

Knowing what people are buying today always relates to one of four possibilities:

1) The product or service that will increase their profitability within the current fiscal year or enable them to reach another ultimate objective (say, health) as soon as possible.

Here a couple of things need to be pointed out. As you'll notice, I have again added the notion of product here. One of the tricks of the trade for successful advisors and independent professionals is to consider whether you would be better off putting your knowledge into the form of products and so help ourself break out of the Time Trap. For most of us, the answer is a resounding "Yes!"

Secondly, American enterprise and Americans as a whole are very much geared to short term thinking. This is part of the contemporary view of time. We have largely deleted our past and we continue to ignore the consequences of our contemporary actions upon the future. We have snuffed out heaven and hell and have reduced the richness of time to whatever is happening now. Americans are notoriously "now" oriented. This is both good — and disastrous.

It is good for those of us who can pitch our product and service as the solution to a problem which our client prospects have now. And the longest state of "now" is the current fiscal year of a corporation. As my father used to say (admittedly in a different context), "Tomorrow never comes." Or, "Eat, drink and be merrie for tomorrow we die!"

For advisors, our objective is to so position ourselves that we have a product or service which meets an ultimate objective of a client prospect in the shortest possible time, or not longer than beyond their current fiscal year.

Being able to offer such a result within the current fiscal year will not only meet our clients' needs for an immediate result but will help them sell the need for us to their decison makers. It is a lot easier to sell an advisor to a body of decision makers if they will see results in the near term. Speed, efficiency, results faster than expected — this is what our countrymen want.

Where the objective is not quantified and precise, such as increased widget sales, it is important notwithstanding to focus on a precise time period in which you can work the result. Thats why a product like "thirty days to thinner thighs" works: it offers a desired result within a finite period of time. The realization of the ultimate objective must be done in the most abbreviated period of time conceivable. Hence "the one minute manager".

2) The product or service that will cut expenses within the current fiscal year.

Please note, this item is not the same as number one, increasing profitability, although it is clear that cutting expenses can be a most important part of increasing profits.

In fact, during periods of prosperity people tend to emphasize point one above. That's because one is a sales and marketing point and when people have more money to spend sales and marketing regain their primacy in enterprises. During bad times, however, (like that in which I am writing) people look for ways to cut their expenses and stay afloat until the good times return. Hence an important point here: depending on the state of the economy in your field, these two items can change places.

Ordinarily, however, products and services designed to increase profitability will take precedence over those designed to cut expenses.

3) The product or service that will increase profitability beyond the current fiscal year.

This item is placed third for obvious reasons. With our notoriously short term thinking, Americans balk at plans that will increase profitability beyond the current fiscal year. It is harder to sell them until the benefits are extremely clear. This doesn't mean, however, that you should not develop a service or product in this area. Not at all. You should, however, realize the difficulties of selling it.

I wrote and published, for instance, two books on fund raising. One is entitled **DEVELOPMENT TODAY: A FUND RAISING GUIDE FOR NONPROFIT ORGANIZATIONS** and deals with how to raise money from corporations, foundations and individuals within a single fiscal year. Its companion volume is **THE COMPLETE GUIDE TO PLANNED GIVING: EVERYTHING YOU NEED TO KNOW TO COMPETE SUCCESSFULLY FOR MAJOR GIFTS**. Both books have been marketed identically and yet **DEVELOPMENT TODAY** has always outsold **THE COMPLETE GUIDE TO PLANNED GIVING**. This is very odd in some ways given the fact that the large capital gifts discussed in the latter book can often be many, many times what one can receive from corporations and foundations. People are, however, short term oriented and are not willing to put the time and effort into projects which may not pay off for ten or twenty years. "Eat, drink and be merrie. . ."

It should be clear to you that I would not advise you to begin your advising practice with a service (or product) in this category. As you diversify your offerings, by all means add items here. But if you are interested in making money early, don't begin here.

4) The product or service that cuts expense beyond the current fiscal year.

What I wrote above is even more applicable here. As you diversify your practice, by all means add a product or service that will help people cut long term expense. Don't, however, expect this to be their top priority. It almost never is.

A Note On Educating Your Client Prospects

In my workshops, participants continually ask me about what they should do if their clients are not aware of their problems. Should they, they ask rather plaintively, begin an "educational process" to alert their client prospects to their needs?

My answer to this question is, again, a strong "No!" Not unless, that is, you have the time, patience and wherewithal to wait until whatever educational process you launch takes hold. For make no mistake about it: if you have to educate your clients to an understanding of their problems, you are in for a very long wait.

I cannot say strongly enough that even under the best of circumstances, your clients will move slowly towards a decision. Let me give you but one example. I represent many community health agencies, visiting nursing agencies and homemaker home health agencies. In one way or another, these agencies are directly affected by the changing funding priorities of the federal govenment. Cutbacks in medicare, for instance, have made it difficult for visiting nurse agencies to offer long term patient care since they are not reimbursed for it at the level of their expenses. This problem has resulted in these agencies beginning to develop quite sizable deficits. This is a problem that is well known in their industry.

I know that the long term solution to this problem is either changing the funding priorities of the federal government or in developing sizable endowment funds for these agencies so that they can sustain their long term care programs. It is difficult, however, to get the agencies to focus on these problems when their immediate needs are so pressing.

Now I could spend all my time working on educating my clients about what they should be doing (and starve in the process) or I could do what I do do, namely focus on the agencies' current pressing problems and offer economical and efficient solutions to them. That, of course, is what I have done.

Each of us as experts will be well aware that our clients and client prospects are not performing up to our mark. That they are continually falling down from our expectations. And that as a result they are failing to achieve their ultimate goals and do the best work they can. One of the glories of our profession is that we are demanding, that we push our clients and our client prospects to do more, to achieve, to realize grander objectives. When it comes time for our apotheosis and entry into heaven's reward, this signal fact should be remembered about us.

You cannot stake your career on it though. Spend part of your time educating your clients for the future. Spend part of your effort in helping to prepare them for the developing world you already sense as palpable and near at hand. But spend the majority of your time working with their pressing problems in the here and now. Specifically those problems that impact on their profitability (or achievement of another ultimate) in the current fiscal year, or most immediate span of time.

Understanding The Next Step In Your Development: Going Top Drawer Or Universal

Truly successful advisors must make a decision about their career objectives and how to achieve them. Most of the advisors, both tyros and the seasoned, with whom I deal fidget around this issue and never quite come to a decision. As a result, they suffer; moreover, ultimately many fail and are driven from the business.

The longer you are in business, you will find that the bulk of advising monies are concentrated in just a few places. Studies show that 20% of your effort produces 80% of your return. I'd go so far as to say that 80% of the advising money will come from the top 20% of the client prospects in your industry. Obviously entering into this top 20% is, therefore, crucial to you. Positioning is what enables you to do so. Here, then, are a few tricks for proper positioning for success.

Entry into the top 20% of your business is not just a consideration of what you know and can do and the result that you produce. When you deal with the leaders of any field, you are dealing with people who have an often inflated view of themselves. They are and act like leaders. Rank, remember, hath its privileges, one of which is consorting with other leaders.

To be successful at the top rank of your buyers means to reflect the image these individuals have of themselves. Or, in short, you must be perceived as being a leader yourself so that by engaging you the leader gains reinforcement that he is himself a leader. Got it?

I well remember, for instance, one of my first sustained exposures to an independent advisor. It was while I was still working for a living. This advisor was retained by the college I was working for to prepare certain documents for its capital campaign. They were documents that could very well have been prepared in house but the job (thanks to the advisor's blandishments) was contracted out. The man's job was, as I came very well to learn, to prepare prototypes of certain key documents and to lunch monthly with the president of the college. What else he did was a mystery, although he did draw down a stipend of over $100,000 a year, higher than any full time member of the staff including the president herself.

I once chided him for this while lunching with him in his office in New York. We were eating lobster salad (paid for by us, served graciously by him), but he only smiled knowledgeably and refused to rise to the bait. Why should he? He was a Top Drawer advisor, and he played his lucrative game very well indeed.

At the top drawer level, therefore, many other factors besides outright competence enter into the reckoning. This is very, very difficult for most advisors to accept, feeling, as we all do, that competence should be the deciding factor in getting retained. Maybe it should be. But, as I can personally attest, it isn't!

The following factors enter into consideration:

- social skills
- personal connections
- education
- dress
- ability to charm and to entertain.

These are skills, in short, which enhance a leader's perception of himself and which provide confidence in the advisor. I don't think I'd be far wrong if, *in toto*, I defined the collective effect of these items as charisma.

My own hunch is that charisma alone will not suffice to sustain an advising practice for long. There must at some point be results. But charisma plus intelligence and the ability to solve people's problems is quite simply unstoppable. If you have the ability to assemble such a breathtaking package, do so because by following the rest of the suggestions of this book, your entry into the upper ranks of advisordom is assured.

Of this one thing I am sure: if you wish to live exclusively by selling a single service, or cluster of related services, you must secure entrée into the upper sector of your market. To be ideally placed, you should be offering a service that increases profitability within your client's current fiscal year and you should personally possess that combination of skills and attributes as listed above (generally defined a charisma) which make you a desirable part of any leader's entourage.

Who are some of the people we all know who have such skills? Henry Kissinger, of course, is one of them, a top consultant. Alexander Haig, advisor to the Amway Corporation, is another. So is Walter Cronkite, who makes more than a widow's mite from advising in his oh-so-gilded retirement.

These are quite clearly people who have pitched themselves at the very top part of their respective markets and who have not only skills (skills such as many, many other advisors can also rightly claim) but the necessary personal attributes, the charisma, the entire package.

Looking At The Top

Here's another thing you should know about this top rank of advising opportunities: money is freer there. I have discovered based on my personal experience and observations that the poorer and worse positioned the client, the more difficult he is about money, the more nagging and proprietary about my time. I try to be understanding about this; I know they need the help. But I often fail. People with less wherewithal and more problems cannot afford the baroque saraband of niceties, the long lunches, the weeks that go by without a telephone call to their advisor, that often distinguishes the upper reaches of the profession. All clients, you see, are not equal, and you must be calculating about where you'll spend your time.

- Deal with the richest organizations and individuals who need your services. When you're starting out, your clients may not be the most advantageously placed. Nonetheless, contract with the best you are able to.
- Work hard to bring yourself up to the level of the richest client prospects, to be perceived as being at their level, to reflect their status. Be the kind of advisor who reinforces their own perception of themselves as a leader in their field.

You will find that a more gracious life awaits you, that your fees will be more satisfying, and that the *sturm und drang* of many smaller clients will not aggravate you.

This, of course, doesn't happen by accident. It happens by positioning yourself properly: by targeting the most select group of client prospects in your market and bringing yourself up to their level.

Again, I must emphasize that mere knowledge, the mere ability to solve your client prospect's problems is not sufficient for success. There is a heavy psychological aspect to the successful advising practice. If you fail to be aware of it — and to profit from it — your practice must suffer.

The Mobile Mini-Conglomerate

Does this mean, though, that you want nothing to do with the other 80% or more of those other individuals and organizations who have problems you can solve? The answer is, "That depends."

- It depends on what your personal financial goals are.
- It depends on what your lifestyle goals are.
- It depends on what you want to do professionally and with whom you want to mix and in what way.

Many of the advisors with whom I come in contact have not answered these questions clearly and don't know what they want to do. As a result, they flounder.

Let me show you what I have in mind so that you won't.

There are approximately 1,000,000 voluntary organizations in this country. Virtually all must continually raise money for their capital, project, and operating expenses. Fund raising is a suitable field for advising, and there are many fund raising advisors in existence.

We can offer a service that returns a disproportionate benefit to our clients compared to our fee within the current fiscal year by raising their needed funds from corporations, foundations, and individuals. Thus we fit into positioning category #1 above. Nonetheless as a fund raising advisor, I have three significant problems to overcome:

- There are many competitor organizations and independent advisors.
- My client prospects are scattered around the nation.
- Even those near at hand, while needing the service, don't always have the funds available to pay for it.

To succeed in this field, one must overcome these problems by helping the maximum number of organizations succeed in reaching their objectives. We already know that there are one million such organizations. Sadly, however, at least 75% of them, while needing the service, will not be able to pay the high cost of an advisor, his daily fee and travel and accommodation expenses. Thus a substantial fraction of your market is not a realistic possibility because while having the problem you can solve, they don't have the means of paying you.

Thus deduct 750,000 from the one million available client prospects.

Of the remaining organizations, there will be a series of already existing specialized advising firms who cater to highly targeted markets: the fund raising advisors for hospitals, private schools and colleges, &c. Begin to deduct these numbers from the total remaining or at least to realize that to gain clients within these categories will take time to bring yourself up to the perceived status level of the top firms within any individual category.

By scanning your market closely, you will likely identify a niche which has not been served or where the existing competitors are new (like you) and not well established. Determining this niche is in part dependent upon what you want to do with your life. Let's say you are married with young children and cannot travel long distances. Based in Boston, you look at the nonprofit market and decide to become an advisor to community health centers, homemaker home health care facilities and visiting nurse agencies because there is no existing firm in your marketing territory catering to these clients. The number of such organizations in the state of Massachusetts is around 200.

By scanning the market, you discover that, yes, there is a niche and that, yes, you can fill it. You calculate, however, that working moderately hard your income will be about $50,000 a year (although to reach this figure you may have to reach into Rhode Island, Connecticut and New Hampshire.) This may be a sufficient income for you and if so, fine. If not, you must decide either to broaden your marketing territory, see about raising your fees (and hence perhaps invite a competitor to undercut you, and /or launch another problem solving service in your territory).

By following these steps you have secured a comfortable niche for yourself and can sustain your advising business accordingly. This is what I did during the first year of my practice, and it worked very well. But, I confess, it was not sufficient for me. This is what I mean when I say that the kind of practice you develop is very much dependent on the kind of lifestyle you want and what you are prepared to do to get it. I developed the Mobile Mini-Conglomerate, which I am now going to share with you, to reach objectives which could not as easily and effectively be met by running the traditional one-on-one client-advisor business.

Understanding The Mobile Mini-Conglomerate

The Mobile Mini-Conglomerate is based on several important points. It begins with your understanding that advising is not something which needs occur between two people, between yourself and a client, situated in the same room and in the same location but is rather a process whereby you, the expert and problem solver, have it within your power to solve the client's problem whether you are personally present or not.

In the Great Age of Information, it is possible for you, the problem solver, to be present in many ways to help people solve their problems not just by working one to one with a client. Advisors who simply ply their trade by being physically on site with a client are, therefore, missing most of the opportunities that come with this age.

Advising, to my mind, is a process that takes place whenever a knowledgeable and well informed expert helps a client prospect solve a problem through the use of the information and problem solving techniques at his disposal. Under this definition my being "with you" through this book is a form of advising in that with my step-by-step techniques I shall assist you in solving the problem addressed by this book: how to establish a successful independent advising business.

Now, as I have already pointed out but wish to reinforce here, you may neither wish nor need to transcend the immediate, personal nature of advising. Top drawer advisors like Kissinger and Haig make enough from dealing with a very few, select clients that their professional expectations (read income) are satisfied. They do not feel the need to create a line of problem solving products to solve other people's problems. At this level, the kind of advising they provide is exclusively tailored: each problem is looked at separately, separately analyzed and separately solved. Such customizing, as those who buy designer clothes have always known, is expensive.

Then there are those who have accepted for themselves a modest rate of return on what they know and can do. They are happy with a lesser income because they are free to pursue, in the spare time that that income provides, other interests. Let me stress: this is not my choice, but it may be yours. And it is acceptable given the way you choose to live your life.

Thus, on the one hand, if you are a Top Drawer advisor, you do not need to explore the possibilities of the Mobile Mini-Conglomerate because you are already among the highest wage earners in the nation. And you do not need to explore the Mobile Mini-Conglomerate if, on the other hand, you are happy having less, not squeezing the full benefit from what you know and can do.

The Mobile Mini-Conglomerate, however, offers an enthralling third possibility of opening the prospect for you of helping not just a few score of individuals and organizations but, literally, tens of thousands in many different problem solving ways. Using the illustration above in my case, for instance, it expands my advising practice in the nonprofit world into a national problem solving firm with many products and services all capable of being managed by a single individual.

Reasons For The Mobile Mini-Conglomerate

- The Mobile Mini-Conglomerate opens to you the entire prospect of your market. Through the Mobile Mini-Conglomerate and its many products and contract types, each individual or organization with the problem you solve can benefit from your advice through the use of a suitably priced vehicle.
- It provides a means of enhancing your standing and so not only opens up an enhanced profit possibility but the further likelihood of raising yourself to the status level of your best buyers. The Mobile Mini-Conglomerate, then, is a way of becoming a Top Drawer advisor!

- It gives you the satisfaction of knowing that you are being helpful to the maximum number of individuals and organizations. Advisors like being helpful. Those who implement the steps of the Mobile Mini-Conglomerate are unquestionably among the most helpful of advisors as measured in sheer bulk of people assisted.

- It breaks you out of the time trap in an often breathtaking way. By this I mean that you are ordinarily capable of being in only one place at a time physically. The Mobile Mini-Conglomerate allows "you" to be in many places simultaneously, dozens, hundreds, even thousands at once. Thus you are able through the Mobile Mini-Conglomerate to transcend the constraints and limitations that confine all people and most advisors.

- You are able to deal with the income uncertainty that is one of the debilitating aspects of being an advisor. One of the things people like about their mainline jobs (or, often, the only thing!) is the security of the paycheck. Independent advising doesn't offer beginning advisors or even necessarily well-established advisors this security. The nature of income is necessarily episodic with peaks and valleys as the work load waxes and wanes. This state of affairs need not happen to you, however. With the Mobile Mini-Conglomerate, drawing income as you will from many sources, this problem ceases to be a difficulty for you, and you will have the many benefits of being an advisor without the uncertainty of income, surely one of the chief drawbacks of this career.

Are there, then, no drawbacks to the Mobile Mini-Conglomerate? Of course not; there are a few! It is, for instance, demanding. You must be able to move back and forth between a variety of demanding occupations. You may find yourself in a single day doing the following: providing on-site advising with a client; working on research for a new information product you are developing; stacking books in your warehouse, and fulfilling orders for them, and delivering a paid evening problem solving process workshop.

People who operate Mobile Mini-Conglomerates lead hectic lives. I know.

I have this to say about the kind of life it is: contrary to what you may believe, it is actually mentally refreshing to move back and forth between a variety of different tasks. People ask me, for instance, why I personally send out the individual book orders. It's because after I've finished an hour or so of this kind of work, I feel mentally relaxed and eager to return to the more tiring tasks of researching, writing, and providing direct client services. You'll see what I mean when it happens to you! The reason why people put up with this degree of busyness is, however, clear: the bulk of the money coming in belongs to you. This, I must say, is a very real inducement and one which I am sure will provide the necessary inspiration seriously to consider the following parts of the Mobile Mini-Conglomerate and how you can make them work for you.

The Steps Of The Mobile Mini-Conglomerate

The Mobile Mini-Conglomerate is made up of the following 10 parts. Please note that the Conglomerate is a circuit and not a sequence; you can break into it at any point and move forwards and backwards until the circuit is complete. The important thing, however, is to consider all the ways of deriving profit from the problem solving information you have at your disposal. The Mobile Mini-Conglomerate allows you to do just that.

Step 1. Billable Time. You as advisor are hired to provide your problem solving advice on an hour, daily or project basis.

Step 2. Retainer Contracts. Under this arrangement, the client pays you a fixed amount of money, usually monthly, in return for your guarantee of availability for a fixed amount of time. Any additional time used by the client you bill him for directly at the end of the month at a previously agreed upon rate.

Step 3. The Supergroup of Independent Contractors. Your clients always have a variety of needs complementary to that being solved by you. A nonprofit organization using my services as development advisor may have, for instance, accounting and bookkeeping needs, legal work to be done, public relations and marketing requirements, computer assessment, various training programs to be mounted, &c. You maintain a list of individuals (other advisors mostly) in these fields and as the client's needs materialize, you market these individuals in return for a percentage of the fee.

Step 4. Problem Solving Articles and Special Reports by you. Articles alone may never be a large source of additional income for you but sold as Special Reports (see Catalog at end), they can well be. Moreover, they will promote your practice, enhancing your visibility and desirability simultaneously. These articles/Special Reports deal with problems your clients prospects need to have solved which you, of course, can handle expeditiously.

Step 5. Problem Solving Newsletters. The newsletters I have in mind are those that you sell nationally to individuals who have the problems you solve.

Step 6. Problem Solving Booklets and Books. Like **HOW TO MAKE AT LEAST $100,000 EVERY YEAR AS A SUCCESSFUL CONSULTANT IN YOUR OWN FIELD,** your booklets and books (usually self-published) are designed to solve the problems of those outside your primary marketing area or those who cannot afford, because of your daily and retainer rate, to hire you directly. Remember: this will easily amount to over 80% of the individuals and organizations who have the problem(s) you solve.

Step 7. Problem Solving Audio And Video Cassettes. This is the same as Step 6 except that you are selling your problem solving information on tape rather than paper.

Step 8. Problem Solving Talk Programs (Lectures, Workshops and Seminars). Again, the same.

Step 9. Cooperative Marketing Agreements. This is the product equivalent of the Supergroup of Independent Contractors. Through Step 3 you offer problem solving individuals; through Step 9 problem solving products. Try as you might, you can never produce all the products your clients need to have. I know. I am an assiduous worker and every day I find another new product, produced by another advisor somewhere in America, which I know my clients can profit from. Cooperative marketing agreements allow you to enter into marketing and sales relationships for any product which your clients need. To give you an idea of how these products can be marketed see my Success Catalog at the conclusion of this book.

Step 10. Capital Diversification Stage. The Mobile Mini-Conglomerate is so named because it is small (hence "Mini"), and can, thanks to the telecommunications and high tech revolutions of our time, be run out of a very small space, even a single room of your home. It is called "Mobile" because, it involves much travel and national contacts. And it is called a "Conglomerate" because, like other conglomerates, the profit you produce from the various divisions (above) can be used to purchase related and unrelated enterprises. This is what happens at Step 10 and why, as the Mobile Mini-Conglomerate becomes successful, you must spend part of your time mastering some of the many available investment vehicles.

The Mobile Mini-Conglomerate is designed to provide your various clients, those organizations and individuals with a problem you can solve, with that level of assistance which they can afford. Granted, the lesser priced services (for a product is a service) will not be particularly tailored to the client's situation. The client will have to extrapolate from what you provide to their own situations just as you must do with the information in this book. This should be acceptable, however, to the client given the disproportionate value of the information compared to what they are paying for it.

It goes without saying that you can be both a Top Drawer advisor and operate a successful Mobile Mini-Conglomerate. You can also be a Top Drawer advisor and not bother with the Mobile Mini-Conglomerate. And you can, ultimately, run a Mobile Mini-Conglomerate and find that one-on-one advising is the least significant part of your income. All this can happen, and you will still find yourself among America's top wage earners.

What must not happen is that you fall between the stools:

- You make no attempt to upgrade yourself and move into the top ranks of advisors and to attract the top clients where the top stipends are paid.
- You do not develop suitable information based products and services and continue to rely upon a single problem solving skill.
- You pitch your services to the bottom end of your market but keep your market territory too small to sustain your income and business operating expense requirements.
- You heap constraints upon yourself about what you will and won't do, even though you don't have the secure income sources to sustain such pretensions.

Advising, as I've often said, is not for everyone. Running an independent professional practice is not for everyone. And the reason is not just because of a failure to master the information of your specialty, as should now be clear.

What should also be clear is that marketing cannot succeed unless and until you have a very precise vision of where you are going, who you wish to serve, who you must compete with to be able so to serve, the ability of the people and organizations to pay for what you are serving, and the kind of income you wish to have and lifestyle you want to lead.

My precision in this regard unnerves many people who seem to find themselves unable to match it. This is rubbish! Your ability to succeed in business, as an advisor or any other independent professional, is directly related to the degree of precision with which you approach the topics in this chapter and this book as a whole. Airy vagueness has no place in your deliberations. If you will not do what is necessary to succeed, you have only yourself to blame if your advising business does not prosper. I follow these rules and prosper. You can do the same, or you can try to charm success from other much less certain ways. It's your decision.

CHAPTER 4

More Preparation

Are you ready to go off now without a second thought and establish your successful business? No! There's more preparation, much more preparation, before doing so.

The activities outlined in Chapter 3 could take you 90 days. The activities in this chapter will take less time but are equally important.

Chapter 3 told you how to position yourself and gave you a number of decisions that need to be made about your business. Here we consider the ways in which you can get business for yourself.

The Problem Solving Process

In a nutshell, an advisor, as should be already clear, is a person who solves other people's problems. As I said in Chapter 3, most people think an advisor is someone who solves problems in person. But that's not true. An advisor, simply understood, is a person who helps solve other people's problems in any way that exists — on the telephone, by letter, through articles, booklets and books, in lectures, workshops and seminars, through audio and video cassettes, and with other people's products.

To solve other people's problems, however, you need a process.

All books on advising tell you that each problem you'll encounter is unique. That no two problems are the same. That, like snowflakes, every situation you face will be different and that you cannot generalize from one problem to the next problem you deal with. This is both true and not true.

It is true that two problems will be different, the people will be different, the terms of engagement and the constraints will be different. Thus, no solution to a single problem can unthinkingly be applied to the solution of any other problem.

But the steps that you go through to solve your problems can and should be the same. That's where the Problem Solving Process comes in. I designed the Problem Solving Process, or rather deduced it, because I found myself with clients going through a series of steps each time, either in whole or part, as I began to deal with their problems. The result is a procedure which I now employ.

It's important to point out a few things about this procedure. The ways in which you implement each procedure each time you use it will be different. That's fair enough. But you've got to consider each step each time you confront a problem and make sure that it has been adequately dealt with. Otherwise you are courting disaster. The Problem Solving Process is an action-oriented sequence that helps you and the client move towards the solution of the problem. It recognizes that you have a part to play in the solution of problems but that in almost no case can the advisor unilaterally and solely bring about success without the direct involvement of the client. Ideally, you would sell the entire Problem Solving Process to the client as a package.

In practice, however, you'll find yourself in different situations selling different parts of the package for the following reasons:

1) The client has already dealt with some aspects of the package himself.
2) Other advisors have already been brought in and already made recommendations.
3) There is inadequate money available just now for dealing with all the problems sequentially and logically.
4) Other constraints come into play.

Remember about the Problem Solving Process, while every step has to be addressed in virtually every problem, you personally do not have to apply every step yourself. You can use your Supergroup of Independent Contractors to do so, to bring in, that is, other experts who can implement their own expert procedures and so help solve the client's problem. What is important is not so much who implements the procedures as that in every case due consideration is given to the fact that the steps are realized.

Here, then, are the steps of the Problem Solving Process. Make sure:

1) The client is mentally prepared to do what is necessary to achieve success.
2) The client is technically prepared to achieve success.
3) Both you and the client understand what the real problem is, the real objective.
4) The client has all the necessary documents for success.
5) The decision makers at the client's office are fully behind the project and will do what is necessary to make it a success.

6) You and the client agree on an implementation strategy for how success will be achieved.

7) You have agreed with the client on how success will be reported and how the inevitable obstacles of any relationship will be reported, too.

8) You and the client have agreed to the fact of a "clinic" following at intervals upon the conclusion of your contract to see how things are coming along.

This is the Problem Solving Process. Let's now see what each of these steps means and why it's necessary.

- **Make sure the client is mentally prepared to do what is necessary to achieve success.**

Clients are people, first, and usually American people at that. We have become, as current studies gloomily confirm, a fat and slothful people. Fifty years into the "American century" we show signs of rampant decay and disintegration. No one likes to hear this. Jimmy Carter got his ass whipped for saying it. Ronald Reagan made hay for ignoring it. It's, however, a fact and the sad evidence of this fact is all around us.

Every client prospect you approach will tell you that he wants to achieve success. Success, after all, is the only thing most Americans believe in anymore. But most of us want our success to be easy, effortless, and certainly not disruptive to our daily lives and routines. Success at such a cost is not acceptable. Hand it to us on a silver platter, we seem collectively to say, or go away and let us seek out a new, less demanding conjuror promising what we seek.

Because this attitude is rampant in our society, you must be alert to it. It is easy to see the advisor as god, and many advisors are quite prepared both to be seen as god and sell themselves accordingly as the people who can deliver whatever the client wants.

Most of us advisors and independent professionals are in no way able to deliver results without the direct involvement of the client. Client involvement is key and lack of such involvement is perhaps the chief reason why so many advisor-client relationships fail to be productive.

In my own advising practice, for instance, nonprofit organization after nonprofit organization comes to me seeking money. There isn't a not-for-profit organization in the nation that doesn't, as a knee jerk reaction, say it wants more and more money. Modeled after Oliver Twist in the workhouse, their collective, plaintive cry is "We want some more, sir!" This much I take for granted: my clients and client prospects always want more!

What, I wonder, are they prepared to do to get it? Are they prepared to:
- work more hours, week-ends and holidays
- mount events which take time and creativity to arrange
- stimulate Board members and remove those past being helpful
- ask and ask again of those who are capable of giving
- learn not to take "No!" for an answer?

I put these questions to my client prospects as directly as I can. I ask them, in short, whether they are mentally ready to do the tasks that need to be done to achieve the success they say they want to have. Time after time, they decide that, while the money would be nice if somebody gave it to them, they really don't want to put themselves out to get it.

Having made this decision, they retire to do whatever they like to do: usually grousing about the difficulty and intractability of the world.

Now, my workshop participants are usually aghast when I tell them this technique. They are upset because:
1) I have discouraged a client.
2) I have lost the business.
3) I have established myself as a stern, unyielding taskmaster.

They wonder why I do it.

Quite simply, the answer is because all people, all putative client prospects are not prepared to work for success, and those who are not should be assiduously avoided.

If I were to take on a nonprofit client who felt I could, by dint of means known only to myself, produce funds miraculously, and who felt that the task of fund raising could be dumped on me and that they could as a result avoid their collective responsibility, we would collectively be setting ourselves up for disappointment. In effect I would be agreeing to be their scapegoat.

Mental preparation, as I said in Chapter One of this book, is always a necessary (if not a sufficient) precondition for success. You will find yourselves again and again confronting client prospects who will tell you, with the best will in the world, unaware of the depth of their own self-deception, just how badly they want to achieve success. As you talk to them, however, as talk to them you must, you will see that they don't wish to achieve success at all. They wish, instead, to be perceived as publicly as possible as working to achieve success without doing any of the things that are actually necessary to reach it.

In this connection, here are some of the assignments I've faced:

1) The board of directors of a summer camp for mentally retarded children (that I had successfully worked with for two years) dropped the fund raising program after I pressed them for a higher level of direct board contribution. They not only refused to give but dropped the fund raising program altogether and significantly scaled back the size and activities of the camp. In this connection, one can only deduce that the governors of the organization cared more about their own pocketbooks than about the children they were supposed to be concerned about.

2) An executive director of a special needs adoption agency (for handicapped and other distressed children) finds he doesn't have the stomach for fund raising after meeting a particularly abrupt and discourteous foundation official who doesn't like him and lets him know it. The executive director discovers he has a very thin hide and his enthusiasm for fund raising wanes considerably.

These people don't understand what it takes to achieve success or, understanding it, will not do what it takes. In any event, they are not mentally prepared to achieve success and ought to be avoided like the plague.

I tell you quite candidly I feel somewhat contemptuous of these people and their softness and slackness. I don't understand how they can continue to deceive themselves into believing that they are doing what is good for their businesses (in this case the people they service) and yet so consistently not do it. Their reaction is, however, entirely characteristic of so many.

I have the gut feeling that a large majority of consultancies do not produce the beneficial results that both parties say they want to produce. I further have the feeling that this is because on the one hand the advisor is not strict enough with the client to say what needs to be done and how, and the client doesn't want to hear about any bitter pill anyway.

Remember, though, where we got the word consultant in the first place. It comes from the British medical establishment. Beginning in the nineteenth century with the rise of the great medical establishment, consulting physicians were those specialists who received cases, difficult, perplexing, vexing cases that other physicians could not solve. They were the ultimate experts — and as such they acted and charged accordingly, just as we, their advising descendants, do today.

Looking back to our heritage, I remind my workshop participants that all we advisors are like these medical specialists and that we must learn from them. It is our job to set forward the best possible advice in the way best expressed for client use. It is our job to help the client visualize the realistic objective (if he is not altogether clear about it, as he often is not) and to put forward realistic steps for achieving this objective.

You will find, as I have found, that there is nothing to be gained by being at all reticent with a client in either expressing the dimensions of the problem or exactly what needs to be done to solve it successfully. If you have been in business but a short time or are only now contemplating going into your business, you may, you will!, be inclined to give the client the benefit of the doubt, to believe what the client tells you at face value about what he will do about solving the problem. The longer, however, you are in business, the more a grizzled veteran you become, you will, like me, take all this verbiage with a grain or two of salt. In truth, clients always secretly harbor the fantasy the the advisor will save them — and save them, mind you, with a minimum of their own involvement.

They want to believe this, they do believe this, even when they know, as professionals themselves, that much of whatever success they obtain will be owing to their own substantial efforts, linked to the advisor, of course, deriving from information and concepts at the advisor's command, but owned and implemented by them. As, of course, it should be!

When I began my practice over six years ago, I believed, as you probably still believe, that people given the opportunity and the necessary assistance would pursue the solution of their problems earnestly and with gusto, with a mind, in short, to their economical and quick resolution. I no longer believe this. In part, I think that all people at all times are on the look out for the White Knight who can and will absolve them of responsibility for their actions and who can take it upon themselves to solve our problems for us — without, of course, anyone being the wiser for it except the courteous White Knight himself who, being the hired hand, will be dispatched elsewhere. I have shifted, in short, from a belief in classical liberal theory to becoming the deepest Hobbesian.

If you think this is sad, that one so young and fair as I should at such an early age be quite so cynical, think again. My success rate has gone up as my expectations about humanity have gone down. A realistic view of humanity as epitomized by your client is of the utmost necessity as you approach the solution of their problem and the ability to look past the honied words and the calm assurances to see what they will actually commit, what they actually mean to do; for make no mistake about it, if your clients can get away with doing less, they will automatically do so because, after all, under such circumstances they have the satisfaction of knowing that, having eschewed all responsibility, they have yet readily at hand that one necessity — the scapegoat, who just happens to be you!

- **Make Sure The Client Is Technically Prepared To Achieve Success**

As I have written above, mental preparedness is a necessary but not a sufficient precondition for success for you and your clients. You, they, must together be not merely mentally prepared but technically ready. In this connection there are three ways of ensuring that the technical assistance which the client needs is available to them:

- Staff training programs
- Assisting the client with staff recruitment
- Using advisors (both yourself and members of your Supergroup of Independent Contractors).

Staff Training Programs

There are two distinct reasons for having staff training programs: either the staff needs to be brought up to a level to effectively work with you and so help the client get the best use of your time and expertise, or the organization wishes to train its staff in your problem solving techniques and procedures and so hope to dispense with the need for using you in other, more expensive, more long-term situations. Both are valid situations for the advisor. I regularly find myself in both during the course of a year.

As to the first point, we advisors are expensive. Moreover, as we move more and more to mandarin status, it is perfectly permissible, and indeed of the utmost necessity, that we not do certain kinds of tasks which can best be undertaken by others. Let me use an example.

In the beginning of my advising practice raising money, you'll recall, as development counsel for nonprofit organizations, I often found myself in a situation writing the necessary documents for my clients: full fledged development proposals, fund raising précis, &c. That was in the beginning. . .

Now I train people, using both training seminars and my book **DEVELOPMENT TODAY: A FUND RAISING GUIDE FOR NON-PROFIT ORGANIZATIONS** in which all the relevant documents are to be found, to do the necessary documents themselves. That way they can make the best use of me in an advisor-client relationship and use me to do what they most need and what I do best: sniff out likely sources of funding for them and set to work with them getting the money they need.

In other words, as their advisor I fix my attention exclusively on the highest and best use of my time which should, and does, overlap with their highest need: their need, in this case, for capital, project and operating funds.

While I could write their documents for them, that is not the best use of either my time or their money, for writing documents is a skill that is easier to learn that the more creative, demanding and, frankly, esoteric business of locating suitable funding sources.

Creative, demanding and esoteric it might be, but, of course, my clients want to learn this skill themselves. Either they wish to do so because:

- they have full time staff who ought to be employed in, this case, raising funds;
- they are too small and too far away to make a long-term advising relationship plausible and likely, or,
- they have the suspicion that my "tricks of the trade" are such that anyone applying a modicum of intelligence can learn them and so dispense with the need for little ol' me.

In such situations, you are training people not to be able to have skills to work with you but to acquire the skills for dispensing with you altogether. These are two very different things, but, need I say?, both necessary in the diversification of your practice and in the implementation of your Problem Solving Process.

Understand this, whatever the client says to the contrary (about your engagement being short term and to train others and so do without the need for you!), you must regard this training assignment as the thin edge of the wedge, as an opportunity, that is, to begin to build a longterm relationship with the client.

Clients are necessarily conservative and cautious when it comes to using advisors. Many people have had a bad experience with an advisor or independent professional of any kind. They have spent their money and achieved disappointing results. Or else, they have heard about this happening to a friend or associate. You must regard such negative feelings as the norm, rather than the exception, and proceed accordingly.

If you are being brought in to do a staff training program, to impart the skills that you have and that the client is convinced the staff can learn (and so dispense with the need for a longterm involvement with you), be clear with the client that:

- the best results come from working with you over a reasonable span of time, in having you there to work through all the stages of the Problem Solving Process, but
- working together you can achieve certain fixed objectives through a training session, if and only if this session is followed up at a later time.

As an adult educator, I can be very clear about this point. Adult learners need to hear what you've got to say about the success techniques you have learned and which you now come to teach them, but they also need time to read any written materials you may have and, more importantly, to work through your techniques on their own jobs.

I give, for example, many, many training seminars on marketing and promotion during the course of the year. These workshops are inevitably favorably evaluated by participants but over time I have become increasingly dissatisfied with them. In the beginning it was enough for me to give a good program, to be satisfactorily evaluated, and to have the knowledge that I gave a sufficient amount of significant, practical information which, if applied properly, would help my clients (for so I regard all those taking the training session) reach their objectives.

As I discovered, however, all too many people taking these training programs regarded the program as the be all and end all of their connection to the topic at hand. They didn't, in short, systematically go about implementing the new procedures they had learned and, having no need to report success to anyone, didn't bother to do much.

As an educator I found this sufficiently irritating that notwithstanding the actual satisfactory evaluation of the programs, I began to tell clients that while workshops and training sessions would be mounted to their satisfaction, the best results would only be achieved by follow-up and reporting of success (and stumbling blocks) at sufficient intervals. In short, there must be a systematic attempt to implement a success system involving the new information.

Sadly, most clients will not agree to a package initially, that is a package consisting of an initial training session and some periodic follow-up sessions. Expect this. Understandably clients wish to see exactly what they are buying. This is true notwithstanding an exalted reputation and a sheaf of testimonials and endorsements from satisfied clients. Don't be insulted, therefore, when the client holds back even while acknowledging the merit of your point.

Do, however, immediately sit down with the client following a successful training session and indicate how you'd like to follow up the day with a half-day mini-program in 90 days, when participants should have had the opportunity to begin implementing your success techniques.

To summarize: clients will be cautious about buying a complete training package consisting of initial presentation and one or a series of follow-up, reporting, sessions. Expect this.

Do, however, set finite tasks in your training sessions and the correct sequencing of tasks against a calendar of dates: what happens, when. If and when you do return, you can structure your next program around these tasks and what participants have accomplished.

Such a subsequent program will, I guarantee you, be a real eye-opener both for you and for your client. You see, the client probably still believes that reasonable people will behave reasonably and that beneficial tasks will be followed to their beneficial conclusion. Any subsequent training session will prove that a more structured approach to achieving success is absolutely necessary and thus plays right into your hands for a longer-term relationship. The client needs to see just how necessary you and your actual skills are, how deceptively simple they may appear to be when initially discussed and shown in your initial presentation but how long it actually takes people to master them. That will pave the way for you and a longer, more sustained relationship with this client.

Remember something else: you may be one of those advisors (like I often am) who thinks that the skills you have mastered can easily be mastered by others. Those of us with a background in humane letters often believe this despite all evidence to the contrary. I, for instance, who am a fast and (don't you agree?) easy-to-read writer, forget that this is not a universal skill.

Thus the fund raising documents that I teach others to write are not quite so easy for them to produce as the ones I myself oversee. If, on the one hand, there is a tendency for us advisors to see ourselves as little gods (a tendency, I need hardly say, that our client prospects themselves are inclined to foster for their own purpose), there is also the counter tendency, equally apparent, to disregard certain of our skills because they are, to some extent, possessed by many people. "Why do we need to hire a professional speaker," as one man said to me, "when everyone in our organization can talk?" That's the problem exactly, and I confess to you that it is important to keep in mind just how valuable your skills are without letting that knowledge lead on to a debilitating hubris and the arrogance which is so endemic in our profession.

Assisting The Client With Staff Recruitment

Often it will happen that the necessary staff needed by the client so as to work with you and help implement your success procedures will need to be recruited. Thus you will find yourself in the position of billing the client for:

- writing the job description
- assisting to launch the personnel search
- assessing the credentials of various candidates
- interviewing selected candidates
- helping in other ways to structure the job and find the appropriate candidate.

I do quite a lot of this. There are several reasons why you should, too:

- You'll be building up your own team within the organization. Although this result is scarcely foolproof, the individual who enters an organization thanks in part to you should be willing to work cooperatively with you to achieve the solution to the problem at hand. And always remember: you are there to achieve success, a success which can be leveraged by you to gather more and better clients who want to replicate this success in their own situations.
- You will, in the candidate in question, get the person with the necessary skills to bring about the success.
- You will be building a beneficial relationship with the client. Remember: client trust builds slowly. This is natural, given previous experiences with advisors and their own reluctance to spend money, no matter how attainable the success. Allowing the client to get to know you better is very much in your interest since you want, after all, to involve the client in the multi-step Problem Solving Process as well as use the client as a happy and satisfied customer and so help promote you to others who are similarly situated and can benefit from your assistance.

Some clients may attempt to get you to provide these services for free, arguing that until the staff is complete, you cannot work and that you will be compensated by being paid when the staff is, indeed, whole. This argument is decidedly spurious. Seeking and finding appropriate personnel is a terribly expensive business both in terms of time and money. Finding the right person, who has the necessary skills and who is prepared to make the necessary commitment to success, is a very important skill and if you are exercising it on behalf of a client you deserve to be compensated at your usual level. But remember: if you are not prepared to stick up for your rights and say this, don't expect the client to do so. As I advise my clients, if you can get the service for free, don't bother to pay for it. Learn, reader, learn.

Because this staff person can be so important for you, I hope it goes without saying that you will give the utmost consideration to who you need and the skills this person must have. Write them down and draft a narrative profile of the candidate you have in mind. Remember: with this person or people in place, the people you want and must have for success, you have a far greater likelihood of in fact achieving this success and making the assignment useful far beyond its current bounds.

Using Advisors

The truth of the matter is that most people haven't got the foggiest idea how to get the best use from an advisor, what they can ask the advisor to do and what kinds of results are possible working with an advisor. That's where you, the ever solicitous problem solver, come in.

From the very first moment of approach to a client prospect and, of course, through all the stages of your relationship, stay helpful. Often times, for instance, I find myself in a competition with other advisors for a contract. The kinds of organizations with which I work may not previously have worked with an advisor, and they have some very basic questions about what an advisor is and what he does. Because these questions are basic, they often feel, quite wrongly, sheepish about asking them.

I know the questions, however, and I don't feel sheepish at all acting like an advisor and helping people. Recently, for instance, I was in a competition to secure the fund raising account of a Massachusetts visiting nursing agency. I am, of course, well known in that market but the agency in question wanted to interview a number of candidates. That's fair enough.

During the course of my interview I asked the people seeing me whether they had had many dealings with development advisors and nary a person had. I then asked them whether they would find it helpful if I put to them a series of questions which they might ask of the advisor candidates. They said they would. And of course, no fool I, I put out a series of questions the answers to which I knew would benefit me and the methods I use and which, as I pointed out, were to be found in my fund raising book. I got the contract, a year's retainer agreement.

It is your obligation, and very much to both the advantage of yourself as well as your client, to act at all times like the advisor, even during the pre-contract phase of the relationship.

Thus, if you are in a competition, help the people; if they are unfamiliar with advisors make sure that they get the person they want, the person who has the information and problem solving processes they need and the one whose operating style will be compatible with their own.

If you are not yourself in a competition, help the organization bring in advisors in other fields who will be right for the task at hand. Needless to say, these advisors can and should be members of your Supergroup of Independent Contractors so that you can get the benefit of their contract.

Is this a conflict of interest? Surely not. Have you taken the time to select these people and assure yourself that they can in fact benefit the client? Would it take time for the client independently to find such people? Would it be expensive? Is this a service you are providing to the client? The answer, of course, to all these questions is "Yes!"

You ought, to be sure, to inform the client that the advisors in question have a relationship with you. There is nothing wrong with that. You needn't discuss with the client the exact monetary relationship you have with the advisor, that goes beyond the bounds of what it is necessary for you to tell. But it stands to reason that if the client has established a beneficial trust relationship with you and is happy with your work, they will take your recommendation in other areas. You'd be a fool not to benefit from that situation accordingly.

- **Make sure that both you and the client understand what the real problem is and the real objective for your consultancy.**

As I'll emphasize again and again, more advising relationships come acropper because the parties are at cross purposes about the purpose of the assignment. Either they are not clear at the commencement of the relationship about what each of the parties is to do, either because it is not convenient to be clear or because they are simply lazy, or they simply get started hoping that things will sort themselves out. This is, of course, a prescription for disaster.

There is always a research component in any advising relationship. The advisor has to work to get a clear understanding of what the real problem is before he can devise means to deal with it. As I'll discuss later, this research can take any of a number of different forms. You can:

- use questionnaires
- use site visits and interviews with administrators and staff
- review documents and past records.

The course you'll take will vary with the situation, what the client has done on his own, and your own expertise. That's fine.

The problems begin to develop when you see difficulties the client doesn't or that the client doesn't wish to solve.

Say, for instance, I wish to function as a development advisor for an organization and help raise needed funds. Before I can do that, I need to take a close look at the organization's ability to raise funds, which always necessarily involves the full cooperation of the Board of Directors in both giving and getting funds. Say, however, the Board refuses to cooperate, wanting to have the funds raised, of course, but refusing to participate in the actual fund raising process. The typical "hands off" situation that so many of us advisors typically confront.

If the Board (and more particularly, the Chairperson of the Board) refuses to see this issue as a real problem, I have several courses of action:

- I could go ahead with the contract hoping (and praying) that the issue will solve itself during the course of our relationship.
- I could opt for a training session with the Board and take soundings following such a meeting and see whether, having been apprised of certain critical facts about the fund raising business, their attitude changes.
- I could meet privately with the Chairperson of the Board and attempt to persuade him to my point of view with a mind towards also changing the minds of his colleagues.
- I could refuse the contract altogether giving my detailed and specific reasons and citing the likelihood of failure if the full involvement of the governing body did not occur.

Before taking any of these courses of action, however, I would necessarily have to spend some time with the organization to research the problem. What I found during the research phase would inevitably influence my findings.

Now, as with all the other parts of the Problem Solving Process, this research phase can be separately contracted. In some instances it may produce results which do not lend themselves to immediately going ahead to the next stage. Say, for instance, that, in my research into the organization and its situation, I discovered that the Chairperson of the Board was entirely disinterested in fund raising and entirely unwilling to be of assistance but that the Board, for other reasons, was not willing to remove him from his post. My research might lead to the conclusion that any major fund raising effort would have to await a resolution of this difficulty.

What is important to point out is that as a result of any of these phases you may find yourself either:

1) not wanting to go on to another stage because the organization is not ready for it, or
2) having the organization tell you it wishes to spend some time implementing the information and findings they have already been given by you (as, for instance, in a training session).

In either case, you need to stay in regular contact with the organization and see how things develop. Throughout the course of this book, I shall again and again be suggesting that you be persistent, doggedly persistent, with any organization or individual with whom you have worked in the past, persistent because, whatever the dimensions and urgency of their problem, it will take them time to think about and digest the benefits of becoming involved with you.

Remember, too: your research findings may, perhaps will, point to the need to have other advisors involved in helping to solve the client prospect's problems. If you yourself cannot go on with the prospect immediately, don't forget the possibility of selling one of your colleagues.

One sad thing I have discovered in the process of building my advising practice is that clients move a lot slower to take action to solve their problems than I'd like them to. One of the very frustrating things about this job is that I can see with excruciatingly clearness that a client prospect has a very definite problem; I can be very precise about what I can do to solve that problem to the client's substantial benefit. I can document that benefit to my own and (I trust) to the client prospect's satisfaction, yet despite all this lowering of their risk, there is still an often fatal hesitation about taking action.

I have come to learn, as I shall discuss later, that taking any kind of action is a terrible risk for many clients. So often they would rather risk the possibility of bleeding to death (The Hemorrhaging Phenomenon), slowly, steadily, than take action to arrest the problem and begin implementing a solution.

Worse, I have come to the realization that I can tell within a very short period of time, a single hour's meeting, whether the person I am confronting has what it takes to be able to tackle a problem head on with the chance for a solution, or whether he doesn't. More and more in such situations I trust my gut hunch about whether to do business with them or not. When I disobey that feeling I inevitably rue the day.

- **Make sure the client has all the necessary documents for success.**

Advising is a paper business. We advisors thrive on producing paper, much of it worthless. Still, to ensure that the client gets the utmost benefit from your advising, help him create all the necessary success documents he can use over and over again after you've departed to your next assignment.

No matter how technical your assignment, you'll find you'll be creating for the client a series of written materials to help them best utilize the information you are imparting. These materials include:

- proposals
- training manuals
- instructions
- précis

- contracts
- diagrams
- plans
- letters

- articles
- media kits
- speeches, etc., etc.

Anything that can be written, can and should be written by an advisor.

You need to produce these documents because the client cannot absorb your technical expertise as quickly as you can put it out. Thus, while it is useful if you can be present to instruct people, whether or not this is possible (and it often isn't), you can still produce the necessary documents that people can use after you've departed.

These documents must be clear, simple, concise and should deal with all the problems that you expect readers to find in implementing your particular technical information. Sadly, much of what advisors produce is vague, highfalutin, pompous and ponderous. This, I think, is partly by design and partly out of laziness. Good writing, as has often been said, is simple writing and simple writing is anything but simple to produce. Lean, taut writing is as much an art as having a lean, taut body after 30: it's difficult, demanding, and needs constant work.

The documents you produce for the client should be sold to the client for one-time-only use. Advisors are often very, very fuzzy on this point. One of the questions that pops up consistently in my advising training program is: "Can I use a training manual that I wrote for Company X a year ago. I want to sell it to another company now."

Leaving aside the question of whether it's a good idea to reuse the same training manual without updating it, let me say this in response:

The company contracting with you for the production of the training manual will presume that it has bought all rights from you. Given the fact that you did not add a specific clause saying that you were selling one-time-only use rights and that any further use of the material beyond the specific terms of your engagement was reserved to you, the creator, and that permission had specifically to be granted, you have probably lost that right. Now, practically, you can go ahead and use the material since it is unlikely (but by no means impossible) that the other organization would sue you, but in fact having failed to specify which rights you were holding, the company would regard itself entirely naturally as having bought all the rights.

This brings up a terribly important problem and one that advisors as a whole are very bad at solving; one that I see, for instance, on a continuing basis with the advisors I encounter and counsel.

- **The Issue Of Separable Rights**

We live in an age of very complicated rights questions and advisors are always and necessarily involved in them, though they often don't realize it. We are all familiar with the multiple rights that come, say, through a new feature film where there may be box office rights, television replay rights, video rights, product rights, song rights, &c. What we are not so familiar with are the various rights questions that may emerge out of the most prosaic advising assignment.

And I mean prosaic, for the more ordinary the problem is that is being solved by the particular materials being produced, the more universal it is, the more important it is that the rights question be addressed and the less likely it will be.

To wit: every nonprofit organization in America needs to develop skills for writing funding proposals for private corporations and foundations. If I write a funding document for an agency and do not specify what rights I am selling, they have the right to use that document not only for their own funding purposes but to sell the format to other agencies that need to master that skill and have the same problem. In practice, you may argue that the agency would not do that and that may be true. It remains an option for them, however.

Thus, be very clear that whatever you produce for an organization be sold to them for use only within that organization and only to solve the particular problem that they brought you in for. If you are producing the training manual mentioned above, for instance, be clear that you are selling what may be regarded as first usage rights and that you have retained all subsequent rights to that material. If such a clause is inserted in your contract, then you know full well that you and you alone have the necessary rights.

This becomes a most important consideration when you begin to develop your own paper profits empire based on booklets, books and other written materials, and when you begin to develop your own information-based audio cassettes, too.

Take my example above. Say that you decide to produce a one-hour audio cassette entitled "Money making proposals" and accompany it with a 25-page booklet packed with suggestions and illustrations, including successful proposals from past advising assignments.

It should be obvious why you would want to do this. There are a lot of organizations in this country, the vast majority in fact, with the need for this kind of skill but which cannot afford to bring you in on a one-to-one basis to offer it. Evening training programs, where many organizations band together, may also not be a feasible way of learning your problem solving skills, so that the only chance you have of helping them solve their problem and bringing the information they need to their attention (in a way that is profitable for you and cost effective for them) is through some product information source. You will, however, be opening yourself up to the prospect of needless difficulties unless you have maintained all the rights in question. This is true for whatever you have produced, including software, one of the new wrinkles in this problem.

Whatever you are producing, however, make sure you reserve the rights to yourself and so use the information you are producing and the solutions that you find working to solve other people's problems to enhance your direct profit potential.

Let me make this very clear to you: no situation should be perceived in terms of its uniqueness but rather in terms of its most universal interest. Every situation will be different from every other situation you confront to some extent. If you perceive problems only as distinct and unrelated, however, you will find yourself frustrated because of your inability to derive the maximum benefit from what you know.

In this regard, I have a recalcitrant former student now practicing his advising business in New Orleans. He helps retail establishments deal with employee theft of property and receipts. Any business that deals with cash receipts has the kinds of problems he addresses and thus the number of businesses that could use his services rises quickly into the many millions.

Nonetheless he is barely making a go of it.

That's because he approaches each problem as somehow autonomous and unrelated to any other problem, while, as I have consistently told him, the reverse is true. He needs to take the lessons derived from individual clients and apply them as widely as possible through all the possible mechanisms available — which means, ultimately, products.

Don't you make his mistake.

Develop documents which are specific to an individual client's situation but retain all but first rights to this material (that is, the ability of the client to use the materials you develop to solve his own problems) and sell them to others who have the same problem but not, perhaps, the same ability to bring you in on a direct one-to-one basis to solve it.

I often wonder why this particular lesson is so difficult for advisors to learn, and yet I see evidence daily that it is so.

- **Make sure the decision makers at the client's office are fully behind the project and will do what is necessary to make it a success.**

It is all very well to have a good idea and even the introductory support of mid-level people about the problem that needs to be solved and even the willingness to proceed to solve it, but unless key decision makers are interested in the problem solving process and committed to its success (which means doing their part to make it successful), you'll find yourself frustrated and success elusive.

In this connection, remember your LaFontaine, the renowned French fable writer. The mice gathering one day unanimously agreed that it would be a superb idea to bell the cat and so have themselves alerted when danger was near. The problem, of course, was that none of them wanted to assume the risk of the job. We might remember this in our assignments. Everyone wants success. Americans are good at mouthing the shibboleths and buzz words of success without for a moment committing themselves to doing what is necessary to achieve it.

This well-known state of affairs becomes terribly difficult for us advisors who do not ourselves have the responsibility to dictate courses of action and ensure that they'll be followed. Hence we must have the complete and unqualified support of decision makers before there is any chance of bringing about the success which all parties say they want and need.

Oftentimes the key decision makers want success — but have their own ideas about how to go about getting it, ideas which may very well conflict with your own operating procedures. You need to know this in advance.

To avoid getting the unproductive results which so often dog advising assignments, you need the utmost clarity at the commencement of a relationship, and that means even before a contract is actually signed. You must be rigorously certain that the individuals who have the power to implement change are actually interested in doing so, or whether they are not.

While writing this chapter, I happened to be reading the life of Margot, Countess of Oxford & Asquith, a well-known English personality earlier in this century, both in own right and as wife of England's World War I prime minister, H.H. Asquith. As the war opened and England's position deteriorated, Asquith fiddled and at least appeared to do nothing. Public opposition grew and ultimately he was removed from power and replaced by the Welsh firebrand, Lloyd George.

Asquith was the decision maker who needed to be convinced to alter his mode of governance but for one reason or another he failed to do so, failing to take advice which was in his own best interest and that of his government. We advisors very often deal with such people in our professional life, much more often than we'd like to admit, too. So let me say this as strongly as I can: discern early on, as early as possible, not whether the client prospect regards change as a good thing (remember LaFontaine's mice) but to what extent the client is prepared to commit resources, including changing his own habitual patterns of behavior, and so achieve the success which he freely admits he'd like to have. Sadly, you'll find it a lot less often than ought to be the case.

- **Make sure you and the client agree on an implementation strategy on how success will be achieved.**

As should be clear by now, I think that diagnosing the problem, while important, is by no means the most difficult part of your advising assignment. Implementing change strategies is far more demanding and frustrating for all concerned. Even those willing to do what is necessary to achieve success and solve the problem at hand may do so in ways which are dilatory, unsatisfactory, meandering and lackadaisical. This is why you must give your sustained attention to the development of an implementation strategy.

An implementation strategy involves settling the means you will use to achieve the success which, by now, all parties are agreed upon wanting. It involves the following questions:
- Where will our meetings take place?
- Who will be involved?
- How long will they last?
- What kinds of minutes will be taken?
- By whom?
- Who will get them?
- How will communication between meetings take place?

As you will shortly see, in the next section of this chapter and in Chapter 8, the answers to these questions enable you to offer a client different contract modules based on different answer possibilities as well as offer a very clear means for structuring success.

I have found that unquestionably one of my highest uses in solving problems is not simply being able to ascertain what a problem is, not merely being able to gather information about this problem, not only getting the full support of executives to implement change strategies but being the unending gadfly, the unsettling burr, the nag who pushes and pushes some more to ensure that there will be some measure of success.

Let's be honest: this is not a role that many people like but it is a critical role in any advising assignment. Merely identifying a problem does not solve that problem. Merely getting the concurrence that executives want to solve the problem and will work to solve the problem does not solve the problem. What solves the problem is overseeing the day-to-day implementation of problem solving procedures, dealing with the many smaller questions which inevitably arise on the road to total success, and being able to communicate, openly, candidly, honestly, your genuine, authentic conclusions about actions which are taking place during the consultancy. Call yourself a goad, a gadfly, a "can do" man, whatever you like. The result is the same: you are a pusher for success. It's a role that is very draining. And absolutely essential.

During the writing of this chapter, I happened to see the film "Gypsy" on television. You remember Mama Rose, the quintessential show-business mother who pushed, pulled, wheedled, argued, schemed and cajoled to make progress towards her dream? Rose, of course, was an advisor; she was willing to do what it takes to achieve the success that she wanted. But her life, while edifying, was scarcely always happy. "Why is it, Herbie," she asks her departing fiancé, "that everybody walks out on me?" The answer is disturbingly clear: mediocre people don't like success pushers, feel uncomfortable around them, acuse them of being workaholics, urge them to lay off, take it easy, have a good day and a million other things except the one thing that the success pusher is there to produce: the process which brings about success.

Mediocre people don't want to know this, don't want to know that getting success often means giving up other things, including the ability to tolerate the sloppiness, inefficiency and foolishness of others, who (for whatever reason) have come to prize other results.

So become resigned to it, you are in the success business, and the achievement of all success needs an implementation strategy, a set of mutually understood and accepted procedures which, when followed, enhance the ability of your client to reach the result which both of you say you want. It should and must be understood by you that while you will approach the solution of the client's problem with as much savoire faire, as much charm, as much bland persuasiveness as possible, you need to realize that if these things don't work (and they often won't), you will have to lay down some law for the client and get them moving along to success.

Don't fail to do this, thinking, wrongly, that such forthrightness will cause you to lose the client. It won't. In fact, the client will often thank you most profusely for what you have done and said to them, well knowing that the role of candid friend if a valuable one, is one that often goes underappreciated. Your job, however, is to be candid, to think through exactly what you must do and when you must do it, and what the client must do and when he must do it, and to resolve yourself that if the client fails in his part, you must do whatever is necessary to motivate, move, persuade and influence the client to take action on his own behalf. I call this understanding the "Guerrilla Theatre of Advising" and, because we have no direct power, but rather influence, you'll find yourself using it more often than you may have imagined.

- **Make sure you have agreed with the client on how success will be reported and how the inevitable obstacles of any relationship will be reported, too.**

This is basically an extension of the implementation strategy, as is the next item, too. I have separated it from the discussion of the implementation strategy, however, because of its importance to the achievement of success and the fact that advisors frequently overlook the importance of this stage.

Successful advisors are proactive, not reactive. In reality, this means that we must anticipate that in the realization of any client-advisor relationship and in the achievement of any success there will necessarily be problems that must be worked out. This is normal and must be expected. While many of these problems can be worked out during your regular meetings, some others will need the involvement of more senior officers of the organization.

In my case, for instance, I work with the executive directors of non-profit organizations. Still, from time to time, it is necessary for me to see the Board of Directors as ultimate governors of the institution. Your contract should allow for access upon both regular and needed occasions, both to discuss with the decision makers why certain matters are not proceeding as smoothly as they might, and why, by the same token, they are — and render up thanks and congratulations accordingly.

Big problems are little problems allowed to grow. Very infrequently does a problem arrive on the scene fully blown. Quite the reverse. Big problems are little problems allowed to fester.

Thus, in your advising relationship it is necessary to bring up all problems, both big and the nagging little ones, too, for solution. If they can be solved at your regular client meetings, well and good. But if they cannot be so solved, then utilize your contractual access to a higher level of decision makers to make a report and point out what needs to be done, by whom, under what circumstances, &c. This is your job, and admittedly it can be tricky if the people you are working with are themselves the cause of the problem.

Under such circumstances, you will have to make a series of decisions:

- Do you want to achieve success, or do you want to play along with the current client?
- Is there a means of opening up the situation for analysis and review without your necessarily being involved in making the suggestion for doing so?

Some of my workshop participants don't like it when I say that advisors must not lose sight of the fact that we all, when on assignment, necessarily work in a political universe. If you discover that the people you are working with are themselves the problem, you are necessarily right smack dab in the middle of a very trying and difficult political situation in which there are very real risks, very real benefits, the very real chance of failure and loss of the contract and professional esteem. That's, as they say, life.

I'll deal with this problem in greater detail later on in the chapter (Chapter 10) dealing with making a success of your client relationships, but let me say now: it would be very naive of you to believe that the professional information and expertise you have at your disposal somehow renders you immune from the very political situation which necessarily flourishes in all institutions. It doesn't, but to assume that it does is a very common mistake in the professions.

Keep a list of the things that are troubling you about the developing relationship with the client. This list should be composed of both specific, detailed items and what I might call "atmospheric" matters, which are rather harder to quantify and catalog. Both are equally valid. Let me say this: merely bringing up your concerns, no matter how valid to the achievement of success, does not necessarily ensure that they'll be solved or even properly handled. Moreover, the responses you get may discomfit you as pointing to aspects of your own professional (and personal!) behavior which the client finds offputting and detrimental to the achievement of success.

Such meetings must, therefore, be pursued in a conciliatory and open manner, a spirit of free and open conversation. I confess that I find this most difficult to do, although I am learning. Like many advisors and professional experts, I find it easier to dish out the (constructive) criticism and advice than to take it. But I have learned that we advisors must be open to the (not always positive) comments of our clients and learn to respond to them without personal rancor or bruised feelings. This is very, very difficult — and yet it is absolutely necessary. If the relationship with your client is going to become as genuine as it needs to be to succeed, you must learn not only to give out information but to accept the comments of clients — and to respond to them in appropriate ways.

By the same token, you need access to decision makers to praise and to compliment. Don't miss the opportunity to praise people in your client organization who are helping to make the relationship a success. Don't hesitate to bring their names to the attention of decision makers. We advisors are in a superb position to be advisors able not only to remove people from organizations but to advance them as well. We are clothed in the garment of candid objectivity, and this has some very real uses for us. We can go to decision makers and commend people, congratulate them and tell why what they have done is in fact important. An advisor who misses this opportunity to help out his client friends is missing one of the benefits of the job and, I might say, one of the best means of developing a good contact network, since those we say good about are often likely to return the favor.

In my contracts I like to schedule at least two meetings a year with the next highest level of decision makers within the organization from the ones I'm working with. Since most of my advising in the nonprofit world is done with executive directors, this ordinarily means meeting with Board members who themselves may only meet monthly or quarterly. You may need more meetings than this; fewer is very unlikely.

- **Make sure you and the client have agreed to a "clinic" following at intervals upon the conclusion of your contract to see how things are coming along.**

In ordinary circumstances, bringing an advisor into any setting begins a change process. No wonder. We advisors are catalysts for change. While we are present things hum: success, however feebly, comes into the picture. People's behaviors change. New priorities are set and old ones discarded. And if we press, and work hard on establishing a meaningful implementation strategy for the client, we do achieve much, or perhaps even all we had set out to do.

When we leave, however, things may, indeed usually will, revert in some measure to the situation before we came on the scene. That's why we need a clinic.

Physicians use a clinic to check on the progress of former patients who are now convalescing. We should do the same. Whatever your contract, you should include a clause that establishes formal meetings and reviews of progress to take place after the formal expiration of your intense consultancy. In any advising relationship, there is always a period when you are working longer and harder with a client. The clinic is for the period following your intense effort.

Do you need to return after 30 days? 60? 180? You decide based on your understanding of your business, its particular ebb and flow, and what you know of the client and his approach to the solution of the problem.

You'll find upon going in that whatever his intentions, the client is probably not living up to the high standards that you brought to the situation and that he has fallen down, with the result that the success he wants is slipping away from him. Thus, in effect, your subsequent meetings with the client, which are, of course, being paid for by the client, become an opportunity for you to sell yourself by saying, "You're not doing it right!" "You are not implementing the strategies we agreed to, the specific success techniques and procedures. You are not allocating the resources we both know are necessary for this job and your commitment has waned." In short, "You're not doing it right!"

The clinic properly understood and properly handled becomes a superb means for you, the advisor in need of another assignment, to return to the client and assess the situation and, as a result, so market and present yourself that your return to the situation is vastly enhanced. This is smart marketing, and, I need hardly say, it is important to the client as well, for it increases the likelihood of their success.

The Problem Solving Process: A Summary

Collectively these 8 steps are known as the Problem Solving Process. They are an action directed set of steps which, when addressed, will enable you to move towards the solution of the client's problems in such a way that ensures the absolutely greatest possiblity for success.

The steps can be sold either as individual modules or as a sequence. If they are sold individually, however, you must at all times keep in mind that your ultimate objective is to sell them as a sequence of success procedures, although it may, with any individual client, take a good long time for them to buy the entire set.

Yet selling the entire set is important because it allows you to have the longest engagement with the client, to work with them most closely, and to bring about the success which they say they want to have. Needless to say, selling the entire sequence also allows you the best chance for maximum profit.

I will say again and will emphasize and reemphasize this critical point: to succeed as an advisor means working as diligently as possible to bring about success with your clients and leveraging this success to attract others who are similarly situated and wish to replicate it. The best possibility of achieving this success is to sell the 8 steps of the Problem Solving Process. If you can do so, you will be in a position to deal effectively with one of the greatest drawbacks facing an advisor: the uncertainty and instability of our incomes.

Determining Fees

Once you've internalized the Problem Solving Process, before you can begin selling yourself, you have several other things to do. One of them is to determine your fees.

Here are a few typically candid remarks about fees:

- The more a client pays, the more civilized your dealings will be and the less they'll try to nickle and dime you to death.
- Getting paid by government money is often like taking a Bahamian cruise. It's languid and often undemanding.
- Your fee should reflect the perceived or desired status of the buyer of your service.
- Once the buyer has understood that you can deliver disproportionate benefits compared to fee, you are well positioned to raise your fee.
- Your fee bears an important relation to your ability to perceive the dream of your client and your ability to help him realize it.
- The stronger your perceived success image, the more a client will wish to have you on retainer (and not necessarily regularly use you) at a substantial fee.
- The less a client pays you, the more he'll expect, because he'll see you less as an influential expert and more as the employee he is already skilled at undervaluing.
- Your fee should be perceived by the client as the least important part of doing business with you, almost as an afterthought.
- Fees are as much (if not more!) a matter of perception than of reality. Good people who can solve problems often draw less money than inept people who understand that fee is as much psychological as it is practical.
- Fee is in no way related to the amount of time you put into a project but rather the results you bring about.

More On Fees

I have learned more about money since becoming an advisor than I ever thought possible, and indeed I have an entirely different perspective on the subject than when I was a regular employee earning a regular wage. The 10 insights I've listed above constitute the heart of what I now know to be true.

Let me begin by saying there is a lot of nonsense written about fees. The discussions in most books on advising approach this matter as if it were somehow entirely objective. As if the question of fee was determined by entirely rational people pursuing entirely objective and rational ends. Well, nothing could be further from the truth.

Almost everyone reading this book begins at the same place: as refugees from the American institutional job market where we put in a set number of hours in return for a set amount of money. This isn't necessarily how things are done in advising, not at all! That's why I've got more than one way of calculating your fee.

Introductory Fee Setting: The Technical Assistant Advisor Formula

Because there are two major kinds of advisors, technical assistants and mandarins, there need to be two kinds of fee-setting formulas. The Technical Assistant Advisor is the knowledgeable individual who not only makes recommendations to a client but also helps implement them directly. The Mandarin, on the other hand, while superbly knowledgeable, ordinarily only recommends action to his client; he does not undertake it directly himself. He is a team builder, working largely through others to achieve successful results.

When you begin your advising practice, you are probably going to be a Technical Assistant Advisor; most people are. You'll most likely be working regular hours solving the problems of your targeted client prospects and drawing in return a reasonable fee. There is nothing wrong with this, except that being a Technical Assistant Advisor pure and simple ordinarily limits your income potential. There are, after all, only so many hours in the day. Still, here's how to set your fee in this situation.

Take your last regular job salary and divide it by 52 (for the number of weeks of the year) and 5 (for the number of days of the week). You now have your current (or last job) daily rate. Now multiply this figure by 2.5. This is the suitable multiplier if you are working out of your home or from inexpensive rented space and don't have heavy equipment and other major expenses to figure in. This multiplier takes into account your loss of employee benefits and the fact that as a full-time advisor fully employed, you'll only be working 14 to 17 days each month. The other working days will be given over to running your small business, marketing, promoting and client prospect meetings, professional continuing education, &c. You now have another number. Round this number up to the nearest number evenly divisible by 25, 50, or 100. This is because advisors, when selling days, charge a round number. This is now your new daily rate.

Let's work this out in an example. Let's say that your current annual salary is $35,000 a year. Divided by 52 and then again by 5 you come up with a current daily rate of $134.62. Multiply this by 2.5 for a total of $336.54. The nearest divisor is 50 and so you'd round the number up to $350, your new daily rate. Now multiply this by, say, 15 (for the number of days you work on average monthly) and by 12 for the number of months of the year. Your new yearly gross is $60,576.92, out of which you must pay all your business expenses including:

- salary
- workman's compensation
- pension
- rent
- stationery
- office equipment and machines
- telephone
- printing
- postage
- copying
- various insurances, etc.

To determine your hourly rate take the figure of $336.54 and divide by 8, for the number of hours in the day. That produces $42.07, your new hourly rate. Round this number to the nearest number evenly divisible by 5, 10 or 15, in this case $45 per hour, your new hourly rate. Note: People who buy you by the hour should always pay a slightly higher rate for your time than those who pay your daily rate, since it involves more of your energy and creativity to shift from subject to subject on an hourly basis.

It goes without saying that all customary expenses such as copying, telephone, postage, travel, accommodation, &c are billed additionally and separately to the client.

This formula is what most people in advising start with. Once you have calculated what you are going to do, how many hours it will take, you can cite your hourly and daily rates as necessary. Don't forget to allow for a margin of error. If you have done the job before and you know how things should be done and how they can be arranged, factor in a 20% margin error; that is, your estimate should be based on 20% more time than you think it will take. If you have not done the job before and are uncertain of how long it will take, this figure should be at least 40% higher than you've estimated. The shorter the period you've been in advising, the more optimistic you are likely to be about how quickly a project can be completed. I talk to many, many advisors during any given year who rue their cost estimates, having failed to understand that projects always take longer than you suppose they will in the palmy days when you are making your bid and estimates. Failure to provide an accurate figure to your client prospects is in fact a psychological error of major proportions. That's why before we go on I must discuss a point or two about advisors and their fees.

On Becoming A Dreamspinner

The wealthier and more powerful the clients you deal with, ordinarily the less they are interested in money *per se*. Money becomes no more than a convenient means of keeping score with themselves on their relative position in the world. Faced as you may be with a stack of bills, a demanding family, and an immediate need for cash, you may find this statement absurd, but I can assure you it's true. People who are powerful and rich are, of course, interested in money, but they are more interested in how money can help them reach their aspirations, realize their dreams, and help them meet their ultimate objectives. They realize, more that those without money, that money is only significant insofar as it assists them in realizing their objectives and that for any other purpose it's meaningful only as a device to secure comfort. Thus, to talk to such people about money first is a great error. That's why you must become a Dreamspinner.

To succeed in the advising business means understanding the dreams, hopes, aspirations and objectives of client projects, to keep inside their heads and to know, often better than they do themselves, *what* they really want to accomplish — as well as *how* it can be accomplished. This is what Dreamspinners do, and the successful advisor is always a successful dreamspinner.

In the beginning of your practice, you'll probably approach your new business like you approached your last full-time professional position: to get paid for doing your task, your task and nothing but the task itself. This is, however, a terrible error. In your previous place, you may have had no clear indication of how you, wherever you were in the organization, fit into the dreams and aspirations of the individual ultimately paying you, the client. As an advisor, however, you have to have a very clear sense of the relationship between the work you are doing and what the client is really trying to accomplish.

Mandarin Fee Setting

It should go without saying (shouldn't it?) that as soon as you possibly can you should move to becoming a mandarin and setting mandarin fees. There are many fewer mandarins than technical assistants in the world but these mandarins are by far the better paid advisors. Here's how to set fees in mandarin fashion:

- What is the disproportionate benefit to the client prospect of the result your information or skill will help bring about?
- What is the client prospect's need to achieve (or desire to achieve) this result and in what period of time must he achieve it?
- What happens to the client prospect if he fails to achieve this beneficial result?
- What is your perceived ability to assist in delivering this result based on your success track record, experience, and general reputation in your field?
- Who else competes with you in offering this perceived ability to deliver the desired result?
- What is his fee?
- What, then, is your fee?

In considering how to calculate a mandarin fee, think of this illustration. It concerns the ten millionaires on board the storied ship *Titanic* and a ship evacuation advisor traveling with them. Upon setting out from Southampton, this advisor, like everyone else, has no reason to doubt the current wisdom that "God himself cannot sink this ship!" and so charges a fixed, flat fee as a technical assistant. Like a good advisor, he lets particularly the First Class passengers know about his evacuation service and the fact that he has a private lifeboat available. He points out in his advertising that the *Titanic* has too few of its own life boats. One cautious soul takes a place in the private lifeboat and a few others sign up for the advisor's shipboard class on "Quick and Easy Exits During Seaborn Emergencies."

This situation remains constant until the advisor becomes aware that the *Titanic* has struck an iceberg. From being before a rather humdrum technical assistant, he is now able to elevate himself into a mandarin, a mandarin, moreover, with an available solution readily at hand — the extra boat. Having never before been in such a situation (which was indeed unique in seafaring annals), the advisor is uncertain what to charge. He is assailed by the following qualms:

- One passenger has already paid a fixed, flat fee for a seat. Is it fair to charge others more, despite the fact that circumstances have altered?
- Under the new circumstances what is a fair price to charge? How can he find out?

The advisor considers the points of the Mandarin Formula:

- What is the disproportionate benefit to the client prospect of the result your information or skill will bring about? As the *Titanic* moves to her tragic, majestic end, it is clear the advisor can in fact deliver life itself to those who use his technical information and skill. What, then, is life worth?
- What is the client prospect's need to achieve this result and in what period of time must he achieve it? The prospect's need to achieve this result (life) is acute, and he must act increasingly quickly (as lifeboat spaces are taken) to achieve it.
- What happens to the client prospect if he fails to achieve this beneficial result? A premature (and highly uncomfortable) watery grave, perhaps mitigated by a mournful paragraph in *A Night To Remember*.
- What is your perceived ability to assist in delivering this result? As the only private evacuation advisor on board (for remember: you are competing with the administration of the ship which offers a similar, and already prepaid, service) it is very high.
- Who else competes with you in offering this perceived ability? As you discover that all the ships in the area are failing to respond to the ship's distress calls, you feel comfortable no one else is competing with you, a situation, of course, which you must continue to monitor.
- What is their fee? As the unique purveyor of a critical service, this item is not applicable.

What, then, is your fee? Well, let's put it like this: if you stay cool and competent, you should emerge with a clear profit (albeit perhaps some sneers from the faint hearted and less well organized). Don't, however, let that bother you.

Commission Fees

Participants in my advising workshops are particularly beguiled by the notion of commission fees, that is, taking a percentage of monies saved, monies earned from the project they are involved with. Now, it is certainly true that as an advisor you can make often substantial sums through commission contracts, but several critical factors must be present:

- Commission contracts are ordinarily not a wise idea for those who are recently in business and who do not fully understand the ins and outs of their client's business.

- You can rest assured that while a commission fee may appeal to your client at the beginning of a relationship (when it looks like an inexpensive form of getting a needed service), after you've done the service and the results begin pouring in, your fee will seem expensive and may produce a very negative reaction from a client. "Is that all he had to do for the fee? Why I could have done that myself!" Thus, a commission fee will often in the long run produce client hostility that a fixed flat fee will not.

- Clients who have enjoyed your service and made good use of you under a commission fee arrangement are not always punctilious about letting you have the information you need to figure your fee. Advisors must always be aware of the propensity of humans to be greedy.

Remember the following points about a commission fee arrangement:

- Don't consider it until you have sufficient other financial resources so that you don't need the money.

- Don't consider getting into one unless you and the client have clearly agreed upon the basis for figuring what you'll get and when you'll get it.

- Make sure, too, that you or your representative will get access to all the necessary records, materials, communications and information sources within the company to make sure that you are being properly paid.

- Don't do commission arrangements with start up companies or other fiscally weak organizations, unless you can afford to take the financial risk. You may find yourself putting in a lot of time and effort and getting little if anything in return.

- Do not consider getting your payment in merchandise of the organization unless you have a clear idea of how this merchandise can be sold, or unless you have a professional or personal use for the quantities you will be acquiring.

Final Thoughts On Fees

One of the significant reasons you are considering advising, why in fact you may already have begun your practice, is because of the fees you can draw. For make no mistake about it: advisors who handle their business properly can get rich. I know. And I believe deeply in the ability of advising to provide inspired, creative, innovative, and hard working people with a very substantial income. Sadly, I see people making significant errors all the time in regard to their fees, and before closing this section of the chapter I'd like to share some of these pivotal errors with you.

- **Move away from nickel-and-dime clients as fast as possible.**

Too many advisors spend too long a period misunderstanding their market. As I wrote earlier in this book, the top 20% of your market, probably controls about 80% of the money available to retain advisors. Thus, you must aim towards this slice of the market, particularly if you do not intend to create a full-fledged Mobile Mini-Conglomerate. If you expect to live on your fees alone, then you must aim for the top of your market, for that is the only part of your market which can pay the kinds of fees which will sustain you.

- **Don't be sheepish about your fees.**

There's nothing to be shy or awkward about in the matter of your fee. If you have clearly thought through what disproportionate benefit you client receives compared to fee, the matter of fee should be nothing significant. If a deal comes unravelled on the matter of fee, it's because your client prospect is not convinced that he can derive a disproportionate benefit from working with you or because he doesn't understand that such a result is possible using your methods and techniques. That's your problem. If you are helping the client get something he substantially wants to have, you deserve to be compensated. If everyone could do everything for themselves, could always and in all circumstances help themselves to the objective they most wanted, there wouldn't be any need for advisors. We are necessary because people cannot always achieve what they desire alone. If we help them get what they want, we deserve to be compensated accordingly. Nothing to feel sheepish about in the slightest.

- **Tell people what a good deal they are getting.**

If your fees are moderate, have thoughtfully been considered, are lower that the industry, or if your track record is better than others in your profession, tell people. Don't expect them to figure out these things for themselves. I'm proud, for instance, that one of the fee structures I've created for nonprofit organizations in the Greater Boston area is less expensive than that offered by others and thus offers an enhanced likelihood of major return on investment. I see no reason to be shy about this contract, its advantages to the client, or its place in my industry.

- **Raise your fees as you can demonstrate success.**

Your ability to deliver success to your clients, a disproportionate benefit compared to fee, entitles you to raise your prices. Remember: knowing how to get a disproportionate benefit compared to fee is a time-consuming thing. It takes much of your mental concentration, your attention and your abilites. As you know how to achieve it, however, you have increased your desirability for others who, being conservative and yet wishing to duplicate the result, will feel more comfortable working with you.

- **State fees, don't discuss them.**

Would you think of going into a grocery store and asking the owner on what basis he charges for his toothpaste? Certainly not. In the same way, simply put your fees forward and let people know what they are getting for their money, specifically, the likelihood of obtaining their desired objective. Unsophisticated buyers refuse to understand that part of what they are buying in your fee is a long term of experience. James McNeill Whistler, when asked by a London judge in a libel action he had brought against the famous art critic John Ruskin how long it had taken him to paint a certain picture, replied, "All my life!" I know exactly what he means.

A client is not merely paying for your current time but all the years, the effort, the intense mental concentration, the innovation, the creativity and patient practice and determination it took you to get to this point, the point, that is, of being able to help the client solve his current and pressing problem. It's a pity so many client prospects never adequately understand this.

- **Don't have a sliding fee scale.**

Individuals who work with poorer and less lavishly financed individuals and organizations often provide them with a lower or sliding scale depending on their ability to pay. I am adamantly opposed to this. For one thing, it is often difficult to determine what an adequate and fair scale is. For another, clients do place a value on your recommendations that is commensurate with what you charge. If you want your clients to pay attention to you, attach a fee to what you say that will force them to do so. To do anything else is no kindness (and indeed certain madness) in the long run.

Instead of altering your fee, alter the amount of time you spend with your client. Don't change your hourly or daily rate for anyone, but do alter the available means of how clients can work with and learn from you. This is where developing all the stages of the Mobile Mini-Conglomerate comes in very useful. If a client cannot afford to bring you to his office (Full Service Contract), have him to yours (Delphic Oracle Contract). If he cannot afford either alternative, set up a workshop. Or publish a booklet or book. Or produce problem solving audio cassettes. Modern telecommunications and new information-generating resources have made it possible for you to assist people virtually wherever they are located. Your job is to provide your information in as many problem solving formats as exist, and, if the client cannot afford you on a one-to-one basis, to let the client invest his own time and determination to solve his problem using whichever vehicle of yours he can afford. However, you must always charge what the information you have is fully worth. Make no exceptions.

- **Determine as quickly as possible what is the maximum amount of money you can make from a client.**

I keep saying and reiterating that you must understand your market, and part of this understanding is knowing to what extent and for what they can pay. If a church calls me from Idaho, for example, I know the maximum amount of money I can make from that organization will be from the sale of a book, and, if I ever have a workshop in their area, sale of workshop slots. That's it. My sales pitch is therefore geared towards realizing this amount of money and not investing any further time or effort in this client prospect since such investment would not be a good use of my time.

Advisors too often invest their scarce time and other resources in individuals who, even if the advisor is successful in getting the client, cannot repay the investment. This is, indeed, a very serious problem in advising ranks, particularly for those at the beginning of their careers when they are more inclined to scramble for new clients, more inclined to look congenially on projects they will later ignore or reduce in importance. I did this, too. But I don't do it anymore. Neither should you.

Determine based on what the organization is, where they are located, the kind of problem they discuss with you, and their ability to pay, what you will sell them, the most you can sell them, and stick to your decision and the level of your investment accordingly.

- **Never apologize for your fee.**

Once you begin apologizing for your fee, a client may well (and quite properly) begin to wonder whether you can actually deliver for them. Questions you raise about fee will lead to deep misgivings about you and your professional service. Once you have determined that the fee you are charging is fair based on the likelihood of achieving the result the client wishes, stick to your guns. Fees are a part of life and if the client wishes to achieve the result, there's no use disguising that it'll cost them.

- **Stress the fee as investment.**

Working with an advisor can and should lead to long-term improvements in an organization. When I go into any nonprofit organization as a development consultant, I am leaving behind skills in key personnel that the agency can benefit from for the remainder of its time in business. We advisors are natural teachers and as such the benefits from our assignments extend far beyond the terms of our immediate engagement. It is important for our clients to realize this fact so they can perceive our fee as an expense to be amortized over a long term of years.

- **Remember that fee is not profit.**

Many advisors make the mistake of assuming that what they bring in in fees is all profit. That's simply not true. Your profit, like any other business, is what is left after all your many expenses are deducted from your gross revenues. It's very easy for others to forget this, too, and to assume that you're getting rich faster, in fact, than you are. People who are not in business themselves, who do not have the responsibility for running and marketing an enterprise forget the many expenses of even the smallest small business. You cannot. Whatever our fees, we advisors are cheap for two leading reasons: in part because of the disproportionate benefit compared to our fee, also because we don't take the customary benefits that institutional employees enjoy. These we must supply for ourselves.

Creating Advising Packages

In this chapter I've asked you to consider the implementation strategy you'd use with clients, how, that is, you'd work in an action-oriented and directed way to help them solve their problems. I also said that you should not offer a sliding fee scale but rather so organize your problem solving procedures that the client could select the best possible option based on his resources and ability to work independently to solve his problem. Not all advising, as should now be perfectly clear, need be carried on at the client's premises with you present. There are many alternatives.

Understanding The Delphic Oracle And Full-Service Contract Options

You will no doubt remember your ancient Greek history and recall the Delphic Oracle, one of history's earliest consultants. This advisor lived in and worked from a cave from which she dispensed salient advice to kings (the chief executive officers of their day) and upwardly mobile warriors intent on success. These clients journeyed to the witch-advisor from around the ancient world to seek out problem solving information of interest to them. The Oracle, perhaps the most sought after advisor of her time, was sufficiently eminent so that traveling wasn't often necessary and so she met with her clients in her office-cave. In the process she created an advisor-client relationship which is well worth remembering, and, indeed, adopting for oneself.

Remember: not all client-advisor relationships need to develop at your client's offices. Some may, and indeed should, develop at yours. It is expensive both in terms of time and energy (to say nothing more) for you to travel hither and yon servicing your clients. As an advisor you need to develop methods which preserve particularly your energy and concentrate your effort in meaningful ways. Moreover, most clients will take no interest in just how exhausting your tasks are. This is something you must do for yourself.

When it comes time to work with a client prospect, you want to structure the experience, right from the start, as close to the actual advisor relationship as you can. That means thinking through answers to the following questions and so structuring not one but a series of possible ways of working together. This allows the client the maximum amount of choice in working with you and so creates for your business a cluster of client possibilities.

Here are the questions which need answering:
- Where will the meetings between client and advisor take place?
- Who will participate in these meetings?
- How long will the meetings last?
- How will contact between meetings be accomplished?
- How will reporting sessions with ultimate decision makers be handled?
- What about expenses?

Here are some answers.

- **Where will meetings between client and advisor take place?**

Under the Delphic Oracle contract, regular client-advisor meetings will take place in your offices. There are several benefits here: 1) it is less expensive for the client to come to you than for you, the Oracle, to travel to them. The fact that the client is willing to spend his time, money and energy in coming to you should mean that the cost of the contract is significantly lower than if you had to expend your resources coming to him. 2) It is better for you since you can focus exclusively on the advising service that you offer rather than expending your resources on the peripheral matters, like travel. As a result you should be a more productive professional.

Now, it goes without saying that some clients will want you to come to their offices. That's fine. But neither you nor the client should automatically assume that this will happen. Whether you go to them or they come to you is, you must know, subject to negotiation and consideration. If the client wishes you to go to them, it will have to cost them more than if they come to you. Let this be clearly understood. The situation which involves you traveling to the client is part of what I call the Full Service Contract.

Let me say this: the richer, better connected and more self-regarding your client prospect is the more he will want the Full Service Contract. Whatever the limitations of money, the one thing it is superb at doing is ensuring one's own comfort. If the client is convinced that he is a superior being, that his time is valuable, that you are there in the capacity of modern day servitor, then that client will want the Full Service Contract, indeed any other alternative is unthinkable because by buying the Delphic Oracle Contract, he admits that he is rather lower in status than you are, a deduction he may be rigidly unwilling to consider. If this is the case, then take advantage of your prospect's need for status bolstering and propose the Full Service option, charging accordingly.

• Who will participate in these meetings?

In my own advising practice, I inform Delphic Oracle clients that they may bring whomsoever they wish to each of the meetings at my office. In practice, however, it is difficult to organize meetings of more than two representatives from the client's. Thus, whereas at the client's offices (under a Full Service agreement) I may deal with more people, under the Delphic Oracle plan the client must take back marching orders and instructions to people he will help organize. This is a rather subtle, though important, difference between the two agreements which is why, in practice, the Delphic Oracle relationship is actually called the Cooperative Service Plan.

The name Cooperative Service Plan suggests that you, the advisor, will do certain things, the decision maker you meet with will be responsible for other things and that this decision maker will yet have to involve others, who do not regularly participate in the meetings, to accomplish still other things. Under all advising relationships the team-building function is an important one, but here it has the added, and often piquant twist, that it must be done at a distance, for whereas under the Full Service relationship you will work at the client's office and with the client's staff, you will, under the Cooperative agreement, work at your office with only the tiniest portion of the client's staff and decision makers and will thus have to work through this, then these individual(s) to bring the problem to a solution.

What I am saying is this: it is a luxury (a perhaps unaffordable luxury, just like any other) to have you working directly with a client and a client's staff on site. If the client is to have this luxury, then they will have to pay for it. If, on the the other hand, the client wishes to save money, to learn from, to have you structure the relationship, and to have to report back to you regularly as tasks develop and are completed, then the Cooperative Service Plan/Delphic Oracle relationship makes sense. One involves much more of you than the other.

What is important to point out is that you provide the client prospect with alternatives. The essence of salesmanship is not selling a client with a problem merely a problem solving process; that is relatively easy. The essence of salesmanship lies in selling that prospect a slightly better problem solving process than he had intended on getting, that is, investing slightly more than he had originally intended. The extent to which you accomplish this desirable objective is the extent to which you have succeeded in sales. And, at least in theory, the extent to which you have secured the support of the client to solving the problem, a support which is often directly proportionate to their financial investment.

• How long will the meeting last?

Learning how to structure a meeting for maximum results is an important part of becoming a successful advisor. Deciding on how long meetings shall be is an important difference between a cooperative service agreement and one that is full service.

I have a Cooperative Service Plan option, for instance, under which I meet for one hour each week for a year with the client. Meetings are very rarely longer than this and often rather shorter due to two leading reasons:

1) the crisp way I march the client through the meetings so that the problems waiting to be solved are dealt with with specific problem solving strategies (up to 10 problems and solutions each week).

2) the fact that at any given meeting several previously discussed strategies have not yet been implemented by the client, thus (so long as conditions remain constant) obviating the need for additional discussion beyond the mandatory Lant-initiated motivational goal, an important part of any goal-oriented consultancy like mine.

Under a Cooperative Service arrangement, the client is actually buying a fixed number of meetings. Beyond the number of meetings, however, they are actually buying a highly disciplined problem solving process which absolutely ensures (so long as they proceed in good faith and with a minimum of obstructions) that at the conclusion of the relationship they will have at least some success, the success being directly proportional to their own ability to implement my recommendations in a timely, efficient fashion.

This is not to suggest that under the Full Service option meetings are not efficiently arranged as well or that set tasks (what I call a Task Action List) are not assigned. Quite the contrary. It does suggest, however, that the amount of meeting time under the Full Service option is greater and that there are fewer restrictions placed on the calling of meetings. Under the Cooperative Service option, as already mentioned, regular meetings would be one hour each week for a year (or whatever the time period you select). Under the Full Service option meetings could be longer in duration (say, twice as long) and could be called as needed when problem situations emerge. That is not the case under the Cooperative Service option. There all problem-related business must be handled in your office at the regular meetings; such an option lacks a "crisis management" provision which executives so often like in the other.

- **How will contact between meetings take place?**

Under the Cooperative Service Plan there can be no between-meeting client-advisor contact (with the one exception to be dealt with next). All business, all problems and all problem solving information must be dealt with at the time of the regular (in my case, weekly) meeting. In fact, the client has bought a block of time to be used in a certain way and if additional time is needed, they will have to buy it as a supplement to the original option. Under the Full Service option, of course, your clients have the right to call you and contact you whenever they have a need. This may worry you.

You will find, however, that those who pay for Full Service agreements do so as a form of insurance. Whereas those putting relatively little into an agreement might very well be inclined to call and call again at the drop of a hat; those who actually purchase what I call the "telephone privilege" do not make excessive, or even allowable, use of it. This is especially true if you are properly arranging your meetings so that the client is left with a "task action list" of things to accomplish before the next meeting takes place. Under these circumstances, the kinds of calls that do take place are brief and to the point as the client calls you for specific and particular information leading to the solution of a well-defined problem.

- **How will reporting sessions with ultimate decision makers be handled?**

As you already know from reviewing the Problem Solving Process, it is critical that there be meetings with ultimate decision makers, especially if these are not the people you are meeting with on a regular basis. In my case, for instance, my weekly meetings tend to be with executive directors of nonprofit organizations. These organizations have, however, boards of directors which are responsible in an ultimate sense for the decisions which are made. Thus, it is important for me to meet with them regularly. Experience has taught me that two meetings a year with the Board are usually sufficient to acquaint them with what is happening, problems that need to be solved, problem solving processes that will be used to solve them, and what they themselves must accomplish, for what reasons, and by what dates. These two meetings are built into the contract between the client and me, the advisor.

On the other hand, with the Full Service option the organization may decide to have as many meetings as it (in consultation with me) deems necessary. In practice, this will mean as few as two or as many as one every other month with decision makers. In my practice, it has never been necessary to have more meetings with ultimate decision makers than this; your situation, of course, may well be different.

Here are two important things to point out about meeting with your client:

- Questions about how many meetings with ultimate decision makers will be necessary will be settled by your experience as an advisor. Don't expect to know the answer to this problem on your first day. It may take you a year or even two to learn just how often you need to meet the ultimate decision makers and how to structure these meetings for best mutual advantage.

- You nonetheless must attempt to address this issue as soon as possible so that you can present your client prospects with options from which to decide. It is crucial that you meet with ultimate decision makers. Just how often you cannot know until you have lived through the solution of the particular problem you have been hired to address, once or even more than once. Thus, you must at the beginning of your advising practice hazard a guess about how much time you need. Don't be afraid to do this, despite the fact that you will probably underestimate the amount of time you need at first to make your estimate more palatable to the client. Remember this: the richer the client, the more well placed, the better connected, the more the client wishes to buy services that will keep the client in this enviable position. Since you know you need to report success and foreshadow difficulties with the client's ultimate decision makers (this is mandatory), the only thing you need to consider is how often such a reporting process is necessary. If uncertain, try once every three months and see how this works out in practice.

- **What about expenses?**

In the Cooperative Service option there will be precious little need for expenses. In fact, with certain of my clients, there have been no expenses for years, just the regular payment of the retainer contract stipend! That's because the client uses his own time and money to get to me. The exception, of course, is when by contract I travel to their decison makers and meetings. This is properly regarded as a billable expense. It is quite otherwise with the Full Service agreement, under which all expenses are fully billable to the client at regular monthly intervals.

Further Words About The Delphic Oracle And Full Service Options

A successful advisor business means developing a cluster of possibilities for your clients and marketing them to the widest possible extent to all those who have the problem you can solve. Some of these advising possibilites, as a look at the Mobile Mini-Conglomerate affirms, are through booklets, books, newsletters, cassettes, and workshops. Others are through a variety of advisor-client relationships. It is most important to have the widest number of possibilities you can so that the client understands there is an available solution to his problem, whatever the amount of discretionary money he has available. If you are only willing to sell time and only willing to sell this time by working at the client's offices, you are creating a tremendous obstacle for yourself, for in such circumstances you are tragically limiting the ways you can reach your income objectives and benefit from your wisdom and problem solving expertise. This is a major mistake!

Your job, therefore, is to create the maximum number of problem solving vehicles. This necessarily includes a vehicle you primarily offer at your office, and one you primarily offer at your client's office. Your job is to think through how each of these will work and to offer them to the client with, of course, your recommendation as to which is preferable given his circumstances.

Offering the client the maximum number of options (with your advice as to which is appropriate for his circumstances) properly positions you as the advisor and allows the client properly to act as the client. You advise on options; the client prospect selects the appropriate option given his circumstances. Thus, right from the start, you are functioning as the advisor, and it is natural to move into other situations with this same client wherein you continue to function in this, your proper, role. This is the essence of client-centered marketing, for the maximum success which can be obtained with this particular client.

Last Word On The Delphic Oracle-Cooperative Service Option

Before leaving this section, I should like to put in a final word on behalf of the Delphic Oracle contract. All advisors, of course, are well aware that they may be called upon to work with their clients in their clients' offices. This is standard procedure. Many fewer understand the profitable possibilities of offering their less well financed clients the prospect of coming to their, the advisor's, office. Yet I have found in my practice that many clients welcome such an opportunity.

Some advisors foolishly think that under such a contract option they'll be losing money. This is very far from the truth. Delphic Oracle contracts make it possible for those organizations and individuals with limited resources to take advantage of what you know and can do. Moreover, because of the ways clients actually work, such contracts ordinarily result in greater stipends to you than your regular hourly rate. Here's what I mean:

I have a Delphic Oracle contract under which Boston-area organizations currently pay me $11,400 yearly for a certain advising service I offer. Under this service, they get one-hour weekly meetings and two two-hour meetings with their boards of directors (decision makers) during any given year. Thus, for $11,400 they buy up to 56 hours of my advising time yearly. Given that my regular hourly advising rate is $250, by purchasing a year's retainer agreement, the client saves lots of money. I offer this savings as an inducement for them to buy the complete contract.

In actual fact, however, these agreements ordinarily return more than $250 per hour to me for the following reasons:

- If a client has not finished his "task action list" of assignments for the week, he usually cancels his meeting.
- A client will not hold meetings during his vacation time.
- A client will not hold meetings during certain seasons of the year: the end of December, during the month of July, etc.

Since clients cannot, by contract, bank hours, time they have bought but not used is time they have subsidized for me, time I in turn use to market to other, would-be clients. This is how, in fact, I can afford to offer such client prospects a "free" hour of my time examining their situation to see whether they would benefit from my advising services. My existing clients have, in fact, paid for that time!

N.B. If I, however, have to cancel a meeting, I must make up that time with the client. That's my fault, not his. When he cancels a meeting, on the other hand, that's his problem, not mine. Collectively I call the reasons why a client cancels a meeting the "Dog Ate My Homework" Syndrome, and I have found over the years that clients are remarkably fertile about the excuses they'll use for avoiding and postponing meetings which are very much to their advantage. Curious, isn't it? And, as you see, profitable to me, for in practice a client, having secured by contract 56 hours, and having paid for about 46 of them at the rate of $250 per hour, will only actually use about 40 during the course of the year, thus nicely raising my hourly stipend over my regular rate and allowing me to provide client propects with time which I otherwise, because I was not being directly compensated, might well begrudge them. To add to all this, clients missing meetings put the task you are collectively working on at risk and should be told so. In this fashion, not only are you paid for hours you do not work, can you prospect for new clients while being subsidized for doing so, but you can put any blame for lack of progress directly where it belongs — on the client — and thereby strengthen your hand in dealing with them. Yes, I like the Delphic Oracle contract option and am frankly amazed so few advisors have anything vaguely resembling it.

It's important to develop as many of these different problem solving packages as you can, to have a line of advising services which can progressivley be supplemented as you move through the various problem solving possibilities of the Mobile Mini-Conglomerate. The more options you have for the client to select from, the better for both of you.

Having said this, let me remind you that once you have these various options available, you need the skill of salesmanship more than ever. For this skill involves not so much selling the client a problem solving vehicle but selling a better vehicle than he had in fact been considering getting. Once you have identified a problem and a client population that has this problem, once you know you can deliver a disproportionate benefit compared to fee, salesmanship is the art of getting the client to buy not merely a means of solving his problem but that means which is the most lucrative to you as well as most beneficial to the client. Fortunately the development of the proper image, a Quintessential American Success Image, and the right documents will assist you in reaching this goal. Read on!

CHAPTER 5

Still More Preparation

By the title of this chapter you are getting the idea, and getting it strongly, I trust, that to succeed as an advisor or any free-standing, independent professional means a vast amount of preparation. Selling the clients, indeed working with your clients, should be almost mechanical for you, since much of the real work happens long in advance of your ever seeing an actual client.

By this I mean, you must have thought well in advance exactly who you are targeting your services to and exactly what you can and will do for them and the ways in which you'll offer your expertise. Without a doubt, one of the chief reasons for failure as an advisor is the fact that too little thought goes into the process of selecting clients and targeting them, making sure that they have the problem you can solve and have the resources to retain you to solve it. There's too much "catch as catch can" in the practices of too many advisors.

Here's some more information so that that doesn't happen to you.

Setting An Image

Much rubbish has been written about images and their role in business. Here are some of my thoughts on the matter:

- Not every advisor needs to follow the rather sterile and unimaginative "dress for success" formulas propounded by the likes of John Malloy in his book of the same name. These formulas may make sense for those attempting to work in Fortune 500 companies, but advisors are to be found in many, many other situations. The problem of image is much more complicated than some of these "image consultants" would have us imagine:

    i. Give consideration to your clients, what they wear, how they look, where they work. Your image must take into account their own patterns of behavior (which obviously includes dress), what will make them comfortable but what will also establish you as a knowledgeable, intelligent, empathetic and, importantly, genuine personality. In such circumstances the standard three-piece suit doesn't by any means always work.

    ii. You must take into account who you are, your own desires and objectives and the image you are trying to propound. Again, most importantly, you need to project an image, indeed the perceived reality, of genuineness and authenticity.

    iii. An image should be clean, crisp and capable of being understood in an instant, for an image is nothing more than a hook which snags the attention of a client prospect and lets that prospect know, in an instant, that you are not only capable of solving his problem but that you are also a person they want to be with. Both of these are important for an advisor for, in fact, with each advisor there are actually two sales to be made: you are selling yourself as an individual the client prospect wishes to spend a sustained amount of time with and you are selling your ability to solve the prospect's problem. If you fail to make both these sales, you will not end up their advisor.

In this connection, I think of a man I saw on the Boston subway yesterday while I was mulling over this chapter. It was late afternoon and he ran into the car. He was obviously a businessman of some kind in his mid-forties. He was dressed in a light brown suit wearing a gold signet pinkie ring, a flashy gold bracelet and picked his teeth with a toothpick. I analyzed this man in the light of what I'm telling you for this chapter and the following things occurred to me:

- Except in Hollywood and the fashion industry, men still cannot wear gold jewelry. It looks decidedly lower class. If you want to inspire the confidence of your buyers, lay off. It smacks of the wrong kind of people.
- Be very careful about the colors you wear and the kinds of material. His businessman's brown was anemic and thin; it looked cheap and nasty. It did not inspire confidence.
- Don't pick your teeth.

Do these things sound obvious? They're not. Day in, day out I face people who have obviously not given any prolonged attention to who they are, who they are trying to reach, do not understand what their clients need to see them as being, or how to approach them to gain the client's confidence. An image, in a fraction of time, begins to provide satisfactory conclusions to these points. It should be complete, thorough-going, concise, and should at once sell you and your ability to provide the kind of professional advice that your client needs.

In my work on this question, I have identified a series of what I call Quintessential American Success Images. These are images which, if properly employed, go far towards making the necessary two-tier sale that satisfies client prospects that you are the right advisor for them. These images are all client-oriented, meaning that while they are about you, they also take into account your client prospects, their aspirations and anxieties, their almost palpable fears, and your ability to deal with them. There's an old saw, "Eat for yourself. Dress for others." Too many people nowadays have forgotten this. In this heyday of the "me generation", people are eating for themselves, dressing for themselves, and generally living for themselves. This is fine if you are independently wealthy and contemptuous of others but not if you expect to make a living and gain confidence and rapport of people who need you.

Quintessential American Success Images

Advisors are people who solve problems. That much is very clear. Therefore any image involving you as a problem solver must exhibit the following characteristics:

- empathy
- intelligence.

These two traits are absolutely important and must be evident in any advising image. To show intelligence without empathy is to focus the discussion on who you are and what you have. That's very detrimental to your interests, since the discussion must focus first on the prospect and his problems and only secondarily on you and your ability to solve them. The precedence always goes to the client and his fixation with his problem. If you show intelligence but not empathy you will be thought to be bright, no doubt, but the client may very well not select you as his advisor, since you failed in the acid test of concern for the client and his problems.

On the other hand, there are those, alarmingly frequent in the aftermath of a wave of California-isms, who can show empathy but haven't the intelligence to make the empathy worthwhile. I see quite a lot of these people. Is it wrong to suppose that there are more of them on the West Coast than the East? Nonetheless, they are deeply disturbing to me because they do evince an almost morbid interest in your problems but haven't the skills, intelligence, or sustained effort to help you solve them. They are as unwelcome as the brand of cool but self-centered intelligence which the other model manifests. Hence the need for the two following images:

The Accessible Expert, The In-Command Technocrat/Infocrat

When people buy you, make no mistake about it, they want an expert. But they do not want a cold, aloof expert spouting jargon and other (generally) meaningless language. They want someone who understands their problems and speaks to them about it in language that is at once clear, precise (without being pedantic), and meaningful. I have a curious hobby of actually listening to professionals as they talk and notice how they obscure the most common concepts and principles in a maze of obscurantist language. It's infuriating, and, as I said at the beginning of this book, it's a sign of an uneducated person, not an intelligent one. For you to do this is a passport to oblivion.

The image of the Accessible Expert meets a profound need for the advisor. On the one hand it meets the need for you to shine forth as an expert, as someone who understands the problem at hand, understands how it has developed and how it stands with the client and how to go about solving it with the client's assistance. But at the same time, you project a warmth and accessibility which assures and reassures the client that you will be there to help them as necessary.

The Accessible Expert is a warm image. It is an image most helpful for clients who are particularly anxious, insecure, who have not previously confronted this problem, who are uncertain about their own ability to solve the problem. Robert Young on "Marcus Welby, M.D." was such an expert, and, of course, he was a much loved figure. The Accessible Expert knows how to use information to solve problems but in such a way that while the problem is in fact solved the client is not overwhelmed by the erudition and expertise of the practitioner. Such an image conforms to the contemporary need for intelligent problem solving skills and the even more profound need for caring consideration, since we live in an age of maximum isolation and diminishing connectedness. The trick to this image is not only providing empathy and intelligent problem solving skills but being seen to do so. That is what an image suggests and confirms: the promise of meeting two deeply felt client needs.

The Accessible Expert is a warm image. The In-Command Technocrat (whom I also call the In-Command Infocrat) is its cool counterpart.

You will find, as you deal with more and still more clients, that in many instances the client's desire to achieve success doesn't begin to approximate your own. Advisors are a success-oriented breed. Clients, paradoxically perhaps, are not always equally motivated to solve their problems. In many instances, they wish only to get credit for looking like they are working on a solution without going through the bother of actually getting one, for this is a much more demanding and often uncongenial task.

Moreover, there are clients who are terribly anxious about confronting the problem, who know nothing about how to do so and who need a hand to hold and an advisor with a powerful kick to help elicit movement. This is where the In-command Technocrat comes in.

I told you before that charm is necessary to a successful advisor, that good manners are essential, the ability to be pleasant and still action oriented. But from time to time with alarmingly regularity you'll find yourself in situations where plain speaking is absolutely called for. I think for instance of dealing with a cigarette smoker who has been told time and again, at first pleasantly, then with greater asperity, to stop smoking. Yet he continues to do so, killing himself by inches. Finally, out of love, remember, out of love and an acute desire to solve the problem that the cigarettes cause, you must lay down the law. This is where the In-Command Technocrat comes in.

Both images evince technical expertise, intelligence and knowledgeability. Both employ empathetic variations for, make no mistake about it, the In-Command Technocrat/Infocrat is no less empathetic than the Accessible Expert, a fact it is often easy to forget when the withering and precise commentary of the latter is being delivered.

The advisor, however, must feel free to employ both as needed, and, depending on who the client is, the client's degree of obstruction of a solution, and the anxieties (real and imagined) which the client faces.

There are many other images, too, which a successful advisor can employ:

- The Maverick. With this image the advisor is seen to be on the cutting edge of change, offering new, imaginative and constructive solutions to client problems. With this image, as with all the images, there must be a degree of highly perceived intelligence (and problem solving) and empathy towards the client's problems. Whatever the image, these factors must remain highly visible.
- The All American Mother. This very powerful Quintessential American Success Image is, of course, limited to women. It taps into our collective desire to be loved and nurtured by Mom. If you want to attract clients who have problems and who need this obvious nurturing, this is a very powerful image to project.

I am not, here, going to list all the possible images for you. I did so in **THE UNABASHED SELF-PROMOTER'S GUIDE**, which remains, as far as I am aware, the most complete discussion on the subject for those of us who work outside mainline corporate America. As you craft your image use this book and **THE UNABASHED SELF-PROMOTER'S GUIDE** to make sure that your image meets not only your needs but also attracts and comforts clients who need to be reassured about your intelligence and problem solving skills and also your empathy for their conditions.

I will say this, however, as you construct your image take into account your perceived negatives, too. No one is perfect, but it is the job of an image to enhance the qualities you do have and diminish the negative impact of those often very obvious drawbacks that you do have, too.

- Do you talk slowly, methodically?
- Do you have a pronounced regional accent?
- Are you a woman or minority in a predominantly white male field?
- Are you very young or old for the advisor work you are practicing?
- Are you physically handicapped?

These, and a thousand other conditions, are facts of life, but they are not necessarily negative facts of life. How they are perceived by your client prospects depends on your ability to craft a Quintessential American Success Image — and to put the proper gloss on the condition in question.

- Talking methodically, for instance, might be perceived as the sign of a slow, plodding mind. It can also, properly understood, be seen as the sign of a deep thinker, plumbing the depths of any given point, methodically analyzing data, seeing connections and patterns, and giving all that you see the benefit of your vast intelligence. What's the difference? Positioning for one thing, positioning and telling people.

When you are dealing with negatives and how to transform them into perceived benefits, don't let the people (client prospects) you are dealing with struggle alone to a proper understanding of your virtues. Help them arrive at the right conclusion. Tell them. Have satisfied client prospects tell them. Address the perceived flaws directly, in the most open and candid way. We used to do this at Harvard with recommendations written about the undergraduates for the major prizes like the Rhodes. Obvious weaknesses of the candidates were not suppressed but were dealt with in the most beneficial way. No one (except perhaps yourself) expects you to be perfect. What is expected is to deal with your faults (or perceived faults, that being basically the same thing) with the utmost candor so as to place them in perspective.

An individual who speaks slowly, ploddingly, gracelessly may be either perceived as stupid and backward or as contemplative, weighing all the alternatives before taking necessary action. It depends on the image you portray and how that image is established in your various documents (which I'll discuss momentarily).

- A regional accent can be a real plus when selling to people in that area, for its says, unmistakenly, "I am one of you. I understand you." It helps to establish a significant degree of empathy with your client prospects. But where you are selling to others outside the area, you had best address the subject forthrightly with a degree of good humor and directness so that what could be a barrier fails to be one.

- Being a woman or minority in a predominantly male field is, indeed, a problem, but it also establishes you, immediately, as a trendsetter, a frontiersman, someone on the cutting edge of change. If you can establish this as a significant trait, you can clearly establish it in relation to other things you are doing, too.
- Are you very young? Then focus on your intelligence. Or on your ability to solve problems. Or on the fact that given your age you are competing against others twice your age and more. People like winners, and youth is progressively more attractive the older one gets and the less of it one has oneself. I found at an early age that people are willing to help me the younger I was so long as I was interested in them and their interests. The image must demonstrate the attractiveness of youth and not it prevailing selfishness.
- By the same token, if you are older, then stress your experience. But remember, being old can be perceived as a prescription for being out of it, too. Here the image must be experience linked to an understanding of what is new and valuable on the contemporary scene.
- A physical handicap can work for or against you, just like these other characteristics and traits. People like to help, like to work with people who are overcoming their disabilities, not giving in to them. Americans, being an inherently fair minded and just people, like helping others and will help you on your way, too, if you have a handicap, if you are perceived as fighting against it, not giving in to it.

This is not a book on image, but in this section I mean to stress just how important your image is. To reiterate:

- An image is your attempt to answer the felt needs, anxieties and aspirations of a client prospect by assuring him that you are both empathetic and intelligent and that you can solve his problem.
- An image is built on your perceived positives and your perceived negatives, transforming the latter into benefits which show you to be both empathetic and intelligent and the kind of person that your client wants to know.
- While each image should be thorough-going and complete, you need *not* adopt a single image and stay with it forever, or even in all situations in a single day. Your task is to be aware of all the images that are suitable for you and your clients and to utilize the maximum number of them as needed. That means that even in a single situation you may find yourself being warm (The Accessible Expert), cool (The Incommand Technocrat/Infocrat), on the cutting edge of change (The Maverick or Frontiersman) or some other combination of possibilities — all designed to show you as intelligent and empathetic.

I must stress and stress again that in any consideration of image, it is of the utmost importance that you be authentic and genuine and that you not seek artificially to blot out aspects of who you are and the way you act. By this I most assuredly do not mean that you have to tell a client exhaustively about yourself. I don't mean that at all! But I do mean that the way you relate to a client must be absolutely authentic and genuine, candid and open within the rather circumscribed limits that necessarily characterize a client-advisor relationship. Thus, I know immediately upon seeing someone in a three-piece suit whether or not that is the correct attire, the right image altogether for that person. They may have read in some book that that is the look, but they have not considered who they are, what their client needs, and how best to establish the necessary link between client and advisor.

In my own case, for instance, my workshop participants and readers of my other books, where I have admitted these facts, are surprised, often amazed, to learn that I do not have a suit, not a single one; that I don't have a car, even the Mercedes Benz that they apparently think I should have! My leading image, the All-American Whiz Kid, with its subsets, including The Accessible Expert (and the In-Command Technocrat/Infocrat, when needed), the Maverick, &c — allows for such peculiarities. It doesn't bother my clients who are not, however, Fortune 500 corporate clients but rather independent consultants, small businesses, nonprofit organizations, professional associations, universities, &c., the kinds of places, in short, where my behavior and offbeat image are acceptable and which enables me to stand forth as entirely genuine and authentic. This, I think, goes far to explain (in conjunction with the success of the consultancies themselves) why my advising relationships are of exceedingly long duration. The people know I can solve their problems and feel comfortable with who I am and the way I present myself. This is the *sine qua non* of any practice.

Once you've got your image (or, I might say, linked images, since one is usually not sufficient for all the situations in which you'll find yourself and will want to draw clients), write down all the descriptive words and phrases that pertain to that image. The reason for doing this is so that in the documents you produce (your first set of promotional materials) these words will be present. I am very clear about this: if you want someone to know that you are helpful, that you are innovative, that you have discovered a new and productive problem solving technique, you've got to tell them. Don't leave it to the (usually meager) imaginations of others to guess your intentions. Attracting business to yourself is really a simple thing, but for such a simple process, it is amazing to me how many otherwise intelligent people fail to get the point of telling people exactly what they need to hear about the advisor, who he is and what he can do for the client.

Thus, if you are attempting to portray yourself as an Accessible Expert, here are some good conjuring words:

- warm
- congenial
- knowledgeable (always this!)
- intelligent
- clear
- comfortable
- non-threatening
- friendly
- neighborly

You get the idea. You want people to know, and all the documents you create must show them, that you are at once technically expert and personally empathetic to the client's concerns. I'll say it again: to succeed as an advisor it is not enough, it is in fact decidedly insufficient, to be knowledgeable, to be intelligent, to be able to solve a client's problem. For if the client feels in any way uncomfortable with you, unless you have an absolutely unique service, the client by failing to buy/accept you will fail to use your problem solving skills.

Make sure you keep this list (and be exhaustive in the words and phrases and related concepts that you keep on it). Make sure, however, that what you are writing relates to the needs, anxieties and aspirations of the client (which you'll learn by working with them, talking to them and asking questions of them) and to a consistent theme that you are promoting to your client prospects.

We live in a society, after all, where we are assaulted by hundreds of competing aural and visual images each week and where our attention spans have diminished as our ability to delete these images has increased dramatically. We hear but don't listen. We see but we do not perceive, and in large part this process takes place because each human needs to maintain a measure of inviolate space and consciousness for the needs of his being. This means, of course, that it is increasingly difficult to snag the attention of our buyers, even those buyers and client prospects who have an acute need for the kind of problem solving skills we are selling. That's why you must be very clear that all the materials you produce must offer a unified image on a single, consistent theme and that you must understand that getting this theme to the sustained and real attention of your buyers is a long-time proposition, not something that can occur overnight.

Basic Documents

Once you've got the image, the right words for the image, a precise idea of the market you are targeting and their problems (as they understand them as well as how you understand them) and have thought through your Problem Solving Process and the contractual options you will use (Delphic Oracle vs Full Service), it is time to begin crafting your first set of marketing documents. But let me say this: any paper put out by you, anything dealing with your firm, its services, you, the advisor, must be considered a marketing document.

This is a point that many advisors and independent professionals forget. Thus, each document should be consistent with your leading image, should embody the key words that indicate your empathy and intelligent problem solving procedures, should have complete follow up information and as much material as the client needs to know that you are the right person to help solve their problems. Different documents may work together, may in fact be placed together in a set, but must be capable of standing entirely alone to make the necessary impression on the buyer.

The Wrong Documents

I see a lot of marketing documents and, sadly, much of what I see indicates that on one or more of the counts above the author has failed, thereby not only wasting resources (which is crime enough for a Yankee like me!) but, worse, lowering the impression of the buyer prospect for you and lessoning his willingness, much less enthusiasm, to buy from you. For make no mistake about it, good documents do help but inadequate and mediocre documents hurt you in not one but several ways, a fact worth contemplating before you do anything.

In this connection, people waste their money in many ways. As a Scotsman in good standing, I aim to spend as little money on my marketing documents (and anything else!) that I can. I delight in finding new ways of reducing costs and getting my message, the right message, into the hands (and, indeed, the minds!) of my targeted client prospects. You do the same!

Beware, then, of the following ways to spend your money:

- cards
- garden variety organizational brochures
- general direct mail
- yellow pages advertising
- other forms of paid advertising.

• Cards

I don't have a card and haven't had one for years. When I did have a card I couldn't point to any good that it did, despite the fact that like every other upwardly-mobile professional I passed them out with gay abandon. I now have another, different way of handling cards.

If someone wants information about me, my products and services I hand him a précis, a two-sided 8 1/2 by 11 inch flyer (described below) which is, in one way of looking at it, a gigantic card packed with information. If I want to keep information about them on file, I ask for their card, which I annotate with the following information: time we met, where we met, what we discussed, interests of theirs, anything I'm supposed to do as a result of meeting them.

On your card make sure that you have not only your name, address, and telephone number (I'm staggered by the number of cards which are incomplete in these particulars, and I'm not kidding!) but some indication of the problems you can solve and the services you provide. This may suggest having different cards for different audiences (a problem solved, by the way, with the précis.)

• Garden Variety Organizational Brochures

The other day a friend asked me to review his brochure, a brochure being used to promote a gardening product. Within two minutes, I had discovered two gigantic problems sufficient to ensure that this $300 investment was virtually wasted. There was no price for his product (elementary, my dear Watson) and no clear description of benefits for the buyer. Instead the product was described rather than the benefits clearly established. His money was wasted!

Ordinary brochures don't work very well and, again, I don't have any. Brochures are expensive, tend to age quickly (especially if you add the names of advising associates) and generally focus insufficiently on the benefits of working with you.

Brochures are a business placebo; having one will undoubtedly (if generally incorrectly) make you feel better, and they will satisfy your client prospects to the extent they need to have something about you in their hands as they hear your pitch. But, for my money, they are a waste of time and cash. Instead, try my question and answer, information dense documents explained below.

• General direct mail

Thankfully this is not a book on direct mail, a subject on which I teach an intensive workshop, but I can and will suggest a few problems with the advisor and direct mail. By ordinary direct mail I mean the situation where you attempt to reach large numbers of buyer/client prospects through the post bringing to them a list of your products and services.

Of course, we live nowadays in an age of exploding direct mail. A quick visit to your mail box is proof of that. But for most people direct mail doesn't work, and it is not a good investment for most hoping to promote advising and other independent professional services. For one thing, it's just too expensive. Instead, a little later, I'll clue you in on how to use what I call personalized direct mail or my success letter sequence, which is very profitable, and a technique that you'll use for the remainder of your time in business.

Remember: when you are selling something, you have a much higher likelihood of success if you can make a face to face presentation with the buyer. You have less high likelihood of success if you deal with the buyer prospect on the telephone. And you have a much diminished chance of success if you must deal with the prospect by mail.

Conversely, because most professionals dislike sales, they think first about selling their services by mail, because it is the easiest to conceive of and is less risky for them and easier for them to deal with the rejection that necessarily comes in sales. They go for telephoning client prospects next and finally opt for direct one on one presentations, or just the reverse of the way it should be.

• Yellow pages advertising

I have an advising friend in New Orleans who (until I met her) was spending over $3000 a year on her yellow pages advertising and not making her money back. When I suggested she stop doing this and turn to some of the mechanisms I'm about to recommend to you, she virtually wailed, "But I'll lose business. No one will know how to find me!" It was the professional version of an atavistic shriek. But it's positively rubbish.

I don't have an ad in the yellow pages. Indeed, I don't even have a business telephone, but this has never mattered. People find me just fine, thank you. They'll find you, too, when you begin using the methods I'll be discussing shortly.

If you do feel the need for yellow pages advertising, get the smallest ad and see whether it draws for you. If you are a compulsive comparer, get a bigger ad in the next issue and see whether that draws better. If neither draws well, drop them. Or take my advice right now, save money by doing other things with your money, as per my impending advice.

- **Other Forms of Paid Advertising**

The same largely holds true for other forms of paid advertising, too. In preparing for my "succeeding in your mail order business" course, I talked to several of the best known names in mail order, people who spend tens of thousands of dollars yearly on advertising, to pick their minds. One candidly told me that he doesn't make a dime off sales resulting from his ads (I took this, of course, with a grain of salt) but rather he makes his money selling the names of people who buy and inquire from him to others who want to use them for their own mail order projects. What an admission! I wish it were on a poster so that every professional and independent advisor thinking of using paid ads could consider this before buying space in publications.

Paid advertising may work, but it works only when you have planned a sustained campaign and where you can convert the names derived (as with inquiries for products) into further cash by selling them through a list broker. If and when you can do this, then consider paid advertising. Otherwise, consider the methods I'm about to share with you now.

Your Success Documents

You have already come to know that as a Yankee in good standing I detest spending money unless I am absolutely certain it will meet my profit-making objective. Set this down as your own rule and behave accordingly. Think about whether what you are sending out accomplishes the following objectives:

- Is your document client centered? Does it indicate a knowledge of the client's problems, the problems, that is, that the client (not you!) wants to solve today and is willing to spend this money to solve?
- Does your document clearly indicate exactly what kind of results your service provides? Before you tell **how** the service works, tell exactly what the client can expect to receive as a result of your service. As a professional you may be (and probably are) enamored of your professional methodology. But the client cannot be expected to share your enthusiasm and is interested in it only to the extent that it provides him with the results he is seeking and which must be as obvious to you as it is to him.
- Does your document lead to an action oriented conclusion? Does it move the client step by step through a series of steps toward a buy decision? Professionals are often too proud (to be charitable) to ask for the sale but a sale is always what you want with a client prospect. Your document, standing in place of you, must move the client step by step to a conclusion, even if that conclusion is only picking up the telephone to ask you for more information.
- Does your document make it easy for the client to act, to move towards a resolution of his problem? I'm infuriated when I want to buy the offering and cannot readily find the means of doing so.
- Does your document validate you as both empathetic and intelligent? Are these traits crystal clear in the materials you are creating?
- Does your document present a lean, efficient, taut feeling? Or are there too many words that do not reinforce your leading image of empathy and intelligence?
- Does your document urge action by demonstrating that others have successfully utilized your service?
- Does your document reinforce your image through the color, ink, and type selection and general lay-out?
- Does your document address the leading anxieties of your clients and let them know that they are in good hands with you? (Do you even know what the leading anxieties are of your clients and why, if they are not dealt with, the client may very well not contract with you?)
- Does your document provide precise information about how you work so the client knows what he's buying?

Whatever you write, whenever you write it, read over these ten points and review the documents below to make sure you get the best results from your documents.

Success Documents Continued

Most people in most circumstances are justifiably cautious. They should be cautious, too, because most people are quite capable of making the wrong decision and their caution is justified because of the frequency with which they do the wrong thing, squander their resources, and end up with less than they should. That's why these documents are called "Success Documents", because they clearly indicate to any client prospect that their money will be well spent and because by working with a reputable, knowledgeable, intelligent and empathetic professional like you there is an enhanced likelihood of reaching their objectives successfully. The problem, of course, arises when you have just begun your business.

At The Beginning

Whether you are now a practicing advisor, independent professional or another offering an advice-generated service, or whether you are only now contemplating beginning such a course, keep a Success Record. Even when I was in high school, I kept a large sheet of poster board tacked to the inside of my bedroom closet door on which I meticulously listed each one of my successes and every one of my failures. It was a useful, if often chastening, experience! These days I keep a journal, which serves the same function, in which I weigh what I am doing, what worked (and why) and what didn't (ditto).

To succeed as an independent professional of any kind means to be consciously aware not only what you do or when you do it (for this is simply historical information) but what kind of success resulted from your direct involvement and what this success means for the person or organization you helped. Now, you may tell yourself that you already keep such a reckoning mentally, but unless these items are consistently written down, consistently weighed and evaluated, consistently analyzed and considered, I'll wager that you have no clear conception of precisely what good you are doing for the people you are with. And this goes, by the way, for your current full-time position as well, which must be so analyzed so as to provide you with suitable testimonials and validation as you jump off for a career as an independent professional.

I call this Success Analysis, and it's a critical prerequisite of fashioning a successful career whether or not you are an independent professional, and in whatever documents you may create for yourself.

Part of the purpose of your Success Analysis (and the folder in which you should log all your successes) is to get away from thinking that merely putting in hours, merely contemplating an issue, merely working (as work is generally understood) are at all meaningful in establishing your independent practice. They aren't. You could put in long hours, engage in profound contemplation of issues, and work hard, even slavishly, and fail to be anything remotely resembling a success — and it could, in fact would, be you own fault.

Instead, you must learn to see what you do exclusively in terms of clearly perceiving a client's problem and applying your intelligence and technical expertise so that this problem is solved and the client achieves the disproportionate benefit he desires. This is the entire purpose of any professional practice, and seeing things in this way enables you to write the most successful possible marketing copy, copy that will decidedly appeal to others who have that problem and wish to gain that solution.

Moreover, each success that you gain must be put in a context, put in its proper situation, so that anyone else contemplating the situation will be clearly aware of exactly what the success means. To wit: as I write I am working with a national professional association that is now 74 years old. In the 74 years it has amassed an endowment of about a million dollars. But in the 11 months I have been associated with the organization, I have helped them raise, one way and another, over a million, including one very large capital gift for a new building, the first real estate they have themselves owned in their entire history. As written in my success log, the bare figures themselves, while perhaps impressive, only become truly meaningful when placed in the context that in a single year I assisted in the raising of as much money as in the previous 74 years combined. *That* is a truly meaningful statistic.

Now let us say that I was not yet an independent development advisor but rather a full-time employee working on this project contemplating a career move to autonomy and free-standing status. The fact would remain the same; its significance would remain the same. People get very confused about this and I hear from grown adults constantly, "But I don't have any advising successes to sell. My practice has just begun!"

Such comments irritate me a good deal. Draw from your life for success data! Draw from the past projects you have handled! The past successes you have had! But be sure of this:

- Avoid merely historical data. People do not simply wish to know where you have been and the sequence in which you have accomplished things. That is not enough!

They want to know the dimensions of the success and the context, the situational significance of the success. And it is only with this information that the success can possibly be properly construed and its vital significance established. Thus at one point I was a member of the Massachusetts Commission on the Status of Women. That was important, no doubt. But what made the membership significant was that I was the only man on the Commission; that provided the fact with situational significance and enabled me to be perceived not only as concerned with the issues but as a frontiersman truly on the cutting edge of change.

Of course, the sad fact is that much of what people accomplish they have no idea of what its situational significance is. You have to do a little work to establish it. You have to contemplate the fact and assess — often assign — its significance. In short, you must do more than do; you must think and craft. The full dimensions of success without this thinking and crafting are, however, impossible to know; you will thus fail to derive the full benefits from what you are doing.

The Précis: Your Basic Marketing Document

The word précis is one I have borrowed from my study of diplomatic history. The précis is a short, concise synopsis document which clearly outlines an issue or topic for discussion. (See Samples, page 281. See also page 283).

I first made use of the term and began developing the form with my non-profit fund raising clients who needed not so much a proposal dealing with their need for funds for a particular project (this being called grantsmanship) but rather a document which set forth clearly and concisely who they were, the organizational and programmatic successes they had recently achieved, a list of their various supporters and those capital, program and operating objectives established by the Board of Directors. A précis is a document which makes a good case as to why an organization (or an individual) should be given money (and for what). It is really an investment document rather than a grant proposal and as such is subtly different from the typical grant request form.

Later I began using this form in my own business, with superb results. The précis has several very material advantages which make it a format no advisor or independent professional should be without:

- It's inexpensive. A two-sided 8 1/2 by 11 inch précis on colored paper costs $85 for 1000 copies here and will be significantly less in other areas of the country where offset photocopying is cheaper.
- It need not be typeset but can be typewritten on a good quality machine.
- It can be treated as a relative of the newsletter for as you run off new copies you can add appropriate messages and client offerings to the copy.
- It can easily be inserted in packages, used as conference registration packet stuffers, etc.
- You can keep a variety of different précis available depending on the various clients you wish to attract. Thus, in my case, different précis would have to be prepared for my for-profit clients *vis à vis* my not-for-profit clients. This is easy to do.

Constituents of the Précis

All précis are based on a perceived client problem to which you have the solution. Précis are most decidedly not merely a list of your services but rather an indication that you understand what the client's problems are and that you have developed appropriate services accordingly.

Address your précis to the most significant problem that your client has and use the steps of the problem solving process to show how that problem can be solved. Here's what I mean.

Every nonprofit organization in America wants to raise money. So let's say I create a précis that helps sell my capital campaign fund raising service, a service I offer to organizations needing to buy or rehabilitate a building, land, etc.

The Problem: If you're like most nonprofit organizations you'll find that from time to time your building will require much-needed rehabilitation work. Or, indeed, you may have even reached the point of needing a new building and the land to go with it. Capital campaigns are a necessary part of the work of most every nonprofit organization, and they can be either a rewarding experience for you — or a disaster. Here are some things to keep in mind as you consider undertaking such a campaign:

Now go into the steps of the Problem Solving Process. Tell your client prospect how to:

- put himself in the right mental attitude.
- develop necessary technical prerequisites for success.
- make sure the right people are really committed to the success of this project.
- see whether the timing is right.
- learn how to develop the documents he needs.
- develop a Coordinating Committee.

All the points up to now have been straight forward information designed to assist the client prospect solve his problem. This section properly handled, you have established that you are both empathetic and intelligent, that you can and already have been of assistance to them and have thus indicated that you can be of further assistance, too. Now for the essential point that you are available to be of assistance. Add this point:

- See whether a management advisor can help you. Use this kind of wording. "We have found that most people in a capital campaign are grateful for the assistance of a professional organization which can assist you in reaching your objectives economically, efficiency, without the difficulties which can often arise and which often make such a project a burden. That's where we at Jeffrey Lant Associates, Inc. can be of the utmost assistance to you, and we hope you'll call for a free one-hour consultation on your project."

Now begin to add the necessary validation:

"Many others have found both our service and this free-consultation very helpful." (Add the names here of satisfied clients for validation.) Also, if you have received any newspaper or professional publication or client publication coverage (which you will after following the suggestions in the unabashed promotion chapter) add quotes here to further validate who you are. Validation quotes can come both from satisfied clients as well as from media sources in a position to know something about your work.

Interim Steps. If you have suitable products dealing with your service, now is the time to mention them. In my case, for instance, **DEVELOPMENT TODAY: A FUND RAISING GUIDE FOR NONPROFIT ORGANIZATIONS** has a clear, precise chapter on how to handle capital fund raising campaigns. This information should be included in the précis along with the price (including shipping).

If you have an audio cassette available ("The 10 Most Common Problems in Capital Fund Raising — And What to Do About Them!"), also indicate the tape's availability.

It goes without saying that at the end of the tape you'll include your name, address and telephone number since, properly understood, both the book and the tape (or any other product you may have developed) is best understood as both an independent profit center (for those who cannot afford your services or who wish to undertake the project largely independently) but also, more importantly, as a very sophisticated marketing device for you and what you do. The person, for instance, who reads and understands the book, booklet, or hears the tape will be much more understanding about what needs to be done, how things should be done and the difficulties of proceeding without the expert guidance of — you!

Production and Distribution of Your Précis

Just where and how you distribute your précis depends on who you want as clients, but consider the following:

- Package and invoice stuffers. Each package that leaves my office (and this includes all book bags) and each outgoing invoice includes a précis.
- Seminar and workshop pass-outs. Never give a program henceforward without providing a suitable précis for the audience in question. I am utterly amazed at how infrequently this is done. I remember being the key-note speaker at a recent free-lance writer's conference at the University of Minnesota. There were at least a dozen other speakers and not one, not one!, despite being locally-based and mostly independent professionals, passed out a single brochure — much less crafted précis!
- Find offbeat distribution channels. My précis for nonprofit organizations are distributed (free!) by the local grants library which maintains an information shelf. Several hundred such précis are distributed in this fashion annually.
- Consider package stuffer possibilities. Individuals with products or distribution channels reaching your targeted audience can stuff your précis (for a flat per thousand fee which is usually $50 per thousand) in their outgoing packages. *N.B.* I maintain such a service in which you can participate.
- Ask other advisors and trainers to have your materials at their programs and reciprocate by distributing their materials at yours.
- Find out from your local convention office which meetings are coming to your community in the near future and place your materials on information tables, &c. during the course of the show or convention.
- Place your précis inside air magazines while flying. What else have you got to do?

While writing this chapter I went to the post office one day carrying a stack of books for mailing. I happened to see a friend in the line who recently had seen me on television. He expressed an interest in one of my books and I whipped a précis out of my briefcase and handed him one. Never be without these materials!

Later I shall discuss more about how to use précis in connection with radio and television shows, too; it is one of the things you can send out to those having the problem you go on the air to discuss.

While writing this chapter today, a friend called to discuss promoting a seminar he puts on called "Managing Your Boss." He wanted to know about media possibilities, but I recommended that he consider not only where to promote but the précis that would accompany the promotion. His précis would deal with key issues in managing your boss and would be sent out to all those who wanted to have tips, "tricks of the trade", for successfully doing so. In addition, he'd be selling four things along with this précis:

1) his own workshop on the subject (with precise follow-up information)
2) the book of the same name on the subject. Now this is not his book and to be able to offer it (as he does in his workshops) he needs a distribution deal (drop ship) with the publisher.
3) a 60 minute tape (one cassette) packed with more tricks of the trade
4) his own advising service dealing with the subject.

As I'll say again and again in the self promotion chapter, the media source will be happy to allow you to promote the availability of this précis so long as it's seen as information rich and solving the problems of a targeted population (those people who work and who want to work better and more productivity with their bosses in this case). It is then seen as a public service and not as self-serving promotion.

Variations on the Précis

- Consider crafting a two sided 8 1/2 by 11 inch précis listing all your products and services and explaining who needs them. You may have seen the précis I use for myself in this connection. It always ends with a special conclusion specially titled, "Persistent Reader Reward" or some such. I give those who read to the end of my précis the chance for some special offer that will be to their advantage. This way I ensure that my whole précis gets read (and there's a lot on it!), and I make another sale, too, while benefitting the reader/buyer/client. (See Samples, page 285).

- Consider putting together your own special précis/catalog (as per the example at the end of the book). As you work you'll be identifying books and other products (tapes, newsletters, booklets, &c) that will be of interest to your clients. Make distribution agreements with these people. The customary (but not universal) percentage share is 50-50% between manufacturer and vendor. You'll find that a single sale from one of these mini-catalogs can pay for the cost of producing 1000 pieces. I highly recommend it and would be glad to be a part of yours.
- Consider placing a whole article by you (always assuming it directly relates to the targeted client population) or about you (assuming that the targeted client population would be interested) on the reverse of your précis as validation of you and your service. The question often arises as to whether you have to use all of the article in question and the answer is "No!" You can have set in type the following phrases: "As seen in" "Excerpted from" &c and use them as necessary. You don't need to use the date (after six months any article begins to seem dated) and can snip out bits of the article you don't like and use what you do. Use your imagination! You don't, by the way, have to secure the permission of the publication to use the article either. So long as you identify from whence it has come, the publication will be quite happy to use it: after all it promotes them, too!

Other Success Documents

As an outgrowth of your Success File, you can begin to create what I call the Mini-Case. Much of your prosperity as an advisor and independent professional will come from replicating your successes with other individuals and organizations who suffer from the same problem (wholly or in part) and wish to solve it. Your experience in handling something comparable makes you all the more desirable to those who must also face this situation. Hence the Mini-Case. (See Samples, page 279).

The Mini-Case is, as its name suggests, a very brief document of about 300-350 words. It provides a client prospect with the following information about a comparable situation you have already faced:

- the name of the organization
- individual you worked with
- the exact nature of the problem
- the success you had in solving it, as specifically as possible
- the amount of time you worked with the client
- any professional recognition you secured as a result of solving this problems (including awards, write-up in company newsletter, other, outside publicity, &c.)

The Mini-Case, like every success document you create, should be placed (typewritten or typeset, if you prefer) on a sheet of your stationery which contains complete follow-up information: your name, address, and telephone number.

The only problem you will face in creating this document is in situations where the client does not wish you to mention his name, for you have to secure the client's permission to use his name and situation. This will not be difficult to do if you are working with organizations and individuals who are not directly competitive with the client. If you are, then the client will quite naturally not wish his exact particulars cited. In this case, you will be reduced to using generic information that gives an idea of the client's situation but without the precise information that is best for you.

You may conclude this document with the client's name, address and telephone number so that client prospects may call direct for further information. I prefer instead, however, to keep this information on file and to alert client prospects that when the discussion of a contract becomes serious, I will provide this reference as I see fit. I don't like to trouble my clients (and past clients!) unnecessarily and neither should you.

You should produce no more than about 50 to 100 copies of your Mini-Case, and you should feel (as your success record space grows) free to stop using them as you develop new, more impressive successes. But never throw them all away. Keep one for your own file as an illustration of materials you produce and to remind yourself, in your years of prosperity, how far you've come from your beginnings!

Mini-Case Variation

Consider using the reverse side of your Mini-Case for an article by or about you, quotes from other, satisfied buyers of your service or a variation of the précis (problem solving process) as it relates to the problem you have solved and which others would like to solve. You've paid for the paper, so you might as well get the best use of it!

Successful Projects Description

One more variation of the Mini-Case I call a Successful Projects Description. If you have handled several successful projects dealing with a common theme, you may wish to cite them on a single 8 1/2 by 11 inch flyer. Make sure to include all the information that goes in a Mini-Case including the situational context for the success you helped obtain. Remember: don't leave the client prospect to attempt to figure out exactly what your success means. Provide the relevant context for them. People cannot be expected to know, because you know, exactly what your success means and its significance. If you want them to know, tell them!

Success Letters

As should be entirely clear to you by now, advisors succeed by helping to bring about success with their clients and by bringing this success, and their ability to help create it, to the attention of other individuals and organizations similarly situated, wishing to duplicate the success. Sadly, too many advisors and independent professionals look upon their activities as somehow distinct, autonomous, and unconnected to each other. Thus they fail to get the maximum advantage from each assignment. No successful assignment has been successfully completed until such time as you have used it to leverage further business from those organizations similarly situated and to derive the maximum amount of promotional and public relations advantage. If, upon the conclusion of a successful assignment, you simply walk away from it without making further use of it to enhance your career, raise your standing in your field and garner new clients, you are ensuring the wasting away of your business.

Hence the need for a complete understanding of The Success Letter, which is a tool to be used again and again.

I have previously advised you to consider most seriously the advisability of using direct mail to promote your business and gather new clients. For most advisors, for most independent professionals, standard direct mail is a complete waste of money and resources and should be avoided. Until such time as you are ready to generate names in masses of at least 5000 (for that is a convenient unit for further sale), you must be very, very cautious about how and when to use direct mail.

There is, fortunately, an intermediate step to take which I very strenuously recommend to you. I call it "Personalized Direct Mail" and it rests on the leveraging of a successful project and a follow-up Success Letter. Here's a superb illustration of how a success letter sequence works:

I happen currently to represent (as I usually do) a Massachusetts visiting nurse organization, a not-for-profit agency assisting with various kinds of home health and nursing activities in a Boston bedroom community. I have previously represented other organizations in this industry and will, as a result of these activities, represent still others. Here are some things you must know about successfully using Success Letters in such an environment.

- You must identify all the organizations that have the same kind of problem as the current client. That is easily done in this situation, because there is a statewide association of these organizations and a booklet which lists their names, addresses, telephone numbers and the name of the executive director.

- Once you have made the decision that this clientele will sustain your income expectations (either in whole or in part) you must realize that on the basis of any single letter you will not do any better than a 1 to 2% return. That, therefore, whatever the perceived need of the organizations/client prospects in question (which must be, by the way, as clearly perceived by them as it is by you), you have to be prepared to make a longterm commitment to generating clients from within this industry even if you have no direct competitors and especially so if you do.

- The chances for a successful result are significantly increased if you can factor in some or all of the following:

    i) testimonials from satisfied clients known to those you are addressing.

    ii) publicity generated within publications read by your client prospects and information and promotion about your successes with organizations they recognize and know about.

    iii) telemarketing follow up to letters.

    iv) sale of products on subjects of their interest which will help to reinforce your own availability to solve their problems.

    v) a series of Success Letters which alerts prospects to your continuing success with any single client known to them.

    vi) a training program (perhaps sold by their own professional or trade association) which allows you to meet client prospects face to face and, through pre- and post-program publicity, be promoted to them, activities which reinforce your expert status and availability to the client prospect on an individual basis.

In short, the Success Letter is best seen as only a part, though a very significant part, of a train of possibilities which reinforces in the client's mind the fact that you are an empathetic and intelligent problem solver who is available to deal with their pressing need.

Writing Your Success Letter

Writing a persuasive Success Letter, one that causes the client prospect to feel that this letter addresses his problem and which motivates him to take prompt action, is unquestionably an art (See Samples, page 296). It is an art which takes into consideration the following critical points:

- the tone of the letter
- the look

- the length
- the inserts which accompany your Success Letter.

Whenever possible the Success Letter should be addressed to the person who has check signing and project authorization power. How do you know?

You have got to be sufficiently aware of your market (you are, aren't you?) to know who is the proper person to address your letter to. This seems obvious doesn't it, and yet scarcely a day goes by that I don't hear a story of such a letter sent ignominiously to "To whom it may concern" or some other obviously impersonal, obviously incorrect individual. If you don't know, if you cannot find a suitable directory, if an appropriate list does not exist, you need to create one for yourself. Start by telephoning. Yes, telephoning is expensive. Yes, it takes time. No, it always isn't easy and effortless. But the information you have still will be useful, if you have truly identified a client prospect's need and have the appropriate problem solving process and technical skills to resolve it. (Need I say, by the way, that once you have such a list, don't share it?)

Contents of a Success Letter

The opening paragraph of a Success Letter should speak directly and forcefully to that problem which is currently causing your client prospect concern. Remember that this problem may not be the one which you regard as most significant. But it is the one (and you know it from client discussions, your professional readings, &c) that is currently exorcising them. To indicate your empathy and identification with the prospect, use the exact language that he uses to describe his situation. This is one time when it is perfectly permissible to use the client prospect's own idiosyncratic words and jargon: after all, you want him to know that you understand him, and what better way is there than by literally speaking his language?

In Paragraph 2, indicate that there is a solution to his problem. Often this can be a simple one-sentence paragraph which says simply, "Fortunately there is a solution to this problem!"

In Paragraph 3 introduce your problem solving skills which deal with the client's plainly perceived problem. "I have been working for the last several years to develop an inexpensive, most effective solution to this problem and I'd like to tell you something about how it works."

In Paragraph 4, introduce the name of an individual or organization known to the client who has already used this problem solving process and achieved a disproportionate benefit compared to your fee. "But don't take our word that the service works. Let me refer you to (name of client). They can attest to its benefits." In this paragraph you must be as specific and detailed as possible about the exact results the client obtained over the period of time. And, as in all documents, you must put this result into the proper situational context so that the reader understands (and does not merely have to deduce) how significant they are. Don't desert the reader at this point! He needs you to tell him exactly how significant your success has been!

Add the past client's name, address and telephone number. But do so only after you have secured his permission to act in this fashion and shown him the letter you are intending to send out. In this situation, the past client cannot be kept in the dark; that is very much against your interest.

As with the Mini-Case, if a past client cannot or will not cooperate with this venture, you'll have to include less specific, less detailed (and hence less useful) information. In this situation, address the reason for your lack of specificity and put the best possible gloss on the situation. "I wish I could provide you with more specific information on who we worked with and precisely the results that we achieved, but as you can imagine I respect our client's wish to remain anonymous, just as I will respect any particular wishes you may have of me during our relationship."

Paragraph 5. Tell people what inserts you have included and recommend any other problem solving products or related services that you have. In any letter I send to the visiting nurse associations, for instance, I never fail to point out the availability of several of my books, including, of course, my fund raising book, which will help them solve their problems. It is always in your best interest to promote your information and problem solving products as they serve as very effective and long-lasting marketing devices for you and your company.

Also, inform the reader about how you will follow-up this letter. Tell them, too, about any particular offer you are now making available (e.g., a free hour's consultation to discuss their situation, &c). I like to send out batches of letters that I intend to follow up by telephone in tens. Ten at any given time is as many as I can deal with, given the number of calls it may take until we connect.

Finally, always ask for the sale. Let people know that you want their business, that you have the means of helping them to solve their problems and providing a disproportionate benefit compared to your fee. Tell them, again, that you are ready, willing and able to work for them. Americans still respond well (thank God!) to people who really want to work for their money. Don't put the client prospect in the unfortunate position of asking you whether you are ready to assist them.

Let them know in no uncertain terms that you are absolutely ready to help them out. And mean it!

The Success Sequence

I shall later expand upon portions of what I'm going to write about here, but let's begin to talk about The Success Sequence and how you can profit from it. Sadly, even people in need don't always (or even often) act expeditiously to get what they want and must have. That's why you must reinforce in the mind their own need and your ability to deliver a solution to their problem. That's where the Success Sequence comes in. Here are the steps:

- Clearly identify a target market which has the specific problem(s) to which you have the solutions.
- Find or create a mailing list of these individuals/organizations.
- Create a mailing package to them which clearly indicates your ability to solve their problem and that you fully understand their need.
- Mail the package.
- Determine your post-mailing follow up. Consider the advisability of:
  telemarketing
  workshops and seminars.
- Work to gain a single client from the targeted population
- Gather a success working with this client.
- Use the success as the basis for unabashed promotion and marketing to attract similar clients with comparable problems.
- Bring the success to the attention of these comparable individuals and organizations through another targeted mailing followed by telemarketing, workshops, seminars and further unabashed marketing and promotion.
- Continue the process until you are indisputably recognized expert in your field.

This is the Success Sequence, and I shall be expanding upon it throughout this book.

There is an important principle which needs to be recognized here. Don't think that a single letter, a single mailing, a single lecture, a single telephone call, a single success will be sufficient to ensure the profitability and longevity of your business. It won't. Success is built on the recognition that even people with substantial problems (and the money to solve them) often move excruciatingly slowly to solve them. Businesses are built slowly, steadily, only through your patience and your continuing ability to identify the problems of a highly targeted market and solve them. This is exactly what the Success Sequence enables you to do. Let me give you an example of the process.

I have, as you already know, as one of my highly targeted markets for advising and other services the visiting nursing organizations of Massachusetts. This is a very specific group of organizations with very specific problems.

The first problem is how to get the mailing list. Since there are only about 125 such organizations in Massachusetts, it is highly unlikely that any mailing house will keep it on file. It's too small and not sufficiently profitable. Thus, the only practical way of getting the names and addresses of both executive directors and organizations which I desire is to get a friend to lend me the association membership list from which I can work. This can also be done through networking.

N.B. Occasionally it is a good idea to join an organization where you can get this information and to meet your client prospects, but in a case like this that's not possible: the organization is designed exclusively for executives of visiting nurse organizations.

The next step is to create a suitable mailing package. Here's what I put in mine:

- cover (sales) letter (after you've had a client in this universe, this letter follows the standard success letter format).
- precis of services and products of interest to visiting nurse organizations. The more fully actualized your Mobile Mini-Conglomerate is, the more things you'll have to discuss here.
- contract options (Delphic Oracle vs Full Service)
- validating documents including articles by and about you from publications of interest to the targeted population and testimonials from those known to the affected/designated population.

Once the package is mailed, I follow up with selected telephone (telemarketing calls, and in addition I occasionally do a workshop or seminar on a subject of immediate interest to the population ("The Ten Things You Need To Know To Successfully Raise Money in 1992.") It should go without saying (but probably doesn't) that you'll pass out complete packets of information (precis, contract options, validating documents,) at any such meetings you have.

Once a client has been successfully snagged, the next step is to get some success. This is where your technical and problem solving skills come into play. But once you've had a success which is meaningful to the affected population then bring it to the attention of others who would like to replicate it for themselves. This suggests that as successes begin to pile up, you can generate a succession of success letters and success packets to others. I suggest quarterly letters to client prospects.

In Chapter 6, I shall go on to describe some of these techniques in sufficient detail to make the best use of them. But for now let me tell you what lessons are to be learned here:

1. Don't put your money into expensive all-round documents like brochures. I haven't had a typical brochure in years. I've saved the money and met the needs of my client prospects and soon-to-be customers through other materials which are cheaper and more nearly suited to their situations.

2. Produce fewer of these materials rather than more. If you think that 1000 brochures is just a few, you won't as soon as you have to consider how to distribute them. Do your documents in multiples of 50, or 100 if you're an optimist. Rework them as often as necessary until you are absolutely confident (because a client tells you!) that you completely understand the problems of your audience and that you have tailored your solutions (and hence, your documents) to the people you are trying to sell to.

3. Focus. Focus. And focus again. You don't need to sell your product or service to everyone to become wealthy and well off. You simply need to make sure that you have a complete understanding of a single, specific market and that you are sure you are meeting their needs.

4. Don't consider anything you do in isolation. Part of what you are getting from a successful assignment is the ability to replicate it for others who are similarly situated. Thus at all times while you are helping your clients create the successes they so much want, consider the opportunities for leveraging this success to your benefit. A success has many uses but for you one of the crucial benefits is its ability to get you further business. Who, however, can know about your successes if you don't consider how to use personalized direct mail, unabashed promotion and marketing, workshops and seminars and the other means through which you can bring a complete realization of the success to others who want to replicate it?

5. Keep your investment in materials small, very, very small. The challenge of successful marketing is how many people you can reach by spending very few dollars.

Understanding that you must continue to reinforce your client prospects' knowledge that you exist, that you understand their problems and that you can solve them is a critical aspect of business success for the advice giver. Ultimately, if you continue to do these reinforcing activities daily, as I do, your success will be assured, for you will pick up not only the clients who are responding to today's marketing efforts but also those who, on account of the cumulative effect of all your efforts, finally, slowly, respond, too. At which point, you know you have truly arrived and that your success is sure and unbounded.

To make this system work, however, you must have success. And to have success you must get clients. In the next chapter you'll find more information on how to achieve this necessary condition.

CHAPTER 6

Beginning To Get Clients

I am absolutely convinced that all-too-many advice givers maintain this unproductive attitude: "I'm good," they say and say again. "Therefore people will find me."

I don't believe this, never have, and hopefully never will. It's the most self defeating of attitudes — and it's rampant.

If you want clients, you have to put into effect an action plan to get them. You most need this action plan when you are just beginning. That's all right. You'll have the most time then to invest, more than you'll ever have again. And, of course, your need is self-evident.

Using Your Current Position

Most people know that their present job can be done in much less time than it now is. Whose law is it which says that the job expands to fill the available time? Well, that's very, very true. The solution? Make a deal with your boss to continue as an advisor offering the heart of your current services in return for between 40-60% of your current wage.

What you are getting with your current job should be very clear: the security of a paycheck. Most job surveys show time and again that what people like about their jobs is the regularity of the money. For most people most jobs are dissatisfiers, not satisfiers. But you can structure things so that you get the bulk of what makes you happy about your current position and use it as a springboard for launching your advice business.

Your current employer, however, must be convinced that he is not losing anything substantial in the transaction, that you will be there to provide the most necessary of your current tasks. You will be, of course, if you are prepared to give up the inessentials of your current position: the annual picnic, the fare-well lunches and dinners, the gossip sessions at the water cooler. All these must go. You must function like an advisor, and when you are there work to solve their problems rather than fill up the time by working to look busy as most employees currently do.

Think about this situation carefully. If you inform your boss that you are interested in transforming your current job position into an advisor assignment, he's sure to know that you are dissatisfied with your current job and will rightfully suppose that you are considering other options. Your current tenure may be short! Ordinarily you'll have about 6 months to work out the details, but it's very likely that you'll be out of your current job as a result of your creativity. So be sure you're ready to be independent!

Network

Advice givers are great networkers. We have to be. Sadly, networking is widely misunderstood and misapplied.

Networking is an action, goal oriented process that seeks to move you from where you are now to where you want to be through the intermediary of a third (or even a fourth) person, known or not known to you. The key to networking is understanding that you need not necessarily know well the person who ultimately helps you, as well as always keeping in mind exactly what that individual can do for you, if he or she chooses to do so.

I use networking constantly and I recommend it to you. It's a very efficacious means of making useful contacts. There are, in fact, three different networks: The Mandarin, Self-Promotion, and Next Check.

The Mandarin Network is composed of those individuals who offer you, the advisor, services on a fee-for-service basis. They are generally themselves advice givers and service providers, and they exist solely to reduce the amount of peripheral activity in your professional and personal life and so enable you to maximize your profitable professional activities and what leisure time you will have.

If you've read any other of my books, you'll remember that I took the word mandarin from Chinese history. The mandarins were those powerful individuals who grew their fingernails to outrageous lengths to indicate to an overburdened world that they did no work. Their job was to think, to advise others, but not to overburden themselves with the draining minutiae of life. If you are to succeed as an advisor you need to move yourself to mandarin status.

In the olden days the Chinese emperor himself, Brother of the Sun, Uncle of the Moon, conferred mandarin rank. Today you confer it on yourself. You must make the decision that you are a mandarin and that you are best employed doing three simple things: delivering your products and services, promoting and marketing your products and services, and creating new products and services to market and deliver. Anything else that you do is inessential and should be rigorously weeded out of your life.

When I say this in my workshops, at this point the participants roll their eyes in their heads. "You can't mean this!" they wail. But I do. Whatever else you do should be a conscious decision. Most people let their lives drain away from them; they are controlled by time (and badly, at that) rather than controlling time. But you, as the mandarin advice giver, must have a complete understanding both of your personal and professional objectives and how best to realize them in the very limited time that you have. Thus, you must work hard to root out all the nagging inessentials of life — and get others to perform them for you.

It would be nice if, like Tom Sawyer getting his friends to paint the white fence, we could always merely entice and cajole others into doing what we needed to have done (and wanted them to do), but we can't. In most instance, we're going to have to pay people to provide us with these services, and that's where the Mandarin Network comes in.

The Mandarin Network is composed of those individuals who are available to you on a fee for service, independent contractor, advising basis to provide you with what you need when you need it. This network is composed, in part, of the following people:

- bookkeeper
- accountant
- lawyer

- financial planner
- office and home maintenance keeper
- chauffeur

- plumber
- electrician
- carpenter

And on and on.

As you'll notice, each of these people is available to you on an independent contractor basis. Each is an advice giver or technician who himself has the same business problems, maybe the same business set-up, that you do!

Time is the ultimate resource. In establishing your Mandarin Network you arrive at the realization that this resource is frighteningly finite and that the tasks which you need to perform are as alarmingly infinite. Thus, you shear and shear away again the inane inessentials and deal with only those things which help you meet your ultimate objectives.

This is what the Mandarin Network can do for you — and you must have one. You can consider yourself a truly successful and fully actualized professional when you have in place a network which has raised you in all ways (but the three daily advisor essentials) to the desirable eminence of complete dependence. That is where I am now: I am, thanks to the Mandarin Network, almost completely dependent upon a horde of other independent contractors (mental and technical). As a result, I spend my time exclusively on the three necessary prerequisites of my success: product and service delivery, product and service promotion, and product and service creation. My income and affluence have increased in direct proportion to my dependence on others. I am not, please note, a do-it-your-selfer. But I am a mandarin.

The Self-Promotion Network

As its name suggests, the Self-Promotion Network is made up of individuals who can help promote your products and services, the problems that you solve, to those individuals and organizations who have need of what you do. With over 1,000,000 people now working in the media in some capacity or other, it's plain that there are myriad opportunities for networking here.

One day while I was writing this book, I decided I needed a pick-me-up. I knew a media story about my book **MONEY TALKS** was just what I needed, and I got on the telephone to my friend Ed Golden at the Associated Press in Boston. I met Ed through my friend Jim Cameron (one of my advisors for this book) who I met years ago while he was public affairs director at a Boston radio station. I never had to convince Ed that I was worth a story: Jim did that. All I had to do was stay in touch. I did, and as a result, last summer I appeared on the 1,200 member Associated Press Radio Network into which Ed feeds stories. This is all as a result of networking — and the pay-offs can be very, very substantial.

As the accompanying Pyramid of Contracts demonstrates, your task is to motivate an individual to assist you in getting to the person who can say, "I'll take care of it for you." That person either is the decision maker or knows the decision maker well enough to move matters smartly along.

The Pyramid of Contacts allows you to plot your next steps, quickly, efficiently. Here's what it looks like:

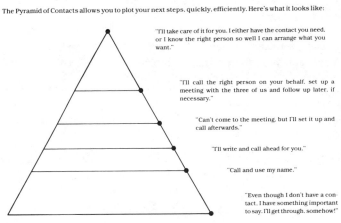

"I'll take care of it for you. I either have the contact you need, or I know the right person so well I can arrange what you want."

"I'll call the right person on your behalf, set up a meeting with the three of us and follow up later, if necessary."

"Can't come to the meeting, but I'll set it up and call afterwards."

"I'll write and call ahead for you."

"Call and use my name."

"Even though I don't have a contact, I have something important to say. I'll get through, somehow!"

The Pyramid of Contacts is a sifting device. It enables you to determine whether:

- the individual you are talking to could offer you, the mandarin, necessary services;
- he could provide a useful media contact (directly or indirectly), or
- could provide a direct or indirect contact to the individual who can authorize your next check for a product or service you have that will solve their problem.

I shall discuss the Self Promotion network further in Chapter 7. For now I'd like to focus on the Next Check Network.

Understanding and Profiting From The Next Check Network

It's very clear to me as I travel around the country that very few would-be advice givers have a lucid understanding of who can authorize payment to them of their next check. Thus, I have created the Next Check Network, which is designed to solve a very important problem for any one who wishes to profit by giving advice.

Getting The Best Use From Your Next Check Network

The Next Check Network only works well when you have a complete understanding of exactly who can buy your products and services. And I mean exactly. One problem advice givers consistently have is wasting their time with individuals who do not have the authority to buy from them or who are being asked to purchase a product or service which is in advance of their authority. Having just read my views on the importance of time, you will understand that I regard such waste as an outright crime.

How can you solve this problem? Before approaching a single individual, write a brief (not more than 250 words) narrative profile of the exact individual who can buy *each* of your products and services. Visualize this person. Write down his title (which may vary substantially from another person in the same industry in the same position who also has the authority to buy) and discover the extent of his authority to buy. You must know this information as well as your subjects do themselves.

The key to making the Next Check Network work for you is not attempting to sell the person you are with more than he is authorized to buy, or more than he can afford to buy. You must know in advance of the presentation the exact limits of this individual's purchasing authority and pitch your product or service accordingly.

If you are unsure of the extent of the individual's authority, ask. There is no crime in this. It can be done in a genteel fashion; ("I wonder if you'd tell me if you are authorized yourself to make this decision or do you have to have it approved elsewhere?"). As I've so often written before, the key to handling this matter is briskly and professionally. Don't assume. It does neither you nor your would-be buyer any service to over- or under-state his purchasing authority.

Once you are at the top of a network (with a person who has said or can say, "I'll take care of it for you."), you should stay at that level, that is, the person who can say that for you should (and usually does) have business associates who are at a comparable level. Networking from one top-placed person to another is called Parallel Networking, and you'll find that so long as you are in business you'll use it.

You already know, for instance, that I contract to provide products and services to a variety of health organizations. Each time I work with an executive director I ascertain what other executive directors this person knows, for at that level a large percentage of the individual's professional contacts are at a comparable, executive level, or, in my terms, to other people who can say, in reference to buying my products and services, "I'll take care of it for you." Thus, my task is to get my original executive director contact to parallel network me to others who are at the same, or higher, level. This is not difficult.

Not difficult, that is, if you understand that networking is decidedly an action process, not something to be approached passively. Thus:

- Listen actively. Listen to the names and contacts reeled off by your clients, your friends and associates, your professional colleagues. As they talk, complete an Imaginary Questionnaire based on the people they know and the contacts you need. You need never feel awkward or guilty about doing this (though you probably will, at the beginning). After all, if you believe in your product and service, and know that they have the capacity to solve vexing problems for your clients, then you have a responsibility, an outright moral responsibility, to listen carefully, to log the information and to use it — not merely for your own benefit, but for those who have need of what you're selling!

- Write down what you hear. People have remarkably short attention spans, and even shorter memories. Try writing down a précis of last night's dinner conversation, for example. Can you even remember what was discussed?

I mistrust my memory, although it's a good one. Thus, I keep reams of notes. So should you. In fact, if you are ever with me telling me something, and I don't write it down, you can be sure I don't regard it as significant no matter how attentive I may appear!

- Ask people to help you. Powerful people like to be asked to assist others, for it reminds them that they are, after all, influential and can make things happen. So you are doing them a favor by asking for a favor. But remember: savvy networkers understand that their influence is not infinite. Like all resources, it's finite and can be exhausted (even if later renewed). The savvy networker will thus be trying to push you down the Pyramid of Contacts while your job is to push the person with the contact up. In this regard, networking is a game: a game, however, with very real, important prizes.

85

Sometime in the last year, I read the line that to want is a human right, and if that's the case, then I am the compleat human, for I want daily and ask people to help me get what I want. So should you. Don't wait for someone to offer a networking contact; ask for it. But remember that you are opening yourself up to the possibility of a deal, of being asked for something in return, for the person you are asking for something has himself an infinite capacity for wanting, which, to a certain extent, may be satisfied through you. Networking is thus deal making, and you should be aware of it.

- Review your notes. Just because you don't want the lead today, doesn't mean you won't want it tomorrow. I maintain an ongoing log book with "editions". As I meet people, as I conduct workshops, as I work with clients, as I have telephone conversations, I write down information in my log for future reference. Then, from time to time, I review this information in an attempt to make good use of it. Just because you cannot make use of something today, doesn't mean that you should discard it. Your job is to file it and know when the perfect moment for using it is.

- Never stop networking. As long as you are in business, you are in the networking business. After all, if you have satisfied a particular client, odds are that the client knows somebody else who can use your service and product. It will ease your marketing considerably if you can approach this individual through a friend who can vouch for you. Vouching for you in this way becomes what I call an Alternative Credential.

Understanding And Using Alternative Credentials

It should be very clear by now that advice givers do not get positions in the usual way that most middle management (and below) employees do. For these people, résumés and such standard employment credentials are significant. For us they are not. Thus, rip up your résumé and look to a variety of alternative credentials including:

- the Success Letter we have already discussed.
- being networked to the attention of a decision maker (as above).
- being promoted through the media and hence becoming the perceived expert in the field, ready, willing and able to solve a client's pressing need.

Traditional thinkers misunderstand this important point about Alternative Credentials, believing, quite wrongly, that they get their jobs because of historical credentials, licenses, degrees, and the like. This is ridiculous!

The only time in which I myself use a résumé or traditional employment document is when applying for a federal or state grant, where such materials are required. Even then these documents are tailored to the individual request for proposal.

I have now been in business as an advice giver for over 12 years, but I can count on the fingers of a single hand the number of times I have been asked for a résumé during those years outside of the circumstances mentioned above. What people want is a reasonable assurance that you can provide a disproportionate benefit compared to fee, a success, a solution for their problem. Networking is one very powerful and influencial means of providing them with just this information.

I was well into adulthood before I realized this salient fact of success. Upon graduating from Harvard in '75, I sent my résumé (with cover letter) out far and wide in a largely vain, costly, and increasingly frustrating attempt to find a job. In most cases, my résumé didn't secure even the honor of a response. In most other cases, the response was a form letter with the wrong content. I was, to put it mildly, incandescent with smouldering rage.

One of the places I applied was a large university in Kentucky, where I had the common dismissive experience. This also happened to be the first place outside Massachusetts where, just a few years later, I got a consulting assignment. For that I was networked in by a senior vice president. We laughed about the experience, but the truth is there is a salient lesson here to be learned. Initially, I had submitted a full vitae, letters of recommendation, transcript, résumé, the lot. And got nothing, not even the barest consideration of a response.

In the second case, I simply knew the decision maker who had read nothing, literally nothing about me, but who hired me anyway as an advisor based on what he had come to know and see with his own eyes. The first contact yielded nothing but frustration, the second a lucrative advising assignment which lead, too, to workshops and seminars and, through the Success Sequence, future assignments in other states. Yes, I believe in networking very, very much!

Begin Networking Today

If you're like me, you are beginning your advice business with very little capital, very little financial capital, that is. For you must consider your talents, intelligence, time and energy your very considerable assets. And your contacts, for they, too, are a form of capital which, like any other form of capital, must be constructively and consistently employed to produce a good result.

Perhaps at some level you already know this, but I bet my bottom dollar you are not effectively using this form of value. Right now, sit down and begin to brainstorm with yourself about who you know and what kinds of contacts they have in each of the three necessary networks. But don't suppose that a single brainstorming session of this kind will be sufficient. It won't be. I've been networking for years and yet at intervals I return to my lists, the names, my workshop participants, students, clients, past clients, friends, professional colleagues of every kind and mull them over to see where their leads go. I'm exhilarated by the possibilities, and so should you be, for they will take you wherever your clients are, and hence to the achievement of your grandest objectives.

A Word About The Base Of The Pyramid Of Contacts

People often ask me whether I rely exclusively upon contacts to get sales. What a question! Of course not! You do not necessarily need a contact to make a sale if you have one necessary precondition for being heard: a success that the client prospect wishes to replicate. Success is a door opener. People who have already achieved success help you get access to those who want such success, whether or not these people know you. Thus, if I have helped a Massachusetts home health agency raise $100,000, you can bet your life that other executives in the industry will see me, contact or no contact, simply to find out whether my methods will work for them. Thus, while networking is always important, it is perhaps most important at the inception of your career when you haven't yet the dramatic success record which will, at a later date, ensure your reception.

Making A Preferential Deal (Which Can Be Leveraged And Replicated)

When you're running a Mobile Mini-Conglomerate you are necessarily in the deal making business. I relish this. Personally, I like making deals, like putting together a series of win-win proposals which will benefit the client (often in new and nontraditional ways, at least as regards their own situation) and benefit me, too. If you think as an advisor that you are simply in the business of advising, you're wrong. You're in business, and being in business means being in the business of making deals.

Thus, even if you are placed in the position of getting those early clients through a preferential agreement, or even volunteering for a job, you should do so on the basis of a deal and an assignment which can be replicated. Here's what I mean!

Last year I was asked by a friend if I'd like to participate in a special program at a local Boston organ store. As it happened, this store was part of a chain of organ stores nationally, the parent company of which had just gone into bankruptcy. While the parent was insolvent, however, the subsidiary was not; the parent looked to the subsidiary, in fact, to relieve them of a substantial portion of their current embarrassment. Problem: the bad publicity the parent had received was causing organ buyers, who were usually institutions such as churches, to postpone their purchase, feeling that their organ would not receive proper servicing. As a result, the sales people, who worked largely on commission, were being placed in a difficult position.

Enter the White Knight advice giver.

The company had decided to put on a special one-day program for institutional organ buyers, the program to include a special introduction to the organs (which started at $25,000), a fund raising lecture on how to raise the funds to purchase such a major acquisition, a special catered luncheon, and an afternoon recital on one of the leading organ types sold by the company. I was invited to provide the fund raising lecture.

In this case, I was networked into the assignment by, of all people, the caterer, who was a friend. But after reading this section, you'll be able to take a much more active role in getting the assignment and in making it pay off for you, even if you are not paid directly!

Assume for a moment that I had been asked to give the lecture but that no fee had been proposed. Would this have been an assignment worth taking? The answer is, that depends on the following variables:

- Are the individuals being invited through direct mail client prospects for you; can you, that is, work with them on a one-to-one basis? (I could.)
- Is the list of names and addresses of those invited available to you for your own follow up? (It was.)
- Can you be promoted in such a way that your products and services are promoted through the initial mailing? (Yes.)
- Can you get a complete list of all those attending the program (qualified prospects) for follow up? (Yes.)
- Can your literature be distributed to those in attendance? (Yes.)
- Can you use the event as an opportunity for unabashed promotion? (Yes.)
- Can the event be replicated in other places? (Yes.)

Given that the answers to these questions indicate there are indeed future possiblities, you would be warranted in taking this assignment on a reduced fee or even a volunteer basis, especially as it does not involve you in a sizable time investment. Thus, whether you do take it or not depends on your ability to work a deal with the client prospect, in this case an individual retail store.

In return for making a presentation without fee (or for a reduced fee), you want the mailing list of those invited, so that you can follow up with your own materials and a Success (sales) Letter. This is easier for the client prospect to arrange if the names and addresses are available on computer or can be photocopied from labels they have. *N.B.* If the mailing list has been rented (not bought!) from a commercial firm, it will be a violation of the rental terms to allow you to photocopy the addresses.

- You can and should write your own promotional copy for the mailing. This copy can promote you in the exact way which is best suited for both attracting people to the event and, later, signing up with you as a client. In this your objective is the same as your client prospects; the problem is that they won't necessarily see it that way.

I remember on one occasion, for instance, a South Carolina university removed all mention of my books from the promotional materials they distributed, to my deep shock and dismay. Their reason: because it promoted the books! I pointed out that the fact that I was an expert in the field, as demonstrated by the books that I'd written, was a very considerable selling point and that they had reduced me to the level of any other garden variety expert by their self-defeating excision. I can only hope they got the message!

As I've pointed out in **MONEY TALKS**, you cannot leave the writing of something as important as promotional and marketing copy in the hands of those who don't understand it and do not know you. But you can, under the guise of Assertive Courtesy, write it yourself and hence get what you must have out of the deal: superb marketing copy which will entice your future clients.

- You can, and must, get a complete list of anyone attending the program, any program you give. Those attending are called Qualified Prospects, for they have self-selected themselves as individuals interested in your service. *N.B.* In this case, the interest in your service is indirect since they have come to see and, with luck, to select an organ. But, once having selected the organ, they will need, in my case, a fund raising expert to help them raise the money to pay for it. This is why they are qualified prospects for me and why getting ahold of a list of who attended is most important.

- You can make sure that your Success Package is distributed to everyone present. Don't allow anyone to come into your presence, anyone, that is, who is a client prospect, much less a Qualified Prospect who, by his presence, has admitted the need for your service, without receiving all the relevant materials. Remember: people don't necessarily (or even usually) make their decisions to buy after a single contact with the advice giver, service provider. They need to hear about what you can do for them over and over again: you must aim for repetition. First, hit them in the initial mailing; second, mail to those who couldn't come (and use the other appropriate follow-up mechanisms); third, hit those who did come and so launch a sequence which will end in a contract.

- You can use the event as an opportunity for unabashed promotion. Although Chapter 7 is our chapter on this phenomenon, I want to get you in the spirit by referring now to what you can get even from a free assignment.

Most media is local. That means it deals with local people and covers local stories. The individuals coming to this particular activity were largely directors of choral music, music directors, &c, that is people who professionally dealt with organs. But they were also people with media connections, in this case church newsletters and the newspapers (usually weekly) in their communities.

That's where a Photographic Reception Line comes in. A Photographic Reception Line, fully described in **THE UNABASHED SELF-PROMOTER'S GUIDE**, is a process whereby all those attending an event are used to secure additional publicity for those giving the event who have products and services they wish to promote and publicize. As far as this event is concerned, it included the store manager (with his organs) and me (with my fund raising books and consulting services). Thus, each person attending the event should be photographed individually (or in individual congregational and community groups) with these two people. These photographs get what is called a Standard Narrative Caption:

This caption should contain the following information: who, what, where, when and a sizzling quotation, thus:

On Saturday, May 21, First Presbyterian Choral Director Bertha Jones attended a special program at the Boston office of the Electra Organ Company at 521 Boylston St. Here Bertha meets Store Manager Bob Jones and featured speaker Dr. Jeffrey Lant, Cambridge fund raising consultant and author of **DEVELOPMENT TODAY: A FUND RAISING GUIDE FOR NONPROFIT ORGANIZATIONS**. Lant spoke on "Raising the money you need for the organ of your dreams." Said Bertha, "What a superb day!"

You get the idea.

As people go through the Photographic Reception Line, someone has to ask them for the name and address of their church newsletter and the name of their weekly newspaper. Some people may know the address, but you'll have to follow up with a standard newspaper listing like *Gale Directory of Publications and Broadcast Media* (available in libraries) to get the addresses. This is the only really difficult part of the entire operation — but, sadly, it often defeats the whole activity.

Don't forget the other promotional opportunities, too. Does the parent company have a newsletter or house organ? If it's large enough, the answer is yes.

Here's where an understanding of who is interested in solving this problem comes in. Remember that the Boston store of this company was not the only store in the chain having this problem. They all were, for the publicity was national. Hence, you can rest assured that the parent company would welcome any creative suggestions about how to deal with it.

Once the story appears in the parent company house organ, you're a member of the family and as such should find out who can authorize a series of comparable programs nationally, all, this time, with a fee for service for yourself, now a proven White Knight.

Are there other leveraging opportunities? Yes, there are. As it happens, in Ohio there is what amounts to a church department store, a place where institutional representatives come to buy any product needed by churches. It's called Church Mart, and like the organ company they need programs informing people how to raise the money to buy their products.

And so it goes.

I've taken just a moment to give you the flavor of this one illustration so that if you are thinking of taking an assignment for less money than you usually get or for nothing at all, volunteering for it, you can see that it is still possible to profit from the experience if you are willing to work and structure the assignment for future benefit and to assure yourself that you will get these benefits through a letter of intent or other contract option.

There is nothing wrong with volunteering, with taking a reduced fee on any individual assignment so long as you have the reasonable assurance that, through the kinds of options I've presented above, you will profit in the near term with the things that spring from your initial engagement. But you must visualize this outcome from the first and structure your engagement to achieve your desired outcome.

Using Telemarketing

There isn't an advisor who doesn't use the telephone, and yet I know how few use it correctly. Properly utilized, the telephone is one of your best assets in getting new clients. I use it regularly and so will you. To learn to use it properly I called upon my my telemarketing expert friend Art Sobczak (who, like all those who assisted with this book, is listed in my "Rogues' Gallery of Absolutely Must-Use Experts on page 276). We pooled our knowledge of the subject to come up with a list of suggestions on how best to handle your telemarketing.

- **Understand where telemarketing fits in the client solicitation paradigm.**

If you are really anxious to sell to a client prospect, you are almost always better off in a face to face meeting. If an individual agrees to see you, they have to acknowledge that their precious time was wasted unless they come to some kind of agreement with you. It is easier to come to this kind of agreement in a meeting, because you can shift your tactics in response not only to what the individual says but how he says it, both verbally and nonverbally. These cues are usually missing a telephone conversation. Further, it is harder to end a face-to-face meeting than it is to end a telephone call. I know.

Like all people who get telephone calls, I have learned a series of steps which make it easy for me to get an individual off the phone without hurting his feelings and without chipping my image as the Accessible Expert, which I want to remain intact. Thus, when someone calls me selling something (at least once an hour), I say in my sweetest voice, "I'm terribly sorry, but I'm in conference right now. I wonder if you would kindly send me your information so that I can take a look at it."

I am relying 1) on the other person's level of disorganization (i.e. that they won't follow up, and thus I can blame them for the failure to establish a substantial contract), and 2) on their probable reluctance to call me again when I have done nothing more than say I'd like to review the literature. But throughout this maneuver I have maintained through voice and action my demeanor as the Accessible Expert.

It is more difficult to do this without greater effort when the person is with you face to face and that's why I, like all successful advisors, make direct access so much more difficult than telephone access.

Thus, remember this: face-to-face meetings are the best for selling to your clients, but such meetings are the costliest in terms of your time and resources. Telemarketing is the next best type of communication, and finally direct mail letters, which, while the least expensive form of contact, are also the least likely for a substantial, profitable return to you. Here are the steps which will ensure the success of your telemarketing efforts:

- **Target your client prospects.**

Throughout this book I have urged you again and again to target your client prospects. This most people, particularly those new to the advisor business, find most difficult to do. Moreover, even when they feel they are targeting, their targeting is so imprecise as to be virtually valueless. Thus, to say that you are targeting "nonprofit organizations" or "small businesses" or "the private sector" as my students (who, after all, are all adults) often infuriatingly say, is utterly useless, worse than useless!

If you want to begin meaningful targeting, ask yourself very specifically where you have had success in the past (either as a full- or part-time employee or as an advisor) and what other individuals or organizations — specifically! — would be interested in replicating that success. And remember: there are two different kinds of successes to consider in this regard:

- the final success, the result that is of your information processes. For example, a homemaker home health agency that wishes to raise funds for a hospice program and comes to me because I have helped raise funds for a comparable project at a comparable agency.
- the success procedures themselves. In this example, you are selling success procedures, the means, that is, of achieving a success. Thus, an arts organization might well hire me to raise money because of my mastery of fund raising processes, despite the fact that my previous clients have been health organizations. The skills, you see, are transferable.

So ask yourself: have I a final success to sell, a success that can be replicated for a comparable individual or organization, or have I success processes to sell, a set of information or technical procedures which is transferable from one situation to a quite different situation? The smart advisor, of course, sells both.

- **Write down a list of your targeted prospects and determine how you will reach them initially.**

The success of your telemarketing effort rests in large measure upon reaching the right people, the people, that is, who can authorize your next check. You must know who these people are, and, as I've already said, you must know as much about them as they know about themselves so that you will be perceived not as some alien salesperson but as one of them, as an outside advisor who knows not only about their problems (as they know about them) but who offers the superb advantage of being able to solve those problems, too — which is something they cannot do.

One of the tricks to successful telemarketing is being very precise about who you are mailing your initial packet of information to, for, of course, telemarketing is but a step in the long chain of contacts you must make with a prospect client before making the sale.

In this connection, successful telemarketing means calling your client prospects in advance to ascertain the name, title and telephone number of the correct individual within the organization who can authorize your next check. This process is long and dull, but it is absolutely necessary. Write this information down, for, remembering the success sequence, you will not be in touch with these people once but a series of times, so long, in fact, as you are in business. You will not, please note, secure them all as clients now but you stand a superb chance of getting a goodly number of them as clients over time, if you follow the steps of this book, which means having the information about them readily available to you. Those of you who have a good word processor, for instance, can easily keep this information readily on file and available for your next contact, but even if you don't have this machine, it must be at your finger tips for future use.

- **Assemble your sales package.**

Before you can telephone anyone about anything, before you can make an apt sales presentation, you have to assemble a convincing sales package and get it into the hands of those with whom you'll be dealing by phone. This package should include:

- a cover/sales letter. No surprise to you, you'll be better off if this is a Success Letter, if, that is, you can apprize the client prospect that you've already solved a similar problem for a related organization and wish to replicate the results.
- a précis of your products and services. If you are selling products, don't forget to include an order blank for them. Make it easy for your customers to buy them from you! If you do not have 5 or 6 pieces (depending on the weight of a single piece) to make up the one ounce you get for the price of a first-class stamp (for you are sending these first class), consider adding a catalog of books and products produced by others. Whenever possible, and certainly in all my mailings, not a packet leaves my office that is not stuffed to the brim with materials, and if I've got the space I enclose my success catalog. Since the rules of direct mail apply here, I'll always secure a response of 1-2 % here and thus offset the costs of the mailing.
- a standardized proposal form for either a Delphic Oracle or Full Service plan.
- testimonials and third party validation (including media pieces) from others who have successfully used your services.

The tone of all these materials should be brisk and upbeat. No matter how difficult the problem and the circumstances you are addressing, you must indicate that you have a solution to the perceived problems of the buyer. This must be very clearly apparent in all your written materials: problem, solution; problem, solution. The telemarketing call simply reinforces the fact that you are available with a solution to the client's perceived problems. Again: the telemarketing call can never be seen in isolation, as somehow disconnected from the necessary sales steps that precede and, then, follow it. They are inextricably bound up as a sales sequence and must be perceived in this fashion.

- **Mailing Your Packets**

The more of an ingenue advisor you are, the more packets you'll send out, thinking it easy to make fifty or sixty follow-up telephone calls and, thereafter, schedule attendant meetings, send further letters and materials, &c. But this is quite absurd. My advice is to send no more than 10 packets at a time, for your business does not conclude with a telephone call but rather with an entire sequence of follow up activities.

Since all advisors must continually use the telephone, it's important to consider how best the telephone can be used for your business. Remember: particularly when you are starting out in the advice business, what you have to offer is yourself; you are your most expensive product. On the whole, people do not buy expensive products or services by telephone. You wouldn't, for example, buy a car on the telephone unless you had already test-driven it. Thus, telemarketing to sell cars to those who had not previously expressed an interest in the product, who had driven it, &c., would be ridiculous. So it is with advisors.

Thus, you must know in advance of any call what is the highest degree of sale you can make with this call. If you are selling advice only, yourself as an advisor, the best thing you can usually hope to accomplish is to schedule a meeting, a meeting at which you'll have a more sustained chance to identify the client prospect's problems and to sell an appropriate product or service for solving it.

If you have the Mobile Mini-Conglomerate in full or partial operation, you may be able to sell the client prospect on 1) the need for a meeting (at which you can sell your more expensive service and 2) an immediate product sale. Thus, when a client prospect calls me about retaining my fund raising service, I cannot do this on the telephone despite a long and distinguished track record in the field. I can, however, sell them on the need and benefit for a meeting. I can also sell them on the benefits to be derived from reading my fund raising book **DEVELOPMENT TODAY** before the meeting, and hence can derive revenue from this contact.

Thus, always remember that, in this business, it is a mistake to focus simply on the prospect's immediate problem in a linear fashion. During a telephone call, you should be closing on a series of desirable objectives, one a final (as in the book sale), one a step to a final (as in scheduling the necessary client prospect-advisor meeting).

Note: This sequence even applies when selling products. People often call me nowadays requesting one book or another. "Do you have **THE CONSULTANT'S KIT** in stock", they'll ask.

There are several ways of handling this call.

On the one hand, I could say, with the utmost civility, "Yes, I do. It's $38.50, which includes shipping." And end the conversation happy that I got this sale. It's infinitely better, however, if I apply the rules of telemarketing to this prospect call and make a series of sales; thus, going into my Assertive Courtesy mode:

"Yes I do. Are you aware that **THE CONSULTANT'S KIT** is part of a series of books that are helpful to advice givers?", I'll begin.

Client prospect: "No, I'm not."

"**THE CONSULTANT'S KIT** is part of a seven-volume series of benefit to advice givers. Could you tell me what you do?"

"Well, yes, I'm a financial planner."

"Then you'll find the other six books in the series, **THE UNABASHED SELF-PROMOTER'S GUIDE, MONEY TALKS, HOW TO MAKE AT LEAST $100,000 EVERY YEAR AS A SUCCESSFUL CONSULTANT IN YOUR OWN FIELD, MONEY MAKING MARKETING, CASH COPY** and **HOW TO MAKE A WHOLE LOT MORE THAN $1,000,000 WRITING, COMMISSIONING, PUBLISHING AND SELLING 'HOW-TO' INFORMATION**. If you bought each one separately they'd cost over $220, but you can get the complete set shipping included for just $200.

At this point the prospect will either ask for additional information, which you can send, or indicate that he wants one or the other and will be placing an order.

But, please note, such a conversation shouldn't be ended until you write down the prospect's name for addition to your mailing list (and for later rental to others who can make use of getting access to this individual).

What is especially pleasing about this conversation is that: 1) it has clearly established you as the Accessible Expert, someone who's going out of his way to help someone else solve their problems, and 2) it's being paid for by the prospect! The more you are the perceived expert in your field, the more often you will receive such calls and the more you can, in a very few seconds, reinforce your leading image and help yourself by making not only the limited sale the prospect originally intended, but the more extensive one which is even more to your mutual benefit.

Think how powerful this is — and how little you've seen it used. I buy many things by telephone, and I cannot recall a single time within the last year when the individual on the other end, purportedly in business, even knowing I was placing a considerable order for anything from crystal to jiffy bags, ever directed my attention to another, related item in which I might also be interested. If I'm lucky this ne'er-do-well might do what he's asked, but surely, most assuredly, nothing more. This is what I call "clerkism", and it's part of what's wrong with commerce in this nation.

Now, though, you won't fall into this, will you? If the client prospect wishes to buy one thing from you, one solution, that is, to his problem, chances are that he'll want to buy other, related items and services if you bring them to his attention. Never forget this! Press on, press harder, keep the client prospect moving to yet another sale. Even as you do so you won't be perceived as some grasping salesman but rather as the Accessible Expert, doing all you can to help the client meet his objectives. You'll do more business and you'll be regarded as a swell person, too. What could be better?

• Script Your Call.

Henry Kissinger used to say that the only meeting worth having was a meeting where he knew what the conclusion would be. I agree. And no where is this more true than in telemarketing, which is, after all, simply a specialized form of meeting. Thus, to get what you want from this meeting, don't go into it unprepared. Once having decided what should transpire from it, script your call so that you are ready for any eventuality. Your script should deal with the following points:

- Client's availability. You must always ascertain whether the client can speak to you at the moment of your call, or whether it would be better if you called back at a later, more convenient time. If the latter, don't ring off with the prospect until that time has been mutually established.

- Client prospect's receipt of materials. Ascertain that the prospect has in fact received your sales materials and has actually read them. If he has, two things should already have occurred: many basic questions will already have been answered and his interest already aroused, a critical point if there is in fact to be a sale.

- Ability to establish empathy. I receive calls continually from salespeople who are like automatons. They obviously have no idea who I am, what my problems are, what I might need, or any knowledge that someone I know might successfully have utilized their product or service and thus excited my envy and desire to replicate the success. Such a lack of preparation might be acceptable if you are selling ball point pens by the gross, but it is most assuredly not acceptable if you are selling a personalized, costly advisor service of the kind you, dear reader, are selling. Thus, it is important for you to establish, as early as possible, empathy with your client prospect.

- How do you do this? Through entering a networking connection, if one's available. If you have the permission of a former or present client to use their name to establish this empathetic connection, do so early on in the conversation. Or let the client prospect know that you are just finishing (or have finished) an assignment with a similarly situated client who may be known to the prospect.

It's terribly important that you differentiate yourself from the mass of telephone salespeople who are themselves faceless and who treat the prospect as if he were faceless, too. You want the client prospect to know that you are like him, that you have links that he has, that you know the problems he has, and have already successfully dealt with them (as per the initial sales/success letter you've sent and which the client prospect has admittedly already received); in short, that you are part of the client prospect's world and as such worthy of consideration.

- Having once established empathy, that you are member of a similar universe of people, you must begin to ascertain the client's problem, for the success of this conversation, where you are selling a costly advisor service, rests on prompt, early (if necessarily incomplete) identification of the client's problem and an indication that you can solve that sort of problem. Even if the conversation is an abbreviated one, you must discover whether the client prospect has a problem you can solve.

"I know you are terribly busy, Ms. Prospect, but I wonder whether you might also have need for some building improvements in the next few months?"

What the client prospect says at this point is terribly important in your determination of what to do next.

Possible responses:
- "No, our building is in pretty good shape, but we are thinking about establishing a new health corner for the elderly."
- "Yes, but I'm not quite sure what we need. I'm looking into some possibilities now."
- "Yes, we need a new roof, as a matter of fact."

Identifying Opportunities

Whatever kind of sales business you are in (and every advisor must necessarily become a sales expert or risk an early retirement from business), you have to train yourself to be alert to the openings that a client prospect creates. Remember: every client wants to spend his money, either today, tomorrow or next week. Money *per se* doesn't interest most people and having money doesn't interest them either. What interests them is using their money to solve their problems, meet their needs. You have to indicate to them that you understand what these problems and needs are and that, using your services, they have a good chance of solving the one, meeting the other. To do so necessarily means staying flexible in your conversations. This flexibility must be in you and be possible of being introduced into your script. Here's what I mean:

- In the first illustration, the client is indicating that there is an opening for a fund raising service. The client has a need. In this illustration you must shift from success result ("I've raised capital funds in the past") to process success ("The skills which allowed me to raise money successfully for capital campaigns will be useful in helping you raise project money.")

- In the second example, your responsibility is to find out what kinds of needs the client may have, whether you can help them clarify their needs and when the client might be ready to meet with you.

- In the third case, the client simply needs to be assured that you can help them meet their objective and that a meeting would be in their best interest, for, remember, the service you are selling is too expensive to be bought sight unseen over the telephone. The meeting in each of these cases remains the intermediate objective, although, of course, it is the final objective of the telemarketing conversation.

Do you think these examples are too easy? That people don't tell you these things on the telephone? Well, if so, you're mistaken. If you have properly identified your client prospects, have properly ascertained what they need, have properly identified the right person to contact (the person, that is, who can authorize payment to you and can sign you up as the advisor) and have properly crafted a good sales packet packed with information about the client prospect's problem and your success in dealing with it, these telemarketing conversations should be rather easy — not least because you are not yet actually asking for the sale, but rather for a meeting at which you can move further towards establishing a relationship.

Other Telemarketing Tricks

- Place your calls early in the day. When you want something from someone, as you most decidedly do when you are using telemarketing, place your calls early in the day. There are several reasons for doing so:
  — An early call gives your prospect an entire day to get back to you.
  — By placing your call early, you are perceived to be interested in the client, enthusiastic about representing the prospect. This is to your advantage. Enthusiasm is a great motivator. People like to work with those who are enthusiastic about being around them.
  — The individual you are contacting is fresher and not yet discouraged by the vicissitudes of the day. Morning is always a time for new beginnings.
- Dress the part. Telemarketing is a form of meeting. You'd dress for a face-to-face meeting wouldn't you? So do the same for your tele-meeting. It'll help you sustain the part you are playing.
- Pump up before making the call. You must transmit in your call enthusiasm, empathy and intelligence. You are, however, understandably nervous and your vocal chords are affected by this nervousness. Remember: on the telephone you can project any image you want to through your voice alone. Do a few jumping jacks or otherwise get ready to sound "up and ready" before you make the call.
- Make the calls from your desk. Have all your papers, script, information about the client (if you've called in advance for it), &c. near at hand before making the call. It sounds elementary, but make sure you have your log book and pens readily available, too, to keep notes. You should never have a telemarketing meeting without keeping notes of who you spoke with, the date, the substance of the meeting, possible ways in which you can work together, and a time to call back. This is called the log, and it is an essential outcome of any tele-meeting.

Move The Tele-Meeting To Its Objective

Even before you've placed this call to a client prospect, you know what you want from it. Perhaps your ultimate objective, of course, is to sign them up as a client, as an organization or individual you can work with to help solve their problems and help create a success. But that objective probably will not be reached in your tele-meeting. You may not yet have sufficient information about the client's problem and the client probably doesn't yet have enough information about you to trust you as the solution agent yet to make a deal. That's all right. Don't be affronted by this. A lot of money and much working time is at stake.

Once, however, you have discovered 1) that the client does have a problem you can solve, 2) that the client would benefit from your services, and 3) is preliminarily interested in moving ahead to a meeting with you, ask for such a meeting. It is very much your responsibility to take the lead in this particular.

This means that you will, far in advance of this call, have had to think through your meeting policy. As you know, mine is that for a one-year retainer agreement with a client, I will give a client prospect one free hour of time. If the contract in which they are interested is my less expensive, Delphic Oracle contract, the meeting will be at my office in Cambridge; if the more expensive, Full Service contract, it can be at their offices, so long as they pay travel costs.

Don't be coy about this matter. Your ultimate success as an advisor to this client prospect has its roots in how you behave right from the start of your relationship, before you have even signed any agreement to work with them. Thus, to have a successful relationship behave as the consummate professional right from the start. After all, the client prospect is expecting you to know what you're doing, expecting you to have thought through the policies with which you deal with clients. It would be detrimental to your standing not to have such policies, rather than, at this moment, to tell the prospect what they are. Too, as you tell them, don't be shy or coy about your policies. The client understands that you are a professional problem solver and that money or other consideration will change hands in the deal. Your job at this point is simply to inform the client prospect how this is done in your case.

When You Don't Need A Meeting

The more expensive the service (or product) you are selling, the more probable a meeting will be. But you don't always need one. Keep that in mind. Moreover, you may discover during the course of your tele-meeting that the client currently has no need for your service and that the top sale you can make today is one of your workshops, books or tapes. To sell this product you most decidedly do *not* need a meeting! If this is the best you can do for now, do it and follow up later if there is a chance to do more business and establish a more lucrative relationship with the client prospect.

Always Follow Up

Whatever result you have reached, follow up appropriately. The truth of the matter is that most tele-meetings do not secure for the advisor any sustained advantage. This is unfortunate. I go into a tele-meeting expecting to make a sale of some kind, either now or in the very near future. This confidence is not misplaced: after all, I've done my homework and I know what the client's problems are, the solutions I have available (and there are always more that one of those), and what the objective for this particular meeting is. To continue the good relationship which this meeting has helped secure, good follow up is crucial. Thus:

- If the client prospect has indicated they are not currently interested in your service, send the individual you spoke to a note and thank them for having spoken to you, and indicate that you'll be back later to see about their situation and hope to be able to work with them. The truth is that people are not always standing ready, willing and able to buy your service right now. Even so, if you know that at some point they will need what you've got, it's your responsibility to create a relationship. People like to buy from people they know even if those people are not necessarily the best and the brightest. Better to buy from a dolt you know than from a brilliant firebrand you do not. So cultivate the illusion, at least, of a relationship. This means thanking the individual for what he gave you, at the very least for his time, which is truly irreplaceable.

- If the client indicates an interest in any of your services, but is not prepared to buy yet, write a follow-up note and suggest when you'll call again. Put the information in your log, on your calendar and do what you said you were going to do. People are impressed with good follow-through, and you'll benefit by doing what you say you are going to do, especially in an age as careless and casual as this one is.

- If the client has agreed to a meeting, put a note in the mail confirming the details of the meeting, the time, place, people to attend, subject to discuss and your hoped for outcome. Don't be shy about stating what you hope the outcome is to be: not just a contract for you, but rather a constructive working relationship between the two parties.

- If the client has purchased something from you (like a book), send it at once along with your invoice. I am unusual among publishers in that I invoice for books and products and do not necessarily wait for a purchase order. I confess I use my discretion about doing this; I won't, for instance, invoice a post office box. But where I feel I can do myself some good by hastening my product on its way, I do so. I am not very often disappointed, although even this does occasionally happen.

One Final Word About Telemarketing

Telemarketing must not be seen as something distinct and separated from what goes before and after it in the sales sequence. That is because for most of us in the advising business, what we do on the telephone will not necessarily close the final sale and make the prospect a client. Moreover, you must be prepared for the fact that most of those you deal with on the telephone initially will not become clients of yours in any form. But that as you have success with others similarly situated the rate of return for those with whom you have in the past been in contact will increase. This is where the Success Sequence comes in.

Let us say that I send out 20 letters, in two batches of 10, to visiting nursing agencies in Massachusetts and get a single client. This would be considered a good return. Now, as I help that client achieve successes, I would use the Success Sequence — letters, mailings, future tele-meetings along with unabashed promotion (soon to be discussed) — to indicate to the other 19 client prospects that now is the time for them to act. Given the dimensions of success, it is very likely that you would pick up yet another client from within this group, and so on until you had increased your representation within it substantially.

In my experience, people in the advice business, those with information and advice for sale, expect too much too soon from their client prospects. They do not allow for the justifiable hesitancy and caution of even those client prospects who have the problem and who understand that you can provide a solution. Nor do they make the continuing investment in returning again and again to those who have the problem, thereby minimizing their fears and cementing their relationship.

Sales people, and that includes advisors who expect to be successful, must expect to spend a considerable amount of time cultivating (in many different ways) their client prospects. You must ask them, first, to buy in to you and your Mobile Mini-Conglomerate, into the solution of their problems that you have available, at a low level of expense. As you prove to their satisfaction that you can do what you say you can do, you will gradually increase their commitment as they feel comfortable doing so.

Since this is the case, you cannot afford the luxury of rushing your prospects to a decision, much less the luxury of telling the slow, the recalcitrant, the dim-witted who do not perceive as clearly as you do what their problem is and how your problem solving solutions apply, what you think of them. For this is detrimental to your success and must be avoided. I have learned all this painstakingly for I have a hot temper, an assertive manner (which grates on many) and the ability, by telling the unvarnished truth, to wound with a word. But I have learned. And so will you. As you learn, your prospecting will be more and still more successful and your ultimate success assured.

Resource

For further tips about telemarketing and how to use this vital marketing technique successfully see Dr. Gary S. Goodman's book *You Can Sell Anything By Telephone* (Prentice Hall).

The Role Of Workshops And Seminars In Getting Clients

Before people will buy your advice they need to know something about you, need to feel comfortable with you and be attracted to you, need to have a reasonable expectation that they are not throwing their money away. You can meet all these objectives by successfully using America's talk circuit. Sadly, however, most people in the advice business woefully misuse and misunderstand this circuit and are often wasting their time on it. Therefore the following tricks of the trade.

Don't Begin With A Self-Sponsored Program

Time and again people I know come to me with the brilliant inspiration of hosting their own free-standing advice program, in part designed as an independent profit center and in part as a means of attracting clients for their professional practices. In almost every case I act the part of the mournful Cassandra, urging them to cease and desist from such ruinous nonsense. And I'm going to tell you the same thing. Here's why:

The workshop and seminar business is, of course, a multi-billion dollar business, but as I showed painstakingly in **MONEY TALKS**, it is a complicated business and one which offers the potential, not merely for profit, but more often for substantial loss for those who offer free-standing, independent programs. The reason for this is plain: until you know your business inside and out, until you understand your market better than they do themselves, including the ease of identifying clients and the ease of motivating them to action (i.e. enrolling in your workshop), begin your business on someone else's money.

Although I do more than 100 programs yearly, I only offer one or two independently each year. The reason for this is clear: rather than put up any upfront money myself, I want to diminish the risk to myself to nothing (not investing a dime) and instead get myself hired as an independent contractor to some of the more than 2,800 college and university continuing educational programs nationwide, the more than 60,000 associations and the hundreds of thousands of businesses nationwide which offer training and other programs.

My rules in this regard are very simple: I either make a deal with a prospecting service (which is all a college, for instance, is) which has the means of attracting an audience or with an organization (such as an association) which has an assured, built-in audience, and thus an assured built-in audience for me. Either way I minimize my investment. My job, however, is to maximize the amount of money I draw from each experience. With over 200,000 programs given each business day, there's no absence of opportunities, and I can affirm that this is a very lucrative business, properly understood, properly managed.

Clearly Identify Your Target Groups

Before you begin to put together a seminar or workshop, clearly identify who you want to attract and why. If you are now in an advising practice, take a close look at the individuals who supply you with the most substantial portion of your income. You do this for two reasons:

- You already have a track record with these people. (I hope a good one.) Thus, you should be in a position to leverage your successes in order to attract others who are similarly situated and would like you to replicate these successes for them.

- You already know the problems of these people and should be able to profit more readily by attracting these individuals since you know what problems they have and how to solve them. Thus, you need not go to the expense (both in terms of time and money) to prep yourself but can make use of what you already know.

The real question you have to ask yourself is whether there are enough of these individuals (or organizations) in your marketing territory as yet unserved to justify a program sponsor in mounting a course and hoping to snag them. Just what you find out in response to this point will determine what direction you go. Here's what I mean.

There are approximately 125 visiting nursing-type agencies in Massachusetts, one of my prime marketing territories. I already have a track record working with these agencies and can leverage this record to attract more business. Let's say that I wanted to draw additional income and exposure to new client prospects from this group (as I often do). There are several ways of proceeding:

- an arrangement with a college or university continuing education program
- an arrangement with the VNA state association
- a free-standing program.

In this instance, the market is very clearly targeted, 125 agencies. Once having targeted the market it is necessary to ascertain what their problems are and what they are buying today to solve these problems. This is your task. Whether you mount a free-standing program or whether you associate yourself with an institution or professional or trade association, you, the expert in the field, must supply the technical, marketing personnel at the institution or association with the information about the problem being solved and the market's willingness to buy a solution just now. This is always your responsibility.

Having done so, analyze the three alternatives above and see which applies, and why.

- An arrangement with a college or university continuing education department.

Such an arrangement might be considered if the institution were willing to mount a special one-day program promoted through its own flyer and if they were willing to extend the focus of their operations beyond Massachusetts, in this instance, to, say, the New England area. 125 is a very small market unless one has a very pronounced indication that the market is ready for this program (which would be done through client prospect ascertainment in advance of a final decision to mount the program). In this case, you might be interested in an institute, which is a program extending beyond a single day and perhaps featuring a succession of individuals. Before any final decision is taken in this regard, you would have to check with the state association to see whether the program you have in mind is one that they themselves are considering doing (for with such a small universe of prospects competition would be disastrous). You might also attempt to create a situation where the program was jointly sponsored by the state association *and* the educational institution.

The attraction of this joint sponsorship is that it enables the association to use the technical expertise of the continuing education department for help with marketing, registration and conference set up without negatively impacting on their own (usually quite small) staffs. The draw-back, of course, is that the educational institution has to be contracted for on a fee basis.

- An arrangement with the VNA state association.

Most associations nowadays offer educational programs to their members. Even smaller associations like the one in this illustration characteristically have an individual whose assignment is to produce programs of interest for their members, programs that is of both personal and professional interest (thus, a program on "Financial Planning for VNA Executive Directors" is as appropriate as one entitled "Raising Money To Provide Care for the Indigent").

Such associations also characteristically contract (as do continuing education facilities) with outside experts (like you!) to provide programs on a straight fee for service (independent contractor) basis.

One of the benefits of working directly with such a professional association is that they should have information from their members about programs which would be of interest to them. If they don't, they can easily take an ascertainment survey to find out what programs their members would come to.

Note: Clever entrepreneurs looking for new sources of revenue have begun to contract with such associations (associations where their own client prospects are, of course, members) for the "seminar rights," the right, that is, to produce programs. In this way they have an ongoing source of income, for, of course, they derive revenue from arranging the entire seminar program, can put themselves on the program, and can make deals with their colleagues who will also be presenting programs. Yes, this is very clever.

- A Free Standing Program

You can always, too, attempt to offer your seminar as a free-standing program. This means, of course, that all the profits would be yours. But then, so are all the expenses.

Particularly when you are just starting out such a course is most inadvisable. Whatever may be the merits of offering such free standing programs later, they are minimal at the beginning of your advising career, when you are least known to your client prospects. Then you are amply repaid by your association with an educational institution or professional association by the credibility which you derive from this association. Thus, I would urge you most seriously not to consider a free standing program until you are well known by those who may attend such a program and have helped your clients achieve a substantial measure of success, success which can be leveraged to attract others to your programs.

Base Your Workshops On A Problem To Which You Have The Solution

I read many educational brochures ostensibly promoting programs, and I am continually disheartened by what I see. Most people who assemble programs have backgrounds in education. As such they are dazzled by one's formal educational training, by degrees and certificates, by what I call the historical data — where one has been rather than by what one has accomplished.

Personally I have a one-man mission to perform: I aim to transform the way such program planners approach their work. People who offer programs where advice of any kind is being given ought to be asked — and as regularly re-asked — about what they themselves have done to help realize their own advice, thereby proving that they are competent to provide it.

Educators and those with the standard, hum-drum educational turn of mind, do not seem adequately to care about such results. Instead they spend too much of their over ample time worrying that those they deal with have the proper credentials, as if that piece of paper proved anything beyond the fact that its holder has successfully learned how to manipulate the educational system.

Thus, the catalog descriptions that you read are characteristically dull and boring, beside the point. They should, instead, focus on the excitement (and anxiety) of the client prospect's problem, the designated instructor's capacity to solve that problem, and the expected outcome of the program.

Now, it should probably go without saying (but probably doesn't) that there is no point in your offering such a program unless some or all of the following points apply:

- You are making outright profit from the event, either through an instructional fee and/or through direct product sales.
- There will be sufficient outside promotion so that you have, at least, the chance of securing clients from those hearing of you in this fashion but who are unable to attend the program.
- There are client prospects in your audience who can afford to buy your individual advising services.

Unless some or all of these conditions apply, don't waste your time getting involved in the program. You can see this means that I, for one, do not believe in doing programs simply because they offer the opportunity of raising one's prestige or because there's a general chance (a disorganized chance) for visibility. On the other hand, at the commencement of one's career, I do believe it advisable to do programs and perfect one's platform skills and one's motivational and client procurement skills so that at a later time one has become quite the master of these essentials. But even in this situation, I only approve of it to the extent that the complete seminar success sequence is followed.

Arranging Your Ideal Seminar

As in so many things, I find that advisors who wish to use seminars as direct or indirect profit centers (that is, whether they expect to profit from them directly as events or through relationships which will come about as a result of the event), approach the experience severely inadequately. I see this regularly, and I confess such an approach infuriates me.

Your Seminar Success Sequence

As I have said before, to get an individual to buy your advice service, no matter how desperately he needs it, is not ordinarily a matter of a single hearing about what you have to offer. Reinforcement is most necessary. This process of reinforcement is built into the Seminar Success Sequence. You must conceptualize this sequence before you approach any possible program sponsor 1) because you stand to gain the most from its implementation, and 2) because, while program planners ought in theory to provide you with this service, my long association with them convinces me that most are unable to function in the problem-solution mode of seminar production that must distinguish you, the successful advisor. Here, then, is your Seminar Success Sequence:

- Identify your target market. Write down the problem they have, the solution you offer (as offered in your program), the number of individuals or organizations within the sponsoring organization's market who suffer from this problem, and the ease of gaining access to them (a key point for any program planner).
- Write the program description as a problem-solution statement. The program description should have three parts: title, description body, and instructor biographical information.

The Title

The title should be divided into two parts: the Grabber and the Descriptor. The Grabber should be an attractive phrase either dealing with the client prospect's program-related anxiety or aspiration. The Descriptor is a phrase (usually following a colon) which provides a straightforward factual description of what the prospect gets in the program.

The Description Body

This portion of the copy deals either explicitly or implicitly with the problems the client prospect (program participant) has and how the course will deal with them (process and outcome information). This section must be very closely connected to the client's problem, the reason that is why he is coming to the program, and the processes which will produce a desirable outcome for him. The language here must be taut and action oriented, for what the client prospect is coming for is movement towards his desired outcome, the outcome you understand as well as he does.

Instructor Biographical Information

Try as I might, I have the most difficulty with this section, since standard educators insist on selling my degree credentials instead of my demonstrated success in solving the similar problems of past participants. Thus, add only that information which demonstrates that you have at your disposal information which works to solve the problems of your designated market. Consider using the enthusiastic testimonials of past participants and client endorsements as a form of instructor biographical information. This is more important than the insipid information about where you took you baccalaureate degree. The former indicates that you are the master of problem solving expertise; the latter is only a bit of insignificant historical data.

Thus, each portion of the program description must, in its own way, reinforce the one overriding theme of problem-solution, that you, the advisor, know what the program participant's problem is and that you can — and will! — solve it. This is the one message that people must get both before, during, and after the program.

A Word On Selling Your Program To A Program Planner

Program planners are, or should be, in the marketing business. They are interested in offering programs that work, that solve problems and make money — for them! You have to convince them on all counts. If you can do so, you'll have no problem getting your programs adopted and, importantly, making money from them over and over again wherever you can draw participants, just like I do. The program planner wants to know, from you, the following information:

- What is the problem you are addressing?
- How many organizations/individuals in our (that is, the program planner's) territory have it?
- How seriously do they rate it? (That is, how likely is it they spend money to solve it?)
- How do you know?
- How do you propose getting access to these people? (This is a dramatic problem that you must think about and specifically answer, in as much detail as possible, before approaching a program sponsor.)
- What program format do you envision? Over how long a time?
- Who are you? Why are you qualified to offer this program? Does this program fit into our current offerings? Does it duplicate or compete against something we're already doing?
- What financial arrangement do you want?

Dealing With Program Planners

As I said in **MONEY TALKS,** which is a book you must master if you plan to use workshops or seminars in any way, it is not difficult to get access to program planners. Their job is continually to scout for new programs and to attempt to open new markets for their employers.

Accessible as they are, however, they do not ordinarily move quickly to a decision. That's why you have to stay in touch with them, often over a long time, to continue to urge them to adopt your program. If you are certain that both the need and market for your program exist, it is your responsibility to continue to press the program planner for action. Remember: unless and until you sell the program planner on the need for your program you will not have the opportunity to use this vehicle to put you in touch with your other client prospects. Thus, unless you are prepared (unwisely, as I have already said) to risk your own money, this is a sale you *must* make.

Obstacles In Working With Program Planners

Even if the program planner accepts the need for your program, there will still be problems. Although program planners are meant to be innovative in their search for programs, they are innovative in almost no other way, a situation which has been both disheartening and frustrating for me and which will probably cause you come aggravating moments, too. Here are some of the obstacles you are likely to encounter and what to do about them:

- Program planner objects to having you sell the course books direct to the students, whether you have made a deal with another publisher or whether you are yourself the publisher. Remember: program planners are in most ways very traditional, unimaginative thinkers. They are, moreover, all middle or lower middle management employees and thus are usually being slowly consumed by a slow rage about the frustrating circumstances of their stunted lives. They are not themselves entrepreneurs and on the whole they mistrust — and sometimes outright dislike — those of us who are. But remember, this is usually their galloping envy at work!

Remember, too, the program is taking place to solve three interrelated problems:

- the need of the program participant for a solution to his problem
- the need of the program sponsor to be perceived as offering a helpful service in their community or to their members while simultaneously making the sponsoring organization a profit, and
- your own need for a profit either directly or indirectly from this program.

In this connection, your ability to supply books to your program participants should be perceived as an Assertive Courtesy, since these books and materials selected by you, the expert, must be perceived as part of the problem solving process. It may be nontraditional for you, the program instructor, to sell books, but it is all a necessary part of the one overriding image you are establishing — as the Accessible Expert who works to solve the problems of your designated client population in all ways. The mere fact that other instructors do not behave (and profit!) similarly means, or should mean, nothing to you.

- The program planner says it's against regulations to provide you with a list of program participants. Yes, even this absurdity will take place! So find out in advance, and if there's to be no cooperation on this point, collect the facts from participants directly by sending around your own sign-up sheet. But remember: this is information you must have — or else you cannot follow up.

- The program planner will not allow you to mention your advisor service or products in the program promotional materials. This is regrettably most common, and you must be continually alert for signs of this madness which sometimes is the result of sheer stupidity on the sponsor's part and sometimes shows his disinclination to be used by you in a promotional manner. Recently, for instance, in the program brochure being sent out for one of my fund raising training programs by a state agency, the sponsor included among my credentials my book on Victorian pageants but deleted any mention of either my fund raising consultation service or the many books I have written which contain helpful information for nonprofit organizations. Such idiocy is by no means uncommon.

On the one hand, inform the program planner that this information is relevant for participants. It gives them a justifiable feeling of security that you are indeed an expert who can help them. In short, it's just the kind of credential which is meaningful, despite the fact that, true, there is a promotional advantage to be gained by you. (And, really, what's wrong with that?)

- The program planner sees no advantage to be gained from having media people attend the program. If a media person does come and cover your program, the coverage can spur attendance at a future program if this kind of line is added to the copy: "Dr. Lant will again be presenting his consulting program in the fall. To get on the mailing list call . . ." The article itself provides validation of you the expert and excites the interest of others who want to come. Of course media people should be in attendance at all your programs, but with the decided understanding that they will in fact notify their readers/listeners that another program is happening, with the date if you know it.

- Program planners often feel shy about using participant comments in their subsequent promotional pieces. Unbelievable, isn't it? But it's very, very common. It seems to me that program planners would be ecstatic about having this means of reducing the anxieties of those pondering the advisability of spending their money to attend your programs, but it just isn't so. I have to plead with program planners to add a line to their standard, unimaginative program evaluation form eliciting good comments from program participants to be used in promoting future programs. You should ask those completing the form how they wish to be identified, and you have to inform them that, yes, you may be using their quotation. But that's it. Insist upon the sponsor gathering such endorsements — and using them to your mutual advantage. Don't expect them to follow this sensible advice unless you prod them, as I must do.

Getting The Best Use From The Program Itself

During the course of the year I speak at program after program, often sharing the bill with other experts and advisors. Just what they think they're doing there often escapes me since they do so little to get a good result from their speaking and attendance. If you consider that reinforcement is what you're after, here's what has to happen:

- If you are speaking at a trade or professional association, make sure there is an article by or about you in the organization's publication both before and after your appearance. If you wish to become The Inevitable Expert in your field, the one person who offers your advice service, this is absolutely necessary. The exact form of this article is discussed in the next chapter.

- Make sure that everyone attending the meeting has the opportunity of getting your material whether they attend your session or not. Of course leave information in the standard places, like literature tables, only don't leave all of it at once. Such places tend to get clogged; you need to go back from time to time with small amounts of your material and so arrange it that it is indeed seen. Use, too, unusual means: leave a few pieces of your literature on top of the cigarette machine, at the telephones, and on the tables in other people's seminar rooms. The cost is trifling. If there is a "speaker ready" room, leave a few copies there, too. It never hurts for opinion leaders to know who you are.

- Using the same problem-solution format, create a précis for distribution to everyone attending your program. Make sure this information clearly indicates that you understand their problem and that you can solve it.

- Tape your programs and sell the cassettes to your audience. Make sure you leave enough space at the conclusion of the tape for your name, address, telephone number and complete purchase information (if you are selling books) or a notice about the advice service on which this program is based. The tape provides you with validation but you must remember that each item you send out must be complete in itself. Make it easy for the purchaser, your continuing buyer prospect, to follow up.

Follow-Up Your Program

There are several different kinds of program follow-up you need to be aware of. Thus, you can follow-up to those who would be interested in working with you to gain the success result that was the purpose of the program (in this case the program participants), and you can follow-up with those who would like to replicate the success process itself, namely other program sponsors. Both kinds of follow up are significant. Thus, if I have once given a successful program to Massachusetts visiting nursing organizations I can follow up:

- to the organizations themselves, the organizations who attended the program, offering my advisor services, and

- to similar associations in other states where the problems I have dealt with in the original program remain to be solved.

Such follow-up is critical if you wish to derive the maximum benefit from any single engagement. Why then don't most people do this?

Sadly, most people do not see success as part of sequence. Do not see that the importance of any single event, any individual program lies in large measure in the extent to which it can be leveraged to secure future benefit. Thus, they seem content to see a single program as just that, single. But this is absurd.

Look at the powerful success sequences that have been strengthened by a single successful program:

- You get to return to organizations and individuals who need your advisor service and now, thanks to your program, know you.

- As you help create successes within this universe, you can return to its members again and again alerting them to this progress — and to the fact that it is available to them, too — if they work with you. Each time you have a success, each time you notify them of it, you reinforce your image as both the Accessible and the Inevitable Expert.

- If the program has been either programmatically successful (as evidenced by participant evaluations) and/or financially profitable, you can entice other, comparable organizations to offer it, too, to their members, members who have a similar set of problems to be solved.

- And, of course, as we shall soon see in detail, you can use each event in its turn as a source for unabashed promotion, and so, depending on the media source, either reinforce your perceived success with your original audience or with other, new audiences who would like such success, too — and the opportunity to work with you, the undeniable expert.

CHAPTER 7

Unabashed Promotion: Its Role In Getting You Clients And Publicizing Your Practice

In the previous chapters I have presented a variety of ways to help you get clients and prosper. In a phrase, the keys to these ways have been:

- targeting a client population
- identifying their problems
- working to solve their problems
- leveraging the success you've had in solving the problems to get more clients who currently have such problems.

In successfully completing this sequence of possibilites, do not lose sight of the value of unabashed promotion: the ability, that is, of bringing your problem solving skills and successes to the attention of thousands, even millions, of client prospects — all for free!

The Author & Unabashed Promotion

As you have by now gathered, I dislike spending my money if I can think of ways of achieving the same result for diminished expense or even no expense at all. That's why I like unabashed promotion, for I can achieve my aim of reaching millions for trifling expense while at the same time allowing the media to burnish my reputation and so enhance the desire of my client prospects to buy from me, work with me. It's a truly magical system, and it's most effective.

I have been using the techniques found in this chapter and in my book **THE UNABASHED SELF-PROMOTER'S GUIDE** for years now. I have an advertising budget which is frankly insignificant in size, for I achieve most of my publicity and promotional results through the free media. On average, nowadays, I get one kind of media mention (article by or about me, &c) daily; this has been going on for years. And I expect that it'll continue for many years to come, each article, each media mention reinforcing my image as the Inevitable, Accessible Expert and Problem Solver.

Why Others Don't Use These Techniques

Despite the fact that I've set down hundreds of promotional gambits in **THE UNABASHED SELF-PROMOTER'S GUIDE** and that I write and lecture frequently about this subject, I am distinctly aware of how few people actually use these techniques. There are several reasons, some bona fide, for their reticence and reluctance to do so:

- They write badly. Unabashed promoters have to produce good, solid English prose. It need be nothing fancy, but it must be serviceable.

- They don't speak well. You cannot appear on radio and television shows without having the ability to appear personally engaging and to string sentences together pleasantly.

- They don't understand what the individual media source to whom they are pitching their story (their service, themselves, &c) wants. Each media source has a slant, a point of view, if you will, which you as the promoter has to understand. If your objective doesn't coincide with what the media source is attempting to do, you'll be ignored. *Tout court.*

- They take no for an answer. Media people are in the business of changing their minds. If you are willing to accept the "No!" they give you today as a likely answer they may give you tomorrow, you will have problems in getting your message out through the media.

I regard these as technical problems which will be solved by mastering the essentials of unabashed promotion. But there is another set of problems which are mental, and these are, perhaps, the more significant, the more trying to deal with.

In my travels around the country, I have now dealt with thousands of people who would benefit from the techniques of unabashed promotion. Yet only a fraction of them are doing so. Some of the reasons, to be sure, are technical. They don't know how to do it. These, it seems to me, are the less significant problems, the more easily mastered. More distressingly, many are handicapped by other obstacles which make it difficult, if not impossible, for them to succeed as an unabashed promoter. These obstacles largely revolve around matters of esteem and entitlement.

Let me say this at the very outset: no one in the media is going to discover you. Certainly you can never have a sustained relationship with the media, a mutually productive symbiosis, by being passive and disinterested in what the media can do for you and your practice. This book is about energy, about activity, about being goal oriented, and about movement to achieve your objectives. So it is in your relations with the media. If you want something to happen, something beneficial for you and your clients, then you must take the necessary action.

This will probably mean getting over feelings of insecurity which you may have, getting over a deep-seated belief that you are not entitled to the coverage because you do not do anything particularly noteworthy and unique, getting over the debilitating condition that what you do is not sufficiently important to warrant media coverage. For if you cannot make progress on these matters, you cannot enter into the kind of symbiosis which is absolutely necessary for you to succeed as an unabashed promoter.

Understanding Unabashed Promotion

The magic of unabashed promotion is that if you do it properly you need never be perceived as either unabashed or as a promoter but rather as a completely empathetic problem solver, eager only to solve the problems of a targeted group of individuals and organizations (who happen to be, coincidentally, the people you want to contract with.)

It is only the awkward and unintelligent promoter who ever opens himself to the charge of being an unabashed promoter, of seeking, that is, to use the media source as a means of free advertising for his advisor practice. This need never happen to you, for once you have mastered the essentials of unabashed promotion, the end result will be a perception by your client prospects (for these are the people you are attempting to reach through your promotional tactics) that you are the consummate, empathetic problem solver. Now, isn't this exactly what you desire? And isn't it particularly marvelous that what you want can happen for a trifling cost?

Understanding What The Media Wants

To succeed with the media, you must understand what media sources want. To speak generally, there are only two kinds of media stories: problem stories and problem-solving stories.

The first of these deals with something urgent, something fraught with drama, tension, and anxiety. Media people love these stories because with them they are able to transcend their own puny insignificance through the importance of the urgent story they are covering. Thus, the more dramatic, the more tense, the more anxious the better they like it, for media people who cover these stories have a need for a continuing adrenalin high, the kind of high which can only come by confronting something truly momentous.

Thankfully, not all media stories are about problems. Many are also about solutions to problems. Needless to say, most people in the media prefer the former kind of story as more colorful and engaging, although when they are being sensible they realize that they should prefer the second.

Fortunately, as advisors we can make use of both kinds of stories, those about problems and those about solutions to those problems, and in the process promote our practices and gain clients, which is, of course, the real reason why we want a relationship with the media at all. Our success in building a symbiotic relationship with the media rests on our ability to deliver what they want (problem stories and problem solving stories) and to avoid being perceived as an unabashed promoter. To the extent that we give media sources what they want, we will in return achieve the truly magnificent results of unabashed promotion without being tagged by that tainted label!

A Word About Image

I have previously discussed the importance of image to your advisor practice, but I must raise the subject again here. In dealing with the media, in dealing effectively that is, you will need a tight, compact image, an image designed to appeal to your designated client prospects and establish you in an instant as the kind of effective problem solver they need. I am not going to reopen the subject of image here. Suffice it to say, instead, that the image must be designed to appeal to your client prospects, must take into account their anxieties and aspirations, and must be capable of being understood by them in the flickering of an eye. You image must always be composed of empathy and intelligence components, for you must never forget that it must assist you in making a two-tier sale: the prospect must be persuaded to buy you as an individual and to work with you, and must know that you have the necessary problem solving skills to be an effective addition to his life and business. Nothing which detracts from this objective must be allowed, which is why the most powerful images are always the simplest.

Producing The Standard Media Kit

The key to working with the media is to do most of your thinking about who you are trying to reach, what their problems are, what your solutions are, and who you are in advance of approaching any individual media source. Actually contacting a media source and working with it to bring yourself to the attention of your client prospects should be largely mechanical and automatic. To achieve this objective means to prepare a complete Standard Media Kit.

This kit should consist of the following basic documents:
- a Context Document
- a Standard Biographical Feature Story
- a Précis
- Head and Action Photographs
- a Standard Media Release.

The Context Document

Most media people are process people, that is, they are good at processing information, putting it into the right form for the vehicle which is dispensing it. But they are not very good at assessing the importance of information. It would be very much against your interest if you allowed the media source you were approaching to attempt to conclude on his own the value of the material you were presenting. So don't.

Media people play god every single day. They like it. They make decisions about what kinds of stories play and in what way. Because they have no effective basis on which to make their decisions and because they are themselves often misinformed and run in a pack, many important stories are not covered, and legions of insignificant ones are blow out of proportion. You will diminish the chance that you'll be caught in this unfortunate situation if you write a good, thorough, cogent Context Document.

This document is designed to sell the media source you are approaching on the importance of your story, why it matters. Don't make the assumption that the source knows what your story is about, why it's important, or who it affects. This is information that you have and that you must present in an appealing way to the source so that in the end he, too, understands the significance of what you're doing and why it matters. Remember: if you cannot sell the media source on the importance of the issue you are dealing with, you will not be able to get the media attention you want and you will be forced to fall back on less desirable (read: costly) alternatives.

The Context Document need only be a very short document, no more than 400 words, or about the number of words which appear on this page. It should provide information on:

- the problem you address
- its dimension within the marketing territory of the media source
- how the problem relates to the particular readers or viewers who tune into the media source you're approaching
- a definition of terms if your subject if not likely to be well known
- any other important information which will indicate to the media person reading the Context Document just how important the problem is in his area
- information on who you are, the perceived solver of the problem which the media person now understands is important.

Here's what a Context Document can look like. This one is for a financial planner with a Boston-based practice:

A COMFORTABLE RETIREMENT OR A CRIMPED ONE: IT'S UP TO YOU

Each year in Massachusetts, over 250,000 workers retire. That's one in every fifteen workers. For many of these workers, retirement is a long awaited opportunity to rest, travel, explore their hobbies and interests and generally take advantage of life. But most of the rest of these people are in for a rude awakening!

About 75% of these people, or nearly 190,000 individuals, will only have Social Security benefits to live on. The rest have company pension plans of various kinds. Still only about one worker in ten will retire with his or her current income, a devastating blow to those who now have the time to do what they want to do — but won't have the money. Now or ever.

Morever, given the fact that at least fifty per cent of these people will also experience a major medical problem within ten years of retirement and that they will not possess adequate health insurance entirely to cover the bill, their prospects of a prosperous, busy retirement seem unlikely to be realized.

Fortunately, this result need not be true for everyone. Melrose financial planner Jim Smith has developed a series of options for those who want to be in a position to realize their lifelong dreams. These packages are designed to be implemented at different ages. Jim can show your audiences how to go about planning at ages 25, 35, 45 and 55 to achieve any lifetime financial objective.

Jim's been in the financial planning business for 8 years and has assisted several hundred Boston-area residents and professionals begin to take the necessary action so that they can have the time of their lives at retirement, just as they want to! Jim's knowledgeable, friendly, approachable and a good interview. He has both the information and personality your audience will relate to and will want to hear again and again.

A Few Points About The Context Document

This document must point out the problem, its local ramifications and the fact that you, the advisor/expert, can solve it. The document should reflect your image, that is the image that is the meaningful hook for your client prospects. As you can see, in this example Jim Smith is the Accessible Expert and his Context Document is warm and empathetic and includes words which reinforce his selected image.

Every document that you send out should have:

- a 24 hour number where you can be reached
- your complete name and address for follow-up.

Each document that you sent out to any media source (or anyone else, for that matter) should be complete in itself.

Biographical Feature Story

Unlike other cultures, Americans have never been very good at thinking abstractly about issues. That's one of the reasons why we are so interested in people, because, for us, people come to personify in themselves either a problem or the solution to a problem. In your case, it's got to be the solution!

You need to indicate to the media not only that within any individual source's territory there is a problem to which you have the solution but that you are an interesting, compelling, engaging and sufficiently attractive personality who deserves the coverage. It won't matter how important the problem is if you are perceived as an unattractive troll. To get the coverage you must yourself be seen as being engaging. This is the purpose of the Biographical Feature Story. It portrays you, first to the media source and then *through* the media source (who will use the same document) to your client prospects, as an attractive personality who also happens to be expert at solving a pivotal problem of a significant portion of the media source's audience.

Before you go on, turn to the samples section of this book and read one of my Biographical Feature Stories (See Samples, page 290). In doing so, remember: you can have one of these stories for each audience you are attempting to reach, for each service you offer. The important thing is that after seeing or hearing these facts your audience will identify with you, for one of the most important motivators in selling (which is, after all, what you are going through this to do) is having your audience associate with you, understand you, empathize with you and, of course, like you. This the Biographical Feature Story should accomplish.

Now that you've read the document, let's analyze what's happening in it and why.

The document you've just read is designed to establish an empathy between me and one of my several targeted audiences, the multi-million person market of small business people, home-based business people, independent professionals and others who want to break away from the standard 9 to 5 routine, begin realizing their own version of the American Dream, and find happiness and contentment through autonomy. This is a very large, diverse, and, for me, wealthy market.

Before you approach your market write down both your strengths and weakness regarding it. No one is without weaknesses *vis à vis* your market. And I am certainly not.

Here's one of my very significant weaknesses, which has to be dealt with before the necessary degree of empathy can be established. Having gone to Harvard and Oxford, having four college degrees, having written 10 books and been featured in many more, I might find it difficult to be regarded empathetically by a very large segment of my target market. "Sure," a home-based crafts maker might say, "it's all easy for him with those credentials. But I don't see that what he says is at all applicable to me." If that attitude is allowed to predominate, it would be equally bad both for the crafts maker and for me, since we'd both starve. Therefore I must work especially hard to establish a clear rapport, a sense of empathy between us when, in fact, there is at least some truth in her feelings.

The Biographical Feature Story has as one of its most important objectives the establishment of a strong rapport between individuals who are otherwise not connected.

Let's take a look at how this important connection is in fact made:

Paragraph 1. This is The Hook, and just like a fishing hook it's designed to hook your audience. But remember: in fact you must always be aware that you have two audiences, the media source who books you and the client prospects you are really there to connect with. You should consider the media source the representative of his audience and keep this audience firmly in mind at all times. The opening line, the opening paragraph as a whole, is designed to establish the undeniable fact that you are arresting and that you are at once interesting and have information at your disposal that is useful to his audience, your client prospects.

Note: any adjectives or adverbs which you use to establish the compelling image should be consonant with that image and not at variance with it. Think of the audience that I'm wanting to connect with in the sample Biographical Feature Story you've just read. The fact that I'm "different" should be appealing to them, for they want to be as different, and as successful! But it's not the fact that I am "different" which makes that the right word to use; it's the fact that it's the right word for the audience I'm targeting.

Paragraph 2. This paragraph should be a quotation validating the impression left by the first paragraph. It should continue to build upon the now-existing link between you and your audience by reinforcing the perception that you are "one of them." But not just like them, for if you were just like them there would be no point to dealing with you, but like one of them who has succeeded in realizing a significant objective that your clients have. One of them, surely, but several steps ahead in life's race.

Paragraph 3. Deal with one of your possible weaknesses in this paragraph. Let's analyze the example. Many people who run home-based businesses are perceived as less professional because they work from their homes. Rightly or wrongly, this is a criticism that is often made about those working at home, and I'm as subject to it as anyone else. Thus, in this paragraph I bring forward weighty credentials intended to establish my professional standing, on the one hand, and demolish a possible common objection.

Note: you'll notice that in this paragraph and in paragraph 2, my name is modified, in the former paragraph with a warm adjective ("expansively"), in the latter by some standard biographical information. Don't lose an opportunity to reinforce your image (in this case, I'm a mixture of The Entrepreneur, The Maverick and The Accessible Expert) and to provide facts which round out who you are.

Beginning with paragraph 4 you can mix empathetic quotations about yourself and information designed to polish off perceived weaknesses. The trick is to do so without appearing to, conveying the information in a Conversational Accessible tone, the tone, that is, that you want to use in the interviews with you and the articles about you.

Look at how many of these weaknesses I deal with: the lack of an M.B.A. degree (while teaching business courses no less!), the lack of a headquarters and assistants, even the lack of knowledge about driving (a fact, by the way, which is almost always used in interviews and which virtually every reader recalls, too!).

Your job in the Biographical Feature Story is to co-opt the reasonable ground, to tell people (first the media personnel and then your targeted client prospects) why you're interesting, and to deal with your perceived weaknesses, and to advance the most plausible, cogent arguments in answer to potential critics.

A word about those critics: it is true than when you present yourself to any media source, you do open yourself up to criticism. Most of the time there isn't any, but occasionally there is. Your job is to expect it, to anticipate it, and to prepare for it. Figure out where your critics are likely to attack you, what they are likely to say about you, and work up your arguments accordingly. Remember: it is not your job, nor even a reasonable expectation, to convince your critics of anything. That's usually beyond hoping. But what is possible is that by presenting the most reasonable counterarguments to whatever your critics are saying you'll be able to persuade your client prospects to hang in there with you. I know for a certain fact that the American public is inherently fair minded. They are also, like most people, interested in a good argument, a good show, so long as it's not an argument in which their interests are affected.

This being the case, all you have to do is put your best case forward and hold tight to your designated client prospects and ignore the rest. It's a very comforting thought, and one I've enjoyed on many occasions, that to become a multi-millionaire in this country you have only to convince a very small slice of the people to do any single thing and can comfortably ignore the rest. Keep it in mind!

A Précis

We have already talked about the précis, and I will not reiterate all I have previously presented. The précis, however, has a very important place in the Standard Media Kit. Remember: either you are going on the air or being interviewed by some print media source to indicate a problem, or you are doing your media stint because you have a solution to a problem. The précis, of course, indicates that you have a solution.

Let's return to the illustration of the financial planner. Let's say that Jim Smith wanted to attract as clients independent professionals between the ages of 30 and 50. These need not be his only clients, of course, but let's assume either 1) that they already provide him with a substantial portion of his income, a portion which he'd like to increase, or 2) that he wishes to diversify his client base by adding such a group to it.

The précis that he would put into his Standard Media Kit, for a program or interview designed to attract this group, would deal with the products and services at his disposal designed for these client prospects. It might start with a series of the characteristic problems of this group (how do you save when you're just buying a house, beginning a family, &c?) and tie in his services and products with the answers to these questions.

Personally, the précis I use is composed of all the products and services I have available, and I tailor any individual document I send to a media source in the cover letter. This I find saves time and has been, on the whole, perfectly acceptable.

The précis is designed to show the media source just what you've got to solve the problems of the designated audience. Whereas the Context Document establishes that there is a problem and the Biographical Feature Story shows that you are the attractive, intelligent, compelling expert who can solve it, the précis shows in detail *how* the problem of the targeted audience can be solved. It is therefore process oriented. Thus, consider these documents as three p's in a pod:

- The Problem: Context Document
- The Personality: Biographical Feature Story
- The (Solution) Process: The Précis

There is also a fourth "p", the photographs.

Photograph Essentials

You'll need two kinds of photographs for your Standard Media Kit: a head shot and an action shot. Both must reinforce the image which you've decided is appropriate for you and to corral your client prospects. The head shot is simply that, a shot of your head and shoulders. In considering this photograph, however, remember the basics: what you wear must reinforce the image you are striving to create and if you are after a warm, personable image (and you probably are), you'll want to make sure you are leaning into the photograph, through the photograph into the arms of the viewer. This photograph should be either a 5 by 7 inch, black and white glossy or an 8 by 10 inch, black and white glossy. No color, please!

The action shot should show you doing that which reinforces your designated image. If you are being an Accessible Expert, have yourself photographed helping someone else, an existing client, perhaps, who will speak well of you if asked. This shot, too, should be in the same standard sizes as your head shot.

Order about a dozen of each. That'll be sufficient for a time. Make sure that you place an appropriate caption on the reverse of each photograph. The caption should include your complete name, address and telephone number (don't forget the area code!) and the name of your company, significant service(s) and/or product(s), thus: "Dr. Jeffrey Lant, President of Jeffrey Lant Associates, Inc., 50 Follen St., Suite 507, Cambridge, Ma 02138. 617-547-6372. Author of **DEVELOPMENT TODAY: A FUND RAISING GUIDE FOR NON-PROFIT ORGANIZATIONS** and other books." This caption should be typed on a label, not written on the back, as any attempt to write directly on the photograph will be seen on the obverse.

Note: Although you can request that these photographs be returned by media sources using them, chances are you'll never get them back. Just what media sources do with these pictures remains a deep mystery to me. But they certainly don't return them. Act accordingly.

The Standard Media Release

Hitherto the forms I have recommended to you are those which I have pioneered myself. That is not the case with the media release, hence its designation of "standard." The Standard Media Release is the form you'll use when seeking a news or feature story in a printed media source. Take a look at the example on page 288. Several things should be immediately apparent even from a quick reading.

- The story is written about you in the third person (just like the Biographical Feature Story). Thus the release reads as if it were written by someone else.
- The Standard Media Release should read *exactly* as you want the actual story to read. It should require the absolutely least amount of editing by the media source and should be capable, indeed, of being run just as it is. This means that you've got to think and write like a journalist. The less work you ask of them, the more likely it is that your media release will be run.

This means that you have to think through not only the actual story itself but provide the media source with complete organization and follow-up information. Thus the following:

As in the sample, your Standard Media Release must include:

- a contact for further information, including name and title
- company name and organization
- address
- telephone number (business)
- telephone number (after business hours)
- a release date (usually media releases are marked for "immediate release", but not always)
- a summary headline typed in caps, giving leading facts about the story
- a dateline providing the city of origin of the release.

All this information precedes the actual body of the release which contains the story.

The Body Of The Release

The first paragraph should contain what is called the "5 W" information: who, what, where, when, and why facts about the story.

Paragraph 2 should include a quotation by you, the principal of the story, elaborating on the facts presented in the first paragraph. Note: your chances of having this story printed are dramatically improved if you insert the name of the media source to which you will be sending the release. This indicates to the media source that you are giving them an exclusive. Clearly this also means that you must make minor alterations and changes in your quotations and the arrangement of facts before you can send the same story to other media sources.

In introducing your own name into this paragraph, make sure you modify it with a significant fact relating to your professional standing ("the Harvard-educated Lant . . .") or biographical information ("the 44-year old Lant . . ."). Your job is not merely providing the facts for a story but the complete, interesting story itself. This means providing your readers, your client prospects, with compelling information about you and any others featured in this piece. Always remember that any information you provide about yourself (or others) should take into account what would be of most value in connecting you to your client prospects, what would enhance their interest in you, or diminish their anxieties.

In paragraph 3 provide further significant information about yourself, or about the organization or event being featured. This paragraph should add a further noteworthy fact about the featured item and another pithy quotation. Don't forget: if there is more than one individual being featured in this release, now is a good time to add an apt quotation from the second principal.

In any further paragraphs (and there should probably be no more than 10), provide additional, less important information that is still of interest to the targeted population.

In concluding, make sure to include all the necessary follow-up information that your client prospects will need: how much your product, service, or event costs. How the reader can get involved. Who does he call? When? Look at the final, concluding paragraph as a free ad and write it accordingly. But remember: this is not advertising; it is promotion. Leave out the hype and just include the facts.

Tips About The Standard Media Release

- Keep it short. 500 words, two single-sided, 8 1/2 by 11 inch pages, typed, double spaced should be more than sufficient for your story.
- Use only one side of the page. Media people get very frustrated when they see a release on two sides. It assuredly indicates an amateur at work and makes it very difficult for the editor to edit, hence diminishes the likelihood that what you write will in fact be used. This is true of any document you write!
- Write your release exactly like the story you are seeking. I cannot stress this sufficiently. Most media releases end up in the circular file, and while there are many reasons for this waste, the chief one is that the writer forgot what he was about. If you want media coverage learn to write — and act — and think — like someone in the media.

Using The Print Media

You now know what should appear in your Standard Media kit. Or, in fact, kits, for as many different client prospects as you are trying to reach for so many will you have media kits. Thus, I need a completely different set of documents when I am selling my fund raising consultation services as I do when trying to make hay with home-based businesses &c. So will you.

Now let's talk about how to get any print media source to carry information which will alert your client prospects to the important fact that you are an empathetic, intelligent problem solver available to help them. In this connection there are three basic article formats for you to master. Having done so you can get access to your client prospects at will and in just the right way to convince them that they need you. These three formats are the Problem Solving Process Article, The Sentinel Article and The White Knight Article, and they conform to the media's primary interest in problems, first, and, then, solutions.

The Problem Solving Process Article

You are in the business of solving problems for your (very specifically targeted) client prospects. If you cannot solve their problems and are not perceived to be able to solve their problems, you cannot make a success of your advice practice. Fortunately, the Problem Solving Process article allows you to be perceived as just the right person for your client prospect, the person, that is, who knows how to solve their problem.

The Problem Solving Process article is ordinarily divided into ten paragraphs, although you may freely deviate from this number so long as you remain faithful to the form and structure of the article. What is important is that having read this article your client prospect (your reader of primary importance) be convinced not only that you understand his problem but that you have a process for solving it.

I have selected ten as the appropriate number of paragraphs for a very good reason: this structure allows you to follow the 8 points of the Problem Solving process and to have an opening paragraph and a concluding one. The opening paragraph should explicitly confront the anxieties of your targeted client population and/or its aspirations. Most decidedly this opening paragraph should be a grabber, smartly pulling in your prospect, either through his fears or the prospect of overcoming them. Thus: "One out of every two people who retire will have to make do exclusively with Social Security. Thus, when they've got the time to have the time of their lives, they won't have the money." This is a grabber, and it suggests that by reading on, the anxiety they have of being in this position will be dealt with and the aspiration they harbor of avoiding this condition of affairs will be realized.

The next 8 paragraphs exactly parallel the 8 parts of the problem solving process, thus:

Paragraph 2: developing the right mental attitude

Paragraph 3: developing the right technical skills

Paragraph 4: understanding the real problem, finding out the real question

Paragraph 5: selling a solution to the decision maker

Paragraph 6: developing the necessary documents

Paragraph 7: developing an implementation strategy

Paragraph 8: reporting success and dealing with failure

Paragraph 9: the clinic stage/review.

Not every paragraph will be pertinent for every problem solving process article, but in most cases most, most if not all, will be.

Let's diagram one illustration. Say I want to sell my fund raising services to community health organizations, one segment of my market. The article I write is designed to be read by executive directors and trustees of such organizations, for they constitute the "next check network" for this segment of my market. The service I aim to sell is my capital campaign fund raising advice service, a high ticket item. Let's see how the Problem Solving Process article would look aimed at these people.

Paragraph 1 deals with the fears of such agencies about their financial stability in the wake of federal government budget cuts.

Paragraph 2 assists them in developing the right mental attitude for fund raising success.

Paragraph 3 alerts them to the technical skills they need for successfully raising money and how to secure such skills through training in-house staff, recruiting new personnel, and working with professional fund raising counsel.

Paragraph 4 helps them understand what the real problem is (in this case that while the boards want the money, the boards do not ordinarily want to work).

Paragraph 5 tells the executive director how to sell a fund raising plan to his board of trustees.

Paragraph 6 explains what kinds of documents are necessary for a successful fund raising campaign.

Paragraph 7 details an implementation strategy for pursuing successful fund raising, including who must be included, where and how often meetings must be held, &c.

Paragraph 8 deals with the question of how and to whom success should be reported and likely failure dealt with.

Paragraph 9 advises the targeted market on how to go about reviewing progress to see whether things are being done right.

The final paragraph can either be in the body of the article and/or in the author biographical tag. That is, you can either add a final paragraph of exhortation, the equivalent of a flick of the whip on the flanks of a recalcitrant beast, or you can conclude the body of the article at the end of paragraph 9. In either case, you must make the best use of the biographical tag to which you are manifestly entitled. Here you'll include information about you, your products and services and, if you are writing this article for a newsletter or specialized magazine, your telephone number and address. This is the free ad. Thus, "Dr. Jeffrey Lant, the noted fund raising advisor, will send you information about his fund raising books and consultation services if you write him at . . . . or call . . . ." You are entitled to a biographical tag of this kind with the Problem Solving Process Article, and you should insist upon it. Just how explicitly promotional it is, however, will depend on the nature of the source publishing it. Newsletters are always the most amenable to providing all that you want, but they also pay little, if anything, in outright payment for your article. They reckon that the biographical tag (and any fame you happen to acquire through writing the article) should suffice.

Variations On The Problem Solving Process Article

The Problem Solving Process Article has, in fact, three forms. The one above I call The Positive, because it set out both briskly and in a no-nonsense fashion what your client prospect needs to do to achieve success. It is very much an "Accessible Expert" format. But as we already know, you need another, strong format to be used with those individuals and organizations who, having a defined problem (and even knowing it quite well) still refuse to take beneficial action on their own behalf. That's where The Negative comes in.

The Negative uses, in fact, the same information that The Positive does, but it reverses it for emphasis. Thus, where the example above might be headed, "Raising Money For Your Community Health Organization: 8 Vital Secrets." The Negative would say, "Here's Why You're Failing To Raise Money For Your Community Health Organization: 8 Vital Secrets." This article is more hectoring, more minatory: it has the aura of fire and brimstone about it. It is written, of course, in the In-Command Infocrat mode. It should only be used when you have discovered that sweet reason works no more. Sadly, you will come to use it often.

Finally, the second variation is The Sequel. This, as its name suggests, is simply an additional set of suggestions, more recommendations about how the client prospect can solve the problem originated in the first article. Thus, "8 More Secrets For Successfully Raising Money For Your Community Health Organization." If you take a quick look down the list of the Problem Solving Process you are sure to see that all items cannot be dealt with in the initial article; there are simply too many points needing a word or two. Hence the need for the sequel.

More Facts About The Problem Solving Process Format

People continually ask me whether the Problem Solving Process doesn't obviate the need for you, the advisor, by providing the client prospect with sufficient information so that he can dispense with you. Actually, the reverse is true. No media source ever provides you with enough space actually to provide your client prospect with everything he needs to know about the process you are imparting. And the more technical and difficult the process, the more true this is. Thus, all that the client prospect learns from the article is exactly what you want him to learn: namely that the problem he has does have a solution and that you know how to implement it, quickly, efficiently and in a way that meets the prospect's expectation. The biographical tag which concludes the article makes it easy for the prospect to take immediate action, hence the importance of this part of the article.

A Few Hints About Problem Solving Process Articles

- Keep them short. A good problem solving process article can easily be written in 1,500 words, about 5 typed, double spaced pages. If you write longer articles in this format (as I very often do) they lend themselves nicely to a series, and thus further reinforcement with the client prospect.
- Problem Solving Process articles can be broken up into short, fact filled bullets which can be run in newsletters. Remember: you are looking for reinforcement with your client prospects. Thus, if a newsletter decides to take your 10 point article and run it as, say, a bullet in ten monthly installments of their monthly newsletter, you are actually much better off than if they ran it as a single feature. Many of my articles are so broken up. Remember: the aim of the Problem Solving Process article is not to solve the client prospect's problem but to indicate to the prospect that you know what the problem is, that you have the technical expertise to solve it and that you are available to do so. Reinforcement helps you meet these objectives. This is not, please note, an attempt to disseminate useful information; it is rather a very clever means of snagging the prospect's interest and getting him to take action on his behalf, and, of course, on your own.

Note: As I already mentioned, while some publications do pay for Problem Solving Process articles, many do not. Whether they do or not, consider the advisability of getting paid in ad space by the publication. Most publications are cash poor and would rather pay their writers in ad space, which is relatively less costly for them. Take advantage of this situation. But if you are paid in space, ask for twice as much ad space as what you would have been paid for the article. Thus, if you were getting a $250 stipend, ask for a $500 ad. The publication might froth a bit, but in truth they are still saving a substantial amount in outright cash.

The Sentinel

Most professionals find sales degrading, decidedly *infra dig*. That is, of course, because they are doing it quite wrong. Properly handled, sales exalts the seller and saves the buyer from a vexing problem. The Sentinel article is a good illustration of what I've got in mind.

In the trade, the Problem Solving Process Article is called an "Evergreen" format. This means that under ordinary circumstances, there is no necessary and special reason to run the article today instead of tomorrow. So long as the information is pertinent (which is ordinarily for a while), it doesn't much matter when the piece is run. This is both a benefit and a drawback for you. It's a benefit for you since the ageless quality of your advice ensures that you'll be able, with minor adjustments and revisions, to use the material over and over again. It's a drawback, of course, because you can't quite dictate to a publisher as to when it must be used. It's rather timeless quality makes that impossible. It is quite otherwise with The Sentinel, a format which meets a media source's need for something urgent and exciting.

Aspects Of The Sentinel

The Sentinel article is designed to establish you, the advisor, as the guard of your clients' interests, as the individual, that is, who, as their (self) designated leader stands alert to the changing conditions of life and how they affect your client prospects. You can use this format anytime something beneficial which your clients currently have is about to be lost to them or anytime something which might benefit them may not come to pass through lack of attention to their interests. It is a natural format for a leader and, of course, if you can establish yourself as your prospects' leader you can sell them anything you want and make them glad of your consideration!

Here are its parts:

Paragraph 1 should set forth the catastrophe that is about to overtake your prospects or the opportunity which is about to be lost to them. This paragraph is an anxiety paragraph, in that it basically says, "If you don't take action now you will be worse off."

Paragraph 2 provides what I call the current facts about the situation set forth in paragraph 1, that is, what's happening now.

Paragraph 3 begins to provide the immediate background and, with paragraph 4, the long range background. That is, how did this situation develop both in the immediate past and beyond. You may need three or four paragraphs to present all this information.

Having dealt with the immediate situation and the facts which lead up to it, you need to canvass the pro's and con's for what is happening. Just what side you'll be on, of course, depends on which side your prospects are on, or should be. You are, after all, the sentinel of their interests! Do present, however, the arguments of those who stand on the other side of the issue, if only to demolish them by presenting those that bolster your client prospect's point of view.

Having once done so, give your prospects some marching orders, tell them what they need to do on behalf of their interests and by what time. In short, act like the leader you have now become.

Conclude the Sentinel Article, like the Problem Solving Process Article and, indeed, the White Knight which follows, with the strongest possible free ad about who you are and the services and products you have available to solve the prospect's problem.

Variation On The Sentinel Theme

Once you have designated yourself the sentinel of your prospects' interest, you cannot abdicate the role, but must continue to act on their behalf. Given the fact that this is very clever marketing and promotion, this really isn't so very onerous for you. What it means, however, is that as other issues arise, including new twists and turns in the original issue you wrote about, you must keep abreast of developments and continue to rouse your followers, your client prospects. Thus, Sentinel leads to "Son of Sentinel," a follow up article either alerting the faithful to continuing (inimical) developments on the subject of interest to them, or, should this subject cease to be germane, a new subject altogether.

Sources Of Information For Sentinel Articles

There is no absence of good information sources for Sentinel articles. Check out:

- public information sources, including commissions, state and federal regulatory agencies, political sources such as legislatures and the Congress
- labor unions
- trade and professional associations
- experts who produce information but are not knowledgeable about how to benefit from it.

There is, in fact, no absence of opportunities for Sentinel articles. Quite the reverse. Your job is to link up with those who produce information of interest to your client prospects and to use it to indicate, through the Sentinel format, that you are *en garde* for them.

The White Knight Article

Each of us needs to be perceived as a White Knight by our damsel-in-distress clients, the expert, that is, who swoops in to preserve them from confusion and mayhem. But remember: no dragon, no knight. The value of the White Knight Article rests on a very important insight. Namely, that without the fire-breathing, destructive dragon there is no need for the knight. Hence, the white knight and the dragon are forever linked in this essential marketing tool.

The White Knight Article is made up of four essential components:

- the anxiety section
- the problem solving process section
- the shame switch
- the white knight section itself.

The Anxiety Section

This section of the article makes good use of the essential insight linking the dragon and the white knight. Thus, your White Knight article should begin by sowing the seeds of a considerable anxiety among your client prospects. The reasons for this anxiety should be stated as clearly as possible and should draw from as many reputable sources as are available to you, including government reports, expert testimony, your own work in the field.

While it is certainly true (as evidenced by the Problem Solving Process Article) that you should not be providing your clients with specific problem solving information, information, that is, that would allow the prospect to do without you, it is also true that as regards anxiety, you should give them as much as is necessary for them to realize they need you, the white knight. Thus you must ensure, by hearty infusions of anxiety provoking material, that the source of their confusion and disruption is very close at hand. Your sources need to provide proof positive to the client prospect that if they don't take action now, their interests will be severely affected.

The Problem Solving Process Section

We Americans are not so constituted that we can live with anxiety for very long (even though we have problems with threaten to exterminate the race). We want solutions, solutions, solutions! That's where you, the expert advisor, come in, with the problem solving process section of the White Knight Article.

In this section of the White Knight Article, you select a few from among the many solutions you have available for the client prospect's problem. You cannot in this section, which will probably not be longer than 200 to 500 words, give too many solutions and, of course, you'll not be able to give them in too much detail. Which ought to be fine with you, since you want to be paid directly for providing them to the prospect.

What is important here is what is important in the Problem Solving Process Article itself: namely that the prospect be made to see that, yes, his problem does have a solution and, yes, you can help provide it, if only the prospect takes the appropriate action to connect with you.

The Shame Switch

Many things motivate people. Anxiety about what will happen to us personally, if we don't take action, is certainly one of them. Hence the first section of the White Knight Article. But shame is also a powerful motivator, that is the knowledge that if we don't take action the adverse consequences will fall on others, others for whom we are responsible and who look to us for their safety. Although we live in an increasingly disconnected and selfish world, shame, the feeling that we do have a responsibility for others, still remains a very powerful motivator. Hence the reason for including it in the White Knight Article.

In this section you suggest that if the prospect does not take the actions you have now suggested and outlined in the problem solving process section of this article, then the consequences will not fall only on himself but on others for whom he is responsible, including: his family, professional colleagues, co-workers, his town and fellow citizens, &c. This section is called the Shame Switch because when you flick it on, your client prospect should be sufficiently motivated to move, to do what in any event is in his best interests and, as you have now shown, in the best interests of many others as well.

The White Knight Section

The White Knight Section is not a part of the body of the actual article. It is actually the biographical tag that follows the article. While it is implicit in the actual article that you exist to solve the prospect's problems, the White Knight Section makes it very explicit by providing your prospect with complete follow-up information. As before, you will be allowed to provide the most complete follow-up information, including your name, address, telephone number and, where products are involved, pricing information, in the more specialized publications such as newsletters. Ordinarily general interest newspapers will offer you only the barest tag line.

Using The White Knight Article

The White Knight format combines certain evergreen qualities of the Problem Solving Process Article and certain urgent characteristics of the Sentinel. Like both these formats, the White Knight Article also lends itself nicely to a sequel, the "Son of White Knight" in which you put forward additional anxieties, additional problem solving processes, again flip the Shame Switch and, as usual, indicate your availablity to solve the prospects' problems.

Using And Reusing Your Standard Article Formats

Looking back at the various articles in these formats that I've written over the past 12 years, I am amazed at how much of what I have written can be brushed up and used again today with very minor modifications. Certainly the problem solving process article formats can be used profitably today with very minor modifications, and even the urgent information in a Sentinel Article can be reused by becoming the long range background for articles which begin with a new catastrophe about to overtake the prospect, a new opportunity about to be lost. In short, you'll find, as I have done, that by following these formats you will be able to use and reuse a good deal of what you write, now and so long as your clients suffer from the same problems, which may very well be for years to come.

The trick to making these article formats work for you is to keep using your material so long as your prospects continue to suffer from the same problems. Too many professionals think (quite, quite wrongly!) that every word they write has to be new and original. I suffer from no such feeling. If, after your professional analysis, you find that your prospects continue to suffer from the same kinds of problems and continue to obstruct the solution to these problems in the same ways, don't feel a morsel of compunction about reusing the same material. Tighten, of course, the anxiety screws and move into the colder mode of the In-command Infocrat. After all, if we as people have learned comfortably to avoid the ultimate anxiety of our possible total destruction, you can rest assured that any more minor problem (no matter how pressing it seems to you, the expert) can also be comfortably ignored. Our task as marketing genie is to ensure, through the apt and continuing use of these formats, that it is not.

Identifying Suitable Media Sources

If you are going to succeed in using the media to promote your business and attract clients, you have got to have a good understanding of all the media sources which are available to you and the ways in which they can be useful to you.

No one knows exactly how many media sources there are in the country, but the number is well over 100,000 newspapers, magazines, newsletters, radio and television stations. And, of course, in actual fact this number is very low since any individual source is made up of sometimes dozens of features and departments, each a possibility if you can pitch your story correctly. There are in fact over one million people now working for the media, one million people, that is, who have as the sole purpose of their lives — promoting you and your practice! Think of it! Each ready, willing, and able to connect you with your targeted prospects.

The problem is that you probably are not aware of even 1% of the media sources that are available to you. This is a great mistake. I cannot here provide you with the extensive list of nearly 200 directories of media sources, some containing as many as 90,000 entries!, which exist. That remains the purpose of **THE UNABASHED SELF-PROMOTER'S GUIDE**. But I can point out some of the most useful sources for advisors, sources which I myself use regularly and profitably to ensure that my message will be brought — free! — to the attention of people who can buy my consulting services and information rich products.

Here's a good directory of media resources:

Gebbie Press All In One Directory, Gebbie Press, Box 1000, New Paltz, New York 12561.

Information on associations and their publications is provided in *Encyclopedia of Associations* and in *National Trade & Professional Associations of the United States*, addresses previously provided.

For information on getting publicity for your products try *Bacon's Publicity Checker*, Bacon's Information, 332 S. Michigan Ave., Chicago, IL 60604.

Two good sources for print media resources are:

Gale Directory of Publications and Broadcast Media, 835 Penobscot Building, Detroit, MI 48226.

Standard Periodical Directory, Oxbridge Communications, 150 Fifth Ave., Suite 636, New York, New York 10011.

Your best source on newsletters is also published by Oxbridge Communications and is entitled the *Oxbridge Directory of Newsletters*.

Don't forget your own local media directory. If you live in a large metropolitan urban area one almost certainly exists.

Finally, the best general list of directories and publications in field both broad and specific appears in my own **UNABASHED SELF-PROMOTER'S GUIDE,** which is a book you really need to master!

The Trick To Getting Media Attention

The trick to getting media coverage is to familiarize yourself with as many different, likely sources as you can. Obviously, you'll have to flip electronic media dials and learn to browse through printed sources. Equally obviously, you'll have to write to publications to request a sample copy. When these materials come back, carefully pursue them so that you understand the kind of publication it is and begin to consider the kinds of openings that it has for you.

The key question to ask is: does this media source reach my client prospects in sufficient numbers so that they'll be interested in my problem solving processes, the kinds of information that I have available? Would they also be interested in me, either as the embodiment of the particular problem solving process, or as an interesting personality? If the answer to either of these questions is yes, then it is your obligation to proceed with the assumption that the media source will be interested in, and cooperative with, you.

At the beginning of your career working with the media (please catch this wording!), you'll not be as supple in thinking about the various alternatives available to you. There is a good deal of necessary stretching that must take place before you can take full advantage of the media opportunities available to you. Thus, review each division of the media source and see what you have available for that section. Write down the information that you come up with.

As I write I have picked at random from among the hundreds of publications which surround me the current issue of a newsletter for home-based entrepreneurs. Like you, I approach each source with the hope that it will feature me or my work, my products or my problem solving processes in a way that will take my message — for free! — to its market, my targeted client prospects.

The lead article of this issue is on publicity. Thus, I know that that is a subject that interests them. I write down the fact that I have a book on the subject that they can excerpt from.

On the second page is a book review feature. Since I'm both an author and publisher, this is obviously a feature of interest.

Then there is an entrepreneurs' corner focusing on an individual business owner and how she made a success of her business. This too is obviously pertinent.

On the next page is a list of news items which will be of interest to the small business owner, tricks of the trade provided by those who are themselves publicized by providing them.

And so on.

For each department, I have something appropriate to offer. Thus, it well becomes me to sit down and write the editor a letter with a series of suggestions on how we can work together for our mutual benefit and, of course, the benefit of the people we serve, her readers, my future clients and buyers. This is truly how a symbiosis is born.

It is your obligation to:
- find the source
- study the source
- find appropriate openings for you, your problem solving processes and problem solving products
- notify the appropriate editor that you've got a good article angle, or are a good story yourself
- follow up the initial contact
- be persistent: remember, it's in the interest of three parties (editor, readers/client prospects as well as yourself) that the deal be struck.

Note: I set as my personal objective contacting between three and five media sources each day. You needn't be as obsessive about this as I am but then I want my problem-solving information and processes to be in the hands of millions of people who can make good use of them. I am, after all, on a mission. And it works: at least once a day I get the — free! — coverage I crave. Do, however, set an objective for yourself even it it's only a single media contact each month. Remember: you can't reach your goal unless you have a goal. It's your obligation to set it!

Getting Articles About Yourself Published

It's as easy, and indeed often easier, to get articles about yourself published as it is to have articles by you printed. And, I must say, it's infinitely more pleasuring to one's galloping ego! Here are some suggestions about how to go about getting this kind of coverage:
- As above, identify an appropriate source, a source, that is, which reaches your client prospects *and* which has a feature designed for covering you. Don't ask a media source to do that which they cannot do. If they don't do personality profiles or articles about people, don't bother them with a request for the feature.
- Either write yourself or get a friend to do so to suggest the article. If you are the squeamish sort, enter into a pact with an enterprising friend whereby you'll suggest to editors articles about each other. This should cover your need for (false) modesty! Make sure, however, that you are the one to follow up your friend's letter. There's no reason to keep the charade going longer than necessary.
- Call the media source to follow up. If the source is not available, leave a complete message. Indicate when you'll call back. If the source is still not available, call again. If still not available, write a note and say how disappointed you are that you have not yet connected. If the source still doesn't contact you (entirely probable) wait until your next media mention comes out. Then send it to the source and start the process again. Never give up. Media personnel feel themselves above the petty courtesies and manners which, they reason, are beneath them. There will be, I trust, a special cycle of Dante's hell for them but until their blissful burning, I suggest you keep the luxury of your honest comments to yourself and play their game. What matter their childish and picayune humiliation if, at the last, you can reach your targeted audience in the right way and at the right price (nothing at all!)?
- Once you have connected with the media source, made an appointment (and confirm it, please, since media personnel are blithe about their engagements), think through the kind of article about you that you want. Articles about you follow the three formats of the articles by you: there are Problem Solving Process interviews, Sentinel interviews and White Knight interviews. The difference between articles by and articles about you is that in the one case you are simply setting out information; in the second you are getting out information with biographical pieces.

Tricks For Getting Coverage

- Give speeches on the "rubber chicken" circuit. Get yourself invited to the Kiwanis, Knights of Columbus, Eastern Star and all the other key professional and civic associations in your marketing area. Of course, you'll not be paid for your appearance, but you can still make it pay off if you do the following:

  — Make sure there is an article about you and your problem solving processes in advance of your appearance (The Advance). Make sure your photograph appears, too. In all cases write the article yourself, send the photograph, and write the appropriate caption. This takes place under the rubric of Assertive Courtesy. And remember: to reach your promotional objective you need reinforcement with your audience.

  — Follow up your talk (at which you distributed précis and other materials, no?) with a second article, a news article which provides information about what you said in Problem Solving Process, Sentinel or White Knight format. Remember: as an admirable expert people want to know what you are going to say (and do) before you've done it and, of course, they want a full report afterwards, too. Note: make sure that in the second, follow-up article you add appropriate color, including the number of people attending, the place where the meeting was held and an indication of the fervid, undeniable enthusiasm of your audience for you.

  — Invite local media sources to attend your lectures and appearances. If they don't come, don't give up! Tape your presentations and drop off a cassette at the local newspaper office. Stop on your way to your appearance and give an exclusive interview; (bring along a media release with all your quotes written down and leave that!) Drop in after your presentation. You must assume that you are newsworthy, long before anyone else does. If you don't, you should learn to cherish your obscurity and hope that you have enough money in the bank to cover the advertising purchases which are now quite inevitable.

Making The Best Use of Print Media

The uses of print media extend well beyond the actual appearance of the article. In fact, if you only derive the benefit that comes from the original appearance of the article, you have failed to extract as much benefit as you can. Don't let this happen to you! Instead, consider the following:

- If the article has been good (and it should have been!), consider turning it into a leave behind. Consider, that is, using some or all of it (you are under no obligation to use the whole article) to reinforce your précis. Offset the article on the reverse of your précis to give you further validation as the perceived expert.

- Send the article to other, non-competitive (please!) media sources with your suggestions for how they, too, can cover you. It is an absolute fact of life in the fast lane that the more media you get the more media you'll get. As soon as you have been validated by the media as someone worthy of coverage, other sources will want to cover you, too. Very often they'll seek you out directly. But don't wait. Seek out these sources yourself with your suggestions about how you can work together.

- See to the reprint possibilities. Newsletters, for instance, will be happy to run articles, or pieces of articles, which have appeared elsewhere. My rule of thumb is that an article has not been truly squeezed for its benefit unless it appears in at least 10 other sources. Occasionally, of course, you'll have to modify the piece in accordance with the targeted audience (thus, while my techniques for promoting pizzerias may be pertinent to promoting aerobic dance studios, the illustrations certainly will not be). That shouldn't take long, however. Ask yourself whether there are others beyond the readers of this publication who could benefit from the problem solving information and expertise you have imparted. If so, identify the publications which reach them and the appropriate features in them and carry on.

- Write to others featured in the publication, if you think it beneficial for you (now or later) to have a connection with this person. I call this the "family connection." I am assiduous in writing to all people who are featured in publications when I am, trying to establish useful connections. The theory here is extraordinarily simple and compelling. The world is divided into two parts: those who are media worthy (as evidenced by coverage) and those who are not. Once you get the coverage yourself, it's infinitely easier to connect with those who are also getting coverage. And if you're going to want them for some reason, the moment of your own transcendence from the state of the merest mortal is the moment to act.

Making The Move To Electronic Media

Electronic media has provided me with some of the thrills of my life. Now, with advanced telecommunications procedures, it is possible for me to talk into my telephone in Cambridge, Massachusetts and reach millions of people around the United States after the radio signal carrying my voice has bounced off the nether side of the moon. There is something deeply exciting, and, I must tell you, entirely appropriate about this. And knowing I am getting this extensive coverage for free — for free! — is just the sugar-rich icing on the cake.

While you may not, just now, need this continental coverage, most of you will surely want and benefit from some electronic exposure. Here's how to get it and how to use it.

Your move into electronic media will be infinitely easier if you wait until you have received print coverage. For even the slightest print coverage (a mention, say, in a fraternal newsletter) establishes you as media worthy (if not perhaps to the extent you'd like). And once you're deemed media worthy by the print media, it is much, much easier for you to secure electronic media coverage. Here is the sequence to follow:

- Consider whether the problem you are addressing, the problem you can solve, is one which large numbers of listeners/viewers of the electronic media source you are interested in appearing on have. Not every expert needs to appear on the electronic media. For many, print media really will be sufficient. But if your client prospects tune in in sufficiently large numbers to the media source, then it is your obligation — for them as well as yourself! — to get the exposure, to bring your message to them. And, if the program director can be assured that there is a sufficient group of people interested in your message, then you will get the spot.

- If you have once made the decision that the media source, radio or television, is right for you because large numbers of the audience would be interested in what you have to say, call up and ask for the name of the program director for the particular program you have targeted. This person may be called public service director, director of public affairs, talent coordinator, or any one of a number of other names. Write this information down. Your objective is not, after all, to appear on the program only once but as often as it works for you — and so long as members of the audience seem to be interested in what you're talking about. Remember, too, that your link to both program director and host constitutes a form of currency, for your friends and colleagues will want to appear on this show, too, and you can trade your connection for other things that you want. Knowing how to get access to valuable media time is a thing of value in its own right and should not be denigrated by you.

- Write this program director a spirited letter not so much selling yourself as the fact that you have problem solving information of interest to his audience. Not being a celebrity just yet, what you are talking about is more important than who you are. What the program director wants to know about you is your ability to help carry the program, how good, that is, you are as the talent. Thus, it is perfectly sensible to give him some indication that you are entirely comfortable in that role, that is, that you are warm, empathetic, a good talker making a good presentation. If you have done other electronic media, tell the host this. If you've been invited back, say so, too. This fact should tell the program director all he needs to know about you and your ability to make the show a success. Of course, offer to send a copy of a tape if you're got one (and you should if you've already been on the air!).

Needless to say, send along selected pieces of your Standard Media Kit with this letter, including: the Context Document (very important to sell the program director on the importance of your issue), the Biographical Feature Story, and the précis of how you professionally go about solving the problem that you'll be addressing. This is usually sufficient, although if you've been in the print media lately send along a clipping. You begin to look quite like The Inevitable when you have been vetted by the electronic media and have a recent clip. Such a celebrity as you clearly are cannot be denied.

- In dealing with electronic media personnel, remember what you have learned from working with the print media. Telephone calls will not usually be returned, and if you are to get the coverage you desire you will have to work for it. This used to bother me terribly but now I reason that if I work like a navvy with the media personnel, it matters not so long as their presentation of me to the rest of the world makes me look like the titan of my own reckoning. Again, if a series of three telephone calls are not returned, write and point out, with sweet suavity, the omission. If this still doesn't work, wait until you've been on another (but not, please, directly competing) station, or until you've again been featured in print before reopening the matter.

- When once you have the program director on the telephone, find out whether he has read the material you've sent. Chances are he hasn't. If this is so, don't attempt to explain all that is in the papers you've sent. You'll probably be a little nervous; the other individual, I can assure you, won't be paying full attention, and you'll come out the worse in the encounter. Instead, find out how long he'll need before you can call back. Arrange a definite time for you to connect and prove that you are well organized by calling back just then. One of the things all media people value (perhaps because they have so little of it in their own lives) is regularity, the ability to count on others to do what they say they're going to do. So, surprise them with your admirable manners.

- After following these procedures, you will get your time booked. But remember: until you are actually in the studio, primed to go on the air, this engagement cannot be considered definite. Everything in the media business is subject to being changed without notice as circumstances change. Thus, don't leave for your appointment without confirming that, yes, your interview is actually going to take place. Don't be surprised, or affronted, if you are put off to another time. Sadly, this is the way of the business. But don't be put off without trying, just at that moment, to reschedule. Remember how difficult it was for you to get the appointment in the first place.

- Make sure in confirming your appointment that you check with the program director about the following:
  - You'll want a tape of your radio show. Can they provide the cassettes or must you bring it yourself?
  - You'll want your telephone number (and perhaps address) flashed on the television screen while you're talking. This ordinarily must be arranged in advance.
  - If you are planning on showing slides or other audio visual aids make sure that the ones you have can indeed be used. Different stations have different technical requirements.

- Dress the part you are trying to play whether you will be on radio or television. The television requirement will not, I suppose, surprise you, but why dress for radio? It was Lord Reith, the founder of the British Broadcasting Corporation, who used to insist that those reading the news wear black tie, so important was it that they sound the part. Looking the way you want, even for radio, will help ensure that you sound the part. Trust me.

- Try not to drive yourself to the studio. Facing the menace of rush hour traffic or trying to locate a parking space close to the station in the teeth of a gale are, to put it mildly, off-putting. Take a taxi or have a friend drive you and drop you off, safe and warm, in front of the studio. Then you'll arrive as chipper as you can be.

- Make sure to bring a complete duplicate set of all papers to the studio. Rest assured that media people are the most disorganized beings you'll ever meet, and it is very unlikely that the program director will have on hand all the materials you want. So, plan ahead. Bring: an introduction written about you so that it can be read on the air (that is, written in the third person); a telephone number which can be read on the air, a Context Document, the Biographical Feature Story, and a list of questions which you can be asked. Allow 20 questions for a 30 minute interview. Half these questions should be generic in nature, designed to cue the audience about the topic which is being discussed, to provide sufficient background information so that even the least informed person (well, perhaps not the *very* least) can follow the discussion. The other ten can be outright promotional in nature. Hand all these materials to the program director before you go on the air and, if there's time, describe exactly what's in your packet. Don't make the assumption that they'll know. Tell them.

- Whether you are going on the radio or television, prepare a telephone answering machine to record the names and addresses of those responding to your invitation to inquire about your free information. My answering machine is always primed to take orders. So should yours be. In this regard, I prefer a machine to a live answering service, because I can make sure that with my machine the exact message I want to have delivered will be.

Tell the host that you're going to be sending a free information packet (a problem solving packet) on the topic you're addressing to whoever calls or writes you. Say that you'd like your telephone number and/or address given out over the air. This information can be provided every 8 minutes on a television show (that is, once in every segment) or about every 8 to 10 minutes on radio. Ordinarily, the host will be most happy to provide this information as a service to his audience; if he doesn't, however, you must. Getting a qualified prospect list of those interested in your service is the primary reason why you're going on the show in the first place and if no follow up number or address is given the chances of your profiting from the experience are diminuitive.

Handling Your Electronic Media Interview

Always remember that as a sales person you have in fact two distinct kinds of sales to make to your prospects: 1) yourself and 2) your problem solving abilities. If your prospects don't buy the first, they'll never get a chance to use the second, and you'll both lose. That's why you must do all that you can to come across during your interview not merely as knowledgeable, an intelligent problem solver but also as empathetic, as the person who understands your prospects and deeply cares whether they are able to reach the objectives. Please note: this does not mean that you need to come across as saccharine or unduly amiable. The In-command Infocrat mode, a cool, commanding presentation, can be as effective as the Accessible Expert, if your client prospects need to be taken in hand by an authoritative expert. But they must feel that you are being cool and commanding because you truly care for them and that that is the best way of handling their peculiar situation.

Here are a few other tricks:

- You are likely to be nervous before facing the radio microphone or going on television. That is perfectly natural. What is not, however, natural is leaving things that way! Go into the toilet and do a few quick deep kneebends or otherwise work out for a moment so that the blood is surging. All media appearances go very quickly, and you don't have the luxury of warming up on mike or camera. That's a waste of your time and remember you are now in a business where first impressions are more important than ever!

- Have a glass of tepid, room temperature water near at hand for two reasons. When you're nervous, your mouth is drier than usual, and this makes a mellifluous presentation the more difficult. Also, you may find yourself at a loss for words at one point or another. This can be a problem unless you have a prop readily available. Your audience will give you the benefit of the doubt as you reach for your water and sip slowly while attempting to get back on track. Make use of this prop if you need to!

- Practice leaning into your audience. Electronic media is so powerful because it creates the illusion of intimacy and immediacy, the illusion, that is, that an individual perhaps thousands of miles away is as near as your fingertips. We are so used to this illusion that we overlook its power. To further this sense of intimacy, lean into the microphone, into the camera as if into a passionate embrace, or into a warm greeting with a dear friend. Simulate the desired effect, and you will create it in the minds of your audience.

- While you're on the air, expunge all pronouns from your speech, or any noun that stands in place of the full name of your service. Thus, never talk about "your specialty" or "your service" but your "Capital Campaign Nonprofit Fund Raising Plan". The reason for this is obvious: reinforcement. You are trying to turn each phrase you utter into a complete mini-ad and so reinforce in the listener's mind the availability of your specific service. Now, mind, real people don't talk like this in everyday speech. It takes practice. But it is a great error to miss the chance to reinforce the name and problem solving aspect of your service in the minds of your potential buyers when you have the chance. Please note: this must be done in the most conversational way possible so that although you are speaking in a very precise, very goal oriented, action fashion the listener is conscious only that you are the image you have set out to be. They must see, in short, your mentioning of your service not as promotional but as an assertive courtesy for their benefit, designed to help them solve their problem.

- While you're on the air, modulate your voice. There's nothing more boring (and thus detrimental to your interests) as someone who speaks in a dreary monotone. Don't do it! Practice reading lines (your own précis, for example) in such a way you impart an intense interest to it. You'll be nervous, of course, but you must remember that both radio and television have their theatrical dimensions and that you must take advantage of that fact to your own benefit.

More Tips

- Learn to speak in short, crisp, upbeat sentences. The electronic media are as active as they are intimate. It is very difficult for people to deal with long, cumbrous, difficult sentences, and you must pare your presentation to the bone while practising making it conversational. Speak *to* your host, speak *through* your host to the prospects you are trying to motivate to take action in your mutual interest as if speaking to your best friend, only instead of using slang and half completed sentences you must speak in complete sentences without an abbreviation, jargon, or pronoun standing in the place of the full proper name of everything you are presenting.

- Although most people worry about being attacked on the media and coming across as a fool, the chances of this happening to you, presenting as you are information that is of direct interest and value to a substantial portion of the host's audience, is less than one in a hundred. Far more likely than an attack is the likelihood that the host will prove garrulous and will interrupt you or hog the available time retailing information that is of no value to you or your audience. This is a terrible disaster! In such a situation you must learn to bridge, that is, to construct a means of moving from an unavailing conversation to one that will produce a benefit all round. I remember one show I appeared on, for instance, where the host was not only rambling, garrulous, but also a longtime friend well known for being difficult to shut up. On this particular occasion he was grousing about the poor service he'd had that afternoon at a drive-in restaurant on Cape Cod. He went on and on to my despair as I saw my time melting away. "The service was terrible!" he sniffed into the microphone. And with that I made my move. "Of course, David, today service is often bad. That's why when I'm working with a nonprofit organization to raise the money it needs, I work extra hard to give them the service they need." That's a bridge. And, thankfully, it usually works, unless the host is downright obtuse, which, sadly, does happen.

- If you are attacked (and even this will happen), pause for a moment and think before you respond. Your job in a situation like this is not to lose your temper and your cool but to co-opt the reasonable position, the position that makes sense to your client prospects. Remember: don't waste any time trying to persuade the host that you are right or wrong. That's frankly immaterial. What matters is that your client prospects understand the reason for your point of view and see you as reasonable and forthright, the kind of person who's not afraid to speak up for himself in a genteel way. Under no circumstances get into a shouting match with the host. This is most detrimental to your interests. If you cannot think of anything else to say, pause and say, "Reasonable people differ about this matter, Paul. Let's just agree to disagree about it." And move the discussion on to safer waters. If the host continues to browbeat and oppress you, consider yourself lucky. After enjoying the scent of blood, the crowd, your client prospects remember, will switch their point of view to feel sympathy with the oppressed. Just stick to the reasonable position and don't deviate from it.

- If you are not being asked the questions you want to be, take advantage of a commercial break to advise the host about what you'd like him to ask you. That's perfectly cricket. Don't expect him to read your mind. Be courteous but be firm. You have a right to get out the information that you've come on to present. *N.B.* If by some chance the host isn't pronouncing your name right (a problem I often have despite prompting) don't correct him on mike or camera but wait for a break and, after advising him of the correct pronunciation, proceed without comment.

- It will happen when you are on a radio call-in program (a very good format, by the way, for the advisor-expert) that you'll be called by a certifiable idiot. Count on it. In this situation, you've got to learn how to get the offender off the line without damaging your precious image and turning off your audience, who must, remember, come to like, trust, and accept you.

In this connection, I remember about a year ago on New Year's Day appearing on a Boston-based, 17 state, clear channel radio program with an audience in the millions. I was there to promote **THE UNABASHED SELF-PROMOTER'S GUIDE.** An elderly, obviously inebriated woman called and after a good deal of rambling confessed that a friend of hers had committed suicide over the holidays and left a note blaming her for causing the fatality. "What did I think about suicide as a source of self promotion?" the woman asked me. What indeed!

This is a situation fraught with peril. If you want to be perceived as an Accessible Expert, as warm and empathetic, you cannot insult, cannot ignore, cannot be perceived as treating inconsiderately the query of this obviously-in-pain individual. But to get into a further discussion with her is obviously not in your own best interests. Thus the following words:

"I can tell that you are obviously in pain about this incident, and I don't blame you. But rather than discuss it with you now, with so many people listening, why don't you call me tomorrow — collect — so I can talk to you. My number is 617-547-6372." Pause. "Did you get that, 617-547-6372? This number rings right on my desk and when you call I'll be there to talk to you."

At this point the perceptive host casts the woman off and goes on to the next call. Your image as an empathetic problem solver is confirmed. You have also, of course, gotten your telephone number out two more times to your client prospects in the audience.

People regularly ask me how many times under such circumstances the individual actually follows up. In their mind's eye they picture the phone lines clogged with collect calls to the utter disruption of their business and pocketbook. But in truth neither did this woman call, nor has *anyone* else under similar circumstances. The chances are similarly strong that they never will, for then they get just too close to you for their comfort. Thus, you get not only to preserve but to strengthen your empathetic image without being called upon to pay the price, even of a collect telephone call!

Wrap Up

Towards the end of the program the host will very likely ask you if you have anything you'd like to add. Give yourself a plug! Remind people to call you, right now!, so that you can send them your problem solving information. This is not the moment for undue modesty. As the show dwindles down to a few moments, don't forget to thank the host, on air, for the opportunity of appearing. You should be glad, after all. If you are having a seminar or lecture, invite him to attend as your guest. This is just the kind of thing a warm, empathetic friend would do.

When you're off the air, the host will see you to the door, perhaps to the lobby. During this time again thank him his consideration but make use of the opportunity to suggest one or two other topics for future shows. The host (or program director) will very likely express some interest, and thus, after a few weeks, you have an opening to follow up. Remember: as soon as you are in the studio for your current program your thoughts ought to be on how and when you'll be back for your next one.

Before you leave the building leave your name, telephone number and précis with the receptionist. She very often gets calls. If your show is being broadcast later, explain this so the materials will be kept to the proper time. Very often people don't have a pencil handy at showtime to take down your number and will call the station for the information. Thus the receptionist becomes a key person.

Upon getting home, write the producer and/or host a thank you note. People seldom extend this necessary courtesy. You'll be reinforcing your desirable image if you do so.

Last Words About Unabashed Promotion

As far as I'm concerned, as long as you're in business you are in the business of unabashed promotion. Having read this chapter, the benefits of this endeavor should be perfectly obvious to you:

- Your message, information about you, your products and services, will be carried for free to those who have need of your problem solving expertise.
- The media source will validate you as an expert. Faster than a speeding bullet, media can establish you as a sought-after advisor.
- As your status as the perceived expert grows, you can (and should) increase your fees and target more affluent client prospects. You are in the process of becoming, after all, a celebrity in your own right, and those who are successful like to deal with those who are also successful.
- The more coverage you get, the more you will get. Once you have been dubbed media worthy, other media sources will want to cover you. This is as close to a perpetual motion machine as there is.

Since these benefits await you, don't dawdle. Get started. Whatever fears and anxieties you have about the media are, in fact, illusory and experience will dissipate them. But remember, too: a single media mention will not be sufficient for reaching your objective. You must make unabashed promotion a regular, ongoing activity of your professional life. Only then will you reap its considerable, undeniable advantages. As you do so, however, let me know. As you become the media validated, recognized pacesetter of your business, you become just the person I want to know and do business with!

CHAPTER 8

Developing The Successful Client Relationship I: The Pre-Contract Stage

The success (or failure) of an advisor-client relationship long antedates the actual signing of any contract. Just how your relationship will develop is in large measure determined by such variables as:

- how the prospect heard about you
- what he heard
- your perceived ability to solve his problem and offer a disporportionate benefit compared to fee, and by
- how the introductory phases of the relationship process are handled, especially the contacts leading up to the contract.

Take a look at this unfortunate (though common) scenario. Do you see yourself?

As an expert in one or several fields, you are no doubt interested in bringing your expert information to bear on the solution of a client's problem. That's only natural. Also, you may need the money that such a relationship would bring you. As such you may exhibit the characteristics of the over-eager contract searcher and, in the process, lose your objectivity about a client and his ability to work with you to bring about the desired solution. This is very, very common.

A key constituent of any successful client-advisor relationship is your ability to ascertain that the client prospect is in fact as willing as you are to work towards the solution of the problem. That is, that he has the mental readiness, the technical preparation, and the support of other branches of management, all of which are in fact necessary to success. If these are missing, then the likelihood of achieving success is diminuitive, and you, too, should consider absenting yourself.

Let me say this as strongly as I can: in virtually no advisor situation can you singlehandedly bring about success. In virtually all cases the client must work with you step by step to achieve the desired objective. This means that right from the start it is your responsibility to structure the relationship with the client (and before this, with the client prospect) so that maximum success is a distinct possibility and not a far-fetched goal.

Many new and untrained advisors fail to achieve this necessary precondition for success for reasons which seem persuasive to them but which, in fact, ensure the lack of success of their client relationship. You, for one, may be someone who says:

- "I need the money." Taking on an assignment for money may make preeminent good economic sense to you, but it can be bad for the development of your reputation (and thus your business) unless you are reasonably assured that you and the client working together can achieve success.
- "The people I'm working with are disadvantaged. It's unfair to impose success criteria on them." This is nonsense, although it's an argument I hear constantly. People, whether they be minorities, women, &c., with whom you may be working deserve to be given the best possible advice that you can give them so that you can help them to achieve truly meaningful success. It's the height of folly (and severely destructive to the people you are trying to help) to lower your standards and shield them from the realities of a situation.
- "If I tell people what's really entailed in achieving success in this assignment, they probably won't hire me." Let me tell you this as straightforwardly as I can. People who have achieved success (and I mean achieved it, not inherited it!) understand that to get what they want entails work, hard work, arduous, often unremitting work. They expect to work hard. It's only the dreamers, ne'er-do-wells and fainéants, who think they can achieve vast success on a pennyworth's effort, with whom you have to gild the pill; I can tell you such a gilding is a critical mistake. If you want to achieve success as an advisor, it is your responsibility to tell people exactly what it will take to achieve success, and if (as will inevitably happen) some people do not feel themselves up to that effort, that's their problem, not yours. In such a situation, you do not want the client and, having failed to get him, you must feel no remorse about the lack of a paycheck. Make it your goal only to work with those who are capable of achieving success and who will work with you, happily, to do so.

- "I'll tell them what's entailed after the contract begins." This is really a variant of the above point. I'll say it again and again: if you want to help people achieve success, really and truly want to help them, then you'll help them determine a reasonable (that is challenging but obtainable level of) success and, set forth the means of reaching this success. You'll tell them the pros and cons of the several available courses of actions and what you do and what they must do to realize this level of achievement. And you'll do it as early as possible in your relationship (so long as the time when you get into exact procedures is, in fact, billable time). Anything less is an acute dereliction of duty and inimical to achieving the success you say you want to help the client achieve. Remember this: as an advisor you have limited actual power. Moreover, whatever actual power you have will be diminished if the client perceives that you have acted dishonorably, have in fact withheld vital information (and information about what actually must be done and how it must be done is most assuredly vital) until after the commencement of a contractual relationship.

- "Knowing what they have to do will demoralize them." It is the unknown not the known that demoralizes people, or, as FDR said, "The only thing we have to fear is fear itself." We Americans are the most practical of people, but we also spend a good deal of time chasing shadows, shadows which terrify us until we see precisely how insubstantial they really are. Again, your job as an advisor is to tell people, with as much precision as you are capable of mustering, exactly what needs to be done and exactly what the ramifications will be of not doing things in one way or another. Don't fall into one of the characteristic advisor traps, namely of making the decision that your clients are not up to deciding for themselves what to do. Perhaps they really are not. You do them an acute disservice, however, when you, an outsider, take on the making of decisions which may affect the client for years to come. Your job is to advise. Their job is to make the actual decision.

Qualifying The Prospect

In the beginning of my advising practice, like most people I was too concerned about whether the prospect would:

1) like me
2) be impressed by my technical skills
3) buy me.

I handled the resulting meetings like standard job interviews. I came prepared with *my* résumé, *my* track record, *my* brochures and handouts.

Today things are vastly different.

Today I am more concerned about the client prospect's ability to work with me as a team member to achieve the success which I know I want and which I only surmise (at this point) the client prospect wants. In other words, whereas in the beginning of my advising practice I worried about whether I was acceptable to the client prospect, now I try to see whether the prospect is acceptable to me. It's a very significant difference.

This does not mean, I hasten to add, that I don't have at least some of the prior paraphernalia (although I don't use the résumé anymore, focusing instead on the success documents you've previously read), but it does mean that the focus of all contacts with the client prospect are significantly different. Now I spend the bulk of my time qualifying the prospect, sometimes ostensibly, always implicitly. This qualifying process begins from the very first moment you contact a prospect, and, if you are successful with it, you are heightening the possibility of a successful client-advisor relationship and, thus, the likelihood that this will be a relationship you can leverage to get future clients, a very, very important part of any relationship so far as you, the advisor, are concerned.

The First Qualifying Decision: Not To Take Everyone

You will regularly encounter people (whom you might, in an unguarded moment, be inclined to consider client prospects) who say they have a problem and who say they want to solve it and achieve success. You will learn, bit by bit, to become increasingly skeptical about such people. Americans learn the success language with their mother's milk but most people only mouth the clichés of the language without remotely understanding what they are talking about. You, however, as an advisor are necessarily committed to success and you must come to know what you are talking about. Which means, by definition, subjecting all people, however grandiose their success language, to a rigorous proving process. You can only afford to work with those who wish to achieve success and are willing to work as hard as you do to achieve it.

Most people, I've come to believe, are victims and enjoy being victims. They regularly position themselves to fail and then have the satisfaction of rejoicing because they have failed. Particularly at the beginning of your practice, when you have not yet formulated a network of successful people (who eat, sleep and breath success as they must the air itself) you will be encountering far more victims than you will when you finally succeed. Victims also talk success language (being Americans they can hardly help it), but they delight in masochistically positioning themselves to fail to achieve any success. Watch out for these people. They are poison!

Most people want someone else to deliver success on a plate. Unwary advisors (particularly the ones who are already prone to believe they are godlike) will have no problem being sucked in to the vortex of this syndrome. People will come to them and say, "Save me!", and the godlike advisor will fall for it. Remember: most people are lazy, slothful, néer-do-wells. Since they live in the success society, they have learned the success language, but, being human, they don't want to work very hard, certainly not as hard as they need to, to achieve success; therefore they are always casting about looking for someone to achieve success for them and give it to them without their having to work very hard themselves. These people are legion, and they are anathema to the successful advisor. As an advisor your job is to become the preeminent team builder, to be clear about what needs to be done and how to do it and to set out the tasks for all the players, including yourself. You are not a god. You are not even particularly godlike; certainly you are not immutable or indestructible. But you can and must be a superb team player, even if the team consists exclusively of you and one person with whom you are working one on one.

Man, as can be abundantly documented throughout history (including our own troubled times), spends a disproportionate amount of time seeking out gods so to eschew responsibility for events. "It's god's fault," men will utter at the drop of a hat and so take themselves and their own fatuities off the hook, when in actual fact it's usually our own fault or simply an immutable inevitability. As an advisor, you can very easily fall into this god trap and allow yourself to be exalted into the great problem solver. But the flip side of this scenario, of course, is easy to foresee: if you fail to bring about the desired results, you will be as richly condemned as you were previously exalted. And since in most instances you cannot sufficiently control the problem solving process to ensure success, such failure is predictable. Take heed.

Your first task as an advisor, therefore, is to develop a means for qualifying your client prospects, ascertaining whether they mean to do more than talk the heady language of success.

If The Prospect Calls You

Once you are an established advisor, people will regularly call on you for assistance. This is, of course, a comfortable way of doing business since, in theory, you don't have to stoop to conquer. Fortunately, if you follow the various marketing means I have previously discussed you will find yourself in the enviable position of getting calls and letters from people who want to make use of you. In such a situation, you must be rigorous about applying your success criteria.

If an individual seeks my assistance, I ask that person to write a 250 word (single page) description of his problem and the desired outcome. As I say, I will either deal with the problem directly (if I feel I have the technical expertise and the client prospect exhibits the necessary dedication to a solution), or I pass it along to someone in my Supergroup of Independent Contractors.

Along with this document, I ask for other pertinent materials. In the case, for instance, of a nonprofit organization seeking to raise funds I ask for:

- current development proposal
- copies of last three fund raising letters
- annotated list of Board of Directors (that is, not only names but also the positions and qualifications of the members)
- list of corporations and foundations applied to in last year with results
- list of fund raising objectives for capital, projects and operating expenses, &c.

I review this material looking for several significant factors:

- Is the client being realistic in his objectives?
- Does the client have technical skills, or does he need to get technical skills?
- Has the client owned the problem? (I ascertain this in part from reviewing the level of Board contributions.)
- Has the client been working on the solution of his problem or must we begin from scratch (and hence with a plethora of client nostrums which it is my sacred duty and need to obliterate)?

Depending on my answers to these points, I make a decision as to whether to go ahead and offer the prospect a "free" hour's consultation or not. This hour is given to what I call "qualified client prospects", that is, people who not only have a problem but who are willing to work with me as a team to solve it. Not only must I have certain technical skills, but the client must have, or be willing quickly to develop, a level of receptivity about solving the problem before I deem it possible to go ahead to the next level.

If You Must Approach The Prospect

The best way of approaching a prospect is with the Success Letter format previously discussed. To send out a cold letter merely saying that you exist and have certain technical qualifications to solve their problems is, to my way of thinking, a complete waste of time. Your job is very clearly to indicate that:

- You know they have a problem.
- You have the necessary skills and problem solving processes to solve that, and
- You have already solved the problem (if you actually have!).

As I've already said, in your Success Letter you advise the prospect of your limited availability and your willingness to work with them *if they are serious about wanting to solve this problem*. Right away, even in this ostensible solicitation approach, you must indicate you are a serious professional and that you are looking for other serious professionals with whom to work. Others must look elsewhere for their sustenance.

Sadly, many, many professionals prospecting for clients spend their time making cold calls to those who may or may not have the problem and have not expressed an interest in working with a professional to solve it. This is generally a waste of time, and I cannot recommend it.

It is better, far, far better, when you do have extra time to invest it in creating a success that can be replicated for others who have the same problem. After which you can use the available media sources to promote both the problem and your success techniques.

Personally, if I were just starting out again, and were entirely unknown, here's how I would solve this problem:

- I would analyze my professional life and ascertain the success modules. What had I done professionally? What difference had it made? Who had benefitted from this success?
- I would then utilize the steps of the Problem Solving Process and write an article of interest to a designated client population that had a precise problem I could solve. I would indicate to them, perhaps through a professional publication, that there was a solution to the problem.
- I would bring this article to the attention of client prospects in a direct mail letter and indeed a series of direct mail letters until such time as I had a contract and a success. (It goes without saying that I would also be using my networking contacts, &c). As soon as I had a success, I would continue to use the specialized publication and direct mail to promote this success to those who wanted to replicate it, over and over again so long as the problem was in fact a problem and so long as I needed clients, in other words, forever. As I moved from being merely another advisor on the horizon to the eminence of The Inevitable I would qualify all prospects using the screening techniques we have discussed.

If The Prospect Doesn't Qualify

In many, many cases the individual approaching you for assistance or the organization seeking out your advice, is not yet ready to embark on a serious problem solving process. They may simply be fishing for free advice. They may want to pick your brain. They may simply want to get some sympathy for their problem. Remember this: you are in no way obligated to provide any advice to these people or to fall in with their petty plans. Every professional has had the unpleasant experience of going somewhere and having some would-be client pick their brains for free. Those who are newly in the advisor business may feel hesitant about not answering the many questions put to them about what they do and how they do it for fear that they will get the reputation of being difficult and unfriendly. Don't you believe it for a minute!

People seeking freebies, of course, will not be grateful to you, but what difference does that make? To be perceived as a professional advisor means to act like a professional advisor at all times. If someone is trying to get you to provide them with free counsel, simply say, "I'd be delighted to help you. My policy is that I need a 250 word description of the problem you want solved and the objective you are trying to reach. If I can solve it, I'll get back to you; if I'm not the best person to solve it, I'll provide this information to someone in my contact network who will contact you."

It's that easy.

If the prospect is a freebie seeker, you'll probably never hear from him again. Freebie seekers don't write their objectives: they don't have any beyond getting something for nothing.

More serious people will write to you. You can then ascertain whether or not they are worth bothering with. But let me say this as strongly as I can: all those who say they are prospects are not prospects; you cannot build a practice while worrying that you have offended people by not catering to their every whim. People who are serious about achieving success will look for signs that you are serious about achieving success, too, and they will understand that you have means for qualifying them as they have means for qualifying you. Never forget this!

It often horrifies the soft headed (not, please note, soft hearted) when I talk in my seminars about these qualifiers, but they are absolutely necessary. You will find, as I have, that every one in America has at least one idea. Most are hare-brained and not worth the slightest consideration. Some are not. The more well known you become, the more you will, like me, be subjected to these notions. Notions which so often clearly show that the person having them has paid no attention to who you, the advisor, are, and what you can do. I treat seriously the suggestions of those who have paid me the courtesy of discovering who I am, what I can do, what I want to achieve with my advising practice. But I treat with cool professionalism and detachment the rather more irritating suggestions of those who pay heed only to what they want and who so clearly have not done their homework before approaching me. I make no apology, none whatsoever, about that. Neither should you.

If the individual or organization does not now qualify and you cannot find someone in your Supergroup of Independent Contractors who can profitably work with them, you have two options:

- You may write back to them and tell them that at the present time your client list is complete but that you'll contact them if an opening should occur.
- You may write proposing a one-hour meeting so that you can outline, on an advising basis, exactly what they must do to prepare themselves for working with you, that is, positioning themselves so that working with you will be a mutually successful and beneficial experience.

I use both of these means. I use the first in situations where I decide the prospect is hopeless, utterly hopeless, and I want to have no further direct dealings. Even in this situation, however, I always point out that certain chapters of certain of my books (or a workshop) will be valuable to the prospect, if indeed this is the case. Never miss the opportunity for a product sale once you have the means of doing so.

I use the other means where the client, by assiduous study and preparation, can raise himself to take advantage of the skills and training which I have. A nonprofit organization, for instance, may be advised they will need to have an effective working board of directors in place before it is advisable to work with me. In this case, my one hour (or more) of consultation may be spent advising them on how to achieve this beneficial result. Achieving this result is a necessary precondition of success and constitutes the basis for a new, constructive (albeit short-term) consultancy. This relationship, I need hardly say, if successful helps to ensure a future, longer-term consultancy to begin at that moment when they have realized their initial success and are grateful to you for structuring the conditions which have brought it into existence.

Note: It goes without saying that these remarks are based on the presumption that the person with whom you are dealing is in fact the decision maker, the person, that is, who can commit the necessary resources either personally or for his organization and so move towards the solution of the problem. If the person you are dealing with is not the decision maker, it is necessary for you to notify your contact, as soon as possible, that for both the prospect and you, the advisor, it is necessary all future contacts involve the actual decision maker.

There's no need to be sheepish about this. Either an individual has the power to commit or he doesn't. If he doesn't, there is no point in spending much time with that individual, not much, that is, beyond an early notification that the actual decision maker must be involved in future for the good of both parties. Certain advisors feel squeamish about being as direct as this, feeling they will "hurt the feelings" of the person without the ability to commit. Remember: you are not running for Prom Queen. Part of being a successful advisor means spending your time with those who have the power to commit, and if your initial contact does not, it is simply the essence of good sense and good professional behavior to do what is necessary so that you will in future deal exclusively with the people who must be involved. You'll be sorry if you don't!

The Prospect Questionnaire

Completion by the prospect of a Prospect Questionnaire will also help you satisfactorily structure both the time before you and your prospect enter into a formal agreement and the time after you do so. Such a questionnaire involves the prospect providing you with information you need to have in advance of any introductory meeting and which you must have before actually presenting a formal proposal. Even if you have standardized proposals, like I do, the information on the questionnaire helps you decide which proposal to give the prospect.

The Prospect Questionnaire includes questions on:

- prospect name
- address
- telephone number
- person to be dealt with
- title
- does this individual have the power to authorize commencement of project?
- if not, who else should be involved
- prospect's description of problem(s) to be dealt with by advisor

- specific outcomes desired by prospect
- dates when they are needed
- others who are working towards these outcomes: 1) within the organization, 2) outside the organization
- name(s) of advisor(s) who have previously dealt with problem(s)
- specific outcomes achieved by them
- if specific outcomes were not at level desired by prospect, can prospect suggest reasons for failure?
- materials which exist dealing with this problem and its solution.

  (Prospect needs to be specific in answering this question and by listing every possible document created by both internal and external sources. *N.B.* Even if you do not wish to review these materials now, knowing about them will prove tremendously helpful once you get the assignment.)
- in-house training sessions held to solve problem. Provided by (name of trainer)
- external training sessions attended. Name of trainer/training organization
- what is the first thing you would like advisor to accomplish?
- amount of time you would think task(s) should take to accomplish
- range of money you are prepared to commit to the solution of this problem

     ☐ Under $100   ☐ Under $500   ☐ Under $1000   ☐ Under $2,500   ☐ Under $5,000
- commitment of management to solution of this problem
- obstacles you see to achieving solution of problem
- need for work to be carried on on your premises
- prospect comments or additional information.

Your Prospect Questionnaire can and, will, of course, be altered in response to the differing situations of your prospects and your own need for certain information. It goes without saying, however, that the more information you get the prospect to provide, the more able you'll be to help structure a mutually profitable and useful first meeting which will, in turn, lead to a constructive client-advisor relationship.

I must stress most strongly that there is no need for you to function in the dark. You cannot, and it's stupid to try. There's no need to say what you'll do until you get a distinct sense from the prospect about what his problem is, what he's previously done to solve it, and what resources (both in terms of money and personnel and spirit) he is prepared to commit to solve the problem. Functioning otherwise makes you a committed advocate to the Shot In The Dark School of Advising, one I am not partial to myself.

You will find, as I have found, that those clients who are most interested in solving their problems, most committed to solving them in a reasonable period of time, who most understand that what they are trying to achieve needs not only the help of a knowledgeable outside advisor but their own rigorous commitment to a solution, will be delighted with the seriousness with which you approach their problem and will understand your need for detailed information.

A prospect who is unwilling (or indeed unable) to complete this Prospect Questionnaire, or to otherwise provide you with the information you need, wishes at the very least to thrust the burden of solving the problem onto you, whether or not it is necessary for them to be involved. They are looking for the advisor as god and not the advisor as a critical — but not solitary — problem solver. Be advised! If the prospect is signalling you so early in your embryonic relationship that he wishes to eschew responsibility, can you really afford to take on such a client, especially when your own success as an advisor is dramatically linked to your ability to achieve success for your clients, success which others similarly situated wish to work with you to replicate? Think about it!

Structuring The Mutually Beneficial Relationship

Once you have received the Prospect Questionnaire and other prospect-sent information materials, you are ready to make a preliminary judgement about what kind of contract may make sense for this prospect. After all, you now know something about:

- the client's interest in solving his problem
- the amount of time and trouble he has already invested in trying to solve it
- the resources he has already committed to solving it
- his immediate need for a solution.
- management's commitment to a solution.

You have learned how much money they wish to expend and the seriousness with which they regard the problem, their involvement in it, and your time as an advisor.

If, for instance, I discern that a nonprofit organization wishes to raise $2 million, has no idea about their ability to do so, and wants to spend under $1000 to achieve their objective, I can make a preliminary decision about their attractiveness as a client. I know they are certainly not knowledgeable about the field (to raise $2 million for $1,000!!!), that in fact their experience is decidedly limited, and they have not yet made on their own a serious attempt to solve the problem, thus having no prior background as to what will be needed — from them as well as from me. (I am not picking this example out of the air, either: it happened in my practice in the last year.)

Any meeting that takes place with this information background between the prospect and me cannot be directed to the realization of their unrealistic objective. That is impossible. Instead, any meeting that transpires must assist the prospect in preparing to realize a series of intermediate steps which will, in due course, help them to achieve their objective. Any time we spend together (which, of course, they pay for) can be spent profitably:

- advising them on how to set a realistic objective
- training them in the steps needed to realize such an objective.

In point of fact, since in my case both these items are comprehensively dealt with in my book **DEVELOPMENT TODAY: A FUND RAISING GUIDE FOR NONPROFIT ORGANIZATIONS,** I would inform such a client that no meeting right now is necessary, but that their mastering this definitive guide is. This is my considered advice to them. This saves the prospect the time and money of a meeting. It also saves me the time, preserves our connection *and* places in their hand (for a fee) one of my most sophisticated marketing devices, for so I rate my problem solving process books. Moreover, once the prospect has finished mastering the information in this guide, they really will be ready for a profitable client relationship with me.

Once you have studied the Prospect Questionnaire, you'll know how much of your time to invest in this prospect. Your advising and your sales task at this point is presenting the prospect with the right problem solving vehicle which will meet his need for helpful information at a price he can afford and which properly makes use of what you know and can do. You must, therefore, be able to act as their advisor in the appropriate format which they can afford (which, remember, in the above instance is less than $1000), make progress towards solving their problem, and profit yourself. This can all happen.

One of the most significant errors an advisor makes as regards a prospect is to attempt to sell the prospect the wrong thing. This happens either because:

- the advisor has too few problem solving products and services available for sale and must, therefore, urge an inappropriate sale if he is to make any sale at all, or
- he is not aware of the prospect's limitations, especially in terms of commitment and funds available for the solution of this problem.

Your task, my task, as advisors is to gather as much information about the prospect as you reasonably can. We must then attempt to discern in it the seriousness of the prospect to move towards a solution and his ability (in terms of knowledge and resources) to do so, and then we must offer the appropriate problem solving vehicle. Thus I do not spend time speaking about the problem of an organization when I discern (in one way or another) that the organization is only willing to spend $100 on solving them. Instead, I offer them the appropriate combination of problem solving products and services, booklets, books, cassettes, and workshops, which will give them as much of the substance of my techniques as possible for the level of commitment they are prepared to make. Even for this price, they will get superb problem solving information, but they must spend a disproportionate amount of their own time and resources attempting to understand and apply it. For more money they will have enhanced access to me, who will work with them directly to solve their particular problems. Otherwise, they must themselves take the problem solving information that deals with their general situation but which is, necessarily, not tailored to that situation and attempt to implement it themselves.

Your task in selling advising products and services is to ascertain (at the earliest possible moment) how serious the prospect is about solving the problem and how many resources he is prepared to expend in solving this problem, and to derive a spectrum of problem solving products and services and a range of investment for this particular client prospect. This spectrum once having been determined (and, as you become experienced, you will be able to derive it oftentimes in the flicker of an eye), your task is to sell this particular prospect the maximum amount of problem solving expertise within his own range of dollar commitment. Once you have done that you may rest assured that you have done the best you can for this particular prospect at this particular moment. It goes without saying that to make this sale may or may not involve a meeting; if limited dollars and a limited prospect commitment are involved, it is not to the advantage of either of you to meet. But if a more major expenditure is likely (say, over $1000), then such a meeting will probably need to take place.

Introductory meetings: To Fee Or Not To Fee

The great question, of course, is whether such a meeting should have a fee or not. In my book, a meeting always has a fee attached to it. Anytime an advisor meets with a client or a client prospect, any time, that is, an advisor is advising (which surely happens in a prospect meeting) a fee should be attached. That is not the issue. The issue is who pays the fee. Let me explain what I mean.

As I told you before, I offer for sale a contract that offers certain of my nonprofit clients 56 hours of consulting time a year for a fixed, flat fee of (right now) $11,400 yearly. These 56 hours are divided into 52 one-hour per week for a year advisor meetings and two two-hour board meetings each year. These hours are not bankable. Unless I am prevented from having the meeting, the client must use one each week. If they don't, they have lost that time, which, however, they have still paid for. In point of fact, the average client under this scheme only uses about 40 hours each year. At my current $250 per hour rate, they have thus subsidized 6 "free" hours which I, in turn, extend to client prospects considering retaining my services. I use these hours to:

- gather necessary information from client prospects
- send and review Prospect Questionnaires
- receive qualified client prospects either at their offices or my own
- develop tailored proposals in those circumstances where my standardized proposals won't do.

These activities, while "free" to the prospect, are in fact all paid for — by someone! The only time in my advising career when this was not the case was at the very beginning when I had no retainer contracts. Then, and then only, was I truly providing free time.

Whether you are at the beginning or somewhere in the middle of your advising career, however, you must create strict guidelines for how much "free" time you'll provide a prospect. As you'll see from my standardized proposals, I am willing to give one "free" hour to qualified client prospects. Thereafter my time is billable at the rate of $250 per hour. In fact, I usually end up providing my prospects with more than this one hour, usually twice as much. The one free hour under consideration is what we spend together after the determination is made that they are, in fact, a qualified client prospect.

I urge you to inform the prospect as early as possible not only that you have some amount of free time available to him once he is a qualified client prospect but what limitations and restrictions you put on the award of this time. It is exceedingly important not only for the proper use of your time but for the development of your client-advisor relationship that the prospect understand that your time is valuable. If you seem to have no concern on this point, rest assured your prospect will have none either. One appropriate time to inform your prospect about a fee is when you are ready to schedule a meeting. State your policy as simply as possible in this way, "Our first meeting, which will be held at my Cambridge offices, will be without cost to you for up to one hour. Thereafter my time is billable at my regular rate of $250 per hour." If after an hour the client prospect (or you!) has made a determination that no business is possible right now, either of you can comfortably conclude the discussion without a substantial loss on either side.

Meeting the Prospect

Now, now at last!, you are ready for a meeting. You have gleaned useful information from the Prospect Questionnaire and from other documents the prospect has provided. The prospect knows of you (from information you have provided to him) that you can solve problems like his, that you have done so in the past, that you are an expert advisor who is not approaching him idly. You know of the prospect that he has a problem, is committed to solving it, and will do what it takes in terms of committing personnel and funds to reach his objective. A meeting is thus an indication that there is on both sides the kind of high seriousness both you and the prospect have the right to expect of each other.

The message, therefore, is plain: do not rush into a meeting. Do not offer a meeting without sufficient mutual preparation. Treat a meeting with a prospect as an important, indeed pivotal moment, in the establishment of a mutually beneficial client-advisor relationship.

Right from the start, it is important that you act like the advisor you wish to become (you are!) and that the client act like the client. That is, that you advise and the prospect be left to make decisions from among a variety of options. These options may include the following:

- Where will the meeting take place? If the prospect is prepared to commit only a small amount of money to the solution of the problem, then he may be a candidate for a Delphic Oracle Contract. Let him know, of course, that a Full Service Agreement is possible, but only if that kind of agreement makes sense given what you know about the client prospect and his circumstances.
- Who will participate in the meeting? Even if the prospect is likely to select the Delphic Oracle option and the initial meeting will be at your office, suggest that all the people necessary to solving the problem are present at this introductory meeting. Again, this will enable you to gage seriousness of intent. If people necessary to the solution of the problem are missing at this time, then indeed the prospect's seriousness may well be suspect.
- How long will the meeting be? The approximate length of this introductory meeting should be made clear in advance, and also what your policy is regarding "free" and "fee" time. Once having presented your policy, allow the prospect to determine how many "fee" hours he wants after the initial free period. Of course, you should feel free to advise him on what course of action makes sense in your opinion.

Handling The Meeting

As Henry Kissinger once said (in an eminently sensible *bon mot*), the only meetings worth having are the meetings where you know in advance what will happen. Run your meetings this way. Thus, before meeting with a client prospect write down a list of obtainable objectives for this encounter. You cannot reach an objective unless you know what objective you want. In point of fact there are two leading objectives: getting a clear and distinct sense from the prospect of what the problem really is and also a clear and distinct sense of what the client prospect is really willing to do to solve the problem. It is not enough to know, no matter how precisely, exactly what the problem is. You must know, in as much detail as possible, precisely what the prospect is willing to do to solve the problem. Then you will get a sense of the solvability of the problem and can also provide a much more detailed indication of what you can do as the prospect's expert advisor.

I wish to say as strongly as I can that there is no need for a sheepish squeamishness in connection with this meeting. If your Prospect Questionnaire (and other materials) are not perfectly plain about what the problem is, what the client prospect is willing to commit to solving it, including what has been done in the past (and it is very unlikely that you will have at this point a sufficiency of detailed information on these points), then make it a point to ask extremely detailed questions. Remember: people enjoy talking about themselves. Most people suffer from a general lack of interest in their problems. Thus, you may be one of the few (perhaps the only individual) who has given your total, undivided attention to the prospect about this pressing dilemma. You are, therefore, in a very satisfying position and should take full advantage of it.

This means, first of all, properly positioning yourself physically to reinforce this advantage. Need I say that you should position yourself closely to the prospect, that you should lean into the prospect to reinforce the message of interest, that you should not station yourself behind a desk (which imposes an unnecessary obstacle between you and the prospect) and that you should maintain steady eye contact? You want the prospect to know, and to know clearly, that:

- you are interested in his problem
- you are available to solve it
- he has your full attention, and
- that you want, are indeed eager, to solve it.

Your meeting with the client prospect will be a success if:

- the bulk of the meeting focuses on the client and his concerns.
- the prospect understands that you can solve the problem and that you want to solve the problem (are interested in taking the assignment).
- your body language and positioning reinforce all the words you utter.

Remember: people derive their impressions (which are vital in sales situations) from a variety of means. What you say is often not as important as how you say it and the sincerity and genuineness with which you say it.

All too often professionals sabotage these crucial meetings by attempting to dazzle the prospect with *their* credentials. They want it to be clearly understood that *they* are smart, that *they* have been around, that *they* are well respected. Well, you can easily persuade the prospect of all these things and lose the sale. What the prospect, conversely, wants to know (and know as profoundly as possible) is that you understand the problem he has, can solve it, have solved it in the past, and exist to serve him. Everything else is superfluous.

What you want to know is that the client prospect can and will give you what you need to solve the problem, including (if he is not directly involved in the problem solving process) his continuing support of your efforts.

Use the meeting, then, to ascertain from the prospect the following kinds of information which both clarifies and extends that initially provided on the Prospect Questionnaire:

- When did the problem begin?
- How did it begin?
- Is the problem better or worse than last year?
- Do you anticipate that it will be better or worse next year?
- How much is the problem costing you?
- Are others in your industry suffering from the same problem?
- What are they doing to combat it?
- What have you done (be as specific as possible) to deal with the problem?
- How successful has each of these efforts been (go through them individually)?
- Who is involved in your organization in the solution of the problem?
- What kinds of documents have they produced (be specific) and what kinds of recommendations have been made?

- Who has been brought in from the outside to deal with this problem?
- What kinds of recommendations have they made?
- What has happened when these recommendations have been implemented? (Review them individually.)
- What kinds of documents have they produced relative to dealing with the problem?

If it helps you, draw up a page with these questions on it and simply work your way down, *writing* the responses. Remember: the more you handle this like an actual advising assignment, the better off you are. Then, if you do not already have this information, make sure you get the following:

- What is it, specifically, that you wish to accomplish?
- When do you wish to accomplish this objective?
- What are the obstacles that may impede the realization of this objective?
- What happens if you do not realize this objective?
- What is your own personal commitment to realizing this objective?

You should have this information in advance; it should come from the Prospect Questionnaire. But if it doesn't, or if the information you have is relatively sketchy, then use this opportunity with the prospect to get the information you must have. I cannot stress enough that you are looking for not only a clear definition of the problem but a very clear indication of the client prospect's willingness to work with you, to do what is necessary to solve the problem. All advisor-client relationships are necessarily collaborative. Each of you, the advisor, the client, has (or should have) precise, specific tasks to accomplish so that the mutually agreed upon objective can be reached within a finite period of time. Let me say again and again: it is not enough, can never be enough, merely to have a clear definition of the problem and clearly to indicate to the prospect that you have the right credentials and expertise for solving the problem. The prospect must be committed to the problem's solution and must be willing to take all the necessary steps (as outlined by you, the advisor) to reach the agreed objective. Without this critical ingredient the advisor relationship will falter and fail.

More On Successfully Handling The Prospect Meeting

The bulk of the meeting will be taken up with getting answers to the kinds of questions listed above. Several other things must also take place at this meeting, too.

You must clearly show the prospect that you have the ability to solve his problem. You cannot show this ability unless you have a very clear indication of what that problem is. Therefore, wait as long as you can to discuss in detail your ability to solve his problem. Just what credentials and experiences you will bring to this task may vary as you come to learn more about the prospect and his situation. As the prospect speaks, therefore, write down what you have done in the past (and the name of the appropriate contact person who will provide you with the appropriate reference) and how it relates to the problem the prospect has. Advisors sell their services because they clearly hear and understand what the client prospect's problem is and because they put forward what I call the appropriate "context credential," that is the credential (be it degree, license, successfully completed assignment, &c) that is most meaningful for this prospect, this problem, and this situation. Not all credentials are meaningful in all situations. You must pick and choose, selecting the appropriate "context credential" which is meaningful to this client prospect at this time. Never forget this.

Note: it may be that it will take you some time to draw up an appropriate list of context credentials for this client prospect. That's perfectly acceptable. If you cannot immediately provide the relevant credential (including referee, organization, address, telephone number, &c) at the conclusion of this meeting, don't let it worry you. What is important is that you demonstrate mastery and control of the situation; that you show, in short, that you know what you are doing. Inform the prospect that you will have such a list by a certain time (usually at the time the follow-up proposal is submitted) and that it will conclusively demonstrate that you have the right context credentials, the certain ability, that is, to solve this problem.

N.B. Telling a prospect you can solve his problem and providing references to others for whom you have solved this problem is *not* the same as telling him how to solve the problem. Your specific problem solving techniques are proprietary and should be reserved until such time as the prospect actually hires you.

When The "Free" Time Has Expired

It may be that the "free" time you are providing the prospect will expire at some point during the meeting. If this happens, it is your responsibility politely to inform the prospect that this has happened and to ask whether the prospect wishes to continue the meeting on a paid basis. My experience indicates that if the meeting is going well, if you have handled it in a professional manner and have been working to ascertain the extent of the prospect's problem and his willingness to solve it, if, in short, there is a distinct possibility of this meeting evolving into a client-advisor relationship, then the prospect will in fact signal his willingness to continue on a paid basis. Congratulations! You are now well along to turning this prospect into a client. The prize is yours to win!

Successfully Concluding The Prospect Meeting

No meeting should be ended until there is firm agreement on the following critical points:

- Do you both agree (at least in a preliminary manner) on the nature of the problem to be solved?
- There should be a reaffirmation of the prospect's willingness to work with you to achieve a solution to this problem.
- Have you made a clear statement about your ability to help solve this problem? Both what you can do and what you cannot do?
- Give a precise indication of how this meeting will be followed up and at what times about the following items:
    - Will there be a formal proposal?
    - To whom will it be sent?
    - When?
    - At what point will you, the advisor, follow up to ascertain final interest and close the sale that begins the formal relationship?
    - What other materials does the prospect need to make a decision?
    - What people would the prospect like to check with to ascertain your ability to solve the problem?
    - When will you, the advisor, send him a list of these people?

If it helps, develop a form with these questions and write down the answers. You can keep this form in a three-hole binder called a Prospect Book which can be regularly reviewed for easy follow-up. A substantial part of your ability to get and keep meaningful client relationships will be the success with which you demonstrate to prospects your organization, your mastery over the situation, and your desire and enthusiasm to work with them.

Some Hints For A Successful Prospect Meeting

Remember something about Americans. We are a nation with incredible riches. Americans are not, as surveys conclusively demonstrate, a saving people. We are a spending people. We like spending money. It's one of our national thrills. We are also a service people. Americans will pay, and pay well, to get service. These two things are worth remembering. Your task is to demonstrate in a prospect meeting that you are a good investment for the prospect's money (money, remember, they want to spend and which they will spend soon, whether or not they spend it on you!) and that you can provide them the service they need.

Remember something else about Americans: we are very skeptical about the claims made by providers. One study I've just read suggests that something like 80% of Americans disbelieve the claims made by commercial advertisers. 80%! Thus, when you are in the midst of a prospect meeting you are confronting two opposing tendencies:

- On the one hand, the person you're with wants to be convinced that spending money on you is a good thing. He really wants to believe this. Really wants to spend his money on you.
- On the other hand, he's deeply skeptical about whether the investment is worth it, whether it will pay off, whether in fact he's not about to fall into a characteristic position: being made a fool and wantonly throwing his money away on something that really won't do much good.

You have to deal with the buyer's skepticism at the same time you are reinforcing his native American desire to spend his money. Right now.

In this situation, many things can assist you:

- Don't sit behind a desk. Sit close to the prospect and subtly lean into him.
- Have your calls held during the meeting. In my case, I simply turn on my answering machine. But I don't merely turn it off, I tell the prospect I am turning it off with the implication that this is something I am doing for him because he is important. If you are going to do something nice for someone, let him know it!
- Get up when the prospect comes into the room. At least act as if you are glad to see him. By the same token, when the meeting is over, walk the prospect to the door, or, in my case, down the corridor to the elevator. Press the elevator button. You are in a service business and everything that you do should emphasize to the prospect that you will provide whatever service you can to make his life easier.

Following Up A Successful Prospect Meeting

What should now be clear is that there are many steps to beginning a successful client-advisor relationship and that the development of this relationship can be adversely affected by neglecting any one of them. Moreover, remember, it is your responsibility, as the person primarily urging the relationship, to make sure that these steps are in fact achieved. It is not the prospect's task to follow up. It is always yours.

The first thing that needs to happen is your sending an immediate follow-up letter to the prospect. This letter puts into writing the various points determined at the conclusion of the prospect meeting. In it you will again:

- Stress your desire to work with the prospect.
- Indicate the problem that you and the prospect have (at least preliminarily) agreed upon which needs to be solved.
- Advise the prospect on when your proposal will be forthcoming (if it is not a standardized proposal or cannot be completed in time for this immediate follow up).
- Provide the prospect with the names, addresses and telephone numbers of those who have satisfactorily used your services in similar situations.

Conclude by providing any other information that you agreed to do at the end of the prospect meeting.

The purpose of this letter is clear: by meeting with you, the prospect has signalled at least an introductorily serious level of interest in solving his problem and has indicated some level of interest in you as the potential problem solver. These signals are a more substantial addition to the trend that began with your introductory prospect contacts. Now there is reason for thinking there is momentum. This momentum, of course, must be exploited, for as Shakespeare wrote in *Julius Caesar,* "We must take the current when it serves/or lose our ventures." Now, then, is a pivotal moment for you to indicate that critical, that essential mastery, that control, that enthusiasm which you have and to move things nearer to the close which will benefit both you and the client prospect. For make no mistake about it: that close is now what you are seeking, for without it both you and the prospect will suffer, the one bereft of an assignment, the other losing out on the use of your essential wisdom and problem solving skills. That would be a tragedy for both of you.

Ideally, of course, your formal proposal would accompany this letter. If you cannot complete it with 24 hours, however, then send your immediate follow-up letter and indicate when the proposal will be forthcoming. But let me say this: if you follow the steps in the proposal section which follows, you should be able to follow up this introductory prospect meeting as quickly as possible with the formal document which embodies your understanding of the problem and your (at least introductory) suggestions about how you can be used to solve it. This being the case, let's move on to the proposal.

Fashioning The Persuasive Proposal

A proposal is just that, a suggestion from you, the advisor, about how the client prospect can solve his problem by working in conjunction with you. Because it's a suggestion, every proposal implicitly has within it the seeds of a counter-proposal. If your proposal is to be successful you must, therefore, not only present your best case, but you must simultaneously deal with any counterpoints which the prospect is likely to put forward, or which he may already have put forward in your introductory dealings. To be sure, the prospect may simply take your proposal lock, stock and barrel, but don't bet on it. Expect a counterproposal. Don't be offended by it. Learn to deal with it with as much equanimity as possible. Therefore, as you write the proposal always keep in mind the prospect's likely response and see whether you have, in fact, understood any possible objection and have adequately responded to it.

To be able to respond quickly to a client prospect, use the following modules and tailor them to the specific situation of this prospect. Here are the leading sections of most proposals:

Title: Provide a one-sentence description of the project. Make this an Action Title, which suggests movement to the client prospect's desired objective.

Project Synopsis: Provide a 100-250 word (up to one page) synopsis of the problem, the desired outcome, the target date of the completion and your role in the solution.

Purpose: List the leading reasons for the project, what the prospect expects to achieve with it.

Need: Write down, in as much detail as possible, why the problem must be solved now and why the project should be undertaken as soon as possible.

Don't forget that you are the doctor. Bring the full weight of your professional standing and understanding of the problem to bear here. Remember: the prospect may have some understanding of why the problem needs to be solved now, but you, as the expert, should add another dimension to this. You should present the most compelling reasons for beginning the project now, reasons that will persuade the prospect to act, or which the prospect can use as he approaches his ultimate decision makers with the need to take action now. Keep in mind the question is not simply whether or not to go ahead with this project. That's relatively easy, but whether, out of all the other problems that the prospect has, to spend some of his scarce resources on this project at all. You provide the answers here and make it easy for the buyer to act by presenting cogent reasons for action *now* and an indication of what will happen if he fails to move *now*.

Suitability: If you are proposing something new to the prospect, you may need to address the issue of the prospect's suitability to undertake this project. In many cases, of course, it is perfectly obvious why the project is suitable for the prospect, and this section can be skipped.

First step: Now that you have assessed the Prospect Questionnaire, reviewed sundry of his documents, and met and talked with the prospect, you should have a fair idea of not merely one prospect problem but a series of them. As I get to know a prospect better, I keep a list of all his problems because, of course, these problems will be the basis of future assignments for me and for members of my Super-group of Independent Contractors. But unless you have fallen into the universe of a prospect with Eldorado in his treasury, the person you are dealing with will have more problems than (immediately available) resources to solve them. Thus it is your responsibility to set down a series of finite, definite, specific steps that are reasonable considering the kind of dollar and other resource commitments the prospect is prepared to make. It may be that the prospect wishes to build a new building (a common objective in my advisor practice) but at present should do no more than raise the money for a can of paint for his present facility. Yes, by all means keep in mind what his ultimate objective is. Yes, by all means let him know that when the time comes you are available to help him reach it. But don't confuse the issue and possibly demoralize him by suggesting that he work on a (perhaps now) impossible objective when he can very well achieve a reasonable (if modest) intermediate objective and so begin the process of moving to the ultimately desired objective.

There are very good psychological as well as business reasons for keeping the objectives reasonable and for helping the client achieve them through reasonable steps. Setting a reasonable objective and reaching it will increase the client's sense of self and thus make him a better client for you to work with. Setting and reaching a reasonable objective will also increase the esteem with which you are held by the client and so increase the likelihood that you will get further assignments and that you will be able to recommend other members of your Supergroup of Independent Contractors at times when the client has available discretionary resources.

I can scarcely sufficiently stress that one of the great problems of particularly new advisors is that they present their prospects with (perhaps laudable but) too demanding objectives. The prospect realizes that these objectives, while no doubt ultimately desirable, are not attainable just now and so rejects the advisor who proposes them. This is not, I should point out, an at all unreasonable action on the prospect's part. He has quite rightly decided that you are the wrong advisor for him based on your inability to present him with a project which lies within his current means of solving. Hence he is right to reject you. I sum up this situation with a client prospect by sometimes saying, "You have a million dollars worth of problems and $5000 worth of solution. Let's work together to see how that money can best be spent using my talents in pursuit of your ultimate objectives."

Time: Ingenue advisors are often guilty of one of the primary sins in proposal writing, that is of grossly underestimating the amount of time it will take them to finish the job they are proposing to do. Don't make this mistake. In fact, I beg you to reconsider the whole matter of the amount of time you propose to devote to the assignment.

If you're like many advisors, you want to project the image of a superhero, of someone who can come in and make any difficult assignment a piece of cake. "The difficult we do at once," as the old saw has it. "The impossible takes a little longer." By following this maxim you get into trouble, because every problem, no matter how often you've dealt with it, always takes longer to solve than you estimate in the halcyon moment when you are merely proposing to solve it. And you might as well make your time calculations accordingly.

In his connection, remember Caesar's *Gallic Commentaries*, the book you probably hated so much in Latin II. Caesar, as you will remember, was at the time an ambitious politician anxious to develop a reputation as a problem solver, and like all clever advisors he wanted to leverage his campaign against the Gauls to achieve further success. In this connection, you may read the *Gallic Commentaries* as a sort of extended early day Success Letter. Thus, instead of pooh-poohing the difficulty of dispatching the pesky Gauls, he built them up into paragons of military sophistication and brute strength. So that when he had finished wiping his feet on what was a bunch of disorganized savages he emerged as a master tactician — and hence the stuff of which heroes are made. Given Caesar's masterful mind, I should very much have liked to see his early letters to the Senate in which he proposed how he would deal with the Gauls. I am sure he didn't begin to underestimate the task. And neither should you.

If the task is difficult, tell the prospect it is difficult. If it has unusual features, inform the prospect what they are. Remember: you are the doctor. It is your responsibility to inform the patient, your prospect, in the most specific detail precisely why the contemplated assignment is a tasking one, even if you must err on the side of emphasizing the difficulties. Don't forget august Caesar's ploy.

In this connection, therefore, even if you have previously dealt with the assignment in question make sure you factor in an additional 20% of time beyond the amount of time you have first estimated it will take to solve the problem. This is if you know what you are doing, have faced the problem before, and can reasonably anticipate smooth sailing. Call this the Murphy's Law factor, if you will, but things will go wrong and you should anticipate them in advance.

If you have not faced this precise problem before and cannot be sure of precisely how long it will take you to solve it, factor in an additional 40% of time beyond your original estimate. Tell the prospect what peculiar conditions about the assignment make this calculation a sensible one.

Also, you can always provide a range of time which must be made available, that the assignment is unlikely to take less than "x" amount or more than "y" amount. But be generous in your time allotments so that the prospect, once a client, will not be shocked once the clock starts ticking.

Cost: Clearly the prospect wants to know how much it will cost to realize the objective which both you and he have now agreed upon as the immediate task at hand. This is only reasonable. Yet before going into the whole matter of cost with the prospect (which may very well be the first thing he wants to discuss) try and keep the discussion focused on what the prospect wishes to achieve, your ability to help him achieve it, and the desirability of achieving this outcome now. If you begin your discussion with a client on the matter of cost, you have a diminished likelihood of getting the assignment. Instead, the prospect's appetite must be whetted and stay whetted about what he is getting from the transfer of funds. Having said this, when at last it is time to talk about money, do so directly and without being squeamish about it. If you are indeed offering the kind of service you say you do, if you are indeed solving the prospect's problem (a problem he very much wishes to have solved), then you have no reason to apologize about the fee.

N.B. As you already know, I do my advising all over the United States and Canada. I have found that in traveling to faraway places, it is inexpedient to charge by the hour or to charge a special fee for traveling. In effect, therefore, I charge a project fee, a fee based on the number of hours of advising I shall do and the travel time between my base in Cambridge and their's. Let's say I'm traveling between Cambridge and Columbia, South Carolina. To determine the fee I do the following:

- Estimate the number of advising hours I shall be spending directly with the client (or otherwise on the client's business). Multiply this estimate by 1.20 if I have previously handled such an assignment (20% margin of error in advance of my estimate) and by 1.40 if I have not (a 40% margin of error).
- Call my travel agent and check the schedule regarding air transportation both to the destination and back.
- Add two hours for ground transportation (one hour estimate in each city).
- Add any time which may be necessary for a follow-up report.

Then I make an estimate of the fee and present it to the prospect as the overall cost of the project, not including customary expenses.

I have found that clients get justifiably anxious thinking that your meter is running while you are stalled in traffic, while you are flying, while you are checking into a hotel, &c. It is better, far, far better whenever possible simply to quote a project fee which (except for customary expenses) is sufficient to meet the cost of the project.

A note on expenses: All customary expenses are payable by the client. These expenses include: transportation, photocopying, postage, secretarial services (when used exclusively for client business), long distance telephone calls and the like. In the fee section of your proposal, simply insert a line to the effect that such expenses are billable to the client. In the actual contract you can insert language dealing with what expenses are reimbursable and how you will bill the client for reimbursement.

Future Steps: It is a good idea to let the prospect know (based on your conversations with the prospect, his objectives and your assessment of his situation) where your relationship will go once the current assignment is completed. This can be done in the "Future Steps" section of the proposal. List here the next one or two projects that should be handled based on what you now know of the prospect's circumstances. In fact, this section of the proposal is an indication that you wish the relationship to develop and begins the marketing process that will, in due course, result in the next assignment which will be to the mutual benefit of the (now) prospect and you.

Follow-up: Indicate in the body of the proposal just how and when you'll be following up this document. If you have been following my suggestions, throughout all your dealings with the prospect you have been demonstrating your mastery and control over the process, thereby not only giving the prospect but reinforcing in the prospect a feeling that you know what you are doing. Don't blow it now! Write down a precise date (*not* time) when you will call, generally ten days hence. Or otherwise specify precisely what you intend to do and when you intend to do it. Then do it.

Prospects rightly feel nervous about dealing with new advisors. We (for I as a buyer of advisor services rightly include myself) wonder whether we are truly dealing with the most reputable and knowledgeable individuals, and we doubt (because of our own lack of expertise) our ability to find out before it is too late. We therefore judge you not only by what you say but by how you say it and by, in a general way, how you handle your relations with us. We are therefore perfectly right to eschew an advisor because he fails to follow through on even the smallest things that he says he will do. We are right to reckon that if he fails now, when he is on his best behavior while seeking our business, so won't he fail again, and again, and again, at the moment when we are, at last, in his clutches. No, we reckon, it will be better to do nothing even though we may indeed be losing the benefit. Losing that benefit is an unhappiness but not having the anxiety that attends dealing with an uncertain advisor is a considerable compensation.

As I write these words I am thinking about a recent encounter I had with a financial advisor. I had a series of (sometimes quite basic) questions about the deal in question and the more I learned the more uncertain I grew as to whether it was truly in my interest. Then a small, very subtle psychological point turned the argument irrevocably against the advisor. In a general discussion of the deal he said, not once but twice, "I've got to make money. And you've got to make money." Of course, the point itself is irrefutable. Both parties to any transaction that is worth its salt must benefit. But the fact that the advisor kept stressing himself first of all, above all, was just the piece of information I needed to make my final decision. On the basis of the advisor's own presentation I made it against him. I reasoned that an individual who would in a sales situation focus so heavily on his own rights and benefits would always function thus and that later, when I didn't have the leverage of not yet having presented a check, I would be at a distinct disadvantage. Think about it.

Presentation Of The Proposal

Different subgroups of the advising profession will, of course, have their prevailing ways about the presentation of proposals. Much has been written about the benefits of presenting them in colorful folders with the prospect's name embossed in golden letters or having them delivered by winsome houris with rubies in their touch-me navels. As a parsimonious Scotsman with every pinchpenny trait of my race, I reject these notions and never employ them no matter how urgently I want the assignment. If, on the other hand, the prospect has laid down certain specifications for how the proposal is to be submitted (as in the case of government agencies) then I am equally rigid about following those particular specifications to the letter no matter how absurd I personally find some of the regulations.

Proposals should be professionally presented on your letterhead with easy-to-read paragraphing and arrangement. I prefer that each page is on letterhead because pages do get separated even in the best run offices.

The proposal should be accompanied by a cover letter. If you are presenting the proposal immediately following your prospect meeting, then this letter will need to be more elaborate than any second letter. Follow the specifications already provided. In the case of a second letter you need say no more than this:

Dear Mr. Prospect:

This letter follows my recent letter to you in which I said that I would be presenting my proposal to you by this date. Please find it enclosed.

As you see, I have indicated in the proposal that I will follow up this submission with a telephone call ten days hence. I look forward to talking to you then and to beginning our formal relationship.

Sincerely,

Advisor

If You Are In A Competitive Bid Situation

If you are competing for an assignment within the private sector (this technique will not work where most government work is involved), make sure you ask the prospect to keep you abreast of developments in the proposal review process. It is easy for a prospect to become confused and overwhelmed when reviewing a host of proposals even though all deal with the same set of facts and are attempting to provide the prospect with the same result. Make this situation work to your advantage.

Inform the prospect either during your initial meeting or in the cover letter that you are available to provide additional information during the proposal review process. Arrange, too, with the prospect that if your bid looks higher and less competitive than others that you would like the opportunity to explain why this may be the case, provide further details and, if necessary, to alter the bid should this be necessary.

Remember: the proposal process is necessarily a rather fluid one. You should not approach it as if your initial proposal were set in cement nor should you expect the prospect's initial response to be final. There is always give and take in the proposal process, and you must let the prospect know that you can and will be flexible if need be. I hasten to point out that this does not necessarily mean that you have to lower your price to the level of the lowest bidder. Perhaps if you review that bid you will be able to point out to the prospect that the other bidder is not providing certain services that you are. If this is the case, should the prospect continue to want these services then the other organization's bid will very likely have to be raised. If the prospect no longer wishes to have them, then you can probably lower you bid. In short, there must be discussion.

Too many advisors treat the proposal process as something fixed and immutable. It isn't. It must involve communication between the parties; you must insist upon this communication taking place. Otherwise you are unwisely placed in a "take it or leave it" situation which can be very detrimental to your interests.

Again, make sure you get the prospect's agreement on this kind of discussion. Always ask the prospect (the prospect meeting is a good time) whether a formal or informal competition is under way to fill the advisor slot. If it is, tell the prospect you can and will be flexible and wish to be fully consulted during the bidding process. At the end of the meeting, when it comes time to enumerate the things on which you and the prospect have agreed and to list who does what when, make sure you secure final agreement on being kept informed. Then insert it into the prospect meeting follow-up letter. You cannot, of course, absolutely ensure that this vital communication takes place, but you can advocate it. And should. Any advisor-client relationship necessarily demands a good deal of communication. If you firmly point out even from the earliest moments of your developing relationship that such communication is in your mutual interest, you stand a better chance of getting it straight through your relationship than if you merely wish and hope for it.

Following Up

Nailing down the prospect can involve much, often frustrating, effort. It is very irritating to me clearly to identify a prospect's problem, clearly to get the prospect's affirmation that this is indeed a serious problem and one he wishes to solve expeditiously, clearly to ascertain that the prospect has the necessary resources to solve the problem, and then wait and wait and wait while the prospect dawdles. The best advisors are very focused on movement and on the achievement of client success (which helps them, of course, achieve their own objectives). Often, however, even the best prospects are severely less focused than we are.

In these circumstances, it is easy to take out your frustration and growing irritation on the prospect. This is fatal. Thus, expect prospects to move less swiftly to a resolution of their problem than you do. Prospects will regularly evince behavior traits worthy of a mugwump. Anticipate it. Thus, for your own salvation (both personally and professionally), develop a network of other advisors with whom you can let your hair down and complain, complain, complain about the inadequacies of the human race and your client prospects in particular. You must expect the stress in these situations to build, and you must have a safe way of letting it out. Keeping a punching bag marked "Prospect" in your office might work, but it might also attract curious judgements from would be clients calling on you. Try other means instead.

Opening Gambits In The Follow-Up Game

You are now in a situation where sales closing information is crucial. In this connection I should like to recommend to you *Secrets Of Closing Sales* by Charles B. Roth and Roy Alexander (Prentice Hall). I find it both creative and realistic about the kinds of people you encounter and how to handle them. Here are my own thoughts on the issue:

- **"I haven't had time to read the proposal yet."**

The first time you call a prospect to nail down the close (and so begin the truly constructive part of your relationship), you are very likely to be told, "I haven't had time to read the proposal yet." In this situation, pin the prospect down to a specific time, if possible within the next 48 to 72 hours, when he will have finished reviewing the proposal and when you can call back to have a substantive discussion on any outstanding issues still remaining to be resolved. Don't attempt to reprise the significant points in the proposal when the prospect hasn't yet reviewed it. This is an exercise in futility, because the prospect can quite rightly respond, "Well, let's wait and discuss it when I've read the proposal." Remember: at all times, in all sales situations (for that is what you are now in) you are much better off anticipating the prospect's reaction and planning your move accordingly. The more you learn to think like a prospect during the sales and negotiating process, the more likely you are to make the sale which will benefit you both.

- **"I've passed the document on to the next level of decision maker for review."**

Again, this is a very common response. Again, pin the prospect down on a precise amount of time this review process will take and plan to follow up accordingly. Also find out from the prospect specifically who will be reviewing the proposal, what particular interests this person has, what objections he may have to what is being proposed, and what additional materials he might want. Ask to be kept abreast of developments in detail so you can respond to the changing circumstances of the case as specifically as possible. Remember: the proposal you have submitted is, in significant measure, in direct response to the individual you dealt with in your prospect meetings and contacts. If the proposal is sent to others for the review (as so often happens in the advising business), then the circumstances have changed and the proposal may need to be changed accordingly, too. This is a fluid situation, and you must be prepared to change along with conditions.

- **"Looks interesting but we're not ready to make a decision now."**

Don't let the "looks interesting" part fool you. Americans love to be loved. As a people we like to keep our options open. This response meets both these objectives. Neophyte advisors continually tell me, with beaming smiles, about proposals they have currently under consideration that have attracted this response. Usually I haven't the heart to tell them that this response is usually a "No!" variant.

Your responsibility here is to find out from the prospect what's really holding things up. If you have adequately gaged the importance to the prospect of solving the problem and have made a reasonable proposal about how this problem can be solved in the prospect's best interests in the near future then you shouldn't be getting this response. You need to find out whether:

1) solving the problem really is a top priority with the prospect

2) the prospect is unconvinced that the methods you are proposing are adequate to the task

3) your suggested fee is a detriment

4) other problems have moved into a higher priority and will get the prospect's discretionary dollars

5) the individual you are dealing with really doesn't have the clout to make a decision after all.

When someone utters those usually fatal words "Looks interesting, but . . .", your responsibility is to push the matter further by finding answers to the above questions. Remember: if the problem really is a significant one to the prospect and if you have convinced them that by working with you they will gain a disproportionate benefit compared to fee, there should be no reason for the prospect to hesitate about going ahead now. None whatsoever.

Consider: you have now put a good deal of time into this situation. You have considered the prospect's situation. You have gathered much information about it. You have grappled with the problem of what kinds of skills and technical information you have and how they could best be put to work in the prospect's interest. And you have made the decision that, yes, a working relationship between you and the prospect does make sense. This all being the case, now is not the moment to rest content with a false lulling produced by the line "Looks interesting . . ." Push here and find out what you need to know to get this contract.

One way of handling this (often frustrating) situation is to draft, as a co-conspirator, the individual you have been dealing with: bring him into the solution of the problem. Ask the prospect if he remains interested in 1) the problem and 2) working with you to achieve a solution. If the answers to both these questions are positive, then ask the prospect what he feels you should do to get the contract signed, sealed, and delivered. If the prospect is not willing to assist you, it is a clear indication that his interest has waned, or that he has previously overstated his ability to make a deal with you and deliver, a problem that many overreaching (but underpowered) Americans have. In this situation say something like this, "It seems to me that what you are telling me is that you are really not as keen on the project as you were before. If this is true, could you tell me why, and let me see what I can do about persuading you that now is a good time to act and that my methods would be a benefit to you."

It may be that what you hear during this conversation will necessitate an updating of your proposal or the filing of a new letter with additional pertinent information. Remember: your original proposal is not cast in cement. Negotiating with a prospect is necessarily an often extremely fluid situation; you must be prepared to react accordingly as circumstances change.

I should also like to point out that if you make the unhappy (albeit rather frequent) discovery during the negotiating process that the individual with whom you've been dealing has overstated his decision making authority, then do not hesitate to ask for an appointment with that individual who can in fact make the decision. Ask your original contact to accompany you by all means, or at the very least ask him to set up the necessary meeting for you. You very likely will not be paid for this meeting, but consider the amount of time and effort you've already put into this project. If you have clearly ascertained that the problem is a serious one for the prospect and that it can be solved using your methods, take this extra step in an attempt persuasively to make your case.

• "Not Interested."

If you hear these discouraging words, something has gone very, very wrong. You need to find out what it is. To begin the reversal process, however, remember the skill of Selective Hearing.

Throughout the course of the development of my advisor practice, I have regularly been the recipient of individuals saying "Not interested" to me. In the beginning I assumed they knew what they were talking about and was willing to accept their judgement as the last word on the matter. Now I very rarely do this. Now I assume they don't know what they are talking about and that they have said these unsatisfactory words because I have failed to make crystal clear exactly in what specific ways they will benefit from working with me. So I ignore the finality of the words and immediately attempt to reopen the discussion and see if I cannot find a way of not so much changing their minds but alerting them to the benefits they are about to lose. Here's what to do:

- Don't take "Not interested" as the final word on the matter of your would-be relationship with the prospect. If you have made a professional determination that the prospect has a serious problem needing to be solved, if you know that you can offer a disproportionate benefit compared to fee, if you know, in short, that the relationship you are proposing is a mutually beneficial and constructive one, don't give up now.

- Ask the prospect for precise information as to why this decision has been made. Find out whether the problem is still a serious one. Find out how else they intend to solve it. Find out whether other advisors are being brought in and what angle they intend to take to solve the problem. Find out whether your fee was the determining factor. Find out, in short, what the obstacle(s) is/are to this prospect making the decision to work with you to solve his problem.

- Having ascertained this information, ask the prospect whether he would be amenable to reviewing an amended proposal, an updated proposal that would take into consideration his current thinking. Unless the prospect has entered into an engagement with another advisor, he'll probably indicate a willingness to review your materials. After all, they don't yet commit him to anything.

- Inform the prospect you are still interested in working with him and you'll do what is necessary to impress him with the need for the problem to be solved using problem solving information and techniques at your disposal.

Avoiding Becoming a Pest

My students worry a good deal about becoming an annoyance to a prospect. I must confess I am less worried about this outcome than they are. We live in a world where disinterest and apathy are the rule rather than the exception. Throughout the entire proposal process, I have stressed and stressed again the necessity for you to be client centered in your thinking and action. This fact remains true especially now that your proposal for working with the prospect has been declined. So long as the discussion remains focused on the prospect and his needs, so long as the problem remains to be solved, so long as no other outside advisor has been retained offering services recognizably similar to yours, so long as you feel confident about your ability to offer the disproportionate benefit compared to fee, you must carry on. It is both to your benefit (of course) and to the prospect's. In this situation you must make sure, however, that your own benefit does not emerge as the predominant reason for your persistence. That is the kiss of death. It's incredible how often this kiss is self-administered. Do what I do to prove this for yourself: listen to those who solicit you and see how often (how ridiculously often) they frame their arguments in terms of their own benefits. It's ludicrous — and sad. If you really want to succeed to the extent of your imagining, you must work and work hard exclusively to focus on the client and his need for your service and not on what you yourself can expect to derive from the relationship. This is very easy to write, I know, and oh-so-difficult to achieve. But achieve it you must.

If The Prospect Persists In Being Disinterested

Sadly, as I have come to know, it is not possible to enter into a sensible business relationship with some people. Some are too timid about committing resources despite the substantial likelihood of a better return. Some are constitutionally unable to make a decision. Some are just plain stupid. For whatever the reason, some people will not go ahead and do business with a sensible person like you. Unless, however, the individual is a complete fool, don't abandon this prospect altogether. If there remains the possibility of doing business with the individual at some future time, if the prospect's problem is likely to prove chronic, then by all means stay in touch with the prospect. Here's how to do it:

- Inform the prospect that you are sorry not to be working with him now and that you hope for the opportunity of doing so in the future.

- Understand that all people do not make up their minds quickly and expeditiously no matter how substantial the benefit you are offering. I honestly believe that if I sent out a 1,000 piece mailing with the free offer of a five dollar bill to anyone who'd respond — no strings attached — a very substantial fraction of the audience would fail to do so. How much more difficult is it, then, to persuade people to act when they have to put up the money and where they have not previously done business with you?

- Put your desire to work with the prospect at some future date into a letter. (See Samples, Page 298). This letter should be upbeat and should let the prospect know that you are, in fact, The Inevitable.

- Keep the prospect on file in your Prospect Book and as you have successes with comparable individuals and organizations let them know. Use the techniques of unabashed promotion to ensure that these successes are publicized in appropriate publications and be persistent about drawing them to the attention of the prospect with a short note indicating your continuing interest in helping them achieve the same, or an even better, result.

- Call from time to time to ascertain their situation and see how they have progressed towards the solution of their problem. You are, of course, in the best possible situation where the problem remains a serious one and where, through inertia, sloth, stupidity and false optimism, they do nothing to solve it. It is likely (though not absolute) that the prospect, by now convinced that you are The Inevitable, will come to see the need to work with you. At which time you will get the contract they should have signed at the beginning. I need hardly point out in such situations that as soon as the first success takes place in this long-delayed relationship, it is perfectly appropriate (in the most genteel way) to point out that this happy circumstance could have been theirs earlier had they only acted beforehand. Delivering this soul-necessary line is one of life's sweetest pleasures.

Why Clients Really Say Yes

I have spent a good deal of time dealing with the delaying lines, the negative lines, because, for most would-be advisors, these are the lines they hear most of all. What is necessary in each of these unfortunate situations is to understand why your needed services were declined, why obstacles were erected which precluded the prospect from benefitting from what you know and can do. In more cases than you'd care to admit, it is not so much the prospect who declines you as you who make such a decision inevitable by the way you handle your prospect, proposalmanship, and negotiating. The prospect, of course, is a convenient scapegoat, but you bear the true responsibility for the failure to connect.

Happily, however, the more you are in business the better you'll (have to) be at getting prospects to say "Yes, I want you!" These, of course, are stirring words. Here are some additional hints for producing this response.

Becoming The Dreamspinner

If you want to get clients, really want to get them, and if you want to succeed, really want to succeed, then pay close attention to what I'm about to tell you. For your ability to succeed in the advice business means successfully becoming a Dreamspinner for your prospects.

You will recall that a Dreamspinner is the person who undertakes to discover in a prospect what his dream is, that is, the underlying motivation that spurs the prospect to do that which you are advising him to do. Let me give you an example. As you know, I am a fund raising and development advisor for nonprofit organizations. I provide professional services in a field which most people dislike and which makes them very anxious: asking other people for money.

They can be induced, however, to overcome their very deep seated aversion because of the benefits that will result to their constituencies (and, by extension, to themselves) through the spending of the monies raised. Thus, the decision maker (a nonprofit chief executive officer) will go through the unpleasantness of raising money (for almost without exception such executives are averse to the task) for the benefit that comes as they spend the money, the chief benefit being the fact that they are confirmed as good, worthy, generous, caring people.

My task when meeting these people is as quickly as possible to ascertain what their dream is and to spin a scenario in which this dream is realized, and they rise to the level of their own expectations. In some situations life has worked in these people in such a way that the spark of their dream burns but slightly. My task in such cases is to foster the flame and make it burn bright again.

Such a realization, of course, involves psychology. It involves stepping back from your own reasons and needs for offering your service and stepping as quickly as possible into the shoes of the prospect so that you can speak with his thoughts about what he really wants to achieve.

Many advisors feel distinctly squeamish about this. They feel manipulative if they go beyond the strict confines of their professional discipline and approach the cosmic verities of their prospects. I don't. I ask people right away what they really want to achieve with the project under discussion. What is their personal and professional interest in it? How much does it really matter to them whether this takes place? Is it a passing fancy, or is the matter under discussion of deep rooted significance?

These are not idle questions, not by any stretch of reckoning. I am in the business of helping my clients realize their fondest and most cherished dreams. I am in the business of helping them become better people, more complete people, happier and more productive people. There is nothing wrong with a frank admission certainly to oneself, hopefully to one's prospects, that this is in fact your real business. I tell them that while there is nothing sacred about any of the means I might employ, there is something sacred about the realization of their dream and using the project at hand (in large or small measure) to do so. If you want to succeed as an advisor, if you really want to achieve your objectives, then catch the prospect's dream and consider how you can help him realize it using the information and techniques at your command. Do not fall victim to any false notions of "professional behavior" which suggest that it is somehow improper to bridge the unavoidable distance between you and the prospect with the compelling linkage that you, like the prospect, value the dream, that you will work for the dream, that you are one of those (perhaps, given your skills, the only one!) who can bring this vital dream into existence. People are not buying advisors. And they are not merely buying the solutions to top priority problems. They are buying what they have always bought: pieces of their dreams. It is you the conjuror, the Dreamspinner, who must not only understand this dream but must, with those who have forgotten that they dream at all, rekindle the dream. It is one of the most important things we advisors do. The more successful we are in doing it, the more successful we are overall.

Developing Standardized Proposals

The kinds of proposals I've been discussing so far are called *ad hoc* proposals, meaning proposals developed in response to a particular circumstance. These proposals deal with a unique problem which you expect to deal with in a distinctive fashion. I hasten to point out, however, that this is not the only kind of problem there is nor the only kind of proposal. Proposals can also be standardized, and the good advisor comes as quickly as possible to develop as many standardized proposal formats as possible, thereby extending his service line accordingly. A standardized proposal, just as its name suggests, deals with a problem (or set of problems) which are not only familiar to you but familiar, too, in the ways you set about solving them. It involves a tried, trusted and tested approach to the problem which you understand very well and can aptly solve.

When To Develop Standardized Proposals

Very, very few advisors can develop standardized proposals right from the outset of their practices. You have to be in business for a while (and, practically, this means at least six months) before you have:

- faced the same problem many times
- developed an efficient and tested set of procedures to solve it
- understand how long it takes to work with and through a client to solve any particular problem, and
- in general worked through the bugs of your own particular advising system and style.

Thus, do not expect, from Day I, to open your shop with a full range of standardized proposal options. It's just not realistic. But do, from Day I, set as an intermediate objective for yourself and the development of your business, reviewing your situation after four to 6 months to see whether you are in fact ready to develop standard proposal options.

Pros and Cons of Standard Proposal Options

As with any business technique, utilizing standard proposal options has both its positive and negative aspects. On the positive side, a standard proposal option clearly indicates to the prospect that you thought through the problem(s) they are facing, that you've faced them before, that you've developed success techniques which they'll find helpful, and that you can apply these techniques through your controlled problem solving process, which is in fact embodied in the standard proposal option.

The standard proposal option very clearly indicates that you are the consummate professional, the complete advisor knowledgeable about the prospect's situation and which techniques will help him achieve the success which both of you want.

On the other hand, unless the presentation of a standard proposal option is properly handled, the prospect may come away with the feeling that you are merely trying to sell a packaged solution rather than one which is tailored to their specific needs. Each prospect, no matter how small and insignificant, deeply wishes to believe that his problem is unique and different from anyone else's. Of course, as an advisor you know differently: I don't think that I've seen anything particularly distinctive in my practice since I ceased being a novice, and you'll soon find yourself in the same situation if you're not already there. Client prospect problems are never as unusual as they'd like us, as their advisors, to believe. Which is not, however, to say that we don't have to take into account their little prejudice on this matter.

This, then, is the magic we must weave: on the one hand we must convince the prospect that the problem they have is one we already understand in full and have previously confronted (if only in part). That, therefore, we have the necessary understanding, technical skills, and expertise to polish it off expeditiously. On the other hand, we must assure the prospect that while we understand the problem and have tested solution techniques we are not forgetting that their situation will, in fact, differ in certain (perhaps critical) particulars from others and that we intend to vary and adapt our methods accordingly. This problem, of course, doesn't exist with the *ad hoc* proposal, for that is clearly developed in response to a particular problem.

There are several ways to assure and reassure the prospect that he is not merely getting someone else's reheated gruel or your own hobbyhorse solution:

- As you come to understand distinctive aspects of the prospect's situation, point out to the prospect that you have seen and assimilated them. Let the prospect know that these can be satisfactorily dealt with within the parameters of your standardized proposal contract.
- Raise the prospect's (usually implicit) fear that he'll be treated just like everyone else and that the distinctive aspects of his situation will not be satisfactorily dealt with. Then show what you intend to do (within or without the matrix of your standardized proposal option) to make sure this worst case scenario does not in fact occur.

Remember: there is nothing wrong with both raising the prospect's (probable) worst fears and addressing them. Let's face it: every prospect always wonders whether the step he is about to take is a sensible one. Most sensible people don't go blindly into a situation without considering the downside risk that is involved in the course of action they are contemplating. So don't pretend that these fears and anxieties don't exist, and do go out of your way to raise them and conclusively to lay them to rest. This is part of developing a genuine, authentic relationship both with the prospect and the client into which he (if you are successful) is transformed. I must stress yet again that there is nothing wrong or unnatural about the prospect having (at least most of) the fears he has. There is nothing professional about you refusing to raise this issue either because you feel squeamish about doing so or because this approach doesn't fit in with your usual sales technique. Dealing with the prospect's reasonable (and often unreasonable) anxieties definitely has a place in your marketing approach, and the sooner you learn how to raise these anxieties in a nonthreatening, problem solving way, the more effective you'll become when prospecting for new clients.

Towards Developing Your Standardized Proposal Options

The first months you are in business as an advisor, you need to be fairly rigorous about keeping time charts dealing with the various problems you are dealing with and all the things you must do (either directly or as the mandarin organizer) to solve them. Without knowing how long it takes you to solve problems, you will have a very hard time creating a standardized proposal option. Be as specific as possible! Here, for instance, is a list of all the things I must do each time I fashion a successful fund raising proposal for a nonprofit client:

- Meet with client to ascertain their capital, project and operating fund raising objectives.
- Review giving for past two years in each area from corporations, foundations and individuals to determine the possibility of reaching these objectives.
- Make a determination about what is a reasonable fund raising objective in each category.
- Outline a basic fund raising proposal document.
- Work with client to gather information suitable for each category of the document.
- Write document.
- Work with client to incorporate client's comments after an initial reading.
- Rewrite and edit document.

- Work with client Board of Directors to explain this draft, which they may wish to change.
- Rewrite and edit based on Board of Director comments.
- Oversee actual production of document.

This just gets us up to the point of having a single document! Similarly, the steps must be laid out for analyzing who to send the document to, what amount to ask for, how to train the volunteer solicitors, how to handle a successful solicitation meeting, and all the other myriad steps which must go into successful fund raising at any level.

The objective in writing down everything that you do as an advisor in the early days of your practice and keeping good time sheets is clear:

- You want to be able to fashion a Standardized Delphic Oracle contract (that is, a contract where you set tasks and the prospect follows them working under your direction) and a Standardized Full Service contract (where you directly do more and more of the tasks needing to be accomplished). Since each of these contract options is in fact based on the amount of time you'll be involved in either overseeing or directly doing tasks, you have to have a very clear sense of how long it takes you. This means keeping good time records.
- You also want to have a very clear understanding of all the various steps that necessarily go into the solution of any given problem. This is helpful not only in fashioning your standardized proposal options but in acquainting the prospect with all that must happen before his desired outcome is in fact attainable. People who are not knowledgeable about a given field may have the very blithest ideas of what it takes to succeed and all that must be done to help them get to where they want go. It is very much in the interest of your successful relationship to disabuse them of any curious notions they may (and probably do) possess.

What Next

Once you have listed all the solution-steps you need for each problem, then create a work sheet for a Delphic Oracle standardized proposal option and one for the Full Service option. Write down on each sheet just what you intend to do directly (Full Service option) and what you intend to oversee (Delphic Oracle option) while the client does the actual tasks themselves. Now write down next to each step precisely how long it takes to accomplish it. (Don't forget the 20% margin of error for tasks you have previously confronted, which ought to be everything on these pages, of course!)

From this list of tasks which need to be accomplished before the problem (or problems) in question can be solved, you can make an estimate of the total time commitment needed and, thus, come up with the cost of this contract option. This cost can either be cited as a fixed, flat fee (as in my Delphic Oracle option) or as a range (as in my Full Service option).

Writing The Actual Standardized Proposal

A proposal, any proposal, is necessarily a marketing document. It must, therefore, always deal with the problem(s) of the prospect (both those he understands and those he may not) and the cost-effective, expeditious solutions you offer. You have to sell:

- the importance of the problem
- the possible consequences if action is not taken now to solve it
- the disproportionate benefits which come with your problem solving methods
- your own standing as the solution guru.

Your first problem is how to present this information in a way that most simply and clearly persuades the prospect that:

- The problem is important.
- It must be faced now if there are not to be adverse, even tragic consequences.
- The benefits of your problem solving methods are indeed disproportionate to your fee.
- You are the solution guru *par excellence*.

To this end, I myself prefer what I call the Question-Answer Standardized Proposal documents. Before I discuss them, take a moment to read the samples on pages 292 and 294.

Constructing The Effective Question-Answer Standardized Proposal

I often call this the info-document because, unlike standard advertising copy or brochures, it is packed with the kind of information that the prospect really needs to make an intelligent decision. With this document you begin to function as the advisor, begin to function, that is, as the informed, knowledgeable, sober, results-oriented problem solver who:

- understands the problem
- has solutions which work
- understands how to get the desired outcomes, and

- has an effective, controlled, problem solving methodology at your finger tips which comes as close as anything can to guaranteeing the much-desired disproportionate benefit compared to your fee.

Start With The Problem

I've stressed and stressed again the need to understand the client prospect's possible problems. Now write down, in either logical or priority order, the problems the prospect may face, may want you, the expert advisor, to assist with. Start the document off with a list of problems that the prospect very likely knows he has and wants to deal with.

Then let the client know (as, in the Cooperative Service Plan, I have done in the box) there is a cost-effective, economical, affordable solution at hand. "Do you have this problem?," you are saying in effect. "A solution is readily at hand!"

Isn't this really what the prospect wants to know? At least to start with?

Now ask and answer the following questions, as in the samples:

- What is this (either Full Service or Cooperative Service Plan)?

Frankly inform your prospects that in the one plan you do more of the tasks directly and in the other you work with them (don't say: "You do the work!") as their ongoing advisor setting tasks for them to accomplish, giving them advice on how to accomplish them and reviewing progress.

- How does it work? Tell people precisely:
    — how often you meet
    — for how long
    — what can be discussed
    — how each meeting will conclude.

Give the prospect a sense of your mastery over the situation: that you not only know what the problems are (and the consequences of not dealing with them) but that you have a precise problem solving plan for dealing with them, perfected in every detail.

- What is discussed? Tell the prospect!
- Where do the meetings take place? If you follow my model, the bulk of meetings under the Delphic Oracle option take place at your office with the key exceptions of one or two meetings (or more, if you decide it is necessary to the success of your undertaking) with the upper echelon of decision makers at their offices. In the Delphic Oracle Standardized Proposal make sure you tell people why the meetings are being held at your office and what the benefit is to the prospect. All prospects like to save money; let them know this is an option.
- Does (your company name) ever come to your client's offices? Tell them under what conditions you go to their offices and why. Again, indicate your mastery over the problem solving process.
- Does (your company name) make any special requirements of (upper management, decision makers, &c)? If you have determined through your experience in solving this problem or cluster of problems that certain people must do certain things, say so. There is no point gilding the lily. There is every reason for being candid if what you want will in fact help ensure success.
- Who will you meet with? Use this section to build your own success credentials. Tell the prospect about the organizations you have worked for, the problems you have confronted successfully, the success (in context) that resulted. Provide the prospect with a sense of your standing in the profession. Your objective is to stand tall as the problem solving guru, not merely someone who has been places but whose presence has made a significant difference in the lives of people like the one who is reading this document.
- What is the cost of the plan? Provide either a fixed, flat fee or a fee range.
- Is all time billable? Set down your "free" versus "fee" time policy. Tell people under what circumstances they get your "free" time. Let them know that not everyone does (hence the wording "qualified client prospects"). Inform the prospect, too, about whether the cost of any billable time they happen to buy before the actual commencement of your working relationship can be applied to the cost of the contract.
- What are the major differences between the Cooperative Service Plan and the Full Service Plan? Always let the prospect know there is something better to buy, or something less expensive to buy (in case you have pitched the more expensive option to a prospect with fewer resources and/or less commitment to solving the problem.) Outline the differences in:
    — travel arrangements
    — the telephone privilege
    — actually doing *vis à vis* overseeing certain tasks
    — the number and duration of meetings with upper level decision makers.

- What is the cost of the Full Service Contract. Provide fixed, flat fee or cost range information and provide information (as in in-state, out-of-state) as to what determines the difference.
- Why would an organization choose the Cooperative Service Plan? Provide the best reasons why the prospect would want this plan. One, clearly, is cost. The other is that it is in effect a training program which will, at its conclusion, leave the prospect prepared to do the task and solve the problem without you.
- What next? Plainly tell the prospect what you want him to do, or what you will do. If you send your standardized proposals out in large numbers like I do, you won't even necessarily know who gets them; they are, for instance, found occasionally in the backs of my books if we find there are extra pages in the final signature. Then you must be quite specific about what you want the prospect to do. If, on the other hand, you are selectively mailing these proposals, then you may wish to indicate that you'll do the following up. At this point in my career, I prefer the first alternative!
- Add an "Anything else?" category. Anticipate what the prospect's reaction will be. Most prospects will not take the first advisor they run into. They are going to shop around. So turn this into an advantage for you. If you are the least expensive in your area, the most productive, the best thought of, say so. Let your prospects know that you, too, keep looking at the competition and that your service is based on what you know of them and on your own significant track record. Don't assume the prospect will know this. They probably won't. If you want it known, say it yourself. There's nothing wrong with this!

Notes On The Cooperative Service Proposal

The Cooperative Service Plan works because you function as a mandarin, providing constancy, oversight, an intelligent matrix, and ongoing supervision; the client works closely with you to achieve his objectives. The document, therefore, must breathe a spirit of cooperation and teamwork. It must be a warm document suggesting that:

- You understand the prospect's problem(s).
- You can solve them.
- You have developed a series of steps, techniques and procedures which, if you do your part and the client does his part, have a reasonable likelihood of achieving success.
- You can offer these steps, techniques and procedures at a lesser cost because most of your client-advisor meetings will take place in your office, thereby putting the onus and expense of travel on the client.

What I like about this approach to problem solving is that you, the expert, get a chance to do what you do best: solve problems, and the client gets the benefit of your expertise at a reasonable cost. The Cooperative Service Proposal should breathe the spirit of this kind of constructive cooperation.

Some people looking at this document insist that there are too many words in it. That it doesn't look like a brochure and that it will put the prospect off because it is so densely written. I strongly disagree.

People who have a particular problem and who have made the necessary commitment to solve it (rather than merely casually reviewing possibilities) will read your info-rich proposal with great and careful interest. These people want to know that you truly understand what their problem is and that you are a reasonable bet for solving it. Don't sacrifice the information you need for slick graphics which may succeed in making a document look nice but cannot necessarily persuade the prospect that you know what you are doing. It's different, of course, if you are in the business of graphic advising and production. Then the medium is the message. For the rest of us, however, it's better to write a dense info-document. I might say, by the way, that my prospects and clients have never complained about the information density of my documents; it's my neophyte students who occasionally do. Got it?

The Full Service Proposal

The Full Service Proposal follows the guidelines I've just laid down but often with a quite significant difference. As you will notice, the Cooperative Service Proposal on page 292 is a warm document. It breathes a spirit of constructive cordiality and camaraderie. The Full Service example on page 294 is different. It is an In-command Infocrat document, cool and commanding. There is a good reason why.

As I mentioned before, it is the client (as much as the advisor himself) who wishes to elevate the advisor to godly status. Many clients wish to thrust their problems and the need to solve them onto the shoulders of a (usually unwary) advisor and say, in effect, "Here, now the mess is yours. Sort it out." Some problems, to be sure, lend themselves to this mode of solving them, but not very many. In most cases the client must be intimately involved (if only to ensure the cooperation of key personnel) in solving the problem. New advisors (and some old ones, too, I must confess) find it easy to take on the mantle of their godhead. It is, after all, a heady experience. It is also a dangerous one, for the god who fails is the god who gets derided, scorned and abandoned. I prefer, therefore, mere mortality to the delights of deitydom. That's why I write cool proposal documents (both *ad hoc* and standardized) for situations where, without great difficulty, the client could thrust too much responsibility on me, thereby weasling out of his own rightful burdens. Such an approach is absolutely necessary when other people (whom, of course, as an advisor you can only advise and not control) are crucial in the problem solving process, as they are in the sample on page 294.

This document begins with a cool, admonitory preamble. This preamble says, one way and another:

- If you have a certain objective, we "may" be able to help. Right in the first paragraph, I want to make it plain that I am not godlike, cannot solve all problems, and may not be able to solve yours. In other words, that I reserve the right to be selective in the pursuit of clients. The prospect must come to believe and to know that your selection of him as a client is the first step on the road to the solution of his problem, that the very process of selection itself is a part of the solution. The good advisor cannot be all things to all people; he must pick and choose. If the prospect clearly understands this, understands that you, as much as he, is looking for a fit, for chemistry (if you will) as well as mutually agreed upon objectives, then your professional relationship will be more likely to flourish and you will be more likely to get the assignment.

- If you proceed without knowing what you're doing, it will be worse than doing nothing at all. This is a very important message to get out to your prospects! Americans tend (quite incorrectly) to equate movement with progress. Nothing could be further from the truth. A situation with present imperfections may actually be better (objectively speaking) than a random and careless attempt to improve matters. Thus, you must conjure up in your prospects a sense of what can happen to them if they proceed without adequate planning and forethought. As I write this paragraph, for instance, I am thinking of a Massachusetts based orphanage which came to me a couple of years ago to save a faltering capital fund raising drive for a new building. Without an overall plan, they had hired architects who had designed an attractive new building for them but at a cost of some $75,000 in fees. Another advisor on the project had taken about $50,000 in fees, for something or other. By the time the board members got to me they had raised just about $150,000 of which all but $50,000 was gone to pay these fees. They were in deep despair. What had gone wrong? What should they do?

The first thing that had gone wrong was that they hadn't considered the possibilities of failure and had proceeded on the utterly characteristic, naive American notion that "We can do it!" without realistically planning how to do it. Utterly predictably, they'd landed up in the soup — to the entire detriment of the ill-housed orphans.

Thus, it is your responsibility to let your prospects know, as coolly as you need to, just what can happen to them if they proceed in ways which are not sensible, are not in keeping with the success techniques which you have available.

N.B. In the case above, my professional review of the situation pointed out that the vast sums the architect had persuaded them they would need for the building could not be raised from their constituency and that a more simple, less expensive rehabilitation of the existing facility made the most sense. The board was forced to buy this diminished expectation which, had they heard it originally, should not have pained them. For, of course, this course of action made all their previous plans — and the expenses that went along with them — worthless. A good advisor — like me! — could thus have saved at least $125,000 for a trifling fraction of the cost. Heed me, reader, heed me!

What Is The First Step?

There are prerequisites to attaining success in any field. You as the expert advisor certainly know what they are in your field — or you are not worth your fee. Now, it is your responsibility to impart the most complete sense of these prerequisites to your prospects. As I've said before, you may feel squeamish about doing so for fear that this knowledge will cause the prospect to draw back, to postpone, or even abandon the project. But that's all right: you should want (professionally and, indeed, morally) to work only with those who can benefit from the experience. In the case of the orphanage, for instance, it is most assuredly the fact that the architects got a lucrative contract. You can be assured, however, that their disgruntled client will not speak well of them. Of course, there will also be for the advisor no success to leverage for future business. Personally, I like to think that some vengeful archangel will later, and appropriately, bring the (at the very least) overzealous advisor to punishment.

As you will see from reading this section of the Standardized Full Service Proposal, I go to address the decision makers of the organization on what will be expected of them. I know as an expert what these people must do, and I know, too, what will happen (or, more accurately, not happen) if they fail to do it. It is my responsibility to my prospect, my profession, and to myself to make sure that this message is delivered as clearly and persuasively as possible. Does this cost me clients? Yes, from time to time it does, but I no longer worry about this: such prospects are merely window shopping and are indulging in the typically American search of trying to get something for nothing. As advisors we can scarcely fail to encounter such people. When we do, at the very least we can put the fear of the Lord in them about what they really should be doing to achieve success. I, for one, take a great deal of positively puritanical glee from this experience — besides getting paid for it, since it is, after all, quite a proper advising role and well worth the money. I should tell you, of course, that in this way I have ended up persuading quite a few (not yet ready) prospects to postpone (and perhaps abandon) their plans, at least until the necessary success prerequisites have been met.

How Should The Decision Maker Prepare Himself?

If you want to be treated seriously by your prospects (and, of course you do!) ask them to prepare for the experience of getting together to meet with you to pursue a solution to their problem. This course of action has several benefits:

- It gives you some feeling for the degree of their seriousness in wanting to solve the problem. You can bet your life that people who will not prepare for a meeting with you, which is a necessary part of the process of moving towards a solution, will be less likely to provide you with the cooperation and assistance you need from them during the actual work on the solution than those who will prepare.

- It provides decision makers with critical background information on what they must do and what you should do to solve the problem. The more detailed this information, the better. This is why I advise boards of directors (nonprofit decision makers) to read appropriate sections from my book **DEVELOPMENT TODAY: A FUND RAISING GUIDE FOR NONPROFIT ORGANIZATIONS**. Having done so they'll have a very good indication of who does what, when and how — including, of course, themselves, the decision makers. As a result their questions are much more precise and professional, their pie in the sky expectations are somewhat lower than they might otherwise have been, and I can assume my role of advising them how they should proceed — now and through a subsequent series of steps — to achieve the objective they say they wish to achieve.

Some of my (more naive) students are quite frankly shocked at this approach. They say things like, "But you are applying for a job and you're asking *them*, your future employers, to prepare for *your* interview!"

It is of course true that I am looking for an assignment, but more than that I am looking for a match. I am attempting to ascertain the degree of necessary seriousness in the prospect. Does he really want a success? Or is he merely talking the usual American success rhetoric, so prevalent, so meaningless? I must find out. My job as an advisor, after all, is to work with the client to bring about success. If there is no success, there can be no leverage for future clients for me and, worse, there may be a disgruntled past client at my rear stirring up dissatisfaction and speaking unspeakable calumnies to others who might otherwise have used my services. No, I have every right to do what it takes to compel the prospect to take this situation seriously. And, of course, they have every right, conversely, to do whatever it takes to reassure themselves as to my ability to grasp their problem and to work with them in solving it. Thus, it is quite right that the decision makers should prepare themselves on points I regard as essential and should require of me materials which they regard as significant.

What Is The Initial Responsibility Of The Decision Maker?

I have found that the realization of success involves the achievement of an often vast number of relatively small and short term steps. It is your responsibility to set down all the necessary steps a prospect needs to take to realize the success he wants and to ascertain, as quickly as possible, his ability to negotiate them in reasonable fashion. Then tell the decision makers just what they must do first. Just as you will tell them, in due course, precisely what must be done next.

What Then?

This short question opens a most important section. This section says that once you, the advisor, have satisfied yourself that the prospect is likely to realize his objectives, then you will be happy to work with him. A contractual relationship can then be begun.

What Does Your Company Do As The Client's Advisor?

List the tasks that you perform under a Full Service Contract. Leave nothing out. If you must do something to realize the prospect's objective, then include it.

Where Do The Meetings Take Place?

Under this standardized proposal option, the meetings take place wherever the client wishes and include those individuals both of you deem essential to the project.

How Often Do Meetings Take Place?

Specify your meeting terms. Meetings are generally longer under the Full Service arrangement than under the Cooperative Service Plan, where I, at least, keep them fairly rigidly to one hour each week.

Who Will You Meet With?

As in the standardized Cooperative Service Proposal, this is a marketing paragraph about you, giving a dramatic sense of your ability to understand and solve their problems based on the advising relationships you have previously had. Do, by all means, put all your successes into a context that makes them meaningful to the reader who has the problem you can solve.

What Happens Between Meetings?

Clients under this arrangement are buying the "telephone privilege", and thus have access to you on an around-the-clock basis.

Note: It has been my experience that clients paying the greater sum for the Full Service Contract will make very limited use of the "telephone privilege." They want it because they prize their access to you, their advisor; this access comforts them. But they will not abuse the privilege. Moreover, if you are properly arranging your regular meetings with tasks needing to be accomplished, the kinds of questions you are likely to get will be short and to the point, often capable of being dealt with in a minute or two, a quarter hour at the most. Your task, however, is to figure out how many hours of telephone privilege you should sell them and how many they will actually use. As a rough rule of thumb, you can sell an hour of telephone privilege for every 10 hours of direct client contact.

What Is The Cost?

You should here offer a cost range, a range which will be different, of course, depending on whether the prospect is local or not.

Are There Alternatives?

It is always possible that the person reading this document is not, in fact, ready for your most expensive (no matter how valuable) contract option. They may not yet have accomplished the necessary success prerequisites, or they may not really have the money. Thus, always indicate what your less expensive alternative is, and give some indication of how it works.

Is All Time Billable Under The Full-Service Contract?

Indicate here how you handle your "free" versus "fee" time, and whether any "fee" time before a formal contract is entered into is credited against the overall cost of that contract.

What About References?

Before I trouble a client for a reference, I want to be absolutely sure that the prospect is both qualified to work with me and serious about doing so. At that point, I will present what I term a "context reference," that is, an individual or organization who has had a relatively similar problem that I have been able to help solve. I ordinarily inform my clients that they will not be troubled with a vast multitude of reference calls on my behalf, but that if they do receive such a call, I would be most grateful if they'd handle it with the utmost seriousness. They do! Use a context reference at the moment it will do the most good: after the prospect has been qualified and needs only the final push of knowing that you can in fact deliver success. Then such a reference can be invaluable.

What Next?

Tell people what they now must do to begin the process of moving to success. As you see, I have advised a prospect to read **DEVELOPMENT TODAY** and, having done so, to see about setting up a prospect meeting. It is also perfectly permissible to invite them to call you and to send those documents (which you should precisely enumerate) you need to review before scheduling this meeting. Lay out the necessary steps for the prospect. At all times your job is to indicate mastery and control, to show, in short, that you have a well-thought out plan which, if the prospect follows it, gives him an enhanced likelihood of realizing the success he says he wants

Anything Else?

As I've already said, prospects will shop around. Since they are going to do so anyway, let them know what they are likely to find and what it means. Be honest with them! The more they find out that what you say is the truth, the more trust in you they will have and the more likely you are to get their business — and to work well with you once you've secured the contract.

A Few Words On The Composition And Production Of Your Standardized Proposal Documents

In these standardized proposal documents, as in all proposals, you should already be functioning as the prospect's advisor, for you are infinitely better off early adopting and sticking to the principal role you will have with the prospect: that of an expert who can help him solve that series of problems which needs to be dealt with before his principal objective can be reached. The documents you produce, therefore, should be warm or cool, as you decide, and should be packed with problem solving information of interest to the prospect. To that point, I've already spoken.

What is clear, however, is that the longer you are in the advising business, the more precise your perception of your prospect's problems will be and the more you will understand about how they should be approached and what needs to be done by whom at what time to solve them. Thus, don't print tens of thousands of your standardized proposals until you are absolutely sure that for at least a year your operating procedures regarding that particular problem (or set of problems) will not change substantially. Consider printing, therefore, no more than 1000 such proposals, and this number if and only if you intend to engage in assertive marketing of the kind I have been suggesting to you. The cost of printing 1000 copies of a two sided, 8 1/2 by 11 inch standardized proposal should be somewhere between $85 and $100, exclusive of typesetting.

Notes On Distributing Your Standardized Proposals

Personally, I use my standardized proposals (like my précis and catalog) in lieu of the business card I do not have. I therefore carry a few with me wherever I go, particularly, of course, to places (be they workshops or conferences) where prospects are likely to be in attendance. I make it a point to give this kind of information to whoever I meet. I reason thus: if I have done my homework correctly and am truly ready and able to solve a pressing problem that my prospect has now or is likely to have in the future, then it is my obligation to bring to his attention my availability to solve that problem. Some people may find this pushy. I cannot agree. I look upon this alerting process as an invaluable service to people who very likely will need me sooner or later and who may (in typical human fashion) need to hear about my problem solving abilities in several ways before they take action. Let this way be one of them and so move the process along to a mutually beneficial conclusion.

More conventionally, send your standardized proposals along in the first batch of information you send to a client prospect. Make sure you include both the Cooperative Service Plan and the Full Service Plan to give the prospect an indication of the range of your services. Inform the prospect that you'll be back in touch after he's had the opportunity to review both options. At that point you can ascertain which is of the more interest and proceed accordingly. Do not begin a relationship with a Cooperative Service client in a Full Service manner, or vice versa. Consistency of approach is of the utmost importance in establishing a productive client-advisor relationship.

So is a complete written contract.

CHAPTER 9

Developing the Successful Client Relationship II:
Contracts, or "Good Fences Make Good Neighbors"

It was Robert Frost, that quintessential Yankee poet, who reminded us that "good fences make good neighbors". All a contract is, in whatever form it comes, is simply a good fence. It sets down what each party will do, when it will do it, its rights, its remedies in case things do not go as planned, and what remuneration can be expected for fulfilling the obligations set forth. It's really quite simple.

Why, then, in my workshops do participants approach the entire matter of contracts with such a heavy heart and with so many questions? Essentially, I think this happens for two major reasons: one technical and procedural, the second, more difficult and burdensome, psychological. Let's, therefore, start with the second.

Developing The Right State of Mind To Develop Good Contracts

I remember when I first went into business. I felt, if occasionally terrified at the choice I had made, essentially free, lighthearted, filled with good will towards my fellow creatures, and enthusiastic about the course I had taken. Sound familiar? People approach their first business venture with something of the same state of mind with which they approach a new lover, the happiness, confidence and optimism that stem from that relationship permeate all other facets of your life, too. So it is when you start a new business.

As a result, you may find yourself pooh-poohing the importance of contracts, thinking instead that like you all others are good, honorable, reasonable people who, equally like you, intend to do what they say they are going to do, when they are going to do it. As a result, you may eschew the cautious notion of writing down these obligations and may feel that contracts are unnecessary, even insulting.

I need hardly say this attitude usually sours and such procedures all too often lead to the destruction, too, of family and friend relationships which would have been better served if more conventional methods were adhered to.

Let me say, then, particularly to those of you who may even now be in that state of hothouse enthusiasm produced by the opening of your new advising business: beware, be careful, be cautious, be conservative.

There's nothing wrong, and much that is right, with writing down the expectations of all parties to a relationship, with exercising good common sense about telling who will do what when, with identifying common problems which may very well arise and suggesting how they will be handled, with clearly outlining how all monetary matters will be dealt with, and what the parties are allowed to do if one or more does not do what he originally said he would. While to those of you who already have business experience, what I am about to say may sound odd, even ingenuous, let me assure you many other of my readers need to hear this: namely, that you are not a suspicious or even a particularly doubting person by suggesting, indeed insisting, on a contract, nor that by having a contract you expect or even suspect the other party will not follow through: you are merely erecting a good, stout fence which makes it very clear just what should happen when, and what will happen if it doesn't. Remember your Frost: more problems arise from the absence of the fence than from its existence.

The Problem Solving Process And Your Contracts

As should be clear by now, the Problem Solving Process has many implications:
- It helps you structure your relationship with a client prospect by giving you a series of tasks which must be accomplished, either individually or sequentially, in order for the client to reach his objectives.
- It helps you structure any proposal which you may send to the client prospect (in contractual language "the offer" which you extend to the client for his possible acceptance). Thus, a proposal should address each of the following points insofar as they are relevant to the prospect's situation:

    — Are you, the prospect, mentally prepared to achieve success?

    — Are you technically prepared?

    — Do you know what the real problem is?

    — Do you understand the real problem and a potential range of solutions open to decision makers?

    — What documents need to be developed to help solve the problem?

- What implementation strategy needs to be followed and is feasible to help solve the problem?
- How will success be reported to decision makers, and how will possible failure be dealt with?
- What arrangements are there for a clinic, an evaluation process?

During the proposal negotiation process, you and the prospect should have worked out detailed answers to each of these points so that it is clear to each of you what needs to be done, why this needs to be done, who will do it, and when this needs to be done. If this has all taken place, the contract that necessarily follows should neither be difficult to arrange nor in any way surprising to either party.

Sadly, however, (or perhaps I should better say, infuriatingly) most contract books either gloss over or entirely neglect several of these important points, thus helping to create later problems for the parties. While I, too, shall not hesitate in a moment to recommend the inclusion of more standard contractual fare, before doing so I wish to point out certain areas which need to be dealt with in most contracts and which stem from a complete understanding of the Problem Solving Process.

Mental Prerequisites For Success

I have previously stressed and must now stress again the question of securing the client's understanding and acknowledgement that there is a proper mental attitude needed in ensuring success. In large measure, this attitude means getting the client to acknowledge that the client-advisor relationship is a cooperative one, namely that there are things the advisor must do to ensure success; equally, that there are things that the client must do. Unlike many of my colleagues, I do not leave this matter to chance: I ask in the proposal, and then in the contract itself, for the client's explicit acknowledgement that he understands he must work with me cooperatively in bringing about the desired success, that I cannot unilaterally ensure and bring about this success, and that should the client fail to work with me then whatever success results will necessarily be limited.

Most seasoned advisors, of course, understand that in most client-advisor situations the parties must work cooperatively to achieve success. Why, then, do they fail to specify in the contract that such cooperation must take place? Often, this omission comes about because the point must seem obvious to the advisor. Watch out for that!!

As I have previously mentioned, in many instances the client, whatever he says to the contrary in the palmy days of contract negotiations and hail-fellow-well-met bonhomie, wishes to thrust the burden of responsibility onto the advisor, to make the advisor the god-scapegoat and so eschew his own burden. But, as you have already seen, in most advisor-client relationships, the advisor is not ideally placed to bear this responsibility, since the realization of the desired objective is necessarily a cooperative undertaking, one in which each party should have clearly defined tasks.

However, if you fail to include in the contract any mention of this need for continuing cooperation, then it is easy for the client to forget the significance of the point, a development which may very well come back to haunt you later when the "Dog Ate My Homework" Syndrome begins to work against you, and other individuals and other problems solving processes seem more alluring than you and your own.

You must remember that the enthusiasm with which the client enters into a relationship with you will wane. That is inevitable. You must remember that a new face is always more attractive than an old face. And that when you are that new face, it's very easy (indeed seductively tempting) to forget that in due course you'll become the old face, the old face who had better have clearly available all the necessary tools to motivate and move your now grudging client to do what is in his own best interests. Secure these tools when you don't need them, so that they'll be readily available when you do.

Thus, your contract must set forth as simply and straightforwardly as possible, the fact that both parties understand and acknowledge that the agreement into which you are entering is a cooperative one. That each party understands that neither party individually can achieve the desired results (unless, in fact, one party can actually guarantee them).

Unless you have a clause stating this point, there may very well come a moment when you need to motivate the client again to become actively involved in the problem solving process but have no mutually acknowledged understanding from which to launch your attack. This understanding must be contained in the contract, for it is unthinkable, of course, that you would ever sue a client to remotivate him!

Reporting Success, Foreshadowing Failure

Another problem generally neglected in the contract literature is the whole matter of how success and failure will be reported and dealt with. Advisors too often make the mistake of assuming that they will be able to get access to decision makers when necessary both to report on the aspects of their projects which are going well and the aspects which are not. This is a mistake. You must think out in advance and secure the agreement of the client prospect during contract negotiations on exactly how you wish to report success and how you wish to deal with reporting (and counteracting) failure should this become necessary during your stint as the organization's advisor.

As you have already seen, in my own Delphic Oracle contracts I allow for two meetings a year between myself, the advisor, and the senior decision makers of my client. This has proven to be adequate for the kind of advising I generally do. Your requirements may, of course, be different; what will not be different, however, is the need for such meetings. Make no mistake about it: be as specific as possible about exactly who you should see and how often you should see this person. If at that moment the meeting is not necessary, so be it. It is easier to postpone or cancel such a meeting than it is to persuade a by then perhaps reluctant administrator to have it at all.

Including The Clinic

The clinic, too, is another neglected area of contracts. Most advisors foolishly conclude a project with a client and go on their way without a backward glance. This is very, very, stupid. Remember: if you have done your work well with a client, you'll get several benefits. You'll get good recommendations, which should lead to future assignments. You'll have the possibility of being invited back when a similar or related problem developes. But the value of these benefits recedes as you do, on the "Out of Sight, Out of Mind" Principle. The client has to see you from time to time, has to remember the value of your work, has to be subtly (and sometimes not so subtly) reminded of all that you did and how valuable you were to them.

Don't just let this happen on a "catch as catch can" basis. Put it in your contract. First of all, it is very beneficial to the client to have you, the expert advisor, come back at regular intervals (generally three times following the formal conclusion of your regular relationship) and review their position. Without the guiding hand of the advisor, it is all too easy for the client to slacken and fail to keep moving toward his objectives as briskly as when you were there. Thus, the client will ordinarily be (if a little sheepish for failing to keep moving ahead as you both agreed he should) very happy to see you, glad to get a shot of your infectious motivation, enthusiasm and necessary reprise of your problem solving techniques.

By the same token, you should welcome the opportunity to return to the client in a familiar role, a role which should, properly exploited, lead to a continuing relationship with the client who, by now, should have a very clear idea of precisely how meaningful you were to the organization.

Advisors of every level of experience all too often fail to understand that maintaining not merely superficially good but contractually continuing relationships with clients is one of the keys to their success. Sadly, outside of this book you will rarely, if ever, find that this point is stressed. An advisor who means to be successful must keep, like the Roman god Janus, an eye firmly cocked not merely ahead, towards future clients, but back, towards past clients who will be, if properly handled, future clients, too. Don't forget it!

More Conventional Clauses: Background

Contracts are made up of five general areas:

- offer
- acceptance
- consideration
- competency
- legality.

Let's take a quick look at these points.

• Offer

The offer can be either the proposal or the contract itself. It constitutes your request to the client to accept you as his advisor and to do certain specified tasks for certain consideration.

• Acceptance

The acceptance comes about when you and the client agree to terms. This agreement need not be be in writing, but for your protection it is better if it is. I am proceeding on the assumption in this book that while, in the earliest days of your new business euphoria you may wish to eschew written acceptance, this would be a grave mistake. Contracts need to be written.

• Consideration

Consideration is something of value which is promised to you or given in exchange for your services. It need not be money, although this is the most common form of consideration. Although a promise to pay for services may be reckoned as consideration, it is better that some fraction of your payment change hands upon acceptance of the contract terms.

• Competency

An agreement can only be considered binding if the people who sign it understand "the nature and quality of their actions". Thus, minors, the mentally infirm, or someone signing while intoxicated are not competent.

• Legality

The undertaking into which the parties enter with the contract must itself be legal. If it is not, the contract cannot be valid. Contracts also specify which state's laws bind the parties. If the parties are in two states, the state laws of the originating party are those customarily followed.

A Check List Of Contract Clauses

I have already pointed out for your particular attention three key contractual clauses all too often overlooked and neglected by contract signatories. Now I should like to continue with those clauses which virtually every authority agrees should be considered. Remember: while not every contract needs each of these clauses, you should consider the need for a clause before cavalierly dismissing it. If you have any hesitation, include the clause. It is always better to be safe than sorry, since at the time of any contract dispute anything not in the document probably cannot ordinarily be considered and is anyway infinitely easier to dispute than the mutually acknowledged clauses of the contract.

- **Parties Involved**

Who is involved in this contract? Name the parties in the contract and state the date they entered into this agreement.

- **Term Of Contract**

When does the contract begin? When does it end? How many hours are you, the advisor, agreeing to provide to the client and in what time period? Most, but not all, contracts have a specific beginning and end. Some rather acknowledge that a continuing relationship between the parties is hereby commenced, the length of which shall be at the pleasure of both parties. Some (not my favorite, by any means) state that a specific task will be performed but do not specify when it is to be completed. This alternative, it seems to me, contains the seeds of an unhappy relationship.

- **Duties Of The Advisor**

It is very important to be specific about all that you intend to do on the client's behalf, and how this will be done. The more specific you can be the better about:
  - what you will do
  - when you will do each task
  - absolute deadlines and those which are merely advisory
  - where the meetings will take place
  - when
  - how long they can be
  - who will travel.

I have said over and over again that the essence of a satisfactory and satisfying client-advisor relationship is contained in the knowledge of what each person will do and when each person will do it. Don't make any assumptions here. Provide an exhaustive list of precisely what you intend to do and when you intend to do it.

- **Duties Of The Client**

Be clear about what the client will do to facilitate the success of your relationship. As I have stressed again and again, it is a huge mistake (and one which distinguishes the ingenue advisor) not to inform the client about what he needs to do to bring about the success he says he wants. Thus, secure the client's agreement about:
  - What access you need to his staff, place of business, office equipment, supplies and other resources.
  - What financial information, ledgers and books, documents and other materials you need to see, when you need to see them, whose responsibility it is to supply them, and any other assistance you must have from the client to make the best use of such information.
  - What personnel the client must make available to you. The more specific the better! Name both specific individuals and/or job titles which must be a part of the problem solving process.

If you and the client need third party information to help solve the problem, be clear about which of you will get it. Either this clause will appear under "Duties of the Advisor," or it will appear under "Duties of the Client." But if you need the material, don't neglect the clause which ensures that someone knowingly has the responsibility to get it!

Don't fall into the god-magician trap often unconsciously set and baited by the client. Be very, very specific about what you need the client to do and when you need it. Write down a complete list of what you need, why you need it, and the likely ramifications if you don't get it. Share this list with the client. A serious client will understand why you need this information, access and the ongoing interest and involvement of the client. If the client doesn't, it's a clear signal that you are going to have problems which may well sabotage the relationship.

- **Payment For Services**

Of course you want to be paid. So don't be coy about this item! Specify on what basis your fees will be rendered: per diem (in which case specify the number of hours in your day or whether you are selling the client an entire day), fixed rate, fixed rate plus expenses, &c.

- **Late Payments**

All clients will not be prompt about paying their bills. Be clear about what will happen if they aren't. Will you charge a late payment for overdue invoices over a specific period (say 1.5% per month for invoices over 30 days old)? This interest charge should be three to five points higher than prevailing bank interest; the objective, after all, is to get the client to pay the money he owes you.

- **Stop Work Clause**

Some clients will either be careless about paying bills, or will simply be unable to do so. When you are the ingenue advisor, you may be tempted to string along with them in the hopes that their situation will change and you'll get paid. Don't do it! Set very clear guidelines for yourself; get the client to agree to them in the contract and once you've mutually agreed to a policy, abide by it. Thus, indicate at what point you can stop work and how this will be handled. My contracts generally say that a client whose monthly invoice is overdue after 30 days gets charged 1.5% per month interest; that that same client whose invoice is overdue after 60 days agrees and acknowledges that I may stop work without penalty until that bill is paid. Moreover, the client acknowledges that if I must take legal action in pursuit of this bill, all such charges will be owing by the client not by me. Further, I include a clause which states that if I stop work, I may, in my sole discretion, declare the entire unpaid balance of payments owing under this agreement immediately due and payable. Let's see what this means in practice.

Let's say that a client enters into a $11,400 yearly retainer agreement with me. $950 of this amount (the consideration) is due on signature, $950 per month in advance of services for the next 11 months. Under the standard clause in my agreements, upon signature the client owes the $10,450 not paid. If the client does not pay an invoice, after 30 days I bill them at the rate of 1.5% per month; if this same invoice remains unpaid after 60 days, I can suspend services and declare the client in default, which means they owe the entire $10,450 plus applicable interest less payments already made. Under this scenario I have considerable leverage for bargaining.

Some of you may consider this "stop work" clause superfluous. I cannot agree. Sadly, there are people who will exploit you if you let them, who will take advantage of your good spirits and good intentions to urge you along, to invest more and still more of your good time and energy in a proposition where you cannot win. Don't let this happen. Being in business occasionally means failing to have a given situation work out. If you see that the client is not ready to proceed, does not have the money to proceed and simply wishes to jolly you along, activate this clause of your contract. As the Godfather said, "It's nothing personal." If and when the client's situation is rectified, you can reenter your relationship with the same feeling of professionalism that caused you to freeze it for a time.

- **Expenses**

In a fixed price agreement (which I personally agree to only with reluctance), you are of course responsible for the expenses. In all other situations, make sure you specify those items which constitute reimbursable expenses by the client. These include (but are not limited to):

- travel (car travel at the U.S. government's prevailing mileage rate)
- accommodation
- meals at which business is discussed or which take place at odd hours due to the client's requirements
- photocopying on client's behalf
- personnel specially hired for client projects
- telephone calls and fax
- postage and shipping.

Clients, of course, are usually very worried about advisor expenses; the feeling persists (not, I admit, without reason) that advisors are all too often a high-living, expense insensitive breed who care only for their own sybaritic delights. To deal with this point, not only write down a list of reimbursable items but write down a limit up to which you have freedom to spend, beyond which you must secure the client's permission. My limit is $5. Clients are very impressed with this figure; it gives them the assurance that they maintain control over the advisor's expense account. I've operated under this rule for 12 years now and have never had any trouble with it; on many occasions my client's have expressed themselves grateful for my Yankee parsimony.

Make sure you include in the contract the means by which your expenses will be handled (invoicing for them at the end of 30 days, for example) and what will happen if the client does not pay for them within a reasonable (say, 30 day) period; I advise using an interest rate penalty three to five points above the prevailing bank rate. Remember: in many cases you have had to expend money yourself in these situations and if you don't charge such a rate, you have in fact made a free gift to the client. Nice, perhaps, for him, but stupid for you!

A word on dealing with the government, universities and other major institutional clients. Sadly, like most advisors, I have discovered that these institutional clients can be sadly negligent about promptly repaying the expenses of advisors. They are called in the trade "slow but sure pays" and that is certainly true. Some of my university bills go for 90 to 120 days without payment. In such circumstances, I flat out refuse to advance any money for expenses. Once bitten, twice shy.

• Independent Contractor Status

The Internal Revenue Service is very particular about this clause, and for good reason. The IRS wants people to be employees, wants them to pay into Social Security and workman's compensation funds and to have taxes withheld. An implacable (though generally ineffectual) enemy of the underground economy, the IRS will always attempt to show that an individual has been a regular employee (whatever you may be called) instead of an independent contractor. Thus, this clause is most important. State that you are an independent contractor, not the client's employee, and that you are not eligible for and are not participating in any benefit programs or tax withholding operations of the client. These you must do for yourself.

• Work Delegation

One of the sore points in the advising business often occurs when a buyer, enthused by you, comes to discover that, lo and behold!, the actual work will be done by someone else, someone not at your perceived level of expertise. All too often the client feels a sense of letdown, even betrayal, and the relationship gets off to a bad start. Don't let this happen. In the work delegation clause, specify who will actually do what work, under what circumstances you intend to bring in assistants, and if you intend to do this, how you will guarantee to the client's satisfaction the work they do. Sometimes, of course, it is necessary to hire assistants to carry out the work. If so, say so. But don't surprise the client; just like Mother Nature, the client doesn't like to be fooled.

• Noncompetition

The client may wish to restrict you from getting access to his competitors, especially now that you have secured privileged information about his situation. In this case, you must reassure the client that the information you have come to know is considered confidential and will not be used by you in any circumstances. If the client wishes to go further and prevent you from undertaking for anyone else this kind of service, fine. Remember: in the early days of television one of the networks did this with Milton Berle who lived for over twenty years on a very nice annuity resulting from a fat noncompetition clause. This, of course, doesn't happen very often and even in Berle's case the network came to see the fatuity of their action and bought him off with a cash payment. Most clients will rest assured with a clause that indicates you won't take the knowledge you have gained in their situation to their competitors. So make sure you include this.

• Additional Work

Time and time again in my dealings with clients, once I have proven myself capable of doing one thing (the thing I was hired to do), the client begins asking me about a whole host of other matters which are usually beyond the terms of my current engagement. You must adopt a policy about this, for it will happen to you, too! Mine is this: when a client asks questions that I can easily deal with during my regular meetings, even if they may be somewhat outside the terms of our current contract, I deal with them. I have learned long ago that it is detrimental to my longterm relationship to make too much of these exchanges, especially when there are things that I shall want myself: testimonials, recommendations, the client to give a good oral recommendation to a would-be client, write-up in the client's newsletter, referral to client's professional association, &c. Why jeopardize these necessary results of a successful engagement by being picayune?

By the same token, enough is enough. I, therefore, protect myself with a clause in the contract that indicates how we may modify this engagement so that these additional concerns of the client may satisfactorily be dealt with. Remember: if either side in a client-advisor relationship becomes resentful, this resentment can permeate the entire relationship and destroy your effectiveness. Don't let this happen. Thus, prepare in advance for that time when the client, happy with your work, begins to request more and still more of you. Thus, include an additional work clause in your agreements under which both parties acknowledge that the initial terms of their engagement may be extended. And that if they are, this agreement can be modified and amended by the parties in writing before such additional work commences.

• Ownership

Of the many clauses in a contract, this is one of those causing advisors considerable grief. So many wish they had had it previously and often deeply lament not doing so. That's because there is no necessary reason why the documents and materials you create, the software you develop (for software is nothing more than a document) should necessarily belong to the client. As they say, it's negotiable. But if you do not specify the rights you wish to retain, the client, not unnaturally, feels he has secured the whole once he has paid you for your work. However, there is no necessary reason why this must be true. Instead, consider the following possibilities:

- You create documents and materials and allow the client to rent them from you. So long as the client pays a rental fee, the client secures the use over what you have created. This I call the "Howard Hughes" clause, since Hughes, you will remember, leased rather than sold his technical equipment to those needing it.

- You create documents and materials and, in return for an agreed-upon (usually one-time only) fee allow the client to use them in his own situation, towards solving his own problems but not in any other situation. Any other use outside the client's situation would involve payment to you of an additional fee, stipend, royalty, or commission.

- You create documents and materials and in return for an agreed-upon fee (which may be made up in part of an upfront payment and in part of some other fee arrangement) you allow the client to exercise area rights in either a certain geographical area or economic sector.

- You create documents and materials and in return for a fee, the client secures all rights to what you have created and may do with these things what he wants.

Sadly, most advisors, not having considered the complete range of applications for what they know and can do beyond the immediate situation with a particular client, are exceedingly careless and relinquish all rights without considering whether this is sensible or not. You must take into consideration whether that which you are creating in terms of documents, materials, memoranda, training manuals, guidelines and on and on can or may have any further applications beyond the situation of the current client. If so, sell the client inhouse use rights and retain all other rights. If, on the other hand, what you are creating has only unique applications for this client, then relinquishing all rights should not be a problem.

But don't make the mistake of forcing the client to think through what is beneficial for you. It is not the responsibility of your client to contemplate in what other situations you may benefit from that which you are creating for him. Nor do clients who so fail to contemplate your future act with some sort of "fleece the innocent" mentality. In most cases, they simply don't think about anything beyond their own interests, and who can blame them?

Thus, just as the client does not wish you to take information about their situation and practices to possible competitors, so you want to limit what the client may do with techniques, practices, materials and information which have been developed and perfected by you. Thus I tell you this: if what you are doing with this particular client can ever be used in solving anyone else's problem, you had better give earnest consideration to protecting your reuse rights and not simply giving them up by default. Whatever protection you wish to provide yourself had better be in the contract.

• No Guarantee

In considering the question of liability, you must be candid with yourself. As a result of your advice, what can go wrong? Begin by writing down each and every possibility which can go wrong, no matter how farfetched it may seem right now. Once you have this list, you must begin to take what action you can to protect yourself.

For many advisors the first line of defense is what I call the "No Guarantee" clause. If you are like me, you will be providing advice, but the client must actually carry out this advice to get his desired result. Thus, as a development counselor to nonprofit organizations, I advise executive directors and board members on how to raise money. But the actual solicitation of money is the responsibility of these people, not me. Therefore, I must include a "No Guarantee" clause in my contracts, because I cannot guarantee that any nonprofit organization will make one dime working with me, despite the quality of my advice. I do not, after all, control the process that will result in the success. What this means is simple: unless you control, absolutely and positively control, the process that will certainly produce the desired success, you must include a "no guarantee" clause in your contracts.

Occasionally my students are dumbfounded when I talk about this clause: "You mean," they sputter, "that people agree to hire you despite the fact that you not only do not guarantee results but include an explicit no guarantee clause?" I mean just that. I am not a god-magician. I cannot as a reputable advisor promise results that I know are dependent on many people doing many things, not just what I can and will do. Therefore, it is absolutely necessary to include this clause, not just to limit my own liability but to move the client to a clearer understanding of just what he needs to do to achieve success while working with me. Personally, I have found this clause sufficient and have not needed to include the following limited liability clause.

• Limited Liability

It is often a good idea to secure the agreement of the client as to the extent of your liability should something go wrong because of your mistake or breach of contract. It is usually acceptable to limit the extent of this liability to the total value of the contract, in other words, that you will not be held responsible for any amount beyond the gross value of this particular contract. If this contract is open ended, then you'll have to arbitrarily pick an amount beyond which you will not be held accountable. If in your situation a "no guarantee" clause will not suffice (because you can in fact be held accountable) then you must investigate the need for errors and omissions insurance, a subject which I'll discuss later. Such insurance is used to cover those situations where your errors or breach of contract have in fact damaged the client. Still, your contracts should set a limit to your liability.

- **Contingencies**

Do you control, really control, that which will produce all the client is expecting and buying from you? Of course not! Therefore you must specify that as a result of accidents, delays, strikes or supplier problems you cannot be held liable for failing to execute this agreement. Moreover, if you yourself may be subject to certain problems that will delay execution, include this information in the contract so that you will not be held liable. If you anticipate no such problems, then assure the client that you have complete control of the services you intend to render with the exception of those events beyond the control either of yourself or the client.

- **Advertising**

I have stressed over and over again that you wish to leverage your successes with any particular client, to bring them to the attention of others similarly situated who should want to replicate them. However, when you use a client's name, you must secure the client's permission. This clause informs the client that no use will be made of the client, his situation, or any success that develops without his explicit permission.

- **Arbitration**

Disputes will happen. Anticipate them. Usually the parties, even after giving vent to some rather heady language, will settle down and themselves be able to solve their problem. Remember the need for selective hearing. In heated situations, you must remember how to use it! Unfortunately, however, such relatively easy resolution will not always occur. That's why you need an arbitration clause. This clause outlines the procedures the parties must take to resolve their dispute. Resolution, remember, is *always* preferable to submitting yourself to the vagaries and costly procedures of the legal system. Normally provision is made for a dispute to be settled by an independent arbitrator, how this arbitrator will be selected, and how he (an advisor, after all) will be paid.

Most contracts use the language prepared by the American Arbitration Authority, a nonprofit organization which makes arbitrators available at reasonable rates and which exists to settle disputes without the need to throw them into the clogged and expensive courts. Here's their standard language:

- **Standard Arbitration Clause**

Any controversy or claim arising out of or relating to this contract, or the breach therefore, shall be settled by arbitration in accordance with the Commercial Arbitration Rules of the American Arbitration Association, and judgement upon the award rendered by the Arbitrator(s) may be entered in any Court having jurisdiction thereof.

For further information on arbitration write: The American Arbitration Authority, 140 West 51st St., New York, New York 10020. (212) 484-4000.

- **Governing Laws**

This clause simply states that the parties will be governed by the laws of the jurisdiction in which the contract is written.

- **Termination**

This clause sets forth clearly how and under what circumstances the parties can end the contract. Here are some possibilities:
  - There must be mutual agreement between the parties to terminate the agreement. Neither party can independently end it.
  - Either party may terminate the agreement by notifying the other in writing some number of days (usually thirty) before wishing to do so. The other party must accept the first party's decision to end the relationship.
  - Neither party can end the contractual relationship. For the term of engagement, both parties are irrevocably bound.

For myself, I prefer the first of these alternatives.

- **Agreement binding**

State that what is in this document, and in this document only, constitutes the entire agreement between the parties and that in the case where there has been prior contracts, only what is in this one (unless clearly specified to the contrary) shall be binding. This clause normally states that any modification in this agreement must be made in writing and agreed between the parties to be enforceable. In effect, this clause says, "That's all there is, folks!"

- **Signatures**

Each party to the agreement must sign it. Moreover, each person signing the agreement must be authorized to do so, so that this clause must clearly indicate that each signatory is in fact the responsible and authorized individual. Each person's name and title should appear on the document. If a corporation is involved, it's a good idea to affix the corporate seal over the authorized representative's signature.

Is All This Really Necessary?

People continually ask me whether all this is *really* necessary to transact business. What happened to the good old days when a man's word was his bond, when a handshake was sufficient for transactions of staggering value? The answer is that the good old days are not entirely gone and that huge transactions still take place on a good faith-trust basis. Let's face it, there are situations where you know your opposite number so well, have done so much business so satisfactorily and have not had any but minor problems, where proceeding even to the simplest contract would constitute a gross inconvenience and, indeed, an insult. Still, let me reiterate the reasons why a written contract makes sense:

- It's good for your image. When people don't know you and haven't previously done business with you, they will judge you by appearances. A written contract will underscore the fact that you are a sensible professional.

- It helps avoid misunderstandings. Communication is a very tricky process, and it's easy for two people, even two well-meaning and intelligent people, to get things wrong. A contract makes it plain what each party is to do and what happens if they don't. Clarity is the essence of a good advisor-client relationship and at the root of clarity is a precise mutual understanding embodied in a contract.

- It provides recourse against an unsavory client. As I've learned, as you'll learn, not all people are nice. Many are mendacious, untruthful, deceptive, and exploitative. The more lamblike you are, the more you need a contract for self-protection. The more you believe the world is composed of good people, the better off you'll be preparing for the evil ones. As I have learned to my chagrin, there are people out there who'll think nothing of stealing your time, property, ideas and, ultimately, your good nature in hot pursuit of their own goals. *Non illegitimi carborundum.* Contracts help reach this admirable objective.

- It sets out the payment terms. People get buggy about money. Always have, always will. If you don't have a clear, precise agreement about how you'll be paid, expect the client to be difficult about it.

- It confirms you are providing a fee for service. We live in a world where virtually everyone expects something for nothing and will try to get it if they can. I don't blame them. People are taught, one way and another, to regard getting things for free as a game. That's why you had better be very clear and have it mutually understood that your service is being done for a fee, not as a promotion, an advertisement, or as a means of honing and polishing your skills.

- It avoids and limits liability. As you probably are aware, we live in one of the great litigious ages. People thing nothing of threatening each other with legal action at the drop of a hat, or even less. Prepare for this. Many people now understand that winning a legal action can set them up for life — at your expense. This may be, I hope is, abhorrent to you, but it's a stark fact of life in the twentieth century. Thus you must have a document which specifically either avoids or limits your liability in the ways I've already discussed.

- It prevents litigation. This is an extension of the point above. As I have learned to my acute dismay, there are many people in the world who think litigation (at least the threat of litigation) is fun and who will use this threat as (in their mind) a legitimate tool to get their ends. They have coolly assessed the disaster that is our national court system and dare you to sue them for your rights, knowing that such a course of action can be ruinous and is highly destructive psychologically even if you are absolutely in the right. Thus, you must have a means of ensuring that your rights can be safeguarded without getting bogged down in the courts. Hence the need for arbitration as outlined.

- It provides a source for collateral. Contracts may be taken to a bank or other lender and used as collateral for loans. Written promises cannot. It's as simple as that.

- It offers the potential for increasing your income. As I've already pointed out, clients who come to realize your worth (and they will if you carefully follow the steps in this book!) will come to rely on you for more and still more. Remember: all people are looking for a savior and once you have demonstrated even preliminary aptitude for the job, you'll find more and still more thrust upon you as the client comes to realize he can reach his professional objectives through you and get in an afternoon golf game, too. If you do not have a clear and precise contract citing what you will do (and suggesting, at least by implication, what you won't), then the client (with the best will in the world) may very well begin to encroach. The smart clients, of course, will appeal to your not inconsiderable vanity: "You're so clever, I'm sure you know the answer to this (which is not in your contract")." The avaricious client will simply move ahead knowing as they do that you may find it difficult to enforce nebulous boundaries. Either way resentment will build and there will be problems. If a contract has clearly defined tasks, then as you exceed these tasks it is perfectly permissible to extend the terms of your engagement — and make more money.

- It confirms your independent contractor status. Remember: the IRS is out to get you and your money. As an independent advisor, you must be chary about confirming your independent contractor status. Otherwise that may be challenged, leaving you open to difficulties.

- It encourages a client to sign on with you. People, all people, are understandably nervous about doing business with new people. That's only natural. They have undoubtedly been taken in before by those who have not followed through on what they said they were going to do. They fear they could be taken in again. Fast talkers often eschew contracts, or make contracts so vague the buyer has limited protection. If you want to succeed in the advice business, your job is to recognize the client's anxieties, come up with reasonable responses to them, and embody the procedures which will diminish the client's anxieties and help them realize their objectives in the contract. Contracts help build a client's confidence. Do what it takes to build it and to keep it.

Contract Options

There are really four kinds of contract documents you need to master to succeed in the advice business. Each is in fact a full fledged contract, although some are more complete than others. Here they are:

- Letters of Intent
- Full Contract
- Commission Contract
- Independent Contractor Services Agreement.

Let's review each in turn.

Letter of Intent

A letter of intent is the simplest possible contract. Often just a few short paragraphs in length, it is easy to write, contains essential information of interest to the parties, and can be drawn up and dispatched with ease. While any of the above clauses may appear in a letter of intent, this document should at least contain the following provisions:

- parties to the agreement
- date terms agreed to
- precisely what you, the advisor, have agreed to do, by when
- precisely what you need from the client in order to accomplish your work
- agreement as to what you will be paid and in what way
- agreement as to what will happen if you are not paid (interest, stop work, &c)
- agreement as to how any disputes will be handled
- signature of both parties, each party to have a copy of this agreement.

This is basic.

This agreement is appropriate for short-term engagements where the parties have not worked together previously or have not established an on-going relationship.

I am often asked whether you should have such an agreement where the client asks you to begin at once and is under time pressure. The answer is yes, yes you should! Given today's modern communications networks, it is easy to draw up the terms of your engagement and either fax them immediately to the client for confirmation or to provide the terms to the client over the telephone and have him type them up and send them overnight to you. What I have found in practice is this: if you are clear about what you must have from the client to begin business, this begins to create the kind of professional relationship you need. If you do not insist on this clarity at the beginning of your relationship, it becomes ever more difficult to insist upon and get it as events develop. As a result, your resentment may grow in direct proportion to the client's poor habits. Don't let this happen. Occasionally, people I do not know will telephone me and say, "I need you. I need you this minute. Will you start working immediately?" I always say this: "I will be happy to do the work (if indeed I am!) and will commence if you send me a fax with the following information (key information from the letter of intent) to be followed up by overnight mail with a signed hard copy." If they are that anxious to begin, they'll follow these common-sense suggestions. If they are merely high anxiety folk, they won't. Either way, I'm protected. I must stress and stress again that reputable people, people who value their time and professional standing and your own, will understand and appreciate your need for clarity and professional behavior. But remember: if you don't insist on it, don't be surprised if people take advantage of you. It is my opinion that you have invited the violation.

Full Contract

As its name suggests, this document is longer and is used in those situations where a longer engagement is desired by the parties. I need not, I think, tell you which clauses are desirable, for, in fact, you will go step by step through each possible clause and include all those which are relevant to your individual situation. One point I would like to deal with, however, is this: I am often asked by my workshop participants about whether it's desirable to hold out for your own contract, as opposed to signing a contract put forward by the other party. I've frankly never understood this point. What always concerns me is what is in the contract, not where the contract originates. If I am convinced (by going through their contract and making sure that all the key items which appear on the foregoing list of contract clauses have been dealt with) that all has been satisfactorily dealt with both from the client's standpoint and from mine, I have absolutely no hesitation about signing their document. By the same token, if I find that certain clauses do not represent my understanding of our agreement or are in fact invidious to my interests, I have no hesitation about drafting substitute language and presenting that for the client's approval and incorporation into the contract. This I consider standard practice, and there is absolutely no need to feel sheepish about it. Curiously, many people seem to feel that there is some almost mystical advantage to be derived from a contract which has been typed onto their own stationery and which emanates from their office. I've never understood this concern and certainly never shared it. It's the words that matter, not the fact that the document comes from your office and has been graced by the keys of your computer.

A Word About Contract Preparation

You'll find that the longer you are in business, the more your contracts will tend to become repetitive in their language. Until that moment, however, I suggest that you use this book and other books (including **THE CONSULTANT'S KIT**) which contain sample contract language, draft your own documents, and submit them to your lawyer for approval. I must tell you this: lawyers take their contract language from pattern books, too. So there are only two real reasons for doing this: Your lawyer may be able to spot a hole in your contract that is to your detriment, and just the fact that your lawyer is checking your document should lower your anxiety.

And A Word About The Look Of Your Contracts

Print the first page of your contract on your usual letterhead. Print all subsequent pages on plain white paper with your name and the client's at the top of the page and the page number, thus "Lant/Smith Contract, Page 2." If you have more than one contract with this client, give this one a shorthand designation, thus "Lant/Smith Fund Raising Contract, Page 2."

Commission Contract

Purists may not consider the commission contract a separate type of document. But, as you already know, I am not a hidebound doctrinaire. The reason I have broken out the commission contract for singular consideration is easily stated: this type of business arrangement presents much allure to new advisors and is often mishandled. Hence the need for clarity about when to use it and what should be included in it.

A commission (sometimes called a results) contract may be used in situations where the advisor expects to be paid not by a fixed, flat fee (or flat fee with expenses) but in relation to the results he gains working with the client. Such an arrangement often seems particularly fair and sensible:

- The client says to you, in effect, "If you're so good and so knowledgeable, surely you'll take our case on commission, getting paid when you deliver the goods."

- The client says, "We don't have any money, but with your skills you'll help us get a beneficial result and can take a percentage based on what you bring in."

- The client says, "We'll pay you more if you take your remuneration as a percentage of what comes in as a result of your problem-solving procedures than we could pay you upfront. You'll do better with a commission arrangement."

- The client also thinks, "If we snag the advisor under a commission agreement, he'll have to work harder for the money and the burden will be transferred from us to the advisor. That seems like a swell idea!"

The Pitfalls Of Commission Contracts

There are several good reasons for being chary where commission contracts are concerned:

- Clients often relate fair payment to hours spent working on their behalf. They tend to forget that through your years of experience (and all the mistakes you've made acquiring it!), you've learned just how to do things so that you get maximum results for minimum time invested. Thus, if you receive a hefty commission (and the client is likely to regard whatever he has to pay as hefty, by the way) for a short investment of time, the client is likely to feel resentful about the payment, feeling that he has been gulled by you and made a bad deal. He could hold up payment and force you to threaten litigation, a draining process you really want to avoid.

- The client may also be unwilling to cooperate with you in the achievement of the desired objective, feeling that as you are gathering such a significant payment, you really ought to work harder to get it. Under commission contracts, carelessly drawn, the client can often escape his just responsibility and obligations to work with you in achieving the desired result. This is particularly true if the advisor is working on something that would be desirable but is not necessarily pressing to the client.

- The client may set terms which seem attractive but are in fact fraught with the potential for conflict. Say, then, that as a fund raising advisor, I agree with a client to take a percentage of "new" money (that elusive commodity) from charitable sources. (This, by the way, while eliciting the acute disapproval of professional societies in this field, is quite legal). Say with the magic of my personality and professional procedures I induce a sitting board member to up his annual contribution to the organization from $1,000, to $10,000 and I claim my fee accordingly. The organization might well cavil that this isn't new money; we'd be left in the soup with the possibility of budding resentments (and perhaps worse) on both sides.

The solution, of course, to these difficulties lies in the contract, lies, in fact, in having the utmost clarity between the two parties. Here are the key points that must be dealt with:

- Client Involvement. Don't fall into the god-magician trap that can destroy mutually beneficial commission contract relationships. Whatever you need to make this a mutually profitable experience, work to secure the client's understanding of and get it in writing in the contract. Thus, in my (admittedly infrequent) commission relationships, I insist on having reasonable access for me and my designated representatives (such as an accountant) to the client's place of business, staff, books and records in order that I may be sure of the results produced by my problem solving procedures. I insist on myself and my agents having this access at any time during the engagement. *N.B.* If you, like me, may have to wait a significant amount of time for the results of your procedures to become apparent, make sure that you have included the right of access to necessary materials for as long as your system continues to produce results under the terms of the engagement.

This involvement, however, goes farther. If you need certain staff to perform certain tasks, if you need regular meetings with key individuals, &c. then make sure you have your requirements of the client written into the contract. Particularly under a commission contract (where it is easier for the client to escape his just responsibility), you must insist on having exactly what you need to achieve success, and these requirements must be written clearly into the contract, binding the parties.

- Payment Formula. What formula will determine how much you'll be paid for your work? Be clear about this. In the above mentioned case, for instance, what is the precise definition of "new money?" Good fences, remember, make good neighbors; good contracts make for good client relationships. If you are not absolutely clear about how you will be reimbursed, if the client is not absolutely clear about the basis for your payment, then do not enter into a commission relationship.

- Time Commitment. Consummate advisors, like consummate athletes, make the difficult, even the impossible, look graceful and easily accessible. That is the magic of being a professional. But there is a silly notion very much extant that one should be paid by the amount of time one puts in. You and I, of course, sophisticated people with the necessary savoir faire to succeed in business, necessarily dismiss this notion with impatience. You will, however, find that many of your clients do not. Thus, you must secure the client's acknowledgement that while you will work to achieve the objectives they desire (the more successful you are, of course, the more remunerated you will be), you will not be bound to putting in a fixed number of hours or to working in a precise way, unless these conditions are absolutely essential to the achievement of success. It is the essence of the independent contractor that you work in your own way, on your own time, using your own best judgement as to how the best results may be attained. If these results are in fact attained (either in whole or in part), then the client must understand he cannot criticize (or worse) because you did not adhere to his preconceived notions of how things should be done.

Independent Contractor Services Agreement (For Your Supergroup Of Independent Contractors)

The previous three contracts are between you and your clients and are designed to protect your interests in such situations. Now I want to present the fourth contract, the Independent Contractor Services Agreement, which is used in your dealings with independent contractors you hire to do business for you, either for you directly or as a subcontractor in other situations. As you will see, the kinds of clauses remain standard but the wording subtly shifts again in your favor because who you are in this situation and what your objective is has changed. Consider the following points:

- Whereas in the prior agreements you wish to be paid upfront and in advance, in this situation you want to pay by results.

- Whereas in the prior agreements you want to be able to cancel the contract through mutual consent, here you wish the other party to be able to cancel only if your client (from whence the contract originally derives) cancels.

- Whereas in the prior agreements you want the loosest noncompetitive clause possible, here you want the most stringent.

You get the idea.

In the advising business, what you do at any particular moment depends on who you are just then. One of the most difficult things to accomplish in this business is to know who you are just now, what your objective is just now, and how to move deftly from one complex role to another with the utmost grace and without confusion. Thus, if you are the independent contractor facing a client you will have one set of objectives because that person is the temporary employer. When, however, you yourself retain an advisor and become the employer your perspective has significantly shifted and you must behave — and write documents — accordingly. Not surprisingly, many advisors find this absolutely mandatory transformation difficult to accomplish.

There is another key difference between this document and the ones which have preceded it: The Independent Contractor Services Agreement *per se* is not absolutely necessary. That is, its objectives can be reached by including the necessary clauses in a letter of intent, full service, or commission contract drawn up between you and the independent contractors you hire in relation to any individual assignment. Thus, while the actual Independent Contractor Services Agreement is not in itself absolutely necessary, its clauses are and must in fact appear in some contract between you and any independent contractors with whom you are doing business.

However, if you intend to establish an ongoing relationship with an independent contractor, it is usually a good idea — and is certainly more convenient — if you draw up such an agreement. One of its benefits, of course, is that it clarifies the relationship between the two parties, clearly setting out your expectations of the independent contractor. This should help keep your relations calm and professional.

If you do decide to draw up such an agreement, make sure to include at least the following clauses:
- parties to the agreement
- date entered into
- description of your business and expertise
- description of why independent contractor is being sought to assist you
- confirmation of independent contractor status of other party
- precise duties of independent contractor
- payment to be made to independent contractor and in what manner
- how agreement between the parties may be terminated or amended
- confidentiality of materials seen by independent contractor
- noncompetitive clause
- applicable law
- assignability clause preventing either party from transferring its responsibilities to another party without mutual agreement
- term of contract.

There is nothing particularly mysterious about the Independent Contractor Services Agreement. What you must keep in mind, however, is that the independent contractor (himself, of course, an advisor in his own right) will struggle with you to make the best possible agreement to his advantage, the same kind of agreement, in short, you attempt to make in dealing with your primary client. Depending on your need for this advisor's particular service, the scarcity of this service, the availability of others who can provide it and similar factors, you will either have to accede to his demands or can comfortably ignore them. It's all negotiable!

Many of my workshop participants worry about, what?, the moral correctness of being able to negotiate for one set of objectives in one circumstance and for another in different conditions with different people. Don't waste your time thinking about it! It's a futile and unproductive exercise. What should be patently apparent to you as you move through this book is the number and variety of roles advisors are called upon to play in their professional (and indeed personal) lives. Your ability to succeed in this business is directly related to your ability to adopt the appropriate posture at the appropriate moment, be clear about what constitutes your interest, understand what your opposite number's interest is (and see to what extent he can get it), and embody the rest of your objectives in a mutually binding contract. Never forget this.

By this token, it is clear that when you are subcontracting a piece of work to another independent contractor you will want to make sure that you keep a substantial fraction of the contract value. This bothers many people, but remember, if you are subcontracting, you ought to receive consideration for the following:
- the development of your reputation which helped secure the original client
- the fact that you have drawn up the original contract
- that you have spent time finding and screening the independent contractor/subcontractor(s)
- that you have convinced the original client of your ability to deliver a quality product — and must now work to ensure that you (through the subcontractor) do
- that you have the liability in case something goes wrong, and very importantly,
- that you (by taking onto yourself these onerous business matters) allow the independent contractor/subcontractor to do what he does best: his professional work. Most people, remember, dislike the stuff and substance of management and running a small business. In an independent contractor/subcontractor relationship, you take on these responsibilities and leave this advisor free to be a pure professional, an almost indulgent state of affairs. For this benefit, and all the others, you should be amply compensated, and my advice to you is to retain between 20% and 50% of the gross value of any contract being delegated to an independent contractor/subcontractor.

In the ordinary course of events, this advisor will not discover what you are keeping. And frankly it's none of their business. Their business is to get on with what they know and do to the best of their professional ability. On the other hand, if they do find out, they may occasionally express a feeling of, what? outrage that you have kept so much of the benefit of their work. If you feel compelled to explain (and in this case I would be ruled by the intelligent saying, "Never complain, never explain") then do so by citing each and every one of the above responsibilities that you have, and citing, in turn, the high degree of professional autonomy you have allowed the advisor to have. Learning how to induce shame and contrition in subcontractors in a necessary part of succeeding in this business.

On The Matter Of Professional Liability

When you talk about contracts, you necessarily deal with the entire matter of professional liability. It is to limit your exposure to liability claims that you in large measure create a contract. Now I wish to carry this discussion farther since, given the nature of our society, you must always be aware of the possibility that you may be held responsible by the courts for professional misjudgement or a wrongful act or a significant omission. Before I conclude this chapter, something needs to be said about the basis on which such charges might succeed and what you can do about it.

If a client makes a claim against an advisor it will ordinarily be because the advisor has failed to perform his services in a reasonable and prudent manner and that as a result the client has suffered loss. For the client to succeed in this claim against the advisor, the following points must be proven:

- There was a valid contract existing between the client and the advisor. Under the law this contract may either be in writing or be verbal.
- The advisor materially failed to do what he said he would do under the contract.
- The client suffered damages as a result.

Does it matter that what the advisor may have done is innocent, negligent, or willful? Not in most cases. It simply matters whether each of the three points above can be proved. This is why it is so important to be most careful that:

- You understand the problem.
- You have not overpromised a solution.
- Your techniques can in fact help provide this solution.
- You secure the full cooperation of the client in working towards a solution.
- What you can do and what the client has agreed to do is fully embodied in a simple and clear contract.

The client has grounds for an action if:

- You didn't do what you said you were going to do.
- The result you promised didn't happen.
- You said you'd work for a certain price and, failing to get more money when you requested it, refused to carry on the work, thus causing the client to suffer damages.

There are other reasons, too, for claims which can be made against you:

- If the client perceives that you are in a conflict of interest situation, that you have used information gained in their situation and applied it to the benefit of one of their competitors.
- If you have delegated part of the work to another independent contractor/subcontractor against your explicit assurance that you, the mandarin, would in fact do the work.
- If a third party (a creditor, investor or lender) suffers damages as a result of your recommendations.
- If the client has been unclear about his expectations, thinks you promised more than is in fact being delivered, and takes action as a result.

There's still another reason for suit which ought to be cited: when a client sues you after you have sued him. A client will file a counterclaim as a delaying tactic and bargaining chip, in part to wear you down, in part to get better leverage. It's just another business weapon.

Clearly each of these causes for claims against you can and should be dealt with in the contract. I bring them up here for a very simple reason: people in the advising business need to be very cautious about what they do and say. Learn to avoid:

- giving fixed cost estimates. Unless you are selling a finite amount of time (as I often do) and can thereby be sure of what the contract will cost the client (as in a standardized proposal), avoid telling the client exactly what the solution of his problem will cost. Provide, instead, a range.
- free opinions. Yes, even those who are not your clients, even those who understand that you are grandstanding after your third martini, may still consider themselves aggrieved that they followed your advice and came to grief. Anything to avoid responsibility for their own actions and cast the blame on you, the negligent advisor.
- unprepared and inadequate subcontractors. In our society, we are amazingly prepared to believe the claims made by others, in part because we are lazy and don't want to check out their credentials, in part because we are a credulous people. But remember: not only can sloppy subcontractors cost you work and besmirch your reputation, they can cause you legal problems if the client suffers damages as a result of what they do. I get lots of requests from people to go into business with them, to let them become independent contractors working for me and in general to collaborate. I have learned to be very, very cautious about proceeding with such deals, and if you approach me make sure you can make a superb case for why we should work together!

As you can see, succeeding as an advisor is rather like losing one's innocence. Innocence may be a charming attribute, but it is not a very practical one. What I am asking, indeed demanding of you, is that you become as hardheaded and clearsighted as possible — without losing those necessary attributes of charm, empathy, and humane consideration. For one must ask oneself at what point the game is not worth more than the candle.

A Word About Professional Liability Insurance

This chapter has in large measure dealt with just two things:

- working with the client to ensure maximum clarity about what each of you expects the other to do and how your relationship will be regulated to bring about what is mutually desired, maximum success, and
- how to protect yourself against any possible failure in this relationship.

So far I have concentrated primarily on the contract, for the contract is a critical part of your defense system. This system begins with a clear understanding on your part of what is (and is not) possible in terms of solving the client's problem, getting the client to understand and acknowledge that which needs to be done and can be done (both by you and by the client himself) to solve his problem, and embodying your mutual agreement in a clear and precise document. Frankly, this should ordinarily be sufficient protection for you, especially given your contractually mandated meeting with key decision makers at which you can put forward your own fears, anxieties and well formulated professional opinions about what will happen if the client behaves in certain unhelpful ways. As I shall point out in the next chapter, your assessment of the consequences following a client's unhelpful actions is another useful part of your defense system.

I would, however, also like to advise your consideration of professional liability insurance. There are basically two kinds:

- "claims made" insurance which protects you against errors, omissions and negligent acts. Under this coverage, you are protected for claims made against you during the policy period only.
- "occurrence coverage" insurance protects you against claims arising during the policy period even if these claims are made after the lapse of the policy.

Obviously, claims made insurance is less expensive and is preferred by the insurance company. But you have to decide whether something about which you advised today (say health advice) could possibly give rise to adverse consequences years from now, as when a baby grows up.

In considering professional liability insurance you should be aware of the fact that policies are ordinarily made up of seven parts:

- declarations
- exclusions
- insuring agreements
- definitions
- limits of liability
- deductibles
- policy conditions.

Since price will no doubt be a factor in considering this kind of protection, be aware that you will pay less depending on the nature of your deductibles and the extent of risk assumed by the insurance company (as should be clear from the discussion above). Of course, you must also shop around.

As I have discovered, the quality of insurance agents (themselves, of course, advisors) varies tremendously. But you can help them. The first thing you must do is to list all the different kinds of errors, omissions, and misjudgements you could make. This is very, very hard to do, especially if you have clients flattering you into a feeling that you are nigh to God himself in problem solving infallibility. This kind of clear sightedness is crucial.

Then present the list to at least three different full service insurance agents who represent not one but several firms. This takes time. There is no other way of solving the problem, though. I can guarantee you, you will be told things you will not understand by these agents; these advisors, no less than others, are masters of the patois of gobbledygook. Make them explain in common English exactly what they mean, and if your gut tells you something's wrong with what they are telling you, it probably is. Learn to trust your instincts. If, upon consideration, these same instincts tell you you have adequately protected yourself in your client contracts, then perhaps you do not really need this kind of liability protection. But, please, be sure, not cocksure.

On Corporations As A Source Of Protection Against Liability

Every standard business text will tell you that having a corporation is a source of liability protection, too, another piece in your defense strategy. I agree — but only to a point. If you, like me, are running what I call a "very closely held" corporation with a single shareholder, an aggrieved client feeling he has grounds for an action will probably sue you personally as well as the corporation of which you are an officer. Do not, therefore, necessarily assume that with a corporation you have absolutely saved yourself from further liability than that of the assets in the corporation itself. This may not be true.

If The Client Breaches The Contract

While the client, of course, will no doubt worry about the quality of your work and your ability to solve his problems economically, expeditiously, you, in your turn, must worry about the client's ability to uphold his end of the bargain. As you know, I have now been in business 12 years and during that time clients have breached more contracts than I have, and as a result I have had to develop means of coping with unhappy, negligent, and wilful behaviors.

- Ordinarily clients give signs of breaching a contract before they actually do so. Is your client failing to live up to your expectations as clearly outlined in the contract? Then he is a candidate for breaching. In this case, you must be clear with the client that your expectations are not being met. If the client persists in not following through on what he has agreed to do, give notice of intent to stop work. You will do this, in any event, after some acknowledged period if your fees have not been paid, but fees are usually only one thing you expect from a client. If these, too, are not forthcoming, you must, after pleading, wheedling and needling the client, take suitable action.

- Most breaches, but by no means all, involve money, directly or indirectly. This is certainly true in my experience. At the beginning of my practice, I, perhaps like you, was much more inclined to believe in the essential goodness of man. I was a Lockean through and through. Learn, reader, learn! If the client doesn't pay you, follow the guidelines outlined in the contract:

  — Charge interest after thirty days.

  — Stop work after 60 days.

  — Along with your stop work letter, send a letter that asks for complete payment in thirty days.

  — After thirty days discuss the matter with the person at your client's place of business responsible for accounts payable. Ask whether they intend to pay the bill and get a precise date for payment. Ask, as a token of their good faith, for partial payment immediately. Name a sum.

  — If the client pays this portion, they are probably intending to pay the rest. Just how long it takes them to do so is undoubtedly dependent on their situation and your ability to overcome your aversion to being thrust in the role of debt collector, a necessary skill for all successful advisors.

If, on the other hand, the client refuses to indicate an intention to pay the bill, refuses to name a date by when he expects it to be cleared, and doesn't forward any payment, you can assume collection is unlikely. Do the following:

- Send out the "Dog Ate My Homework" collection letter (see samples, page 300). Shame the client into paying you!

- If the bill is for over $25 (and each collection agency has its own floor), turn the matter over for immediate collection. You may be loathe to do this but I wish to impart some truly disturbing information to you.

Essentially, business in the United States (and indeed throughout the world) runs on trust, much more so than I ever imagined before I myself was in business. Where trust is present, business can take place; where it is not, it falters. A person who is breaching your contract by failure to pay you (as he agreed he would) is damaging the fabric of trust, or should I say further damaging, since in many ways this fabric is under serious attack nowadays for many reasons. He counts for his relief on you:

- believing (hoping) that this matter will be settled without further unpleasantness

- hoping that you can do business again and so not wishing to further impair matters

- knowing nothing about the legal process and so being unable to use it against him

- finding the whole matter of collections so distasteful that you'd rather give up the money than subject yourself to the indignities which attend the collection process.

And he is usually right. Vast sums of money go uncollected each year for these very reasons. This is a disgrace. It is also a disgrace that our political and judicial establishment have let matters come to this pass without spending sufficient time trying to rectify a situation which in the long run threatens the whole process of doing business.

The person owing you the money understands that the best technique to employ when he is the perceived aggrieving party, the person, that is, who has breached the contract, is to remain elusive. To answer no mail, take no telephone calls, to avoid you altogether, or, more infuriatingly, to yes you to death, to make promises and remain urbane and cheerful while wilfully committing abuse. That is the worst!

By comparison, your task, as the perceived aggrieved party, the party to whom something has been promised which has not taken place, is to take early and firm action, as outlined by the contract, in hot pursuit of your interests. Ditch Locke; adopt Hobbes, the man who knew the need for and value of the club. This action need not be legal, yet, but it must include the firm intention (communicated to your erring client) that such action can and will take place should he continue to be obdurate and offending. If you do not follow through on this intention, a firm signal will be sent to your client that will undoubtedly invite future violations at such time as this matter has been settled.

More On Collections

I wish I could tell you that the likelihood of getting payment, full and swift payment, was great. But I cannot. Any debt under $5,000 (and many of those above) may well be uncollectable in the United States, given factors such as distance and a client's disinclination to play by rules he previously agreed to. This is a stark, often disconcerting, fact of business life nowadays. As I said, trust in business is a very real consideration. Given this fact, you must learn to protect yourself through the contract and to harden yourself to the harsh necessities of what must (and should) take place once your client has breached this engagement. Thus:

- Find a collections agency before you need one.

- Master the intricacies of small claims court so that you stand a better chance of recovering your money in such proceedings. In this connection you'll find Ralph Warner's book *Everybody's Guide To Small Claims Court* most helpful. You can get it through Nolo Press, 950 Parker St., Berkeley, CA 94710. Ask for a copy of their *Nolo News* by calling 1-800-992-6656; it has lots of materials you'll find helpful.

- Make a mental commitment to doing what is necessary to get the money owed you and to getting people to live up to their commitments. Once people have violated with impunity, they will violate again. And you know it!

I do not, however, wish to end this chapter on such a stark note of bleak prophesy. Properly handled, with the mutual obligations and responsibilities of each party clearly outlined, most client-advisor relationships do produce success and can be reckoned beneficial and worth entering into. To ensure that this is the case, however, read on, for in Chapter 10 I shall discuss the advisor on the job: what you need to know about making your engagement the utmost success.

CHAPTER 10

Developing The Successful Client Relationship III:
The Successful Advisor On The Job

You have now succeeded in getting the client. Congratulate yourself. Getting clients is not easy. Every business day good people, bright people, people with good ideas and client benefits at their disposal fail to get the client, but you haven't. *You*, you!, have now succeeded. You are entitled to feel a rosy glow of good feeling about yourself. So long as you also recognize that you have now entered into a period of great peril: for having won the battle to secure the client, you could well lose the war to secure the substantial benefits that come in working with him.

Given that the period of working together with the client to help the client achieve the results he says he wants is such an important one I have been amazed at the almost tragic insignificance of the work available on this subject. During the writing of this book I had occasion to write to the authors of many books and articles who I thought would have something significant to say about working with clients. It is, I think, instructive that not a single one bothered to respond to these queries, despite the fact that I announced that if they did, providing me with their reflections, experiences and observations, I would help to promote their books and articles through this work. I learned several things from this unsatisfactory experience:

- People are often too busy with peripheral matters to secure a point of their own self interest.

- People with things to promote and market do not grasp at available promotional possibilities with alacrity, or even interest.

- It is easier to talk about how to get clients than it is to talk about how to work with them effectively. Yet if marketing and promotion are essential to the creation of a successful advising practice, the ultimate practice that is developed thereby won't be worth a *sou* if you as the advisor in place cannot work with the client to help solve the client's problems.

Please note the way this sentence is constructed. I did not say "solve" the client's problem, I said *work* with the client to help solve his problems. For make no mistake about it: most situations in which advisors function do not and cannot involve your going in and doing things without the consent and involvement of the client. Thus, dealing with the client is always an integral part of the solution process. You ignore the client at your peril. For this reason successful advisors must become adept at securing the full involvement of the client in the change process. This is difficult.

What concerns me deeply as a professional advisor is how glib much of the literature is about securing change. To move towards positive change is difficult, damned difficult. It is arduous, repetitive, frustrating, often thankless work. It is also absolutely essential. Moreover, it is work that can be successfully accomplished only if the advisor comes to understand how the dynamics of change can take place without destroying one of the critical necessities of this change, which is your own dedication to bringing it about.

Locke vs Hobbes

One of the problems that many advisors bring to the change process is a rather starry-eyed belief that people want change; want change, that is, as much as the advisor does. This is easy to believe given the fact Americans are obsessed with a change language, with the language of movement, transformation, and activity. This is highly deceptive. People understand that they are rewarded by their ability to talk this language and to be perceived as advocating and bringing about positive change. Whether or not they can in fact bring it about is somewhat beside the point, but one must, absolutely must, talk the change game to succeed. Even the most rampant conservatives cloak their designs in change language, for they realize, if only instinctively, that to present their case in any other way is to consign it to defeat and obscurity. Given this situation, it is easy to be deluded into believing that people really want change and will really work to achieve it. But nothing, in my experience, could be further from the truth.

Your clients will work, and work hard, to maintain their old habits even while telling you, with the straightest of faces, that, of course, they are dedicated to the new techniques, procedures and ideas you are propounding. That, of course, they want to work with you to succeed in bringing them into existence. That, of course, they intend to follow through and so solve the problem. What, they seem to imply, do you take me for, an obstinate obstructionist?

Here is it important to look, just for a moment, at the philosophical tradition of our country, for this tradition can make it difficult for you to deal objectively and realistically with the clients you encounter. In this tradition, the name of the eighteenth century English philosopher John Locke stands tall. Locke, as you may remember from your high school civics courses, was a significant force in the general movement which culminated in the American Revolution, a revolution undertaken by reasonable men in (admittedly rather reluctant) pursuit of an eminently reasonable objective: their personal freedom. Locke, to speak in very rude and general terms, believed that reasonable men working together would pursue their reasonable ends in a reasonable way. "Come let us reason together," he might have said, anticipating Lyndon Johnson. Such a sentiment is exhilarating, of course; it makes one feel good about oneself and the world of one's fellow creatures and the possibilities that lie before us. As such, it is the point of view that particularly ingenue advisors are prone to taking, for it suggests that the identification and particularly the solving of problems will be a harmonious enterprise genteelly undertaken by congenial souls with commonly shared objectives.

Like you are now, so once was I. When I began my advising practice I, too, thought that reasonable people would pursue their reasonable ends in an eminently thoughtful, practical, and reasonable way. Why not? I believed what the clients told me: that they wanted a solution to their problems; that they wanted to work with me to secure it; that they were enthusiastic, even eager to commence work and to obliterate the obstacles and move triumphantly towards a triumphal end.

But no more.

Now I am a firmly committed, rigorous, obstinately devoted follower of Thomas Hobbes, a darker guide to the human condition. But with this devotion has come, I have to admit, a much more satisfactory, much more successful advising practice.

Hobbes, writing earlier than Locke, viewed life from a distinctly different vantage point. He wrote at the time of the English Civil War, and civil wars, more perhaps than any other, are likely to produce a distinctly saturnine turn of mind. Still, Hobbes has become immortal with this memorable phrase, that life is "nasty, brutish and short." His general attitude may be generally summed up by saying that men will often act against their self interest and that they must be motivated and moved by prodding, pushing, pleading, and pummelling.

Now, isn't this a terrible point of view? Doesn't it at some level offend you? The earlier you are in business, the more you will probably be forced to admit that it does make you feel, perhaps even fiercely, outraged at such an offending sentiment. But if this is the way you (probably) feel, I have this to say to you: get over it.

As you will come to see during the course of this chapter, it is easy to be deluded by the general success rhetoric which people in this nation customarily speak, in which they cloak their often deeply mulish attitudes and actions. Moreover, it is always easier to get along by going along, to drift away from what needs to be done and bathe in the always-satisfying light of popularity by mouthing clichés, shibboleths, and generally held opinions. Yes, this is easy. It just doesn't happen to be very productive.

In this chapter I have one point and one point only to make, and I shall attempt to make it in many ways: to be a successful advisor means working in all ways to get the client to secure ownership over his problem and, this crucial step having been reached, to work with the client in all ways to move the client towards a beneficial solution. During this process, you will often (indeed should) be clearer than the client about what constitutes the problem to be addressed, and you must be clearer, too, about what must be done to solve it. This level of absolute clarity must involve your understanding of the ways the client will naturally take to elude his responsibility, to push it onto you, and to avoid taking actions that will in fact lead to the solution he says, with boring repetition, he wants.

There will be some of you who read this material, just as there are those who take my workshops, who blame me for letting this djin out of the bottle. This, I'd like to tell you, is utterly fatuous. In the days of ancient Greece when a messenger would rush breathless into the presence of the king to announce a shattering defeat (or even some lesser misfortune) he would as often as not be rewarded for his pains in bringing this sad message by being slain. But before you contemplate doing this to me consider: I am only a messenger. I did not create the world as it stands; I can only tell you to my utmost ability how to deal with it. If you don't like what I say about human nature and the vicissitudes of dealing with even the most well meaning clients, all I can say is that I am giving you what I know you need, not what I know many of you would like to hear. I take satisfaction from knowing that someday you will be grateful for my candor, just, I might say, as your clients will be grateful when you are candid with them. But do not expect, it is too much to expect, that this candor, at first hearing, will be greeted enthusiastically. It won't be.

Let me conclude this opening argument by saying this: Americans have a special, even endearing foible which is much commented upon by foreigners. We want to be liked. We do anything, go to any lengths to be liked. It is, I'm afraid, less a sign of our collective good nature than of our collective insecurity and neurosis but, of course, we don't want this to be generally known. But if you are going to become a successful advisor, you must not make popularity the chief objective of your practice. You must strive instead to be respected and hope that in those you have worked with this respect will come, over time, to be a more sustaining affection than mere transient popularity. Good advisors strive to be respected, strive to have it said of them that they were honest, sensible, fair and client-centered. This is a sufficient epitaph for all of us. Let it be your constant objective to do what it takes to have this be said of you.

Preparing To Begin

By now you will already have a good many thoughts about what to do to help your client achieve his objectives. Most of these will, however, center on you. The ideas you have, the skills and techniques you bring to this situation, your enthusiasm, and the commitment you have made. Yes, these are necessary, but these are distinctly secondary in importance to your ability to motivate and move the client towards a solution. I must remind you over and over again: the advisor, while distinctly necessary as a catalyst in the solution process, is an ancillary part of the process: the client is and always will be the primary solution-agent working diligently, along with you, side by side with you, even under you, but always primarily so. You forget this at your peril. If your enthusiasm, your good ideas, your technical skills and procedures outstrip the client's ability to accept and implement them, then the assignment, and your ability to help bring about meaningful change, will be blasted. There is almost something metaphysical here, and I think, in my wilder moments, of myself as a human alchemist.

You will remember that in medieval times, the alchemist (himself, of course, an advisor) purported to be able to change dross metals into gold and the like. It never worked, but it did engage the avarice and the imagination of generations of the gullible and aspiring. I have cleansed the nefarious practices out of the myth and consider myself as one who can take an advisor fixated on his own ideas and problem solving processes and transform him, by a sort of alchemy, into one who is rigorously, painstakingly client-centered. This is a salubrious alchemy, and one you are hereby advised to practice with assiduity.

To achieve this necessary result, you must plan, but you must especially plan for that critical first meeting with your new client. Here are the questions which need answers. Some, of course, may be answered by the kind of contract you have signed with the client (Delphic Oracle versus Full Service, for example); others will need your decision. The questions are:

- Where will the meeting take place?
- Who should attend?
- How long should it be?
- Who will take minutes?
- What do you want to take place as a result of the meeting?
- What does the client want to take place as a result of the meeting?
- What obstacles do you foresee in getting the result you need?
- What do you propose to overcome them?
- What obstacles do you think the client foresees?
- What can the client do to overcome them?

Each of these points needs specific answers. All too often advisors, now breathing easily since they signed the contract, go into the meeting ill prepared, trying, in that odious phrase, to "wing it."

This is a serious mistake which has within it the seeds of future problems. The first meeting is the occasion for you, the new advisor from whom much is desired (but who has given rise to the not unnatural fear that this will be yet another occasion of *plus c'est change....*), to clearly set forward your expectations, to elicit from the client his expectations, and to work on those necessary procedures, recommendations, techniques and applications which can, to the greatest extent possible, satisfy you both.

Thus, draw up a sheet for this critical first encounter with specific answers to each of the above points. Make them as specific as possible but do not overpromise. The client may well have had bad experiences previously with advisors; most people, after all, have. Advisors who have overpromised. Who have not followed through. Who have, frankly, not understood the client's problem and did not attempt to find an appropriate solution. Who did not seem to care about whether the client solved the problem, but only whether they themselves were paid promptly. Yes, there is scarcely a client in the land who does not have grounds for a justifiable anxiety. If you give early signs that you are going to be yet another of these, then the momentum for change, which is always present when an advisor arrives on the scene, no matter how slight that momentum might be, will dry up and things will revert to their previous, defeating pattern. You will become, promises and enthusiasm notwithstanding, merely another bloated advisor whose reality did not meet his rhetoric. In such circumstances, of course, the chorus of "I told you so" from the exhilarated flatworms is almost palpable.

Therefore, sit down and draft your expectations and objectives, line by line, in time for advance submission to your client. Neither the client nor you should go into the initial meeting unprepared or liable for surprises. In his regard, Henry Kissenger, surely a master of the art, is quite right: there should never be a meeting unless you know in advance what is likely to take place. I quite agree.

By the same token, whatever you may need from the client for this initial session should be made quite clear to him far enough in advance so that there is a reasonable likelihood that these critical materials will be available. If they cannot be made available, and they are indeed critical, then give every consideration to postponing the meeting until that time when the are. This will signal the client that:

- If the client does not do what is necessary to achieve the success he wants, you cannot provide meaningful advice and assistance.
- You are serious about enforcing those standards you regard as crucial towards the solution of his problem.

All this can and, indeed, must be done in a humane and genteel fashion. You need not lascerate the client for his failure to produce materials which you need to help him. Simply say, "I really think we should postpone the meeting until we have these materials/people. It would be difficult to proceed without them." If this is so, stand to your guns.

The client at this point in your early relationship is looking to you for a sense of mastery and control, to show that you know what you are doing, that you know what the client must do to achieve success. Remember: people are lazy. With the best will in the world, your client wants to create you as a god-magician; wants to place the full burden of finding an appropriate solution on you; wants you to be fully responsible for all that needs to take place. *N.B.* It is men who create gods, not gods who create men. The creation of god, of course, is man's earliest and most significant attempt to eschew responsibility for his actions and circumstances. This god-creation is absolutely constant from race to race and civilization to civilization. So, as you must imagine, you are working against a deeply ingrained, profoundly atavistic movement as you attempt to shift the responsibility directly to where it belongs: onto the client.

Remember: you very rarely have the power in the advisor-client relationship to get things to change all by your lonesome. This is why I developed the Principle of Blithe Irresponsibility, so that you would understand that what you can do, the benefits that you bring without working through the client, are necessarily limited. Under this principle, your job is to give the most candid, most thorough, most detailed advice possible. But if the client refuses to take this advice, that is his prerogative. So long as you are paid, you have nothing to worry about, for you are not, and never have been, the responsible party in terms of implementing your recommendations.

It is flattering, of course, that the client wishes to place all the responsibility on you to achieve the desired, the much touted success. Each of us in his own way has a craving to be divinity: this, too, is a firmly established trend in human affairs. You are not, being profoundly mortal, in any way immune from it. But accepting this responsibility would be a great, great mistake. Be clear with the client what you can and will do. Be clear with the client as to what he can and must do. This process begins, of course, in the marketing literature you develop. It is continued in the promotional articles by and about you and your problem solving techniques. It is a theme in the introductory prospect meetings and negotiations with possible clients. It also appears here in the document you draw up preceding your introductory client meeting. Here are some points regarding this document and its use.

As already stated, some of the points of this document drawn up for the introductory meeting should in fact have been dealt with in your contract. This includes: where the meeting is to be and how long it will take. If these are not clear, it is now past time to make them so. As to the other matters:

- **Designate precisely who should attend this meeting and why.**

If you can name the names of individuals who should attend, fine. If not, name the positions. Feel free to contact the client and ask for his advice about who should attend. Make it clear that those with decision making authority must be present. In my own case, when working with a nonprofit organization, for instance, this introductory meeting is a command performance involving the executive director, an administrative assistant (the individual who will work with us to ensure that proper minutes are kept and that individual assignments are in fact recorded and those with tasks to perform are reminded, as often as necessary, to perform them), the chairperson of the board, and other key fund raising personnel as the circumstances dictate. If these people cannot attend, this meeting must be postponed until such time as they can. Thus, these people must come to know, as soon as possible, that each has an important, indeed pivotal, role to play in the creation of those conditions which will lead to success. No one is too great to participate in these meetings if they have a necessary function to play in the movement to achieve success. No one is too minor if their function, too, is critical. Each must understand his role; each must be allowed the opportunity to ask questions about it and to give voice to the very natural and undoubtedly present doubts he has. Flatworms, of course, will either not come at all or will come and suffer in silence, obstinance and willful obstruction exuding from every part of their being. This is unacceptable. And you must say so.

New advisors, those desiring popularity over success, may take such behavior without a peep. But such advisors will have a far higher likelihood of being one of those many advising practices that fail to achieve success, forcing the principal back into the nether world of a traditional 9 to 5 enterprise. Take my word for it: honesty now is worth more than honesty later. Setting clear guidelines now is worth more than trying to impose clear guidelines later. Forcing yourself to focus on the client now (and by this I mean each individual who represents in some way the client in relation to your assignment) is worth more than a belated attempt to focus on the client later, rather than on yourself.

How many times must I say it? The average advisor is enamored of himself. Of his education, of his problem solving techniques, of his wit, and verve, and dexterity in a clutch. He is so thrilled by his intelligence, by his ability to think at all, much less think for profit, that all other considerations are dwarfed into insignificance. It is easy to see the client as somehow insignificant, unimportant, downright loutish and stupid because you are the advisor in this situation brought in like the burnished white knight to save the situation and rescue the endangered damsel in distress. But this is not only wrong; it is worse: it is stupid. Your job, your quite clear and absolutely essential task, is to focus on the client. This means, particularly during this absolutely critical first meeting, focusing on each cog in the wheel that will ultimately turn towards the solution.

I remember in this regard an assignment I had early on in my advising practice. I was working for a major eastern university as the coordinator of a project involving three universities and their complicated attempt to create a massive minority engineering center. It was a major project involving the time, attention and resources of dozens of America's highest engineers, top level college administrators, and a host of equally bright lights. Months went into the project, but like virtually all projects involving government grantsmanship we worked perilously close to the deadline. To ensure that our proposal arrived in Washington expeditiously, a courier was hired to hand deliver it to the government agency and secure the precious time stamp guaranteeing our eligibility. Everything, we thought, was in readiness and while the team worked hard we worked confidently. That is, until we had to input the final document into the one word processor available on the campus.

With time of the essence, with millions in the balance, the operator coolly announced that she couldn't give up her breaks, couldn't forego the necessary pleasures of a lunchtime exercise swim, couldn't conceivably work late, couldn't even (without authorization) displace routine work from other departments to accommodate this project. Grown men and women with international reputations and future glories on the line collapsed, distraught, for they were encountering that most common phenomenon, the latent power of the flatworm. And worst of all, a flatworm who, although a crucial part of the problem solving process, had never been consulted as to her role in the process. What did it take to move this woman who positively exulted in the role she had now cast for herself, the role of avenging fury? It took no less than a presidential order, a bonus (a/k/a bribe), and the promise of an day-off immediately after the document was finished. I can only hope that there is a special cycle of Dante's Inferno for such people, all too numerous. Even so, it is not sufficient.

Suffice it to say that much of this problem, and many of the problems which you will face, can be solved by thinking through in advance just what you need to do, just what the client needs to do, and by dealing with this as early as possible, if possible from the time of the very first meeting with the client. After all, had the wicked fairy been invited to Sleeping Beauty's christening, the world might have been deprived of a marvelous tale, but one cannot but believe that the characters themselves might not have lead calmer, less difficult lives.

- **Taking minutes.**

People are all too prone to tell you that they have wonderful memories and verge on being insulted when you suggest to them that they write things down. Successful advisor-client relationships are based on paper, lots of paper. Not papers which cloud issues, but papers which clarify them. This means dealing with the entire question of minutes.

There should be at least two kinds of minutes: Task Action and Narrative Minutes. Task action minutes are those which list the exact thing which you and the client have agreed upon, a person or people who are responsible for accomplishing this task, and a date by which it is to be done. No meeting, no meeting ever, should take place without expectations about what it should accomplish and without ending with the creation of a complete and accurate set of task action minutes.

This means, too, being clear about who is responsible for taking them. Somehow, in recent years the odd notion has come about that taking minutes is lowly, even insulting, certainly not a fit task for an intelligent man or woman. What nonsense! Throughout history, the individual who has taken minutes has always been regarded, until our own fatuous age, as being in a position of power and authority. And for good reason: securing agreement on what must be done and who must do it is, of course, a necessary but not sufficient precondition to achieving success. Someone must oversee the process of bringing into existence the action desired. This is what the secretary can do, and it is no surprise to me that the grandest officers in our president's cabinet are in fact termed secretaries. Thus, if you are given the opportunity to write down this specific information and be responsible for both disseminating it to the relevant, participating parties and for following up to ensure that the agreed-upon tasks are in fact accomplished, take it. For you have been given a position of power.

The task action minutes, once completed, must be sent to all those participating in the problem solving process and must be filed in a three-hole punched binder which will constitute the Project In Process log. This log is absolutely necessary to the success of the project. I insist upon my clients keeping one for each project they are working on with me (thus, corporate and foundation fund raising in a single log; community fund raising in another; special events fund raising in another, &c). The purpose is clear: in a single place the advisor and other relevant players will find a précis of decisions made, individuals assigned to designated tasks, and indications of how far along these tasks are.

It is frankly appalling to me how few advisors use this method and how many clients while not disputing its need (for none is foolish enough for this) do still cavil at what it takes to secure this valuable tool. Let me say this: keeping this log book is time-consuming. It is also invaluable. It is invaluable because:

- The decisions made are readily available with the reasons for them, the individuals appointed to carry them out, and the dates by which they are done.

- The mere existence of this log helps to inform all future client-advisors meetings. Meetings can start by relating progress towards completion of agreed-upon tasks and by rehearsing and reiterating the need for action, if (as will undoubtedly be the case) there are those who creep in moving towards the mutually-desired solution (if they do not obstruct movement altogether).

- It is easy to see how things have developed and why. There should be fewer questions about the reasons for certain activities. This should help to undercut those who specialize in second guessing based on the firm belief that after-the-fact, armchair experts know more than those who are close at hand. It is always easier after the fact to say that this or that should have been done; it is important, however, for your credibility that the client not have the opportunity to eschew his responsibility by adopting such counsel. A log properly understood is a responsibility book; it keeps the client as firmly in place as the pins that pinion a butterfly in a lepidopterist's collection.

- By the same token, it both lessens the risk that you, the advisor, will be held accountable for everything (when god has declined into a scapegoat) but also ensures that you can and will be held accountable for those actions you did in fact recommend and agree to carry out. Thus, as I need hardly say, it is important for you to know what you are doing within the confines of your technical specialty, for the log book in conjunction with the other papers necessarily generated in an advising assignment will ordinarily be quite sufficient to establish the extent to which you may be held accountable.

On The Use Of The Tape Recorder

Personally, I prefer to have my client meetings taped, unless they deal with very sensitive material. Taping your meetings, of course, means that you absolutely must know what you are talking about once you are prepared to talk. It does not mean that you need to come up with, on the spur of the moment, a problem solving solution to a problem you have not previously considered. In such circumstances all you need say is, "I'm sure I can provide you with a thoughtful response to that question. I'll report back by the time of the next meeting," or some such answer. The fact that a tape recorder is running will probably make you a little more cautious than usual, but you need not become abjectly silent. Simply be prepared to talk about what you know and postpone the rest until a time when you are ready to deal with it. This is, an any case, the essence of being a good advisor.

I like having a tape recorder on hand because it provides the client with a complete running commentary on what took place, the discussion which surrounded the decision making process (or what I shall shortly discuss as the narrative minutes), who took what position and why, and how the matter was settled — or postponed for settlement. Granted that you as the advisor must know your stuff; these tapes are admissible as evidence should your relationship ever end up in court. By the same token, these tapes should show that you provided the client with reasonable and prudent advice, that you didn't give way to any saccharine Lockean delusions but rather spoke as Father Hobbes might have spoken: of the risks, the obstacles, the difficulties and complexities that have to be surmounted (and by whom) before there could possibly be success. When you are on tape, you must speak as Hobbes would speak, not as Locke would (in a transport of febrile joy) carry on.

I have never found it necessary to keep copies of these tapes; that would be a cumbersome proceeding at best. In cases where you are liable for the advice that you give and therefore are at risk, simply place in your contract a clause that states that copies of such tapes (along with other minutes, memoranda, &c) must be made available to you upon request. Also simply note in your own meeting minutes that a tape was made so that you'll have a record of its existence. This is purely your cautious pragmatist speaking; I myself have never had a problem in this regard.

The Narrative Minutes

If you don't tape your meetings and keep only task action minutes, it will often be necessary to supplement these records with what I call the Narrative Minutes. These minutes provide you and key decision makers at your client's with necessary background information about the circumstances which lead to the decision: who said what, why, how, what your impression was, speculation about what this all might mean for the future, &c. Clearly such information can be most important and valuable. Whereas the task action minutes can be kept by a secretary or administrative assistant, you, the advisor, must keep the narrative minutes yourself. You will develop, you will have to develop, a sense of when people are telling you the truth, when they are deceiving both you and themselves, when they say one thing but mean to do something very much different. Body language, of course, is often a consideration. A person crossing his arms in front of his body while telling you that he is open to your idea is in fact telling you something quite different than the words themselves.

What I have discovered is that most people, and certainly many advisors, have pretty good hunches about people, but they tend to downplay their significance and overcredit the words people say. This is a mistake. My first piece of advice to any aspiring advisor is: trust your gut. If you feel the person is deceiving you, lying to you, lying to himself, he probably is. You should proceed sufficiently cautiously until you know.

Who gets to see the Narrative Minutes? If they involve important but secondary players, you can show them to the actual decision makers, particularly if these decision makers are going to have to be involved to alter the behavior of, say, recalcitrant and obstructive players. This will have to happen. Using the example of the woman operating the word processor which I told above, I had no power to alter her behavior. I could only advise. But I could (and did) inform the decision maker in my narrative minutes that we had a problem needing an immediate solution. It was within his power to alter her behavior using the carrots and sticks at his command. He needed to know there was a problem and needed to know its extent. Such information the advisor can provide through these critical minutes.

If, of course, the client decision maker is the problem, perhaps the person who hired you, this is another, more perplexing problem. As such I should like, shortly, to deal with it separately.

- **What You Want To Take Place As A Result Of This Meeting**

This is terribly important. Each meeting should have a finite, precise set of objectives. I cannot stress this enough. Write down as specifically as possible exactly what you wish to take place and what you need in terms of information, personnel commitment, executive commitment, resources, &c. to have this happen. Thus, do not say "Objectives need to be set." Say instead, "We need an 8 to 10 page development document setting forth the organization's capital, project and operating needs for possible funding by the area's corporations and foundations. We need information on the following points and with the following lengths: (specifics). The executive director should begin drafting this document and should allow three weeks to complete it after which I shall edit, review and modify it. A sample of the document we need is appended", &c. You get the picture. Nothing is left to chance, because if it is the imp of confusion, an advisor with a fertile imagination, will promptly take his place on the engine of events.

- **What Does The Client Want To Take Place As A Result Of This Meeting?**

The client, too, has expectations — or at least should have expectations — about this initial meeting with you. Get the client to write them down in as much specificity and share them with you prior to this initial meeting. This sharing of information beforehand is incredibly important. The thought about what should take place at the meeting should take place beforehand; the meeting itself should be used to ratify the decisions, clarify obscure points, and assign responsibility for achieving success. To make this situation work fully, of course, the client's expectations must be set forth in sufficiently precise detail.

If the client's immediate expectation list is (as may well be the case) too optimistic and too vague (a very common combination), you must discuss this with the client in advance in what is, in effect, a preliminary conference to the introductory meeting. Of course, if you are meeting with a single individual and not a group, you my prefer to wait for the introductory meeting; that is satisfactory so long as you will explain to the client exactly why his expectations are too hopeful and why they are insufficiently precise.

Now that I do this, my introductory meetings are smooth, congenial even pleasant encounters between people who are mutually committed to realistic objectives. Previously, there were shocks, often disturbing shocks: shock on my side that the client could have such unrealistic objectives, could in fact know so little about their own situation, their own resources, their own industry, the conditions affecting them, to put forward ideas and expectations that might well be, in my humble estimation, absurdly ludicrous. And shock on the client's side that their dream, what might be their motivating idea and *raison d'être*, was about to be cruelly scaled down and so lose the allure which had provided them with a reason for working. Yes, there were moments when mutual shock prevailed rather than orchestrated harmony and controlled realism.

No more!

The Obstacles You Foresee In Getting What You Need

Be candid. But be candid in a context. Consider who will see your written candor, and whether it might be more advantageous, at least in the beginning, to begin with a verbal assessment of the obstacles. Do not, however, jettison necessary candor to secure a diplomatic triumph. Penny wise. Pound foolish. Take my example above, the example, that is, of the need for creating a necessary fund raising document. If the organization has limited experience writing such documents, has not kept adequate data files about itself, including what it has done in the past with funds donated, what tangible successes it has secured, has meager client records and a limited grasp of what difference they really make in their community, these facts constitute a significant obstacle to writing a truly persuasive and compelling funding document. That's fact. It behooves you, one way and another, to say so. Sugarcoating this pill will definitely come back to haunt you later. Remember: you are the doctor. It is your responsibility to tell the client, your patient, what is wrong and what needs to be done to make things right. Granted, as you know more your original diagnosis may, perhaps will, change. That's fair enough. New facts may produce a new diagnosis. The client must understand this; you, too, must be prepared to admit this and alter your recommendations accordingly. Besides, remember your Caesar and his wars against the pesky Gauls. State the obstacles as baldly, as starkly, as menacingly as you can so that the client will understand the extent of risk. Remember: Americans are conditioned from birth to shuck off difficulties. The risk is not that we will become depressed and unnerved by the difficulties we face, but that, accustomed as we are to progress-speak, we'll regard them as tragically insignificant and beneath our constructive notice. You, the advisor, must not let this happen.

What You Propose To Do To Overcome These Obstacles

Be precise with the client about what you can do to help overcome the obstacles. You are equipped, must be equipped, to institute a problem-solving process which will result in each of these obstacles being overcome, either solely through your efforts (this, actually, can and does happen!), or under and through your guidance (which is more commonly the case). Again, take the illustration of creating a compelling fund raising document. If the organization doesn't now have necessary information, you can advise them on the specifics of how in future to gather and store what they'll need to be able consistently and without undue effort to create such a document. In other words, the problem does have a solution, and you will work with the client to achieve it. But again, don't overpromise. Don't make the mistake of saying that it can happen sooner than you know it can. Do not make the mistake of saying that the lack of a crucial ingredient does not have unfortunate, perhaps even grave, consequences. If it does, say so. Admit that the future can and will better by following your problem solving advice. But do not neglect to point out that the present cannot be as good as it might have been had such advice been implemented much earlier — presumably, of course, under your able guidance.

What Obstacles The Client Foresees

One of the things I have found extraordinarily helpful in my practice is asking people, point blank, about the obstacles that they fear might hamper realization of the success. Ask the client to write them down: the obstacles, fears, anxieties, all the nagging, often cripplingly destructive barriers which can come between you and the client and success. Some of these obstacles will be severely practical: "We don't have the money." Some will be personal: "I'm upset because my wife has cancer." Some will be essentially motivational: "I just don't think I can do this." But each of these obstacles does have a solution. It may not be an ideal solution, I hasten to point out; it may simply be the best that can be done under the current circumstances.

What's wrong with that? Progress, any beneficial change, must start somewhere. There can be change, real, meaningful change despite the fact that there isn't enough money to accomplish all that you and the client would like. There can and indeed must be change despite the fact that a client is threatened with personal grief. Does it seem unduly hard to say that life will go on and that one must prepare for the moment when the future becomes the present? This is nonetheless a fact. A client's hesitations and uncertainties about his ability to learn and to achieve something new can — and must be — dealt with. But you must know what you're up against: whether this is the drably practical and unromantic, or the stuff of high drama (or lowly farce). Some of this information, of course, will come through your own observations; you are a trained observer and you will, I know, come up with your own conclusions on events. But why make it more difficult for yourself than you need to? Have the client consider the obstacles that may prevent realization of the objective and write them down. Make sure that the discussion extends beyond the merely prosaic and that it encompasses personal, professional, and motivational difficulties.

Those participating in this process must be assured, and have an absolute right to believe, that what they tell should be considered confidential by you and by the decision maker. That's fair enough. But in your turn you (and the decision maker) have the right to insist on this information. I think, for instance, of what happened to me in one of the MBA level courses I taught just this term here in Massachusetts.

One of the adult students, an executive director of a multi-service agency, always seemed distracted in class, that is when he even bothered to come. He seemed alternately surly and abject; his classwork was poor, and he simply didn't bother to come the night he was to make his in-class presentation. I had resolved to flunk him; what else could I do? I had expectations about his behavior (and that of all my students) which had been communicated to them both at the beginning of the class and periodically throughout it. He had not met them. My course of action, while lamentable, seemed fixed. Until one of my colleagues informed me that the man had diagnosed just a fortnight before the class began as having leukemia.

What a difference it would have made for both of us had he only told me this information confidentially. I am a problem solver, and this information would have been crucial in determining a solution appropriate to what I was attempting to do, the needs of the college to maintain standards, and the desire of this man to complete the course. How easy it would have been! But who was to blame? Me, of course, for not making it perfectly clear that a good instructor (another name for problem solver/advisor) is duty bound to consider factors which under other circumstances might be considered extraneous. And the student, of course, for making no attempt to communicate crucial information to me as the problem solver. *N.B.* I gave this student an "Incomplete" and assured him that so long as the college's standards and my own were met, he could have as much time as he wanted to complete the course. I also told him that had he told me of his situation, I would always have made this decision. He has since completed the course satisfactorily.

What The Client Can Do To Overcome These Obstacles

You, of course, can *help* the client overcome his obstacles. You can do it directly; you can also refer the client to others who may be of assistance. All this is the normal stuff of the advising business.

What is unfortunately less normal is helping the client understand what he alone, within his own situation, can do to overcome the obstacles he faces. If, for instance, gathering information is crucial for the success of your operation and if this is something you do not wish to do, or cannot accomplish as well as others (including the client himself), then ask the client to write down all the ways that he himself could accomplish this task.

Clients need to be taught to write down what they wish to accomplish in the most specific detail. They need to write down in equally specific detail the obstacles which stand between them and realizing their desires. *And* they need to write down what they can do to overcome these obstacles.

Problem solving is necessarily a thoughtful and a detailed business. What I find over and over again is that many problems arise because people are too careless, too hasty about setting their objectives, overly optimistic about confronting the obstacles which might impede realization of these objectives, and have little or no sense of what they themselves may do to overcome the obstacles using their own resources. In all these ways you can be of assistance to the client. This work can profitably begin even before you and the client have your first formal meeting, although, of course, it will continue throughout the duration of your relationship.

Stagemanaging The First Formal Meeting

The introductory meeting between you and your new client should be a time for celebration and for pointed, controlled movement towards solving the mutually-agreed-upon problem and achieving the mutually-agreed-upon solution. But before you schedule this meeting you need to think through not only what will happen at the meeting, the tangible and not-so-tangible achievements which must come from this gathering, but the circumstances in which this meeting will occur. This means giving consideration to the following points and not simply letting them take place at will:

- precisely where the meeting will be held
- precisely where you will sit
- precisely where the client-decision makers will sit
- precisely where the minute keeper will be
- precisely where audio visual and other necessary equipment will be kept.

Why this bother? Because, as those who create the great ceremonies and pageants have always been aware, people are as influenced by circumstantial conditions, by what they see and by what appears to be the case, as they are by what they hear. This is crucial for you, the powerless advisor, to understand. I must say it again: you as the advisor ordinarily have no direct power. You do not have the ability to say to someone, "Do this." You have only the power to advise others to do something that will ultimately prove to be of benefit to them. This is a vastly different state of affairs from an individual who can tell someone to jump, waiting only for the person addressed to say, "How high?" Thus, as an advisor you must always give consideration to those matters which can help you move people to the achievement of the objective. This necessarily means giving consideration to the context in which decisions will be reached and positioning yourself so that you are seen to be a power player, even when you have actually nothing more than the power of influence (which can be, however, of the utmost importance).

Where The Meeting Should Be Held

If you are meeting at your client's office, find out where most of the power meetings are held. This might be where senior administrators regularly meet, where the board holds its periodic meetings, where the staff is gathered to hear instructions from the administration. This is the place you wish to appear. I have found that this place is appropriate for two very good reasons:

- People coming to this place are already in the habit of listening and of reporting their findings to decision makers. You are thus imbued with the power of place. That infamous Russian scientist Pavlov, who trained dogs to salivate upon hearing a bell, absolutely knew what he was about in the field of conditioning. As an essentially powerless advisor, I am most concerned that the people attending a meeting (people with the power to block me and my techniques as well as the power to implement them) come to see me first in a place which enhances my image as an influencial and significant individual.
- This place, too, not being in constant use is usually easier to obtain for your meeting. Indeed, if it is the board room of the organization, you may find this quite convenient to work from as your regular place of business while at your client's, since it may not be otherwise in use.

Where You Will Sit

You should sit on the right hand side of the most important decision maker in the room. The right hand has always been the most influential position *vis à vis* the key decision maker. This goes back at least to biblical times for Jesus sits at the right hand of God The Father and Saint Peter sits at the right hand of Jesus. Remember this.

Where Key Client-Decision Makers Sit

If the table is oblong or rectangular in shape, then the key decision maker sits at the head. You must be on the right hand side. Make sure of this by arriving early enough and leaving your brief case at this place. Only knowledgeable power players (particularly those antipathetic to your position) will have the sense to move you to a lower rung. Make sure that other key decision makers appear on the leader's left and on your right so that you are clearly perceived as being part of the power players block.

Where The Minute Keeper Sits

Ideally, the minute keeper will be at the left of the key decision maker, on your right, or across from you. This is to ensure that you can keep an eye on what is being written, that things are in fact being written, and that you can nod in the direction of the minute keeper when you want to emphasize that what has been said should in fact be written down. All other participants can seat themselves as they will. Remember: this order is not sancrosanct. As different parts of the project emerge as needing your assistance, it will be necessary for you to reposition the players. But remember: your position on the right hand of the (context) key decision maker remains constant.

Where Audio Visual And Other Necessary Equipment Will Be Kept

Your back must never be turned to your audience. Thus, you must position any audio visual equipment and other accessories in such a way that you can remain facing your audience, particularly the key decision makers of the day. If you have to use slides or other audio visual equipment of this kind, arrange for someone to run the equipment. You cannot present the proper image to this group and run the slides yourself.

Meeting At Your Office

Needless to say, you should have several advantages if the meeting is held on your turf. For one thing, you'll be comfortable with the surroundings, will know where everything is, and can function most efficiently. All this will be of the utmost assistance in conveying the proper image to your client. This does not mean, however, that you should not give consideration to the place, for place always has power, or why else is so much earnest consideration given to where international summit meetings are held?

My own circumstances are a good case in point of a situation where possible negatives have been turned into deliberate positives. As you may recall, I run my advising business from my office-condominium near Harvard Square. I run a one-person business and am always involved in a multiplicity of projects, each of which creates a storm of paper which is never adequately filed or ordered. This is a fact of life, but it might be one with negative consequences for those who would equate apple-pie order with a similar kind of mind. Moreover, I often work in casual clothes and simply do not have adequate time to change into a jacket and tie, much less into a suit for every client. So clients are forced to take me as they find me, which is often very, very casual.

To deal with this situation, I have created an office which leans heavily on ultra-traditional, rich, and indeed museum-quality furnishings. No cost, quite literally, has been spared to create an ambiance which breaths quality, taste and refinement — the kinds of characteristics I want my clients to know I bring to the solution of their problems but which may be less than readily perceived when looking at the often disheveled expert arising in haste from his computer.

Persian rugs, antique silver, old master paintings complete the decor, decor which makes people of quality feel very, very comfortable and at home and which subtly intimidates those who merely aspire to this condition of life. Moreover, there is one more master-touch which completes the scene: a huge, museum-quality lifesized portrait of me done by a well-known artist. Even here the necessary effect has been carefully calculated, because while I am painted in casual clothes, right behind me, on a table strewn with books, is the brilliant crimson of my Harvard doctoral gown. The painting says, symbolically, that while I may appear to be casual, one should not be misled into thinking that I am overly so or that this casualness in any way interferes with my ability to be intelligent and problem solving.

This painting, larger than any other, is currently hung in the room where I hold client prospect meetings and where Delphic Oracle client meetings are held. It is hung next to a well known work by a major English artist featuring one of England's prime ministers and by implication suggests that I should be in such company. Do you find this excessive? If so, consider the fact that my regular casual attire might disturb purists, that running my business from my home might be taken as a sign of undue casualness, that the blizzard of papers might indicate disorganization, and you will quickly see why it was necessary to be so precise about countering these potential negatives.

I am not, of course, necessarily suggesting that you must approach the solution of your place problem in the same way, but I do recommend that you write down every negative you can think of in running a business from your home, every negative of how you run that business, and every one of your personal quirks and write down what a not-too-critical client or prospect might say in response to these things that would be detrimental to your interests. Having done so, take action accordingly to minimize the damage, enhance your image, and provide an acute indication that you are not merely a responsible player but a significant one in your client's affairs.

The Meeting Itself

I have spent much time on getting you prepared for this initial meeting with your new client, because I regard the preparation as more important that the actual meeting itself. That meeting should, in the nature of things, be rather anticlimactic.

- The meeting should be called to order promptly by the chief decision maker present.

- This decision maker should express his delight at having you on board, should reiterate your credentials which have resulted in your selection, and should state his objectives, in precise detail, for this meeting. He should indicate, with the greatest possible enthusiasm and commitment, that he understands the problem that is being addressed, that he understands the obstacles that stand between the client and the solution, but that he himself has made a commitment to solving it and he wishes everyone else to make a commitment to solving it, too. Wishes and expects it. He should then turn over the meeting to you, the advisor.

- First, thank the decision maker by name for this introduction. Indicate that you are glad to have been chosen and that you will do your best to work with the client to achieve a solution to the problem. Indicate how much work has already gone into preparing for this meeting. It is important for people to know, even the lowliest players, that consideration has been given to the importance of their time and that this precious commodity will not knowingly be wasted. Most meetings waste time and accomplish nothing. Indicate that you want things to be different here.

- To show people that you are serious about achieving success, pass out a sheet listing your objectives for the meeting. This should constitute a preliminary list. It is inevitable that questions will be raised at this meeting about some of the objectives and that some modifications may have to be made in this list. Thus, stamp this sheet "Draft." Indicate the objectives you wish to achieve, the date by which they need to be achieved, and the people who need to be involved in achieving them, and the commitment that must be made (by whom) to achieve them. Necessarily at this point, some of these items must be left blank. It is the task of this meeting to fill in as many of these blanks as possible.

N.B. You must understand that this preliminary draft list is just that: preliminary. If all that can be arranged at this point is the implementation of a research project which will in fact determine the problem, its extent, the need for action to solve it, &c., then deal only with this. Don't rush ahead precipitately. Move slowly, deliberately. What is important for this meeting and indeed for all meetings is not that every problem of the client's be instantly solved (for some of their problems will have existed in one form or another for years) but rather that you indicate that a problem-solving process is being implemented that will, in due course, result in progress towards solution of all those problems which constitute a part of your engagement.

Once the list has been circulated, allow people a minute or two to read and study it. Then begin. Go through each item on the list point by point. State the reasons why you wish to do this thing in brief specificity. State the result that will occur when this thing is finished and why this is desirable to have. State how this task is to be accomplished, by whom and when. Ideally the person to whom the task is assigned, or will be assigned, is present. This person should then be allowed to express his understanding of the problem, confirm that it is in fact a problem, address the desired result and confirm that, indeed, it is desirable, and give his opinions on the ways the task may be accomplished, how he will be involved, and on the desired deadline.

As you can see, this is a long, sometimes awkward, and rather cumbersome process. But this is what gaining the relevant person's support is all about. Gaining assent is tricky. It is time consuming. It is often meandering and ungainly. There is, however, no other way short of outright, absolute authoritarianism. Of course, as authoritarian regimes have found, those assigned tasks against their will find all the resourcefulness of the flatworm in making their displeasure known.

As this discussion proceeds from necessarily involved person to necessarily involved person, the task action minute taker must be at work. People must not only have the chance to discuss matters; they must be moved to closure, to commitment. This closure, this commitment must be written down, placed in the Project In Process Log, and circulated to participants. There is no other way of doing things if you want to minimize confusion, irritation, vagueness, lack of concrete instructions, and all the other problems which regularly defeat advisors and cause clients to wax furious at their inadequacies.

One of the reasons I have very, very few problems with my clients, despite often acute stylistic differences, is because the client understands and acknowledges that these procedures, though time consuming and often deadly dull, make sense and are in their best interest.

Dealing With Opposition

If you have done your homework, if you have understood what a realistic solution is, what you can do to help reach it, what the client can and must do to help reach it; if the client has done similar homework before a meeting and if both of you are in major agreement on significant points, this introductory meeting should be well-run and cordial. People should leave it feeling that:

- continuing thought is going into the problem, into obstacles standing between the client and the solution, the problem solving techniques recommended by the advisor and those capable of being implemented by the client.

- the opinions of all those involved have in fact been solicited and will continue to be solicited, that they have had the opportunity to have their say, and that while they may not like everything that is contemplated, may not agree, even the most recalcitrant and difficult will be forced to admit that there is an organizing intelligence at work.

- there has been progress towards the desired objective.

Moreover, this should all be confirmed when the Task Action Minutes are drawn up and submitted to all participants. *N.B.* Before this is done, of course, you and the principal client decision maker should check them over for agreement and accuracy.

As you move towards these desirable objectives, of course, you can scarcely expect everything to be sweetness and light. There will be people who will object to what you are saying. There are those who make it a point to cross-question all decisions and to play the annoying devil's advocate role. There are those who will, let's face it, come up with better solutions than the ones you are advocating. As a facilitator moving towards the problem's solution, this should not irritate you. Your job is to help move the client towards a solution; allow for the fact that even the lowest placed player may have the capacity for a good idea. Thus, you must learn to present your ideas frankly, thoroughly, always giving the best reasons you can while advocating a course of action, but you must also learn how to give way gracefully while complimenting the person with the idea by indicating what a good one it is!

Still, there will be difficult moments, even perhaps in this early introductory meeting.

- If a person seems skeptical about what he is being asked to do, say, "You seem skeptical. Care to share your thoughts?" In other words, push a bit, gently at first. Perhaps the individual really doesn't understand and needs a second brush with the information you are presenting. Perhaps the individual really has something substantial to say and deserves to be heard. Perhaps the individual will give voice to what you'll know, because you've confronted situations like this before, to be a common concern, one easy enough to deal with. Or perhaps this person wants to voice opposition. Before doing anything, hear the person out.

In every group, no matter how small, there is always a moderate consensus that can be formed. If you are perceived to be the kind of person who stifles other people's opinions, others will turn against you, and make it difficult for you to function later. Your job is not necessarily to agree to every point that is raised (you must always remember that indeed you may be right: after all you are the tested advisor!), but it is to respond in a reasonable fashion to the points being raised and so co-opt the reasonable position and hold it.

Thus, you can be assured that some people will not understand what you have just said and will need to have it said again. Don't assume that just because you have presented your information clearly it has been understood clearly. As a professional speaker, I am continually appalled by how little of what I say is clearly, really clearly, perceived by my audiences. Thus, welcome the opportunity to make a second, briefer presentation which is directed both to this particular questioner and to all those who need another rendition of the information.

But beware of becoming glaringly redundant. This can turn-off the brighter members of the team. If your audience starts evincing evidence of boredom (coughing, shuffling papers, looking at their watches, pushing their chairs back from the table in expectation of a quick get-away, &c) then inform the individual that you'll be happy to drop by his office and provide further information about his role in the solution of the problem. Be cheerful and client-centered when you say this, for remember the latent power of even the most lowly-placed flatworm. If you're going to need this person, you must go through these steps.

- If a person suggests alterations to your plan and you are not certain that they'll work, indicate that you will give the matter your earnest and utmost consideration. If you are not ready to make a decision about a point now, don't be rushed into doing so. Even in a situation of the utmost emergency, you can usually take a moment or two to clarify your thoughts and make a cooler decision. Your job is not to make a snap-judgement. It is to make an informed judgement. If you can make the decision now, well and good. If you cannot, your job is to indicate how and in what way that decision will be rendered; to channel the discussion, in short, and to indicate that you, the expert advisor, know what you are doing. If indeed the suggestions that have been made to you are ludicrous and are never likely to be implemented, then especially use this procedure. It is never a good idea to humiliate someone unless this is your policy and unless you are absolutely certain that you can expunge this individual from the human record. Since this very rarely happens, if an particular idea must be soundly rejected, then seek out the individual privately or have the client-decision maker do so and explain why this plan cannot be advanced now. Remember: as Winston Churchill so rightly said, if you are going to hang a man, you can afford the white gloves.

- If the person attacks you, let him. First, imagine the worst things that could be ever be said to you. And then remember, as Jerry Brown used so rightly to say, "It's just words." Yes, the words may be humiliating, offensive, degrading, inflammatory. But they are in themselves just words and have not hurt you. It is how you react to them that matters. Let's say an individual releases an attack of unmitigated profanity on you. You'd naturally be upset. Say so. Turn to the individual saying this and say, "Frankly, I'm not used to hearing these words and they offend me. I'd like to keep this discussion rational and on the topic at hand. Can you do this?" And then pause. It is certainly not your job to defend yourself, and it would be a perilous mistake to respond in kind to this kind of attack. Play for the moderate consensus, co-opt the reasonable position and hold it. Make the person attacking you make a fool of himself. It always happens if you do not lose your cool. What amazes me is how often people do and how easy it is to do. But remember, if those whose interests may be adversely affected by what you are proposing (after all: you are suggesting that people work, aren't you? and even this may be considered a low blow by you and the client-decision maker) can throw you off balance by a few words, what have they got to lose by doing so?

I might also say that it is perfectly permissible to use humor. Humor defuses plenty of situations, and I have learned to use it more and more in my work. I'm not talking about side-splitting, thigh slapping humor. I'm talking about a short, deft comment made to turn an encounter to your advantage. Thus, to an individual shouting abuse against you and your proposals, you might simply say, as if to the group, "Dave, of course, is always known for understating his case. And today is no exception." Your job is to realize at all times that communication, which is what this meeting is all about, can and should be used both to advance a certain point of view and to impede the opposing point of view without the discussion threatening your position in the problem solving process.

Thus, your job is to:

- explain again your current recommendations
- answer questions that arise about them
- allow for the possibility that others in the problem solving team may come up with better solutions than you and to adopt them gracefully
- answer doubts, and
- turn and isolate hostility.

Also make sure that people criticizing or adversely commenting are never allowed to do so without being asked, quite precisely, what they would do instead. Being critical, grousing, grumbling, groaning, is an American sport, far more popular than football. I abhor it; I abhor it in myself, and I despise it in others. And I have found means of dealing with it, not necessarily eradicating it, mind you, but containing its debilitating influence. Whoever criticizes a plan, must and should be allowed to do so. Every technique, every procedure, every problem solving step can and should be open to the most intense inspection and the most probing examination. All those involved in moving towards the solution have the right to participate in this process, have indeed a moral responsibility to do so. On the other hand, if they criticize, if they find fault with, if they wish to stop something from happening, they must propose an alternate way for reaching the desired solution. This is an absolute, a cardinal rule of mine which I advise you, too, to adopt.

Turn to your opponent, your critic, your low-grade grouser and say, "I understand that you are not happy. I would therefore be glad to hear your *precise* alternative to what has been proposed."

If you are dealing with a smart player, he'll ask for time. Request a recess. Ask to be able to report back next meeting with additional facts. If he's not such a player, you'll find what is said to be vague, diffuse, irritatingly irrelevant. Try not to let your irritation show. Let the decision maker, let his colleagues see that what is being said is not pertinent. Then once it has been put forward, respond to it, reasonably, in detail. If the points have any merit, say so. If you don't need a sledgehammer to kill a fly, don't use it. If some of the points are not feasible, point out why. In short, do not merely address the individual, co-opt the reasonable position and show the group how they, in their turn, can expect to be treated, how their good ideas will be received, and their less brilliant dealt with in a nonthreatening way. It has taken me a long time to learn this, for I am naturally a rather peremptory and brusque individual, but as I learn it I see that this is truly wisdom.

Moving To A Conclusion

By the time you have completed the round robin of participants, whether there is only one or whether there are a score or more, you should have moved substantially closer to what you and the client need on the following points:

- agreement as to what the problem is
- on how the problem will be approached
- on who will be involved in helping to solve it
- on what this individual will do, and
- by when progress can be reported.

These points can then be enshrined in the permanent proceedings, the Project in Process log and in the Task Action Minutes which must emerge from this and from all meetings.

Before this meeting can break up, however, you have still more to accomplish:

- Sum up all that has been agreed and check to make sure that the individual taking the Task Action Minutes has recorded this information correctly. No meeting can be considered over until the person running it has concluded by summarizing all that has been agreed, even if the agreement is to hold a question open for later decision. Even this may be, in fact, a decision, for as Alice Roosevelt Longworth, who never opened her mail, used to say, "They eventually answer themselves."

- Tell participants that you have all had a productive meeting. If you've run it like this, you have. People are used to spending a lot of time in meetings that are pointless because there is no very good reason for having them, because they are run sloppily, and because no substantial result ensues. This will not be the case with your meetings, not after mastering these points. You should let people know that this is how you'd like matters to continue and that you anticipate that they will.

- Indicate when the next meeting will be and who among them needs to participate. Not all people involved in the problem solving process need to be with you at every meeting, only when their part in this process is under consideration.

- Get the agreement of the task action minute taker as to when these critical records will be disseminated.

- Indicate how participants can get in touch with you between meetings by providing them your telephone number and address. Or, if you have a Delphic Oracle contract without a telephone privilege, be clear they understand that contact with you is limited to these meetings.

Having said what you came to say, having heard what you came to hear, having secured agreement on that which was necessary to be agreed upon, it is now time for this meeting to end. A healthy, constructive pattern has been established. You have acted in the proper role of the facilitating advisor. You have moved a considerable distance to securing the respect to which you are entitled and which will, in due course, provide you with a real, not an ephemeral, popularity, the kind which will translate into other clients. You can congratulate yourself. And you should.

Just make sure, however, you don't remain in this contented state too long. After all, now is the time when the flatworms truly begin to come out and do their undermining work.

Understanding The Flatworm Principle

What do I talk about flatworms for? Perhaps you've been wondering as you've encountered the word here and there in this book. Did you wonder what I was talking about and why? It is now time to tell you.

If you remember your college biology you will recall, I'm sure it's on the tip of your tongue, that in the Kingdom Animalia the Platyhelminthes, that is flatworms, are the most primitive groups of animals to have primary bilateral symmetry. This, I need hardly remind you, is the symmetry assumed by all higher animals (like man). Bilateral symmetry is much more suitable for active movement, like active crawling or swimming, than is radial symmetry. All animal groups higher in the evolutionary tree than the Platyhelminthes are bilaterally symmetrical or have been derived from bilateral ancestors.

What this means is quite clear: flatworms find it difficult to move and so have come to abhor movement. They have remained essentially unchanging throughout the entire historic record. And they have as their unchanging task eradicating change, retarding movement, making certain they have to do as little as possible to remain in the exact position they currently occupy.

Just like the human flatworms that you, the progressive advisor, the enthusiastic catalyst, will have to work with on your assignments.

Now consider for a moment what I am saying. Flatworms, the most primitive of animals, have stayed the same through all the great ages of man. They remained just as they are when Jesus taught. They remained just as they are through the great ages of human discovery. They remained just as they are throughout every significant moment of human aspiration and longing. And they shall remain just as they are through all that you can do or contemplate. Horrifying, isn't it? For the flatworm's task is to obstruct, defeat, and obliterate change, to make sure that nothing alters its successful niche, and to ensure that the present ways, no matter how generally defeating, continue.

Catalytic advisors, of course, are the natural opponents of flatworms and always have been. We are dedicated to change. We strive for perfection. We are expending our life to the last breath on making things better, on improving and altering the condition of things as we find them. But the tragedy is that the flatworms always win. In the end, we advisors live with the sad realization that the flatworm always defeats the best and the brightest, always undercuts our ability to function successfully, always manages to obstruct progress because its objective is so rudely clear: it is to be and do nothing, nothing at all. Merely to exist in a state of damning obstructiveness.

Advisors may come, advisors may go, so know the unreasoning flatworms, but I, in my gripping obstinance, shall remain exactly as I am: a thing void of action or beneficial intent.

Every advisor who enters into any situation replete with hopes, enthusiasm and problem solving techniques, needs to know this about the flatworms — and deal with what is, in fact, a cosmic problem of the most grave and profound kind; what is at issue is nothing more than our ability to cope in a situation which, ultimately, will defeat us, for the natural tendency of events is to decay, dissolution, and dissipation. The flatworm knows it and smiles his unnerving smile to celebrate yet another victory over constructive change.

This Flatworm Principle, then, is clear. It is as the Myth of Sisyphus, fated plodder damned by the gods to push a boulder to the top of a hill, damned to have it thrust down just as he reaches the summit. Our task is the struggle, and as advisors we find our supreme reason for being in the fact that we have struggled and struggled again against the most obstructive forces of a cunning primitive, always knowing that the best that we wanted could only be the slenderest aspiration, always knowing that we were beset on every side by forces which existed for only one reason — to create a void out of everything, not the paradise that we so ardently desire.

Knowing this, living with this as we do, day to day, project to project, we should take time and remember that our contest against the wearing flatworm is an immemorial one that cannot and will not be won by us or in our time. But it is the only battle worth taking on. For it is the very essence of nobility, and what we, as change agents, must do.

How do we fight this battle day by day?

The Client Obstructs You: By Testing You

In the Lockean universe, clients are reasonable people who wish to realize a desirable objective. They rationally seek out advisors with relevant skills and problem solving techniques and work with them, enthusiastically, closely, to get what they want as quickly as possible. These situations are alarmingly infrequent in the actual world of the advisor and his clients, for clients are not always or even necessarily rational people and, whatever they say, they work overtime to defeat both you and the achievement of their own desired objective. If you doubt this, it's because you have not been an advisor before, or because you have just arrived from Shangri La.

One of the ways the client will obstruct progress is by testing you, attempting to discover how much you know, and seeing what will happen if he doesn't follow your advice, whether the consequences you predict will in fact actually occur. You must expect this testing, must clearly state the consequences of not following your advice, and must then sit back and await results.

I think, for instance, of one of my clients. This happens to be a respected scientific organization I represent in a fund raising advisor capacity. The client decision maker is a highly-trained astronomer, but when first working with me understood nothing about development work. Nonetheless, as we began to approach corporations and foundations, the client developed the usual urge to test the advisor, that is to ignore my advice and continue on her own path despite very clear indications from me that no beneficial result would be forthcoming (none, that is, except the one I never mentioned: that she would come to understand and accept that my advice is more often right than wrong).

Against my recommendations, she selected a large series of corporations and foundations across the nation to apply to for assistance for various projects. I carefully examined their guidelines and proclaimed that it was most unlikely any of those selected by the client would in fact return donations, that is, that my client was proposing an exercise in futility. Nonetheless she persisted. Had I done the same thing, of course, in the field of astronomy, she would have roared with laughter, for what did I know of that? My comments about this exercise were on the tapes of our regular weekly meetings along with an equally precise recommendation that one foundation in particular which had previously granted a generous donation to the organization in years past be approached at once. The letters and proposals to the new sources went out long before the letter and application to the past supporter, despite weekly attempts to move the matter along.

Week after week for the next two or three months, the refusals to her applications came in regularly. Some of them must have been sent on the day the proposals were received. Week by week the client became more discouraged. "No one is funding us," she said. "We'll never raise the money we need." I resisted the ever-stronger urge to say, "I told you so." Like a fine wine, this is a sentiment which must be allowed to mellow to be quite, quite right.

Rather less promptly, our proposal was dispatched to the foundation which knew the organization, although no cultivation had occurred for some years. And in the same period of time, they made a donation for $10,000. The amount of work this had taken was a tiny fraction of all that had been undertaken with the other possible funding sources. The return substantial. The wine was ripening.

I then asked the director to turn her attention to her major interest, namely getting a new building for the association, a very substantial undertaking and a very expensive one. We selected an individual with a long-standing interest in the cause with the means to make this possible and in due course asked for his assistance. The result was staggering: a contribution of well over one million dollars. The wine was ripe.

While the client was in transports of joy over this marvelous development, I took the opportunity to point out that all our activities had turned to gold this year (the year of my advisorship) with one significant exception: the vast numbers of proposals sent to corporations and foundations. And that this was, quite frankly, a waste of time and money. I didn't need to prod this valuable client too much. She understood that she had been attempting to practice my trade and ignore my advice. She didn't have to promise never to do it again. I knew that her forays into my domain would be fewer and less taxing. We had, in short, come to recognize each other as critical members of a winning team, each doing the thing we were most suited to doing to achieve successes which by any reckoning are substantial.

N.B. I received a tidy raise when they retained me again for a second year — because I asked for it (for it was not offered) and because the client at last understood my value.

What can we learn from this example?

- Anticipate the moment, early on in your relationship, when the client seeks to play your role as advisor.

- It is very unlikely that you can dissuade the client from playing out this role simply by reasoning. He has to find out by results that you are correct.

- Let the client lay out the course of action he'll follow. If you do not agree, cannot agree, find the suggestions a ludicrous waste of time, say so with the utmost diplomacy but using frank and direct language. Tell the client you disapprove and tell the client why. Keep the discussion on the highest plane possible, which is harder to do if the ideas are especially foolish.

- Make sure your point of view is written down or can be found on the tapes of your meetings. Note the date you provided this advice and the relevant circumstances. Things do change. Try not to use absolutist language. In the example above, it would have been foolish for me to say of the corporations and foundations the client approached that they would "Never!" give them a donation, for I myself was aware of means (which the client could not yet employ) which might well provide the desired result. Say that "Under the current circumstances, it is most unlikely you will achieve what you wish to achieve." Lay out your reasons.

- Don't belabor the point. One of the things all advisors must come to grips with is that the client makes the decisions. Advisors can only advise. Advisors, sure of the superb wisdom of what they are saying, can and will be put out when clients make choices which are not what the advisors wish. But the advisor-client relationship is a very clear instance of the man who pays the piper calling the tune. You can only suggest which tune it will be. Moreover the client must see that you will give way with a good grace; that even if you do not support the activity in question you will assist it in going forward, so long as you are not doing anything illegal or directly detrimental to your interests. Once the client had decided to approach corporations and foundations I thought unlikely to produce the desired result, I dictated the cover letters, wrote the guts of the proposals, and structured the submissions. That's, after all, part of what I was retained to do, disapprove or not of how my specialized knowledge was being used. For make no mistake about it: had I not gone along with the client's (admittedly wrong) decision, I might never have been allowed to use these skills after the client truly came to realize how valuable they are.

- As events move towards realizing the prediction based on your expertise, do not crow. Humiliating the client is not in your interest and may prevent you from ever exercising your technical skills. Tell the client you are sorry things are not working out as he wished. After all it is sad, very sad, that the new ways people use, even if they fly directly in the face of our own experience and advice, don't work. We might all learn something if they did. As catalysts ourselves, we should be sorry when a person's ideas fail, even if we knew in advance that they would. All people, and especially clients testing their advisors, must be allowed to make mistakes and so learn what it takes to achieve success.

- Once it is clear that the client's way of proceeding will not work, ask the client what he has learned from this situation. It is very likely that he will tell you things based on the very reasons you originally cited. In other words, the client has learned something — something, I must add, which is very much to your advantage, for the client has now learned that your advice is valuable and should be followed. The client has come, tardily no doubt, to understand that there are things he knows and things that you know and that it might very well be mutually beneficial to let each of you operate effectively in the sphere in which each of you can. This, I submit, is when the effective problem solving team really begins to come into existence. As you see it happening it is your responsibility, as an individual who understands how difficult it is to achieve constructive change, to be gracious and generous to the client. For it is never easy to admit that one has been mistaken, and there is nothing to be gained by forcing the client to own up to his error. For, in such an admission, lie the seeds of your severence from the client who will remember even the slightest taint of hubris and humiliation.

The Client Obstructs You: By Sabotaging You

People in organizations often have conflicting agendas. The most serious of these situations to deal with is where they actually believe in each agenda and pursue them equally vigorously. In such situations an individual participating in the decision making process can come to sabotage you and to sabotage you citing the very highest motives: that you are wrong, that what you are proposing is destructive, that it is in the best interests of the organization and its employees to ignore you. This happens regularly.

Here are the signs of sabotage:
- If the saboteur is clever, he'll agree to what you are proposing and then do nothing, or even worse, do things directly opposite to what he said he was going to do.
- If the saboteur is not particularly clever, he'll show evidence of surliness and blatant opposition to what you are proposing.

One way of dealing with this situation is to set the individual exceptionally clear tasks with exceptionally clear deadline dates. Make sure the individual agrees to the tasks and the deadlines and make sure the individual's supervisor understands and acknowledges that there has been such agreement. Make sure that this agreement is written down and is in the individual's hands as well as the decision maker's. You want everyone to be clear about what is required, what has been done to secure agreement, and when the task must be completed. Lack of clarity on your part effectively aids the saboteur. And if by chance you are merely dealing with the more common muddler than the less frequent obstructer, if you are anything less than clear you'll be responsible for any resulting confusion.

If the saboteur is clever, he'll agree to the terms (although taking his sweet time in doing so) and then move slowly, painfully slowly, towards implementing them, while advancing a series of plausible explanations as to why they cannot be implemented on schedule. ("Gosh, the boss also asked me to do this report and I had to do it." "There was the annual meeting to prepare for." &c) As time goes by, of course, these excuses become less and less plausible, but the saboteur is counting on you being too timid, too polite, too anxious and uncertain yourself about your position to risk any kind of substantive confrontation. Besides, the flatworm always knows that the energy of momentum, the thrust for change, is necessarily a short thrust, that after a very little time this thrust runs out of steam and comes to a screeching halt and that most practices will then revert to pretty much what they were before. In other words, the flatworm instinctively understands that change comes in bursts and that after change there is always a declension to reversion. His job, therefore, is to stall and to gain time, hoping that you'll lose interest, influence, be otherwise distracted, or merely give up (or be pushed out by the collective weight of the flatworms, who are always hoping for this exact result).

Because you, the advisor, are definitely working in a situation with constraints, a situation that in the final analysis will fail to move as far and as fast to progressive resolution as you would like, you have got to do what is necessary when you have the ability to do so. For make no mistake about it: when you come into a situation seeking change you bring with you a momentum, however slight that may be. But, as I've said before, this is a momentum that naturally does not go far and which will, in due course, stop altogether. Thus, you must move with it immediately.

This means being perfectly clear in your own mind about what you'll do to achieve the change you must have, the change which can result, if circumstances are properly handled, in bringing about the desirable end result to which you and the client are purportedly moving. Thus, you must be prepared to call the flatworm, the likely saboteur, on his behavior as soon as you spot it:

- If deadlines are not met, if excuses are given (no matter how plausible) go to the flatworm and urge him, at first warmly, then (as time goes on) more and more coolly toward the realization of the task that he has agreed to perform. At this point, you can see how important it is that the individual has agreed to the task and to the deadline for without this agreement, the flatworm will give you a version of the old "No taxation without representation" line. "Nobody asked me; if anybody had I would have said it was impossible. I'd like to help, but I cannot." And on and on. Preclude this by gaining the individual's acceptance of the assignment and the deadline.

If the flatworm still fails to respond, go to the next level of decision maker and urge this person's involvement. Remember: you have only advisory powers. You have influence, to be sure, but the obstructive powers of saboteurs and flatworms can always defeat you. You must go to the individual who has the power to order change, and you must insist that this change be forthcoming. Many decision makers, despite wanting the title and the emoluments, feel distinctly uncomfortable actually exercising their power. We have become, on the whole, a society of responsibility avoiders. This is something the flatworms instinctively understand, and they work hard to accelerate the trend towards an emasculated universe. You have to know this. Therefore, as you find that reason doesn't work, that a warm, personable attitude gets you nowhere (as you turn, in short, from Locke to Hobbes), you must seek to gain the necessary and substantial adherence of the decision maker who can force change by apt use of the sticks and carrots at his command.

Many, many advisors, being essentially well-educated, reasonable, well meaning people, don't like this part of their vocation. They don't want to be put in the position of having to fire people, to alter their habits and their lives, to force people to make substantial changes. But let me say this to you: Reason alone is insufficient in the advising business. Reason alone will not always, not even usually, result in the achievement of substantial change. You must be prepared to use the appropriate, the necessary, the, may I say, inevitable, tool to bring about the result that you desire, and that the client says he desires. Hobbes understood this. Now you must, too.

This means going to the client decision maker and letting him know that an aspect of the project, portrayed in the most distinct and dramatic terms, now hangs in the balance because of the lack of cooperation of one of the key players, a player, you would like to point out, who has agreed to the task in question, agreed to a specified date for completing it. Point out what will happen if this task is not completed, how other aspects of the project will be adversely affected. Point out how your own ability to operate effectively will be severely undercut if this task is not completed. And, importantly, advise the client decision maker on what to do. Do not leave the matter open ended. Surely by now you have a sense of the individual flatworm, you know what he is doing, why he is doing it, what it matters that he is doing it. By the same token you should have a clear conception of what you want the decision maker to do. So advise him to do it and keep the matter on the task action list of things to accomplish until it is in fact done. For make no mistake about it: if the task is unpleasant, if it actually involves exercising his authority (as opposed merely to being seen to have such authority) the client decision maker will wait as long as possible to carry out the unsatisfying task. We are a society where people nowadays do not like being perceived as having power and feel distinctly guilty about exercising their power if they can be held accountable for doing so. What a triumph for the conquering flatworms who revel in this disgusting state of affairs.

In dealing with this problem of the obstructing client, I have come to find myself in many curious situations in my advising career. Let me share one with you to give you an indication of what we must do to realize the result we wish to achieve (and which the client says he wants to achieve). Not so long ago I represented a Bible college in the western United States. I had a long and generally productive relationship with this institution as a development counselor until a problem arose I had never faced before and frankly did not expect to face in my practice. All personnel of the college, from its board of trustees to the janitorial staff, were born-again Christians. I was the first person hired by the institution in any capacity for merely technical skills who was not ideologically of the right persuasion; in fact, my ability to function in such an environment was one of the questions asked of me during the prospect meeting.

In the middle of my engagement, the president of the institution and his wife decided to separate. According to certain key Bible verses, this meant that the man no longer had control of his own house and could not, until this situation was rectified, take a leadership position in any other. Hence the need for his resignation. Rather than approach the problem head-on and attempt for an early (if painful) resolution, the college's board of trustees (made up of the president's friends and supporters) characteristically waffled. One of the ways they did this was by keeping me at arm's length for a period of nearly 8 months, during which time they paid my retainer fee but did not make use of my services, despite weekly reminders from me about the need to take strong, immediate, fair action.

Finally, I could stand it no longer. Instead of asking their permission to come, I told them I was coming to the next Board meeting and demanded a meeting with the Chairman of the Board. I was reluctantly accorded it. The man could not have been surprised by what I said. I reminded him that this was a biblical institution. That the injunctions from the Bible were very clear on this matter. That because of the Board's failure to take action, the college's financial position was drifting to disaster, two rival and warring camps had formed among the students and faculty, and that the Board itself was split between the ideological purists and those who thought a more sympathetic approach was warranted. I told the chairman, in a meeting which we conducted behind locked doors, just the two of us, that that evening at the Board meeting he had only one course of action, namely to ask the Board to request the president's immediate resignation. I supplied him with the reasons why this was not merely an advisable but an inevitable course. I then proceeded to supply him with information about who should govern the college in the interim until a new administrator was named, how the resignation should be announced to the student body and faculty, and other pertinent information. In other words, I stepped into a situation in chaos and made the most stringent recommendations possible.

That night at the board meeting I sat next to the chairman of the board and continued to urge this course of events. And at last a substantial measure of what I had urged, including the unanimous request for the president's immediate resignation, was secured.

What can we learn from this situation?

- The president was the man who was primarily responsible for retaining me as development counsel. But ultimately when I came to see that he and his situation were making it impossible to realize the objectives for which I was hired, I felt quite correct in urging, indeed moving, his ouster.

- Although I was not ideologically in tune with the beliefs of the institution, at a critical moment in its history I was the individual who urged, indeed demanded, that the institution live up to its public and publicized beliefs, for to do otherwise would fatally undercut its ability to present a credible image with the people I was working with.

- I waited too long act. In those days, now fortunately long ago, I was more of a Lockean than I am today. It is now clear to me that at the first signs of drift, of rival and warring camps springing into existence, at the first signs of weakness and aimlessness among the decision makers, I should have made stronger and progressively stronger representations about what was happening and what needed to be done to correct matters. But in those days I was not as aware of the injurious influence of flatworms as I am today.

My responsibility, as is yours, is to procuring the success, in working with the client in the best way you can to overcome his obstructive behavior, and to get what you both say you want. As this situation clearly shows, the client early on forget about his previous commitment to securing the success. It was my task to remind him and to press him, ultimately to pressure him, into again taking up that necessary task.

I wish this story had a happy ending, but it does not. Without going into the muddled details of this story, I can tell you this: that the president, even having been forced to resign, would not vacate his office or official home, that the board continued to refuse to take resolute action, that the necessary steps were not taken to unite a divided faculty and student body, and that the appalling Cassandra of the situation, yours truly, found at the end of two years his contract was not renewed. Shortly after that the college went bankrupt and its few remaining assets were merged into another.

Could things have been different? Yes. Yes, they could have been. Do I hold myself responsible? Only to the extent that I should have known the insidious, all pervading influence of the flatworms and taken earlier, stronger action against them. These flatworms, ensconced in positions of power, might not have done anything other than they did, but I should have been freed from wondering what else I might have done to preclude the ultimately unhappy result.

So I say this to you:

- Expect obstruction.

- Work to secure the adherence and agreement of individuals as to what they should be doing and when they should be doing it.

- When they fail to meet the agreed-upon guidelines, call them on it immediately. A bad habit is more difficult to break than it is easy to create a good one. You can do this, at first, calmly, reasonably, but you must be prepared to escalate the discussion faster than I did at the Bible college, for after a certain point the forces of dissolution become too strong to overcome.

- Go from the offending party, the saboteuring flatworm (whose entire being is wrapt up in the necessity to obstruct change) to the next level of decision maker, a level which, most likely, is also made up of flatworms, flatworms who speak progress-speak but who live for obstruction.

- If this doesn't work, if you still cannot secure the necessary assistance you need, the full cooperation of the decision maker to make matters change, to move the flatworm saboteur to movement, the thing he most abhors, then go to the next higher level.

- Remember: your commitment is to achieving success. To get this success, to retain intact your reputation as a meaningful catalyst, you must be willing to risk the loss of the client, however painful that may be at the moment, for by continuing in a situation that is not productive to you or to the client, to continue to aid and abet the lie of progress when you are actually working as the agent of obstruction, will ultimately destroy your soul and hence the joy of your life. Work to be meaningful must be joyful. Advising work, properly understood, is among the most joyous work there can be. But by the same token, caving in to the mediocrity of the flatworms, going along because it is convenient to go along, will produce nothing but a debilitating ennui in your life, undermining your confidence, causing you to question your mission. No, the struggle against the obstructors, doing what must be done to move them to success, is not always easy, not always pleasant, but for the sake of your soul, it is always necessary.

The Client Obstructs You: By Yessing You To Death

Equally destructive to a good advisor-client relationship are those clients who yes you to death, who agree to everything but who do nothing. This is yet another destructive form of obstruction, and a very infuriating one.

I have, for instance, a client who writes down every word I say, quite literally. He has notebook after notebook (for I have represented his organization for nigh on to four years now) filled with my pithy reflections, recommendations, reasons for acting, suggestions about what must be done, in what order, by what date, and by what people. Over the course of some 175 meetings or so, he has scarcely ever disagreed and has at most cavilled at minor points. An ideal client? I'm afraid not.

He is likeable, intelligent, well meaning, ostensibly committed to the success of the organization — and unable, it seems, to take solid, purposeful action to realize the objectives he says he wants and which I aim to help him get. What can be done in such a case?

Unlike the previous case where the flatworm saboteur is unlikely (if he is smart) to admit that he is obstructing you, here the situation is the reverse. My client quite cheerfully admits that I am right when I point out that he is obstructing realization of the objectives he says he wants. I point out that tasks from the previous weeks have gone without action. He tells me (with a smile) that that is true. I point out the need for action and point out why. He can only agree — and does. I rage. I try anger. I plead and wheedle. Whatever I do, he smiles and admits I'm right and leaves with a positive lilt in his step, feeling somehow cleansed by the fiery experience of being immersed with me for an hour a week confronting his many foibles.

I have thought long and hard about this case which, given time, you, too, will confront: the client who is happy to be pushed and pulled by you, delighted to have the benefit of your earnest consideration, wondrous at all your energy and good ideas, but who, in the end, continues to plod along exactly as before — while, I must point out, contentedly paying your bill.

What can be done?

First of all admit, advisor, admit you are not god. There was once a time (now virtually gone) when I thought I could solve every problem I set my mind to. Now I am thankful if I leave a thumbprint on the face of chaos as a mark that I have tried to improve matters.

This individual's problems go way back, and I can only hope to make a beginning in solving them.

- Admit your own limitations. Obviously I have not managed to solve the infuriating management style of this individual and obviously I have not managed to overcome all the problems of his organization. This, I'm afraid, is beyond me.

- Equally acknowledge that you have made a difference. Working with this organization, despite its manager's curious style, we have managed to raise more money that was ever raised before. This is a lively testament to the fact that something positive is going on. Yes, things could be better. But are they better than they were before? It's important that you answer this question and important that you understand the affirmative results that have taken place.

- Keep striving. I have come to the conclusions that American have the need to be told on a regular basis how they could do better, how they could strive harder, how they could be improving themselves. Perhaps this goes back to the blissful days when they were immersed in the security of their families, when all the big decisions were made for them, when they merely had to be cheerful. Clearly I have come to see that for some of my clients I perform a decidedly parental function which cheers them up no end. Look, that is, to what else the client may be getting from the relationship beyond realization of the ostensible objective for your being there. In my very green, very ingenue beginnings as an advisor I quite wrongly, quite naively, thought that people wanted advisors only to do what they say they wanted to do: that is, achieve a mutually agreed-upon objective. Nothing could be further from the truth. One of the things that I have come to see that I provide to people is structure, a channel for achieving success. People who are not self-directed, not self-motivated, not self starters need to be around a person like me and are often sensible enough to realize this and to pay for the structure they must have. I didn't know when I began my practice that this would be one of the things I'd be selling; but it is certainly one of the things people are buying from me. *N.B.* This has lead me to the conclusion that one of the most valuable functions that we advisors in fact provide to our clients is structure: working with a client to clearly set attainable objectives. To work with them to get these objectives acknowledged and understood by all the players in the problem solving process. Working with the client on a regular basis to make sure that these objectives are realized and that the problems which inevitably arise in all problem solving situations are in fact solved. What I call the Implementation Strategy is at the heart of a successful client-advisor relationship.

There are, too, other things you can do with the client yessing you to death:

- Keep the tasks precise and highly structured.

- Secure agreement with such a client as to his ability to perform them by a particular time.

- Check in frequently with the client, more frequently that you would have to with a highly-structured client, a highly self-disciplined and motivated client, to see whether progress is being made. The client will very likely agree that such checking in is in his best interests. Charge him for it accordingly. If your are going to have to spend an extra half hour to an hour a week checking up on the client, bill for this time. This investment by the client should pay off in increased progress towards the desired success.

- Have the client review his task action list of things to accomplish at least a day (or more, if necessary) before the next meeting and to make progress moving towards the completion of each task. Have the client write down in his calendar, in your presence, the fact that this review will take place. Call him a day before this meeting to ensure that these tasks are in fact being accomplished.

In short, bird dog this client. Charge for whatever you do. And do not complain that you must do it. It has been hard for me, a very self-directed, self-disciplined person, to understand the mindworkings of others who do not share these traits, traits which I feel are absolutely crucial to achieving success. Moreover, I have been inclined, as a good Calvinist, to ascribe moral worth to those who possess these traits and the worst human failings to those who are without them. This is perhaps unfair.

If you have these traits and your client does not, you must tighten up the implementation strategy with this client and aim for small, short success assignments which are overseen by you with vigorous energy and determination. In this way there will be progress and, if you are very, very lucky, there will be a marked improvement in the work habits and discipline of the client. But don't hold your breath.

The Dog Ate My Homework Syndrome

One of the things that most irritates me is when clients say, as they so often do, "I didn't get around to the tasks for this week because:

- my kid is sick

- it snowed

- the car broke down

- I had to go to the dentist

- my mother in law is visiting, etc., etc., etc."

This is both pervasive and destructive of your attempt to help move the client successfully to realizing the desired and mutually agreed upon outcome.

I have several comments I would like to share with you about this penetrating and as yet medically untreatable ailment:

- This will happen to you. With the best will in the world, your clients, being human, will put off working on the project you have been retained to assist with because of a whole series of what you can only regard as trifling excuses.

- If you are in a retainer relationship, as I have pointed out before, if the client cancels the meeting which is scheduled for the week (or whenever) then they pay for it. I, as an advisor, sell time to my clients. My clients arrange to buy a block of it. If they arrange to buy it weekly, as they do in my case, and if the client cancels the meeting, the client still must pay for that time. (It goes without saying that if I cancel the meeting I must make it up.) If you do not have this sensible precaution, you can rest assured the client will abuse your time. Since he thinks nothing of putting forth the jejune and flimsy excuses as to why he cannot do his work, he can scarcely be expected to be reasonable and sensible on the matter of your time, can he?

Being human, and being yourself subject to the "Dog Ate My Homework" Syndrome, you will probably rejoice when a client calls to cancel one of his regular meetings, knowing you'll be paid for it anyway. Who doesn't rejoice in a paid vacation? When this happens occasionally, you might as well enjoy yourself. Even you, the most stringent advisor, deserve a busman's holiday from time to time. But don't make a habit with this:

- You succeed in the advising business by helping the client achieve a disproportionate benefit compared to fee. If there is no measurable or significant success at the conclusion of your advising stint, then you will miss out on one of the most significant benefits of the relationship: your ability to leverage this success, bringing it to the attention of others similarly situated who want to duplicate it. You will, thus, have solved your short-term need for a profit-producing engagement but not your more important long-term need to build a sustaining practice. This is why you must not let the client continue on this self-defeating course for long: it is as bad for you as it is for him.

Could you say this? Yes, and you should — but not as your primary reason for urging the client to abide by the terms of your engagement. Americans tend to love guilt and indulge in it frequently; it's one of our most popular national pastimes. You might as well get your share of the benefit of this phenomenon as anyone else. Thus, tell your client at some point, after several meetings have been missed and at the moment when you are discussing your disappointment and the fact that the client's own objectives will not be reached should this destructive behavior continue, that you, too, have objectives for this relationship, objectives beyond the actual terms of this engagement. That you wish, that is, to use it to help you build a meaningful practice. It is important for the client to understand this. For you to say this is an appropriate, genuine response to actions which are, face it, destructive both for the client and for you. Why shouldn't you raise the subject and get the client to acknowledge this as a legitimate issue?

Of course, I must say again: in the final analysis if the client wishes to spend his money on you and not follow your advice, not meet with you, not change his behavior and so move toward success, that is his right. We are advisors and advisors only; we have influence, to be sure, but we do not operate from an authoritarian perspective where we could force people to do our bidding. Thank God! There are problems with the alternatives that we now have available, but there would be many, many more problems, much more destructive problems in any alternative system.

To help cure the "Dog Ate My Homework Syndrome" you must:

- Keep before the client the desired objective. This must not be seen as something impersonal, bland, or uninspiring. Advisors must have the ability to help the client see, taste, feel, experience, and enjoy the success that will come through doing the task on which you both are now working. This is called Visualization, and advisors must possess this ability in spades. Too often, far too often, people lose sight of the objective towards which they are working. They see it as too far off, too dull, too bland, too insignificant. Thus, when the comparatively minor matters that are the habitual constituents of the "Dog Ate My Homework Syndrome" arise, it is easy to jettison the important project while wasting time with relatively less significant things.

- Tell the client what they have lost by not keeping the meeting; depending on how many meetings they have in fact missed, paint the loss in progressively darker colors. This is not just theatre. People must see, must come to understand, that by doing something they have in fact given up something up, or at least jeopardized the possibility that they will in time achieve that desirable something. It is your task to make the client understand this. One of the necessary tasks advisors face is to keep the pressure on the client. To make sure the client visualise the success. To increase the palpable sense of pressure and anxiety when no progress is made towards the mutually agreed upon objective. We cannot simply say to a client, "Tsk. Tsk. Don't do it again!" If a client once perceives that our heart is not in our work, if we are not seen to be deeply devoted to the success (and of course the client's interests), then why shouldn't the client say over and over again, "The Dog Ate My Homework"? They say that enough anyway.

We must continue to let the client know, in small and in major ways, that something important is at stake, important both for the client himself and for the population served by the client. If, for instance, I am representing, as I have, a community ambulance organization raising money for a new ambulance, and the executive director comes to regularly skip meetings, not only does that organization suffer but so do the people, the ill, sick, disheartened individuals, who must ride in the old, dilapidated ambulance. As an advisor I have responsibility not just to my client but to those who are being served by my client and for whom, in a larger human sense, I am actually working.

It is easy for the client, while dealing with the nagging trivialities inherent in the Dog Ate My Homework Syndrome, to lose sight of why he works at all, of who benefits from what he does, of why it matters at all that the task we set out to achieve with such high hopes is in fact important. But you, my fellow advisor, you must never lose sight of this objective, of the several constituencies you must serve at all times. Does this sound excessively high minded to you?

If so, consider both the moral and the practical aspects of the case. Morally, we advisors have an important role to play in the universe, for we are gifted with intelligence, energy, imagination, and enthusiasm beyond the common realm. Not everyone can be an advisor. Not everyone has the ability to work with others and achieve with them the desired objective. This is a task reserved for an élite, and with your role in this élite comes a commensurate responsibility.

By the same token, practically it behoves you to remind the client, especially at moments when they are not living up to your expectations (or, we should hope, their own), that there are others in the equation, those whom the client exists to serve. We live in an age that is morally numb but not morally dead. Thus, understand it is your responsibility to prod the client to remember his role in the grander design. It is certainly true that the man who pays the piper calls the tune, but if the music is delayed, or not played at all, think how many will be deprived. Remind the client. And then remind him again when his inevitable, his damnable, his all-too-human backsliding begins.

The Client Declines Your Advice

It would be nice, wouldn't it?, if the client simply agreed to your recommendations and worked with you to carry them out. Surely by now you know that such infrequent situations constitute the Elysian Fields of advising. More ordinarily one of these other, often irritating, certainly frustrating, situations occurs. One of these is when the client declines your advice. In such a situation you should follow these steps:

- Don't get irritated. Remember, you are only an advisor.

- Determine whether the client is attempting to reach the same objective as previously agreed. Perhaps the objective has changed without your being informed (yes, this does happen). Thus, it may be appropriate for the means to change, too.
- If the objective is the same, rationally and without prejudice consider the measures proposed by the client. Do they make sense? If so, then enthusiastically adopt them.
- If they don't, point out to the client, as dispassionately as possible, why they don't. The client must be at all times treated as a normal and rational human being, even though this may be a howler.
- If the client does not accept your advice, then it is your responsibility to help the client realize his objective. Work with the client to do so and don't be bitter. Remember what I said previously about the client testing you: if the client is wrong, your day will come and be more glorious for the postponement.

Having written this, there are circumstances where you can and should ignore the fact the client has declined your advice. In this situation it is important to see who on the client's side is ignoring it and what you can do to move matters ahead.

I think in this regard of one of my clients, a community health organization. We had embarked on a vigorous fund raising drive, the first general drive in their 86-year history. As part of this drive we were not only continuing but increasing the extent of their annual Christmas fund raising appeal. Neither the executive director nor I anticipated my problem on this front when we went to her Board for final approval; after all, the Board had agreed with the objectives for the fund raising drive and understood we'd have to carry on profitable tasks from the past and add new profitable items in the future.

But the Board balked, determining that this year instead of a profitable fund raising letter with selected community telephone follow-up, they'd engage in something they called "public relations," whatever that might have meant. (Isn't a good fund raising letter good public relations, too?)

The executive director called me up distraught. What could we do?

Ignore the Board's decision, said I, and proceed right on the course we had adopted with the letter, letting those who opposed the course take what action they might.

Isn't this dangerous? Yes it is, a bit:
- The Board might have criticized the executive director for not following their advice (for theirs was not a formal condemnation of the letter, merely a recommendation) and might, too, have criticized me as the organization's advisor.
- The disgruntled partisans of the "public relations" scheme might have decided not to do anything, withdrawing from the Board in high dudgeon.

Yes, something like this could have happened. But it didn't. Instead, what occurred was most instructive and something all successful advisors must come to appreciate — and profit from in their own practices:
- I asked the executive director to bring a few key board members to our next meeting at which the subject of the letter would be discussed as if all was proceeding on track. This meeting duly occurred. Necessary tasks were parcelled out to all those present, and they agreed to take them on. No one said, as they might well have, "But haven't we already agreed not to do this thing?" No, the thrust was too strong in the opposite direction that, of course, this beneficial thing was too important to be abandoned. So the matter moved ahead — without a peep of opposition.
- I had to report to the Board of this organization on a variety of other matters and when doing so inserted a short, organized paragraph about the Christmas letter and told how well it was going and to what ends the funds would be directed — all necessary social services provided by the agency. No one said, as well they might, "But we agreed not to do this." They simply carried on as if, of course, such an admirable project, promising such necessary results, had to be carried on. Even the individual who proposed the "public relations" scheme was swept along by the inevitability of the matter.

But what, my students have asked me, would you have done if someone had in fact said, as they certainly could have, "Wait a minute, Lant, we said we weren't going to do this this year"? I should have:
- Asked why.
- Asked what *specific* alternative they proposed to get the money for the services.
- Shown how profitable the project had been in the past and why it would be equally profitable and even reasonably more profitable this year.
- Pointed out that if something isn't broken, it doesn't need fixing.
- Clearly indicated that this was in fact not merely a fund raising project but one with public relations and indeed distinct marketing factors (for we always ask people receiving the letter to refer people to use the service, a nice warm touch and a beneficial piggyback on the main purpose of the letter).

As I've said before, selective hearing is a necessary part of being a successful advisor. Now, I am well aware, from much wayward experience, that people can and will make stupid mistakes, mistakes which fly in the face of their clear self interest. But the really stupid mistake is to tax them for having done so. If possible, if real damage has not been done, it is often conceivable to ignore such decisions, to overlook them, indeed to benefit from them. For the executive director who wailed at me over the telephone about what she would do without the funds she needed to raise from the Christmas letter now thinks, and quite rightly too, that I am a superb and admirable fellow for having gotten the project through in exactly the way she and I originally wanted it.

People, you know, make idiotic decisions regularly. They make them and then, having fulfilled their momentary need to do that stupid thing, they retreat from them. My job as an advisor, as yours, is to make it easy for them to do that, by acting as though they originally made the right decision, by complimenting them for having made it, and by proceeding right on the sensible course, your course, without even so much as a "by your leave."

This admirable tactic works. Hans Christian Anderson knew it, too, and that's why "The Emperor's New Clothes" is such an admirable tale for advisors. People thought that the emperor was in fact clothed, that the clothes were exquisite, that they were in fact incomparable, did believe all this — and the emperor's clever advisors proceeded apace with their work. Why the tale is necessarily incomplete from an advisor's point of view is that we do not know how the advisors in the story, the men who persuaded the emperor to adopt such a notorious fashion, might have dealt with the crisis in their affairs when the little boy on the pavement blurted out the truth of the matter. Perhaps I shall have to write an updated ending myself, for there are always ways to turn a crisis into yet another opportunity.

More Thoughts On Obstructive Clients

Believe it or not, time after time you will come into contact with clients who will make the realization of their stated objectives difficult if not impossible. In these cases you must always keep in mind the three benefits that will come to you if this relationship works:

- You (and the client!) will be able to point to the existence of a certified success.
- You will have the opportunity to work with this client again and so achieve other successes.
- You can leverage this success to get other engagements with clients similarly situated.

These outcomes are all valuable, and it is worth doing what you can to get them. This often means using your considerable ingenuity and creativity in ways you may not have bargained for. Let me give you some advice about doing so.

The Dreamspinner Principle

Too many advisors (full of themselves and their expertise) go into a client's business, or work individually with a client in an attempt to get the client to follow *their* advice, without making an earnest attempt to understand what the client wants. Advisors, clothed in the full majesty of their technical skills, want to impose order on the client, whereas the client, whether he says so or not, is only interested in using you to gain his own ends.

Thus, the first thing that an advisor must do is seek to gain as complete an understanding as possible of what the client actually wants and how badly the client will work to achieve this objective. The advisor's job, your job!, is to understand this aspiration, translate it into a finite, tangible, substantial end, and to advance methods which will result in its actual realization.

But first and most important you must understand the client's aspiration, his dream. The way in which you do this I call Dreamspinning. In the process you become that most crucial person of all, the Dreamspinner, for you may be the first person not only to understand the dream but perhaps the one to work with the client to give it tangible form, a name, and then to provide the necessary technical and problem solving expertise to bring it into existence.

Most advisors make the huge mistake of merely doing their job with the client. Of working with them to bring into existence the short-range objective that the client currently wants. Advisors who do this are advisors who stunt their own growth and limit their own possibilities. I work with decision makers to find out why they want this task done, really why. That is, when I work with an executive director of an agency attempting to raise money, I understand they need these sums for certain project needs. But why are these projects significant? What do they say about the decision maker? Why these projects instead of other projects? How do these projects define the decision maker? How do they lead to the realization of any ultimate objectives the decision maker may have? How do they relate to getting the decision maker a better job? To giving him an enhanced community image? To helping him realize his own inner needs as a human being? To merely go in and write a development proposal, no matter how good; to merely advise the client on where to send this development proposal, no matter how technically accurate my advice, is to ensure that I will have limited influence with the client and most likely a short-term engagement.

My objective is very clear when working with a client: I want to establish a long, long-term relationship. I want to become part of the client's continuing movement to realize his grander personal and professional objectives. I do not wish merely to be perceived as a technical assistant advisor offering advice on finite projects; I want to be, instead, the client's dreamspinner, that person who helps get inside the client's mind, helps the client visualise, and ultimately make tangible his deeply-felt objectives.

As such I have very lengthy relationships with my clients, three to four years is commonplace. And no wonder. How few people are there in your life to whom you can speak about your aspirations and not be stopped with an avalanche of reasons as to why they are impossible. My job is to be a midwife to ideas which might under other circumstances in other hands die a-borning.

There are ways, which I am about to share with you, which will help in this process. I lump them together under what I call the Open Bourbon Bottle Principle.

The Open Bourbon Bottle Principle

At regular intervals, you need to meet with the principal client decision maker behind closed doors to discuss:

- how the current project is coming along
- whether the resources you have at your disposal are adequate
- whether you are getting the help you need from key personnel involved in the problem solving process
- which of them may be blocking you and what you propose to do about it
- what modifications you need to make in your original recommendations, etc.

These meetings need to be held behind closed doors for one very good reason: members of the problem solving team need to see that you have continuing access to the decision maker, access which they may be denied. For remember: in all institutional settings, familiarity breeds contempt. You need to show people not only that you are not treated contemptuously, but that you have the kind of access they wish they had. Because you do not have actual power, you must make certain to be chary of your perceived influence.

During these meetings, which in my own office are often held over my very good bourbon (owned by the corporation: for I only drink on the job), I also get the principal client decision maker to talk about more that the current project. For if the client talks only about the current project, you will be perceived in time just like the employees who are involved in this project, not as that special incarnation, the advisor.

Ask the deeper questions, the probing questions, the *"Quo vadis?"* questions about where this project stands in relation to the client's grander aspirations, aspirations which because of the daily slog of life can become submerged, even obliterated by events. You need to be that crucial person in the client's life who reminds him of the connectedness of events, of how these events work together to achieve his ultimate objective.

If you are dealing with younger people, with people who have not yet met their financial objectives, you will find that these "ultimate" objectives may very well deal with money. But for almost no one is a financial objective truly ultimate. Usually the pursuit of money is an intermediate objective which, in due time, gives way to other, stronger objectives: the need for community, the need for recognition, the need for personal renewal, the need for spiritual satisfaction, the need to be loved. These are the stronger, the far stronger, needs and you must cater to them whatever you do.

Indeed you will find, whatever your technical specialty, that as you deal with people who have met their lifetime's financial objectives, who have more money than they could possibly spend, they still have very deep and profound needs to be met and to be met quickly as they approach the end of their professional and, indeed, human live. To them, money is no object; other things are. Your task is to find out what these other things are and to work with these clients, who are legion in their number, to help them to what they wish to achieve.

This means spending time with the client. It means taking a real interest in what the client wishes to achieve through this project. It means gaining a clear understanding of where the client wants to go and how you can help him get there. It means being open to the need for dreams and aspirations in a human life and knowing both how to nurture them until they are born and then how to bring them into substantial existence.

The ability to dreamspin, to be the dreamspinner, is one of the key factors which distinguishes the drab employee from the highflying advisor. Employees come in and do their jobs: theirs is but to do or die; theirs is not to reason why. The advisor must reason why and, once knowing why, must work to bring the dream to reality.

Employees and other uninspired workers say things like:

- "We don't do things like that around here."
- "It's never been done that way before."
- "You don't have the right degree to do that."
- "This isn't part of my job!"
- "I can't make that decision myself."
- "Not today."
- "If I let you do it, everybody will want to do it, too!"

Advisors, really good advisors, understand the destructive power of such damning phrases, understand how fragile good ideas are, how loath people are to share their ideas for fear they will be ridiculed or told how impossible they are to bring into existence, understand how the world, a conspiracy of flatworms, denies, destroys, demolishes, all because it is easier to do so.

You cannot do these things.

I recall in this connection a dinner party I attended years ago at which I talked about my role as an advisor and why it was important, indeed critically necessary, for such people to exist. After dinner a most seductive blond woman, in the first bloom of her radiant beauty, came over to where I was by now taking my brandy, knelt down in front of me, put her head on my knees and with the most piercing blue eyes looked up at me and said, "You're dangerous." "You're dangerous," she said, "because you make people believe in themselves."

Yes, that's it, of course. As a good advisor you and I are responsible for letting the genie of hope, inspiration, aspiration, and desire out of the bottle, of letting people who may be bored, run down, trapped know that the best is yet to come. But as good technicians, as problem solving masters, we do more than provide this mad elixir. We also provide the technical skills that these people need to realize their dreams. This is what distinguishes us from the television evangelists, for our kingdom is very much of this world, and we work with our clients to bring them to betterment now. We are not the preachers of an otherworldly waiting game. We are the purveyors of now. It is a critical difference.

I tell you all this now for one very good reason. If the client is obstructing us, it is perhaps that we, his advisor, do not understand what it is that the client wishes to achieve and that his hidden agenda is at odds with the public one we are working toward. Our task is to find out. And then to see if there can be a reconciliation between the two objectives, or whether we in our turn can live with the true state of affairs once we realize what it is, given that we, too, have an agenda we wish to realize beyond the terms of this engagement.

The Guerrilla Theatre Of Advising

In working particularly with obstructing clients, you will find that traditional professional behavior is often inadequate for moving them along towards problem solution. I have been amused, and often disheartened, in recent years as I have seen growing up a substantial myth about how people, in particular aspiring people, should dress, act, and comport themselves in their offices. Most of this advice is all right as far as it goes, but the problem is it doesn't go very far at all. In response, I have created what I called the Guerrilla Theatre of Advising.

A good advisor must realize that to motivate and move people to do what it in their best interest takes more than the limited spectrum of options presented by the notion of "professional behavior."

Professional behavior is essentially a Lockean notion; that is, that you can address a client rationally in his best interest, and he will promptly do that which you have advised. All advisors with any experience realize that this notion is essentially fatuous.

During the opening years of my practice, being then deeply in a Lockean phase, I addressed clients as if they were always reasoning, sentient, rational beings in reasonable pursuit of reasonable objectives. But, as I quickly discovered, this was insufficient. What could I do, where did I turn when such rational behavior failed, when the client ceased to act in pursuit of his own self interest? It was then that I began to use, without yet having even a concept, the notion of Guerrilla Theatre.

Guerrilla Theatre, you may remember, was a concept that came into its own in the 1960's at a time of social unrest and upheaval. It was designed to take great ideas and bring them, through every conceivable means, to the attention of people. Those in the guerrilla theatre movement were not to be found in traditional dramatic settings. Nor did they move in traditional ways, use traditional props, or find it in any way necessary to be bound to traditional theatrical procedures. They did what was necessary to make people sit up and take notice of what they had to say. So do I as an advisor.

I will:

- beg
- cajole
- wheedle
- shout
- tug
- scream
- cry
- badger
- push
- irritate

Or do anything else to get the client to pay attention to what I am saying. It is not enough for me to sit in my office, or the client's, and have periodic rational discussions on what needs to be done and how we are to do it. It is not enough for me to behave rationally, "professionally," and assume that the client will do the same.

189

In my advising practice, as in yours, there are grave and weighty matters at stake. As I have said before, I have a responsibility not just to the client but to those in the client's service population. I may be helping to do marketing and fund raising for a community health organization providing services to low income people. If the agency fails in its task, needy people will fail to get the services they must have. There are very real issues, very weighty, terribly moral issues at stake in these situations. It is not enough for me to say, "I was professional. The client didn't listen to me, but I was professional." As the world disintegrates around you because you would not extend yourself, will you be satisfied to say, "I failed, but I was professional."?

It certainly isn't enough for me.

I remember, in this regard, one memorable day with one of my client's, the executive director of an inner-city black elementary school. Due to mismanagement (prior, I must say, to my stint as an advisor) the school had lost its federal funding. Its financial condition was grave. It was a situation where the likelihood of continuing was not great but there was a chance, at least a chance, if all of us worked together expeditiously. The school was, however, riven with problems. The executive director was white; the board was black. The executive director was slothful and overweight. The board was argumentative and factious. The executive director was afraid to make decisions for fear of the repercussions, but real and vital decisions had to be made almost daily in a situation where one crisis emerged after another. Yet I took the assignment because I believed in the cause.

On one particular afternoon, the executive director and I were having a particularly stormy meeting. Decisions, hard decisions had to be made soon so that the school's hemorrhaging could be stanched. But the director was loath to take them. I had previously tried reason. I had failed. Now, on behalf of the client and her service population, I had to try more. I let her have it with a barrage of largely personal reasons about her leadership and personal styles, about what she was failing to do and what the repercussions would be. When I concluded I said, "If the school fails, I personally will write on its tombstone that you killed it." Whereupon she burst into tears and said, "No one has ever spoken to me this way before."

What did I say? Was I chagrined? Was I sorry to have made her cry? Did I feel I had gone too far? No! No! No! I said, "I am speaking to you this way because I am your advisor and your friend, and I shall continue to speak to you this way either until we have saved the school, or until there is no point in trying any more."

Was this professional behavior? I submit to you that it was, professional, authentic, and moral behavior, the kind of behavior you must use with an obstructive client when circumstances warrant. I say to you with the utmost pride, you will not find this kind of statement, this kind of recommendation in any other book about problem solving. That's because those authors and those books approach the entire notion of problem solving as if it were somehow a disembodied experience taking place between value neutral robots in outer space. It isn't. Problem solving, which necessarily involves the hopes, fears, anxieties and aspirations of real people, is a messy business, an absorbing and often confusing business. It often involves, usually involves, severe constraints and gross limitations. It involves flawed people attempting to assist flawed people. It means attempting to do too much with too little and not losing heart because the results achieved are not dramatic but only adequate. Yes, problem solving, working with clients, is indeed a noble undertaking and you will be more successful with it if you resolve, here and now, that you will do what is necessary, whatever is necessary, to help the client achieve his objectives, even though this means going beyond the commonly held, foolish notions of what constitutes effective "professional behavior." Friend: I can only wish that the right color tie was enough; that the right introduction word was sufficient; that enough reason reasonably applied would suffice. I should be a man delighted. But if I believed this I should be a man deeply deceived, and I should as deeply deceive you if I told you otherwise than I am.

Looking Realistically At Breakdown

Sadly, all client advisor relationships don't work. Most people who have used advisors will tell you that at some time or another they have had an advisor they parted with unsatisfactorily. Indeed, I suspect there are as many of these unhappy partings, if not more, than there are satisfactory ones. I want to examine a few situations where either you or the client want to end the relationship and what needs to happen to preclude further problems.

The Client Keeps Pressing You To Do Things Beyond The Terms Of Your Engagement

Let's take a relatively easy problem first, a problem which, properly handled, can be constructively solved. As clients come to work with you and discover how good you are, they will often ask you to do more and still more, all of which is generally beyond the terms of your current engagement. In this situation it is you, the advisor, who must act to save the relationship. Inform the client as politely but firmly as you can that what he is proposing is something you are interested in doing (or it is something which you can find someone else to do) but that it is not included in your current agreement. Suggest terms, if you are able to do so, under which you could do the task and suggest an early meeting to work out an agreement. Be positive. Be upbeat. But do not let the client run over you. If it happens once, it will happen again. If the client continues to press you, you will have to make the decision about what to do:

- If you give in, you will probably feel resentment towards the client, and this will certainly affect your relationship even if it doesn't affect your current work.

- If you don't give in, the client may be irritated with you and feel resentment. In this case, defuse the issue by stating your point as authentically as you can. Tell the client how important this relationship is to you, how much you want to keep it, but that, if pressed, you are prepared to give it up, even though that's the last thing you want, or the client needs. Don't just say these words: mean them. Remember: you are a professional, not a marshmallow.

The Client Is Dissatisfied With Your Work

Clients will not always be satisfied with what you do. Plan on it. There are clients who, as a matter of course, always nit pick and find fault with what an advisor does no matter how good it is. Then there are those who are congenitally unable to say anything nice about anything or anyone. You know the type.

The first thing to do is to see whether you can accommodate the client's wishes within the terms of your contract. Does the client have a point? Can the work be improved? Can this be done within the terms of the contract and without causing you loss?

Remember: you want this relationship to prosper. You want to build a sustaining relationship with this client. You have worked hard to do so. You want to be able to leverage it to secure new clients who want to replicate the problem solving model you have implemented in this case. Don't jeopardize this without good reason.

- Don't take the matter personally. Much criticism is impersonal and not meant for you. Try and see whether this criticism has any merit or whether it's just talk. Remember: it may be possible to make quite minor modifications, approach the client at another time, and get the agreement you need. Don't rush to extremes just yet.
- If the client's criticisms are reasonable and the work within the terms of your engagement, you will very likely have to do what the client wishes. Remember: I told you to build in a margin of error of at least 20% for situations you knew; 40% or more for situations you didn't. This is what that margin of error is for.
- If the client's criticisms are beyond the terms of your engagement, say so. This is what contracts are for. Be polite. But be firm. Of course, the client will try to get you to work for nothing. Of course, the client wants to turn you into a slave. This is a well established notion. If you let this happen, it's as much your fault, if not more, than the client's.
- If the work that needs to be done is beyond the terms of your current contract and the client still demands that you do it, give serious consideration to not proceeding with the contract.

This is a very hard thing to do, especially when you need the money. But is the aggravation worth it? Only you can be the judge. Before you take any action under your contract, however, tell the client that you are distraught. Be authentic. Tell the client why you feel you should not do the extra work, why the work is beyond the terms of your engagement, and that you still want to keep working on the other projects but are threatened by what's happening. You can do this, make your point, and not come across as whiny or weak. You have an obligation to try.

If the client is himself a reasonable individual, he'll understand your dilemma and attempt to accommodate you. Where two people are intent not on obstruction but on accommodation, there will be accommodation, if not a perfect harmony. But if the client at this point does not wish to compromise, you can be sure his behavior is an indication of a salient personality trait which will cause you grief over and over again. Sad though it is to lose the contract with its present and future benefits, you'll probably be better off without it.

The Client Won't Pay

This should be an easy one, shouldn't it? But it isn't. I've been confronted over and over again with advisors who are in anguish at this situation, a situation which any school child could advise them about. My advice to you is clear: do no work on credit. Either the client can pay you or he cannot. If he cannot, seek work elsewhere. Why is this so hard for so many advisors to grasp?

I think the answer lies in the fact that you want to be popular, do not want to lose a client if there is any possibility, no matter how remote, about salvaging the relationship, do not want to be thought hard or harsh. But let's look at the other side: if you don't get paid for your work, you'll be resentful, and this resentment will come through one way or another. Either you'll be difficult with the client, or, worse, you'll be difficult with your family and friends.

Take my advice: if the client won't pay, stop providing services. If you have already provided the services, resolve (à la Chapter 9) on exactly what steps you'll do to collect, and/or to take legal action. Do them and don't worry about it. At some point you'll either collect, or you'll have to give up the matter because it's costing you too much psychic energy. I am a good Calvinist; I know the world is filled with mean-spirited, hostile, even evil people who will take advantage of you. You have to learn this, too, and proceed accordingly. Even when you like the client, especially when you like the client, it is your responsibility to lay down guidelines for what you will do and what you will not. Then, when the client has agreed to them, too, to abide by them.

One of the most irritating situations in my advising career came when I worked with a client who had run out of money but in whose cause I believed and kept working to advance. It was my own personal Viet Nam: payments were always delayed and erratic. The client was pleading. I became sullen and resentful. Finally, in a burst of clarity, I simply stopped providing the service and watched the organization go bankrupt — owing me thousands of dollars. But at least I had the, admittedly belated, good sense to pull out when I did. Learn, reader, learn. Set clear guidelines for yourself about what you'll do when prompt payment is not forthcoming and abide by them religiously whatever your personal friendship with the client or your degree of commitment to his cause.

The Client Makes You His Scapegoat

One of the reasons why organizations hire advisors is because the client decision maker needs a scapegoat for a decision that has already been made and which he needs to camouflage. This is reality and if you walk into this situation knowing what needs to be done and accept the challenge of the assignment, you should be prepared for what follows. If, on the other hand, the client is an obstructive client who will not follow your advice and then decides to blame you for the lack of satisfactory results, you should consider the following:

- Point out privately to the client that your advice has not been followed, and therefore that it is not cricket for you to be blamed for the lack of success. Tell the client that you want success as much as, if not more, than he does and that you are willing to shoulder your share of the responsibility for not achieving it if such responsibility is warranted. But that in this case it is not.

- If the client still persists in blaming you, you must make a decision. Is there a court of higher appeal, such as a more senior administrator or the board of directors, that you can go to and quietly, off the record, make your case? If so, go this route. While you do not wish to lose this client, you also do not want to have your professional reputation besmirched unfairly. Talk to the chairman of the board off the record. Don't go without a specific plan of action to be followed. When you go to this meeting, go in with a specific request, a specific objective. It is not enough to say that you are dissatisfied and disgruntled.

- If there is no higher court and if the client decision maker persists in making invidious charges against your professional competence, you'll have to withdraw from the relationship. As you do so, make sure you have as complete a list of the charges against you as you possibly can and a comparable list of your responses to them. It may be that if the charges continue and you hear rumors from professional associates (or if, horror of horrors, they break into a professional publication in your field) you will have to approach the client's lawyer with a notice that you are contemplating legal action unless these palpably false charges are stopped immediately. Given the state of our legal system, of course, you will not really want to go through with this course. But you can hope that this bluff will stop matters from escalating; it all depends on how badly the client needs a scapegoat to divert attention from his own failings. One good thing: if you have performed your work competently and have been seen to perform it competently after a while the client will look pretty foolish in what he is saying.

When You Want Out, When The Client Wants Out

If either of the parties to a client-advisor relationship wants out of the relationship, my advice is to end it as promptly as possible. There can be no good resulting from a relationship which is carried on against the expressed wishes of one of the parties, particularly where the parties are the principal decision makers themselves. It is different, of course, vastly different, if one of the minor players on the problem solving team wants to end the relationship. In that case, use one of the techniques I discussed above.

Even in the best relationships, there comes a moment when one of the parties feels that it's time to conclude his involvement. This can either be because the project you were working on has been satisfactorily dealt with — or because it is manifestly improbable that it can be, given the unsatisfactory state of your relationship. Either way, face the inevitable and wind things up, even if the contract period still isn't officially over.

I had some experience in this kind of situation a couple of years ago, which I think most instructive. I was retained by a social service agency to take over a capital campaign which had been mismanaged by another firm of advisors. I worked with the organization for 18 frustrating months at which time it was perfectly clear that the mistakes made by the previous firm could not be rectified and that the project would have to be significantly scaled down. The client asked me to stop work, even though we had another six months of my contract remaining. I did so, but it cost them two months of retainer fee, an amount they were not entirely happy to grant, but was agreed to since I had a contract. Were strings severed forever?

No! It took about a year, but the main individual I worked with called and placed another order with me. And just as I was writing this chapter he called again to place another and to intimate that the same organization wanted some further work done on an advising basis.

The reason this happened, I submit, is because I recognized the client's previous plight, agreed to what they wanted to do (although at a cost they considered higher than they wanted to pay), and behaved throughout in a thoroughly professional manner. They know they can rely on me, relied on me before, and still feel comfortable both recommending my services and using them themselves. I can think of no higher praise given by a client with whom the relationship was not entirely positive or entirely productive. This is how even the least satisfactory relationships should end.

On Success

By now you are probably thinking that life as an advisor is infinitely more difficult than you anticipated. But remember: I am no masochist and would not remain for an instant in a painful situation. It's not my nature, and I hope it isn't yours.

In fact, despite the difficulties in any advisor-client relationship, if you follow the techniques outlined in this book your relationships will be productive, will produce results that are satisfactory, even stupendous. Don't think this will happen overnight. Don't think it will not happen without much study of this book and my other books and much experience. It won't. But more and more the satisfying results will be the ones you will achieve. I promise you that. Thus, you had better be aware of how to deal with success, for this can be as unnerving and unprofitable as dealing with failure.

Reporting Success

I have discussed at great length how you should handle difficult, obstructive, obstinate and sabotaging clients in an attempt to move them along the road to success. Now it is time to give you some advice about handling success, for success, no more than failure, doesn't handle itself. Success is a lever you use to achieve more success, to make the client feel better about his ability to achieve success, and to announce to related professionals, who may have a similar problem, that you exist and can help them, too.

- Keep a list of each person who has helped the project achieve success. As success is reported, alert that individual's superior to the fact so that the helper can be thanked by name and specifically for the work he has done. No thank-you should be merely general. It should be as specific as possible

- If the success achieved has been truly above and beyond the call of duty, has been particularly creative, meaningful, or extensive, alert the editor of any inhouse publication to this fact so that an appropriate story can be published. If the success achieved is of interest to the wider professional community, alert the editors of such publications. (*N.B.* It should go without saying that you can be quoted in these articles, too, as a reputable and knowledgeable source on the situation.) Such articles should be placed in the employee's personnel file and posted for general notice.

- Players in the problem solving process should be stroked by being taken to lunch, given free time, generally being made much of. Employers will not come up with these suggestions themselves. It is your responsibility to make these suggestions; the time you spend with the principal client decision maker beyond closed doors from time to time (either the last quarter hour of any day or at other regular intervals) is perfect for such suggestions.

- When you yourself are reporting to senior administrators and board members, always present a list of people to be thanked officially by them. You must be seen as thanking people, just as you must be seen (where appropriate) as having the influence to block those who are not helping.

When you advance these names do so enthusiastically. Don't forget, when you are reporting to board members, the principal client decision maker. I am, for instance, usually the one who recommends to the board of directors of a nonprofit organization official recognition of achievements of their executive director. This seems obvious, of course, but you'd be staggered by how few senior administrators get much praise either — and how desperately they want it. I am a means of getting them that praise, and in the process I underscore my own indispensability.

- For yourself, as soon as there has been any success in working with this client, success which would be meaningful to others who are similarly situated, then it is to your benefit to send a Success Letter to them and to use the professional publications on your own behalf. Remember, however: if you do this (as you should) you'll have to have the permission of the client. The time, of course, to ask for this permission is when he is happy with you.

Take the opportunity, too, when success comes to bring up some of the nagging bits of your relationship to get them cleared up. You'll notice, for example, in my previous illustration when my client was testing me, I didn't bother to point out that what she had done brought about the only significant failure in our relationship until we had much more significant success. That is the moment to act, to deal with those things which, if improved, would leave the relationship in better shape.

Final Words About Success

As you see, the success section is infinitely shorter than the problem section. There is, however, another thing I must say about success: get some of it in your relationships as early as you can. Understand that the client, whatever he says to the contrary, doubts your ability to deliver as you say you can. He has had promises made to him before, promises which have not been kept. We are, of course, a trusting people, but we are a trusting people who have been disappointed before. It is, therefore, your responsibility to deliver a success, however slight, as soon as you can, to do something which helps in the realization of the client's desired objective.

When this success has in fact been achieved, tell people it's a success. People specifically need to be told when something has been accomplished. They need to be told, too, what their own role was in this accomplishment and what, of course, was yours. Success to be meaningful must be broadcast far and wide. Do your part to ensure that it is.

In The Doldrums Of A Long, Generally Satisfactory Relationship

Even the most successful advisor-client relationships go into the doldrums after a time. You have ceased to be the bright new face, ceased to offer the possibility of magic and an end to all care that you did when you were fresh and new; you have become part of the old, familiar team and, in a sense, the old, familiar problem. This is a dangerous moment for you and for the client.

When you sense that you are being taken for granted, try the following:

- Ask for a special meeting with the client to reaffirm the original objective, both the specific objective and the client's cosmic objective, that is, what he is really working for. It is easy to forget in our day to day existence what we are working for and why, and it is equally easy to forget how the people who are working with us can help us achieve our ultimate ends. Thus it is necessary to take a moment and clarify the situation, to remind the client what he wants and how necessary we are to attaining it.

- Make sure both the immediate objective and the client's goal are written down. Take advantage of this opportunity to make sure the client sees how indispensable you are to getting what he wants.

- Bring the other members of the problem solving team into a similar meeting. Ask them to comment on:
  - what they think they are doing
  - why they think they are doing it
  - the obstacles they are facing
  - the fun they are having doing it, and
  - what they could suggest about doing things better.

Remember: people get bored. Even people achieving success get bored. They, therefore, need to have a sense of renewal. In part this sense comes from thinking about the future. In part it also comes from getting a just appreciation of the past.

When in the doldrums, ask the client to hold a session at which you can comprehensively review progress, to remind people of where you started, with whom you started, and of the progress you have made — and the mistakes you have made which didn't kill you! People forget these things. It is terribly easy to lose a sense of where one is if one has no comprehension about where one has been. It is your responsibility to provide this sense and so give people a renewed sense of pride and enthusiasm in what they're doing.

This meeting should be supercharged with a feeling of accomplishment, and at the same time you should use the confidence that this sense provides to ask for both criticism and suggestions about what can be done better. These items will be useful to you in working with the principal client decision maker to restructure your assignment and recapture some of the necessary enthusiasm and commitment. Try this. Very few people in the middle of an assignment take a moment to see the forest; instead they let the trees get in the way until such time as they are again lost, bored, or despondent about their lack of progress. I say, and not so facetiously either, that I keep some of my oldest friends around so that they can remind me of what and who I was in years past. In this way where I am now comes to be the sweeter to me, for they, even more than I, have the capacity to remind me of how far I have come and how worthy I am. You must do this in your own life, and you must do it with your clients, too.

Client Endorsements And Testimonials

At some point, the project you are working on will be finished. If you have followed the steps in this book it will be very much the success that both you and the client want. The client will be happy with you but will be equally happy to dispense with your services, feeling sure that he can carry on using what you know and have taught him and his staff. In this moment of cheerful termination, you had best keep your head clear, for there is something more that you want: the possibility of using this successful experience as a lever to attract new business.

At this point ask the client to write down specifically what you have managed to accomplish for him. Ask him to make this as detailed and precise a list as possible for each of the things that you have accomplished here you will obviously want to do for others — perhaps at an enhanced fee now that you are, indeed, the bona fide problem solver and expert.

To get the client's creative juices going, provide a partial list yourself as inspiration. Is there something immodest in this? Perhaps, but so long as I can eat well and often, I care not that someone, somewhere may judge me immodest. That is merely a word. The food is real.

When this list is finished, ask whether the client has any objections to your sharing this list, and the kind words which should accompany it, with others who may be interested in using your services. Even if you have engaged in doing proprietary and secret work, the client can still write many, many worthwhile things about you. The client does not have to tell precisely what you did. He can address himself to the difference that you made. That, for marketing purposes, may suffice.

At this point, also ask the client if you may refer client prospects to him for a recommendation. If you have achieved what the client wanted, it is very unlikely he will gainsay you this. But it is as well to get the client's permission in advance, before you need the service.

Don't forget that if the success has been meaningful for this client, it may well be that others in the industry would also welcome some knowledge about it. Ask whether the client would be willing to write to a trade publication, or have you do so, and propose a story. It is difficult to resist having one's peers discover that one is successful. Say that you'll write the story, or at least propose it, if that will help. Because, remember: the story is very much in your interest, too, and with the proper footwork you'll be quoted in it as a pivotal source.

If you feel that all this is immodest or somehow *infra dig,* GET OVER IT! If you are in the position to glorify the client's achievement, it is your responsibility to do so. If you are in a position to help others, then it is your bounden duty to let them know you exist.

Profiting From The Clinic

The day you ask the client for testimonials and the like is not, of course, the last day you'll be officially working with him. No, you'll remember you'll be back at periodic intervals with the clinic. Let's be clear about what the clinic is: it is an opportunity for you to review the client's progress towards reaching objectives which were unfinished at the conclusion of your ongoing working relationship, and it presents you with the opportunity to remind the client of exactly how valuable you were, exactly how much he needs you again.

My experience shows that at the end of a formal client relationship, the client is very likely to say something like, "We've loved working with you, Jeffrey. It's been very profitable for us. But now we know everything you know. We've learned from our regular meeting. We've learned from your books, your tapes, your workshops. And we're ready to go it alone now."

At this point, I nod my head sagely and ask for the testimonials I have already suggested to you. But I know inwardly that if I play my cards right, I'll be asked back again shortly, that is, within less than a year.

Thus, your first clinic should be scheduled for between 30 and 60 days after the ending of your contract, unless you have very fast-moving business in which case you'll want to come back sooner. By this time the client should already have begun to fall away from your demanding standards; the system you have been responsible for creating should still, of course, be working, but it should be working less well than when you were on hand to monitor its progress.

At your first clinic meeting, continue to make your suggestions about how to improve matters but subtly point out the difference between where the client is now and where the client was at the formal conclusion of your engagement. This is enough for right now, although if the situation has become truly alarming in its decline by all means suggest right then a recommencement of your formal relationship. But if things are merely functioning less well and not catastrophically so, the client may still need additional time to make up his mind to the necessity for bringing you back.

Continue with these meetings until such time as the decline in standards seriously begins to impede on the client's ability to realize his objective. That is the moment to strike.

You see, the real purpose of the clinic is to allow you, the advisor, to market your indispensability but to do it on the client's time and money. Of course you'll be helpful during these meetings; you're always helpful, aren't you? But more than that, the client needs to be periodically and forcefully reminded of exactly how useful you are. Otherwise, it will be easy for them to forget and very likely fall victim to the blandishments of some newer, fresher face promising what every client wants: the ability to be the god-magician and hence an escape from responsibility.

This is less likely to happen, however, if you make good use of the time for which the client has paid you after the end of your regular ongoing relationship.

Remember: marketing is something you probably don't like, something you may not do very well (although after you've finished this book you should be much, much better at it). Therefore take advantage of the clinic, which is intended to keep you working with more clients longer than those foolish advisors who don't use this clever means of marketing. The longer you can stay with a good, paying client, the more profitable the marketing you did to get that client in the first place and the more real money you are in fact making.

And since making real money is what the advising business is all about, it's now time to explore the rest of the system of how to do just that: The Mobile Mini-Conglomerate.

CHAPTER 11

Understanding And Profiting From The Mobile Mini-Conglomerate

So far I have dealt in this book largely with finding and working with clients on an individual, one-to-one basis, with identifying a client who has a problem and working with him to solve that problem. This is the way most advisors run their businesses, and it is fine so far as it goes. If you follow the advice of the preceding pages you will do well, often very well. I know. My first year in business as an advisor, at the moment I knew least about marketing, promotion, client identification and targeting, sales closing and the entire business of advising, I made about 5 times my previous salary as a college administrator. Not bad. But not enough either — for me. This is one of the significant questions you must ask yourself: how much do you want?

Setting Your Personal Objectives

One of the pivotal mistakes too many advisors make is simply to go about setting up a business without answering the following questions in precise detail:

- How much money do I want to make this year? What does this objective mean in terms of hours I must work, clients I must be retained by, &c.? It's not merely enough to set an income objective; you must be clear about how this objective is to be achieved, month by month, category by category.

- What am I willing/unwilling to do to make this money? Write down whether you want to travel; if so how much and how far. Whether you'll consider working nights and week-ends to assist your clients, or whether you wish rigidly to adhere to 9 to 5 hours, &c. This question has more to do with determining the lifestyle you wish to lead as well as the income you want to have.

When I ask aspiring advisors to take a moment in my workshops and to write down their answers to these questions, the answers are invariably vague and imprecise. This indicates a lack of clarity about the role of their advising practice in their lives and what kind of life they wish to lead. This lack of clarity, more than the lack of technical skills and expertise, effectively sabotages the development of a successful practice.

In part this lack of clarity comes about because, perhaps for the first time in their lives, people are actually being asked consciously to shape their life and to mold their own objectives for both income and lifestyle, instead of taking what someone else happens to offer them. As I said at the very beginning of this book, one of the reasons people become advisors is to gain freedom of control over their time and their lives. But taking this freedom, really living with it, can be an awesome, even terrifying experience for people who have previously been told when and where they had to work and how much they could make as a result. Now you are being asked to set, and to be held responsible for, these decisions yourself. It is a thrilling, a jolting experience. As you consider it there are several key pieces of information you need to think about:

- As an advisor your market is national, even international. You can go wherever people exist in sufficient numbers with sufficient resources to pay your fee.

- As an advisor with in-demand skills and problem solving abilities, you can work 7 days a week, 365 days a year.

- As an advisor you determine the range of income that you want. Never again will income be something others impose on you. It is something you achieve for yourself based on your ability to identify people's problems and your ability to solve them using the steps of the Mobile Mini-Conglomerate.

- As an advisor you can make deals and gain clients at all times and in all places. There is no clear time, unless you so determine, as to when you are on duty, when you are not.

- As an advisor it is your responsibility to come up with the appropriate problem solving device that falls into the price range of your buyers. You should not be offering merely one service but dozens, each geared to the price concerns of a different layer of your market.

In short, you must do nothing less than alter the way you approach life, time, your objectives. I am asking for nothing less of you than your rigorous consideration of who you are, what you want to be, where you want to go, and what you are prepared to do to get there. All the questions, in short, that most people never ask themselves, preferring instead to drift aimlessly through a meaningless existence. The life of the good advisor is an examined life, a self conscious life (in the best sense of this misunderstood phrase), a life to which you have given the utmost in consideration and which has forced you to make significant choices, rather than have these choices made for you by others. Advisors are responsible for what happens to them, and this acute sense of responsibility for our actions, our directions and our objectives make us some of the most perceptive people on the planet. This chapter is part of the process of making sure that you derive the utmost benefit from what you know and can do and making sure you realize what is and is not possible for you.

Breaking Out Of The Time Trap

I am now 44 years old. In 186 months I shall be 59½, legally able to retire. This is so little time. There is so much to do, so many people to help. It is a problem that each and every one of us has and to which the grim reaper ultimately provides a macabre solution. The question is: what do you want to do in your own life to deal with it satisfactorily for yourself? It is one that man has dealt with from the beginning of his consciousness and one that he will always wrestle with. In this chapter I wish to add my mite to this ongoing debate.

Face it. There is only one of you, and there are millions, even billions, of people in the universe who could benefit from what you know and can do, depending on your technical skills and problem solving expertise. But you won't know how to deal with this situation until you honestly answer these two questions:

- Do I want merely to do enough to get by, to meet my own limited income objectives?
- Or do I want to create a means of breaking free of the time trap, of taking my problem solving expertise to the largest possible market, and at the same time making me a truly significant amount of money?

This was the problem I was confronted with 12 years ago. I had during the first year of my advising practice discovered that with reasonable assiduity, simply by selling project and retainer contracts I could catapult myself into the top 5% of American wage earners. At that moment of satisfaction there were certain grave questions to be answered, the questions that you will have to answer, too: What were my income and lifestyle objectives? Here's what I decided and here are the questions you must decide, too:

- Will I be able to rest content just helping a relatively few people, working directly with them on a labor intensive one-to-one basis? If I run my practice in this fashion, will I be able to meet the precise income objectives I have set for myself?
- If I decide that this kind of advising practice will not satisfy either my personal need to assist more people with what I know and can do and will not meet my income objectives, what are the obstacles I place on myself that will make it difficult (if not impossible) for me to realize my grander objectives?

In this connection, people are always telling me over and over again that they want to help more people in more ways and want to earn more money. Then they turn around and in the same breath say things like:

- "Of course, I won't travel out of my city."
- "I have to have a four week vacation every year."
- "I can't leave my home because of my young children."
- "I feel uncomfortable marketing and promoting my practice."
- "I'm not sure I can succeed."

And dozens of other excuses. For make no mistake about it. People impose their own obstacles on themselves. There is no obstacle in history that has not been surmounted; there is no obstacle, however small, which has not provided for others the exact excuse they need to avoid striving. In which camp will you be?

My own answers to these cosmic as well as intensely personal questions were and are clear:

- I wanted to help people wherever they were located and whatever degree of discretionary funds they possessed to move towards solving the problems to which I had helpful experience and answers. Since all these people could not afford to hire me on a daily, one-to-one basis, I determined I would create appropriate problem solving vehicles for them so that (adding their own creative juices, time and energy) we could still work together to solve their problems — even though I might not be there in the flesh.
- I would impose no artificial barriers on the use of my time. I would work and live as holistically as possible, that is, without saying that such and such a period was for work and that such and such a period was for leisure. I would merely live, but live in a disciplined, directed fashion ever moving onward to understood and acknowledged objectives.
- I would impose no artificial barriers on my income. I would work as fully and completely as possible to reach as many people as possible with problems I can help solve, understanding that being clear about what their problems are and what I could do to help, linked to making contact with the vast numbers of people who have the problems I exist to solve, would make me a millionaire.

Out of these points the Mobile Mini-Conglomerate was born. It was invented to solve finite, tangible problems — most notably the need to reach large numbers of people who have problems I help to solve and in ways that would cost effectively enable them to work with me, whether I was physically present or not.

What's In A Name? The Meaning Of Mobile Mini-Conglomerate

People often ask me where the name itself came from. The word "mobile" is there to indicate that you, in one form or another, will go to wherever there is someone with the problem you can solve. You will not merely stay in one place, in one small area, but will creatively seek out and help people wherever they are to be found who need your service. "Mini" comes from the realization that you are either one person or one small group; that is, that you will work solely or with only a few others in a small space from whence you and your products and services will go out to touch the lives of your customers. In an age of advanced telecommunications and electronics, you don't need a lot of space from which to operate; you need to work smart, not large. The word "conglomerate" is there to remind you that, in the final analysis, you'll behave like any other business entity (however large) which has many divisions and different tasks to accomplish. Your income, just like that at General Motors, will come, if you follow the steps, from many sources, not just one, and some of these sources will not even be related to the main theme of your business. For at some point you will use your profits to buy (and sell) related and nonrelated business enterprises, as the economics and profit potential dictates.

Sections Of The Mobile Mini-Conglomerate

The Mobile Mini-Conglomerate is made up of 10 parts, including:

- Billable time
- Retainer contracts
- The Supergroup of Independent Contractors
- Writing and selling articles by you
- Creating newsletters
- Writing and producing booklets and books
- Profiting from lectures, workshops and other talk programs
- Producing audio and video cassettes
- Creating cooperative marketing (drop ship) product agreements
- Diversifying into related and nonrelated enterprises.

To begin with, the Mobile Mini-Conglomerate is a circuit, not a sequence. You can begin at any point and move backward and forwards to complete the circuit. Most people, to be sure, begin at "billable time" and move ahead. That's not necessary. You can begin with a workshop on your problem solving specialty and move quickly to complete the circuit and so gain maximum profit. The important thing is that you understand how many ways there are which exist to get you out of the time trap and help you meet your humane objective of helping as many people as you can and your income objective of maximizing your profit.

Let's begin by looking a little more closely at each of these points to ensure that you know what they are and how they can fit into your scheme of things.

Billable Time

Here you work with a client on an hourly or project (time) basis helping to solve a designated problem. Most advisors begin by selling their time. The problem is that there are only so many hours of the day that you can sell and that time is, for most advisors, the single most expensive thing they are selling. Thus, people entering into the advisor business with only their time to sell quickly find that while people may have the problem they can help solve, these same would-be clients do not have the necessary resources to hire the advisor. Thus, advisors find they may be needed but cannot be paid. This is especially true when one's possible clients (as in almost every case) are widely dispersed across the country and the world. Yes, they have the problem but not the resources to bring you in to help solve it. Selling only billable time is dangerous for advisors because it limits the number of people who can benefit by working with you. It provides your client population with too few options about how they can profit through your knowledge. It gives you no flexibility about what you can offer. If you've only got billable time to offer, the clients will have to be fairly well off to afford the fee, and you will have only a limited number of ways in which you can work with them (Delphic Oracle vs Full Service or on a project basis). The objective, of course, of the experienced advisor is to provide his client population with the maximum number of ways possible in which you could work together, as evidenced by the first 9 steps of the Mobile Mini-Conglomerate.

Retainer Contracts

All advisors drool at the possibility of getting fat retainer contracts. No wonder. A retainer contract is a relationship between advisor and client under which the latter guarantees the former a certain fee, usually paid monthly, in return for the advisor's fixed availability during that period. The value to a retainer relationship from the advisor's point of view is that it provides him with a certain, predictable income during a certain period of time (a very soothing benefit for anyone whose income is necessarily a patchwork quilt), allows him to work with the client in overseeing and implementing his problem solving suggestions (thus increasing the likelihood of a success and hence the possibility of future clients), and, if the client has bought more hours than he is likely to use, provides the advisor with time which he can place without handicap at the disposal of client prospects. Remember what I said before: no time that you provide a client prospect should be uncompensated time as far as you're concerned. The prospect may not pay, but someone must. If you have only billable time contracts, you will not be able to make this happen. If you have retainer contracts, you will.

Clients buy retainer contracts for related reasons:

- It assures them of access to your problem solving process skills. Once clients have been reassured that you can, in fact, help solve their problems, they want the security of knowing that you are available to them. A retainer makes this possible.

- It assures the client that you can and will be available to them on a regular basis to help them work out often quite small (but tricky) problems that arise as they move towards a solution to their problem. The more anxious they are to secure a solution, the less they have the technical skills available on staff, the more likely they are to want a retainer agreement.

- It is more cost effective to the client. Whereas hearing or reading your problem solving processes may be helpful and a sensible investment, actually working with you on a regular basis, although more expensive in the short run, may make more sense as an investment since they can thereby be better assured that there will really be meaningful results. A longer-term, more expensive retainer contract may thus make more economic sense than one of your less expensive problem solving process vehicles. As I say to my students, not so facetiously, a $12,000 yearly retainer contract with me may be in fact cheaper in the long run than buying a $35 copy of one of my problem solving process books. It depends to what extent the client values his own time, needs an immediate solution to his problem, what kind of opportunity cost he'll have for not acting now, etc.

The Supergroup Of Independent Contractors

Your clients do not just have one problem. They have dozens, even hundreds. Your task is to help them get solutions to these problems through the independent contractors you know and who may work with your clients either directly or indirectly through you. In this connection, it should already be clear to you that you need to listen to what people tell you in terms of the Problem-Solution Metronome. What is this individual's problem? How seriously does he rate it? How much does he want a solution and how quickly? As someone talks, anyone, you should be attempting to discover whether you know someone who could be of assistance in solving the problem. The more the individual indicates that it is a problem he wants solved soon, the more consideration you should give to finding the person who can solve it if, indeed, you cannot solve it yourself.

As I have said again and again, you want your clients to achieve success. The more of their problems that you can be instrumental in solving, the more likely there will in fact be success, the more likely, then, that you can leverage this success to attract others who want to replicate it. Thus, it is good for both you and for the client to work to place individuals connected through you to the client.

These independent contractors may or may not, of course, have contracts through your company. These days, I generally ask the people I refer to the clients to make their own arrangements contractually and to give me consideration in return, be that money or some service. I don't want the bother of having to draw up the contracts, and I don't want the responsibility or the liability either. These I prefer to leave to the independent contractor.

You will find, as I have, that your clients will come to rely on your advice about who to contract. This makes sense. People have problems, to be sure, but they are not necessarily experts on how to find people with solutions. If you can help them, it will only strengthen your position with the client, help others with whom you can do further business, and result in some kind of consideration for you. It's very much a win-win-win situation.

Articles By You

Writing articles by you will never be a huge direct profit center for you. But it nonetheless does deserve a place in the Mobile Mini-Conglomerate for a couple of very good reasons:

- Writing these articles diminishes the amount of money you need to spend for advertising, since, properly handled, they are a better source of promotion.

- These articles enhance your reputation as a perceived expert in your field and hence the kind of desirable person an individual with a problem to be solved should be working with.

As you already know, there are three kinds of article formats that you must master (see Chapter 7):

- The Problem Solving Process Article
- The Sentinel Article
- The White Knight Article.

Each has certain variations and sequels as already discussed. The important thing is that you factor in these articles as part of your marketing and promotional activities. You will find that you will be paid for them in several ways:

- directly by the media source
- indirectly through attracting clients and through the enhancement of your professional standing.

As you will not be surprised to learn, I am a fanatic about writing and publishing these articles — and not merely once but over and over again. The mistake that advisors make in relation to this category is trying to create articles which are new and different. My articles, by contrast, are filled with solid, reliable, sensible information, nothing flashy, just good meat and potatoes on the common problems facing the client population to which I am targeting any particular piece. I learned long ago that so long as any given population continues to have this problem, then the articles, no matter when they were written, continue to have validity. Your task is to write articles which indicate to your client population that you can help solve their problem and to use and reuse these materials until such time as the problem no longer exists or until it no longer makes economic sense for you to deal with it.

Newsletters

With this category we are now breaking some new ground, for previous sections of this book dealt with the first four steps of the Mobile Mini-Conglomerate. Now it is time to discuss the first new division of your company, the newsletter division, and whether this makes sense for you. In this regard, I must tell you that I myself do not have a newsletter. I skipped over this stage to concentrate on the next one, producing books, instead. Therefore, I have sought out the advice of many newsletter owners and would like to share what they have told me along with my own views on the matter.

- The Free Client Newsletter

It will surely be no surprise to you that advisors need a way of staying in regular touch with and being seen by both present and past clients. One of the means they regularly employ is the free client newsletter. In this regard, one of the best I have seen ("The Levison Letter") is produced by my friend and admired colleague San Francisco-based marketing communications advisor Ivan Levison. He estimates that as much of a third of his new business is generated by this letter for the following reasons:

- It makes sure you're remembered.
- It positions you as an expert on topics of interest to clients, thereby causing them to value you the more and to extend your contract into new areas they may not previously have considered.
- It gets routed to others in the company and to people whom the recipient knows (but you do not) are interested in the problem you are addressing.
- It causes you to be quoted in other media sources as an expert. After all, anything in print helps establish you as a perceived guru.

Advice On Free Client Newsletters

- Send it to everyone you can possibly think of who might be useful in getting you business. Levison suggests you should send at least 200 to make it worthwhile, but you'll quickly find yourself sending more and still more.
- Make it short. Levison's client letter is a short, two sided 8 1/2 by 11 inch single sheet with pithy information in an eye-catching context. People these days ordinarily prefer brevity. But don't be too brief. Deal with the subject you have selected in satisfactory detail, thereby indicating your mastery of it. This means including complete follow-up information for anything you provide the client. Your objective, of course, is to get the client (or prospect) not merely to read your free newsletter because it contains valuable problem-solving information but to save it because it is packed with names, addresses, telephone numbers and other essential information of value to him. If the client learns to use your newsletter, surely learning to use you, too, will follow in due course.
- Send your newsletter out regularly. If you can only do it twice a year, that's fine, but be regular. Again, you wish to indicate mastery and control to both clients and client prospects. It isn't necessarily how much you do that makes the difference; it's doing what you say you're going to do, when you say you're going to do it, and producing a quality product, even though this product be a short one.
- Use your own name in the title of your newsletter. This isn't presumptuous. Either you are an expert or you're not. Either people should listen to you, or they should avoid you. You decide. Being in the advising business means enhancing your perceived reputation as the expert. Why not face up to this and begin to live and work accordingly?

- Make sure there is an action subtitle for the newsletter. Levison correctly suggests that each newsletter have an action subtitle clearly indicating both to clients and prospects what kinds of subjects you'll be addressing in the newsletter. His own says, "Action ideas for better marketing communications." Personally, I like words like "success", "action," "problem solving information," etc. to be included in this descriptive phrase.

- Hire a graphic designer to prepare your format. This will cost money, but it'll be worth it. (Cost: about $300.) Once designed, of course, you can use it over and over.

- Keep your newsletter simple but with impact. This may mean using a second color. In this connection, run your second color on, say, 5000 sheets; then every month run your issue copy (in black) as a second pass. Levison has a master board with the headline and his photo already pasted up. Each month his assistant pastes up his typewritten copy which is then run over his pre-printed second color masthead.

- Make sure to include: your masthead (the newsletter's name), your subheadline, the date of this letter and your business name, address, and telephone number. Each newsletter should offer complete follow-up information to the reader, who should never be asked to rummage through papers to find out how to get to you. This sounds obvious, but you'd be amazed how often the obvious is overlooked.

- Make sure, too, to include a brief biography about yourself and a selling message about something you can do to solve a particular prospect problem. These selling messages should change each time you send out your newsletter. Also add a copyright and "all rights reserved" line. You don't want others to use your ideas without your permission. And, as Levison suggests, consider closing with your signature.

Some Production Tips

- Use a typewriter to produce copy. I agree with Ivan that this gives your copy a "hot off the presses" look that is hard to beat. Years ago I even produced my catalog on a typewriter for this reason, although today I use a desktop publisher.

- Keep your mailing list on computer.

- Word process your envelopes. Ivan is adamant that labels look tacky. He's right, but as he knows when you get to the point of sending out more than 500 pieces, word processing envelopes may just be too expensive. You'll have to play this one by ear.

- Send your newsletter first class. Americans are in a love affair with speed. We want to be the first on our block to know something, to use something. So submit to the inevitable. Bulk rate postage is cheaper, of course. However, if you are aiming to portray yourself as an individual with crucial success information exclusively available to a select group, first class postage is in your best interest. Besides, it indicates to both clients and prospects that you are serious about your business.

- Use instant printing services to produce your newsletter. Again, there's no need to use an expensive printer, and you want the client again to feel the urgency and importance of what you are sending.

- Don't do the paste-up/production yourself. If you are as uncoordinated as I am, you don't need to be told to avoid this unpleasant task. Unless this is therapy for you (in which case don't give it up!), hire someone else to paste-up your newsletter for you. You worry about the substance; let someone else (at about $20 to $25 per hour) worry about the look.

Costs

Let's be frank. Putting out a free client newsletter is not particularly cheap. Ivan's sharp looking newsletter costs about 70 cents a piece to produce when the following expenses are taken into consideration:

- graphic designer — format development
- postage
- envelopes
- quality paper stock
- typing time for secretary
- fee for paste-up person
- printing
- word processing envelopes
- any special typesetting costs (for headlines, &c) done each month.

For this cost, you are getting a two-sided, two-color newsletter — and as Ivan can enthusiastically attest, a superb reputation and excellent professional visibility.

Note: Don't just take my word for it. Ivan will be happy to send you a sample of his excellent free client newsletter, "The Levison Letter." Write him at Ivan Levison & Associates, 14 Los Cerros Drive, Greenbrae, CA 94904. Tell him I sent you!

Newsletter As A Direct Profit Center

As I've already said, I do not operate a newsletter. I chose instead to concentrate on books. There are several reasons for my decision, which you may share:

- I operate a one-man business (with the help of my subcontractors) and travel frequently. Running a newsletter would tax my time resources considerably, what with both editorial and marketing functions to perform.

- I can meet the same marketing needs through my books.

This doesn't mean that I do not value newsletters or am not aware that with the house list I possess of buyers of my books and participants in my seminars I may be overlooking a likely source of additional income. That's why every year I agonize over whether now, at last!, the moment has come to launch my own newsletter.

To see whether you (or I!) should do so, I called in two of my top newsletter advisors: Howard Penn Hudson, the national newsletter guru, and my friend Barb Brabec, editor and publisher of the *National Home Business Report*, an Illinois-based newsletter targeted to people like me who run a home-based business. Both know what they are talking about. Here are the kinds of things they suggest:

- Be clear about your market.

There are more than 100,000 newsletters nationwide. The best ones are rigorously targeted to a very precise market. To target this market, use the same steps as you would to target your advising business. Remember: a newsletter, properly understood, is merely another form of advising service that you offer to those who may not, for lack of resources or geographical distance, be able to take advantage of a one-to-one relationship with you in the flesh. Nonetheless, if people are willing to pay you to offer such a service directly, they will probably do so, too, to have the information you make available in a newsletter.

- Write down the dramatic need.

The newsletters which succeed are the newsletters whose publishers are very precise about the dramatic needs they are fulfilling for their target market. These publishers, like you, of course, want to make money, maintain maximum control over their time, work from home, &c., but they never say so in their publications. Everything that they — and that you! — do has to be targeted to the precise and urgent needs of your target market. Remember: in business you are not merely competing against other newsletters. You are competing against every other thing that exists that could help solve the need of your targeted reader prospect.

- Know your universe of prospects.

You must be clear about how many people/organizations have this dramatic need. A universe of prospects is properly understood as the total number of individuals who could buy your newsletter because it solves their problem. The more precise you can be about this universe the better. "Small business people" is not a universe. It is very unlikely that a newsletter could be effective trying to cater to the needs of a business with 100 employees (the uppermost limit to the category) or one home-based Cambridge advisor. Be precise. Most newsletters fail because their publishers want to cast their net too broadly, are afraid of missing someone and losing out on some source of income. This is a mistake. Newsletters can be rigidly targeted to ultra-precise markets. The key is figuring out what percentage of this market you need to reach so that you'll produce the revenue you need to make this venture a success.

- Get ease of access to your targeted prospects.

Once you've identified a target population and discerned how many prospects there are, you must spend time discovering how easy it is to reach these prospects. Some groups are easy to reach (Alabama funeral service directors); some are hard. The trick to creating a profitable newsletter is to identify a group which is easily reached, identify their most palpable, pressing problems, and create a product which is a lively problem solving process vehicle producing for them a disproportionate benefit compared to fee.

This is what Barb Brabec has done with her superb publication the *National Home Business Report*. Her market is crystal clear: America's home-based entrepreneurs. She is one herself and understands the problems of running an exceptionally demanding small business. She keeps her hand on the pulse of other home based entrepreneurs' problems and is alert to plausible, profit-making solutions to them. *National Home Business Report* is just the kind of newsletter I would recommend for your consideration, because it is an advisor between sheets. While Barb does advise home-based entrepreneurs directly and through her workshops, the *National Home Business Report* is just like having her (and a bevy of other advisors, including me!) on hand to tackle their specific problems. It does not just contain news *per se*; it contains problem-solving information, hands-on how-to details geared for immediate use and specific application by the readers. This is the essence of a successful newsletter product as far as an advisor is concerned.

Once you've identified the market and assessed their needs, you need, of course, to check out the competition. But let's be clear about what we mean as competition. Competing vehicles are not merely those offering information about inns. Competing vehicles are those which are specifically attempting to function as an advisor between sheets: that is, who function as a direct, one-on-one advisor might. This is your real competition. This means that there could in fact be other publications in, say, the innkeeping field which are not yet competitors. If they offer views and not problem solving process information, techniques and procedures, they are not, in my strict definition the real competition. You must keep this in mind.

One of the problems in the newsletter business involves a differing understanding of what the newsletter is there to do. People with a journalistic background are apt to feel their job is done when they have imparted facts, news, straight information, the "here's what happened" details. I do not agree. For an advisor, someone who is anxious to solve the problems of a targeted audience, a newsletter is necessarily incomplete until such time as it actually helps provide, in precise, specific detail, an individual with the problem being addressed the right kind of information so that he can in fact solve it. Thus, for me, most newsletters fail in their primary reason for existing.

Once you have in fact determined that you have an audience, that this audience has problems of pressing urgency, that you can identify and reach this audience with relative ease and with problem solving information they can immediately apply but which is not easily available elsewhere, you are ready to carry on. The precise details of what you do next, from an editorial and marketing perspective, are really beyond the terms of this book. But let me provide you with some information you'll find helpful:

- Before beginning, make sure you have a complete sense of the matters of pressing urgency to your client population. If you are not appealing to their "hot buttons", they'll have every reason to ignore you. Face up to it: even if you do have such an understanding, you'll be lucky, given people's slothful habits, if you get 5% of your designated market to sign up as subscribers in the first year.

- Develop an action name that includes your surname somewhere in the title. Use the advice previously rendered for a headline and a descriptive subheadline, as in *"The Lant Letter: How To Build Your Six-Figure Independent Consulting Practice."*

- Keep the copy short and action oriented. Don't just supply information. Tell people precisely how to use it. It's not enough to give your readers facts. Every day, in every media source, we have fact after fact thrown at us. It's insufficient. Tell your people how to use this information. How it affects them. When they should act. Why they should act. The pitfalls of acting incorrectly, &c. This is the sole point to a newsletter: providing your readers with hardcore, action-oriented information they cannot get elsewhere without expending vast amounts of their own limited time and resources.

- Develop a style. Don't be afraid to be unique. You are not trying to be an impartial journalist (as if that rare animal actually existed). Remember: you are an advocate for your designated client population. If something that is happening is against their interests, say so. Tell them, precisely, what to do about righting matters. A newsletter as published by an advisor should be as personal as your advising practice itself. Wax warm. Be cool as your client/readers' interest dictates.

- Make sure every item printed has complete follow-up information. Infuriatingly, there are many newsletters which do not give you complete follow-up information for every source they cite, every book they quote, every expert they feature. This is ridiculous. You want your newsletter not only read but used. I read my newsletters (and I get many!) at my computer. As I find something of interest, I write for it immediately. I cannot do this (and thus come to doubt the intelligence and, often, the paternity) for newsletter publishers who do not provide this information. Remember: a newsletter is merely another form of advising vehicle. Would you be this vague in your professional practice? Then don't be that vague in your newsletter either.

- Tell success stories of people using your newsletter. I like success stories. They inspire me and incite me to duplicate the success. Other people like them, too. Why, then, are there so few newsletters that ever say how successfully their readers apply their advice? Does this sound like patting yourself on the back? Well, what's wrong with that? People always like reading about themselves, particularly when it's something good. Keep a file of your success stories, of people who have benefitted by using what you told them to do. Envelope yourself in a success aura. People will always want to work with people who are successful, who can help make them successful. These success stories prominently featured in your newsletter will help create this necessary aura.

Other Benefits From Newsletters

- Newsletters are superb promotional tools. Because you have industry-specific information, other journalistic and media sources will want to know what you know. In this connection make sure you send information about your newsletter (including a sample copy) to journalists who cover the industry. Any time any media source mentions anything about your industry, drop that source a note indicating that you are available for future interviews, etc. By the same token, release your stories as news immediately following notification to your members (you must continue to show them that they are getting privileged information before it is generally available). If your population is national (as it will probably be) make sure you especially keep in touch with the wire services and national news media. Cultivate the impression that you are the ultimate source of problem solving process information for your designated buyers. (I need hardly say that **THE UNABASHED SELF-PROMOTER'S GUIDE** is essential reading here.)

- Don't forget the other steps in the Mobile Mini-Conglomerate. Newsletters are, of course, only one of 9 ways to help your targeted buyers solve their problems. When you are in the newsletter business you should be moving step by step into these other businesses, too. Thus, you should offer your buyers problem solving process advising services (both project and longer-term retainer relationships), books, cassettes, seminars and products produced by others. There is nothing wrong in this. Unless you have a complete monopoly on every single problem solving vehicle of interest to your readers, it is your responsibility (as well as to your profit) to make such offers to them. Sadly, newsletter and other publishers don't really understand this fact of life and often create unnecessary obstacles. One of the things that I do is to persuade these publishers to make their readers special offers of various kinds, reminding them the real business they are in is not merely putting out information but offering to work with people to solve problems through the proper utilization of information, which is precisely what an advisor does. *N.B.* In this connection once you've got your newsletter, I'd like to hear from you. I've got deal possibilities which will be good for your market, good for you, and (I breathe this quietly) good for me, too.

- Newsletters should be the basis for booklets, books, audio and video cassettes, and talk programs. Nothing that appears in your newsletter should appear there once and for all. Nothing. But don't be lazy about this. It is not enough to reprint your newsletter and bind it as a book. The information must be recycled, updated, and made to conform to the peculiar necessities of the book, the booklet, the cassette, the workshop. I abhor books that are titled "The Best Of Newsletter X." This shows that the compiler is slothful and not client-centered.

There is nothing wrong with reusing information. There is everything wrong with making it seem dated, no longer up-to-date, and centered on the client's immediate problem. As you develop your Mobile Mini-Conglomerate, it is your responsibility to make sure that each scrap of information is considered in relation to being used in each part of the cycle. Too many people with information make the wrongful and foolish assumption that just because information has appeared once somewhere, they cannot, indeed must not, use it again. This is just plain stupid. Have all those with the problem seen this information and understood how to apply it for the solution of their problem? Will anyone ever have this problem again? Of course, everyone with this problem has not seen your problem solving solution; of course, others have it and will have it in the future! In that case, it is your obligation to use and reuse every scrap of problem solving information you have — to help others and to profit yourself.

Key Sources Of Newsletter Information

The treatment of newsletters in this book has necessarily been brief. Fortunately, good, solid follow-up information is readily available to you, including:

- Barb Brabec's *National Home Business Reports*. Write for a free copy to P.O. Box 2137, Naperville, IL 60567 or call (708) 717-0488.

- Howard Penn Hudson's *The Newsletter On Newsletters and Newsletter Design*, 44 West Market St., P.O. Box 311, Rhinebeck, New York 12572 or call 914-876-2081. Howard is also the author of a critical book on newsletters entitled *Publishing Newsletters: A Complete Guide To Markets, Editorial Content, Design, Printing, Subscriptions, And Management.* (Available through his firm or through Charles Scribner's Sons, New York.)

Also check out:

- The Newsletter Association
  1401 Wilson Blvd., Suite 403
  Arlington, VA 22209
  1-800-356-9302

Frederick Gross is the executive director. Among other benefits, members receive "The Guidebook to Newsletter Publishing."

- *Editing Your Newsletter: A Guide To Writing, Design And Production* by Mark Beach. Coast to Coast Books, 1115 S.E. Stephens St., Portland, OR 97214.

Each of these resources should help. Tell them I sent you!

Writing, Producing, And Profiting From Booklets And Books

For me, a booklet and/or book is merely another way of assisting a designated client with a precise problem or set of problems. These products are perfect to:

- solve the problems of those who cannot otherwise afford you

- alert would-be buyers who can afford the more costly kind of client-advisor relationships that you do in fact exist and can in fact solve their problem.

- promote you to the widest possible extent.

Booklets and books are what I call "profit making brochures." They are profit centers in their own right, of course, but also exist to market you and your other advising services. Booklets and books can be used by the buyer to solve his problems directly. But remember: most people are lazy. After reading one of my books, for instance, people always call me to see if I can help them directly, in a one-to-one client relationship. The reason is plain: they now know just what it will take to solve the problem satisfactorily, and they don't want to use their limited time and energy to learn the things they know I already have mastered. Thus, from your standpoint a book becomes a marketing document, profitable in its own right, which helps secure you other, more profitable clients.

A Snare: Books Published By Mainline Publishers

In the beginning of my writing career, I like most authors published with mainline publishers. Like most authors, my experiences were not entirely happy. I had then (but remember I was younger!) the curious notion that the job of an author was finished once the book was written and accepted by the publisher. Now I know how ridiculous that idea is — and how prevalent. As is well known in the book trade, some 55,000 titles are published each year. Of these, fully three out of 10 lose money; 3 to 4 titles break even. The remainder make some kind of profit, often minimal. Yet I must tell you, as strenuously as I can, that this is largely because of the most stupid management and marketing procedures imaginable. Now that I publish books myself, I am prepared to tell you that every title I have ever published has made money, often lots and lots of it. The reason is very plain: publishers suffer from a one-season mentality. Self-publishers do not. Thus, if you want to work with a mainline publisher, you had better understand what you are getting into and protect yourself accordingly.

Publishers are in the business of manufacturing books. (It is often debatable if they even care whether the books, once produced, are in fact sold. I kid you not.) Advisors are in the business of solving people's problems through the apt use of information. These businesses are in no sense necessarily incompatible, but you had better be aware of how to get what you need from an industry which is operating on a different wavelength. Understand that most people publishing with mainline houses will not secure their objectives. They will not recoup the investment they made in writing their book. They will not make further profits beyond the initial advance. They will not secure sufficient recognition to enhance their professional reputations. They will not get lucrative clients as a result of their books being extensively marketed. So long as you realize that this is the likely result, you can prepare yourself accordingly — and protect yourself in your dealings with the publisher.

- Make sure any book you publish with a mainline publisher has a complete listing of all your advising services and who they are meant for. Don't just say you are a financial planning advisor. List the kinds of specific services you provide and who they are meant for. Provide information about your audio cassettes, newsletters, seminars, &c. Give people your name, address, and telephone number. Invite them to contact you for further, follow-up information (and a place on your mailing list). In short, use your book as what it is meant to be: a prospecting tool. Now go to any bookstore in the land and leaf through the books written by advisors. Their number, of course, is legion. But I challenge you to find a single one that acts as a prospecting device for the advisor-author. Why not?

Authors have the curious notion that people will take the time to hunt them down by writing to their publishers and then having the publisher forward their mail. They also possess the maddening idea that the mere existence of a book, as some kind of hallowed token of their intelligence and expertise, will necessarily lead to clients. Nothing could be more idiotic — or more common. If you want to make the best use of a book, you must be client centered; you must tell the client that you understand what his problem is, that you have created appropriate problem solving vehicles, and that you have made it easy for him to follow up and get in touch with you.

Publishers, of course, may resist the notion that you are using *their* book (for that's how most consider it after you've handed it in) for such base purposes. They may oppose the notion that you be allowed to include, in effect, a marketing brochure in the book. Authors, they'll reason, should not be allowed to make a book so blatantly commercial. This reasoning, of course, is blatantly anti-client, the client in this case being you — and the people you have written the book to help. Publishers are no more client centered than anyone else, and arguably less so. Nonetheless, you've got to stand your ground — or go elsewhere to someone who understands what you are trying to accomplish. Give in and you'll become like the rest of the authors who hoped for good results — and failed to get them because they did not make it easy for their clients to follow up.

- Insist on seeing all material written by the publisher's publicity department. The material sent out should follow the problem-solution format. Your book should be seen as a solution to a problem (or cluster of problems) of your targeted client prospects. Most materials developed by publishers are not only deadly dull; they are positively inimicable to the success of the book. They provide information about the book but not about the problem solving information in the book. Remember: most people are not interested in books. They do not regard the book itself, as publishers do, as a sacred item. And frankly, most people are right. There is nothing necessarily worthwhile or admirable about the book *per se*. Thus, all materials emanating from your publishers should zero in precisely on the targeted audience, their significant problems, and how this book addresses them in a way to produce a disproportionate benefit compared to fee. Sadly, most publishers, even if their lives depended on it, could not write this kind of copy. Thus, you have to. You must, too, effectively appoint yourself promoter-in-chief for your book. You will deeply come to regret your relationship with a publisher unless you come to understand that publishers are primarily interested in manufacturing books, not in selling books, whatever they say to the contrary. If you want to derive benefits from the book beyond the mere fact of seeing it as physical object, you must make the commitment to it that will ensure these benefits.

- Count on the publisher not being able to sell all the copies of your book that he prints. Thus, make sure there is a clause in your contract giving you first refusal over the remainder copies and the right, too, to purchase the plates from which the book was printed. Remember: if your designated public continues to have the problem you address; if the book continues to have useful material in it, the mere fact that it was not published this afternoon is not pertinent. Americans have such a love affair with the present, with the impetuous here and now that we forget we should care only with what works, not necessarily with what is new. You as an advisor cannot afford to forget this, especially where your book is concerned. So long as your information is useful to your designated client group it should be available to them.

The Profitable Alternative: Producing Your Own Booklets And Books

Unless you are writing a book that must get quick distribution to be successful, as an advisor you are probably going to be better off not merely writing but manufacturing and distributing your own products. I know what I'm talking about. Without training, without detailed information on publishing, without a background in book manufacturing or distribution, I set up my own publishing company in 1980. Since then the books I have published have grossed well over two million dollars. They have become an independent profit center for me, provide me with a solid annual income, act as the basis for extensive, continuing promotion of my various advisor services and products, and bring me to the attention of those who want to work with me more directly. No wonder I am so keen on the self-publishing alternative.

The trick, of course, is to realize that a book written by an advisor and meant to solve the problems of a designated client is different from other kinds of books. Other books, like fashions, come in and go out in a single season, if not less. Books written by advisors can stay current so long as your clients have the problem and your information remains relevant for solving it.

A Booklet Or A Book? Which Is It To Be?

I have no bias whatsoever in favor of or opposed to a booklet *vis à vis* a book. This is vastly different from many authors who feel that a booklet is beneath them, somehow demeaning to their dignity as an author and authority. For these poor benighted folk only something between hard covers will do, whether they have enough material for such a book or not, whether or not that format really meets the needs of their clients. Remember: the decision about whether to go with a booklet depends on several factors very much including which format really makes sense given the needs of your buyers. The rules of client-centered marketing apply as much in this area as anywhere else. Writing and producing a booklet makes perfect sense to me if the following conditions apply:

- You are targeting a very specific problem that can effectively be dealt with in the compass of 8 to 100 pages. Length is not the pertinent factor to consider in publishing. It is whether you have effectively identified a client population, effectively targeted a vexing and urgent problem of that population, and provided this population with exactly what it needs to know about solving that problem. For instance, there are one million nonprofit organizations in the nation; virtually all at some point or another have to write proposals for funding to foundations and corporations. A good effective booklet could easily be written on how to do this. Such a booklet could be short and yet most meaningful.

- Your market wants information, problem solving process information, as quickly as possible and is not particularly interested in packaging. People who produce books are usually as concerned about the way a book looks as what's in it. That's all right if you are a book lover. But if you are a problem solver, this concern with packaging may (rightly) strike you as misplaced. In booklets as in newsletters, people are interested in information. They want to work with someone who understands their problems and has developed timely solutions to it. Their concern with beautiful packaging is definitely way down their list of priorities.

- You expect to reach your market through direct mail sales, seminars and workshops and catalogs rather than bookstores and other retail outlets selling books. In bookstores and other retail outlets, you need to be concerned about packaging, about how your book stacks up against all the other pretty packages in the store. This is much less true in direct mail and other forms of information selling, where targeting the audience and understanding their problem (and letting them know you have the solution) is infinitely more important.

- You want to keep your investment low and see how this new enterprise goes. Fools rush in where angels fear to tread. If you are going to succeed in the information selling business, to succeed as an advisor between sheets, it will take some time and some tinkering.

No one has as precise a picture of their market and its problems on day one as they do on day 365. So plan on it. Booklets allow you, for a fairly minimum cost, to produce a profit-making product, to get out problem solving information (including information about the other advising services and products you produce), and to learn what you need to know about the publishing and marketing business. With booklets, your initial investment (that is direct expenses) can be kept low. Given the value of the information and problem solving techniques to the targeted market, the price of the booklet can be set high, often very high. In trade book publishing, books are generally priced at about 5 to 6 times cost. With booklets, always given the critical caveat about importance of the information to the buyer, you can price your product at up to 50 times cost and do proportionately much better than mainline publishers.

Given this fact, you'll not be surprised to find that I am now turning my attention to the creation of a booklet series of interest to my target markets. Why now and not years ago when I established my own publishing company? In a word: the existence of my own house mailing list. Once you have a list of several thousand buyers of your products (whether they be books, tapes or newsletters) you need to think of new ways to cash in from the existence of these proven buyers. Here booklets can be invaluable, especially booklets clustered around a common theme and priced not according to the usual publisher formulas but according to the value of the information to the buyer and the degree to which it is difficult to secure elsewhere.

Other Advantages Of Booklets

- Booklets are easy to store. Even a spare closet can become the headquarters for your embryonic publishing empire. (Yes, you can have your publishing company pay you rent for this service. This is a legitimate business deduction. How many of you have your closet producing income anyway?)

- Booklets can be typewritten and offset printed. Thus, when it's time to go back to press they are relatively easy to update.

- Booklets can be used as a source of unabashed promotions just like newsletters. They can be sent as review copies particularly to newsletters and publications dealing with the affected population. They can be excerpted in these publications and made the basis for how-to stories which piggyback information about you and your other problem solving products and services.

On To Books

At some point, however, despite all the merits of booklets, you are probably going to move on to the writing, production, and marketing of books. In fact, this is where I began. As with booklets, there are ways of effectively easing in to this business so that you can learn while you earn. In this regard, here are two varieties of books for you to consider:

- typewritten, offset print, GBC spiral bound workbooks
- typeset, perfect bound books.

Spiral Bound Workbooks

The first of these is an easy extension beyond booklets, and it is the kind of book I began with when I first published **DEVELOPMENT TODAY: A FUND RAISING GUIDE FOR NONPROFIT ORGANIZATIONS**. The value of these workbooks both to you and your clients is considerable:

For your clients

- Workbooks are designed to be written in. I find that my client/readers very much appreciate not just being advised what to do but having examples on hand of what they should be producing and very specific guidelines of how to achieve the desired result. Workbooks are designed to be used, written in, actively considered. They are an important variety of the advisor between sheets, for the advisor is at his best not when he merely tells the client what needs to be achieved, but actively shows him how to do it and works with him to achieve the desired result.

- Workbooks are not intimidating. Many, many people have unhappy memories about books. Books are symbols of a time in their lives when they were trapped and miserable in school. For those of us who were happy in school, of course, this is a great tragedy; nonetheless it is a reality. Your books, therefore, need to be easily accessible to your users.

For you

- Workbooks are a learning experience. They are relatively easy to put together, can be produced in short runs, and yet be profitable because of their disproportionate benefit compared to client fee.

- Workbooks are relatively inexpensive to produce and a good place to begin learning the publishing and marketing business.

- Workbooks allow you to tinker with your product. For the average author writing a book, the book once completed is in fact finished. It would be foolish, for instance, to have Charles Dickens rewriting his novels every year in response to what he heard his buyers say about them. To this kind of writer, a book is a book is a book. But this is definitely not true for us. For advisors using books as a means of reaching their clients and helping them solve their problems, a book must be perpetually updated and revised. I liken a book to a stew which must continually have new vegetables and other nutritional ingredients added to it. So long as people are hungry, it is necessary to keep working on the stew, even though the stew is continually changing. Tinkering is a necessary part of developing a successful advising practice. So it must be with your books. Just as problems change, so your approaches to these problems will change, if only because year by year you know more and more about how to solve them. Workbooks provide you with an easy means of handling this necessary updating process.

Drawbacks Of Workbooks

So long as you are prepared to forego the traditional retail book establishments, you can probably stay with workbooks for years and years. Indeed, using direct mail, catalogs, sales to seminar and workshop participants, drop shipping relationships with other book sellers and your own house list, you can make a very good profit from your workbooks and may decide never to go on to the next step. There is nothing wrong with this decision. Don't fall into the usual trap set by snobs and fools who say that unless your information is behind hard covers and sitting on a bookstore shelf you have somehow failed. Remember: most books are in fact returned to their publishers about 11 months after being placed on the shelf; 95% of books fail to live beyond one year. It takes most authors far, far longer to write their books than it does for the publisher (and the bookstores) to kill them. Thus, for most people writing a book does not make economic sense; it only serves to inflate their already too large egos and lead to a diminution of any client centered marketing they may have been doing. In this regard, I follow the lead of my esteemed countryman Benjamin Franklin whose lack of pride and whose deep reserves of common sense made him the very symbol of intellect and humanity in his times. This is what I would like people to think of me. This means approaching each problem to see what works, not with any preconceived notions, especially those based on the disturbing notions of pride, arrogance, or inflated self worth.

Still, if you have material that would be of interest to a wide popular audience and once you have perfected your problem solving methods and refined what you are publishing through your workbooks, you may well find it advantageous to move on to the next stage of publishing: typeset, perfect bound books.

Perfect Bound Books

What is a perfect bound book? A perfect bound book has a flat spine. You are looking at one. It is a completed statement by an advisor who has a precise conception of a targeted market, has made a point of ascertaining the problems of this market, and has come up with a set of problem solving procedures which will produce a disproportionate benefit compared to fee for this market. That is what is happening with this book.

Perfect bound books have several advantages:

- They can be sold through bookstores and other retail establishments selling books. Most such establishments do not carry booklets and avoid spiral bound books because you cannot put the name on the spine. Thus the book must be displayed face outward, taking up a disproportionate amount of their precious shelf space. Moreover, bookstores often quiver about the prices that you as an advisor put on your books because they are out of line with the other merchandise they are carrying.

I can well remember in the first days after the publication of **THE CONSULTANT'S KIT,** when it was an immense spiral bound workbook, the dismay of local booksellers who thought it would not sell at $30. How wrong they were! As they quickly discovered, people can and did pay that price because of the disproportionate benefit of the information compared to fee and the difficulty of meeting their needs in any other way.

- They are easier to store than spiral bound books. The spiral on those books make flat stacking difficult.

- They can be sold to libraries and other permanent book repositories, as workbooks and booklets usually cannot.

- They are a much, much better source of unabashed promotion, since they have the look and feel of "real" books. Neither booklets nor workbooks will ordinarily be reviewed in major newspapers and magazines or by major on-air publicity sources who do not regard these formats as sufficiently book-like. Workbooks are usually reviewed by newsletters and trade publications. Perfect bound books can get general media attention.

- Catalogs and book clubs are more likely to take an interest in perfect bound books appropriate for their markets.

What, then, am I really saying? If you have a relatively small, precisely targeted group of clients you may well be better off with a booklet or workbook-style book. If you have a much larger market (as, say, all nonprofit organizations needing to raise funds in the private sector, hence **DEVELOPMENT TODAY: A GUIDE FOR NONPROFIT ORGANIZATIONS,** or all people wishing to break into the talk business, hence **MONEY TALKS**), a market that can be reached in many ways including retail establishments, then and only then should you consider writing, publishing and marketing a typeset, perfect bound book. But if you do, and are willing to keep this book updated year by year, the results can exceed your most rosy fancy.

Tricks Of The Perfect Bound Book Trade

- Your books should be designed so that all the numbers and timebound illustrations can easily be updated or so that, if necessary, a section can be deleted and rewritten without necessitating huge amounts of typesetting.

- You should not even consider writing and publishing such a book, unless you are prepared to spend at least as much time marketing it as you did writing and producing it. Do not make the mistake that regular publishers make: if you are going to write a book, then you have to make the commitment to marketing it. If you really have solved the problems of your designated client group through this book, you have, too, a moral obligation to do this, for as your book sells you will be commensurately solving deeply-felt problems of people who need your problem solving skills.

- Make sure that (as with your booklets and workbooks) you promote the availability of your other advisor services and products. Don't just say what you've got. Say who should use it and what they can expect to get out of it.

- Include a catalog of other people's products (from the sale of which you benefit; see cooperative marketing agreements below) at the end of your book. Don't just try to solve one problem of your designated buyers (and so get one check). Attempt through a single vehicle to solve as many as you can, profiting accordingly.

Key Book Publishing Resources

- **If you insist on publishing with a mainline house.**

If you want to brave the problems of mainline publishing, at least have the good sense to do so after having consulted the following books:

- *How To Get Happily Published: A Complete And Candid Guide* by Judith Appelbaum and Nancy Evans. A New American Library paperback, this book is must reading for the aspiring writer or self-publisher.

- *How to be Your Own Literary Agent* by Richard Curtis. Published by Houghton Mifflin ($10.95), it gives you the low-down on how to represent your own work with the best chance to make the sale!

- **On publishing booklets.**

There is really just one good book on this interesting and highly profitable subject. *Writing And Selling Simple Information* by Jay Barnes is available from the author at 330 Route One, Fort Ann, New York 12827. This book is not terribly prepossessing in its packaging. It merely contains exactly what you've got to know. I've found it very helpful.

- **On publishing books.**

Two books between them contain all you need to know to get started in this lucrative part of the Mobile Mini-Conglomerate:

- *The Self-Publishing Manual* by Dan Poynter, Para Publishing, P.O. Box 4232-37, Santa Barbara, CA 93101. Dan Poynter is well known as the guru of self-publishing. He goes out of his way to provide helpful information. Each time I publish a book, I reread this one.

- *How To Make A Whole Lot More Than $1,000,000 Writing, Commissioning, Publishing And Selling "How-To" Information.* If you're really serious about turning your problem-solving information into a multi-million dollar info-empire, you'll want this 7th volume in my series. Over 550 pages long, it contains detailed information on how to make real money from books, booklets, audio cassettes and special reports. In case you think I'm a biased source on this volume, here's what Dan Poynter said about it: "The exhaustive, absolute last word on information creation and selling. This books says it all and is the best there is. Highly recommended." Purr

More Resources

While there are literally thousands of additional sources of information available to those wishing to succeed in the publishing business, here are a few of the very best places to look for technical assistance:

- Ad-Lib Publications, P.O. Box 1102, Fairfield, IA 52556. The knowledgeable Marie Kiefer and John Kremer publish many helpful directories and guides for self-publishers, including a list of over 60 key resources on the subject. Write for a complete list of publications, including *The Directory Of Short Run Book Printers* which provides a unique list of book manufacturers. Call 1-800-669-0773.

- *Book Marketing Handbook* by Nat G. Bodian, published by R.R. Bowker. Volume One deals with tips and techniques for effectively selling your books. Volume Two weighs in with over 1,000 more tips. These books are expensive and rather dully written. Nonetheless they've got a lot of information if you're really serious.

- COSMEP, P.O. Box 420703, San Francisco, CA 94142-0703. An organization of over 1,500 independent publishers nationwide. Headed by Richard Morris, a well-known author in his own right, COSMEP offers essential marketing and production information monthly. (415) 922-9490.

- *How To Make $6000 A Month Selling Books By Mail.* This 64 page booklet is just $1 (that's what I said!) and comes from that innovative marketer Russ von Hoelscher who's always got something cooking. Get if from Profit Ideas, 254 E. Grand Ave., Escondido, CA 92025.

- National Association of Independent Publishers. This organization headed by Betty Wright, one of the most generous people in publishing, offers workshops, a spiffy newsletter, and constant encouragement to the independent publisher. Write them at P.O. Box 850, Moore Haven, FL 33471.

- Publishers Marketing Association, 2401 Pacific Coast Highway, Suite 102, Hermosa Beach, CA 90254 (213) 372-2732. Another organization of independent publishers, this one, too, publishes a fine periodical packed with industry news and profit-making tips.

And One More Pivotal Resource

If you're really serious about promoting your books (as well as your practice as a whole), you're going to need to master my own **UNABASHED SELF-PROMOTER'S GUIDE.** Yes, I'm the author, but that doesn't mean this recommendation isn't sensible. Take it.

Talking For Money

Every business day over 200,000 lectures, speeches and workshops are given across the country. The vast majority of these are given by advisors like you and me who understand the value of the talk circuit in creating an independent profit center in its own right, providing the opportunity to capture new clients, and enhancing your image and reputation. Yes, there are many good reasons for breaking into this market. The problem is that the competition is fierce. Yet if you follow my advice you'll find yourself easily able to make thousands of extra dollars yearly and to meet your several other objectives, too. Here's what to do:

Start Small, Start Local

As you probably know, in poll after poll Americans say that public speaking is their greatest fear, far and away beating death, nuclear war, or any of the truly significant issues of our time. You probably share this fear; it's natural. Getting up in front of an audience means placing yourself in a situation of vulnerability, one where you can and will be judged. Such a situation is an opportunity, of course, but it also provokes anxiety. Your job is to make sure you make the most of it. But you won't be able to do that until you've mastered certain essential techniques of making persuasive presentations. This takes time and that's why you need to start small and locally to learn what you need to know to make yourself an effective, compelling speaker.

Fortunately, most communities in the United States now have some type of adult education facility, be it a free-standing center or one connected with a high school or community college. Collect the catalogs of these facilities. See what they are offering and whether they have a gap in your field. Since advisors provide eminently practical, immediately usable information you'll have little trouble making an opening for yourself.

Contact the program planner with a stirring marketing letter. Point out why your topic is of interest now, how you know this, where the audience is, how easily they can be reached, and why you're the best person to teach a program. This letter should be easy for you to write; after all it's really no different from the other marketing letters you are now doing regularly. Once the letter is sent, call the program planner and make a personal presentation. Remember: program planners are deluged with suggestions. Most of them are of ridiculously poor quality. Their chief fear is that yours won't be any different. Surprise them. Bring in:

- a course outline

- a course description heavily stressing the benefits, the ultimate and practical benefits, participants will receive

- a 50-word write-up on your qualifications to teach the course

- a media release packed with reasons why the media should be interested in what you're doing.

Make Sure This Course Is A Success

Assure the program planner that you'll work as hard as he will to make this course a success. Too many people on the talk circuit, particularly those at introductory levels, assume that once their suggestion has been adopted, they are off the hook and don't have to do anything else. False. If you want a new course to succeed (and you do!), you've got to help. Send flyers to your friends and business associates. Tack up notices on bulletin boards everywhere you go. Volunteer to contact relevant media sources, including calendar departments and individual programs and columnists, to get some coverage. Remember: at least half of all new programs are cancelled for lack of sufficient enrollment. If your initial program fails, a program planner is necessarily a little less enthusiastic to do business with you again. Make sure this doesn't happen. Your task is to get this going, to make it a success, so that you can leverage it and get more speaker business.

Using The Program Itself In Your Interest

As you should by now know, there are many ways to make money on the talk circuit. Your speaker honorarium is only one. You'll make more money by:

- Making sure each participant in your programs gets complete information about your advising services and products, including a précis. You shouldn't be offering a program unless you can make more money from selling your professional service and/or advising products than you can from the speaker fee itself. But you must make it easy for people to buy from you.

- Showing your advising products to be clearly useful. If you are selling such products, don't just have them available for inspection, refer to them in your program. Selling is an active, not a passive process. Thus, if you have a problem solving process book like this one, hold it up and tell people about what's in it in relation to a problem in which they are particularly interested. If people see how your product can solve their problem, they'll want it. Remember: people don't buy seminars; they don't buy books. They don't buy any advising product because they like it: they buy solutions because they must have them to reach their own objectives.

- Asking participants what other programs on related themes they'd like to see offered. Take their suggestions to the program planner and work out future programs based on what your buyers have said.

- Getting participants to write down their reactions to your programs. Candidly inform them that the best of what they say may be quoted in future brochures using their names. At the end of a program that has met their needs, people will be enthusiastic about you and about the experience and they'll say so. You can then use what they say in future brochures to attract new customers and to prove that you are successful at what you do.

- Taping the program. Tape it for two reasons. If you were good, you can sell it both to participants (at about 50-75% of the original admission price) and to those who couldn't come but are interested in the subject. If you need improvement, you need to listen to your presentation to see where you can make beneficial adjustments. Keep taping until your program is perfect.

After The Program

- Meet again with the program planner. Discuss when the program you have just successfully completed can be repeated and when the other suggestions made by the participants can be implemented. Thank the program planner for his cooperation and tell him you want to continue to work with him. Your task in the talk business is clear: to keep the engagements you get, to turn them into regular profit centers (for all your advising products and services) and to use the successes in these programs to leverage new talk business — and hence new business on every front!

- Identify all the other noncredit adult education facilities, including community and other colleges, where you could offer your advising programs. A good list is available when you join The Learning Resources Network (LERN), a consortium of over 5000 producers of continuing education programs nationwide. Tell Bill Draves, executive director, I sent you: 1554 Hayes Drive, Manhattan, KS 66502.

- Now write and request the catalogs of the other possible sponsors. If *they* have a gap, not offering the kind of advising program you can produce, then write and tell them about your success at the original location and mention the name of the individual program planner you worked with. This is a small universe and the planners may well know each other. If they don't have a gap, write and say you'll be happy to stand in when they do. Don't expect your first letter to achieve great results. Program planners are not good about answering their mail and are often not as entrepreneurial as they should be about welcoming new programs, particularly when they think, horror of horrors!, that you'll be making money from them. Many program planners in academic institutions maintain the foolish notion that instructors should be offering their knowledge for the mere love of their subjects. Don't forget, too, program planners work at least 6 months in advance. Thus, you should be preparing for fall programs in the winter, for winter programs in the early spring.

Notes On The Lower End Of The Talk Market

- Starting out on the talk circuit, you won't be in the same league as Cronkite, Stormin' Norman Schwarzkopf, and Kissinger, who get over $25,000 a speech. It just won't happen. How could it? Nonprofit adult continuing education facilities pay little; $25 to $50 per hour is common. Instead, set a realistic profit objective for yourself. $5,000 a year is sensible. But remember: you can make much, much more from your other advising products and services that can be promoted through these presentations and through the catalogs of your sponsors. Remember: it's very sensible to use their money to build up your practice and enhance your image. This is what clever marketing is all about.

- Stay at this lower end of the market only until such time as you have perfected your speaking skills, have a clear sense of your audience, and what it wants to buy, and are ready to move into the higher paying markets. This will probably take at least a year.

Moving On, Moving Up

Too many advisors who do produce programs make the mistake of staying too long at the low paying end of the talk market. This is an error. This end of the market is valuable, of course, as a training sector for you, but once you know what you're doing and who can substantially benefit from what you know, it's time to move on. Here's how to do so:

• Set A Greater Dollar Objective For Yourself.

If you really want to turn yourself into a professional on the talk circuit, set yourself a professional objective: making at least $10,000 a year from your advising talk programs. No objective: no arrival, no success. If you find it relatively easy to reach this objective, it's too low.

• Keep A List Of All The Problems You Can Solve.

These problems, of course, should be related to your advising business. There's no point telling people how to solve a problem if you do not have a problem solving service in that area. But the more such services you have, the more programs you are capable of offering; the more diversified you are, the more likely you are to keep getting engagements.

• Draw Up A List Of The Various Talk Formats You have Available.

Not only do you have to be aware of your client/audience's problems, you should have the maximum variety of ways to solve them. Thus, you need:

- a 50-minute speech (good for after meals and for meeting keynotes)
- a two and a half hour workshop (suitable for morning and afternoon convention sessions)
- a 6 to 7 hour workshop (suitable for one-day convention sessions or to be offered as a pre- or post-convention special or through continuing education facilities)
- a two-day intensive workshop (offered by trade and professional associations as continuing education for their members)
- a five-day institute (sponsored by colleges and trade associations).

The shorter the program, of course, the more you tell your audience *what* to do. The longer, the more you show your audience *how* to do.

• Identify All The People Who Have These Problems Who Are Easily Reached.

The key to succeeding on the talk circuit is to go where people are already assembled, not to try to attempt to generate your own audiences. This means being aware of certain key resources including:

- *The Encyclopedia Of Associations* published by Gale Research Co., 835 Penobscot Building, Detroit, MI 48226. Provides information about over 20,000 U.S. associations, about one third of the total.
- *National Trade And Professional Associations Of The United States* published by Columbia Books, 1212 New York Ave, NW, Suite 330, Washington, DC 20005. Fewer associations than Gale but includes many not found elsewhere.
- American Society of Association Executives, 1575 Eye St., N.W., Washington, D.C. 20005 (202) 626-2723. Publishes a membership directory. Also has available a number of means speakers can use to get to the association executives who make the buying decisions, including a card-deck where you can list your topics and other pertinent information.
- *Standard Periodical Directory* published by Oxbridge Communications, 150 Fifth Ave., Suite 636, New York, New York 10011. Indexes about 80,000 publications, including many published by newsletters and associations.

Note: You don't simply have to do your speaking business with trade and professional associations. Not by a long shot. I work with many newsletters who quickly come to realize (after I've urged them along!) that they have an unexploited source of income in their readers if they are not already using talk programs. Get information about this group, in addition to the *Standard Periodical Directory*, through:

- Howard Penn Hudson's Newsletter Clearinghouse at 44 West Market St., P.O. Box 311, Rhinebeck, New York 12572.
- *Oxbridge Directory of Newsletters* published by Oxbridge Communications. Indexes about 9,000 newsletters.

• Find Products (Or Create Them).

Whatever advising program you are offering should have supplementary materials included. For two reasons:

- Adult learners need reinforcement to be able to grasp the problem solving techniques you are talking about. Thus such materials are absolutely crucial in helping these learners achieve their objectives.
- They constitute an important profit center for you.

If you don't have such problem solving products, you need to make arrangements with those who do. I shall explore these arrangements shortly in my discussion of Cooperative Marketing Arrangements, but suffice it to say for this moment that you should not be offering any advising program unless you have available a suitable advising product (often a book or cassette) either through a distribution agreement with the manufacturer or directly available through you. Each time you have contact with a client who needs your problem solving information, you should be attempting to sell him as many items from your Mobile Mini-Conglomerate as possible based on his discretionary resources. The extent to which the problem is important to him (something, of course, which you should know in advance) will depend to what extent he'll commit these resources to the purchase of your problem solving products and services.

• Don't Leave These Sales To Chance.

Your job is to negotiate with the program planner to make sure all people attending the programs receive your problem solving books and/or cassettes. The mistake too many people on the talk circuit make is to sell from the platform. This kind of hucksterism detracts from your professional image and distracts the audience. Instead, make a deal with the program sponsor so that the price of your book (reflecting, perhaps, the usual 40% trade discount) is included in the price of admission to your program. This way you don't have to hustle (as much!), and you reap the benefit of the sales.

N.B. If you cannot get this concession from the sponsor, then make sure information about your advising products and services is placed in all the registration packets, not just for your session but for the entire conference, even if you are only presenting a single program.

• More Hints To Improve Sales, Enhance Visibility, And Develop Reputation

- Make sure there's an article about you (and your problem solving products and services) in the sponsor's publication before the program. If the sponsor is (as usual) pressed for time, offer to write the advance article yourself.
- Get the books and services reviewed either before or after the program in the sponsor's publication.
- Make sure there is a write-up on your problem solving presentation after it occurs. People need reinforcement before they take action. Make sure they get it!
- Too, see which other publications in the field would be interested in the information you've presented at the conference. Aim for multiple use. Smart advisors use and reuse every word they write until their public finally wakes up to their existence and the importance of what they are saying.

• Following Your Presentation

- Get a complete list of all the people who helped make your program possible. Send them thank-you notes and ask for the opportunity to work with them again.
- Get a list of all the participants in your sessions. Send them a letter with information about your products and services. Ask them to refer you to organizations they are active in and which need your kind of expertise.
- Get to reference guides like *The Encyclopedia Of Associations* and identify all other associations whose members have similar problems and could be clients for you. Send them a Success Letter about this presentation including a spiffy quote about you and your presentation from the program sponsor and from a couple of program participants.
- Take time to sit down with the current program planner or next year's designated program planner (at a conference) and discuss new programs and new ways you can work together. Once you've got an association, don't lose it!
- Request a warm and personal testimonial letter from the program planner and/or president of the organization sponsoring you, attesting to your many virtues and the worth of your presentation. Make this available to people who could hire you.

Benefits

How much can you make following these guidelines? That clearly depends on the size of your audience and the extent to which you have correctly identified their pressing problems and are offering a service to solve them. But conservatively you should be making between $500 and $5,000 a day on the talk circuit. I have many, many such days during the year, for I currently make over 100 presentations annually, each profitable. The other perks aren't bad either: public acclaim, articles about you, deference, and fans all increase the attractiveness of this line of work. I recommend it to you.

One More Thing

If you are really serious about breaking into the talk circuit, creating it as a substantial profit center and using it to attract new clients, then get my book **MONEY TALKS: THE COMPLETE GUIDE TO CREATING A PROFITABLE WORKSHOP OR SEMINAR IN ANY FIELD.** And then take off!

Profiting From Audio Cassettes

I read recently that there are at least two audio cassette players per household in the United States. What a source of potential profit for us advisors! But here, as elsewhere, there are some tricks of the trade you should know before jumping into what could be either a lucrative profit center for you — or an unqualified quagmire sapping your resources. Here's how to make it profitable for yourself:

- Tape your speeches and workshops first. As should be clear to you by now, I aim to have multiple profit from each thing I do. Thus, if you are having a workshop you can make money by:
    - getting a speaker honorarium
    - including your booklets and books in the price of admission
    - selling other people's products at the site
    - gaining clients from among those who attend, and
    - selling cassettes of the program both to those attending and to those who cannot.

Thus, from a single experience you have succeeded in making a handsome profit. This is working smart! As far as the tape portion of this scenario is concerned, tape your programs on a simple Panasonic recorder in 55 minute segments. Allow a couple of minutes for program introduction and a minute or two for cassette wrap-up. Sell these programs as is without editing for at least 50% of the cost of admission to the program or not less than $15 per cassette. You can produce labels in advance or type them as need be. Don't forget to include complete follow up information on your cassettes, including your name, address, telephone number and copyright information. That is a "C" in a circle, the year and your company name. Each thing that you send out about your advising practice should be complete in itself.

- When you're ready to move on, tape 55 minute problem solving cassettes on subjects of maximum interest to your clients. Follow the outline of the problem solving process to give these cassettes structure. Speak in a warm conversational way, but don't be afraid to inject cool language on issues where clients tend to backslide. Don't act any different on tape then you would in person. Price these cassettes at at least $15 per cassette.

- Before you go any further in the cassette business, you've got to consider the problem of tape distribution. Before you consider doing a more professional job with your cassettes, going to a professional production house, &c., make sure that you have given adequate consideration to how you will distribute your cassettes. It is vastly easier to produce cassettes than it is to sell them. Thus, make sure you have some of, if not all, the following already in place:
    - a house list of people who'll buy your problem solving advice
    - a catalog of problem solving products and services into which you can insert your tapes
    - an existing classified or space ad program eliciting queries from interested buyers on the subject(s) of your cassettes
    - an existing talk program or programs attracting people interested in the subjects of your cassettes
    - your own problem solving booklets or books on the subject of your cassettes and into which you can insert material about these cassettes
    - substantial interest from audio cassette catalog houses.

Unless several of these distribution possibilities are already in place, your consideration to go further into the audio cassette business is premature. If you have such distribution channels, however, then you are ready to proceed.

Going Pro

Here's what you need to do to make professional audio cassettes:

- **Produce a script.**

Don't just "wing" your presentations. Script them. A good script gives you control over what you're doing. This script should be heavily action oriented, immensely client centered, focusing on problems the client wishes to solve and providing this client with problem solving process information which will clearly prove that you are the expert in the field.

Your script may be in straight lecture format, in which case you must learn to modulate your voice so that the listener will not be bored. Or it can be in question and answer format.

- **Generate A Master Tape**

Once you have written your script and spoken it through several times to make sure it is conversationally accessible to the listener, it is time to rent a studio. Up until now your costs have been fairly minimal, of the "sweat equity" variety. From now on, however, they mount up quickly, so again I beg you: if you don't have an adequate conception of how you are going to sell the product you are now producing, refrain from going ahead until you do.

Check the Yellow Pages under "recording service, sound & video." An in-studio session makes more sense than a live audience taping since, under ordinary circumstances, you'll have more control in a studio and the resulting tape will need less editing. This, of course, saves you money.

In-studio time will cost you between $30 and $75 an hour. You should plan on being in the studio for at least two hours for every hour of finished program time you want. What you are paying for is the use of the studio and its engineer.

In working with the studio, plan to have your remarks recorded directly on to a 1/4″ open reel recording in one direction only. This provides better quality and allows you to go directly into the editing process without any additional transfers. Moreover, make sure the engineer records your session with simultaneous cassettes. This will cost slightly more, but you'll have cassette copies to listen to right away without the additional cost of reel-to-reel cassette transfer. Remember: when recording directly to cassette only, an additional "generation" or transfer is required to go to open-reel format for editing. You will need to use one 7″ tape for each thirty minutes of recording at a cost of between $12 and $20 per tape.

Getting Your Cassette Advisor Into The Act

Before you have produced the master tape, it's time to get a professional involved in editing and manufacturing it and producing the right kind of packaging. Here's what this professional will probably have to do:

- Editing. Your tape can be improved with basic editing or it can be worked over until it's perfect.
- Sweetening the master. This means adding music and sound effects.
- Adding professional voice narration. You know, James Earl Jones.
- Equalizing. This process enhances the quality of sound.
- Creating dubbing masters. These are the tapes from which the final copies will be run.

As these processes are taking place, you must consider, too, the packaging for your product. You may wish to have a vinyl album with either silk screen printing or a clear overlay with insertable graphics. In either case, you'll need suitable copy for the front and back covers, the spine and the identification labels, and the assistance of a graphic designer.

How much does all this cost? That depends, of course, on many variables, but you can figure that professionally to produce 250 four one-hour cassette album packages with a 10-page supplementary booklet, including information about both the program and you and your advising products and services, will demand between $4000 and $5000. In this case, you'd have to sell these albums for about $50 each so that you could glimpse some profit on your initial order. Clearly, as in all such matters, your profit goes up the more cassettes you can produce, the less extra marketing and promotion you have to do, rather piggybacking this profit center onto other advising activities and products you already have.

Audio Cassette Resources

Four leads will get you started in this potentially very lucrative field:

- Audio Tape Catalogs, published by Evon Publishing, Rt #1, Box, 658, Elcho, WI 54428. This is an example of a large cassette catalog offering both a possibility for your own products and a source of those cassettes you might also like to sell.
- Cassette Productions Unlimited, Inc., 5796 Martin Road, Irwindale, CA 91706-6299. (818)-969-6881. Bill Guthy, my audio guru for **MONEY TALKS,** is the owner of this aggressive company which offers one-stop shopping for anyone interested in producing a quality cassette package. He'll treat you right. He produces the "Taping Yourself Seriously" audio cassette by Toni Boyle which provide further information on how to produce your cassettes. ($39.95)
- Dove Enterprises, 907 Portage Trail, Cuyahoga Falls, OH 44221. 1-800-233-3683. A good place to look for information on tape duplication, cassette accessories, and blank cassettes. Start here when you want to handle matters yourself.
- **MONEY TALKS: THE COMPLETE GUIDE TO CREATING A PROFITABLE WORKSHOP OR SEMINAR IN ANY FIELD.** The most complete book now on the market offering information on designing, producing and marketing audio cassettes, including complete guidelines for producing your own if you're so inclined.

Cooperative Marketing Agreements

We are now at step 9 of the Mobile Mini-Conglomerate. You should have a clear conception of how many ways there are to serve your clients, to provide them with the problem solving information they need, at a price they can afford, and to create for you a mechanism which will produce profit every single day from a wide variety of sources. Never before has this concept been put forward so clearly so that every advisor, whatever his field, can serve his maximum audience and derive the maximum profit. Now we are at yet another link in this golden chain.

The concept behind Cooperative Marketing is a very simple one. It assumes that there are others besides yourself who have created worthwhile products or who offer worthwhile services to your clients and that it would be beneficial to these clients, to these manufacturers, and to yourself for you to offer them for sale. The key to such agreements, also called drop shipping agreements, is that you do not manufacture the product, you do not warehouse the product, and you do not ship the product. Where a service is involved, you do not provide the service, you only sell it. In other words, you must simply identify a client's need and let the client know that you have a product or service available which can solve it. Remember: the objective in dealing with your clients is to help them solve as many of their problems as you can and to profit accordingly. Cooperative marketing agreements help make this possible. Drop shipping is the vehicle.

The first problem, of course, is knowing what your client's problems are. That has been a *leitmotif* of this book. As I said, they are legion. Every time a client or prospect expresses a problem, write it down. Find out whether this is a problem others have and whether they'll pay to solve it, and how badly they need the solution. If the answers look positive, this may well be something for you to consider. Consider, too, whether you can cluster this problem and its solution with the other problems and solutions you are already dealing with, in other words, whether this is a logical extension from what you are already doing. Your objective, after all, is to create yourself as a one-stop-shopping place for clients who have particular sorts of problems and who need particular sorts of problem solving products and services.

Once you have identified problems and ascertained that clients are willing to pay to have them solved, begin to find people with products and services who can in fact solve them. Where are these products and services? They are everywhere. Everything that is manufactured, every service that is offered can be offered cooperatively. Think of the staggering possibilities. Of course, there are some guidelines you should be aware of:

- The product or service should not be commonly available. If it is, it is unlikely that you can offer it at a better cost than people can already find it.

- The product or service should not be commonly marketed. Again, this suggests that you cannot be competitive.

- The product or service should be rigidly targeted to a specific group, a group that will find it difficult to get the solution it needs elsewhere.

This, then, is the key to profitable cooperative marketing agreements:

- that the problem be a severe one for a precisely targeted market, a market you are serving in other ways with other products and services

- that the solution to this problem not be commonly or readily available through others.

If these points can be satisfied, then you are in business. Still, where should you begin looking for leads?

- *Books In Print* published by R.R. Bowker Co. This and *Forthcoming Books*, a companion volume, list all the titles in print. It is available in nearly every bookstore and all libraries. If you want to help people solve problems through books, this is a crucial place to look.

- The annual fall books issue (usually published in August) of *Publisher's Weekly* (also published by R.R. Bowker). An amazing catalog listing all the new releases for the next 6 months or so of all major publishers. Supplemented by smaller spring and summer catalogs. At least 90% of the books listed in these sources will not get adequate promotional exposure and can be prime targets for you.

- *Drop Shipping News* published by Consolidated Marketing Services, Inc., P.O. Box 7838, New York, NY 10150. They also publish the book *Drop Shipping as a Marketing Function: A Handbook of Methods and Policies* by Nicholas Scheel ($42.95).

- *American Drop-Shipper Directory* published by World Wide Trade Services, P.O. Box 283, Medina, WA 98039. Lists thousands of product possibilities and how to get in touch with their manufacturers.

What You Want From The Manufacturer

Once you've identified a problem solving vehicle (product or service) for your targeted market, you'll need help from the provider. Here's what you need:

- ready-to-use sales and marketing literature
- a suitable incentive to make it worthwhile for you to get involved
- assurances that your orders will get prompt consideration.

Marketing Literature

If a manufacturer is interested in having you sell his product (or service) to your buyers, he should provide you with ready-to-use materials into which you simply have to insert your name and address to be in business. Such materials are called stats and are, in fact, camera ready artwork from which the printing (which is usually your responsibility) can be done. If the manufacturer is smart, he's already thought through the problems of your market (which is, of course, his market) and how his product solves them. He may already have produced the necessary sales letters and order materials, thus making it very easy for you to do the most important thing of all: working to get access to the ultimate buyers.

N.B. When you in your turn become a manufacturer, you have to produce these materials for *your* dealers. I have. If you are interested in representing my lines of problem solving books, both those for nonprofit organizations and entrepreneurs like yourself, I have all the materials you need ready and waiting. Just let me know!

Suitable Incentive

Unless you can make money by telling your clients and prospects about these problem solving vehicles, there's no reason to do it. Each industry is based on a discount structure. Ordinarily the more items you sell, the better your discount becomes. But here's some advice:

- If you are going to sell books, request a 50% discount from the retail price. Independent and self-publishers will ordinarily be happy to provide you with this discount. Mainline publishers balk, usually offering no more than a 40% discount. But keep pressing. Mainline publishers handle these situations through what is called their Special Sales Department. Many of the people staffing these departments are chuckleheads without the power to make decisions. My advice to you is that if the discount is anything less than 40%, do not take on the project. But don't just drop it silently. Inform the publisher. Maybe if enough of us entrepreneurial types do this, we'll get some positive change.

- If you are going to sell products besides books, check with others selling the product to see what discount they get. Then request between 10 and 20% more. Just because someone else hasn't made the best possible deal doesn't mean that you can't.

- If you are selling professional services, you'll have to negotiate your percentage on a case by case basis but make sure it's not less than 20% of the client fee.

In each case, make sure that all orders and inquiries are returned directly to you. Don't trust the honor and good faith of the people you are doing business with. It's too easy to "forget" to tell you about a few orders or a few inquiries. Have the customers send you their checks directly, and where you are handling professional services, have all inquiries go through you.

Assurances

Don't do business with people who will not fulfill your orders and handle your client inquiries promptly. Monitor this for a time until you are satisfied. Remember: all complaints about fulfillment and service will come back to haunt you. If one of your suppliers is negligent or just plain slothful, it's going to hurt the customer relationship you have with a client. If a supplier doesn't supply your orders promptly, send a gentle but firm note to the president of that firm expressing your concern and asking for his assistance in solving the problem. If things do not improve at once, drop the firm from your repertoire and look elsewhere for a solution to the client's problem.

Creating Your Own Catalog

As you probably already know, I have created my own catalog. It's what I call a "Cluster Catalog" or a "Theme Catalog" because all the items in it, whether they are produced by me or by others, deal with a series of problems around a certain theme, in this case Small Business Success. Just as I advise you to do, I identify all the problems of my target market and then assiduously seek out solutions in the form of books, newsletters, association memberships, and professional services. I update this catalog quarterly, adding new items, deleting those which have not been as popular as I thought they might be. The costs are kept to the bare minimum by inviting others who want access to my market to join me through my "stuffer program", adding their own flyers to my outgoing packages at a per thousand rate. In this way, I keep my own direct costs ridiculously cheap and ensure the profitability of this enterprise, which my buyers have praised as offering them timely problem solving vehicle at a cost they can afford.

Let me tell you one or two things about this catalog:

- It's very profitable. I use my own house list, including book buyers, seminar participants, and those responding to my unabashed promotional articles and classified ads as the main groups to be solicited. As is well known in the mail order trade, house lists produce the best response. Why not? These people have already heard of me.

- I write very warm catalog copy. My catalog continues to be typewritten by me and each description is a warm, friendly, accessible one that my buyers can easily relate to. This has been, I feel, most significant in producing its success.

- It is easily produced and easily updated, unlike most catalogs which are major undertakings. If something doesn't work, I can more quickly delete it than the major houses. If something does, I can keep it in indefinitely.

All this is done with drop shipping. Except for a single sample of the items in my catalog, I personally keep no extras on hand. The manufacturer bears the responsibility for production and storage — and (though the customer pays for this) for shipping, too. I do what I can do best: promote, market, and help solve my client's problems through the apt selection of materials to be included in the catalog.

N.B. If you'd like access to this catalog, to my market, please let me know. I am always on the look-out for good materials which will help solve the problems of my get-ahead buyers, people just like you. Send me a sample of what you've got in mind with hot copy stressing the problems of the targeted market and why your product solves them. Keep my own problem solving materials in mind when you get your own Success Catalog off the ground, as I'm sure, now, you'll do — successfully!

Step 10: Diversification

The first nine steps of the Mobile Mini-Conglomerate are income producing. Using them will regularly increase the number of people whose problems you can solve and so regularly increase your income to the time when, even working alone or with part-time clerical and administrative assistant help, you'll be billing upwards of half a million dollars a year, as many top advisors regularly do.

This final step is an investment step and as such I have little to say about it — in this book! The first 9 steps of the conglomerate will produce regular profit for you, year in, year out so long as your target groups have the problems you are solving. The more you target the most pressing problems of these groups, the more profit there will be, and hence the more to invest here at step 10. Remember: to as you produce profit, you'll have the same problems and opportunities that any other conglomerate has. You'll solve them in the same ways: by acquiring related and unrelated properties to the theme of your main business. And, when the time comes, by selling them off for yet more profit. This is what diversification is all about: it shields you from recession and from the cycles that occur in all businesses and provides you with additional sources of income.

What is important to remember is that with the Mobile Mini-Conglomerate you must learn to think like a tycoon:

- You must think globally about wherever your buyers exist.

- You must create a product and service line so that whatever your client's ability to pay, you have something appropriate for them. My line runs from $3.95 at the lower end to upwards of $12,000 a year at the top, with a lot of other choices in between.

- You must aim to produce profit from each division of your company.

- You must invest the proceeds in such a way that you become recession proof and so solve the most taxing problem advisors have: the lack of certain income, the lack of a comfortable guarantee.

Properly managed, the Mobile Mini-Conglomerate will supply you with a secure daily income. It will produce income for you on the days you are ill and cannot work, on the days you have office paperwork to attend to, on the days you are just having too good a time to attend to your business. (Yes, even these happen!)

To make the conglomerate work for you, each step should have an annual income objective. This objective should be divided into the number of activities that can take place within the objective and each of these should have its own sub-objectives. Thus, if the category is Retainer Contracts, you should have an annual income objective for Delphic Oracle contracts and an income objective for Full Service Contracts. If the category is books, you should have income objectives for each book based on the following:

- direct sales to buyers (you get 100% of the purchase price)

- short discount sales (you get 80% of the retail price for books used in, say, college courses)

- regular trade discount sales (you get 60% of the retail price for books sold through book stores and other regular retail outlets)

- non-bookstore vendor discount sales (you get 50% of the retail price for books sold through non-retail outlets, like mail order book dealers and catalogs)

- deep discount sales (you get 20-25% of the retail price for books sold to a wholesaler who sells to non-retail book sellers).

You get the idea.

Too many advisors do not have a clear picture of what income they want and precisely what they have to do to get it. If you do, you can arrange your life accordingly and check your return month by month. Personally, I have monthly income objectives for each of my categories, and I translate these into daily objectives. I organize my life so that this objective is met, and usually exceeded, each day. If it isn't, I spend a portion of my afternoon (and sometimes beyond, for remember when it is five p.m. on the East Coast it is only 2 p.m. on the West Coast), trying to put together a deal which will push me over the top of my daily objective. I am firmly of the belief that one must have a precise dollar objective for the year and must monitor the achievement of this objective daily. Big successes are always made up of bite-sized successes rigorously pursued. The various divisions of the Mobile Mini-Conglomerate allow you to do this.

Last Words About The Mobile Mini-Conglomerate

Over the last several years, I have seen thousands of advising businesses get launched, often to an uncertain start, frequently to founder. This will not happen to you if you think through the pressing problems of your target market and provide it not with a single advising service, but with a wide variety of options, all resting securely on your problem solving expertise, on options, that is, which ask the client to do more and still more himself to solve his problem. Let me say this as strongly as I can: unless you are very much at the perceived status level of your most affluent client prospects, you must consider moving as quickly as you can to implement the various stages of the conglomerate. For here you will find the solution to one of your own most difficult problems: the lack of a certain income. With this certain income will come the confidence you need to be able to tell your clients and client prospects what they ought to be hearing, not what you think they want to hear (so that you'll get the contract you desperately need to keep afloat). The Mobile Mini-Conglomerate is a moral and a profitable machine. It gets your much-needed problem solving information into the hands of the largest number of people possible and so helps move them to the achievement of their desired objective. It provides you with the income you want and need (often very, very substantial) and thus ensures that the advice you give can be the complete, hard-hitting, precise, and substantial advice that your clients need to hear, thereby ensuring that you are behaving in the most candid and moral fashion possible. And so, for all of these reasons, assisting you sleep soundly at night with the comfortable assurance that you are doing well by doing good.

CHAPTER 12

The Business Of Business

So far we have dealt with how to get and service clients for best results. Now it is time to move on to equally essential, though often overlooked, questions of how to structure your business, and, indeed, your life so that you are able to meet both your own and your clients' expectations.

Advisors, particularly good advisors, as by now must be perfectly apparent, have the ability to shape and structure their lives to a far greater extent than most people. We have a pronounced need for autonomy, for freedom to build the kind of environment which most nearly allows us to be the person we want to be. The need for such autonomy is one of the reasons we become independent advisors in the first place and is a *sine qua non* of our existence. This chapter is about various possibilities open to you, various choices you need to make so as to be able to structure the kind of environment you need and which also provides clients with the kinds of constructive assurances they need about you and your ability to help solve their problems.

Establishing Your Mandarin Network

You will remember my telling you that the mandarins of ancient China grew their finger nails to outrageous lengths to indicate to an overburdened world they did no work. This is the congenial universe all successful advisors hope to establish in their own lives. To do this, you need a Mandarin Network, a network, that is, of people who exist to provide you with independent contractor services so that you can concentrate on what you do best:

- helping your clients solve their problems
- marketing your problem solving abilities to new client prospects
- diversifying your offerings so that you can provide more problem solving processes to more kinds of clients.

Successful advisors concentrate only on doing those things which directly relate to making them more successful advisors. All other things must be considered as of secondary importance. This necessarily means that successful advisors rely heavily on other successful advisors to provide them with the services they need so that they, in turn, can maximize the potential of their own problem solving abilities. Thus, to be a successful advisor you must learn to give up many of life's nagging responsibilities, for you, like all of us, have only so much time, and if you squander this time on less essential, if prodding, details, you will never succeed in becoming the complete advisor you want to be. Thus, advisors *you* should consider having include:

- a bookkeeper
- an accountant
- a tea drinking attorney
- a leg breaking attorney
- a financial planner
- a graphic designer
- a printing jobber
- a go-fer/house cleaner.

All of these people are, of course, independent contractors, advisors like you are. The need for some of them is obvious; for others, perhaps less so. Let me spend a moment on each of them:

- A bookkeeper will help keep your financial records, balance your company checking account, and handle your state and federal tax forms. Cost: about $20-40 per hour.
- An accountant is helpful with business planning decisions and in assisting you reduce your taxes, both corporate and personal, to the lowest possible extent. Cost: about $100-150 per hour.
- The tea drinking attorney is the individual who can maintain all your company and corporate legal papers, be the secretary or clerk for your corporation, call the annual meeting to order, and review contracts. This person should be a competent lawyer, someone with whom you can discuss both current problems and potential risk. Cost: $100-175 per hour.

- The leg breaking attorney is the individual who is useful in handling matters like larger debt collection, breaches of contract, and other matters which may lead to litigation. I have discovered that one attorney is generally not useful for providing both these necessary functions. One is adept in handling the nicer points of law and contracts; the other is a master of psychological harassment and deal making. Cost: $100-$175 per hour.
- A financial planner is absolutely necessary. A good financial planner seeks to understand your long term objectives and to advise you on the various means available to help you get to them. Cost: varies widely.
- A graphic designer is the person who helps you with the look of your materials, designs logos, arranges your documents, etc. Cost: about $40-60 per hour.
- A printing jobber is the person who can help you find the most advantageous printing prices. Different kinds of printing establishments give you advantageous prices on different jobs. It is perfectly clear to me that there is not a one-step shopping center for printing. Prices vary widely depending on the job. The jobber's cost varies but figure about $30 per hour.
- A go-fer/house cleaner. Unless you find housework therapeutic (in which case, keep doing it since everybody needs an outlet for life's little frustrations), stop doing it. Stop doing errands, stop shopping for your own food, stop buying your own typewriter ribbons. Learning to delegate is one of the most important things you can learn about running your advising business. Your time is frankly too valuable to do these things. You concentrate on doing what you do best: helping other people solve their problems. Cost: about $10-15 per hour.

This list, of course, is by no means exhaustive. You'll add people as you need to. The important thing is that you:

- Make the decision not to do everything yourself.
- Decide which things you wish to do because they are therapeutic and make you feel better, more fit, rested and ready to go back to your crucial problem solving work.

The people within this network should be compatible with you, should understand what you wish to accomplish, and should be available (for a fee, of course) to help you do just that. Everything which I have previously said about client-centered marketing applies here, too, only now you are the client and the members of your Mandarin Network, your advisors, even the lowliest go-fer. Thus, to begin with, you ought to have them read this book so that they know how to treat a client. In recruiting people for your network, take the trouble to inform them:

- what your objectives for them are
- what you expect from people working with you in an advising capacity
- what you hope they'll accomplish for you
- how you hope they'll accomplish these things
- that you want a long-term relationship with them
- whatever idiosyncracies you have in relation to this job.

Now that you are yourself the client, don't behave like the typical client you despise so much: stupidly. Write down what you want from each advisor. The more you can tell this person about who you are and how you operate, the more likely the relationship will be successful. Don't make the wrongful assumption that the advisor can simply walk into your life and help you without your helping him in return. Just because your objective is clear to you doesn't at all mean that it will be clear to your advisor. Remember this and act accordingly. In practice you will find that many advisors are not sufficiently flexible to be able to take into account your desires. They want, without necessarily saying so, you to pay the bill and to let them do what they want, in the way they want, in the time they want. Just as you may wish with your own clients. This is a mistake, of course, and if this problem is not dealt with early on in your relationship it probably presages an unhappy result.

Finding Members Of Your Mandarin Network

It takes time to create a Mandarin Network, often years until you have it in prime working order. This is to be expected. Members of this network need to reflect your objectives and need to feel comfortable with each other. That's why you should use referrals as much as possible. But beware of how most referrals are made. People understandably like to provide you with the names of their friends and business associates, feeling that in return they will get referrals from them. Unfortunately, as I have discovered, most people making these referrals know little or nothing about the people they suggest. Thus, you are left in the position of having to discern for yourself that which the person making the referral should have discerned for you: the putative advisor's credibility and usefulness. To avoid this irritating problem, when looking for a referral draw up a check list of what you want to accomplish. Provide this and any other relevant information to people you are asking to make referrals. This perhaps laborious-seeming task is actually to both your advantage and that of the person making the referral, since it is undoubtedly the case that an individual making an inappropriate referral himself is lowered in your esteem. Or should be. If the person being asked for the referral values your business and really wants to help you achieve your objectives (and, in the process, his own) he'll take the time to provide you with the right kind of referral or simply admit he doesn't have one to make. Which is, of course, a preferable response to making an incorrect recommendation.

Handling Problems In The Mandarin Network

Just as in any advisor-client relationship, there will be problems in your Mandarin Network; people will not always do things the way you like, even reasonably close to what you like. You may begin to feel resentful, irritated. Before this situation grows to flash point, take a moment and tell your advisor what is bothering you. Put your irritation into a short, friendly memo. Keep a copy. I got irritated with my accountant, for instance, because he was not itemizing his work for me; I had no way of knowing what I was buying and this was irksome. Rather than continue to be silently irked, prey to a growing feeling that I was being taken advantage of, it made more sense to put my feelings into a direct, professional, but friendly note letting him know how I felt. Do this with all your other advisors. The reason for this is plain: if a relationship has been in place for a time and is generally meeting your objectives, try to keep it. It is time consuming to try and establish a new relationship with new people who may, in the final analysis, prove to be as fallible and irritating as the advisor you are leaving behind.

But this doesn't mean that you should put up with poor service if the advisor cannot answer your sensible objections. Remember: you are paying for a service and if you don't get it, you should not hesitate to go elsewhere. This is one reason why in the Mandarin Network you should always keep the names of two or three others who could, if needed, provide you with the service. Test these people, if possible, by giving them short-term tasks to perform. See how they do with them. There should never be a need for you to fall back entirely on someone you don't know.

Home Sweet Home

One of the nice things about being an advisor is that you have the increased likelihood of working at home. Personally, as you by now know, I prefer this. New England has foul weather. People spend hours commuting, often arriving at their place of work frost bitten and incensed. I have a 10-second commute each morning. I arrive in my office, a brilliant sun-filled room, if not necessarily cheerful, at least not morose and suffering from commuter malaise. This saves me hundreds of hours each year which I can devote to the three primary tasks of any advisor's business: servicing clients, getting new clients, and diversifying to get more clients still. Think about this and think whether you can do as well, as inexpensively, by setting up an office outside your home.

All is not, however, necessarily clear sailing as far as setting up your home office is concerned. To begin with, you need satisfactory answers to the following very practical questions:

- Do I have a convenient space where I can work? While you do not necessarily need a self-enclosed space for tax reasons, you really ought (for professional and personal salvation) to have a room of your own in which you can maintain your business.

- Is the space at my disposal large enough for all the tasks that will need to be done in it? Having a self-contained space is one thing; having a sufficiently large space is something else. The more divisions of the Mobil Mini-Conglomerate you have in operation, the more space you'll need. As I can attest with all my heart, one's business has a way of overrunning any amount of space and intruding into the other, supposedly "private" quarters of your home.

- Is my home client accessible, or will it be difficult for my clients to come here? Many people set up home-based businesses with the understanding they will only see their clients at their clients' offices. This, of course, effectively costs you an important kind of business option: Delphic Oracle contracts, where the client visits your office. Since Delphic Oracle contracts are lower in price and therefore more attractive to certain kinds of clients, such a decision may not be in your economic interest.

- Are there zoning or other town regulations which preclude operating a home-based business in my neighborhood? Most towns maintain some kind of regulation precluding home-based business. To be sure, most of these regulations are antediluvian and foolish, but they still exist. You can, of course, decide to ignore them. If you are running a quiet advising business (as opposed to, say, giving rock music lessons) and are going to see only a few clients at home, perhaps it won't matter what you do. But there is still a risk. Still, taking risks is what being an entrepreneur is all about.

These problems are technical and are usually (if not always satisfactorily) answered. Either you have the space or you don't. Either you can and should be seeing clients at your home or you shouldn't. Either way, there are fixed, finite answers to be had. It is quite different with the crucial psychological points that must satisfactorily be resolved before your home-based business can be a success.

Credo of a Home-Based Business Advisor

The following points are the *sine qua non* of a successful home-based business, although clearly several of them apply to any business at all. Flout them at your own risk:

- I shall keep regular business hours. I shall not give way to the temptation to watch "just one" of my favorite soap operas and so creep away from my desk.

- I shall not talk to my friends and neighbors during business hours. I am running a business! I am not available for small talk until after the shop is closed. This includes my spouse and children, too. They must be trained to respect my need for time and space so that I can run my business. On the other hand, when I am with them, I must resolve to give them my full attention and not attempt to deal with lingering business problems. Fair's fair.

- I shall answer my telephone in a business way. ("Jeffrey Lant speaking"). If the call does not concern immediate client business, future client business, or the diversification of my business, I shall put off dealing with it until it is convenient.

- I shall structure a part of each day for marketing and promotion so that I shall have clients tomorrow.

- I shall set aside at least a quarter hour each day to think about what I'm doing, what I want to do, what is making me happy (and how I can continue this) and what is not (and what I can do about it). I deserve the luxury of thought!

- I shall set limits to when I am "in business at home" and when I am simply at home minding my own business. And I shall abide by them. I don't want anyone to think I'm merely a drudge.

Specific Issues Of A Home-Based Business: Qualifying For The Home Office Deduction

One of the chief reasons for working in your home (particularly at the beginning of your advising practice) is because it lowers your expenses. Assuming you meet the relevant government criteria, you get to deduct certain costs as legitimate business expenses. Moreover, if you are incorporated and your business rents its quarters from you, you'll be able to deduct the cost of the rent as a business expense (thus lowering your possible taxable liability). Of course, in this case you must declare the sums received as income and hence liable for personal tax. Here are the leading things you must know to be able to get the maximum benefit from your home office:

- Get a copy of IRS Publication #587 entitled "Business Use Of The Home". Things change in relation to using your home as a place of business. You can be sure the IRS keeps up on what's happening, especially if they are likely to get extra income from the changes. Call the IRS for this free booklet: 1-800-829-3676.

- Know the IRS' definition of what constitutes a home-based business:
  - A home is at once your family's place of residence and your principal place of business.
  - It's a place where you meet clients, customers or patients, and/or
  - a separate structure near your home.

Here are the exact words from the IRS:

"If you use part of your home exclusively and regularly as the principal place of business for a trade or business of yours or as a place where you meet or deal with customers in your business, you may deduct the expenses for the part of your home used for business. Also, you may be allowed to deduct expenses for use of part of your home as a day-care facility or as a place to store inventory you sell in your business, even if that part of your home is sometimes used for personal business."

- You must use these premises regularly and exclusively for your business to qualify for the home office deduction.

This space must be used regularly for your business. This does not necessarily mean daily. You can, after all, have a part-time advising business. But it does mean continuing use after a clearly-established pattern.

Two Notes

1. The IRS fairly recently changed its mind about whether your home-based office must be in a self-contained space. Now it says no. This means that you can use a part of a room, without a permanent partition, for your headquarters. Frankly, while this may be perfectly legal, I think it would be fairly devastating for your business if you were trying to live and work out of a rather limited space. Legal? Yes. Sensible? Not very.

2. My colleague Dr. Katherine Klotzburger has written a superb little book entitled *How To Qualify For The Home Office Deduction: 31 Legitimate Ways To Save Money On Your Federal Income Tax*. Get it from Betterway Publications, P.O. Box 219, Crozet, VA 22932.

Specific Issues Of A Home-Based Business: Insurance

We live in a litigious society, and you must prepare yourself for the worst. That's why you need insurance. Here I'd like to point to the kinds of insurance you especially need in a home-based business, although some of these are not without their relevance wherever you are located:

- liability to clients. You must prepare for the possibility that one of your clients may trip and fall while visiting you. Given our New England winters, this isn't such a farfetched possibility either, although, knock on wood, it hasn't happened to me yet! Still, I'm prepared, and you should be, too. You will need a rider to your standard homeowner's or apartment dweller's policy. You can get such coverage even if your area isn't zoned for business purposes. Such a policy costs about $250 yearly.

- general liability. You'll also need a policy that will cover you should you break or damage something while visiting a client or should a client at, say, one of your workshops, fall and break a leg and sue for damages. This is a general liability policy and is available for about the same price as the client liability policy mentioned above.

- business property coverage. You need a policy which covers the contents of your office as distinct from the contents of your home in the event of fire or another catastrophe. I suggest a policy which gives you at least $15,000 worth of coverage on your office equipment and furnishings and at least as much on the basic contents of your home. You'll want more, of course, if you follow my advice and purchase superb furnishings for both office and home. For these, though, you need a special fine art rider which enumerates these items specifically. The cost here varies, of course, on what you are insuring, but you should probably allow between $200 and $500 a year.

Specific Issues Of A Home-Based Business: Isolation

One of the chief problems of working at home as a solo advisor is that you may feel isolated and get lonely. Of course advisors have a high need to be autonomous, to do their own thing, but this can be carried too far! Solve this problem by allowing for rest time when you can contact professional colleagues either by telephone or in person, but do be cautious about this. I am myself the kind of person who works best in the morning up until about 2 p.m. I try very hard to reserve this time for new creative work: my writing and for thinking. I dislike scheduling meetings in this period and try very hard not to see people at this time. Moreover, I almost never (except when traveling) eat lunch away from my office.

But there comes a moment, usually about mid-afternoon, when I've created enough for the day and when I'm ready for more routine tasks, including seeing clients as well as colleagues. The latter I schedule, usually over generous libations in my office, after 5 p.m. and often extending into a convivial dinner. This way I meet my need for human contact and profitably extend my day, for such sessions are for brainstorming, which is for me a salubrious kind of relaxation.

It goes without saying that you should join relevant professional and networking associations. However, I say this to you: have a motive and an objective for going. Having fun and relaxing, of course, is a start. But see if you cannot make deal making and prospecting a form of relaxation, too. If you enjoyed Monopoly as a kid, I'm sure you'll be able to get into the fun of making real adult deals.

Specific Issues Of A Home-Based Business: Becoming A Self-Organizer

It is easy to become slothful working at home. The refrigerator, a natural enemy of the upscale advisor, is steps away. The television is near at hand. All the comforts of home become adversaries as you attempt to reach your objectives. Don't let them. Use the advantages of a home-based business to help you reach your objectives; don't give way before them.

In all businesses, of course, but particularly in a home-based business, where it is so easy to get distracted, you will find the GNOME system useful. GNOME is a five-step system which you can use to structure any given day as well as to arrange longer periods of time to your advantage.

- G is for "Goal". A goal is a general target towards which you are aiming. Making money today is a goal.
- N is for "Need." Why do you need to make money today? Because on any given day you have the following kinds of expenses which must be met:
  - rent
  - office machine costs
  - insurance costs pro-rated day by day
  - tax costs pro-rated day by day
  - costs of professional advisors regularly used by you
  - cost for your pension and financial planning, &c.

Whether you are aware of it or not, each day in your life is a spending day. Therefore each day in your life had better be an earning day, too.

- O is for "Objective." This is the specific amount of money you need to make today so as to be able to meet your needs.
- M is for "Method." This is the specific means you will use, and the emphasis is on the word *specific*, which will enable you to meet your objective.
- E is for "Evaluation." How will you know whether you have reached your objective? Your evaluation will tell you.

As I have consistently said throughout this book, big successes are made up of thousands of little successes. Each day should be organized for success, whether you are working at home or not. Each day you should reach the objectives you have set for yourself today which should be used to help you reach the objectives you have set for yourself tomorrow.

When you reach these objectives you deserve a reward, and you should give yourself one. One of the sad facts of life today is that people don't know what kinds of things make them happy and even if they do, stupidly wait for someone else to give them to them. This makes no sense at all! If you want something, give it to yourself — but give it to yourself once you have achieved a notable objective. Just what this notable objective is will vary by the day and the circumstances. But each time you successfully achieve one of your objectives, give yourself a suitable reward, something which will meaningfully mark and acknowledge the achievement.

Unfortunately, in a home-based business it is all too often too easy to give yourself the reward, the soap opera, the extra piece of cake, merely because it's present and not because you've done something to earn it. You have to assume responsibility for your actions, for making sure that you do get a reward but for ensuring that the reward is for something that truly should be rewarded.

Final Words On Working At Home

Working at home can have its negative points:

- Your clients may regard you as unprofessional because you are not working out of a standard office setting.
- Your family and neighbors may never regard what you do as "work" because it's being done at home.
- You may find it difficult to move between your various roles, being (as necessary) the creative, aggressive entrepreneur in business and the nurturing, yielding partner in a humane relationship.

Yes, these are problems. Fortunately, each of them has a solution. The question is: are you willing to do what it takes to make a home-based business succeed? If you are, then nothing will stand in your way as you become the home-based advisor *par excellence*. Fortunately there are wonderful resources at hand, beyond the wonderful resource now in your hands, to help you. Here are two of them, must reading if you want to operate a successful home-based advising business.

- *Homemade Money: The Definitive Guide To Success In A Home Business* by Barbara Brabec, published by Betterway Publications, P.O. Box 219, Crozet, VA 22932. Barbara runs a home-based business herself, knows what she's talking about, and has written a masterful book which is jam-packed with useful follow-up information.
- *Working From Home: Everything You Need To Know About Living And Working Under The Same Roof* by Paul and Sarah Edwards, Jeremy P. Tarcher Publisher, 5858 Wilshire Blvd., Suite 200, Los Angeles, CA 90036. Good solid information including material on husbands and wives working together and on computerizing your business.

Moving On, Moving Out

Some of you may not want to work in your home, some of you may have done so and found it distracting, or found that you have outgrown a home-based business. The real question you need to answer in each case is this one: Can you realize both your own objectives and your clients' adequately by working from home or do you need to expand to another space? Each of us advisors must answer this question for himself. I can only tell you how I feel — today. For now, a home-based business continues to meet my needs; it has not curtailed my business in any way and has provided me with the comfortable, quiet environment I need to be able to produce the several problem solving vehicles of my Mobile Mini-Conglomerate. You may decide differently.

Before taking a long-term office lease, however, and investing in a considerable amount of furniture, make sure your business can sustain the extra expense. I decided early on in my advising career that I didn't need either the prestige or the reinforcement which came with a "real" office, that I could satisfactorily achieve my objectives without them, and thus pocket the profits saved. For make no mistake about it: going out into a distinct office is a considerable expense, not least because it usually leads to the hiring of other personnel to manage it when you are yourself away or otherwise engaged.

I want you to be perfectly clear about one thing: you need not operate a formal office away from home to make very substantial income objectives. Now, in the great age of information, with modern telecommunications and electronics technology at your disposal, you can be connected with the farthest points of your market at a moment's notice and be very much within the comfort of your own home. If your clients do not need the reassurance of having you in an office, you must make the decision as to whether such an office is an unnecessary expense. There is no need for you to take on more expenses unless and until you are absolutely convinced it will be an investment that will return several times its cost in profit.

At such time as you have made the decision to look for new quarters, however, consider an intermediate step: renting space in one of the several companies, usually found in major cities, which for a monthly fee will provide you with an office, access to a conference room, and secretarial and clerical services. These are expensive, but if they prove to be unnecessary or excessive, at least you haven't made an unnecessary investment in a long-term lease and office equipment.

Deciding On The Form Of Your Business

Wherever you locate your business, you still have to decide on its form. Will you establish yourself as a sole proprietorship, a partnership, or a corporation? This is an important question, and one that demands your full consideration.

Pros And Cons Of A Sole Proprietorship

The easiest form of advising business to establish is a sole proprietorship. In this arrangement you are the sole owner of your business and are as such fully responsible for all debts and liabilities of the business. In return, you have the sole right to all profits generated by the business.

You are in business as a sole proprietor the minute you select a name. You don't even have to open a separate bank account for your business, although you'd be foolish not to. You're in business (as it were) because you say you're in business. You start generating income and start making note of your expenses, usually (at the beginning at least) more of the latter than of the former.

These expenses may include (but are not limited to):

- accounting and bookkeeping charges
- advertising
- briefcase
- business books and publications
- business-related entertainment
- Christmas cards for business associates
- computer
- consulting fees
- conventions and trade show expenses
- delivery charges for your business
- donations
- dues to professional organizations
- educational expenses, including seminars, workshops, and materials
- electricity used by your business (half of your regular monthly household charges would be a good estimate)
- equipment leasing
- freight and shipping
- gas (a percentage of your regular household charge, say one third)
- insurance premiums
- interest on business loans, late tax payments and business charge card payments
- independent contractor stipends
- legal and other professional fees
- licenses and permits
- mail list development, rental and maintenance
- maintenance contracts on office equipment
- membership fees in business-related organizations
- office furniture (to be depreciated)
- office maintenance help
- office supplies
- postage
- product displays
- professional services of artists, designers, copywriters, free lance writers, &c.
- rent
- research and development expenses
- stationery and printing
- taxes, including sales, state income, &c.
- telephone, including long distance services
- travel expenses connected with business, including gas, oil, and percentage of car maintenance expenses.

These expenses should be kept and tallied monthly, and monthly you (the business employee) should be reimbursed for any sums you have advanced the business to pay these costs.

Your obligations as a sole proprietor include:

- Filing a "doing business as" declaration with your state's secretary of state should you not be using your own name for the business. I urge you most seriously, however, to name the business after yourself.

You, as the advisor, are the chief product of your business, whether you are doing your advising one on one or through a series of problem solving process vehicles. Any means that helps enhance your standing as the expert should be utilized.

- Paying social security and federal income tax withholding payments. As an unincorporated sole proprietor, you'll probably be filing what's called Schedule C along with your 1040 tax form. This is the "Profit (Or Loss) From Business Or Profession" form. As soon as your profit on Schedule C is at least $400, it's time to file a Self-Employment Form along with your regular income tax form and pay into your personal Social Security account. Don't forget: as a self-employed individual you'll be paying roughly twice as much Social Security as your friends who work for regular corporations. This, of course, is discriminatory against the sole proprietors, and you should let your elected representatives know you are outraged by this state of affairs.

Your Social Security payments must be made quarterly as part of what are called Estimated Tax Payments. These payments from self-employed people are due on the 15th of April, June, September, and January. There's a penalty for not paying taxes when due as well as for underestimating them by more than 20%.

Your accountant can help you figure out what's due and how to file the papers, or you can read the excellent book by Bernard Kamaroff entitled *Small Time Operator: How To Start Your Own Small Business, Keep Your Books, Pay Your Taxes & Stay Out Of Trouble*. It's available from Bell Springs Publishing, P.O. Box 640, Laytonville, CA 95454. You should also review IRS publication #505 "Tax Withholding And Declaration Of Estimated Tax."

Further IRS Information

For further information from both the Small Business Administration and the Internal Revenue Service, you can get the following publications. The SBA publishes "Steps In Meeting Your Tax Obligations" along with other business management aids, many of which are free. Call 800-368-5855 and ask for their complete title listing. Two IRS guides list their assistance titles: #910 "Taxpayers Guide To Free Tax Services" and #552 "Record Keeping For Individuals." #334 "Tax Guide For Small Business" will also be helpful. You can obtain these and other free publications by calling 1-800-829-3676.

On Your State Level

As far as your individual state is concerned, you will have to pay your state income tax based on the figures you are reporting to the IRS. You will ordinarily not have any unemployment taxes to pay as you do if you maintain a corporation. If you are selling products, however, as you will do if you have a complete Mobile Mini-Conglomerate, and unless you live in Alaska, Delaware, Montana, New Hampshire and Oregon where there is still no state sales tax, you need to apply to the department of revenue for what is called a Resale Tax Number. This number "permits" you to collect sales tax on products produced by you for sale to in-state customers. Once you have applied for this number, the Revenue Department will send you quarterly the forms on which you'll report sales and remit payment for applicable taxes withheld.

Considering The Benefits And Drawbacks Of Sole Proprietorships

Clearly the chief benefit of a sole proprietorship is that it is quick and easy to set up and relatively easy to operate as compared to a corporation. You have the least amount of oppressive paperwork with this business form and a kind of operating clarity and ease which sometimes becomes elusive when operating another format.

Moreover, under the tax laws passed in 1982, the Tax Equity and Fiscal Responsibility Act (TEFRA), you are no longer at a disadvantage when it comes to pensions and long-term financial planning. Previously your company could only invest 15% of your yearly salary or $7,500 (whichever was less) in a Keogh Plan as a legitimate business deduction and for your long term benefit. Since 1982, however, you are eligible to have the benefits of a professional corporation pension plan even if you don't have the corporation itself. This means your company can invest on your behalf up to 25% of your yearly salary (up to a maximum amount of $30,000 annually); $120,000 is the top salary for which this deduction currently applies.

Given this benefit, there are now fewer good reasons to incorporate than there were before 1982. If you run an advising business where you can include strict "No Guarantee" clauses in your client contracts; if there is a very limited risk of legal action against you for the advice you've given; if your gross income for the company will be under $150,000 a year, it may make as much sense for you to remain a sole proprietor for the duration of your time in business as to incorporate. You need to ask your accountant, of course, and you need to be certain about the legal risks you face, for with a sole proprietorship all that you own is at risk, but this way of doing business is more viable nowadays than before 1982.

The Partnership

Despite the more attractive features these days of a sole proprietorship, you may want to enter into a business arrangement with a colleague and establish a partnership between yourselves. The primary reason for setting up a partnership is because you feel you cannot do all that needs to be done and that you need regular, ongoing assistance from someone who has a sufficient stake in the business to work for its success. This is what partnerships are all about.

I'm going to be frank with you, a bad partnership has the same effect on you as a bad marriage. Unlike a sole proprietorship which is easy to establish and easy to dissolve, a partnership, involving as it does one or more people, can be a good thing to establish — or a nightmare leaving you shaken and uncertain for months after it ends. That's why you should approach a partnership, any partnership, with the seriousness that you give to establishing a marriage or any other important relationship.

The benefits of a partnership include:

- Help! There are other people at hand with a substantial interest in the business who bring supplementary skills to the enterprise. All the responsibility, unlike in a sole proprietorship, is not on you.
- The partnership itself is not taxed. Whatever the partners take out in compensation (usually called a draw against profit and paid monthly or by some previously-arranged formula of the partners) is taxed in accordance with the individual partner's tax situation.

Overcoming The Main Drawback Of A Partnership

The main drawback in a partnership is in the area of partner relations. In a sole proprietorship, if you want to do something, you do it. If you don't, you don't. Personally, I like this level of freedom — and responsibility. I like being the autocrat of my breakfast table. In a partnership, on the other hand, there is always the likelihood that one partner or another will not do what he says he's going to do, or, worse, will do things which he explicitly agreed not to do, thus obligating the other partners. Make no mistake about it: all the partners are responsible for what one of the partners undertakes in his business capacity.

This is why the single most important document in a partnership is the partnership agreement. As partnership experts Denis Clifford and Ralph Warner have pointed out, this agreement must deal with the following points on each of which you need to secure precise agreement between the partners:

- name of the partnership (and names of individual partners)
- term of the partnership (indefinite, or for a set, limited time) and date started
- purpose of the partnership; the type of business to be conducted
- personal business objectives of the partners and partnership
- cash and property contributed to start the business
- what happens if more cash is needed
- skills to be contributed (hours to be worked, work duties of partners, management rolls, possible other business activities, &c)
- distribution of profits
- losses (how divided)
- salaries, guarantees, or drawing accounts and how regulated
- withdrawals of contributed assets/capital by a partner
- duties of partners, acts restricted or authorized by partners
- general management provisions (power to borrow money)
- expense accounts
- accounting and check signing rules and procedures
- disputes (rule by majority voting, provision for arbitration or mediation)
- sale, assignment, &c of a partnership interest
- admission of new partners
- continuing business if a partner withdraws, dies, becomes disabled, or retires
- determining value of a departing partner's interest, provisions for payment of that interest
- dissolution, winding up, and termination.

Settling Partnership Disputes

The disputes that arise in a partnership are not always obvious; often they are subterranean, as is often the case in human relations. Thus, just as in a good marriage, you must take regular provision for meetings between the clients to iron out the "tooth paste tube" issues, the small, irritating, potentially explosive issues which can destroy any relationship. Oftentimes these issues emerge because one of the partners may not have the same commitment to the business as the other partners yet is equal to the others. This can and does cause smoldering resentment which, if not dealt with expeditiously, can lead to the dissolution of the partnership. That is why there must, simply must, be a means for bringing out difficulties into the open and dealing with them as quickly as possible for the good of all concerned. I say this particularly to you if you are the partner who offers the greatest enthusiasm to the relationship: make absolutely certain that each task that needs to be done in putting the partnership in to good working order and keeping it in that order is written down and assigned to a partner and that that partner explicitly agrees to take care of it. As surely must be clear to you by now, in getting your advising business successfully started and in successfully maintaining it, there are literally thousands of things which must be done and which in a partnership must therefore be assigned to one of the partners. The more enthusiastic you are, the more you may be inclined to project your enthusiasm onto others and to let the necessary agreements slide; thus, the more you need a very clear and precise rendition of duties which need to be attended to and who will, in fact, do them.

Further Information On Partnerships

The best book now available on partnerships is one by Denis Clifford and Ralph Warner entitled *The Partnership Book: How To Write Your Own Small Business Partnership Agreement* available from Nolo Press Self-Help Law Books, 950 Parker St., Berkeley, CA 94710. I'm very impressed with the thoroughness of this book which is must reading for anyone even contemplating getting involved in any kind of partnership. I mean it!

To Incorporate Or Not To Incorporate: That Is The Question

Despite the situation where the benefits of incorporating are not as clearcut as they were just a few years ago, incorporation remains a precise objective of many aspiring advisors. Their minds swirl with visions of write-offs, deductions, perks of every kind — all the benefits, in fact, of tycoondom. Unfortunately, reality is a little less glamorous, although there are still substantial benefits from your corporation:

- Limited Liability. A corporation is a defence, although not an absolute one, against personal liability. In theory, if you are a corporate owner and officer, your liability is limited by the extent of the corporation's assets. In practice, if yours is what I call a "very closely held" corporation (that is, of one owner, or, perhaps, two partners) it is quite possible in the event of legal action that the plaintiff will take personal action against you, too. Still, limited liability is one part of your defence.

- Financial Planning. A corporation to be of the utmost usefulness to you for financial planning purposes must maintain a different corporate year than the regular calendar year on which the IRS figures sole proprietor and partnership taxes. If you have a different fiscal year for your corporation, you will have a certain amount of financial flexibility.

Say you wanted to buy a real estate tax shelter to diminish your personal tax liability in any given year. Instead of taking the money out of your corporation as salary (and hence opening yourself up to paying additional taxes), you could take the money as a loan from the corporation. Let's say your corporate year began April 1st and you took the loan out immediately and purchased the tax shelter. You would begin as of the 1st of April getting your depreciation deduction and would thereby lower your personal taxes for the present year. But you would not pay tax on the loan until the *next* calendar year by which time you could have secured another loan, purchased another shelter, and so lowered your personal tax liability. Yes, the corporation does have a use for personal financial planning.

- Less Chance Of Being Audited. Once your sole proprietorship's income goes beyond $150,000 gross annually, you are open to the enhanced likelihood of being audited by the IRS. Whether your accounts are in apple pie order or not, you're still likely to need representation by an accountant. This will be costly. The chance of your being audited when you have a corporation with this income gross is much, much less, for in such a situation you will be small by corporate standards, for one thing, and for another you'll simply be a salaried employee with your own 1040 form. Maintaining a corporation reduces the likelihood of an IRS audit.

- Easy Accounting For Bills And Expenses. With a corporation, you can easily handle your expenses and bills. All the worry, for instance, about whether you qualify for the home office deduction, so much a part of running a home-based sole proprietorship, will depart. The corporation will simply pay you a rent based on the square footage of your dwelling that it uses. It can reimburse you monthly for a percentage of your heat, electric, gas, and telephone bills. All these bills can and should be maintained in your personal name with the corporation making its payments directly to you. Moreover, the corporation will reimburse you directly for your travel and entertainment expenses, expenses which often cause the IRS (and then you!) such problems. This is easy, simple, and effective.

Drawbacks Of A Corporation

While there still are benefits from having a corporation, there are most decidedly drawbacks. You have, let me tell you!, a lot of paperwork that must be assiduously dealt with. This is because once you have established a corporation you cease to be merely an owner and become an employee yourself and thus subject to all the various forms of federal paper harassment, including:

- Getting a Federal Employer Identification Number. Apply for this through the IRS, which has published Circular E, "Employer's Tax Guide", with information you'll find helpful. You do not need an employer identification number if you are a sole proprietor.

- Fill out IRS Form W-4 or W-4E. These forms are used to determine the amount of income taxes to be withheld from an employee's wages.

- At the end of the year complete three copies of a form entitled "Wages and Tax Statement" (IRS form W-2), if income tax has been withheld from your employee check. One copy of this form must be sent to the IRS along with IRS Form W-3, Transmittal of Income and Tax Statements; the second copy goes to the state to be used in determining the amount of money you owe for state income tax.

- Set up procedures to withhold federal income tax and Social Security (F.I.C.A.) tax from your wages. Each month in which you've paid yourself a salary, you'll be responsible for paying the Social Security tax and the federal withholding tax on your salary. As of January 1, 1991, the maximum Social Security tax again went up: your corporation must now pay 6.2% of your salary up to a maximum of $53,400; you must pay the same amount, which, of course, is effectively double taxation where you are corporate owner and employee, too. You must also pay in 1.45% of your salary (until $125,000) for Medicare. These payments must be made on the 15th of the month following salary payment unless the tax you owe is under $500. If, on the other hand, you've had a particularly good month (and you will if you faithfully follow the directions of this book!) and find yourself owing more than $3000 in tax, you must pay what you owe within 3 days.

- Pay federal unemployment tax. In 1984, the IRS instituted a new coupon book for ease of paying its various taxes including your federal unemployment tax. This tax is paid during the first quarter of your corporate year during which you'll be paying .008 of the first $7000 of your salary to the government to handle your unemployment — should you ever decide to lay yourself off.

- Pay corporate income tax. The feds, of course, want their share of your prosperity, their reward for the fact that you have succeeded in making a profit despite all the obstacles they created for you! Monies that are maintained in the corporation are subject to double taxation as corporate profit and as personal income to you if they are removed from the corporation. The corporate income tax rates change almost annually; new ones were determined in 1986. Don't worry about getting the necessary forms. The government will be sure to send them to you towards the end of your corporate year. Then, because they are complex, you'll have to employ your accountant (a subtle form of taxation in its own right) to fill them out.

This is only at the federal level! On the state level, you'll also have unemployment taxes to pay (apply to the Division of Employment Security in your state for the necessary forms) and, of course, your state's corporate income tax and yearly corporate maintenance tax, too. Whatever is left is yours — until the powers that be think up some new way to confiscate our earnings.

Forms And Records For Your Corporation

In each corporation you must also concern yourself with creating and using the following necessary forms and records:

- Record of initial incorporator's meeting
- Articles of Organization (also called a Certificate Of Incorporation)
- Corporate by-laws
- Corporate minutes.

Record Of Initial Incorporator's Meeting

Whether you are the sole share holder of your corporation or not, there must be an initial meeting to call the corporation into being. This meeting, called the initial incorporator's meeting, must take place before you file the articles of organization (or the certificate of incorporation) with your state. The minutes of this meeting should be maintained by the clerk or secretary of the corporation (ordinarily your lawyer or accountant) and should include the number of directors determined upon, the election of the directors and the corporation's officers, the adoption of the corporate by-laws, the date of incorporation, and the term of the corporation's fiscal year. Make sure this fiscal year, as I stated above, has a different term than the calendar year so that you'll have maximum financial flexibility. Also, even if you reside in a state which only requires you to have one officer — yourself — make sure you make your attorney or another trusted advisor a director. To do business in many states, the corporate secretary or clerk must witness the signature of the corporate president and in these situations one individual may not witness for himself.

Articles Of Organization (Or Certificate Of Incorporation)

This form is available in kits which may ordinarily be purchased at your state's Secretary of State's office, in form books, or from your lawyer. When completed, it should be sent to the Secretary of State's corporation department with the required filing fee (yes, another tax!). The certificate should include the following information:

- corporate name. The Secretary of State will inform you whether the name you have selected is unavailable. Should it be your own name, this problem will ordinarily not arise. (Yes, there are occasions when you cannot use your own name!)
- corporate location. This includes the state of incorporation and the address of your business. If you use a registered agent, his name and address should also be included.
- nature of your business. Do not restrict yourself. Use language like this:

"To have and to exercise all the powers reserved for a corporation organized under and in accordance with the provisions of Chapter 156B of the Massachusetts General Law, and to do any or all of the things hereinbefore set forth to the same extent as natural persons might and could do, and in any part of the world."

This sweeping language will cover any of the activities you may be doing and will do using the many steps of the Mobile Mini-Conglomerate.

- stock. This covers the amount of authorized capital stock and its appropriate par value.
- name and mailing address of the incorporator. This may be your name and address or that of your agent.
- initial directors. Make sure, as stated, you have two, even if you are to be the only employee and only shareholder.
- powers of the directors. The powers and rights assigned to the directors usually include creating and amending the corporation's by-laws, examining corporate books, managing capital stocks, specifying the manner in which the corporation's accounts are kept, fixing the directors' compensation, &c.

- officers. The standard officers include a president, a treasurer, and a secretary or clerk. Again, you can hold all the positions except for the latter office.
- dates and signature. In addition to the incorporator's signature and that date, there may be space designated for your fiscal year and the time of the initial annual stockholder's meeting.

Corporate By-Laws

Your corporate by-laws set out the basic rules by which your corporation operates. Standard sets can be purchased as part of sample books, or you can follow the example fully detailed in **THE CONSULTANT'S KIT: ESTABLISHING AND OPERATING YOUR SUCCESSFUL CONSULTING BUSINESS**. Either way you should include these points:

- Section 1. By-laws and regulations of your business are subject to the provisions in your articles of organization or certificate of incorporation.
- Section 2. Stockholders. Provides information on the annual and special meetings, voting, quorums, actions by vote or by writing, and proxies.
- Section 3. Board of Directors. Deals with their number, tenure, powers, formation of committees, meetings, notice of meetings, quorums, and action by vote and writing.
- Section 4. Officers and agents. Their powers, election, tenure and responsibilities.
- Section 5. Resignation and removal of officers and directors.
- Section 6. Vacancies on the board of directors and of officers.
- Section 7. Issuance and replacement of capital stock certificates.
- Section 8. Transfer of stock and methods of distributing dividends.
- Section 9. Indemnity of directors and officers. This section protects those parties to the extent legally permissible against the liabilities of the corporation.
- Section 10. The corporate seal. This can be purchased as part of a kit or separately from a stationer.
- Section 11. Execution of papers. Identifies the signatories for all legal transactions.
- Section 12. Closing day of the fiscal year.
- Section 13. Means of amending the by-laws.

Final Thoughts On Corporations

Corporations, make no mistake about it, are a lot of work. They cost money to operate and their relative advantages have rather dwindled in recent years. Yet there are still benefits to having one. I recall being invited, in my role as a corporate president, to a meeting in Boston of my fellow presidents: the chief executive officers of John Hancock, Raytheon, Gillette, and the like. About twenty of us attended, and I confess myself to having been delighted to be treated as the equal of these corporate giants. It must have been rather as the Prince of Hohenstauffen-Lundkriegen-Sauerbrautten must have felt among the Great Powers at the Congress of Vienna. It's a feeling you will very much enjoy. Do so. You've paid the price for it in many other ways!

A Useful Resource

Besides the materials in **THE CONSULTANT'S KIT**, which you'll find most helpful in setting up and operating your advising business, check out *How To Incorporate: A Manual For Entrepreneurs And Professionals* by Michael Diamond (John Wiley & Sons).

At Your Office

Whether you establish your office in your home or outside it, you must give consideration to what you'll have in it and to spending the least possible amount of money to best effect. Unlike large spend-thrift corporations, you probably don't have unlimited funds at your disposal for office equipment, supplies and decoration, yet you rightly want to get the best value for your dollar. Fortunately, there are smart ways to organize your office purchasing so that you can achieve the effect you want within the budget you have available.

To suggest these winning ways I contacted one of America's leading buying experts, Tod Snodgrass, whose superb *The Office Buyers Manual* tells you how to save up to 50% on office supplies, furniture, business forms, printing, office machines, and equipment. I very much appreciate Tod's go-ahead ways and the detailed thoroughness of his cost-saving information.

As Tod rightly points out, most people buying supplies and equipment for their offices are just plain dumb about what they're doing. They are:

- Complacent about prices, not looking very hard to get the best prices and not understanding that the extent to which they save money on such expenses directly relates to their business profit.
- Unacquainted with formal quote/bid methods to make sure they are getting the best prices on a regular basis.
- Likely to entrust the buying particularly of office consumables (paper, pen, typewriter ribbons, &c) to the least experienced person available. A recent survey shows that the vast majority of consumables are purchased by secretaries who are given no guidelines about how to do the job right, which means inexpensively.

Yet as Tod points out, the art of buying what you need for your office is really quite simple:

- Determine what you need, how much, how often.
- Identify specific quote information for the products needed.
- Initiate Request-For-Quotes (RFQs) from competitively priced vendors.
- Consistently purchase from the lowest priced vendors.

As Tod says, you should have a buyer's guide for the following six categories of vendors:

- office supplies (paper clips, pads, folders, pens)
- machine supplies (ribbons, disks, paper, toner)
- printing (letterheads, envelopes, brochures)
- business forms (invoices, purchase orders, checks)
- furniture (desks, chairs, file cabinets)
- equipment (computer, copy machine, postage meter).

To make this buyer's guide work:

- Identify and list potential vendors. Just start with the Yellow Pages of the telephone directory, and come up with at least three for consumables, at least 6 for major office furniture and equipment.
- Create a product item list for competitive price quotes. Draw up a sheet with the items on which you want quotations so that you can send it to the various vendors.
- Send potential vendors the selected item quote list. Ask them to fill in the form on each item for prices good for at least 60 days.
- Obtain the most competitive price quotations. You'll find in practice that different vendors will give you the best prices on different items.
- Record information on vendor service performance. Purchasing from a vendor is not the end of the road. You need to check the vendor's service performance. Is this a company that really deserves your business? Are they really working for it?

Snodgrass' Strategies For Enhancing Company Profits

Tod has 14 specific hints for enhancing your company's profits in dealing with supply vendors:

- Build good vendor relations by visiting the vendor's location. Yes, it helps if they know you and like you!
- Try new, untested products before using up the current, reliable product. A buyer must consider changing brands if lower prices, faster delivery, or better quality is possible. However, it is important not to exhaust the current supply. Maybe you won't like the new product.
- Maintain a minimum inventory level. A good rule of thumb is to keep on hand a one-to-two week supply of standard consumable items and a one-to-two month supply of forms and printing.
- Avoid over-ordering. More than a one-month supply of consumables or more than a six-to-twelve month supply of business forms (or printing) could be excessive.
- Initiate a minimum/maximum inventory control reorder system. The strength of this monitoring procedure is that it:
  - Provides an inventory list by type, stock number, and/or other identifying characteristics.
  - Identifies critical reorder points to allow time for additional product to be shipped.
  - Pre-determines the amount to be ordered.
- Carefully control critical items. Specific products, like checks and invoices, warrant extra precautionary measures.
- Affix a form sample to the outside of each carton.
- Do a most-used-items analysis of supply products. In most cases, 20% of the items represent 80% of the total purchases.
- Initiate a Purchase Order System.

- Become a "house account" and save 14-25%. A self-sufficient company that works up its own orders, maintains its own inventories, and monitors its own usage may not need a commissioned sales representative calling.
- Pick up will-call orders from vendors for extra cost savings. Delivering to you costs money!
- Request catalogs from vendors.
- Retain empty boxes. Empty vendor boxes provide product descriptions as well as reorder information.
- Return incorrectly ordered/shipped items in the original manufacturer's carton. Failure to retain the manufacturer's carton may mean the item cannot be returned.

A Few More Buying Hints

- Don't purchase all your supplies from a single source. If your supply seller believes he has a monopoly, the chances are good your prices will go up.
- Do not believe the word "wholesale." Look beyond discounts. Look only at the actual cost of the item. Make sure, too, you have factored in tax, shipping charges, and other relevant costs in determining the bottom line.
- Do not disclose bid/quote information to vendors after the fact. Informing a vendor he was a low bidder by a certain percentage may result in your prices being raised next time.
- Do not divulge to competing vendors what the firm is presently paying for items. Remember: commissioned salesmen will sell for whatever the traffic will bear. If they are informed of the price a company is willing to pay, that is the price they will charge.
- Buy your consumable products from contract stationers whenever possible. These vendors usually offer better prices to you than walk-in vendors.

Your One Necessary Resource For Office Buying

I can't think of an office of any size that wouldn't profit from having on hand, studying and really following Tod Snodgrass' advice. Get his *The Office Buyers Manual* from Cost Control Consultants, 2464 Rue Le Charlene, Palos Verdes, CA 90274 (213) 831-2770.

Your Personal Protection Plans

So far I've spent this chapter advising you about the location of your office, the form of your business, and giving you effective ideas for handling office purchasing so that you'll have more profit at the end of the year. Now we come to a critical area that all too many advisors overlook with very, very serious consequences: disability insurance coverage and personal financial planning. Both are absolutely mandatory aspects of your successful advising business and for providing you with the security and lifestyle you aspire to.

Securing The Right Personal Disability Coverage

As an independent advisor you are in a vulnerable position, and you might as well recognize it. Like all other professionals, according to the Society of Actuaries you stand one chance in three between the ages of 35 and 65 of being disabled for three months or more; on the average such disability lasts over 5 years. Thirty percent of individuals becoming so disabled never recover their full working potential. Furthermore, a person who is 37 years old is 3.5 times more likely to become disabled than to die.

The ability to perform your advising function and earn an income stands out as the most valuable asset you have. The following chart illustrates the potential income you would earn to age 65 based on the monthly salaries from a given age.

Potential Earnings To Age 65

Monthly Salary	$2,000	$5,000	$10,000
Age			
25	$ 96,000	$2,400,000	$4,800,000
35	720,000	1,800,000	3,600,000
45	480,000	1,200,000	2,400,000
55	240,000	600,000	1,200,000

As these figures clearly show, loss of this future income would be devastating. That's why I've asked my insurance guru Allan Oxman, CLU, ChFC for information on how to select the right disability insurance policy so that you can have the mental security you need and, God forbid!, the income you'll need to maintain at least some significant semblance of your lifestyle and also meet your family responsibilities should something happen to you — as it will to one person in three reading this book.

Factoring In Social Security

As Allan points out, everyone working and paying the Social Security tax is eligible for disability benefits so long as you've worked for the required number of quarters. As a rule of thumb, if you have worked for 5 of the last 10 years, you are eligible to apply. To find out, call your local Social Security office and ask for a pamphlet labeled "Request For Statement Of Earnings." You'll find out by return of post your record of earnings with notification of disability eligibility.

Social Security disability benefits are paid to individuals after a five month period of continuous disability; this is called the (Waiting) Elimination Period. The monthly benefit amounts are contingent upon your age, whether or not you have dependents, and what your present annual earnings are.

Monthly Benefit Estimates

Your Age in 1991	Who Receives Benefits	Your Present Annual Earnings		
		$20,000	$30,000	$53,400+
40	You	$ 696	$ 932	$ 1,139
	Child (or Children and Spouse)	$ 348	$ 467	$ 569
	Your monthly disability benefit:	$ 1,044	$ 1,399	$ 1,708

Ordinarily the proceeds are not taxable except where a single person has outside income above $25,000 and married couples filing a joint return have outside income above $32,000. In these cases part of your Social Security benefits (but not more than half) will be included in taxable income for income-tax purposes.

As Allan Oxman rightly points out, being eligible for Social Security benefits is relatively easy; qualifying, on the other hand, is not. Social Security will only compensate you and your family if your disability is so severe that you cannot perform any substantial gainful work. Normally your disability must be expected to last at least a year and/or result in early death. Qualification depends on you filing your application immediately as well as medical evidence which must be approved by a state agency designated by the Social Security Administration. Note: although it is important to know where you stand as far as eligibility and procedure, the fact remains that 7 out of 10 people who apply *never* collect Social Security disability benefits on their claim.

Workers' Compensation

Workers' compensation requires employers to provide benefits to employees for accidental occupational injuries arising out of and in the course of employment. Substantial variations exist in state laws. Generally, in order for an employee to collect disability benefits under worker's compensation laws, you must meet one of the following four categories of disability:

- Temporary Total Disability. Here, you cannot perform any of the duties of your regular job, although you expect full recovery. Most workers' compensation claims are paid for this kind of disability. Benefits are normally paid after seven days (except in the case of hospitalization) for as long as it takes until you return to work.

- Permanent Total Disability. You will never be able to perform any of the duties of your regular job or any other job. Benefits will be paid similar to temporary total disability with the exception that benefits usually continue for life. *N.B.* There are states where a 10 year maximum exists.

- Temporary Partial Disability. You can only perform some of the duties of your regular job but are neither totally nor permanently disabled. Benefits are calculated as a percentage of the difference between your wages before and after the disability.

- Permanent Partial Disability. You have a permanent injury, such as the loss of an eye, but may be able to perform your job or be retrained for another job. Some states provide for lump sum payments to employees for such losses.

As long as you have earnings records, meet the definition of one of the four categories above, and are covered by your employer (yourself in most cases), benefits are available. Benefits received under a workers' compensation plan are excluded from gross income, although there is discussion in the Congress to change this. Note: if you receive disability benefits through Social Security, you will probably receive less through workers' compensation. Benefits under the two programs may not exceed 80% of your "average current earnings". Workers' compensation will also reduce most group long-term disability benefits. This, however, is not the case for individuals who acquire individual long-term disability contracts for themselves.

For additional information on the listing of workers' compensation administrative contacts from state to state write or call:

Alliance of American Insurers
1501 Woodfield Road, Suite 400 West
Schaumberg, IL 60173-4980

(708) 330-8500

Ask for *Survey Of Worker's Compensation Laws.*

Other Alternatives

If you don't qualify for Social Security and/or worker's compensation, there are just a few other alternatives:

- borrow from a lending institution
- sell off your assets
- have your spouse support you.

Are you prepared for these alternatives? In any event, the ramifications of a prolonged disability can be frightening. No one who has spent a lifetime using the kinds of skills we advisors do wants to see their estate dispersed or diminished because of their disability. You don't. I don't. That's why all of us advisors need a disability income contract tailored to our individual situation.

Finding The Right Agent/Broker

I'm very fortunate in having Allan Oxman for my disability broker, and that's why I unhesitatingly recommend him to you. But suppose you don't have Alan Oxman already in your Mandarin Network (and for some foolish reason don't follow up this chapter by contacting him). What then?

- Make sure you find out from any agent or broker you may deal with on this (or any other insurance-related) subject about his institutional affiliation. There are hundreds of companies nationwide that offer disability coverage. Your agent may be connected with only one or a few of these. You need to know what his connections are.
- Ask how long he's been in the business, specifically in marketing disability coverage. I can tell you from personal experience that many agents and brokers offering disability are startlingly inexperienced about the business. This is shocking as regards their own professional specialty and can have the most severe consequences for you — if you ever do get disabled.
- Inquire about the agent's education, training, and/or professional designations.
- Ask why the agent or broker represents the companies he is talking to you about. You should hear that these companies have a solid financial history, have been in business for a sufficient amount of time to have qualitative figures for future claims experience, and have expeditious and equitable handling of claims.

Doing Your Homework

The *leitmotif* of this book is doing your homework, knowing what you need to know to most successfully structure your client prospect and prospect experiences, and to make sure you get what you need from your own advisors. This advice holds true here. Despite the fact that you may be (indeed should be) comfortable with what your disability insurance advisor has told you so far, go to the next step. Check out *Best's Insurance Report* (Life/Health Edition) or their new condensed version called *Key Rating Guide* (just $85 compared to the full report's $505). Both are available in your library or by writing:

A.M. Best Co.
A.M. Best Road
Oldwick, New Jersey 08858
(908) 439-2200

This publication is issued independently of any insurance company. It provides information on a company's overall financial position by rating them "C" to "A+". Only companies with an A+ rating should be considered. A.M. Best also carries *Best's Agent Guide*, a condensed version of the above book. One of the most important things to check is for claims incurred compared to premiums earned. You can discern what percentage of premium dollar goes out in claims. Companies which have been in business for some time and are rated A+ and have claims to premiums of around 50¢ to $1 are your best bet. Also, you may want to write your state's insurance commissioner and ask for Schedule H which will confirm the payout ratios of premiums to claims. Companies with payouts consistently in excess of 90% are likely to be considering getting out of the disability business or may be having potential claims payment problems.

What To Look For In Your Contracts

Here's what to look for in any disability contracts you may be considering:

- Non-cancellable and guaranteed renewable. This feature Allan rates as very important. As long as you pay your premiums on time, the company cannot cancel or change your policy. They cannot change the premium rate either, even if you decide to change occupations. Some contracts are just guaranteed renewable which may save you money now, but it does not guarantee that the premiums will not be increased later. Note: stick with non-cancellable and guaranteed renewable contracts so long as your status permits.

- Definition of total disability. Undoubtedly the most confusing aspect of a disability contract lies in understanding this most important part. The definitions will determine whether you will qualify for benefits. Different companies offer different definitions to individuals in different occupational classes. Professionals like us, because of favorable statistical experience, ordinarily qualify for the First Class of disability, an important point in our favor. However, such qualification is not necessarily automatic. Because our income may be derived from many sources, will be if you follow the procedures of the Mobile Mini-Conglomerate, it is very likely the individual agent to whom you are speaking may not be able to categorize you within a single occupational class. Therefore the agent may have to inquire directly of the underwriter as to where you can be categorized. To make a decision the underwriter will need financial information about you and your various sources of income, percentage of income from each distinct kind of task you do, a completed application form, and probably a medical examination. Just what you need to do will be contingent on your age and the amount of the monthly benefit you desire.

- The "Own Occupation" Clause. Normally if you have this provision in your definition of disability, it removes the requirement that the insured not be engaged in any gainful employment while disabled. Insurance companies may require you to be under the regular and personal care of a physician.

You should be advised that some insurance companies may have the "own occupation" clause built into the definition itself, or that it may be acquired as a policy rider. Ask! The "own occupation" rider offers the most liberal definition available. Be sure, however, to check and see if gainful employment is permitted after you meet their requirements for the total disability benefit. You may find that because of the specific nature of your work, insurance carriers will only cover you in your "own occupation" for five years. After that you must be able to work in a reasonable occupation, that is, using the education, training, and experience you have. Note: be advised that what seem merely like subtle differences in wording to you could greatly influence whether or not you receive benefits. Find the definition which will offer you disability benefits for your "own occupation" and where it is your decision whether or not to work elsewhere. This is what you want, isn't it?

- Residual disability benefit. Like the "own occupation" clause, the residual disability benefit may be included in your definition, or it may be available as a rider. Residual disability insures your income, not occupation. It takes into consideration the fact that individuals may be disabled and are therefore unable to perform some but not all of the duties of their occupation.

For instance, suppose your disability only permits you to work 20 hours a week, or about half the number of hours you regularly put in. In this case, the insurance company would pay for 50% of your total disability benefit. Most companies require that you sustain at least 20 to 25% loss of earnings to qualify. If, in fact, you have greater than a 75 to 80% loss of earnings, most companies will pay the full total disability benefit.

When determining the benefits you receive during periods of residual disability, most companies look at prior earnings. It is not unusual for companies to give you a choice of your monthly earnings prior to disability or your highest average earnings for any two successive years during the five-year period just before disability begins, whichever is most favorable to you. Also, ask the agent if the prior earnings are being indexed to offset inflation. They should be! Note: Watch for policies requiring you to be totally disabled before residual benefits are payable. Ask the agent if the contract has a "0" day qualification period.

Other Important Riders To Consider

- Supplemental Social Security. This rider is designed by insurance companies so that you will not be overinsured in the event the company and Social Security pay your disability claim. It also has the effect of reducing your premium cost because the risk of insuring you is shared between Social Security and the insurance company. At a $20,000 income level, most companies will only insure 30 to 40% of your income. Therefore, a Social Security rider would be desirable in that it will provide the added protection to insure up to a more realistic 60 to 65% of income. Conversely, at a $30,000 to $40,00 income level and up, many companies will insure up to a 60 to 65% percentage. Since professionals in this income range can purchase long-term "own occupation" with realistic issue limits, there is no great need for this supplemental Social Security rider.

- Cost of living. This is relatively new in disability contracts. It provides for an indexing of benefits for residual and total disability to offset inflation. This benefit will cost you more, but without it in a surge of inflation your disability benefit may shrink into insignificance. Note: ask if the cost of living rider has a cap (e.g., two or three times the original benefit amount). If you are going to pay for a cost of living benefit, you shouldn't have a cap on the amount you'll be paid.

- Guaranteed insurability. By purchasing this rider, you can increase your monthly coverage (if your salary increases) regardless of your current medical condition. Thus, if you happen to acquire a condition during the time you have the contract, you may still increase your coverage to the limit of the company's policy. The rider will not provide you with price breaks, but it is offering you the possibility of additional coverage which would otherwise not be available to you. If your salary increases markedly while you are in excellent health, you should consider having the contract revised to reflect that. If many years have gone by since you originally wrote the policy, it will probably not be advantageous to rewrite the entire contract but only to add an additional policy for your new income.

- Presumptive disability clause. Regardless of whether or not you are working in your regular occupation in some capacity, presumptive disability means that if you suffer the loss of use of your sight, speech, hands, or hearing the company will consider you to be totally disabled, thereby qualifying you for full benefits.
- Recurrent disability. If after a disability you return to work full time and then become disabled again from the same causes, the company will not insist on your waiting the full elimination period again.
- Waiver of premium. Once you have been totally or partially disabled for 90 days, the company will waive further disability premium payments for as long as you remain disabled. Note: ask the broker if the company requires you to be at claim time (or at the end of waiting period) in order for the premiums to be waived. This is important if your waiting period is longer than the waiver period.
- Return of premium or cash value provision. This rider costs you between 50 to 75% above and beyond the basic cost of the contract. It provides for a percentage return (around 80%) of the premiums you have submitted over the contract years if you have not made claims. This is not recommended, because disability income should be utilized for protection, not investment. The contract should not dissuade you from making claims when you need to.

Cost

And what, pray, will all this cost, you must be asking? Cost is always, of course, a consideration. Yet you must take into account exactly what your income and current lifestyle are worth to you. Here are factors over which you have little or no control but which do affect the policy's cost:

- your age
- your sex
- your occupation
- your current health
- your personal habits and what the companies call your "morals".

Here, on the other hand, are those factors you can control and which may well reduce the cost of your policy:

- the elimination period
- the benefit period
- the benefit amount
- the various riders on your policy
- type of policy — level premium or annual renewable disability (ARD).

The most significant of these is the elimination period. Here's the example of a 39 year old male non-smoker with a $3,000 monthly benefit and an "own occupation" total disability definition (including residual disability) and a lifetime benefit period for sickness and injury.

30 day elimination period	90 days	180 days	365 days
$1790.00 annual premium	$1398.60	$1268.10	$1147.60

(These are 1991 figures of the Ohio National Life Assurance.)

As you can see, the cost differs significantly with the various elimination periods. But you must ask yourself not only whether cost is a consideration, but whether you have the personal resources to sustain you through whatever period you choose before you begin to receive benefits. That is the real issue. If you only have two month's worth of savings, a 365 day elimination period, while less costly, is not more sensible. Also, note that the difference between 90 and 180 days is only about $53 or just 3%. Some people believe the difference in cost is not worth the savings and recommend a waiting period of not more than 90 days.

Key Resources Available For You

I have spent much time on the disability issue, because it is a most important one for independent advisors, and one which you must solve for yourself. However, there is much else to learn about this pivotal subject. To do so contact the following:

- Allan Oxman, my insurance guru. You'll find Allan, a Chartered Life Underwriter and Chartered Financial Consultant, both knowledgeable about the issues and generous with his time in helping you solve particularly your disability and life insurance problems. Contact him at Gilley, Oxman and Riggins, 1043 East Morehead St., Suite 301, Charlotte, NC 28204 (704) 342-2277. He can also give you a superb deal on term life insurance!
- The National Insurance Consumer Organization publishes a helpful booklet entitled *Buyer's Guide To Insurance: What The Companies Won't Tell You*. This deals with disability and many other kinds of insurance coverage you should consider and some impartial tricks of the trade. It's $3 from 121 N. Payne St., Alexandria, VA 22314.

- If you really want to pursue the disability question on a company to company comparison, consult *Disability Income: The Sale, The Product, The Market* ($31.95) by Jeff Sadler. Published by the National Underwriter Company, 420 East Fourth St., Cincinnati, OH 45202.

Financial Planning

No chapter on the business of the advisor would be complete without some frank words about you and financial planning. Financial planning is an essential ingredient in assisting you to reach your business and personal objectives. You cannot do so without such planning and the earlier you start planning, the better off you and your family will be.

A recent study has shown that there are now about one million millionaires in the nation, just about one for every hundred households. Contrary to the usual glamorous, high-living scot-free image perpetrated by the media, most millionaires are people just like you and me. Indeed, the fact that you are reading this book indicates you have a higher than average likelihood of becoming one of America's new millionaires (or, of socking away another million on top of the one you've already got!). For the truth is that most of America's millionaires are self-made, self-employed, hard-working people providing services to people — just as you and I do.

It is also true that these millionaires make the best use of their money and of the existing tax structure to help them reach their objectives. You must do the same, for a substantial portion of your wealth — and your security — will come by using your money wisely and having it work as hard as you do while you are simultaneously building your advising business as the substantial multi-part profit center it can and will be if you follow the suggestions in this book.

Start Today

If you have done little or no financial planning, don't wait any longer. Start now. The truth is that by using the available personal and business deductions, compound interest and time, you can have financial security and outright wealth. There's no mystery to this. If a million other Americans have already discovered this, so can you! This means, of course, that the younger you are the more likely you are to reach your financial objectives by following these suggestions. Obviously, one of the best things you can do for your children, parents, is to explain this to them so they can begin to realize objectives which may not, the younger they are, yet be very meaningful.

The sad truth is that the younger a person is, the less need he sees for financial planning because he is very likely under the ridiculous (but generally prevalent) illusion that he'll stay young and carefree forever. Each of us has at some time (hopefully long ago) given way to this nonsense. More practically, the younger one is the less disposable income one probably has and the more need for what one earns for present expense. Most people, of course, never move beyond this problem and therefore never achieve financial security. I never said financial planning would be easy. It's just mandatory! The precise moment when it is least easy to invest is the very moment you must begin to implement the following suggestions. Otherwise you will never know the power of money working to breed money, which is the essence of capitalism — and of comfort.

When you begin your advising business, make the following resolutions — and abide by them:
- Resolve that financial planning will be a factor in your business plan.
- Resolve that you will use all the personal and business deductions available to you.
- Resolve that you will utilize these plans as early in the year as possible to achieve maximum benefit.
- Resolve to spend at least some time familiarizing yourself with the various investment vehicles available to you and how they work so that you can protect your money once you've made it.

Secrets Of Successful Financial Planning

There can be no success without an objective. It is always thus. Therefore, to begin your financial planning on the right foot, write down your financial objective and when you'd like to achieve it. Write down exactly how much money you want to earn by what point in your life from your investments. If your objective is financial autonomy (and this is a very good one to have), having your various investments return sufficient funds to enable you to live the way you do now without further work, then write this down.

Say you currently need about $50,000 per year to live comfortably and want to be entirely financially autonomous in 15 years, do the following:
- Figure a constant rate of inflation at about 7%. In 15 years you will need an income of approximately $142,000 to maintain your present lifestyle. If you wanted to be entirely financially autonomous you'd need an investment portfolio of approximately a million and a half dollars yielding approximately 10%.

- To get this portfolio, you would need to invest escalating amounts of money, thus:

  $30,000 for two years

  $35,000 for two years

  $40,000 for two years

  $45,000 for two years

  $50,000 for two years

  $55,000 for two years

  $60,000 for two years

  and $65,000 in the fifteenth year.

At a constant (and I must say modest) 10% return you would reach your objective of being totally self sufficient in 15 years.

Obviously this simple example does not take into account many factors, least of all that you might be able to do much better than an average return of 10% on your investments. Most importantly, however, it shows that your investment burden drops significantly over the years you are investing. $30,000 is a very significant amount to invest on a $50,000 income. $65,000 is a much less difficult burden to bear on an annual income of $142,000.

Know Your Options

Surprisingly few people (but, I would guess, most millionaires!) are aware of what tax deductible options are available to them.

Individual Retirement Account: Your Basic Option

Recent figures show that only 15 to 20% of American wage earners use an Individual Retirement Account. Make sure you are one of them both for long term capital appreciation and to save money on your individual income taxes. Moreover, make sure that you make your IRA investment on the first business day of the new year so that you will get the maximum return for yourself. Over the course of, say, ten years you will be over a thousand dollars ahead (return figured at a constant 10%) of the person who invests on the last day of the year and the difference becomes more and more substantial the longer the investment is at work. The clear deduction: invest as early as you can.

Business Keogh Plans

From the first moment that you begin making money with your advising business you should begin investing money in some form of Keogh plan. Different vehicles, as already discussed, enable your business to contribute between 15 and 25% of your compensation up to a maximum of $30,000 per year (on a salary of $120,000). It is important to point out that this is a legitimate business deduction for your company (thereby lowering your tax exposure) and is an important benefit for you. As with your IRA, you should contribute to whichever plan you have as early in your fiscal year as possible. Do this by setting your salary, making the contribution (which thereby has the most time to compound), and paying yourself the salary thereafter. If you have underpaid your pension (because you've had a good year), you can pay in the balance later in the year. If you find you've been overly optimistic about the money you'll make this year and have overpaid your pension compensation, you can correct the problem in your next fiscal year. The important thing is to contribute as much as you can as early as you can and let time and compound interest do their best on your behalf.

A Few Words On Investment Strategies

Investing, having to worry about money, makes most people very, very nervous. I'm one of them. I wonder, like you do, whether I've invested wisely and whether I'm getting the best return for my money. Taken to an extreme this can lead to a lot of sleepless nights and a new, aggravating form of misery. There are, however, ways to deal with this problem and reduce your anxiety:

- Spend some time familiarizing yourself with the different kinds of investment vehicles. A book like *The Power Of Money Dynamics* by Venita Van Caspel (Simon and Schuster) can help. It's a good introductory guide and thorough reference on the different kinds of investment vehicles available to you.
- Be conservative. I tell my students, by no means facetiously, to invest their first million in very cautious, conservative vehicles, vehicles such as U.S. government zero coupon bonds and similar (though non-guaranteed) investments from major corporations. Nothing exotic and very little risk. Don't let some high-powered broker try to get you into Mongolian sugar futures until you are a power player in your own right. Yes, you'll not get the very best return that some other investors will get that year in much more speculative vehicles (and which they'll brag about at cocktail parties), but you won't have the worry either. After you've got enough for your own purposes in such low-risk investments, then you can try out your speculative wings.

240

- Buy some real estate. Although real estate is not the hot item (in most markets of the United States) it was just a few years ago, it is still just about impossible to beat its tax advantages. I'm not part of the "no money down" school of investors, but you'll find a little book by Hollis Norton a helpful beginning in real estate even if his most optimistic projections seem a bit far fetched (as they do with all those who are so enthusiastic about the no money down line) — *How To Make It When You're Cash Poor: The New Strategy For Buying Real Estate With Little Or No Cash* by Hollis Norton. (Simon and Schuster)

- Keep at it. Investing is not something you do once in a while whenever you have the time. You have to work at it, day in, day out, just like your primary advising job itself. This doesn't mean that you have to become a fanatic trader, shopping for 1/8 of a point advantages. For most of us, that's a ridiculous way to carry on our investments. Instead, it means that you must give them the attention they deserve so that you are not caught totally unaware by tax and market changes that could undermine your present comfort and future prosperity.

- Finally, review your investment strategy yearly to see whether it is still moving in the direction you want to go, whether your expectations for it are reasonable, and whether you are really trying as hard as you can to realize the objective you say you want to reach. Many of my very Yuppie friends tell me they want to be financially independent but are forever caving in on minor points which, taken collectively, make it increasingly unlikely for them to realize their larger objectives.

I recall in this connection a very good friend of mine. Last year when she was a continuing education administrator at one of the universities where I teach, I happened to fall into a conversation with her about her financial situation and her lifetime objectives. Whatever she might say about financial autonomy, her entire lifestyle belied it. Despite a good income, she was substantially in debt and ill-provisioned for the future. An ardent feminist, her lifestyle seemed tailor-made for a dependence which she seemed to court but indignantly denied. Whatever her rhetoric I marked her as a candidate who'd drop everything as soon as she could hook a man, her financial *deus ex machina*. And that's precisely what happened right in the midst of my writing this book. She met an advisor (a doctor, as it happened) with a six-figure income, quit her job in another state, and moved in with him. I await developments, but I tremble. To base so much on something so undependable as an untested personal relationship strikes me as incredibly naive — and yet people do it all the time to the detriment of realizing other, much more certain objectives. Don't you!

The thrust of this book has been entirely towards being deliberate, towards setting reasonable objectives and working reasonably to achieve them. So it must be, too, with your investment policy. By following the suggestions of this book you will find yourself grossing more and more money and cutting your expenses to the barebones so that your profit expands as a direct result. This will, of course, make your need for ongoing financial planning acute. Plan accordingly. And plan now, when this need may not be quite so pressing. The dandy thing about working smart is that if you do it properly you can return all the benefits of this work not merely for your lifetime but for your family's, too. By not using the existing tax system to your advantage, by not using the deductions and other vehicles available to you, and by indulging in unproductive, costly and downright stupid habits, you cannot. So take heed and join the ranks of America's next phalanx of millionaires. Write me when you arrive. I like success stories.

CHAPTER 13

Becoming The Successful Computer-Assisted Advisor

Computers are here to stay, and many advisors can benefit from them. That's a fact. Yet every advisor doesn't need a computer right away. Instead, in each advising business there seems to be a time when it's right to get into computers and, once in, to expand the procedures you can do by getting a bigger machine and more sophisticated software.

I must confess (though it pains me) I am not an expert in this field. That's why I sought out two of the best in the business, my knowledgeable colleagues Jackie Masloff and Katherine Ackerman, the one to provide you with advice on breaking into computers, the other on how to find information useful to your practice via computers and online databases. They are responsible for the information in this chapter. I want to give them full credit and my thanks for helping add this dimension to the successful advisor's practice.

Computers According To Masloff

Before you decide to add a computer to your collection of advisor's paraphernalia, it's best to have an idea of what a computer can and can't do. The greatest asset of a computer is that it does mundane tasks (calculations, arranging information, printing) very accurately and very quickly. So if the nature of your advisory work involves a number of repetitive, mundane tasks, the computer could very possibly leverage your time for more productive (and profitable) tasks.

What would be defined as a mundane task? Preparing correspondence and proposals for one. Keeping records as another. Calculating taxes and client invoices. In short, any function where you really don't use your creative powers, but that requires a minimal degree of attention.

The other benefit of having a computer is that since it greatly simplifies the mundane, you are more inclined to do more because tasks now require less time. For instance, you'll send out more correspondence and follow-up notes in less time. Voilá, increased productivity.

Do You Really Need One? Some Rules Of Thumb

As an experienced computer user, I can, in retrospect, identify several benchmark criteria for non-computer users of when you should begin to give serious thought to acquiring a computer. If you perform the following tasks, you're probably a candidate:

1. Write more than a dozen letters a week of any appreciable length.
2. Write more than 10 feature articles a year, of any length.
3. Write more than one or two 3 - 5 page reports per month.
4. Keep a monthly budget with 10 or more categories and more than 30 entries.
5. Calculate an income statement and balance sheet for a business that pays any appreciable amount of taxes, or where you need to know where the money goes.
6. Do future projections of any kind of figures, for more than 5 periods.
7. Do repetitive calculations that require more than 5 sequential calculations, and do this more than 2 or 3 times a day.
8. Do any kind of 'cascading' calculations. (That is, a calculation where the sequential number is a result of the previous calculation, and is used in the next calculation. Balancing your checkbook is a good example. Calculating the balance on your home mortgage is another.)
9. Manipulate any kind of data, and do frequent 'what if' projections and/or manipulations.
10. Write, calculate or plot (graph) anything that requires a copy or documented record.

If you answer 'yes' to two or three of these criteria, you're a candidate for a computer. If you answer 'yes' to more than three, you'll be sorry you didn't buy the computer sooner.

Another good rule of thumb in making the computer purchase decision is to calculate the payback period. In short, how much time does the computer have to save to justify its cost? It's somewhat difficult to estimate the time savings of a productivity tool with which you have no experience, but you can call a few colleagues and get some rough estimates. Let's say, for the sake of argument, they estimate the computer has saved them between 50% to 70% of their time in the tasks where they now use a computer. Use the conservative figure (50%) to estimate your time savings. Then use your average annual hourly rate (not your billable, since your new 'free' time won't all be spent on billable tasks) which was last year's billings divided by 2000 hours. Determine how many hours you would have to save at this rate to pay for the computer. If the timespan of that savings is less than a year, buying a computer looks like a good bet.

For example:

Last year's billings = $30,000

When divided by 2,000 hours = $15/hour

Hours per month devoted to tasks that could be done by computer, (8 hours per week x 4 weeks) = 32

Time savings = 50%

Monthly hours saved = 32 x 50% = 16

Monthly cost savings = $15 x 16 = $240

Yearly cost savings = 12 months x $240 = $2880

This analysis indicates you could justify approximately a $3,000 system (under rather conservative assumptions). This doesn't mean you have to go out and spend $3,000 on a computer system. It does mean expenditure up to this price level is probably justified by the increased amount of time you would have.

Selecting A Computer

With the smoke clearing from the first micro-computer industry shake-out, many advisors are considering their first purchase of a computer system. Two of the primary reasons for a business computer are:

- to be in control of information, rather than being overwhelmed.
- to be more productive and to make better use of time and talents.

However, even with these straightforward objectives, identifying the best system may seem like an insurmountable task given the choice of software and computers available. This need not be the case. By following a game plan that focuses on your needs, the choices can be narrowed to a manageable number of candidates.

The first step in the selection process is to identify the tasks to be done by computer. Be specific and exhaustive about what you'd like done: next, identify the employees who will work with the computer on a day to day basis. Their (or your) level of previous computer exposure and the amount of training necessary is a major consideration in the selection of a vendor, software, and possible supplemental training.

Armed with this information, you should start to evaluate computer systems and vendors who will address the needs of your practice, based on the following three criteria:

- Training (vendor resources and/or need for supplemental training)
- Software (ease of use, flexibility, special features, publisher support)
- Hardware (the actual computer).

Training

For the advisor who is making the first computer purchase, training is of prime importance. Careful evaluation of the vendor's abilities in this area are well worth the effort. Will the training be done at your location or at the vendor's location? Have they trained others on the software and computer system that is under evaluation? How good is their training? For first time users, proper instruction cannot be overemphasized. An experienced, patient instructor can save you much frustration and aggravation in the training process.

Software

The choices of software can be narrowed to a few prime candidates when evaluated by the advisor's list of required tasks. Very quickly, the choices and tradeoffs (there are always tradeoffs) become apparent. The software should be tested hands-on, or demonstrated in use at an actual user's (preferably another advisor in your line of work) place of business. Involvement of the advisor's staff in the final selection process greatly eases the eventual acceptance of the entire system. One caveat: It is usually less expensive to modify your work procedures to conform to the computer system than to modify software to exactly replicate your method of doing business.

One thing that you should remember is that to get the greatest benefit from the computer, you should probably re-study your work habits after you come up to speed on the computer. For example, traditionally in an office with a secretary, the 'boss' would draft a memo, then have it proof-typed. It would then be edited and retyped. It would be proofed again, then reviewed by others. It would then be revised, retyped, and proofed again. With a computer (or 'word processor') it's often faster to type the draft right into the computer. The manual step is completely eliminated. Also, corrections are quick, and consequently more correspondence can (or should be) prepared.

Hardware

The selection of the actual computer (hardware) should come last. To a certain extent, it will be dictated by the choice of software (because the computer has to be able to run the software). Although the hardware will constitute the largest part of the system price, it should not influence the factors of training and software selection, because the best computer in the world doesn't make up for bad software and lack of training.

One tip for hardware selection: stay with the major brands. Obscure or offbeat machines are like exotic cars — strictly for the enthusiast.

The three priorities of training, software, and hardware are often reversed in the selection process that is advocated by the computer industry. Needless to say, when the computer is selected first, the software second, and final consideration given to training, the results are often disappointing.

The issue of obsolescence is much over-done by the computer industry. A more accurate concern for the business computer purchaser is that of outgrowing the capacity of the initial computer system. There are two ways to protect against this:

- Choose either an IBM-compatible configuration or a MacIntosh-based computer. Time has shown these two to be the industry-standards, as nearly all business and personal computing falls under either category.
- Select a computer system configuration that will initially have ample reserve capacity (memory, both internal and external), with the design feature of supplementary memory. When (and if) the system is "tapped out", increased memory can be added at an incremental cost.

If you select your first computer wisely, it will probably be adequate (or more than adequate) for your needs for at least five years, and possibly ten or more. Even the first generation computer users (1977 vintage) tend to still use their Apple IIs, even when they buy additional computers. The Apple II is still an adequate machine for many uses.

Some System Selection Tips: An Initial Configuration

When you go to select a computer, you have to decide upon the initial configuration of the machine. This configuration is expressed in RAM (Random Access Memory), the type of processor, and disk storage capacity. These are expressed in terms of standards of measure of computer processing power, memory and storage. You should understand what these terms mean so that you have a better idea of what you need and can make your own judgements. Don't feel that you need to know them in detail; some knowledge is useful when making your decision or talking to computer salespeople.

RAM is the working memory of the computer. It's the memory that stores the program and the data you put in and does the specific tasks. Most computers come with 1 Mb as a standard. The "Mb" stands for Megabytes and means a million bytes or characters of data. Each byte is composed of eight bits, or binary digits, which represent the individual circuits in the computer chips and whose combinations create the different characters. Another unit of measure is the Kilobyte which is one thousand bytes.

There are upgrade options, so you can increase the memory over 1 Mb or more; this is called extended memory. You determine how much RAM you need based on the programs you plan to run and whether any of these programs take advantage of extended memory.

The type of processor is one determination in how fast your software will be executed; the more data that is processed at a given time, the more powerful the processor. The early IBM PC's used an Intel 8088 processor which processed 16 bits at a time yet transferred data from itself to memory at only 8 bits at a time. The next IBM AT's used an 80286, which also processed 16 bits at a time yet transferred data from itself to memory at the rate of 24 bits at a time.

The latest technology uses either the Intel 80386 or the 80386SX processor; the former processes 32 bits at a time and transfers data to and from memory also at 32 bits at a time whereas the latter processes the same number of bits but transfers data 16 bits at a time. The 80386SX provides similar performance to a 80386 — yet at 80286 prices! The 80286 itself is considered a "dead" processor by many in the industry.

A hard disk is an essential component of your computer system. It's what is commonly called a "mass storage device" and is usually measured in megabytes. For most applications, you should start your system with a 40 Mb hard disk, although to be on the safe side, 100 Mb isn't a bad idea if you plan to do a lot of writing and maintaining of databases. Besides, the difference in cost is only about $200. (Note: I personally maintain a computer with 200 Mb which is used mainly for my large customer data base and my books, special reports, etc.)

Floppy disks are the storage media that are used to load programs or backup data. The two popular sizes are 5 1/4 " and 3 1/2 ", either high or low density. Surprisingly, the 3 1/2 ", whether high or low density, store more than the 5 1/4 " media. Whichever you choose is a matter of personal preference as just about all software is available in both sizes. To facilitate the exchange of data amongst your business associates, you might also want to consider a computer with both kinds of floppy drives. This is what I have.

One last item to consider is the type of monitor. Monochrome or single-color monitors were very popular several years ago, but color is now becoming a standard at very little additional cost. Popular configurations are either EGA (Enhanced Graphics Array) or VGA (Virtual Graphics Array), the difference between the two being the resolution or the number of dots per inch that appear on the screen.

A good configuration that will handle most everything you'll want to do initially would be an 80386SX-base machine with 2 Mb of RAM, a high density 5 1/4 " drive with a 40 Mb hard drive and a color VGA monitor. Prices for this, as of mid-1991, are between $2000 and $2500.

Resources

For the best prices I've found so far on computer hardware, printers, etc., contact Pierre Kerbage at Total Systems, Inc., 9290 Bond, Suite 101, Overland Park, KS 66214 (800-242-0136). For the best software prices, check out Lilac Akiko Ltd., P.O. Box 4131, Palm Springs, CA 92263. (800) 659-4135. They publish a listing which always shows who has the lowest prices for any program. Ask for Aki Korhonen. Tell them both I sent you!

Computer Choices - Popular Brands

For the independent advisor who is selecting a computer system, if the needs point to a "personal computer", then there are several obvious choices as of the writing of this book (mid-1991).

Computer systems boil down to two choices: IBM and compatibles and the Apple MacIntosh, everywhere called the Mac. The main difference between the two systems is that the IBM and compatibles are character-based and the Mac is graphic-based. What this means is that with IBM and compatible hardware and software, you usually type in commands or use keystroke combinations to enter commands whereas with the Mac, you use a mouse, or pointing device, to point to commands and click on them to execute. This distinction, however, is becoming less defined as the Windows, or graphical, environment is growing on the IBM and compatible systems.

The argument used to be that if you were more interested in applications that required graphics, you should be more inclined towards a Mac and if you were more interested in business applications, you should lean towards an IBM or compatible. These days, with the advent of more powerful Mac computers, the dividing line is less clear. Again, the choice of Mac or IBM is more one of personal preference and price; a Mac equipped comparable to an IBM-compatible being more expensive due to Apple Computer Company being the sole distributor of Mac hardware. This distinction becomes less clear as you move towards using Windows on IBM and compatible equipment; the IBM graphical environment requires an additional investment in memory, disk storage and monitors above the recommended minimum configuration.

Used Equipment

As with everything else, you can get used computer equipment. However, unless you are very knowledgeable about the particular brand of computer and can ascertain the machine's condition fairly quickly, used equipment is usually more problem than it's worth.

Used equipment, as a rule of thumb, should sell for about 50% of the cost of new. If you research the used equipment listings, you will notice that most of it is being offered for only minor discounts from new-equipment prices. There are several reasons for this. The prices of computers have come down rather dramatically in the last two years, but the used-equipment owners are still thinking in terms of what they paid for their equipment, not in terms of the prevailing prices. So the sellers generally have some inflated expectations. Another factor you should be aware of is that there are generally no warranties on used equipment, especially if bought from a private party. And computer repairs can be expensive. The computer stores that offer used equipment with a warranty generally want more than the 50% of new equipment price, to compensate for their efforts and warranty. So why not buy new?

Another factor that you should be aware of is that the older machines may not run the newer software. Much of the newer software requires a lot of memory and the latest version of the operating system software. You might have to 'upgrade' the older units. Often, the cost of the basic machine and upgrade exceed the discounted prices of new equipment. Another factor to consider is that even though you might find upgrades that will fit (such as hard disks for the IBM PC) you find little surprises like the fact that the power supply unit on the computer is too small and has to be upgraded as well. Don't take anybody's word that the software will run on the machine unless you (or a competent user) verifies it. When you buy used (especially from a private party) 'all sales are final'. Remember, compare the total price of the end configuration (hardware and software) and negotiate from there. What you are really looking for is a solution and the best price/benefit combination for that solution.

So where do you find sources of used equipment? Generally, you will find those sources locally (in your area) in the same manner that you would find any other marketplace. Check local classified pages, Yellow Pages, shopper's directories, user groups, etc. If you want to expand to a national search, check the computer magazines. One of the larger used computer equipment exchanges is:

The Boston Computer Exchange
P.O. Box 1177
Boston, Massachusetts 02103
(617) 542-4414

They function mostly as a brokerage, putting buyer and seller together. Their directory is also on-line.

To determine the prices for used equipment, use the guidelines mentioned above. There are also some directories available that will list equipment that is not so common:

Brown Book
Adventure Capital Corp.
10 State St.
Santa Barbara, CA 93101
(805) 965-7544

Orion Computer Blue Book
Orion Research
1315 Main Avenue
Suite 230
Durango, Colorado 81301

Computer Classified Bluebook
Box 3395
Reno, Nevada 89505

Keep in mind that used computer equipment is priced by negotiation, nothing is written in stone. Determine an upper limit and don't exceed it. Start your negotiations from the lowest possible realistic (or unrealistic!) limit and make the seller work you up from there. Remember, it's basically a buyer's market.

There are some caveats about buying used computers and software that you should be aware of, as is true of buying anything in a used condition:

- The best values are easily spotted by a knowledgeable buyer. If you're not knowledgeable about what you're buying, get someone to help you who is, or re-consider whether you should be buying used equipment at all.

- Get the owner's manual or any and all documentation that came with the equipment. It can save you many hours of frustration. If the documentation isn't available, that would make for a heavy discount factor.

- Work out an understanding with the seller that you'll be able to call with questions. If the seller isn't the user of the equipment, find out who was, and how to get in touch with them. Every piece of equipment has its quirks, and someone who used it for any length of time can tell you what they are (after you describe the symptoms).

- Don't buy used unless you have adequate time (immediately after the purchase) to give the equipment a thorough work-out. If there is any chance at all for exchange, adjustment, refund or return, it will be for a brief period following the purchase. So plan really to put some time in putting the equipment (or software) through its paces.

- Be leery of peripherals with moving parts (e.g. printers, disk drives, plotters, etc.). Give them a thorough visual inspection as well as functional check. Look for obvious signs of wear and/or abuse. Don't accept any statements regarding the availability of parts and service until you've verified this information yourself. Check with repair technicians regarding the reliability of various components and models. They repair the equipment; they can tell you if certain brands and components have a good or bad design and/or repair history.

- If you're buying a number of components that are supposed to work together, insist that you get a functional demonstration. After all, if the seller can't make it work, you probably won't be able to either. Also, once you get a satisfactory functional demonstration and negotiate a sale, note the serial numbers of the equipment at the time of the demonstration. This ensures that "what you see is what you get".

The issue of the business computer purchase need not be a high risk situation for the advisor. By following the steps discussed above, the issue becomes similar to other business challenges, and if the choice is made wisely, the benefits should far outweigh the cost.

Software Selection Techniques

This section is a recommended search and evaluation technique for the advisor who wants to select software that is appropriate for his needs or would like to keep abreast of some of the new software releases.

As an independent advisor, I have use for general and special purpose software, specific application software, and a requirement to stay abreast of what's on the market. The task has not been easy! This requires reading many industry magazines, attending meetings and trade shows and talking to a lot of people (like Jackie Masloff!). I also learn a lot from my own clients and their experiences, successes and failures.

So if you want to locate the software that will perform the tasks that you want to automate, or improve your productivity, these guidelines will save you time and money.

First, however, here are some general comments. When looking for software, try to stay with popular programs supported by major software publishers. This tends to ensure that you will get a program that has been well developed and tested and that support is available. The more obscure the publisher, the less likelihood you will get the necessary support or information.

So begin your search with a list of the popular bestselling software in the area of your need. Only if your criteria aren't met by these should you begin to look at more obscure programs.

Also, be aware that for some specialized applications, the software program that you buy may not do the whole job by itself. It may be a series of instructions for another program, which creates specialized displays and performs specific calculations. These types of programs are called 'templates', and they serve a useful function. But be aware that you might need the underlying program to make it work. For instance, say you purchase a personal financial planning program that is a template for the popular program 1-2-3 by Lotus Development. In order to run it, you need to have 1-2-3 software on your machine.

Determine Your Needs

This is the critical first step in any purchase transaction. It's impossible to optimize any situation unless you know what is the optimum. Review your current requirements. List the functions/performance that you actually use and how often. Then draw up a list of what you *want* new software to do and what you would *like* it to do. This is called a 'must have' and 'nice to have' list. Then put down how much you would be willing to spend on your 'wish list'. Just this exercise alone will probably eliminate 75% of the software. It also serves to narrow your focus to the real candidates.

The Search

Once your 'wish list' is drawn up, start assembling data on what's currently on the market. There are several sources that can provide specific information on specific programs. One caveat: unless you're simultaneously going to embark on a total system upgrade, you're limited in your search to software that will run on your computer. So the first criteria is software compatability with your computer. If you don't have a computer yet, have the computer selection follow this software selection, not the other way around.

Some sources for information on software

- Ask your professional peers. One of the quickest and easiest ways to identify appropriate software is to ask your professional peers what they use for the task you have in mind. Go through the directory of your professional society or even the Yellow Pages and make a few calls. Make a special note of those professionals who appear to be helpful. You may want to ask for a demo of their system later.

- Review back issues of trade journals. Most trade journals now review software that is specific for that industry (e.g. consulting, financial planning, farming, portfolio management). Also, the advertisements will give you an idea of what's available on the market. Collect these reviews and advertisements, and review the features for your particular needs.

- Check out issues of computer magazines. These provide detailed evaluations of software, and often review several programs for a specific application (for instance, a special issue on word processing software). The magazines oriented toward your specific hardware (e.g. make of computer) are usually the best, followed by the large circulation publications. Software reviewed in general interest computer magazines is usually not specific to your business, but for general purpose programs, the reviews are a good benchmark. Usually the last issue of the calendar year or first issue of the new year has an index. Get the index and start from there. As a particular matter, only review the last two years, with emphasis on the last 12 months. Anything that hasn't been released or upgraded in that time period is probably out of date.

- Collect literature at computer stores. You know, the give-aways at the front of the store! Again, this pertains to general purpose software. One caveat: they are often annoyingly shallow, and, obviously, don't give objective comparisons. They, however, provide a sample of what's available, and the price is right. If you need more information, write to the software publisher.

- Read "The Business Computer"™. This is a useful newspaper column that reviews computers and software. Syndicated weekly since 1983, an index of reprints is available.

    The Business Computer ™
    3006 Gregory St.
    Madison, Wisconsin 53711
    (608) 271-0220

- Collect software catalogs. These provide a mind-boggling listing of goodies, but are often restricted to write-ups that seem to come from sales literature. They also list programs that are distributed by smaller, more obscure publishers that you might not otherwise hear about. One of the largest is *Datasources:*

    Datasources
    Ziff-Davis Publishing Co.
    1 Park Ave.
    New York, NY 10016
    1-800-289-9929

    This three volume sets sells for about $500 a year. There are volumes on software, hardware and data communications. Available in libraries.

- Join user groups and professional societies. Local computer groups often have user's groups that are knowledgeable about software. Also, professional societies often have technical subgroups. If the society is national in scope, the national publication often has advertisements for software. One of the largest user's groups in the world is the Boston Computer Society, with over 30,000 members, and many special interest subgroups.

    The Boston Computer Society
    1 Kendall Sq.
    Cambridge, MA 02139-1562
    (617) 252-0600

- Try salespeople at computer stores. This is a source, albeit a dubious one. They will often try to steer you to that which they stock, or claim that it doesn't exist, or they've never heard of it. But sometimes you can get a good lead. It doesn't hurt to ask questions.

The Evaluation

Now comes the fun part. You've identified several likely candidates; now you want to see what each one does, and how *you* like them. For general purpose software, find a computer store that has a demo. Make an appointment to have the program demonstrated. (Always try to make an appointment in advance, and stress that you would like a demo from the salesperson most knowledgeable about the program. The quality of the demo will tell you if you can depend on the store personnel for support after the purchase.) If the store doesn't stock the program you want, sometimes they'll order it. Doesn't hurt to ask. If no store stocks it, call the publisher and ask if they will provide you with the names of anyone locally who has ordered the program. Software demos by a knowledgeable user are infinitely more useful than demos by store personnel. Not only will a user probably give you a thorough demo, he will probably be quite candid about the program's strengths and limitations.

Take some time to work with the software yourself, performing some typical tasks. This, more than anything, will give you a feel for working with the software.

For professional-level advising software, you'll probably do best to make an appointment with the local dealer or agent for the software. The more sophisticated programs usually need some degree of support and therefore have a local representative. It's also in your best interest to see them in action before you make a commitment. For that matter, visit several installations where the software is installed and running. If you have some sensitive questions regarding the software and/or the dealer, don't ask them during the visit (when you will probably be accompanied by the dealer) but during a telephone conversation afterward.

Once you're in a position to actually operate a program, the following guidelines will make your evaluation time more productive:

- Draw up a list of tasks to be demonstrated. This can come from your 'wish list' containing both 'must haves' and 'nice to haves'. Your collection of literature may have yielded some checklists. For instance, Pacific Data Systems, publisher of Money-Master™, an accounting software program, has a booklet titled "11 Secrets You Must Know Before Choosing Accounting Software". To obtain a copy, contact:

    Pacific Data Systems, Inc.
    48021 Warm Springs Blvd.
    Fremont, CA 95439
    (800) 421-4706

- Create a small demo problem or task that does everything that you need to do, preferably in the same fashion that you're used to doing it.

- Take notes on how well each program does what you want. If assistance is available, get each program's specific features demonstrated. Examine the documentation for thoroughness. Try to find answers to your questions on your own.

- Make careful notes of each program's limitations and strengths.

- For some specialized programs, you may not be able to find software available for a demo. In this case, try to get a copy of the user's manual, even if you have to buy it. The user's manual will give you an indication of the complexity of the program. On one occasion, I had need for a specialized statistical program. I narrowed the choice to two candidates, and ordered the user's manuals for each. The choice became clear once I had the manuals: one was obviously written by a Ph.D. for other Ph.D.s; the other was designed for users like me.

If you get into a situation where you feel that you need some professional assistance for software evaluation, you might want to contact a computer consultant. One source is your local chapter of the Independent Computer Consultants Association:

Independent Computer Consultants Association
933 Gardenview Office Pkwy.
St. Louis, MO 63141
(800) GET-ICCA

The Choice

Is it really worth it?

Only you can answer this, of course. If you've done everything outlined above, you will have more knowledge about specific software capabilities than do 90% of the users. And you should also have some opinions. Is it worth the cost? What additional costs, in terms of learning, changing, or modifying your work habits, will be incurred? Are your current files (if you have a system) upwardly compatible with the new software?

At this point, whatever decision you make, it will be a well informed one.

Peripherals, Equipment and Supplies

Printers

After the selection of the computer and software, the choice of a printer is the next significant decision. The options include dot-matrix or laser, either Hewlett-Packard or Postscript.

The term dot matrix printers comes from the design of the print-head on these printers, which is a series of small wires (dots), from a 5x9 matrix to the higher end 24x24 matrix. Each letter is generated by the appropriate configuration of "dots". The resulting effect looks computer generated for the lower resolution matrix but almost presentation quality for the higher concentration of wires. Their speeds range from 80 cps (characters per second) in near letter quality mode to 300 cps in draft (regular computer) mode. Dot matrix printers can either be narrow-carriage for standard 8 1/2" by 11" paper or wide carriage for 14" wide paper. (Keep in mind that you need the larger paper if you plan on doing cheshire mailing labels.) Prices range from under $500 for a narrow-carriage near-letter-quality printer to $1,200 to $1,500 for a wide-carriage higher speed printer.

Laser printers have become more popular recently due to their reduction in price. They are based on the Canon photo-copying engine and generate high quality hard copy at a resolution typically of 300 dpi (dots per inch). They are generally much faster than a dot matrix printer, producing eight to ten pages per minute. The two popular categories for laser printers are the Hewlett Package (HP) Laser Jet and Postscript-type printers. HP printers and compatibles can be purchased for under $1,500 whereas a Postscript printer starts at over $2,000. The difference in price is due to the fact that Postscript printers are typically used for more complex graphical and desktop publishing applications and may offer higher resolutions. Laser printers warrant serious consideration these days for the business user due to their speed, quietness and quality of output.

Several computer magazines have annual or biennial 'printer directory' issues. One of these issues can give you some quick side-by-side comparisons to narrow down the choices. Also, there are now stores that specialize in printers and allow you to compare many printers at one time. One of the national franchises that specializes in printers is called Orange Micro. For a directory of their stores write:

Orange Micro, Inc.
1400 N. Lakeview Avenue
Anaheim, California 92807
(714) 779-2772

Your local Yellow Pages is also a good place to look to determine if there is a printer specialty store in your area. Ask the printer dealer who will service the printer. If it's a third-party service agency, a call to the service technicians could give you some pointers on the reliability and dependability of various printers.

Hard Disks

A hard disk is a data storage device for a computer. The term "hard disk" comes from the fact that the data is stored on a sealed, hard disk. (The disk is sealed in a vacuum, and you connect the disk to the computer via a cable. You add and delete data via keyboard commands without touching the disk.) This is in contrast to the 'floppies' which are the small 5-1/4″ disks that are commonly used for data storage. These are inserted and removed from the computer's disk drives. There are also 'micro-floppies', the 3-1/2″ high density micro disks. The advantages of a hard disk is that it can store many times the data that can be stored on a floppy, for instance, 20 to 30 times the amount of data. Also, the programs and data on a hard disk can be accessed more quickly by the computer.

Hard disks are a requirement for today's computer usage. The question now is how much disk storage to purchase. Price is not a determining factor here as the price diffential between a 40 Mb hard disk and a 200 Mb hard disk is only $500. You need to decide what software you want to use, how much space it will take up and then allocate additional space for data and future growth. Frequently, the main computer system unit provides compartments or slots for the addition of more hard disk units.

Modems

A modem is an electronic device that allows you to transmit and receive data over telephone lines. Modems are usually rated in terms of their speed of transmission or baud rate. Standard speeds used today are 1200 baud (1200 characters per second) and 2400 baud. Modems can be either boxes external to your computer system or cards internal to the system unit. Prices start at under $200 for a 2400 baud modem, either internal or external. The industry standard for microcomputer modems is generally considered to be Hayes Microcomputer Products, Inc. For more information about their products:

Hayes Microcomputer Products, Inc.
5953 Peachtree Industrial Boulevard
Norcross, Georgia 30092
(404) 441-1617

Buffers And Spoolers

Buffers and spoolers are devices which allow you to dump your data to be printed and print out the information while your computer is freed up to do other tasks. Normally, the computer is "frozen" while the printing is being done. The usefulness of a buffer or spooler is dependent on how much printing you do, and if the printing can be done "unattended". Buffers and spoolers cost about $200 and up, depending on their storage capacity.

Supplies

You can buy all kinds of supplies for your computer, from furniture to dustcovers, but obviously some supplies are more functional than others.

The Basics

Functional supplies should come first. You should have an adequate supply of floppy disks, printer ribbons, and computer paper. Also, a disk cleaning kit and a specially treated rag to clean your monitor screen as well as a surge protector or even uninterruptible power supply (UPS) in case of power outages.

It will also be useful to have a floppy disk storage device and dustcovers to keep the dust off your equipment.

Workstation

The real issue with a computer workstation is that it enhance, not detract, from your productivity. This productivity is accomplished through proper layout and design. Technically, this is called ergonomics. As a rule of thumb, ergonomics becomes important if you spend more than a third of your time in front of the computer. There are three major areas where ergonomics will have an impact:

- the chair
- lighting
- working surfaces.

The Chair

The choice of a chair for your computer workstation should consider:

- Is the seat height easily adjustable once you're seated in the chair? Experts recommend from six to nine inches of travel, a height between 16 and 22 inches.
- Does the backrest adequately support the lower-lumbar region of the spine? It should fit snugly into the small of your back. (About 80 to 120 degrees measured from the seat)?
- Can the backrest be adjusted up and down? Two inches or more is recommended.
- Do armrests interfere with movement? They are important to reduce arm and shoulder fatigue. They should be short enough to allow the chair to be drawn up to the work surface and preferably adjustable in height.
- Does the seat have a rounded front edge? It should be rounded or scrolled so as not to cut into the back of your legs and so cut off circulation to your thighs and feet.
- Is the chair adequately padded? Lightly padded is the key. If it's too soft, it can cause pressure under the thighs and thrust the hip bones forward. The material should breathe, so as not to trap body heat or perspiration.
- Does the chair have a five-legged base with casters? The five legs are important for stability, and casters greatly aid in mobility.

Lighting

Selecting the lighting for your computer workstation is dependent on several factors such as specific room conditions and the placement of your monitor. The lighting must illuminate the screen, keyboard, and documents. The American Optometric Association recommends screen brightness three to four times the lighting level of the room.

Here are some other guidelines for your computer workstation lighting:

- Is the level of illumination adequate for computer use? Ambient lighting should be 30 to 50 footcandles, task lighting about 70 footcandles. (Footcandles are a measure of illumination. Light meters are available; check photographic supply stores.)
- Is the light flicker-free? For this reason, avoid fluorescent tubes. They flicker when the tubes are wearing out or the circuitry gets faulty.
- Is the fixture covered with glare shields or adjustable shade?
- Can you easily position the lamp to avoid glare and reflections? If you use overhead lighting, the incidence (angle) of light should be as close to a 45-degree angle to the monitor as possible to avoid reflections and glare.
- Are windows fitted with blinds or shades to control sunlight? Your monitor should be positioned so the sunlight does not shine directly on the monitor screen, or in your eyes. Also, it's a good idea to keep direct sunlight off of your equipment and supplies.

Working Surfaces

For optimum working conditions, the working surfaces of your computer workstation should be flexible, spacious, and nonreflective. Keeping that in mind, use the following criteria:

- Are there separate work surfaces for keyboards and displays? This is for a relaxed hand position. The keyboard should be lower than the usual 29-inch desk height. The top of the monitor screen should be about 10 degrees below eye height, the midpoint about 15 to 20 degrees below eye height.
- Can you tilt the work surfaces and adjust their height? Work surface is generally about 30 inches. Keyboard surface about 28 to 31 inches, home-row keys about 26 to 28-1/2 inches. Wrist inclination should not be more than 10 degrees.
- Does adequate space exist for storing copies, manuals, documents and supplies?
- Is the work surface deep enough so that you can place your monitor at a preferred distance? Viewing distance should be from 17 3/4 to 19 3/4 inches.
- Is the legroom adequate to accommodate different postures? Leg clearance should be about 27 inches for normal stature.
- Can you rest your arms when you are not typing?
- Can you route the computer wiring out of the way? A multiple-outlet power bar is a good way to minimize cord clutter.
- Are the work surfaces nonreflective? Nonreflective surfaces greatly reduce eyestrain.

For further information on making your office ergonomically correct, see:

"Ergonomic Eyeshades" by N. Sullivan
Home Office Computing
February, 1990

and

"Making Your Office Human Friendly" by S. Wooly
Business Week
August 20, 1990

Resources

My friend Jackie Masloff is one of the most helpful and accessible technocrats on business computers. She's helped people make better use of their personal computers for the past ten years. Her consulting practice specializes in training people on software and its applications for their businesses, supporting people with their day-to-day problems in using their computers, guiding them through the decision making process in the purchase of computers and creating custom applications for their business. Jackie's helped me for years and she can help you, too. Contact her at PC Directions, 47 Abbott Road, Dedham, MA 02026 (617) 326-4744.

Also check out *The Computer Buyer's Handbook: How to Select and Buy Personal Computers for your Home or Business* by R. Wayne Parker. It's published by Fast Forward Publishing, P.O. Box 45153, Seattle, WA 98145-0153 (206) 527-3112.

Profitably Using Online Databases With Your Micro-Computer

Now that you know how to select a computer, it's time to discuss the ways you can derive more profit from it. This means knowing where to find the information you need to solve the client's problem. Remember: all an advisor is is an individual who is trained at finding and applying information for the benefit of the client. Once you've got your computer, therefore, you need to know something about how to find the information you need with the utmost efficiency. To do just that I've asked Michigan online information expert Kathy Ackerman to supply what you need so that you can reach this objective with the fewest frustrations and the lowest cost.

Ackerman On Line

There are basically two major reasons why you'll want to master online computer processes:

- Quickly to ascertain what technical information has been produced on a subject of interest to you and your client. *N.B.* It is now estimated that approximately 90% of everything published in the last decade is cited online somewhere.
- To tap into such communications possibilities of your micro computer as electronic mail, electronic banking, shopping, and airline ticketing.

Benefits Of Online Search

There are 12 leading reasons for knowing how to perform online computer searches:

- Searching saves time. If the information you want is available online, the computer can find and print it quickly. The time lag between print publication date and availability online is constantly decreasing, and some databases are now updated as often as every ninety minutes!
- Searching can save money. It takes you or an assistant less time to find what you need.
- Searching can eliminate research travel. You can do your searching right from your home-based or local office.
- Online data bases are usually more current than other information sources.
- Searching offers you greater flexibility and efficiency in research.
- Searching gives you a greater number of access points to information than a printed index.
- An online data base gives you a wider range of research materials than ever could be provided locally, a real boon if you do not live near a major research library.
- Searching allows you to reduce periodical subscription costs since you can read some publications "cover-to-cover" while online.
- Searching allows you to more easily monitor your field of interest.
- Searching can provide convenient electronic document ordering.
- Searching gives you a competitive edge, for now you know where to look (and how to look!) for the information you need when you need it.

This doesn't mean, however, that searching is easy. It isn't. As Kathy points out, searching can be frustrating and expensive if you don't know what you're doing. She also points out, it can become addictive once you get into it!

Types of Online Databases

There are four kinds of online databases, or "electronic libraries." These are:

- bibliographic. This type of database provides citations to articles or books and occasionally provides abstracts.
- full-text. This type of database provides the full text of the article, law, press release, report, &c.
- numerical or statistical. This type of database provides statistics.
- abstract. This type of database provides an abstract or summary, sometimes giving enough information that you needn't track down the original article in print.

Some databases may be a combination of these types.

CD-ROM and Other Laser Systems

The information industry has been excited about the potential of CD-ROM (Compact Disc Read Only Memory) systems for handling huge quantities of information, such as large databases, or entire encyclopedias, on a single disk. These discs look and operate much as the CDs you listen to, and in fact can incorporate sound and graphics along with data. The information is read by a laser, and on CD-ROM systems cannot be altered.

Information professionals love these systems because the cost is fixed, but since the marketplace isn't huge, that cost can be very high. Not all the bugs have been worked out yet in order for these systems to have large mass appeal, but the time is coming! In the meantime in your local library, you may find business directories, magazine articles, newspapers and the like on laser-based systems.

Directories Of Online Databases

To find out which databases are available check the following directories:

- *Computer-Readable Databases*
  Gale Research Company
  835 Penobscot Building
  Detroit, MI 48226
  800-877-GALE

- *Data Base Directory*
  Knowledge Industry Publications
  701 Westchester Ave.
  White Plains, New York 10604
  (914) 328-9157

- *Directory Of Online Databases*
  Cuadra Associates, Inc.
  2001 Wilshire Blvd #30
  Santa Monica, CA 90403
  (213) 829-9972

- *Federal Database Finder*
  Information USA, Inc.
  12400 Beall Mountain Rd.
  Potomac, MD 20854
  (301) 983-8220

Specific Databases Of Interest To Advisors

Here are 12 of the many, many useful databases for advisors. Remember: there are hundreds of data bases as even the most cursory look through the preceding six directories will confirm.

- *ABI Inform*. A general business database with lengthy abstracts of articles from over 650 business press publications. Dates back to 1971. Available on many systems including BRS, SDC, Dialog, SDC, VU/TEXT and others. (The addresses for these systems follow in the next section.)
- *The Computer Database*. Provides indexing and abstracting of articles from about 70 computer publications. Superb source for information on hardware, software, telecommunications, and networking. Available on Dialog and BRS among others.

- *Corporate Affiliations*. Contains business profiles and corporate linkage for 80,000 parent companies and affiliates. Available on Dialog.

- *Courier Plus*. Contains virtually cover-to-cover indexing and abstracting of articles in over 25 national and regional newspapers and in more than 300 general interest, professional and scholarship periodicals. Available on Dialog and others.

- *Disclosure*. Contains business and financial information extracted from documents filed with the Securities Exchange Commission (SEC) by over 12,500 publicly-held companies. Available on many systems including Dialog, CompuServe, Dow Jones New/Retrieval.

- *Dow Jones News*. Contains news stories from the *Wall Street Journal, Barron's*, and Dow Jones News Service. Over 10,000 U.S. and Canadian companies in fifty industries are covered dating back to 1979. Available on Dow Jones News/Retrieval.

- *Dun's Market Identifiers*. Provides marketing information and company history for U.S. businesses, both public and private, which have more than 10 employees. Coverage includes parent companies, subsidiaries, headquarters information, products and services. Available on Dialog.

- *Investext*. Contains the full text of more than 200,000 industry and company research reports produced by financial analysts of leading investments firms in the U.S., Canada, Europe, and Japan. Available on several systems including the Source and Dialog.

- *Magazine Index*. Provides indexing for articles from over 400 popular magazines. In many cases the full texts of the articles are provided. This includes information on many subjects including consumer information, restaurants, and travel. Available on Dialog, Mead's Nexis System, and BRS.

- *National Newspaper Index*. Contains indexing for articles from such national newspapers as *The New York Times, The Wall Street Journal, The Christian Science Monitor* as well as the *Washington Post* and *Los Angeles Times*. Available on Mead, BRS, and Dialog.

- *The OAG-Electronic Edition*. This is the computerized version of the Official Airline Guide and is available on almost every major system. You can also see hotel listings and get rates and ratings.

- *PTS Prompt*. This is a must for industry information and includes data on both private and public companies. Includes abstracts with citations to the full text covering thousands of publications since 1972. It is international in scope. Available on several systems including Dialog, BRS, and VU/TEXT.

Addresses of Major Vendors Of Business Databases

- BRS
  1200 Rte 7
  Latham, New York 12110

- CompuServe
  5000 Arlington Centre Blvd.
  Columbus, OH 43220

- Data Times Corp
  14000 Quail Springs Parkway, suite 450
  Oklahoma City, OK 73134

- DIALOG Information Services
  3460 Hillview Ave.
  Palo Alto, CA 94304

- DOW JONES NEWS/RETRIEVAL
  P.O. Box 300
  Princeton, NJ 08540

- LEXIS and NEXIS
  Mead Data Central
  P.O. Box 933
  Dayton, OH 45401

- NEWSNET
  945 Haverford Rd.
  Bryn Mawr, PA 19010

- Prodigy Services Company
  P.O. Box 8667
  Gray, TN 37615-8667

- Source Telecomputing Corp.
  1616 Anderson Rd.
  McLean, VA 22102

The Equipment You Need For Online Searching

Most business people make their connections through personal computers. To make the connection with a personal computer, you will also need:

- a serial port
- a modem
- a cable to connect the two
- communications software
- a phone.

A Serial Port

A serial port is the means by which the computer transmits data to an external source, like another computer. The bits are sent into the modem where they are then transmitted over the phone lines. Serial ports are standard equipment in today's computers.

The Modem

Before you actually start communicating, you need one more piece of equipment: a modem (or an accoustic coupler, but since they aren't used much anymore, we'll stick to a discussion of modems). "Modem" stands for "modulator/demodulator" and is the device that translates the signals from your computer into a form that can be transmitted over standard telephone lines. It also translates the incoming signals into a form that your computer can understand. In order for two computers to communicate, there must be a modem at each end.

The first decision to make in selecting a modem is to decide how you will be using it. If you need to make your calls through a central office switchboard, you may need one which offers dialtone sensing features that will make it easier to get an outside line.

If you will be calling many electronic bulletin boards (BBS) you will want a modem offering automatic dialing, since these lines are so often busy. (A BBS is a computer that is set up for others to access. Most are run from private homes, computer stores, or are operated by publications or by computer hobbyists. A BBS resembles a bulletin board in that users may post or read messages. Many software programs are available on these systems for "downloading," or retrieving on to a disk.)

Nearly all direct connect modems are able to answer an incoming call. There are other features which you may also find useful. However, if you just need a basic modem, here are some features you'll most likely find useful:

- Hayes Smartmodem® compatibility. The Hayes Smartmodem® has become an industry standard, and most communications programs will assume that the modem on the other end is Hayes-compatible.
- Full duplex 1200/2400 bps capabilities. This allows you to send or transmit at either speed. Slower 300 baud modems can be found at used computer stores very cheaply, but you may find the slowness irritating and expensive.

Modems may be internal or external, stand-alone units. If your modem is built into your computer, your telephone line connection may be a simple plug-in telephone jack. If your modem is a separate unit, you will need a serial interface card installed inside your computer which attaches to your modem via a standard RS-232C connection.

- auto-dial with both tones and pulse. Automatic dialing allows you to dial by typing the phone number on your keyboard and viewing it, before transmitting it for dialing. With many programs, you may store a menu of phone numbers or a "dialing directory." Then, by hitting one key, you may dial the phone. The pulse/tone dual capability is important because it allows you to use discount long distance services which require tone dialing. Since some areas still require pulse dialing, so you need that, too.
- a direct-connect stand alone unit, as opposed to an internal modem or an accoustic coupler. Accoustic couplers aren't used much anymore, since they require that the phone receiver be placed into rubber cups and therefore are quite susceptible to line noise. (See glossary that follows). After reading further, you may decide that you would like an internal modem as opposed to a stand alone unit. This is a personal decision.

Modems meeting these criteria will be a bit more expensive than the most basic modems, in the $200-$300 range. You may also have additional needs which would change the type of modem you'll need to consider:

- If your computer is portable, you may want to consider a modem on a card which mounts inside your computer and makes it more easily transportable. However, they do take up one of your computer's expansion slots and add more heat to your system. On the other hand, one advantage of an internal modem is that it's compact and you don't need another piece of equipment!

Modems can operate at varying rates of transmission or "baud rates". The first modems could only operate at 300 baud, or roughly 30 characters per second. This is now considered quite slow by the pros. The most common modems on the market now operate at either 300 or 1200 baud, and new 2400 baud modems are becoming common. Many of the online services do not yet accommodate 2400 baud, and some add a surcharge for the faster speed. Also take into consideration that the phone lines don't handle 2400 baud transmission very well either since more data must be packed into the same amount of time. Data errors are common. Compability with other 2400 baud modems may also be a problem. Right now the additional cost of a 2400 baud modem (between $700 and $900) probably isn't justified, since with any online communications, much of your time is spent waiting for a response. Since these faster modems have become available, the 300/1200 baud modems have dropped in price, and you be just as well off acquiring one of these.

Communications Software

Communications software is necessary when you are using a micro computer. This is what lets your computer "talk ASCII," which stands for the "American Standard Code for Information Interchange" and is the standard almost everyone uses. This software allows the computer to communicate in letters instead of only in numbers. Many good commercial programs are available such as Smartcom II or III, ProComm Plus, Telix SE, Crosstalk XVI, White Knight, HyperACCESS, and many others. There are also Shareware programs available at little cost. A local user group for your type of computer can help you with this. Take a look at Dvorak's book listed in Resources, or contact Margaret Killeen at Paradise Software, 7657 Winnetka Ave., Suite 328, Winnetka, CA 91306 (800-709-4666). Margaret has a catalog of many helpful shareware programs.

Useful features of telecommunications software are:

- A break or "interrupt" function so that you can interrup your output without being dropped from the system;
- A "print" function which allows you to print your results;
- A "save" function so that you can save what you've seen on the screen to a disk;
- PC status indicators which will let you keep informed of the status of your printer (on or off), whether your disk drive is saving information, and how full your memory buffers are.

N.B. Besides your equipment, you also need to obtain passwords from the vendors you wish to utilize. Each vendor has its own fee structure. Most require start-up fees, although some do not. Many have monthly fees or monthly minimums.

Equipment Needed For CD-ROM Systems

Many of the databases listed here are available on CD-ROM systems for a one-time fixed charge, and others will be available soon. CD-ROMs can be great to use if you can afford the initial cost. In order for your computer to accept a CD-ROM drive, it must have an SCSI (Small Computer System Interface) connection. These connect to a card or printed circuit board that is either already connected to the computer (as in a Mac) or is inserted into an expansion slot (as in IBMs and compatibles). IBM compatible computers may also accept drives using a different interface, but the installation process is similar.

On a DOS system, you will also need MS-DOS extensions, which "extend" their operating system's environment so as to support a drive with the physical storage capabilities of the CD-ROM. In addition, many CD-ROMs require their own software for researching. You'll need quite a bit of memory if you wish to use CD-ROMs — at least one megabyte of RAM is recommended, more if you'll someday be using multimedia applications. Some applications may require a mouse, and you'll certainly want a printer.

A Brief Information Retrieval Glossary

Now that you've selected your equipment and have some idea about the kinds of databases available, it's time to introduce you to some of the terms which will help you become "information literate."

- Acoustic coupler. A device for transmitting data over phone lines using a standard telephone handset. The phone receiver nests in the acoustic coupler, which converts electrical signals into audio signals and vice versa. An acoustic coupler can cause errors in the data being sent or received.

- Asynchronous communication. This is a physical transfer of data to or from a device that occurs without a regular or predictable time relationship following the execution of an input/output (IO) request. This is also known as "start/stop" transmission. It is one of the two techniques used to ensure that the receiving data terminal equipment begins reading the transmitted data at the correct character. This means you can send characters in irregular bursts as you do on a keyboard and the timing of the two communicating computers doesn't need to be synchronized. When searching online databases, we use asynchronous rather than synchronous communication.

- Baud rate. A unit for measuring data transmission rates. The transmission speed is generally measured in bits per second (bps). At 300 baud, 300 bits are transmitted per second.

- Boolean operators. The most basic technique of online searching which involves combining search terms by using three words: AND, OR, or NOT.

- CD-ROM. Compact Disc Read Only Memory. A disc which can hold more than 1000 times as much data as a floppy in digital format to be read by a laser. This may become the preferred method of distributing databases.

- Database producer. The company who has the information to begin with, in many cases a print publisher. The producer makes the information available to one or more vendors who distribute the information electronically and usually pay royalties to the producer based on use.

- Database vendor. The companies which make many databases available to subscribers. This allows a searcher to use all that vendor's databases with only one password and one bill. All the databases offered by a vendor usually are searched in a similar manner, although each can and usually does have its own idiosyncrasies.

- Downloading. This means capturing information from the host computer and putting it into your own computer, usually onto a diskette. Downloading is the subject of many conversations in the online field, because reusing information pulled from a search can be illegal and can deprive the producer and vendor of revenues. On the other hand, downloading from many electronic bulletin boards is encouraged!

- Full duplex. This data is transmitted in both directions at the same time. All of the research-type online services operate at full duplex.

- Gateway systems. These are fairly new services which attempt to make it possible for people to search databases without having to learn all the protocols of that system.

- Half duplex. This method of communication allows transmission only one direction at a time.

- Information broker. A search intermediary, usually trained as a librarian, who conducts research for a fee. (Like Kathy Ackerman!)

- Modem. The device that translates computer information into sound so it can travel over the phone lines, and translates it back into computer-readable information at the other end.

- Parity. A type of error checking which is a function of communications software. For online searching, parity is usually set at EVEN or NONE.

- Protocols. A set of methods or procedures that govern the transmission of data between data terminal equipment. They are the rules governing the transfer of data and make communication work.

- SDI. Selective Dissemination of Information is a service offered by many information professionals such as librarians and information brokers which involves searching a topic on a regular and frequent basis providing updates in the form of documents or search results.

- Telecommunications carriers (or "Packet-switching networks"). Such carriers lease lines for use in data transmission. This eliminates the need to pay long-distance rates from terminal to the mainframe which stores the data. Online database users select a carrier such as Telenet, Tymnet or Uninet and pay an hourly rate for the amount of phone time used.

- Terminal trembles. A condition known both to beginning and experienced searcher as they log on to expensive databases. The ony way to combat this condition is to know exactly what you are going to do BEFORE you log into the service. Of course, your plans may change in the middle of your search which is one of the advantages of searching.

Ackerman's Online Tips

Here are nine things to keep in mind as you use online computer searching:

- Try to anticipate all your communications needs when you purchase your computer system. You'll be able to get a better price from the dealer on necessary hardware and software.

- If a night-time service has what you need, use it. It pays to get your practice on the consumer services like the Source and CompuServe, before moving on to the more complicated systems.

- Keep track of the times you are kept waiting for unusually long periods of time. Request a credit.

- Before attempting difficult searches on services like Dialog read the documentation and call the database producers' customer support lines to request assistance or check your strategy.

- Check with the vendors and the database producers to make sure you have all the available documentation. It's important and will save you money online.

- Plan out your search BEFORE you log on and plan what you will do if you find that there is too little information on your subject — or too much.

- Don't sign up with six services at once. Learn one or two at a time. Otherwise, you may get confused.

- If you aren't interested in research, don't find it thrilling as a game, you'll probably never be very good at it. Use an intermediary to help!

When to Hire An Intermediary: Your Online Advisor

If you don't plan to use online databases extensively — or just have too many other things to do — you'll probably be better off using an intermediary service like Katherine Ackerman and Associates. Such an intermediary can:

- keep you up to date on the latest developments in your field without wasting time and money.

- work on a retainer basis tracking fields of interest to you and your clients, or

- can be called in as you and your clients have need. In your Supergroup of Independent Contractors, it very much pays to have an online specialist available. Remember: this is the Great Age of Information and such specialists are a good way of tapping into what's available.

Resources

Kathy Ackerman is not only a knowledgeable professional in the area of online computer searching. She's also fun to work with! She maintains her own computer-based research and information service, runs The Telecommunications Bookstore reviewing and recommending current titles of interest in the information field, and offers workshops nationwide on such topics as "The Ins And Outs Of Information Brokering" and "Introduction To Online Business Databases." Contact her at Katherine Ackerman & Associates, 403 Oxford St., East Lansing, MI 48823, (517) 332-6818.

In addition to Kathy, you'll find the following resources helpful:

- *Business Guide: The Professional's Guide to Electronic Information Sources* by Jean Scanlan, Ulla de Stricker, Anne Conway Fernald. (John Wiley & Sons)

- *CD-ROM Collection Builder's Toolkit* by Paul T. Nicholls (1990). Published by Pemberton Press, 11 Tannery Lane, Weston, CT 06883.

- *CD-ROM EndUser* published monthly by Helgerson Associates, Inc., 510 N. Washington St., Suite 401, Falls Church VA 22046-3537 (703) 237-0682. Free upon request to qualified subscribers worldwide.

- *CD-ROM Librarian*, published monthly by Meckler Corporation, 11 Ferry Lane West, Westport, CT 06880. The best source of reviews of new CD-ROM products.

- *CD-ROM Professional* published 6 times yearly by Pemberton Press, Inc.

- *Competitor Intelligence: How To Get It; How To Use It* by Leonard Fuld. (John Wiley & Sons)

- *The Complete Handbook of Personal Computer Communications* by Alfred Glossbrenner (St. Martin's Press).

- *Directory of Periodicals Online*, Published by Info Globe, 444 Front Street West, Toronto, Canada M5V 2S9 (416) 585-5249. One of two recommended databases which contains full magazine article texts. Fulltext Sources Online (below) is the other.

- *Disc Magazine* published monthly by Helgerson Assoc.

- *Dvorak's Guide to PC Telecommunications* by John C. Dvorak. (McGraw-Hill)

- *Fulltext Sources Online*, published by Bibliodata, P.O. Box 61, Needham Heights, MA 02194 (617) 444-1154.

- *Online and Database*, Online, Inc., 11 Tannery Lane, Weston, CT 06883
  Aimed at information professionals, these cover online databases and the online industry.

- *Telecommunications Directory*, published by Gale Research. Gale also publishes a *Directory of Online Databases*, a *Directory of Portable Databases*, *Online Database Search Services Directory* and a *Dictionary of New Information Technology Acronyms*, among many other helpful resources. Call 800-877-4253 for a complete list.

CHAPTER 14

Mastering The Life Of The Advisor

Success as an advisor is now within your grasp. You have now familiarized yourself with, and will no doubt master, the information which precedes this, our last, chapter. Having done so, however, there are still three areas you must consider. For succeeding as an advisor means not only mastering your subject field, not only identifying your clients and their problems, not only creating and implementing problem solving procedures which will bring disproportionate benefits beyond your fee, not only learning to market these benefits successfully. No, succeeding as an advisor also means adapting to the curious, demanding, often debilitating lifestyle of the advisor.

As we come to be in-demand problem solvers, as our territory expands to its greatest dimensions, as we come to be not only on the cutting edge of change but the perceived change masters, more and still more will be asked of us. Being who we are, with our need to bring the benefits of what we know to the greatest number, we will want to accept this escalating challenge. To do so, we in our turn must master three critical areas in the life of the advisor, for if we do not we may well become casualties of our increasingly fast-lane existence. Here are those areas:

- time management
- travel management
- stress management.

It has long been a concern of mine that no other book on advising treats these subjects as an internal part of the successful advising practice. Failure to deal with them constructively, however, ensures problems which may well result in undermining your ability to develop a successful practice. It is true that all aspiring people to some extent must interest themselves in these matters. Advisors, however, given the nature of what we do and how we do it, must master these subjects. Following the advice of this chapter, you will.

Time Management

Time is our ultimate resource. Without it there is nothing else. Yet how profligate we are about time and how much we take it for granted as if it were an expandable, renewable commodity. Nothing, of course, could be further from the truth. That is why the first concern of any aspiring advisor should be mastering ways which ensure this apt use of time, rendering him conscious that this is the most finite of resources, one which it is criminal to waste, and which by its very nature is irreplaceable. If you consider yourself any kind of environmentalist concerned about the dwindling nature of the earth's resources, I say to you: start with yourself and with the time you have available. This is the one commodity you should strive to preserve and protect. For without it, you do not exist.

In this connection, I sought out time management expert Gary O'Malley, who has developed procedures which can help you get the most out of every day. This is particularly important to advisors who ordinarily have to manage several different projects, both for their clients and their own small business, simultaneously. Since all these projects are at different phases of development, it is important to develop techniques which allow us to move each of them ahead with the least delay and the utmost expeditiousness. Gary O'Malley's techniques do just that.

To begin with, Gary suggests a goals clarification exercise. Write down, he says, on a blank sheet of paper the six most important things you want to do today. Write down, too, what your long-term goals are one, five, and 10 years from now. As I have said over and over again in this book, unless you have clear, readily understandable goals, you cannot, by definition, have a success. You are a wanderer without an objective.

Now visualize yourself reaching the goals, having them, enjoying them. Visualization is used by successful people to connect themselves in a direct, almost palpable way with the goals they are striving to realize. If you want to make a million dollars a year from your advising business (as some people already do who have implemented the various stages of the Mobile Mini-Conglomerate), write down the goal. Then *see* yourself as a millionaire. Experience your life. See yourself getting the clients that will enable you to generate the receipts. Walk yourself to the bank and back the day you've made a substantial deposit. In short, project yourself into the experience you say you wish to achieve. Over and over again, I confront people who tell me they want to achieve success but have no substantial, readily identifiable goal they want to achieve. For them getting through each day is all they are capable of doing. Realizing any of their greater, vaguer goals is, therefore, almost an impossibility.

Don't just do this exercise once and forget it either. Do it regularly. Do it until the thing you wish to achieve is as clear as a snapshot. If your powers of visualization are atrophied at the beginning when you first do this, cut out photographs from magazines which represent your vision. Your power to visualize is not dead. But it may well be dormant from lack of use.

Having once written down your goals (which, of course, must be updated as you realize them) then create three interlocking planning lists:

- The first list you create is a long-term planning system. This should deal with items that need to be accomplished four weeks and beyond. If you know that your disability insurance premiums must be paid quarterly on the fifteen of the month, then write this down when your first think of it. Most people try to burden themselves with extraneous information. Instead, learn to write down what needs to be accomplished, when it needs to be accomplished, and where you have put the information about this matter if you need to refer to other materials before accomplishment can take place.

- Your second list is a short-term planning one. This contains what you want to accomplish in the next four weeks. In the case of an advisor these tasks will ordinarily fit into the three areas in which you work:

  — working directly with your clients

  — marketing and promoting for new clients

  — diversifying your problem solving process line into new services and products.

Ideally, you should be working on something in each of these areas daily, although this will vary a bit depending on the stage of your career. A new advisor, for instance, may have fewer clients and more time for marketing. An advisor with many projects now in hand may concentrate on these to the detriment of marketing for future clients and the creation of more lucrative products and services. The key to making this short-term list work is to ask yourself: "What should I be doing in each of these three areas day by day over the next four weeks in order to help me reach my one year, five-year and 10 year goals?" If you cannot contemplate creating this list in any other way, begin the task by laying a blank sheet of paper in front of you, dividing it into sections for weeks and sections for goals. Then say the question out loud and begin to fill in the blanks. If you do this regularly you will inevitably find yourself moving towards the realization of your goals.

- Your third and final list is the daily planning one. As with all these lists, start with a fresh piece of paper. Write down the six or seven (not more) things you wish to accomplish today. Things not accomplished today should be carried over until tomorrow. These items should be directly connected to your longer-term goals which should in turn connect to your longest-term, lifetime goals.

Once you have written down these items put them in priority order, not order of urgency. Something may in fact be urgent today but rank relatively low among the things you want and need to accomplish to reach your considered objectives.

The creation of these lists, all these lists, is most important in your realizing your objectives. Do not treat them frivolously. Do, however, revise them as necessary. Advisors are profoundly forward looking people. We need to be moving ahead, need to be progressing towards an object. This is what we are retained by our clients to help them accomplish, and this is what we must do in our own lives and businesses.

Keep these lists where you can look at them. Look at them, regularly, checking off the items you have finished. Take a look at them, particularly when you have finished your day. Were you honest with yourself? Did you set goals which were realistic for yourself, realistic, that is, but challenging? Or did you just go through the motions?

Don't throw these lists away. Keep them for yourself. Keep them in a three-ring binder. At the end of a week, at the end of a quarter, at the end of a year, &c., look back at what you have accomplished. The human memory is a wonderful thing; it blocks out reality. It helps us to forget. This is useful, of course, when dealing with tragedy, but it is fatal for when dealing with accomplishment. We need to know how far we've come. We need to know that we achieved what we set out to achieve. It is all too easy to forget not only what we wanted to achieve but that we achieved anything at all, thus helping to create that debilitating "Is that all there is?" feeling which can creep up on the best of us.

Make sure, as I have said before, that as you realize your goals you reward yourself for doing so. Rewarding yourself is a necessary part of time management. Not only should you receive the intermediate and ultimate rewards for which you have been striving, you should reward yourself for mastering the process which in fact produces the successes. If you set yourself a reasonable task action list of assignments for today, and accomplish what you set out to do, reward yourself commensurately tonight. If you do the same this quarter, give yourself something correspondingly meaningful to yourself.

What I have found is that people are afraid, positively afraid, to reward themselves, feeling somehow that they don't deserve whatever they want, that they have to ask permission of their colleagues, their spouses. Even of me, a total stranger! That you need this crutch is unfortunate, and in due course you must learn to live without it. Only you know whether you have been honest enough with yourself in setting your goals and working towards them. If you give yourself the reward without in fact doing the work, you have cheated yourself. Unless you are entirely disconnected from yourself, this will and should bother you. The fact that it bothers you is actually a good thing, not a bad one, and you should encourage it.

By the same token, if you have worked hard and not rewarded yourself, this should bother you, too. Although this is something it took me quite a while to learn, as a human you have the right to gratification. I am much less worried about the individual who gratifies himself and doesn't work than I am about the individual who works hard but does not gratify himself. For this latter person, by far the more worth saving, is in fact in far greater danger. Don't let this happen to you! If you need permission to do that which will recognize your achievement and reward yourself, I, your guru, hereby give it to you.

Handling Interruptions

Once you have considered your goals, written them down, and placed them so that you can review them as necessary, you must guard against those nagging interruptions which, as effectively as anything else, sabotage your ability to reach them.

As Gary O'Malley rightly points out, more valuable work can be accomplished in one hour of uninterrupted time than in two hours which are interspersed with just 8 to 10 two-minute interruptions. It's quite clear why this is the case: interruptions destroy the mental head of steam and concentration that you've worked up. It takes time to restore your former state. Thus, it is important for you to establish a policy on interruptions and to stick to it so that you can in fact achieve the objectives which you've decided are important towards reaching your ultimate goals. Here are some ideas:

- Ascertain which period of the day is most productive for you. For me it is the period from around 9:30 in the morning until around 2 p.m. in the afternoon. This is my quiet time. During this period, concentrate on the tasks which need to be done, particularly those tasks demanding your highest energy and greatest creativity, the most depleting tasks, in short. During this period allow your answering service or machine to take your telephone calls. Tell your colleagues, friends and family that during this time you are unavailable for chats. Do what is necessary, in short, to preserve your most valuable time as sacrosanct for the things which you really need to accomplish.

Telephone Management

Particularly for those of us who work at home and allow no walk-in traffic, the telephone is the greatest culprit in terms of interruptions. Therefore, part of learning how to contain the interruptions in your life is a question of learning how to control the telephone.

Gary O'Malley and I have drawn up the following list of things which will help you do so.

- Realize that you are under no obligation to take a telephone call the minute it is placed. You should control the telephone rather than the telephone controlling you. I can tell you for an absolute fact that in virtually all advising practices, if you are on top of what your clients are doing and what you have promised to do for them, a four or five hour delay in returning a telephone call isn't going to matter.

- If you have an answering service, make sure it takes a complete record of the name and telephone number of the caller. I am infuriated when someone leaves a message and says, "You have the number." Inform your answering service in no uncertain terms that you must have the complete follow-up information as part of every message. If you use a machine as I do, ask people to leave you a complete message, too. Those of us who travel a lot (and don't carry a bulky roladex) and use devices which allow us to retrieve our calls from far-away telephones must have complete information.

- Messages must include the reason why people have telephoned. Insist on people leaving a short line about why they have called you. This is incredibly important when you are dealing with someone like me whose telephone number is on literally millions of pieces of paper. If I don't know the person, if it's not clear why he's called, and if the number is long-distance, you can rest assured I probably will not return the call. This hasn't caused me any loss of sleep over what might have been, and I advise you to adopt the same policy.

- Make all your calls at the same time. It is destructive to your schedule to take calls as they come. It is productive to deal with a batch of them at once. I find in practice that most telephone calls can be dealt with in three minutes or less. This may not be true when you are trying to sort out your love life, but it certainly is when you are handling matters relating to your advising practice. If people are rambling (and, God, how they ramble!), say "I'm under a bit of a time constraint right now, Mr. Smith. How can I help you?" It's more civil than saying what you really want to say, but usually cannot, namely "Get to the point!"

- Keep an egg timer on your desk. Your objective is to finish the call in three minutes or less *and* to make the biggest possible sale to this client-prospect or help the client to the greatest extent in this time. Did you do it?

- Use conference calls instead of face-to-face meetings. Moving from place to place is physically draining and disorienting. A well organized tele-conference is often vastly preferable to traveling to such a meeting. If all parties have a clear understanding of what this meeting is to accomplish and are working with necessary documents in front of them, all you'll be missing is the rancid coffee that usually accompanies such meetings and the unsavory atmosphere of their smoke-filled room.

- Speak standing up and use gestures. Telephone conversations are often dull and meandering. Don't consider you are speaking into an instrument. Think of the telephone as a representation of another person and treat it like the individual himself. You will come across more strongly and more persuasively.

Proper Delegation

We all know that time is money. We don't, however, treat it as if it were. This is where delegation comes in. I guarantee you that if you have mastered this book, your time is going to be worth more both to yourself and to others than before you started. If, however, you continue with the same defeating practices, you will be functioning as an eleemosynary institution for you will be giving away something of value.

Some kind of delegation is necessary to all advisors. I have learned this early and have created a system where I am dependent on dozens of other people. The only things I do myself are those which I find personally therapeutic and like to do and those which I am the best person to do.

This question of therapy is an important one. Each of us needs things in our (personal and professional) life which soothe and restore us. I find, for instance, writing itself (which is ultimately satisfying) terribly draining at the moment of execution. When, therefore, people tell me I should spend 8 to 10 hours a day writing, I must laugh, just as I do when simpletons advise me (for, you see, I am always getting advice myself!) to do day after day of exhausting 8-hour intensive workshops. No, friend, we all need to find some activity which is soothing and restorative — and I hope — useful and necessary, too. In my case, I find typing my letters and packing book bags highly therapeutic. All other things should be delegated through both your clients (where client business is involved) and your own Mandarin Network. Here are Gary O'Malley's steps towards securing proper delegation:

- Determine which jobs should and should not be delegated. Don't forget to retain those which are soothing and restorative to you!
- Assess what person has the right skills for the job.
- Mutually define the task being delegated with the person doing this task.
- Mutually agree to the details of the assignment.
- Mutually outline the objectives of the task. What is this task supposed to accomplish?
- Grant sufficient authority to the person doing the task. "Entrust," says Gary. "Don't assign."
- Mutually agree to the manner in which performance will be measured.
- Mutually agree to the extent of ongoing support and back-up assistance you will provide. In other words, if you've delegated, delegate.
- Mutually determine a schedule for checking on progress.
- Mutually agree to a deadline.
- Identify the rewards and benefits for doing the task successfully.

Tackling Procrastination

With the best will in the world, having considered and written down your goals and objectives, having kept your lists up to date, having cleared your schedule, and learned effectively how to deal with the telephone and with delegation, there are going to be days when you just can't get going. Even Napoleon, one of the most task oriented of men, had them; towards the end of his career, in fact, he was overcome by lassitude and disinclination to act on fields of battle (surely one of the least convenient times for a general to be so struck)! *He* would very much have benefitted from knowing about the causes of such debility. But you have the far greater benefit of now knowing what to do about it. We call this disease procrastination, and it is rampant.

Who among us has not experienced procrastination? Who among us has not felt guilty giving way to it, feeling somehow lessoned by the gnawing feeling that we should, we really should, be able to do something about it? The next time you feel yourself giving way try the following: determine the cause for your procrastination.

As Gary O'Malley rightly notes, there are really only four reasons for procrastination: fear, feeling in awe of the task, dislike of the task, and boredom. Which of these are you feeling?

- **Identify your fear.**

Fear, of course, is the primary reason why people procrastinate. They are afraid their work will be found inadequate. They are afraid they will be severely judged. They are afraid they will be somehow humiliated. They are afraid, in short, to be found as flawed as we all are. This fear is normal, but it is unnaturally debilitating. Nothing worth achieving has ever been accomplished without someone first overcoming his fear. You should, therefore, acknowledge the fear. Write it down. Face it.

- **Analyze the task.**

Big successes, I say at the risk of repeating myself, are simply a compilation of little successes. The realization of big tasks is no more than the realization of many smaller tasks. This has always been and will always be true. If you are avoiding a major project (of the kind we advisors so often face) because it seems too great to know where to begin, develop a task analysis. Divide the project into as many smaller components as are necessary to achieve the overall result. You may not, of course, even have to do the tasks in order. Just begin. If you get bogged down on one, go on to another on the list. Reward yourself for making a start. And carry on until the whole is finished.

- **Weigh the consequences.**

Ask yourself what the best and particularly the worst things are that could happen with this project. First, visualize the best. Project yourself into enjoying the success that you, with your problem solving skills, can help bring into existence. Keep this vividly before you. Do the same with the worst possible consequences. Gary suggests making a written list of these consequences and comparing them with the list of roadblocks which are preventing you from doing the task. Having this list in writing in front of your helps point out how irrational — and how manageable — your fears and excuses are for not doing the task.

- **Do something.**

Try creating an outline. Sharpen a pencil. Type the date on the top of the letter you've been meaning to write. Draft the submission cover letter to a report you can't quite get started. Do any sub-task that forces you to focus on completing some part of the total task. Once you have begun, go on to another part of the whole and so on until you have built up a momentum that carries you through completion. All of us have probably been daunted by grand projects which when broken down into their myriad components we have polished off quite nicely, thank you.

- **Do nothing.**

Procrastination, of course, is a particular kind of doing nothing. It is the kind of doing nothing where we are anxious about what we are not doing, concerned about the consequences of our failure to act, perhaps wallowing in a tepid bath of self-pity about our manifest inadequacies as a human being. Gary O'Malley's "doing nothing" is nothing like this! Physically push your chair away from your desk, he advises, and sit with your hands folded in your lap for five minutes. As you sit, ask yourself a whole series of questions about what you are procrastinating on and what techniques you can try to begin the task. Then, when you push your chair back to your desk, begin the task. This technique works well because it creates a radical change from your typical and possibly compulsive work habits. Typically in the past you may have reached for some less important task to do just to feel busy at your work. In this case, however, you confront your procrastination head on and behaviorally manipulate yourself into positive action.

- **Create a deadline.**

No task has a sense of urgency to it without a deadline. People who know me, who know that business over the last many years has gone very well, are sometimes amazed (and unsympathetic) about the deadlines I set for myself to finish projects, particularly my in-progress book. "Why", they ask "does it have to be finished by that date?" The reason, of course, is that if there is no firm deadline, we find many rationalizations for procrastinating. Put the deadline in writing and force yourself into accountability by coupling this with a public commitment. I do this by announcing, months before one of my books is nearly completed, when it will in fact be available. I have never, knock on wood, missed a deadline either.

- **Make a public commitment.**

As I said, letting people know when the project will be finished forces you to work towards its completion in a task-oriented fashion. Don't just tell your mother, either. She's very prone to forgiving you your trespasses.

- **Do the task early in the day.**

Work towards completion of your daily tasks, those tasks which move you towards realization of both your short- and long-term goals, as early as you can. Completing this task will give you a sense of exhilaration and accomplishment which will pervade the remainder of the day and cause you to have a sense of accomplishment. In this connection, I well remember how when I was writing my first book I had a terrible case of bronchitis. Because I had a deadline and because I intended to honor that deadline (as much for my own sake as the publisher's), I wrote my quota each day, every day although I well remember the sweat pouring down my face and the discomfort. I felt well compensated, however, by the saintly aura which emanated from me the remainder of the day. Set your most important, your most pressing, and your least savory tasks first. Then polish them off.

- **Slow down your arm.**

Here's one of Gary's creative ideas! As you see yourself placing that item you're putting off one more time into the "pending basket", physically slow your movements down and catch yourself in the process of procrastination. You will often find this helps you to bring the time back into your focus of attention. As with the "do nothing" technique, it works because it's a different behavioral manipulation from your old self-destructive pattern.

- **Create a game.**

Many tasks are boring even though they are crucially necessary. If it's a repetitive task you're tired of doing, try challenging yourself with breaking a speed record, or focus on a constant improvement in the quality of the product. I do this and it really does help!

- **Write the instructions.**

Pretend that you have hired someone else to do this noxious project. That you have to write extremely detailed instructions for him on what to do. Write down what must be done first and how to do it. What must be done second. And so on. Then instead of giving these instructions to someone else, see if you can carry them out yourself. After all, following your own instructions should be easy.

- **Reward yourself.**

Proscrastination, while a very human failing, exacts a pitiable toll on our lives. Once you've overcome it, even in a single project, you deserve a reward. The more important the project, the more difficulty you have faced getting it started, getting it finished, the better your reward should be. Consider this reward carefully. Make it commensurate to the task involved. Write down this reward. Visualize it. Think of how much you want this and how much you'll deserve it for finishing this hated task, getting the monkey off your back. Now dig in. After all, being the good person you are, you'll only be able to get this reward by finishing, right?

Resources

- Gary O'Malley is someone whose services you may well need in your life. He teaches a fine time management workshop nationally and works with both individuals and organizations who need to master these necessary skills. Contact him at LTS. Inc/Time Systems, 400 Interstate N. Parkway, Suite 750, Atlanta, GA 30339 (404) 952-9448. Tell him I sent you.
- Read *Procrastination: Why You Do It, What To Do About It* by Doctors Jane B. Burka and Lenora M. Yuen. These ladies approach their topic with both seriousness, good suggestions and infectious good humor (they even admit they were late in turning in their manuscript to the publisher). It's published by Addison-Wesley Publishing Company. Don't put it off!

Travel Management

Good advisors ordinarily travel frequently. I myself travel very frequently and am well aware of the toll travel can take on your life both physically and in other ways. Like many advisors I can relate travel horror stories by the score: about the four days in New Orleans where I had workshops to give — and only the clothes on my back to give them in. About the three days hopping from Oregon to California to New Jersey, each day marked by a cancelled flight and the need for immediate reshuffling of my plans. About endless quick marches down soulless airport corridors attempting to catch, just barely!, the last plane back to Boston. As every frequent traveler knows, the distance to the gate you want is inversely proportional to the amount of time you have. Why, thanks to stupendous airport personnel stupidity (of which I keep constant note), I have even been put on the wrong plane (but scrambled off in time)! Yes, we can all share such tales. While we may laugh at them today, collectively they take their toll. Travel burn-out (and hence diminished business prospects) is a reality in our business. That's why I sought out travel expert Jonathan Kean and stress management advisor Dr. Jack Curtis for advice on what to do about traveling smart.

Traveling smart, it seems to me, breaks down into the following management areas:
- anticipating travel and preparing for it
- booking travel
- avoiding smoking while traveling
- ensuring restful productive in-flight travel
- handling between flight situations
- dealing with post-flight stress management and facilitating rest.

Anticipating Travel And Preparing For It

If you follow the suggestions of this book conscientiously, it is most likely you'll be doing more business-related travel in the near future than you have done in the recent past. This means you should begin to prepare for this eventuality now. To do so, first of all find a good commercial travel agent specializing in business travel. Some people still foolishly believe travel agents charge more for the same service than airlines or hotels. This is false. Moreover, such agents provide services that can save hours of unnecessary waiting, telephoning, and negotiating. I can honestly say that my own agent is often a godsend to me; while I am often on the telephone two or three times in a day with him planning complicated, multi-city trips, I almost never telephone hotels and airlines directly anymore. What's the point? Make it a priority, then, to add a commercial travel agent to your Mandarin Network. In your search for the perfect agent consider the following:

- Ask your friends who travel frequently to tell you the agent they use. Referrals are still the best way to make contact with an agent.
- Ask how long your contact has done business with this agent.

- Find out what kinds of services the agent provides. Do they, for instance, have an "800" emergency number or a 24-hour emergency line. Remember, when you are stuck in California at 8 p.m., it's 11 p.m. on the East Coast. Will your agent still be able to help you?
- Test the agent. As I have discovered, agents don't always know the cheapest and most efficient way to get you places. Thus, give them a couple of scenarios and then check with the relevant airline or other mode of travel. Did you get offered the best deals? The better times?
- Don't be afraid to ask for references from the agency. There is a high turn-over in the travel business. You want to make sure the agent not only gets to know you but will be here tomorrow.

Booking Travel

To make sure you get the kind of travel arrangement you require, make sure you provide your agent with information about your likes and dislikes. Write them down and have the agent keep them on file.

- Do you want smoking or nonsmoking?
- Do you have long legs (like I do). If so, you'll probably want an airline aisle seat.
- Do you have a tight connection to make? You'll want a seat on the aisle near the front. (In such a situation ask the agent to find out the configuration of the airport for you and the best way to get to your destination. Knowing this information has been very helpful to me on several occasions.)
- Do you have special dietary requirements (or do you simply hate the usual plastic food that's available)? Tell your agent to call ahead and order something special for you. Among the possibilities are vegetarian, kosher, low sodium, low cholesterol, low calorie, plus on most international flights Hindu and Moslem dishes. Whether you really need this special diet or not, you are probably better off asking for something special since the food will ordinarily be fresher than what is generally available.
- Make sure your agent has all the numbers of all the frequent flyer programs in which you are enrolled. (You have made sure you're a member of them all, haven't you?) These numbers will be entered into his computer and will be printed on your ticket. You must still conform to each airline's peculiar (often very peculiar) rules and regulations regarding flyer mileage programs but in case you forget to use the relevant confirmatory coupon this number will ensure that, in due course, you will get credit for this flight. *N.B.* If you forget your frequent flyer mileage coupon, don't worry about not getting credit for the flight: call your agent when you get back and have him work out the details with the airline. You'll find this much more convenient than doing it yourself!

It is your responsibility to tell your agent about all your likes and dislikes, so that you'll get the most out of travel. It is his responsibility to see that your expectations are met. If you are not happy with your agent, say so. See what can be done about it. Like other members of your Mandarin Network, you should set clear, precise expectations for him. If he wants your business (and the travel market is most competitive), he'll try harder. If he doesn't, go elsewhere. Your travel business is valuable.

- **Avoiding Smoking While Traveling**

Whether you are a smoker or non-smoker you can, and should, inform your travel agent about your preferences. This will ensure that you get what you want. I must say, however, that I am far more concerned that we non-smokers get our preference than those of you who must indulge in the noxious weed. That's why I called upon non-smoking expert Bruce Miller for tips on travel for non-smokers. Bruce is the nation's leading authority in this area, and his advice is top-flight. Like me, he's concerned about the dangers that we non-smokers confront from sidesmoke and proximity to smokers. Hence the following advice:

- Beginning February, 1990, Department of Transportation rules dictated no-smoking on all flights in the lower 48 states. When flights to and from Alaska or Hawaii exceed 6 hours, smoking is permitted in sections designated by the airlines.

Bruce recommends that if you find yourself on a smoking flight in violation of the rules, you should bring the situation to the airline's attention. They have an obligation to deal with this matter to your satisfaction. If they are not accommodating write to the organization Action on Smoking and Health (ASH), 2013 H St., N.W., Washington, DC 20006.

Beginning March, 1990, smoking is no longer permitted on Amtrak coaches. Smoking is only permitted 1) in the bottom of lounge cars, if a lounge car is on the train, 2) in sleeper compartments, or 3) designated smoking cars on the east coast. Complaints should go to ASH and to Manager of Service Development, Amtrak Marketing, Amtrak, 60 Massachusetts Ave., NE, Washington, DC 20002.

Bruce has gathered other important information of interest to non-smokers, including where to stay, where to eat, resorts, and non-smoking resources. Here's just some of what he's found out:

- **Where To Stay**

Ask your travel agent to book you into a hotel with non-smoking quarters. Many major chains now have such rooms, and others are bending to popular pressure to get them. Insist on your having such a room and make sure this preference is in the profile on your likes and dislikes maintained by your travel agent.

If no non-smoking room is available, tell your agent you'd like him to propose that you get an available suite but at regular business room prices. This often works. After all, the management does want to please you and have you return. If you are going to have to suffer, at least you might as well suffer grandly. *N.B.* You should always make sure you get the business rate for hotels and motels. Don't *just* assume that you are getting it automatically when you book yourself or that you are getting it when your agent books for you. Tell your agent that you want this rate. When booking direct from the hotel, ask for it. They may ask you to fill out a special form certifying that you are indeed a business. It's a nuisance, but you only have to do it once. Just to make sure that you have received the best available rate for your class, ask the desk clerk when you arrive. You can't be too careful when it comes to saving money!

Don't forget the bed and breakfast alternative. For one thing, you will generally find the management (usually the owners) of bed and breakfast inns and establishments most interested in securing your comfort. Since my connection with *Innkeeping* Newsletter and the marketing workshops we do for innkeepers across the nation, I have had the opportunity to stay in many of these inns, always satisfyingly so. Moreover, a large percentage of these inns, by now the majority, are in fact smoke free.

- **Where To Eat**

Smokeless eating is now a distinct possibility, particularly in any large city. Your best bet, says Bruce Miller, on finding the names and addresses of such places is to check with the local office of the American Lung Association. Also see the 110-page *Guide To Smoke-Free Dining* available from Environmental Press, Box 701, Ellicott Station, Buffalo, New York 14205. Look in the Yellow Pages for vegetarian restaurants. They're almost always smoke-free.

- **Resorts**

Health spas, of course, offer the most likely opportunities for smoke-free vacations. To get information about them check out *Spa-Finders Guide To Spa Vacations At Home & Abroad* by Jeffrey Joseph. (John Wiley & Sons)

Resources

Bruce Miller is the nation's non-smoking authority *par excellence.* A frequent advisor to individuals and organizations on the non-smoking issue, and lecturer, Bruce is also author (along with William L. Weiss) of *The Smoke-Free Workplace* (published by Prometheus Books). Contact Bruce at P.O. Box 21963, Seattle, WA 98111-3963, (206) 527-8292.

Restful And Productive In-Flight Travel

As we all know, sitting on an airplane (or anywhere else) for any length of time creates:
- reduction of joint flexibility
- circulation slowdown
- reduced reaction and coordination capacity
- stiff and aching muscles
- swelling of hands, legs, and feet.

To avoid these unfortunate consequences of prolonged sitting it is necessary to exercise. This can be done from the "comfort" of your seat. Fortunately, Lufthansa Airlines has a handy booklet available (which is free when you write on your business letterhead) entitled "Fitness in the Chair." To get it write:

Lufthansa Executive Traveler Services
1640 Hemstead Turnpike
East Meadow, New York 11554
(516) 794-2020

Also do the following:
- Wear comfortable shoes, as your feet may tend to swell.
- On take off and landing, suck candies or chew gum to keep your ears clear.

- To overcome the effects of jet lag, keep away from caffeine and alcohol, and drink a cup of water or juice every hour. You may also benefit from the special diet created by Argonne National Laboratory, which must, however, be started a few days before your trip. For full information send a self-addressed stamped envelop to:

> Anti-Jet-Lag Diet
> Office of Public Affairs
> Argonne National Laboratory
> 9700 S. Cass Ave.
> Argonne, IL 60439
> (312) 972-5575

My anti-stress wizard Dr. Jack Curtis, the author of many books on the subject, also has developed a handy exercise which should help diminish the effects of jet lag.

Jack calls this particular exercise "The Exhilation Exercise." It helps establish the exhalation phase of your breathing cycle as the cue for relaxation to occur within your body. As you perform this exercise remember to breathe normally, disregard the inhalations, focus your attention on the exhalation phase of the breathing cycle, and feel, sense, and experience the key sensations as you exhale.

Curtis' Exhalation Exercise For Dealing With Jet Lag

Assume a comfortable relaxation position with as much support as possible. Do not cross your arms or legs. During this exercise, be sure to maintain a passive attitude and to allow relaxation to occur.

When ready, allow yourself to close your eyes and for the first several (two to five) breathing cycles, quietly observe the air as it enters and leaves your nose.

For the next several breaths, focus only on the exhalation phase of the breathing cycle, notice the warmth of the air as it leaves your nose and r-e-l-a-x as you exhale . . . . and r-e-l-a-x as you exhale . . . . and allow yourself to let go as you continue to focus on your exhalations . . . . and r-e-l-a-x as you exhale . . . . and r-e-l-a-x as you exhale.

Now, as you exhale, feel or sense the body sinking down into the supporting environment. This sinking down feeling should continue with each exhalation.

At this time, as you exhale, feel the body slowing down. You may notice the breathing rhythm slowing down, or possibly the heart beat slowing down. Each time you notice any of these sensations, allow the body to let go and relax more and more.

Remain in this relaxed state for several moments and when ready to end the relaxation, take a deep breath as you flex, stretch and open your eyes. You're ready to go for it, tiger!

A Few Words About Productive In-Flight Travel

Being alone in an airplane, on a boat, or train is a wonderful time for me. It is one of the very few times in my life when I am away from a telephone and where my creative work can proceed with minimal distractions. I love it. Use this time wisely.

- Give yourself a task to accomplish while you are traveling. I read client memos, client newsletters, and papers that pertain to the meeting I am traveling to. Or if I'm am going to give a speech, I read through recent issues of the organization's publications. By reading a full year's worth of publications, you can get a distinct sense of the organization. Facts from your reading can be blended into your talk to tailor it for your audience. This kind of tailoring is very much appreciated by an audience. You can also familiarize yourself with leading individuals in the organization, their recent projects and successes, so that when you meet them in person your remarks can be most apropos. This impresses people. Remember what I've said right through this book: an advisor always has two sales to make — himself and his problem solving techniques. Don't forget this!

- Use the time you have available to accomplish a marketing task. Too many advisors push marketing to the bottom of their task action lists. This, of course, is a great mistake. Use your time to draft marketing letters to would-be prospects, draft a problem solving article for a newsletter, or to review a key publication in your industry to see how they can feature you or what you are doing. You can follow up appropriately when you're back in the office.

Don't overlook the possibilities of the travel company's own publications or inflight channel. I make it a point to review these and often send in suggestions. On one memorable occasion I was part of an interesting feature on an Eastern Airlines inflight channel. I had remarked to one of my freelancing friends that I had just had a curious encounter on a morning television show with a singing pooch named Newbury. I was on to discuss my book of the moment; Newbury came to sing a medley of his favorite showtunes. The result was a wonderful interview entitled "Advisor Upstaged By A Dog" which ran for about a month or two. If this can happen merely because of my unexpected encounter with an over-vocal canine, just think what you, with your creative juices, can come up with!

- When you do talk to people, remember to be prepared. Bring your précis and brochures on board with you so that when you talk to people you can give them follow-up information. In this fashion, I have sold many copies of my books to seatmates who I discovered couldn't live without them.

- If all else fails, stuff your précis and other materials into the magazines in the seats around you. It doesn't take long, and who knows what may happen? So far, I've been the only person in America doing this, but this book is designed to let you share the wealth of opportunities.
- Remember: if you travel a lot, you may want to look into the possibilities of a portable computer. My good friend and fellow advisor Jim Cameron swears by his original Tandy Model 100 laptop (cost: about $400) It's about 8 1/2 by 11″ in size, weighs in at about 4 pounds, and produces marvels during his frequent and extensive travels:
  - He can input documents on the road including thank you notes and post meeting follow-up which he prints as soon as he's back in the office. No wasted time.
  - He keeps his telephone numbers in memory and readily available.
  - He sends electronic mail and telexes.

Jim also confirms his portable computer is a wonderful conversation starter for when he's ready to rejoin the world. Since he makes a point of traveling first class, it helps him meet the right kinds of people without undue effort. And, of course, because he's such a wise fellow well ahead of his time, he has used this portable model (which is still by no means commonplace) as a means of unabashed promotion for himself and his advising business, as a recent article in *Success Magazine* (telling others how to duplicate his methods) confirms. This is very smart!

Resource

Jim Cameron is one of the brightest and most accessible advisors I know. An advisor to radio stations, among others, Jim is also director of JFORM, a computer data base for journalists. JFORM allows journalists, among many other things, to gather job and story leads, leave messages for each other, and mutually interview a sought-after source. For information about this service, contact Jim at Cameron Communications, Inc., 55 DuBois St., Darien, CT 06820-5224 (203) 655-0138, CompuServe E-Mail 76703,3010. For information about the FORMs for other professions, contact CompuServe, the parent company, at Box 20212, Columbus, OH 43220 or call 800-848-8199.

Between Flight Travel

Look into the possibility of joining one of the lounge clubs which exist at all major airports. Here are telephones, spacious living rooms, and tables where you can hold meetings. These days many flights make a stop and often have a fairly lengthy lay-over. Make sure you use this time wisely. If you are going to provide adult continuing education programs, for instance, knowing that you are going to be stopping for an hour allows you to have a meeting you might not otherwise be able to afford with a program planner at the airport. The lounge club provides you with space in which to have it.

Thanks to the existing mileage programs it may not even cost you anything extra to belong. You can use some of your mileage credits. And if you don't have such credits? Easy! Jonathan Kean has the answer for you. Companies exist from which you can buy frequent flyer mileage coupons and use them either to purchase lounge club memberships or to take off for more exotic places. Use your travel agent to get such coupons (and, of course, make the necessary reservations) or contact:

Frequent Flyer, Ltd.
177 State St.
Boston, MA 02109
(617) 742-0072

At the very least, once you know what city you'll be in, check out directories like Gale's *Encyclopedia Of Associations* and *The Standard Periodical Directory* for associations and publications headquartered there. You can make any necessary prospecting calls for speaking assignments and promotion and not pay the long-distance rates. The key is to be prepared to take advantage of the opportunity when it presents itself.

After Flight Stress Management And Rest

Travel is exhausting. Because your audiences and clients are paying for your best, you've got to know how to rise to the occasion when you don't have the likelihood of all the sleep you need or the security of your own bed. Fortunately, Jack Curtis has developed exercises which are designed to put you in the best shape possible.

In addition to the jet-lag exercise previously given, try this one when you are finding it difficult (as I so often do) to fall asleep in a strange room in a strange (and generally uncomfortable) bed.

Curtis' Sensory Awareness Exercise

The sensory awareness exercise is designed to help you become more consciously aware of sensory perceptions and sensations existing in your body. As you tune into and develop a more heightened awareness of your body and permit it to set its own pace, a feeling of calmness, slowing down, and relaxation occur.

Whenever you are ready, assume a comfortable relaxing position, allow your eyes to close, and for several breathing cycles, focus on your exhalations, listening to yourself breathe, feeling the warmth of the air as it leaves your nose.

As you continue to focus on your exhalations, feel the gentle pull of gravity as it exerts itself on your body. Feel down and sense your body sinking down, slowing down, and relaxing as you exhale.

Pay attention to everything that is happening within your body. When you identify something happening, such as an itch on the hand, a twitching of the eyelid, or a churning of the stomach, mentally acknowledge this occurrence, focus on your exhalations, and continue to scan the body for other sensations.

Each time you identify something, simply acknowledge the sensation, and then move your attention to other body parts, searching for still more sensations.

After a few moments, you will notice a general quieting of the body, and a calm state will occur. Simply permit the body to set its own pace. After you begin to feel relaxed, go to the breathing cycles, and, as you exhale, allow your body to become more and more relaxed, feeling a sinking down, a slowing down, a letting go.

Remain in this relaxed state until you are ready to terminate the exercise. At that time, you may stretch, inhale and — sleep!

N.B. While you will no doubt recall that purple in ancient times was the imperial color, lines of lavender in the bags under your eyes after a sleepless night will not increase the respect in which you are held. Instead, try this exercise and get a good night's sleep.

A Potpourri Of Kean Travel Advice

My shrewd travel expert Jonathan Kean has supplied me with a list of what he amusingly terms "brieflets" which, when followed, will ensure better travel. I intend to give them to you rat-tat-tat:

- If the flight you want is sold out, ask your agent to put you on the priority wait list.
- When traveling abroad, sit as near the exit as possible. Customs lines can be provokingly long. Get there first!
- Carry an Official Airline Guide in your pocket. If your schedule changes, you can quickly check what the alternative flight options are. Moreover if, like Jim Cameron, you travel with a portable computer you can get access (for about $20 per hour) to the Official Airline Guide database. To place an order for this guide call 1-800-323-3537 between 7 a.m. and 7 p.m. Central Time. Or write: Official Airline Guide, 2000 Clearwater Drive, Oak Brook, IL 60521.
- If you are traveling to another country and will be paying normal fares, ask your travel agent to give you two quotes: first, the price of the roundtrip in U.S. dollars, and second, the price of a one-way ticket from the U.S. to your destination and a one-way ticket from your distination to the U.S. priced in the local currency and converted to U.S. dollars. You can then select whichever is lowest. This is advantageous at times when the dollar is high.
- When traveling overseas, find out from your agent whether the carrier can make hotel and car rental arrangements for you. Since the carriers often own such businesses, you generally benefit by lower costs.
- When staying at a hotel, inquire (through your travel agent in advance) about their frequent traveler clubs. These often connect with airline frequent mileage programs.
- Make sure you have your travel agent book you a room away from elevators and soft drink machines. These are most distracting!
- If you expect to arrive late at a hotel, guarantee your room with a credit card. Otherwise, you don't have a leg to stand on. If the hotel sells your guaranteed space (as has happened to me), you should be accommodated elsewhere for free. If they don't offer, ask for this consideration.
- Have your travel agent inquire about whether the hotel has an airport limousine. Arrange to have this meet you. In smaller cities where the airport is at some distance from the town, if you don't reserve the limousine in advance, you may have a very long wait.
- If you are especially adventurous, try this. If you arrive in a city after 7 p.m. call up the most luxurious hotel and ask the price of the room category you want. Then offer them 50%. Or offer them the price of a regular room for the Royal Suite. If they don't accept, go on to the next best hotel. As Jonathan Kean discovered during a recent survey of ten major hotels in Boston, five agreed to discounts ranging from $10 to $80 off a $200 suite. The rationale for bargaining is plain: if the room doesn't get rented, the hotel gets nothing at all. This practice is more common in Europe, but if enough of us use this gambit we'll start a trend here, too.
- If your flight happens to be very busy and has a first class and/or business class section, give your card to the airline representative at the gate. Suggest that should they need to upgrade passengers, you'd be happy to oblige. This is Assertive Courtesy very much in action!

- Make sure you travel with your night gear, medications, and other necessities in your brief case. If you travel often enough, your luggage can and will be lost. If it is lost and you are more than usually inconvenienced (airlines don't care about mundane irritations), write a letter to the customer service department of the airline and carbon the chief executive officer. Pay your bills by credit card, not cash, and ask for a free flight or some kind of credit. Don't pay your bill until the matter is resolved. I am sitting here right now as I write, having done just as I advise you, with a free one-way ticket anywhere on a particular airline's system. Rio sounds nice, I think.
- For information on new airfares, ways of saving travel dollars, and other crucial traveler information see *Consumer Reports Travel Letter*, P.O. Box 53629, Boulder, CO 80322 1-800-234-1645.

One final note: if things go wrong, complain. Bad experiences while traveling affect us in many ways and can throw us off balance while we are doing business with clients and would-be clients. I have found in practice that travel bureaucracies will respond to complaints if you press hard enough. When United Airlines cancelled a flight of mine out of Oregon recently, I told them what an inconvenience this was and the meetings I was missing in San Francisco. They gave me use of a long-distance telephone line. When a cruise ship I was on developed problems, I pressed for free tickets — and got them. Unless you get the service you've paid for, it is your obligation to yourself and the rest of us to press the company for appropriate compensation. Like I say, if you pay your bills by credit card this gives you just the leverage you need to make them sit up and take notice.

Resource

Jonathan Kean is my travel authority, and a most satisfactory one he is, too. If you are not yet being helped by someone as well versed as Jonathan in the intricacies of comfortable travel, give him a call. He'll treat you right. Contact him at Going Places Travel, 225 Friend Street, Boston, MA 02114 (617) 720-3660.

Stress Management

Stress seems inevitably to accompany the successful careers of fast-paced, in-demand advisors. You feel stress while traveling. It builds when you have to make a presentation to a client prospect, or to a client who is not entirely happy with the progress being made toward his objective. It is present when you have to speak before a large group. Fortunately, you can learn to deal with situations just like these.

To help you do so, I sought out Dr. Jack Curtis, one of the nation's leading authorities on stress reduction. You've already benefitted from his advice on handling travel-related stress. Here's what he suggests for other characteristic situations in an advisor's career.

Confronting The Stress Accompanying A Client-Prospect Or Heavy-Going Client Meeting

The rest of your advising career you'll be dealing with client prospects. To be sure, the more experienced you become the less stressful the situation is. There will always be an element of stress in it, however, because there is always an element of uncertainty about what will happen. By the same token, there will always be clients who are less than satisfied with how their account is being handled, with the results you are helping them achieve. In both situations, in which you must cope successfully, you need to know how to manage your stress so that you can better manage the presentation you'll make. Here's a good suggestion from Jack Curtis about how to do so:

With a total of four normal breaths, body parts are relaxed sequentially within thirty to forty-five seconds. Allow your eyes to close if desired.

As you exhale from the first breathe, allow your jaw to relax (let go, become heavy and loose).

As you exhale from the second breath, allow your shoulders to relax.

As you exhale from the third breath, allow your arms and hands to relax.

As you exhale from the fourth breath, allow your legs to relax.

Do this in the washroom. When you're finished, splash some cool water on your face. Comb your hair. You're ready to go. Remember: if the meeting proves to be difficult (as meetings will), ask for a short adjournment and repeat the process. Your job is to stay cool and in command at all times. This exercise will help.

Confronting The Stress Of Public Speaking

Advisors make many, many public presentations both before large and small groups. Yet, as we know, public speaking is always at the head of the list when Americans are asked their greatest source of anxiety. The following Curtis exercise can help you relieve this often-crippling tension.

Jack calls this exercise the "Deep Breath Technique." It is a one-breath technique that can be repeated if desired. Each successive breath should be a normal breath and not a deep breath.

To do this exercise, simply take in a deep breath and hold it for a count of five. As you exhale, feel the body sinking down and becoming heavy and relaxed.

Do this until some of the butterflies go away. My advice to you, however, is not to eradicate them all. An adrenaline edge is, in my opinion, necessary to peak performance.

Confronting Stress In Your Office

There are people you would like to cuss-out, but you cannot. There are days when your clients really do deserve a good whipping, but you cannot provide it. There are, in short, situations of stress which confront each and every one of us in our personal and professional lives. In such situations you need ways of dealing with the stress so that you do not take out its ill-effects on your family and clients, even though they may deserve it. Try the following:

Visualization Of Relaxed Scenes

On a day when the world seems too much with you, stop a moment. Visualize a relaxed scene or return yourself mentally to a relaxed moment in your life. When you select a scene, the following criteria are important:

- It must be a happy scene, one that focuses on an enjoyable experience.
- It must be a scene in which you are relaxed.
- It should be a scene in which you are inactive.

These criteria are based on the mind/body relationship. Thus, if you visualize running a marathon or hiking up a mountain, the subliminal motor movements are taking place. The muscle action sequence is being fired, and this will hinder — not help — relaxation. However, if you visualize yourself after the race sitting relaxed, contented, fulfilled, and basking in the sunshine, this will help the relaxation.

Having one of those days today?

Then close your eyes and visualize a relaxing scene. Picture, for instance, the state of solid contentment you'll have as you return from the bank having deposited a nice round sum that you've secured from mastery of this book.

Resource

Dr. Jack Curtis, my stress expert, has written many fine books and articles on the subject of stress management. An advisor, author and lecturer, Jack has most recently assembled a superb 14-day "Learn To Relax" program which contains a book, an audio-cassette, and a most intriguing stress indicator card. Get this and a complete list of his other publications and workshops from Coulee Press, P.O. Box 1744, LaCrosse, WI 54602-1744 (608) 788-8464.

Last Words On The Life Of The Advisor

People very often ask me how I, without a formal staff of any kind and only a part-time go-fer, can be doing so many things simultaneously. Often during my advising workshops I see people dragging a bit, wondering how they, too, can make use of so many good ideas and do so much without overburdening themselves, threatening their existing relationships, and giving way to unbearable tension and stress. Let me tell you something: you can do it.

Part of what will ensure your success, your ability to manage so many disparate pieces of an increasingly complicated puzzle, is making sure you understand the goal towards which you are moving. My life, contrary to what many people may think, is a very simple one. Unlike many people who are continually distracted by many warring elements, I have reduced these pesky matters to a minimum. I am focused on just three things:

- providing problem solving products and services to my clients
- marketing and promoting my problem solving products and services to would-be clients
- diversifying my line of problem solving products and services to be able to serve more and still more people.

Other things which I regard as of lesser importance, which do not help me achieve my considered objectives, are left to a more convenient moment, or simply not done at all. I feel comfortable about this state of affairs. That there are others who do not agree with my choices is of no concern to me.

What matters, then, is this: you must make a decision about where you are going and how you want to live. Once you have so decided, then the other parts of your life as an advisor will, bit by bit, fall into place — if you insist that they do. Your life as an advisor will be a wholly successful and satisfying life if you concentrate. If you concentrate, that is, on knowing what you want and doing what is necessary to achieve your goal.

Those who are most successful as advisors are those whose lives are the most simple, the most goal oriented, the most willing to shuck off life's nagging inessentials in favor of their truly significant, truly grand aspirations. Now you must do the same. As you do so, you will find not only success in your advising career but deep contentment, too.

Conclusion

You and I have come a long way together. And some of you who have traveled with me before, through other books and through my lecture programs, have come far indeed! I thank you.

As I am sure you now see, **HOW TO MAKE AT LEAST $100,000 EVERY YEAR AS A SUCCESSFUL CONSULTANT IN YOUR OWN FIELD** is not merely a book to be read through once quickly and set aside. It is a book designed to be read and returned to as you have the need. It will take you, if you use it conscientiously, from the beginning of your career in advising, from the moment when you are a technical assistant advisor not merely offering advice but implementing your own suggestions, to the exalted status of the mandarin, the individual who not only recommends what must be done but who helps generate a perception of when a condition is in fact a problem which can and should be solved. For make no mistake about it: there are many conditions of mankind which are not yet recognized as matters which ought to be dealt with. Fortunately some mandarin somewhere, perhaps you!, is even now working on how to change any given situation and so make the world a better place for us all.

This is, of course, the telling reason why we advisors exist. Ours is the ultimate credo of change. We may not always succeed to the farthest extent of our aspirations. Don't worry. Without people like us there would be precious little change at all. While others may cavil at how far we have fallen from what we set out to accomplish, we must remember how far we have come from the futile predictions of the nay-sayers who exist everywhere and in such profuse numbers. With **HOW TO MAKE AT LEAST $100,000 EVERY YEAR AS A SUCCESSFUL CONSULTANT IN YOUR OWN FIELD** in hand, we have at last a guide to lay these despicable flatworms low.

I take this opportunity to remind you that people like us are bound to fail now and again. Those who promote and work for change will. Nonetheless, people like us are essential if there is to be a better world. On days when you are weary. On days when clients may berate you. On days when there may indeed be fewer clients than you would like, remember how profoundly essential you are, how truly rare your admirable qualities. Then come back to this book, to me, and take what you need to carry on. For you are now a certified member of a necessary élite: a dogged advisor who will stop at nothing, who will try anything, who will jettison all that does not work to bring what you know and can do to the attention of the greatest number and who will then apply yourself diligently to their benefit. I know you can do it. In my turn I am working right along with you not just as your advisor but as your admirer, too, for no one knows better than I the commitment you have made and what it has cost. This is why I am so proud to have contributed to your success and so moved this ponderous, lumbering earth closer to deliverance.

Jeffrey Lant's Rogues' Gallery Of Absolutely Must-Use Experts

Many people have given me the benefit of their advice for this and other books and articles and in keeping my own consulting business prosperous. Many are noted in the text but all can help you with your specific service needs. Call them! Let them help you as they help me. These are some of the brightest people in the nation, and they're ready to help make your consulting business a success. Tell them I sent you!

- Katherine Ackerman, President, Katherine Ackerman and Associates, 403 Oxford Rd., East Lansing, MI 48823 (517) 332-6818. Katherine runs an information consulting and direct response company. She specializes in locating business information for clients, often using hundreds of computer databases. She also locates and orders mailing lists for clients. Her seminars "Marketing Information Services" and "The Ins and Outs of Information Brokering" have been given internationally.

- Robert W. Bly, Department RG, 175 Holland Ave., New Milford, NJ 07647 (201) 599-2277. Bob is a well-known independent copywriter and consultant specializing in business-to-business, hi-tech, industrial and direct response marketing. He is author of 19 books including *The Copywriter's Handbook*. Bly is one of a handful of how-to authors whose books are really worth reading. Contact him and he'll send a free catalog of his books and tape programs.

- Barbara Brabec, Owner, Barbara Brabec Productions, P.O. Box 2137, Naperville, IL 60567 (708) 717-0488. Barbara's the nationally-known home-business guru and popular spokesperson for the home-business industry. Her newsletter, *National Home Business Report*, is the most important and valuable periodical in its field as is her book, *Homemade Money*. Call and request a copy of her catalog offering a variety of useful products to help make your home-based business more profitable.

- John Cali, President, Great Western Publishing Co., 74 Jefferson St., Westfield, NY 14787. Great Western Publishing Co. specializes in books and services designed to help small businesses prosper. Just ask and John will send you a free one-year subscription to his *Hot Tips For Small Businesses Newsletter*. An author himself, one of John's best sellers is *Strategies For Getting Charge Card Merchant Status At Your Bank (Even If You're Running A Home-Based Or Mail-Order Business)*.

- Jim Cameron, President, Cameron Communications, Inc., 55 DuBois St., Darien, CT 06820-5224 (203) 655-0138, CompuServe E-Mail 76703,3010. Jim's been my pal since the long-ago days when he used to feature me as a regular guest on his Boston radio show. These days he's a well-known media trainer who coaches CEO's, industry experts, authors and celebrities for media interviews, both print and broadcast. He also runs JForum, a computer database/bulletin board for journalists on the CompuServe computer network. You'll find him a joy to work with!

- Gery Carson, President, Carson Services, Inc., P.O. Box 4785, Lincoln, NE 68504 (402) 467-4230. Gery publishes the must-read *Mail Profits Magazine*. It's a leading "how-to" magazine for mail order and direct mail entrepreneurs. He's also an expert in multi-level marketing by mail and is founder of one of the largest MLM networks in the country, The "C" Team.

- Dr. John Curtis, Publisher, Coulee Press, P.O. Box 1744, La Crosse, WI 54602-1744 (608) 788-6253. Jack Curtis is one of the nation's leaders in stress management. Author of *Learn to Relax: A 14-Day Program*, many other books and articles (ask for a complete list), call him when you really want to cut the tension. He also does workshops on stress reduction nationwide.

- Fred and Elizabeth Dent, Jr., Financial & Management Services, 707 Caddo St., Baton Rouge, LA 70806 (504) 923-2422. Fred, one of the grand gentlemen of the South, and his chic and charming wife Elizabeth provide a wide range of organizational development services. Fred, former Commissioner of Financial Institutions for the State of Louisiana, works with banks, savings and loans, insurance companies as well as business, industry and government regulatory counsel. Need financial planning, personal development and ownership and succession plans? These experts can help you with all of them!

- Bruce David, President, Starting Smart, P.O. Box 468, Aurora, OH 44202 (216) 562-2316; (800) 837-6815. Bruce has been a good friend for a long time. Despite the fact that he's authored the rather nefarious sounding (but utterly practical) *Mercenary Marketing: How to Promote Your Business for Less than $1,000*, he's one of nature's gentlemen and one of the kindest people I know. You'll want to ask for a free sample copy of his fine *Starting Smart* newsletter and contact him when you need a marketing consultant, copywriter or client-centered convention speaker!

- Jeff Davidson, MBA, 3713 S. Geo. Mason Dr., 705W, Falls Church, VA 22041 (703) 931-1984. Jeff has written a string of successful management and consulting books including *Cash Traps: Small Business Secrets for Reducing Costs and Improving Cash Flow*; *Marketing Your Consulting and Professional Services* and *Getting New Clients*. Ask for a complete list of his many helpful publications.

- Bill Doerr, William J. Doerr & Associates, P.O. Box 270071, West Hartford, CT 06127-0071 (203) 233-4331. Bill specializes in marketing and management consulting for individuals of companies selling services rather than products. If your services aren't selling or your people aren't performing, call Bill! By the way, you'll find him one of the most enthusiastic and nurturing people around.

- Dr. Rob Gilbert, Head Coach, The Success Action System, 91 Belleville Ave., Suite 7, Bloomfield, NJ 07003 (201) 743-4428. Rob coaches people to become winners, and he does it all over the phone! I've known and admired Rob for years, and I've personally seen the success he's brought to so many people. So, if you're not reaching your goals yet, give Rob a call for a free consultation.

- John Hamwey, Graphic Designer, ABC Publications, Inc., P.O. Box 162, 385 Weatherbee Drive, Westwood, MA 02090 (617) 329-8811. What can I say? John's my right hand man for all my design and printing projects, the books, catalogs, even my card-deck. If you want to design it... if you want to print it, John's your man. Books and catalogs are a specialty.

- Gary M. Haiser, President/Co-Founder, Personal Wealth Systems, Inc., 8535 BayMeadows Rd., Suite 25, Jacksonville, FL 32256 (904) 731-5785. Gary, America's Big Daddy, has an extensive background in network marketing and the direct sales industry. Author and publisher of *Personal Wealth News* magazine and several network marketing training manuals and audio tape training programs, he is frequently asked to help other network marketing companies develop recruiting and training products. His own company specializes in personal and financial development products and consumer benefit services.

- Robert C. Hackney, Corporate Attorney, DeSantis, Cook & Gaskill, 11891 U.S. Highway One, North Palm Beach, FL 33408 (407) 622-2700. Bob is the author of three business books on corporate and securities law matters including finding business financing, buying financially distressed companies, and mergers and acquisitions. He is a former state securities regular and securities fraud prosecutor.

- Herman Holtz, President, HRH Communications, P.O. Box 1731, Wheaton, MD 20915 (301) 649-2499. My friend Herman is the guru's guru. Author of many, many books, he has particularly specialized in writing about consulting and marketing. Write him for a complete listing his mind-boggling array of books including *The Executive's Guide to Winning Presentations* (John Wiley & Sons). He can help with advisor planning, research, writing and training staffs, and developing a speaking profit center.

- Howard Penn Hudson, President, The Newsletter Clearinghouse, 44 West Market St., Rhinebeck, NY 12572 (914) 876-2081. Howard is the leading name in the production and distribution of newsletters. If you're going to do a newsletter, free or subscription, you're going to connect with this man sooner or later. So, make it sooner! Publishes annually the *Newsletter Yearbook Directory* and many other helpful resources.

- Jonathan Kean, President, Going Places Travel, 225 Friend St., Boston, MA 02114 (617) 227-6210. The ever charming Jonathan provides expert meeting, convention and incentive travel service. His travel agency, Going Places Travel, also provides business, leisure and group travel services. Don't leave home without him.

- John Kremer, Publisher, Open Horizons Publishing Co., P.O. Box 1102, Fairfield, IA 52556 (515) 472-6130. John's editor and publisher of the superb *Book Marketing Update* newsletter as well as the author of many books, including *1001 Ways To Market Your Books*, *Book Marketing Made Easier*, *Mail Order Selling Made Easier*, and *How To Make The News*. John can help you carry out your book marketing campaign, locate special markets, and plan all sorts of direct marketing programs. Until recently he was one of the three most eligible bachelors in the publishing world; I am now the only one left!

- Ivan Levison, President, Ivan Levison & Associates, 44 Montgomery St., Suite 500, San Francisco, CA 94101. Ivan's an expert in marketing communications and producer of the fine "Levison Letter" I referred to in the text. If you want to improve your marketing communications, friendly Ivan's your man!

- Norma Leone, President, Lion Press & Leone Associates, P.O. Box 92541, Rochester, NY 14692 (716) 381-6410. Norma is author of *A Mother's Guide To Computers*, an easy-to-understand book that tells what a computer can do for you (even if you're not a mother!). She's also a WordPerfect Certified Instructor, one of just 96 in the US & Canada, and a warm and gracious friend.

- Gary Lowenstein, CPA, 40 Grove St., Wellesley, MA 02181 (617) 235-5001. Gary's been my one and only accountant all the years I've been in business, and I can heartily recommend him to you whether you're local or in Tangiers. Manufacturing rep, proprietorship and independent contractor questions are his specialty, so are payroll tax return, Schedule C, Subchapter S and more. If you find the accounting advice in my books helpful, Gary's been the one supplying it all these years!

- Jackie Masloff, President, PC Directions, 47 Abbott Road, Dedham, MA 02026 (617) 326-4744. Jackie is my own computer guru and pal; she's the person I call, late, on the week-ends, etc., when I've got a computer problem. I've been doing this for years and she still likes me, so you can tell she's got a terrific personality. Her consulting practice specializes in training people on software and its applications for their businesses. You'll find her most helpful with your day-to-day computer problems and purpose decisions.

- Leslie N. Masonson, President, Cash Management Resources, 20 McGarrah Road, Monroe, New York 10950 (914) 783-1231. I first met Les in a workshop I gave. He's now a nationally known cash management consultant and trainer who can help you uncover cash management opportunities or train your staff. He's authored two books (including *Cash, Cash, Cash*), a newsletter and video-training program.

- Barry L. McVay, Vice President, Panoptic Enterprises, P.O. Box 1099, Woodbridge, VA 22193 (703) 670-2812. Barry is the author of *Getting Started In Federal Contracting* and *Proposals That Win Federal Contracts*, both published by Panoptic. A Certified Professional Contracts Manager and a former Department of Defense Contracting Officer, Barry has helped small and large businesses win millions of dollars in Federal government contracts and subcontracts. If this interests you, he's your man!

- Bruce Miller, Box 21963, Seattle, WA 98111-3963. Clean-air pioneer Bruce, the author of *The Smoke-Free Workplace*, advises organizations on the benefits and methods of developing smoke-free travel, accommodations, and workplaces. His services include short presentations, workshops and private consultations by telephone and on-site. He also does computing consulting!

- Eileen & Jerry Monaghan, Association of Bridal Consultants, 200 Chestnutland Road, New Milford, CT 06776-2521 (203) 355-0464. These attractive go-getters have created a full-service international for-profit trade association for people in the bridal industry. I've been priviledged to work with them many times. They're experts in association newsletter production, effective meetings, seminars, creating an information hot-line, professional development programs and direct mail marketing.

- Thayer Morgan, President, Thayer Productions, P.O. Box 459, Belmont, MA 02178 (617) 923-9558. Thayer, a near neighbor of mine, is your source for quality full color printing and graphic production services. Whether you need a sales building post card, catalog sheet or beautiful color brochure, give Thayer a call! I'm sure you'll be as impressed as I always am with his soft-spoken courtesy and gentle professionalism.

- Blaine V. Morrow, 10 Kercheval, Grosse Pointe, MI 48236 (313) 343-2340. Blaine is a librarian and a specialist on CD-ROM systems. Because he reviews new CD-ROMs, Blaine has seen just about everything in this format for business users and also knows how to create friendlier ways to use the technology.

- Tom Muraso, President, TNT Books, P.O. Box 681519, Miami, FL 33168 (407) 790-7495. Tom is the knowledgeable publisher of two of the best mail order publications in the business, *Mail Order Dynamite* and *AdMag*. If you mention my name, he says he'll give you a free issue of either. You'll want to say in touch with him for information about mail order issues and MLM.

- Nucci, President, Superior Publishing Co., 1202 E. Pike St., Suite 900, Seattle, WA 98122-3918 (206) 726-6055. No this is not a misprint; Nucci is the whole name! And though the name is short, what you'll get is not! With a broad range of experience in business start-ups, management, sales and training, Nucci can provide you with information on how to clearly identify the results you want, write proposals that get you clients, create and implement successful marketing strategies and produce profitable training programs.

- Allan Oxman, CLU, ChFC; Gilley, Oxman and Riggins, 1043 E. Morehead St., Suite 301, Charlotte, NC 28204 (704) 342-2277. Allan, my insurance guru, is a Chartered Life Underwriter and a Chartered Financial Consultant. He's your man when you need assistance finding the best disability coverage, life insurance, or to design and implement a retirement plan for yourself or your employees.

- Nido R. Qubein, President, Creative Services, P.O. Box 6008, High Point, NC 27262 (919) 889-3010. Nido is one of America's top professional speakers. Publisher of *The Nido Qubein Letter*, author of many books on sales, personal growth and communication, his books are published by Prentice-Hall and Farnsworth. He has also recorded a dozen popular cassette learning programs.

- Chuck Schuler, President, Applied Training Technology, P.O. Box 972, Boca Raton, FL 33429 (407) 394-3747. Chuck is a professional speaker who does a series of public seminars throughout the country on securing grants and contracts. Nonprofit organizations of all kinds flock to these programs. Always on or between flights, Chuck nonetheless is lightning fast about returning calls & taking care of business, two facts I love about him!

- Barb Schoeneberger, President, Schoeneberger & Associates, 1147 S. 93rd Ave., Omaha, NE 68124 (402) 397-9223. Barb's author of *The Nitty Gritty of Selling*. She is also not only an expert sales trainer and public speaker, but she also has a system to help you find the best match for positions you have open. Save thousands of dollars by making the right hire or promotion instead of the wrong one by taking advantage of Barb's consulting services.

- Art Sobczak, President, Business By Phone, Inc., 5301 S. 144th St., Omaha, NE 68137 (402) 895-9399; Free Telephone Tips Line (402) 896-TIPS. Art knows how to use the phone to sell more of your products and services, and I'm glad to recommend his public seminars, in-house customized training, video and audio tapes, books and *Telephone Selling Report* monthly training newsletter. A generous fellow, he'll give you a free copy of his newsletter and catalog if you give him a call.

- Tod Snodgrass, President, Loss Control Consultants, 2464 Rue Le Charlene, Palos Verdes, CA 90274 (213) 831-2770. Tod can save you money on all your office products and supplies. Read his book *The Office Buyers Manual: How To Buy Better, Easier, and Spend A Lot Less On Office Products, Printing, Business Forms, And Office Equipment.*

- Dennis Strong, President, Dennis Strong & Associates, 1564 Major Oaks Road, Pickering, Ontario, Canada L1X 2K3 (416) 428-6854. I met Dennis at a workshop I gave in New York and knew right away he was destined for my Rogues' Gallery. He has over 30 years experience in communications, organizational renewal and training. His Presentations Skills workshops provide participants with tips and techniques to overcome common presentation pitfalls. You'll also find Dennis a helpful speaker on topics in customer service, membership retention and team-builders. He also offers a mean rendition of "Under the Boardwalk"!

- Joe Vitale, "The Book Specialist," P.O. Box 300792, Houston, TX 77230-0792 (713) 434-2845. Joe is getting better known every single year and no wonder. Author of such books as *Hypnotic Writing*, *Turbocharge Your Writing*, and *The 7 Lost Secrets of Advertising*, Joe's the kind of nuts & bolts publishing and marketing expert you'll profit from. He writes super sales letter copy and can also help you get your book into print fast and easy.

- Dottie Walters, President, Walters International Speakers Bureau; Association Administrator, International Group of Agents & Bureaux, IGAB; Publisher: *International Directory of Speakers Bureaus & Agents*, and *Sharing Ideas* speakers magazine, P.O. Box 1120, 18825 Hicrest, Glendora, CA 91740 (818) 335-8969. Author of *Speak & Grow Rich* and many audio albums, Dottie's the person to contact when you want to make money on the speaker circuit.

Want to be listed among this illustrious crew? Befriend me! Show me how we can make each other more prosperous; tell me about your skills and technical abilities, your publications and workshops. I'm open to your ideas!

SAMPLES SECTION

Essentials Of The Mini-Case

This is a success document. It points out to prospective clients that you already have had a significant success working with another client. Ideally you should be providing your mini-case statements to prospects who have the same kinds of problems. The results that you have already helped another client achieve should be meaningful to your prospect and should help reduce his anxiety about investing in you.

- Be as specific in this document as you can be. If you cannot divulge the client's name for reasons of confidentiality, then say why you cannot. Don't assume anything. Prospects understand that you have confidential relationships; they may wish their relationship with you to be confidential, too. But don't let them make the necessary deduction on their own. Assume mastery of the situation and proceed accordingly.

- Tell precisely what you were retained to do.

- Provide context information. Tell your prospects where your client began and where your client ended having had your assistance. Put all this information into a meaningful context for your prospect.

- If you are still working with the client (as you may well be, for there is no need to wait until the end of an advising relationship to use it for marketing purposes) inform your prospect what you are doing now. Be exhaustive about your duties. Tell *what* you are doing. Don't say *how* you are doing it.

- Provide complete follow-up information. Each document you put out about yourself and your advising activities should make it easy for prospects to respond.

Sample Mini-Case

Since the fall of 1984, Dr. Jeffrey Lant has been retained as development counsel by the American Association of Variable Star Observers. AAVSO is a 75-year old professional association based in Cambridge, Massachusetts. Its 1300 members help chart the movements of selected variable stars (that is, stars which change their positions) and report their findings to NASA and other agencies of the U.S. government.

Dr. Lant was retained to assist with corporation, foundation, and individual fund raising. Over the course of this consultancy he has assisted with:

- securing contributions from each member of the AAVSO Board of Directors.
- dramatically raising both the percentage of AAVSO members contributing to the organization and the amounts given.
- securing new contributions both from corporations and foundations previously supporting AAVSO and new ones as well.
- getting major individual donors to give substantial sums of money to AAVSO.

At the beginning of Dr. Lant's consultancy, the assets of the AAVSO stood at a little over $1 million. Due to the procedures and techniques he helped implement, AAVSO's gross assets have more than doubled to over two and a quarter million dollars. This means that Dr. Lant has been in part responsible for doing in a single short span what it had previously taken 74 years to accomplish. As a result of these activities, Dr. Lant's original one-year contract was extended by AAVSO for another year.

Dr. Lant's duties continue to consist of:

- writing persuasive fund raising proposals to individuals, corporations, and foundations.
- overseeing the direct mail campaign of the AAVSO to its membership.
- training and overseeing AAVSO volunteer solicitors.
- assisting in the preparations for AAVSO's 75th anniversary celebrations and the dedication of its new corporate headquarters.
- providing general organizational development and management advice to AAVSO's executive director.

Further information about Dr. Jeffrey Lant's successful relationship with AAVSO (and other organizations) is available upon request. Suitable references can also be provided. Please contact:

Dr. Jeffrey Lant, President
Jeffrey Lant Associates, Inc.
50 Follen St., Suite 507
Cambridge, MA 02138
(617) 547-6372

Essentials Of The Précis

The précis is an info-document. It is designed for both informational and marketing purposes. It is the kind of document a prospect organization will study because it contains information which bears on its problem and therefore keep on hand. It also, of course, communicates basic information about you and your services.

- The précis should be printed on your organization's letterhead with complete follow-up information (name, address and telephone number as well as contact person if not otherwise clear.)

- A précis is ordinarily divided into 10 parts. 9 paragraphs deal with what the client-prospect needs to know about solving the problem he wants dealt with. The 10th paragraph is outright promotional information about you and your services.

- If you are finding the structure of this document difficult to write, follow the steps of the Problem Solving Process. Remember: a précis is designed to tell a client-prospect *what* they need to accomplish, but does not provide a sufficiency of information about *how* they can do so. For that they must purchase you and your services.

- For every service (and problem solving product) you produce, you should consider having a précis.

- Your précis can be strengthened by including an article about your product and service on the reverse. This provides third-party validation for your service.

- Distribute your précis widely. Use it as a package stuffer; send it out with your invoices. When you appear on media, ask people to call and write you for a copy. (Remember: it contains critical information they need about solving their problem.) Be imaginative! Your client prospects will keep this document on hand so long as they have the problem you can solve. Since this is a qualified prospect list, consider following up the précis within 30 to 60 days with a letter providing further crucial information and reasons why deciding to act now is in the client prospect's best interest.

Sample Précis

What You Need To Know To Raise Money Successfully For Your Organization From Corporations, Foundations, and Individuals

Of course you want to raise money for your organization. You need it for:

- buying or improving your property, building a building or fixing up the one you've already got.

- paying the expenses of new, creative, necessary service projects, the kind of projects your organization is known for.

- covering those nagging ongoing expenses like rent, heat, electricity and salaries.

- building an endowment fund, the kind of capital reserve which will generate much-needed operative revenue.

These are all good reasons for raising money.

Raising money, however, can be a very difficult, frustrating experience for anyone who doesn't know the basics. Here are a few things you need to keep in mind:

Develop your fund raising plans in advance. Don't go out to raise the money you need. Go out to raise the amount you know — in advance! — you can successfully raise. This means planning. You should begin your planning for successful fund raising at least 9 months before an annual campaign and up to two years before a typical capital campaign.

- Get the full support of your Board of Directors. Your Board needs not only to approve what you are raising the money for; it needs to support the objectives by contributing to them financially. Unless the Board — 100% of the Board — contributes to your fund raising campaign in hard cash you are risking its failure.

- Develop persuasive fund raising documents. Bad documents can hurt you. They show that your organization is ill-organized, sloppy, inefficient. Good documents are expected by donor prospects. Learn in advance how to draft persuasive development proposals, fund raising letters, and brochures. Work on them until they sparkle.

- Research the right corporations and foundations for possible support. Too much time is wasted approaching the wrong corporations and foundations in an attempt to get their support. Most corporations and foundations are quite clear about the activities they want to support, and they expect you to find out what their interests are before you approach them. Make sure you do.

- Keep on good terms with past donors. It's amazing how few organizations make any sustained attempt to keep past donors committed to their cause. Don't you make the same mistakes. Develop activities and means of communication — like newsletters — to keep your donors abreast of the good work you are doing now.

- Construct an active oversight committee. A coordinating committee is necessary for successful fund raising. This committee should be composed of the executive director, chairman of the board of directors, chairmen of individual committees, your development counsel, and an administrative assistant. All are necessary components.

- Meet regularly. Fund raising is at best a slow, often frustrating process, but if your goals have been clearly set, your documents well developed, and your prospects reasonably identified you will reach your objectives if you are willing to work towards them regularly. Ordinarily weekly meetings are advisable.

- Develop a series of internal and external community fund raising committees. Internal committees may include those soliciting funds from the Board, the former Board members, the staff, and your service group. External committees may work with area small businesses, churches, committee groups, and special events. Any fund raising drive is actually broken down into many smaller committees, each working towards its objective under the leadership of an energetic and a hard-working coordinating committee.

- Learn how to use direct mail. Too many nonprofit organizations assume that the use, any use, of direct mail solicitation letters will solve their fund raising problems. Direct mail, however, can be a costly snare for many organizations. Direct mail is best used in concert with a highly targeted list of potential supporters, a series of letters (usually three), and telephone follow-up. Direct mail is a specialized art-science. Familiarize yourself with it and how it works before you use it.

- Work with a good development consultant. Each aspect of successful fund raising demands specialized skill and expertise. You can, of course, familiarize yourself with what needs to be done through a book like Dr. Jeffrey Lant's well-known fund raising text **DEVELOPMENT TODAY: A FUND RAISING GUIDE FOR NONPROFIT ORGANIZATIONS** ($29.95 postpaid). You may, however, prefer to work directly with Dr. Lant and the other Associates at Jeffrey Lant Associates, Inc. His is a firm which specializes in helping you raise the capital, project, operating, and endowment funds you need. Consider your immediate need for money and the need to take action today. Then call Dr. Jeffrey Lant at (617) 547-6372. Qualified organizations are eligible for a free consultation session. We want to help. Please let us!

Essentials Of A Project Description Précis

- Document should be typewritten or typeset on your office stationery with complete follow-up particulars.

- Give the document a brief preamble. Raise the questions a reasonably sensible buyer would have about you. Buyers are always wondering whether their scarce dollars are going to be well invested in you. Let them know you know what they are thinking about and how you propose to calm their anxieties.

- Give as many recent (up to 3 years old) illustrations of your success as you can to make a convincing case (at least three — unless you are just starting off!). Make these illustrations punchy. Again: your client prospects want to make sure that their money is well invested. These brief paragraphs about your past successes should convince them that they are. *N.B.* You don't entirely have to be finished with a project to list it as a success. If things are moving along well now, are ahead of schedule, &c., list this project.

- Make sure that each success is put into a context. Don't assume the reader will understand how truly significant your success is. Maybe you only raised 50¢ and it took a year but point out that the organization previously only raised a nickel in the last five years. Context is terribly important in getting the client prospect to understand the significance of what you've accomplished.

- Tell the prospect that complete follow-up information is available, including recommendations and other documentation.

- Don't hesitate to use quotes from client newsletters, other third party validation and snippets from letters of recommendation either alongside the success they refer to or on the back of your project description. Remember: your goal is to project mastery, that you know the client prospect's problem and not only can solve it but have already solved it. This reduces the level of his justifiable anxiety about spending money.

Sample Project Description Précis

Sure you want to raise capital, project, operating, and endowment funds for your favorite charity or nonprofit organization. But you wonder whether retaining a development counselor really makes sense. You wonder whether the money will be well spent, whether the counselor knows his stuff, whether you can't get along without one. Well, don't you?

As you consider these issues, consider the successful track record of nationally-known development counselor Dr. Jeffrey Lant and his firm Jeffrey Lant Associates, Inc. Dr. Lant, author of **DEVELOPMENT TODAY: A FUND RAISING GUIDE FOR NONPROFIT ORGANIZATIONS**, has the kind of track record that should make you confident your money is well spent and that the results you want to achieve are likely to occur. Consider the following:

- CAMBRIDGE VISITING NURSING ASSOCIATION. After two years working on a mixed capital, project and endowment campaign this 75 year old visiting nursing organization had raised $200,000. Previous to Dr. Lant's consultancy, the organization had been dipping into its limited endowment funds. This invidious trend was reversed; the endowment was increased in size at the same time that needed project and capital improvement funds were raised.

- AMERICAN ASSOCIATION OF VARIABLE STAR OBSERVERS. In a little more than a year and a half working with this 75 year old national association, its endowment of just over one million dollars was more than doubled. It had taken 74 years to build up the first million. With Dr. Jeffrey Lant's assistance, the next million (and more!) came in a little more than a year.

- BOSTON COMMUNITY AMBULANCE. This small, 15 year old community-ambulance service assisting in Boston's poorest sections, raised the money it needed for a new ambulance (which cost the equivalent of one year's operating budget) and start-up funds for day-shift operations designed to put the organization in the black permanently.

- HEALTH SERVICES, INC. Dr. Lant handled the first-ever capital campaign for this previously totally federally supported health center. This fund raising drive enabled the center entirely to renovate its premises and to add badly needed equipment and personnel.

- NATICK VISITING NURSING ASSOCIATION. Dr. Lant advised this 90 year old Massachusetts community-based agency in its first ever capital campaign. Significant funds began to arrive only 6 weeks into the campaign. The first year's goal was reached three months early.

- PROJECT IMPACT. Dr. Lant was the advisor to this special needs adoption agency helping them raise corporate, foundation and federal government funds. As regards the latter category, Dr. Lant was the advisor on a special pilot project involving a public-private partnership. The proposal he drafted and helped conceive was one of only 60 selected out of over 5,000 submitted nationally.

Each of these cases can be further documented and recommendations are available to qualified client prospects.

You can rest assured that your money is well invested when you retain Dr. Jeffrey Lant and Jeffrey Lant Associates, Inc. to assist you raise your capital, project, operating, and endowment funds. We don't take your account unless we are sure we can help. We want to achieve the success as much as you do and will work hard to see to it that you get what you want.

For further information, and to see about scheduling a free assessment meeting, call Dr. Jeffrey Lant at (617) 547-6372.

Essentials of the General Précis

The general précis of problem solving products and services of your firm is like a brochure. It is, however, less expensive than a brochure and can be more easily updated as your product and service line develops.

- Print the précis on your stationery.
- Keep the tone warm. It should be written as from one friend to another.
- Consider printing the précis on colored paper. Goldenrod, for instance, is an effective color.
- Provide complete (albeit necessarily abbreviated) information about everything you do to help solve people's problems, including problem solving products and services.
- Offer people a reward if they read the entire précis.
- This précis can be widely distributed and inexpensively so. Use it for package stuffers, take it to conventions, make distribution deals with people who reach your prospective clients.
- Note: Once you have developed your own catalog, the information in the précis can be incorporated in it. A catalog, properly used, is the ultimate précis.

Sample General Précis

*Running a for-profit enterprise? Here's how we can help **you** sell more products and services.*

Running a not-for-profit organization? Here's how we can help you raise the money you need for capital, project and operating expenses.

Ways We Can Help Your For-Profit Organization...

• **Jeffrey Lant's Sales & Marketing SuccessDek.** Want to lower your lead generation cost? And get new sales? Great. Look into our Sales & Marketing SuccessDek. Every 90 days, we reach 100,000 different business decision makers with our post card marketing program. What's unique about what we're doing? Just this: we offer the lowest prices in the industry. Our prices are generally only 1/4 to 1/3 as much as our competitors'. What's more *all* our names are card-deck responsive. Want more? We give you a free second color. Every other deck in the industry charges. Call now for a free media kit and information about how you can join our satisfied customer list and make post-card advertising work for you!

• **Our Sure-Fire Business Success Catalog.** Every 90 days, we present at least 125 recommendations on how you can make more money with your business, solve a wide variety of business problems, develop and market new products and services, and much more. Could you use this kind of help? No problem. We'll be happy to send you a free year's subscription. Just ask for it.

• **Marketing expertise.** Marketing is like kissing. Everybody does it. But some people do it a lot better than others! Let us help. We don't talk graphs, charts, complicated statistical formulas or anything that stands in the way of what marketing really ought to be: strategies to get you more prospects and close these prospects faster. Invite Dr. Jeffrey Lant to spend just one day with you on site... or consult by phone... in a focused, non-nonsense, results oriented session. We'll review and improve all your marketing communications, your ads, flyers, cover letters, brochures. We'll give you a simple, easy to follow marketing program that gets results! And we'll happily provide references from people who swear that this simple, results-only program works... without bankrupting them or tying up their days in unproductive activities!

• **"Get Ahead" Books.** Tens of thousands of people worldwide are using Jeffrey Lant's books right this minute to develop profitable consulting practices, create and sell "how-to" information products, sell more products and services faster, get free time on radio, tv and in newspapers, magazines and newspapers, make really big money through talk programs of every kind and learn how to write marketing communications that get fast results.

Get:

- THE CONSULTANT'S KIT: ESTABLISHING AND OPERATING YOUR SUCCESSFUL CONSULTING BUSINESS (203 pages, $38.50 postpaid). New Revised Edition! Just published!!!
- THE UNABASHED SELF-PROMOTER'S GUIDE: WHAT EVERY MAN, WOMAN, CHILD AND ORGANIZATION IN AMERICA NEEDS TO KNOW ABOUT GETTING AHEAD BY EXPLOITING THE MEDIA (365 pages, $39.50) New Revised Edition! Just published!!!
- MONEY TALKS: THE COMPLETE GUIDE TO CREATING A PROFITABLE WORKSHOP OR SEMINAR IN ANY FIELD (308 pages, $35).
- HOW TO MAKE AT LEAST $100,000 EVERY YEAR AS A SUCCESSFUL CONSULTANT IN YOUR OWN FIELD (315 pages, $39.50). New Revised Edition! Just published!!!
- MONEY MAKING MARKETING: FINDING THE PEOPLE WHO NEED WHAT YOU'RE SELLING AND MAKING SURE THEY BUY IT (285 pages, $39.50) New Revised Edition. Just published!!!
- CASH COPY: HOW TO OFFER YOUR PRODUCTS AND SERVICES SO YOUR PROSPECTS BUY THEM... NOW! (480 pages, $28.95).
- HOW TO MAKE A WHOLE LOT MORE THAN $1,000,000 WRITING, COMMISSIONING, PUBLISHING AND SELLING "HOW-TO" INFORMATION (552 pages, $39.50).

- **International workshop program.** Thousands of people worldwide have now participated in marketing programs by Dr. Jeffrey Lant. These programs focus as unrelentingly as his books and consulting on giving you the precise techniques you need to sell more products and services now. Among his topics are:

  — "What you have to do to sell another $1,000,000 — or more — of your product or service."

  — "How to create marketing communications — flyers, ads, cover letters, proposals, brochures, and more — that get your prospects to buy NOW!"

  — "How to make at least $100,000 a year from your own consulting business."

  — "How to become a multi-millionaire through your own Information Empire."

Ways We Can Help Your Not-For-Profit Organization

- **Development Assistance.** Dr. Jeffrey Lant can help you raise the capital, project and operating money you need with his direct technical assistance. Dozens of organizations over the years have relied on Jeffrey to help them raise millions of dollars. He'll help you with corporation and foundation grantsmanship, community and direct mail fund raising. Like all Jeffrey's consulting, the processes he'll use with you are efficient, focused and dedicated to helping you raise the maximum number of dollars fastest.

- **Jeffrey Lant's Development Library.** Two books published by Jeffrey Lant Associates, Inc. contain the information you need to raise annual and capital gifts. They include:

  - **DEVELOPMENT TODAY: A FUND RAISING GUIDE FOR NONPROFIT ORGANIZATIONS** by Dr. Jeffrey Lant. Precise details on how to raise the capital, project and operating funds you need from corporations, foundations and individuals. The standard book in its field. (278 pages. $29.95 postpaid)

  - **THE COMPLETE GUIDE TO PLANNED GIVING: EVERYTHING YOU NEED TO KNOW TO COMPETE SUCCESSFULLY FOR MAJOR GIFTS** by Debra Ashton. The most detailed book ever written on how to get major gifts through all the planned giving options. Recommended by the National Committee on Planned Giving, American Red Cross, PBS, American Lung Association, Association of American Museums, National Hospice Organization and many others. (422 pages. $54)

- **Fund Raising Training Sessions.** Thousands of non-profit executive directors, directors of development, board members and volunteers have already profited from Dr. Lant's high-energy, intensely practical fund raising programs. You learn exactly what you need to do to raise money now from corporations, foundations and individuals. The focus is on maximum results in the shortest period of time. No theory. Just techniques that thousands of U.S. nonprofits are already profitably using to get the money they need.

Let us get started now helping you achieve the results you want. Call (617) 547-6372 today for further details or to get the consulting, training or products you want.

Jeffrey Lant Associates, Inc., 50 Follen St., Suite 507, Cambridge, MA 02138

Essentials of the Standard Media Release

- The Standard Media Release should be typed on your letterhead and should include complete follow-up details.

- Provide a headline which indicates that there is a solution to the problem you are bringing to the media's attention and that you provide it.

- Your release should have between 8 and 10 paragraphs and should fit on two pieces of 8 1/2″ by 11″ paper single-sided. Double space the release.

- The sample release piggybacks my service onto a current piece of news. This is a good way for you to get publicity. When a story breaks which is detrimental to your client prospects' interests, put out a Standard Media Release showing how they can avoid the worst by adopting certain procedures. Indicate in the release that your firm is available to supply these techniques.

- Modify your name with helpful information about you including age, schooling, professional credentials, publications, awards, &c.

- Write this release exactly as the story you want to appear — or to solicit the interest of an electronic media producer.

- To increase the interest of the media source, make the opening paragraphs anxiety paragraphs. Remember: media people love anxiety-provoking stories. So do you! The more anxious your client prospects are about a given matter, the more likely they are to hire you to correct the situation.

- In your various paragraphs, provide information about the results people should try to achieve, but don't provide them with sufficiently detailed information so that they can achieve them without you.

- Be prepared to follow up this release with a telephone call. At the very least indicate that you are available when further stories on this pivotal topic come out so that you'll be used as a regular media source. In this way you'll be sought out as an expert and publicized as one to your would-be clients.

Sample Standard Media Release

For further information contact:
Dr. Jeffrey Lant, President
Jeffrey Lant Associates, Inc.
50 Follen St., Suite 507
Cambridge, MA 02138

All telephone calls to (617) 547-6372

For immediate release (today's date)

GRAMM-RUDMAN LAW MEANS NONPROFIT EXECUTIVES NEED TO BECOME MORE SAVVY ABOUT FUND RAISING TECHNIQUES — OR CUT OUT PROGRAMS

Cambridge, Massachusetts. In the light of President Reagan's first Gramm-Rudman budget, Cambridge, Massachusetts fund raising advisor Dr. Jeffrey Lant today announced that many of the nation's one million nonprofit organizations and charities would have to begin a "much more assertive" scramble for dollars. The 39 year old Lant said, "Particularly health and human service organizations previously relying in whole or in part on federal funds must now institute rigorous fund raising campaigns to get at least some of the money they are losing. Otherwise they will go out of business or scale down on the vital services they provide."

Lant, president of Jeffrey Lant Associates, Inc., a consulting firm providing technical assistance to nonprofit organization, pointed out that "fund raising is a time-consuming, often frustrating business" that many nonprofit executives are not familiar with. Lant points out that particularly those organizations having previously received government funds have hitherto had no need for private fund raising. "Now they do," Lant says, "but too often they have made this realization far too late."

Lant, Harvard-trained, pointed out, however, that there are "many things" nonprofit executives can and should be doing to deal with a situation "which is only going to get worse for them as Gramm-Rudman progressively takes effect." Lant mentioned specifically instituting an agency-wide planning process for capital, project and operating fund raising needs. "Too many organizations go out to raise money haphazardly," Lant says. "You should only set about raising funds after a complete planning process has taken place." Lant said, "You go out to raise the money you know you can raise not the amount you think you want."

Lant also said the boards of directors of nonprofit organizations "have to be much more involved both in the planning and in the solicitation process." "This means," Lant says adamantly, "Board members themselves must be familiar with what it takes for a fund raising campaign to succeed and must themselves be willing to give money to their organizations." "Charity," Lant says sternly, "really does begin at home. If Board members won't support their own organizations, how can they expect anyone else to do so?" Lant pointed out that he is retained by governmental agencies in both the states of Michigan and Minnesota to help instruct Board members in these responsibilities.

Lant, whose fund raising book **DEVELOPMENT TODAY: A FUND RAISING GUIDE FOR NONPROFIT ORGANIZATIONS** is in its third printing, also says that executives must be "much more careful" about which corporations and foundations to approach for funding. "Too many organizations randomly send their requests to possible funding sources thereby wasting time and money." Lant pointed out that fund raising is a highly targeted process. "Don't approach a funding source unless you have a very good reason for thinking it can and will help you," Lant said.

Lant, whose fund raising methods have been featured in such major nonprofit publications as *The Grantsmanship Center News* and the *Journal* of the National Society of Fund Raising Executives, pointed out that nonprofit executives also need to become adept at writing more effective direct mail letters, organizing special events, and building broad-based community support. "These aren't luxuries anymore," Lant said. "They are now necessities."

Lant pointed out that the number of nonprofit organizations has not been growing as fast in the past five years as in the five years immediately preceding. "This is directly attributable," he said, "to the increased cost of doing business, cuts in government funding, and the ineffectiveness of many of their fund raising efforts." No money. No organization. "It's as simple as that," Lant concluded.

Lant's own Cambridge-based fund raising consultation service has been in existence over 7 years assisting nonprofit organizations get the money they need to survive. "We've learned a thing or two in the this time," Lant said. "I want to share what I know so that good organizations providing much-needed services can go on doing so."

—End—

Essentials Of The Biographical Feature Story

When you're selling advice, problem solving information, people want to know about who you are and how you operate. The Biographical Feature Story tells them. It is also designed to attract the interest of media sources (who can connect you to your buyer prospects): they want to see you as different, unusual, interesting, even exciting. Make sure this is how you come across!

- The story should be typewritten on your letterhead with complete follow up details. Provide this information at the top right hand side of the first page. Note the instruction: "All telephone calls to." This indicates that media personnel can reach you after regular business hours. Even though you may only work 9 to 5, they don't!

- Keep the paragraphs brief and punchy. The opening paragraph is called the "grabber." It snags the readers attention. Remember: with media it never hurts to be less than subtle. Don't just show them you are "distinctively different." Tell them. Otherwise they might miss the point.

- Remember that your Biographical Feature Story should have a theme and that details should illustrate this theme. In my example, I'm coming across as the Maverick and the Frontiersman. I therefore bring in George Washington as the ultimate revolutionary to my assistance.

- A good strategy for constructing this article is to have a paragraph of facts alternating with a spiffy quotation about yourself. Include information about where the "interview" is taking place, how you look, what you are wearing, &c. The goal is to give the reader (or the program producer who represents the audience) a sense of who you are and what you are like down to the smallest details.

- When your name appears modify it with details about your age, your disposition ("expansively"), your mood, your bewitching smile. Again: provide people with am ambiance which underscores the kind of person you are.

- Deal with your perceived negatives. If you are a maverick, it's important to point out that you are *not* a flake. A healthy corporate profit, therefore, is cited as evidence that although yes, you may be different, you are a pathfinder who has found a profitable new way of arranging your business and life.

- Tell people both what you are doing now, how you came to be doing it, *and* what you'll be doing next.

- Your total Biographical Feature Story should be between 8 and 10 paragraphs in length.

- Remember: You can have as many biographical feature stories as there are divisions of your firm. Each story can concentrate on one aspect of your activities.

Sample Biographical Feature Story

Contact: Dr. Jeffrey Lant, President
Jeffrey Lant Associates, Inc.
50 Follen St., Suite 507
Cambridge, MA 02138
All telephone calls to: (617) 547-6372

DR. JEFFREY LANT

As a corporate president, Dr. Jeffrey Lant is distinctly different. High above the historic Cambridge, Massachusetts Common, where George Washington took command of the Continental Army, steps away from Harvard University where he did his graduate work, Lant directs his problem-solving "Mobile Mini-Conglomerate," Jeffrey Lant Associates. It offers to solve the problems of entrepreneurs through its management consulting, publishing, educational training, and public relations divisions. Each bears the distinctive Lant brand.

"I don't own a suit, a watch, a car or a Gucci brief case," Lant says expansively. Clad in Khaki trousers, penny-loafers, an Oxford button-down shirt, the boyish-looking Lant looks more like a candidate for a fraternity party than a seat on the Board of Directors. But looks are often deceiving.

"I'm listed in *Dun & Bradstreet, Who's Who in Finance And Industry, The International Who's Who Of Intellectuals* and more than a dozen other biographical directories," the 39 year old Lant says. He holds up a copy of the new book by fellow ex-humanities major Steve Bennett entitled *Playing Hardball With Soft Skills.* "I'm cited in this book as a role model," Lant chuckles. "I think people are fascinated by the fact that someone who deliberately thumbs his nose at the established patterns of business advancement can be such a success. I'm definitely not the man in the grey flannel suit!"

In 1986 Lant's unusual operating procedures not only gained him a healthy corporate profit — book sales on the first three volumes of his well-known "Get Ahead" Series passed one million dollars in gross sales — but increasing celebrity as a guy who found a way to corporate profit by doing things his own way. Lant points to books like *What Color Is Your Parachute?, The Harvard Guide To Careers,* and *Utilizing Consultants Successfully* by Herman Holtz which all extol his successful business procedures. "I have to watch out," Lant says in mock horror. "Pretty soon everybody will be using these methods and I'll have to go back to the old ways to carve out a niche!"

Lant's success is by any measure unusual, as he clearly recognizes. His graduate work (which resulted in a Harvard Ph.D. in 1975) was in Victorian royal pageantry. "If Queen Victoria ever needs anyone to arrange a coronation or royal baptism, I'm available," Lant quips. "I've never had an economics course, a statistics course, a marketing course, or anything else that resembles standard business training," Lant says. But because of his own success, he's now invited regularly to lecture to MBA candidates at major universities. "They're the guys wearing the suits. They usually think I'm an undergraduate who's wandered in for the lecture!"

Lant's distinctive business methods were first honed on nonprofit organizations. He left academic administration in 1979 to assist such groups raise the money they need in the face of federal and state budge cuts. He's never looked back. As it became clear to him that as a one-man band he couldn't be everywhere at once, he began spinning off his advice in information-dense how-to books (there are now 6 of them), lectures and workshops (over a 100 a year including regular classes at over 20 universities) and tapes. "Yes, my fund raising techniques are available on over 7 hours of video tape. Longer than 'Gone With The Wind!'"

Is he over extended? Lant says, "No way! I know what's important and what isn't. Little things don't bother me much anymore. I concentrate on the big ones and make each day productive, come what may." In this spirit, Lant points out that he's only recently begun his "Sure-Fire Small Business Success Catalog" a selection of over 75 items useful to every small business or professional practice. "There's nothing like it in the country," Lant says with characteristic exhuberance.

What's next for this fast-moving Cambridge intellectual and info-impressario? "Another how-to book, of course," he says. This one (tentatively titled **MONEY MAKING MARKETING**) will help "any individual or organization" market better, more effectively, less expensively. It's due out in 1987. "I'm going to start a booklet series, too," Lant adds. "It'll deal with selected get-ahead topics that need Lant's brand of specific advice but are not big enough for a complete book." The first topic? "Disability Insurance," Lant says.

Is there a secret to the success of this high-energy, off-beat entrepreneur. "Yes," he smiles. "I live right in my office, have a ten-second commute each morning, take all my own calls, and deal with their business right away. Nothing is put off. If you know your business you should be able to handle things right away and go on to the next productive project."

— End —

Jeffrey Lant Associates, Inc.

THE JLA COOPERATIVE SERVICE PLAN
FOR NONPROFIT FUND RAISING AND PUBLIC RELATIONS

From time to time you've probably felt the need for technical assistance in fund raising and public relations. Maybe you've needed assistance in:

- selecting appropriate fund raising objectives for your capital, program and operating needs
- adopting a suitable fund raising goal
- instituting an effective agency planning process
- crafting persuasive development documents
- getting leads from your Board of Directors to potential funding sources
- involving your Board in the fund raising effort and getting them to contribute to it
- identifying corporations and foundations which might be interested in your work
- getting access to them
- knowing what they might be interested in funding
- handling solicitation interviews
- following them up expeditiously
- organizing community fund raising
- arranging successful special events
- interesting media sources in what you've been doing

or any one of a hundred other problems.

Maybe you've felt that the fees you'd pay for technical assistance would be higher than you could afford — or maybe you just didn't know where to look for help.

> ### Now JLA has created a plan to give you the help you need at a price you can afford —
> ### The Cooperative Service Plan.

What Is The Cooperative Service Plan? This is an innovative, unusual plan which involves your organization and ours working together to achieve your fund raising and public relations objectives. Under this plan we act as your ongoing advisers, and you carry out weekly assignments under our expert supervision.

How Does It Work? Under this plan representatives of your organization meet with a representative of ours for one hour each week for a year. During this hour we will advise you on both the strategy and tactics of successful fund raising from individuals, corporations and foundations and assist you with related public relations tasks. While we are happy to use time in *any* way *you* like, we will always advise you on how we think you will get the best results for your money. Each meeting will conclude with tasks for you to accomplish during the week which, if successfully concluded, will help you realize your fund raising and public relations objectives.

What Is Discussed? The topics range from the general to the very specific. We have found that executive directors and chairmen of boards appreciate extremely detailed advice on specific issues, and this is the kind of advise we provide.

Where Do The Meetings Take Place: All meetings take place at the headquarters of Jeffrey Lant Associates, Inc. We have found that consultants generally charge clients for their travel time. We decided we could save clients money by asking them to come to our offices. The savings have been passed on to you in the low cost of this plan.

Does JLA Ever Come To Your Offices? Yes, twice a year we are willing to meet with members of your Board of Directors. During this meeting we have a procedure for eliciting Board links to corporations, foundations and individuals and for training Directors in soliciting contributions. We are also happy to advise them on the level of their own contribution and of any details of the fund raising effort in general.

Does JLA Make Any Special Requirement Of The Board? Yes. We have found that Board participation and involvement with fund raising is absolutely essential. We therefore *require* that *each* Board member make a financial contribution to the organization during the time we are retained and that members assist with the fund raising through committee work, providing leads to funding sources and contacting their friends and associates.

Who Will You Meet With? Ordinarily your account representative is Dr. Jeffrey Lant. Dr. Lant is well known to nonprofit organizations nationwide. His book **DEVELOPMENT TODAY** is used by several thousand nonprofit organizations to raise the capital, program, operating and endowment funds they need. His innovative fund raising methods have been featured in major nonprofit publications including *The Nonprofit Executive*, *Grantsmanship Center News*, the *Journal* of the National Society of Fund Raising Executives and *The Nonprofit World Report*. He has successfully worked as an advisor to such organizations as the Cambridge Visiting Nursing Association, Natick Visiting Nurse, Health Services, Inc., Boston Community Ambulance, Project IMPACT, the American Association of Variable Star Observers, and the American Association of School Administrators, to name a few. He has trained thousands of nonprofit executives in his distinctive management techniques through special federal and state programs. More generally, Dr. Lant is featured in over a dozen biographical references including *Who's Who In The East*, *Who's Who In Finance And Industry*, *The International Who's Who Of Intellectuals* and in such books as *What Color Is Your Parachute?*, *The Harvard Guide to Careers* and *Playing Hardball With Soft Skills*. He is the author of 10 books including **THE UNABASHED SELF-PROMOTER'S GUIDE**, regarded by many as the definitive book on no-cost/low-cost public relations, and **HOW TO MAKE** *AT LEAST* **$100,000 EVERY YEAR AS A SUCCESSFUL CONSULTANT IN YOUR OWN FIELD.** Other JLA Associates are also available to handle selected cases.

What Is The Cost Of This Plan? The economical JLA Cooperative Service Plan costs just $7,800 a year, or $650 per month.

Is All Time Billable? No, to see whether the Cooperative Service Plan is right for your organization we are always happy to meet with qualified representatives of your organization for one hour. Thereafter, however, time is billable at the rate of $100 per hour.

What Are The Payment Terms? $650 is due upon signature of a one-year contract and $650 per month thereafter for the next eleven months. There are ordinarily no further costs.

Anything Else That's Different? Yes, about 60 to 90 days after our formal working relationship has expired, Dr. Lant will return to review your situation and make sure things are proceeding on course. We want you to get a good start and we want to help you continue to meet your fund raising objectives when you're on your own.

What Are The Major Differences Between The Cooperative Service Plan And JLA's Regular Fund Raising Counsel Contracts? Under our Full-Service Fund Raising Counsel Contracts, JLA:

- travels to you
- makes an account representative available to you by telephone on an "on call" basis
- writes all documents for you including development proposals, précis, direct mail letters, &c.
- meets on an "as needed" basis with your Board of Directors
- places no limits on the duration of weekly meetings

What Is The Cost Of These Full-Service Fund Raising Counsel Contracts? These contracts begin at $12,000 per year for Boston-based organizations and range up to $16,000 per year for out-of-state organizations. Travel and accommodation expenses, where applicable, are additional.

Why Would An Organization Choose The Cooperative Service Plan? For at least two good reasons:

1) Cost. The JLA Cooperative Service Plan is very reasonably priced. Indeed, we have found *nothing* like it on the market. Fund raising counsel is often ridiculously expensive; it can cost $10,000 and more *per month*. Under the JLA Cooperative Service Plan, you get the technical assistance you need from seasoned professionals — and it won't bankrupt your organization.

2) Education. The best consultants teach you how to handle your own account and so, in due course, dispense with their services. Under the JLA Cooperative Service Plan you will learn both the why and wherefor of fund raising and public relations — and so be well positioned to carry out the tasks yourself.

What Next? Please call us at (617) 547-6372 and tell us how we may be of service. You may even want to schedule your free hour with Dr. Jeffrey Lant to discuss your needs and our services.

Anything Else? Yes, before you call us, shop around. Look at the other technical assistance services. We already have. We know that the JLA Cooperative Service Plan is both unique, inexpensive and directed to your needs. But we'd like you to feel sure about it, too. Once you are, let's get together and discuss how we can help you meet your fund raising and public relations objectives.

THE JLA COOPERATIVE SERVICE PLAN FOR NONPROFIT FUND RAISING AND PUBLIC RELATIONS . . . ANOTHER INNOVATION IN NONPROFIT TECHNICAL ASSISTANCE FROM JEFFREY LANT ASSOCIATES, INC.

Jeffrey Lant Associates, Inc.

CAPITAL CAMPAIGN TECHNICAL ASSISTANCE
FOR NONPROFIT ORGANIZATIONS

Perhaps your nonprofit organization is considering undertaking a Capital Campaign. Such campaigns enable organizations to renovate, build and acquire facilities, add significant equipment, and begin and enlarge endowment funds. If any of these is your goal, JLA can probably help.

Most nonprofit organizations have, from time to time, significant capital needs. But they are often uncertain how to go about meeting them. Frequently, in a laudable but misguided attempt to save money, organizations undertake insufficient advance planning before a campaign is publicly announced. The result is often significant embarrassment for an organization and its board. The tested capital fund raising techniques of JLA will insure a very different — happier — result for your organization.

What Is The First Step? JLA will work with the board of your organization so that its members understand their part in the Capital Campaign. Ordinarily, Dr. Jeffrey Lant, president of JLA and well-known to thousands of nonprofit organizations through his books and lectures, addresses a full session of the board to acquaint members with the tasks they must undertake for a successful campaign result. Unless the full commitment of the board is forthcoming, in terms of donation and active support, a successful result will be elusive.

Simultaneously Dr. Lant helps the organization examine its giving constituency to see what level of support is likely — and from whence it might come. This information is communicated to the board and helps determine the extent of the campaign and the likelihood of success.

How Should The Board Prepare Itself? Dr. Lant's book on nonprofit fund raising, **DEVELOPMENT TODAY: A GUIDE FOR NONPROFIT ORGANIZATIONS**, contains a concise, thorough chapter on the organization and direction of capital campaigns. This chapter details the role of the board, the Capital Campaign leadership, and individual fund raising committees. Dr. Lant recommends that board members read this chapter before agreeing to begin a Capital Campaign. (*N.B.* A copy of this book is given to JLA clients as part of the cost of their contract.)

What Is The Initial Responsibility Of The Board? We recommend that the board of *any* organization considering a Capital Campaign pledge *at least* 20% of the total sought. In rare instances this figure may be lowered, but as a rule it provides a good guide to the Board's financial commitment to the campaign. Boards whose membership cannot subscribe this sum or where *all* members are not willing to support the campaign with an extraordinarily financial gift are generally not yet ready to embark on a Capital Campaign. In addition to this level of financial support, we also seek the assurance that board members will lend an active hand to the campaign by chairing committees and assisting as committed committee members. In no other way can a Capital Campaign be successful.

What Then? Should these assurances be forthcoming and, in the opinion of JLA, the success of the Capital Campaign be likely, we are most happy to work with an organization. At this point we enter into a contractual relationship with your organization for one year.

What Does JLA Do As Your Campaign Consultant? JLA can assist you in all matters of the Capital Campaign including the following:

- determining your fund raising goal
- determining the campaign objectives
- the means of establishing full Board support
- training Board solicitors
- establishing fund raising committees and objectives
- drafting inexpensive, persuasive campaign documents
- drafting solicitation letters
- recommending corporations and foundations to approach
- how to handle special events
- the design and use of a campaign newsletter
- the use of direct mail
- and many other related items.

Where Do The Meetings Take Place? Meetings generally take place at your headquarters and should involve as many of the leading organizers of your campaign as possible.

Essentials Of A Success Letter

- Letter should be sent on your organizational letterhead with complete follow-up particulars.

- Send it as soon as you have good news to report, news which will be of interest to other organizations similarly situated. You need not wait until an assignment is completed to leverage it for marketing purposes.

- Mention the name of the satisfied client if you can. You must secure this client's permission to do so.

- Open your letter with one of the leading anxieties of the prospect. This should be something which they have told you currently bothers them.

- If possible, tell what the objective was you set out to assist the client in reaching. If the objective has not yet been reached (because your relationship is still in progress), give as precise information as you can about what has in fact been done.

- Do not claim sole responsibility for the beneficial result, unless, in fact, you are solely responsible. This is a Success Letter for a Delphic Oracle contract option. This success was secured by team effort, and it is both fair and sensible to admit it here. Do, however, take the credit for the problem solving process, the essence of the strategy which helped secure the success.

- Tell prospects how many vacancies you have just now. Let them know you can only take on a limited number of clients. Impart a sense of urgency to the proceedings. This will help your case.

- Let your prospects know that qualified client prospects can get "no fee, no obligation" meetings at your office (or at theirs, if you are offering Full Service agreements).

- Don't forget to include a "no guarantee" statement. Unless you can guarantee that every new client will secure the results of the client you are working with, put in a disclaimer. This disclaimer is the more necessary if you are going to have to work through others, as most advisors do.

- If you are going to follow up this letter with a telephone call, say so. If you are going to do this, however, only send out about 5 or so letters at a time. Telephone follow-up increases the likelihood of getting the prospect meeting you want, but it is time-consuming. If you don't follow up a letter after you've said you were going to, it makes you look disorganized.

- Tell your prospects you are looking forward to meeting and working with them. (No doubt, if you need the money, you certainly are!)

Sample Success Letter

Dear Prospect:

Are you worried about your ability to provide long term care to needy lower income individuals at a time when the federal government is significantly reducing its appropriations to visiting nursing agencies? I bet you are!

So was the Natick Visiting Nurse Association, one of your colleagues.

That's why the Natick VNA retained me as fund raising counsel.

Although my year's contract with Natick still has six months to run, I can report very good things to you about what in fact has been happening.

Working with Judi Boyko, Executive Director and the Board of Directors of the Natick VNA, a mixed operating, project and capital fund raising objective was set. The total sought is approximately $80,000. One portion of this is to set up a permanent endowment fund, the income from which can be used to provide long-term care to needy Natick residents, residents whose incomes are too high to qualify for exisiting government programs but who do not have sufficient resources to pay for the care themselves.

In the last six months, we have already raised over $50,000 towards this goal using a variety of means and approaching corporations, foundations and local individuals. Think of it! $50,000! Isn't this an amount which you, too, would find helpful?

It goes without saying that I have not been solely responsible for raising the sum. Judi, her board chairman, her board and volunteers have been most helpful. But I can tell you that the fundraising techniques and procedures are those created and overseen by this firm. You may already know them since they are found in my book **DEVELOPMENT TODAY: A GUIDE FOR NONPROFIT ORGANI-ZATIONS** which is used by thousands of organizations nationwide and many visiting nursing organizations in Massachusetts.

As it happens, there are now two client vacancies on my list, and I am writing today to ask whether you could use extra money for some much-needed capital, project or operating objective? If so, I would very much like to hear from you and see about setting up a "no fee, no obligation" prospect meeting with you here in Cambridge.

I welcome the opportunity to meet with you and discuss your situation, review your fund raising objectives, and see how we can work together to raise more money for objectives you need today.

Since, as you may already know, I only work with a given number of organizations at any one time, if you are interested in beginning your fund raising soon, I would appreciate it if you'd call now. It goes without saying that while I cannot promise you that your own result will be as profitable as the Natick VNA's has been, I can also say that every organization I have ever worked with has substantially profitted from the experience.

I look forward to hearing from you in the near future and to working with you to help you reach your objectives and to serve the people of your community.

Sincerely,

Advisor

Essentials Of A Letter To Client Prospect Who Has Declined Your Services

- Letter should be sent on your stationery.
- It should be sent as soon as you are sure there is no hope of salvaging this engagement. That means this letter may follow a telephone call with the decision maker in which you have finally ascertained that, on this occasion, you will not be getting the assignment. This letter should be sent only when you have exhausted other persuasive alternatives.
- Indicate that you want to work with this prospect in the future. Don't assume he knows this.
- If the prospect has mentioned other possible assignments (or his dreams) during previous conversations which you feel prepared to help with, say so in this letter. Indicate, too, how and when you'll be following up. The prospect should get the strong indication as a result of this letter (and previous contacts) that you are not going to go away.
- Ask to be kept on the prospect's mailing list. Keep the prospect on your own. Prospects often decline to work with advisors because they don't know enough about them. By familiarizing the prospect with your activities (and keeping abreast of theirs) this problem can be solved.
- Make sure you keep the prospect informed about successes you have with other similar organizations. Remember: envy is a powerful motivator!

Sample Letter To Client Prospect Who Has Declined Your Services

Dear Prospect:

I was sorry to learn today that your Board of Directors has decided not to accept my proposal to work with you as a capital campaign fund raising advisor.

I want you to know that I still hope that at some future point we can do business together and that you will again consider my services as you set out to raise necessary operating and project monies. In this regard, I recall during our last conversation that you hope to raise funds in about six months to provide a special training program for your emergency medical technicians. As I mentioned then, I have had experience in this area. I would therefore like to call upon you the beginning of September to see whether we can, at that time, enter into a constructive relationship.

Until that time I shall keep you up to date with the plans and activities of my firm, and I should be grateful, too, if you would add me to your mailing list. As you know, in the past my firm has had very successful relationships with other visiting nursing associations, and it is my hope, in time, to have one with you, too.

Sincerely,

(Persistent) Advisor

Essentials of the "Dog Ate My Homework" Collection Letter

This letter isn't, obviously, the first thing you send to a client behind in his payments.

- Start with your standard invoices.
- Follow up with a telephone call to see whether the client means to pay. If he does, see what the trouble is, when he can pay, and then determine what you should do next. If the client is being difficult about paying and if there is more work for you to do, stop doing it until this situation gets rectified.
- If you have a "stop work" clause in your contract, use it. It is frustrating, of course, to have to use it, but it's better than continuing to work without expectation of payment to which you are entitled.
- After sending three regular invoices, send this one. It is an indication that you are really serious about your rights and you are placing the responsibility squarely where it belongs: on the recalcitrant client. Sadly, all clients are not good, and decent people and well-meaning advisors can find themselves bilked. Your job is to be professional and direct. If the client means to pay — but is merely disorganized and slothful as can often happen — this letter should push him into action.
- If this letter doesn't work (and it should be followed up within 10 business days with a telephone call), then turn the matter over for collection and possible legal action. It's a nuisance but it's a necessary part of doing business. Note: Don't be surprised when clients, having received this letter, return a letter of outraged innocence (often with their check) claiming they didn't know of the matter, had always intended to pay, never got your invoice, &c. Don't let this spurious air of aggrievedness bother you. There comes a point, after all, when you need to shuck off such people and get on with things. Worrying about what they think of you is pointless.

Sample "Dog Ate My Homework" Collection Letter

Dear Delinquent Client/Customer,

You and I have got a problem.

You owe me (amount) for (service provided).

Despite many attempts to bring this matter to your attention, you have not yet paid this bill. I am now on the verge, therefore, of turning your account over for collection, a step which will lead to legal action.

Isn't this foolish?

The bill you owe is a modest one. I delivered the materials (did the consulting work) for you in good faith, and I'm sure you meant to pay my invoice. Now our entire relationship is threatened by, what? Carelessness? Sloth? This is probably just another example of the "Dog Ate My Homework" Syndrome at work.

If you don't clear this up, however, I'll be forced to take action. You won't be able to benefit from problem solving information which you already know is helpful. And we'll both be the losers.

Don't let this happen. Please take a moment — right this minute! — and send me a check and conclude this business which has dragged on for months. It's in our mutual interest and will keep our relationship healthy.

Sadly, if you don't do this, I'll be forced to conclude you are one of those people who mean to take advantage of honest business people like me, and I'll take whatever action I need to ensure that you can't do that with impunity.

It's up to you.

Sincerely,

Aggrieved Advisor

ABOUT THE AUTHOR... DR. JEFFREY LANT

Unlike virtually all other authors, you can reach Dr. Jeffrey Lant directly... right this minute. His phone number — (617) 547-6372 — now runs in nearly 150 publications in this country and abroad as part of his Sure-Fire Business Success Column. Over 1.5 million people monthly get access to Jeffrey this way.

Another 100,000 hear from Jeffrey every 90 days through his Sales & Marketing SuccessDek, a card-deck with prices only 1/4 to 1/3 as much as his competitors!

Another million a year get his Sure-Fire Business Success Catalog, a quarterly publication featuring the best in business "get ahead " information. To get your free subscription, just call or write for it.

On top of this, Jeffrey offers dozens of business programs yearly throughout North America. An animated and often electrifying platform speaker, Jeffrey has become well-known for offering some of the most practical and timely business development programs around. A large number of these programs come through referrals, not least because Jeffrey provides those making the referrals with 10% of the money he makes from his speaker fee and product sales. By all means, call and request the details!

In addition, Jeffrey is a practicing marketing consultant, working with for-profit organizations to sell more of their products and services faster and with not-for-profit organizations to help them raise the capital, project, and operating funds they need. When you need assistance in these areas, call Jeffrey! He can work with you in person or by telephone.

Jeffrey holds a B.A. *summa cum laude* from the University of California, Santa Barbara, a CAGS in Higher Education Administration from Northeastern University, Boston, and M.A. and Ph.D. degrees from Harvard. Author of 10 books and hundreds of articles, he has never had a business course in his entire life and doesn't regret the omission. You'll find him in a paper-strewn home-office hard by Harvard Square in Cambridge where he works without assistance. You can reach him at 50 Follen St., Suite 507, Cambridge, MA 02138 or by calling (617) 547-6372. Yes, he answers his own phone, but if you say "Jeff" when you call, he'll know you are a damnéd flatworm!

Special Edition for

HOW TO MAKE *AT LEAST* $100,000 EVERY YEAR AS A SUCCESSFUL CONSULTANT IN YOUR OWN FIELD

*Hey, consultants. Here are Jeffrey's two must-use money-making resources that ensure your practice makes **at least** $100,000 every year. Both are just out, newly revised and packed with details to help you make more money faster.*

Item #B1 Revised 3rd Edition. Just published!

THE CONSULTANT'S KIT: ESTABLISHING AND OPERATING YOUR SUCCESSFUL CONSULTING BUSINESS

Thinking about consulting or new to the business? Then join the over 26,000 people worldwide who have launched profitable consulting businesses in hundreds of fields with this crucial resource.

With the *only* book on consulting recommended by the U.S. Small Business Administration, you get the help you need to:

- define your specialty to make the most money
- develop a contact network and get business fast
- market and promote your expertise
- upgrade a lead into a contract
- develop contracts (yes, you get the exact language you need!)
- set up shop
- incorporate
- handle bookkeeping and accounting

And much, much more. 203 pages. Packed with ready-to-use forms, contracts, letters and marketing documents to get your practice off to a fast, profitable stop.

Recommended by *What Color Is Your Parachute* (the best-selling career guide of all times), THE CONSULTANT'S KIT gives you exactly what you need to turn your expertise and problem-solving skills into money — fast! $38.50 postpaid

Item #B4

HOW TO MAKE *AT LEAST* $100,000 EVERY YEAR AS A SUCCESSFUL CONSULTANT IN YOUR OWN FIELD: THE COMPLETE GUIDE TO SUCCEEDING IN THE ADVICE BUSINESS

Jeffrey Lant's
SURE-FIRE BUSINESS SUCCESS CATALOG

Helping your organization since 1979

INSIDE...
details on how can raise major gifts for your nonprofit organization with the just-published **THE COMPLETE GUIDE TO PLANNED GIVING: EVERYTHING YOU NEED TO KNOW TO COMPETE SUCCESSFULLY FOR MAJOR GIFTS**

(see page 302)

and the brand new edition of Jeffrey's classic **THE UNABASHED SELF-PROMOTER'S GUIDE: WHAT EVERY MAN, WOMAN, CHILD AND ORGANIZATION IN AMERICA NEEDS TO KNOW ABOUT GETTING AHEAD BY EXPLOITING THE MEDIA**

(see page 303)

Here's the new Second Edition of Jeffrey's companion volume to THE CONSULTANT'S KIT. This is the book for people who won't be satisfied piddling along in consulting but want to learn how to make big money now — and grab at least $100,000 every year from their technical skills.

You find out how to:
- raise your fees higher than your competitors... and still seem like a bargain;
- get the big retainer contracts that get you income every month, whether you're working for the client or not;
- develop a national or even international consulting business — in person & by phone;
- get the best results for the client... so you can leverage them and get more clients in the same field;
- develop the "passive income" sources that enable you to make money every day whether you're working or not... we're talking about books, booklets, special reports, cassettes, and more.

You'll get the low-down on how to use your computer for maximum efficiency (and where to get top hard-ware and soft-ware for rock-bottom prices); how to get detailed problem-solving information fast. There's even ready-to-use information on time management, stress reduction, and traveling smart.

If you're not making at least $100,000 every year consistently, get this resource (previously titled *Tricks of the Trade*). Like everything else in this catalog, if you don't like it, return it, no questions asked. And if you're really broke, get it from your local library. But make sure you start using these tested techniques to make your practice just as profitable as it can be! 315 pages. $39.50 postpaid.

#C8

Get a deal on THE CONSULTANT'S KIT and HOW TO MAKE AT LEAST $100,000 EVERY YEAR AS A SUCCESSFUL CONSULTANT IN YOUR OWN FIELD

Don't wonder how to make money as a consultant. It's all here. Just $68. Save $10!

Special free premiums if you order by April 1, 1993 (See page 309)

#B5
MONEY MAKING MARKETING: FINDING THE PEOPLE WHO NEED WHAT YOU'RE SELLING AND MAKING SURE THEY BUY IT

The new Revised 2nd Edition of Jeffrey Lant's well known book offers relentless detail on how to sell MORE OF YOUR PRODUCT/SERVICE. Jeffrey's become one of America's most well-known marketers by showing tens of thousands of people just like you what to do to make more money now.

In 11 info-packed chapters you find out how to:

- handle your market research — even when you hate market research;
- connect with your prospects in the ways that get them to buy — now;
- find out how to produce marketing communications that generate ACTION and SALES. We're talking about yoru brochures, flyers, cover letters, proposals — anything you're using to get people to MOVE!
- master the intricacies of headline writing, body copy, testimonials, postscripts and more;
- get all the free publicity you want;
- create classifed & space ads that get maximum response;
- handle telephone sales to get appointments and make more sales;
- master the profit-making ins and outs of co-op advertising, direct response cards deck, premium advertising, trade shows & exhibits;
- make money with mail — despite the new, prohibitive postal rates.

And much, much more.

A good product/service and superior marketing skills will make you a millionaire. If you've got the former, let Jeffrey Lant give you the latter — and make you rich. 286 pages. Just $39.50

> *"I'm currently reading MONEY MAKING MARKETING and I've found it more valuable than my entire college education... and I was a marketing major!"*
> Larry Genkin, Rockville, MD

#T2
MONEY MAKING MARKETING AUDIO CASSETTE PROGRAM. It's all here — 18 hours of fast-moving, profit-making information. Now, sit in your car or relax at home, and let Jeffrey share his money-making marketing secrets with you. This is the complete book on tape... perfect for the "scrap" time you want to put to good use. These tapes are packed with information and impart, as only an enthusiastic human voice can do, just, the right note of "up and at 'em" that we all need to get started. Just $125

#C2
MONEY MAKING MARKETING AUDIO CASSETTE AND BOOK SPECIAL OFFER. Now get both the 285-page MONEY MAKING MARKETING book and 18 hours of audio cassettes for the very special price of just $144.95. You save over $20... and get just what you need to implement the profit-making marketing program you've been looking for.

> *"Thanks for MONEY MAKING MARKETING... As always, you've set the standards by which all other 'how-to' books will be judged. Unfortunately, none I've read even come close to your standards."*
> Allan McAdams, Mattawan, MI

#B2
THE UNABASHED SELF-PROMOTER'S GUIDE: WHAT EVERY MAN, WOMAN, CHILD AND ORGANIZATION IN AMERICA NEEDS TO KNOW ABOUT GETTING AHEAD BY EXPLOITING THE MEDIA. New Revised 2nd Edition. Just out!!!
Don't *buy* all your marketing... get free time on radio and television and free space in newspapers, magazines and newsletters... with Jeffrey's definitive guide on how to get the media to promote your product/service for FREE! It's all here... all updated in this revised 2nd Edition. You find out how to:
- craft the right Quintessential American Success Image... the image that'll get you maximum free time and space;

- pitch what you've got to radio and television stations... and editors and columnists, so they'll want to feature you;
- project the right details about your product/service so your listeners and readers will want to buy what you've got;
- deal with loquacious interviewers... hostile interviewers... stupid and uninformed interviewers... and still get the promotional advantages you want;
- turn every aspect of your life into a hook for free media attention. Your spouse... your children... your pets... they can all get you more ink and time.
- get your picture in the papers... get a day in your honor and turn it into a media event...

It's all here in the ultimate guide to getting free time and space. There's even a listing of tens of thousands of media sources you can use right this minute. There's never been such a complete listing of so many print & electronic media sources available to you — right now!

Whether you're promoting books or drain pipes, here's just what you need. Learn the secrets of a man who's been given millions of dollars worth of free time and space by the media. Thousands of people already swear by these techniques. And now everything's newly updated for the 'nineties.

365 pages $39.50 (your book will be shipped in December).

#B3
MONEY TALKS: THE COMPLETE GUIDE TO CREATING A PROFITABLE WORKSHOP OR SEMINAR IN ANY FIELD. Brand new edition!!!
Just out!!! If you want to make money with talk programs of any kind, find out how to use these programs to get clients and publicity, then you need the new Second Revised Edition of this well-known book. It's got everything you need to start making money — really big money — on the talk circuit with workshops, lectures, seminars — every kind of talk program. Find out how to get sponsors — or sponsor programs yourself; make money from "back of the room" sales, even when you don't have a product. And when you do. The Most Complete Book Ever Written On This Subject. Yes, you can

follow these guidelines to make up to $25,000 or even $30,000 a day! 308 pages. $35

#B7

HOW TO MAKE A WHOLE LOT MORE THAN $1,000,000 WRITING, COMMISSIONING, PUBLISHING AND SELLING "HOW-TO" INFORMATION. People just love this book... and no wonder. It's the most complete ever written on how to make money from "how-to" information with profit-making books, booklets, audio cassettes & special reports. It's relentlessly detailed and tells you how to:

- create the information products people want to buy;
- produce the kinds of products you'll make money from for years;
- produce your products fast and accurately;
- make tens of thousands of extra dollars from end-of-product catalogs;
- save money — and avoid problems — by following Jeffrey's product production guidelines;
- turn your personal computer into the most effective customer service center ever imagined;
- get other people to produce products for you so you can make your million-dollar+ fortune faster;
- get all the free publicity you want... so you can reach your buyers on other people's money;
- master the essentials of direct response marketing so you bring your message to just the right people and get them to buy your products NOW;
- make big money through talk programs, bookstores, libraries, overseas rights, exhibits... and

more. Yes, you learn how to make thousands of dollars a day regularly! Dozens of alternatives fully presented so you can start making money immediately. 552 pages. $39.50

#C4

Combined offer for the future information millionaire...

Four fast-paced, densely detailed books by Jeffrey give you a fast start towards becoming a million dollar+ producer & seller of books, booklets, audio cassettes and Special Reports. Whatever your field! Get **HOW TO MAKE A WHOLE LOT MORE THAN $1,000,000 WRITING, COMMISSIONING, PUBLISHING AND SELLING "HOW-TO" INFORMATION; CASH COPY; THE UNABASHED SELF-PROMOTER'S GUIDE** and **MONEY TALKS.** Just $115. You save $23.45!

#C6

Combined offer for the people who want to sell more of their products and services faster...

Now benefit from Jeffrey's step-by-step marketing advice and learn how to sell more of your products and services for the least possible cost. Get a deal on **THE UNABASHED SELF-PROMOTER'S GUIDE, MONEY MAKING MARKETING** and **CASH COPY.** $80 for all three. You save $23.45.

#C7

... when you want to master all the master's profit-making techniques.

Get all seven books in Jeffrey's "Get Ahead" Series, including **CASH COPY, THE CONSULTANT'S KIT, THE UNABASHED SELF-PROMOTER'S GUIDE, MONEY TALKS, HOW TO MAKE AT LEAST $100,000 EVERY YEAR AS A SUCCESSFUL CONSULTANT IN YOUR OWN FIELD, MONEY MAKING MARKETING** and **HOW TO MAKE A WHOLE LOT MORE THAN $1,000,000 WRITING, COMMISSIONING, PUBLISHING AND SELLING "HOW-TO" INFORMATION.** Well over 2,000 pages of detailed step-by-step guidelines on achieving success by creating and selling products and services. No other specialist — anywhere — has ever written such complete instructions on what it takes to make money — lots of money. We'll be flabbergasted if you don't make back the cost of this package many hundreds of time. Get all seven for just $200. Save $46.95! You automatically qualify for a free 60-minute cassette with this order!!!

60 Money-Making Minutes With Jeffrey (on tape)

#T3

HOW TO GET FREE TIME ON RADIO AND T.V. AND USE IT TO GET YOUR PROSPECTS TO BUY WHAT YOU'RE SELLING. Listen as Jeffrey gives you the secrets of getting valuable free time on radio and television so you can sell your products and services without spending any of your money. Getting on *just one* program could return your investment dozens of times! $16

#T4

HOW TO CREATE MARKETING DOCUMENTS THAT GET YOUR PROSPECTS TO BUY WHAT YOU'RE SELLING ... NOW! Since you spend thousands of dollars on your marketing documents, don't you think you should know what will get people to respond to them faster ... to buy what you're selling **NOW**? Here's just what you need to know. $16

#T5
ESSENTIALS OF MONEY MAKING MARKETING: WHAT YOU'VE REALLY GOT TO DO TO SELL YOUR PRODUCTS AND SERVICES, EVERY DAY! Jeffrey shares his secrets of successful marketing, what you've got to do, when and how you've got to do it to sell your products and services. $16

#C3
ALL THREE OF JEFFREY'S 60 MINUTE AUDIO CASSETTES (T3, T4, T5). Just $38. You save $10!

> If there's a ** next to your name on the mailing panel, you're about to be zapped off my mailing list. Buy something. It's for your own good.

Remembering Names and Faces

#T6
New!

ON YOUR WAY TO REMEMBERING NAMES & FACES. There are many things you've got to know to make more sales. But one of the most important is remembering names and faces. Your prospects want to be remembered... and they'll be impressed not only that you know them... but that you remember stuff about them, too. I know. People are often astonished when they call that I remember just their voice... much less (sometimes quite trivial) things about them. My sales benefit from my ability to remember them and come up with just the right information. So will yours. That's why you need this 6 cassette (3 hour) album packed with Bob Burg's easy-to-follow six-step method. You get just the details you

need to master personal information about the people you meet... and use it to build the relationships that make you money. Just $64.95. Now quick! What's the name of the last person you met? Forgot? Get Burg!

Good Fences Make Good Neighbors

New!

#B103
THE COMPLETE BOOK OF SMALL BUSINESS LEGAL FORMS. Attorney Daniel Sitarz hits the mark again with this new 245-page book. Provides over 125 detailed forms valid in all 50 states & Washington, D.C. including contracts, collection documents, employment contracts, leases, powers of attorney, financing agreements, promissory notes, purchase & sale agreements, real estate forms, receipts, releases & many more. This is billed as having "all the legal forms and documents you will need to successfully operate your small business". I believe it! $20.95

Special Reports

We've already sold tens of thousands of these quick and dirty profit-making reports (#R1 – #R72). They're densely written five-page, single-spaced computer print-outs personalized with your name so you know you're supposed to follow the good-for-you directions. Don't expect fancy packaging. Just solid, up-to-date information you can use right now. Each report is packed with use-it-now details so you can achieve what the title promises. No one else in the country offers this kind of instantly available, eminently practical information in this form or gets them to you this fast. Stock up on 'em. Just 5 bucks each, 3 for $12.

#R1
THE SECRET TO BECOMING A MILLIONAIRE SELLING "HOW-TO" INFORMATION: 10 STEPS FOR CREATING, COMMISSIONING, PUBLISHING AND SELLING PROBLEM-SOLVING BOOKS, BOOKLETS, SPECIAL REPORTS AND AUDIO CASSETTES. In honor of his new book **HOW TO MAKE A WHOLE LOT MORE THAN $1,000,000 WRITING, COMMIS-**

SIONING, PUBLISHING AND SELLING "HOW-TO" INFORMATION, Jeffrey lays down the rules for profitably selling problem-solving information. $5

#R2
SIX STEPS TO MORE SUCCESSFUL NEWSLETTERS. If you're putting any money into producing either a free or subscription newsletter... or even thinking about it... don't do anything until you get Roger Parker's steps for designing the product so it accomplishes your objectives. Roger's one smart cookie, and he knows what it takes to get people to pay attention to your newsletter. Here he shares this vital information with you. $5

#R3
WHICH 2% WILL YOUR AUDIENCE SIT STILL FOR? In honor of the publication of her new book, Jeffrey interviews author Marian Woodall on how to find the focus that is appropriate for each audience. Too many speakers try to cram everything they know into their talk... and end up alienating their audience. Not you. Here you learn exactly what you've got to do to give the right talk to the people you're speaking to. $5

#R4
HOW TO ELIMINATE JOB STRESS AND INCREASE PROFITS AND PRODUCTIVITY THROUGH STRESS MANAGEMENT. Jeffrey interviews author Dr. Andrew Goliszek about what you can do to cut stress in the office. Stress doesn't just debilitate and even kill you... it cuts your profits! Here's what you can do to help yourself and break your stress habit. $5

> *"CASH COPY has given me a totally effective way of marketing. Yes, I am a believer in CASH COPY. It has doubled our company sales!"*
> Danish Kazi, Covina, CA

#R5

MEGATRAITS: 12 TRAITS OF SUCCESSFUL PEOPLE. Jeffrey interviews Doris Lee McCoy, author of a new book based on interviews with several hundred successful people, and identifies the crucial traits, the "megatraits", they possess in common that helped get them where they are. $5

#R6

HOW TO MAKE YOUR PR MAKE MONEY. For most businesses, public relations is a useless activity that is not tied to the profit picture. Now Jeffrey tells you how to turn your expensive public relations into a money-making activity that will sell your products and services faster. $5

#R8

OVERWORKED ENTREPRE-NEURS' GUIDE TO LUXURIOUS CRUISE DISCOUNTS. Jeffrey interviews Captain Bill Miller, author of the superb new book Insider's Guide To Cruise Discounts, and provides you with specific information on how you can take some of the world's best and most luxurious cruises for ridiculously low rates. $5

#R9

WHAT EVERY INVENTOR ABSO-LUTELY MUST DO BEFORE CONTACTING ANY MANUFAC-TURER. Jeffrey interviews consultant Arnold Winkelman, author of the new book The Inventor's Guide To Market-ing, about precisely what you've got to do before you show any manufacturer your creation so that your rights are fully protected. Must reading if you're an inventor! $5

#R10

EIGHT SELF-DEFEATING BE-HAVIORS PREVENTING YOU FROM BECOMING THE MILLION-AIRE YOU *SAY* YOU WANT TO BE... AND WHAT TO DO ABOUT THEM! Here Jeffrey lays out eight significant behaviors making it difficult, if not impossible, for people to become millionaires and tells them just what to do to overcome them. If you keep talking about wanting to be a millionaire but just can't seem to get started... or keep failing along the way... these behaviors are probably bedevilling you. Learn what they are... and how to get rid of them. $5

#R11

EVERYTHING YOU NEED TO KNOW TO PREPARE YOUR OWN WILL — WITHOUT THE EXPENSE OF A LAWYER! Eight out of ten people in America die without a will, throwing their accumulated posses-sions and savings into the hands of the court system which then allocates what's available. To stop this idiocy, Jeffrey interviews Attorney Daniel Sitarz, author of the new book Prepare Your Own Will And Testament — Without A Lawyer. Here's exactly what you need to do to prepare your own legal will without a lawyer, securing your estate and saving the lawyer's fees. $5

#R12

WHY MOST CONSULTANTS CAN NEVER MAKE AT LEAST $100,000 A YEAR... AND WHAT TO DO SO YOU WILL. Jeffrey shows you why most consultants fail to make at least $100,000 a year... and provides specific steps to follow so you will. $5

> *"Jeffrey, I'm finding your information very useful and very profit-able. Don't slow down. Keep talking, and writ-ing. There's a lot of information out there that needs to be gath-ered and distributed. And you're doing an excellent job of both."*
> Steve Manning,
> Pickering, Ontario, Canada

#R13

HOW TO GET FREE AND LOW-COST SOFTWARE FOR YOUR IBM AND IBM-COMPATIBLE COMPUTER. Jeffrey interviews John Gliedman, author of the new book Tips And Techniques for Using Low-Cost And Public Domain Software, on how to get your hands on some of the stupendous amount of free and low-

cost software currently available for IBM and IBM-compatible personal computers. Gliedman provides the names, addresses and phone numbers of just where to go to save big money on your software and techniques on how to use it effectively. $5

#R14

HOW TO CREATE CLASSIFIED AND SMALL SPACE ADS THAT GET YOUR PROSPECTS TO RESPOND... AND WHAT TO DO WHEN THEY DO! Jeffrey gives you the low-down on how to create classi-fied and small space ads that get people to respond... and how to create an effective, profit-making program so you can turn your new prospects into buyers... fast! $5

#R15

SETTING AND GETTING YOUR FEE. Jeffrey interviews author Kate Kelly upon the occasion of a new edition being published of her well-known book How To Set Your Fees And Get Them. People selling a service either run the risk of pricing them-selves too low (and working for too little) or too high... and losing the business. Kate tells you just what you need to do so you price your services just right... for fast sale and maximum return. $5

#R16

HOW TO MAKE MONEY BUYING PRE-FORECLOSURE PROPER-TIES BEFORE THEY HIT THE COURTHOUSE STEPS. Jeffrey interviews property investment advisor Tom Lucier, author of the new book How To Make Money Buying Pre-Foreclosure Properties Before They Hit The Courthouse Steps, on just what it takes to make big money in pre-foreclosure properties. New workshops have sprung up recently charging as much as $5000 for a week-end providing this kind of advice. Why pay 5G's when specialist Tom Lucier provides the detailed steps right here? $5

#R17

HOW TO DEVELOP AND USE A CLIENT-CENTERED QUESTION-NAIRE THAT GETS YOUR PROSPECTS TO TELL YOU WHAT THEY WANT... SO YOU CAN SELL IT TO THEM. In this report, Jeffrey helps people who hate making cold calls... and can't figure out how to get their prospects to tell them what they want. If you can solve this problem, you can sell any product or service. Here are the guidelines you need to create this unique client-centered prospecting questionnaire... and how to use it. When you do, your prospects start telling you precisely what they want... all you have to do is give it to them. $5

#R18

HOW TO DO "HOW-TO" (BOOK-LETS AND BOOKS, THAT IS). Here Jeffrey tells you exactly how to produce a how-to booklet or book that really tells your readers how to do what your title promises. Most how-to products are dismal failures, because they don't provide the details your readers need to achieve what they want. Don't let this happen to you. Learn how to create a truly useful how-to. $5

#R19

HOW TO MAKE OVER $100,000 *EVERY* YEAR WITH YOUR OWN CATALOG SELLING PROBLEM-SOLVING INFORMATION PROD-UCTS. Most people in mail order try to make a big kill from a single problem-solving information product... or just a few. Here Jeffrey shows you why that's futile... and how to go about establishing a client-centered catalog selling how-to information products that will make you at least $100,000 every year... and maybe a whole lot more. $5

#R20

HOW TO USE JOB ADS TO LAND THE JOB YOU *REALLY* WANT. If you've ever tried to get a job using classified job ads you know how time consuming and frustrating it is. Here Jeffrey interviews jobs-finding special-ist Kenton Elderkin, author of the new book How To Get Interviews From Job Ads: Where To Look, What To Select, Who To Write, What To Say, When To Follow-Up, How To Save Time. With these techniques answering job ads can lead to the interviews you need... and the good job you want. $5

#R21

YOUR WORST FEARS REALIZED, OR WHAT TO DO WHEN THE CORPORATION OR FOUNDA-TION DECLINES YOUR PRO-POSAL. The competition for corporate and foundation dollars for non-profit organizations has never been greater... and will get worse. You can count on getting turned down, often. What you do next determines whether your organization will ever get the money it needs from these sources. Here are Jeffrey's guidelines for turning a no into a yes, for doing what it takes to build a lucrative relationship with a funding source that has just turned you down. Since this will happen to you (if it isn't happening already), prepare for it now. $5

#R22

IT ISN'T JUST SAYING THE RIGHT THING THAT MAKES A SUCCESSFUL PRESENTATION... OR WHAT YOU'VE REALLY GOT TO DO TO CONNECT WITH YOUR AUDIENCE AND PERSUADE THEM TO LISTEN TO YOU. This isn't a report about speech content... it's a report about how to deal with your audience so they like you and want to listen to what you have to say. Verbal presentations aren't just about imparting information; they're about persuading people to do things. Here's what you've got to do to achieve this crucial objective. $5

#R23

HOW TO CREATE A BROCHURE AND COVER LETTER YOUR PROSPECTS WILL RESPOND TO... NOW! In honor of the new second printing of his book CASH COPY: HOW TO OFFER YOUR PRODUCTS AND SERVICES SO YOUR PROSPECTS BUY THEM... NOW!, Jeffrey tells you how to solve one of the most basic marketing problems of any business: what it takes to create a brochure and cover letter that gets people to respond, instead of being tossed. $5

#R24

HOW TO RAISE MONEY FOR YOUR NON-PROFIT ORGANIZA-TION WITH AN ANNUAL PHON-A-THON. Jeffrey tells you what you've got to do to use telemarketing to raise money for your non-profit organiza-tion... when you've got to work with community volunteers and can't afford professional help. $5

#R25

HOW TO BRING ORDER TO DESK CHAOS, OR ESSENTIALS OF ORGANIZING YOURSELF. Jeffrey talks to organizational specialist Kate Kelly, author (along with Ronni Eisenberg) of the best-selling book ORGANIZE YOURSELF!, about what you've got to do to control clutter and get all those papers in your business life under control. $5

#R26

HOW TO AVOID DESKTOP DISAPPOINTMENT, OR WHAT YOU'VE *REALLY* GOT TO KNOW TO MAKE DESKTOP PUBLISH-ING WORK FOR YOU. Jeffrey interviews desktop design specialist Roger Parker, author of Looking Good In Print, on what to do to avoid the

GET YOURSELF A CHECK FOR UP TO $3,000 FOR THE LEAST IMAGINABLE WORK

How? Just recommend Dr. Jeffrey Lant as a speaker to any college, professional association, trade group, or corporate sales meeting. If your recommendation works, you'll get 10% of Jeffrey's speaker fee and product sales the day of the program. This adds up fast.

Right now, Jeffrey's dishing out big checks to people all over America who have had the brains to pick up the phone or write a letter and say, "Hire this man!" When the people you talk to find out what he talks about, they want him. Here are just some of his popular topics:

- "How to sell another $1,000,000 of your product/service."

- "How to produce marketing communications that get your prospects to respond... and your customers to buy again NOW"

- "How to build the million dollar plus home-based business."

- "How to make at least $100,000 a year from your own catalog & mail order business."

- "How to raise the capital, project and operating money you need for your non-profit organization."

Call the people you know or the organizations in your area... find out if they book speakers. Inquire about their budget. Send in your recommendation. And then tell Jeffrey and/or send him a copy of your letter. He'll follow up. When he gets paid, you get paid.

Wonder why Jeffrey is one of America's most booked speakers? It's because of smart people like you who know his books, like his message, and use their brains to network him into lucrative assignments — and get their cut of the profits. For further details, call (617) 547-6372 or just get started! And remember, you get your commission *every* time one of your recommendations is accepted. Get started. Your checks are waiting!

Cutting Your Property Taxes

New! #B93
DIGGING FOR GOLD IN YOUR OWN BACK YARD: THE COMPLETE HOMEOWNERS GUIDE TO LOWERING YOUR REAL ESTATE TAXES. Gary Whalen's been a tax-reduction consultant to commercial & industrial property owners for years now and he's saved them a pretty amazing amount of money. Now he's laid out his system on how all us residential home-owners can save on our property taxes. In 264 pages, you get simple, easy-to-follow guidelines on how to tell if your assessment should be challenged, how to deal with the assessor's office, 5 different strategies to reduce your assessment (with special directions for condo owners), and how to appeal your assessment and win. Gary offers state-by-state summaries and your local exemption requirements. This book is a steal at just $23.45

SPECIAL NOTE FOR COMMERCIAL AND INDUSTRIAL PROPERTY OWNERS. Let Gary Whalen see about saving you thousands or even tens of thousands of dollars in unnecessary property tax payments. Call him at (708) 985-4550. He'll give you a free, no-obligation consultation. Depending on how much you're overpaying, this should be the most single most profitable call of your life!

Successful Inventing

New! #B86
HOW TO BE A SUCCESSFUL INVENTOR. This new 236-page resource by Gordon Griffin tells you how to "turn your ideas into profit." It's all here: filing for a patent or infringement, licensing agreements and patents; invention pricing and marketing; manufacturing , patent applications and more. Listen, kiddo: you're not going to get rich working for someone else. You're going to have to develop a system for producing the big bucks. This resource tells you one way of doing that. $24.95

Making Money At Home

#B43
If your're running a home-based business and you don't have Barbara Brabec's superb book **HOME MADE MONEY**, shame on you. Barb's the national expert on the topic and was recently featured 5 days running on ABC dishing out info about how to profit from home. Her book's the best there is and covers everything about home-based businesses, including zoning, licensing, marketing, the good businesses to be in and the ones to avoid. What's more there are literally hundreds of specific follow-up sources in this book which connect you to anyone who's anyone in the home-based business world—including me! You'll have to leae home without it! $21.95

Successful Time Management

New! #B89
SUCCESSFUL TIME MANAGEMENT. How are you going to do everything that needs to be done? You're going to manage your time better and specialist Jack Ferner's going to help you. In 287 pages he provides guidelines for analyzing existing time problems; learning how to focus on what's really important to you, developing the daily planning habit, improving methods for dealing

with time-robbers like interruptions, procrastinations & paperwork. Believe me, you can't get rich without better time management and when you get rich if you can't manage your time better (so you have some available for what you want to do), what's the point? Don't put this off. $19.95

Getting More Credit, Paying The Lowest Interest Rates, Cleaning Up Your Credit

New! #B100

DIRECTORY OF MASTERCARD AND VISA CREDIT CARD SOURCES. I don't know about you, but I HATE paying high interest charges on credit card purchases. That's why I love this new 2nd Edition of the one resource you must have if you have — or want — credit cards. More complete than ever, you get 750 pages (that's right!) of up-to-date information on all MasterCard & Visa credit card sources with their interest rates, membership and annual fees (if any), credit amounts, cash rebate information, toll free numbers, addresses, minimum income requirements (if any), what area (regional, national, etc) they serve — and more. If you're paying more than 9.9% APR (current lowest amount in the nation), you need this resource! And if you're looking to expand your lines of credit,

you'll find this staggering, unique guide a must. Just $54.50

New! #B102

ORGANIZED TO BE THE BEST! Subtitled "New Timesaving Ways to Simplify and Improve How You Work", this 434-page book has been selected by NINE major book clubs as a special pick. No wonder. It's awesomely detailed! Author Susan Silver takes on the gigantic task of organizing America — and you! And succeeds! Details about organizing your desk and its paper jungle; getting files up-to-date; organizing IBM personal computer & Macintosh files; work and project management shortcuts; special tips for collectors who "can't" throw anything away... and much, much more including tip after tip for organizing your work environment. People just love this book. If organization isn't your strong suit, get this crucial resource. $15.95

New! #B105

HOW TO REPAIR YOUR OWN CREDIT AND BUILD IT INTO A AAA-1 RATING (WITHOUT GETTING RIPPED OFF BY PHONEY CREDIT REPAIR SERVICES. Got a credit problem? Bad credit? Can't get credit? Then get Neil Brown's practical new resource about establishing the top credit rating, erasing bad information from your credit report (without

having to pay big fees to "credit repair" services), tips for using credit to your advantage, and getting more credit cards. There are lots of credit repair books on the market; this is the best value for the money. The book alone is worth its $41.95 price. But I've twisted Neil's arm for more benefits for you. So... when you order here Neil will also be sending you 7 FREE special money-making reports: "The Lazy Person's Secrets To Overnight Wealth"; "How To Start A Profitable Home-Based Business"; "The Easiest & Most Profitable Mail Order Business of Them All"; "How To Get Free & Nearly-Free Booklets, Reports and Other Helpful Publications About Saving & Making Money from the Government"; "Spare Time Money Making Opportunities that Can Pay Off Your Debts Fast"; "How To Make A Fortune With Government Auctions" plus another secret special report that'll help you make more money in your own business. All this for just $41.95! Truly unbelievable and *only* available here.

pitfalls of desktop publishing and use design to create compelling marketing communications. $5

#R28

HOW TO CREATE A MARKETING PLAN THAT SELLS YOUR SERVICE... WITHOUT COSTING YOU ALL YOUR MONEY. Most people selling a service are "winging it" with predictable results: their marketing is episodic, spasmodic... unproductive. Jeffrey tells you how to create a marketing plan that will sell a service for the least possible cost and greatest results. $5

#R29

TELESELLING: HOW TO GET THROUGH THE SCREEN THAT'S KEEPING YOU FROM YOUR PROSPECT. Jeffrey talks to Art Sobczak, editor of Telephone Selling Report, on what you've got to do to get through your prospect's screens... switchboard operators, secretaries... anybody who stands between you and your next sale. $5

#R30

HOW TO OPEN A TELEPHONE SALES CALL WITH EITHER A PROSPECT OR A CUSTOMER... SO YOU GET THE BUSINESS. Jeffrey again talks to Art Sobczak, editor of Telephone Selling Report, on what to say during those crucial opening moments with a telephone prospect... and how to build profitable relationships by phone with existing customers. $5

#R31

HOW TO CREATE A PROPOSAL THAT A CORPORATION OR FOUNDATION WILL FUND. Jeffrey tells you and your non-profit organization what it takes to create a

proposal that a corporate or foundation funding source will give money to support. $5

#R32

WHAT YOU HAVE TO DO TO SELL YOUR PRODUCTS AND SERVICES THROUGH A FREE CLIENT NEWSLETTER. Jeffrey tells you how to produce free client newsletters that get your prospects to buy your products and services. $5

#R33

HOW TO CREATE INEXPENSIVE, EFFECTIVE AUDIO CASSETTES TO GET MORE OF YOUR PROSPECTS TO RESPOND FASTER... AND MAKE EXTRA MONEY, TOO. Jeffrey tells you how to create inexpensive 60-minute audio cassettes in your home or office that you can use to induce more and faster sales... and sell profitably, too. $5

#R34

HOW TO PROFIT BY INVESTING IN USED AND BRUISED HOUSES. Jeffrey gets step-by-step advice from Florida author and investor Thomas Lucier on how to make money in real estate through affordable used and bruised houses, one of today's smart investments for people with a moderate amount to spend. $5

#R35

HOW TO USE WORKSHOPS AND OTHER TALK PROGRAMS TO GET CLIENTS. In honor of the publication of the new Second Edition of his well-known book MONEY TALKS: HOW TO CREATE A PROFITABLE WORKSHOP OR SEMINAR IN ANY FIELD, Jeffrey tells you how to use lectures and talk programs to get clients. $5

#R36

THINKING ON YOUR FEET, ANSWERING QUESTIONS WELL WHETHER YOU KNOW THE ANSWER — OR NOT. People who can't deal effectively with questions present a poor self-image and can harm a company. Here Jeffrey interviews Marian Woodall, author of a popular book on the subject, about how people can master the crucial "thinking on your feet" strategies. $5

#R38

WHY YOU NEED SPECIAL REPORTS: HOW TO WRITE THEM, USE THEM TO GET PEOPLE TO BUY WHAT YOU'RE SELLING NOW, TO PUBLICIZE YOUR BUSINESS, AND MAKE MONEY! The secret to successful marketing is making people take action NOW to get what you're selling. Jeffrey shows you how to create inexpensive but powerful Special Reports and how to turn them into compelling marketing tools that get your prospects to respond NOW, and that you can also sell profitably. $5

#R39

COPY FLAWS THAT DOOM YOUR EXPENSIVE MARKETING DOCUMENTS TO LINE BIRDCAGES IN SAINT LOUIS. Jeffrey tells you just what you need to know to write marketing copy that gets people to buy. Key rules of profit-making copy. $5

> *"I'm enjoying CASH COPY very much. By far the best book of its kind in existence today. I mean it."*
>
> Nick Hetcher, Marinette, WI

#R40

YOUR GRAND OPENING: HOW TO START YOUR MARKETING DOCUMENTS SO PEOPLE *BUY* WHAT YOU'RE SELLING. If your marketing documents don't draw people in immediately, you — and your next sale — are lost. Jeffrey tells you precisely what to do to begin documents so your prospects read what you have to say — and buy what you have to sell. $5

#R41

COMPUTER-ASSISTED MARKETING: HOW TO INCREASE YOUR PRODUCTIVITY AND MAKE EVERY PROSPECT AND CUSTOMER FEEL YOU'RE DELIVERING *EXACTLY* WHAT HE WANTS. People have computers but aren't using them effectively. Now learn to turn the computer into your best marketing tool. You'll read things here you've never seen before and increase your marketing productivity astonishingly. $5

#R42

MONEY MAKING MAIL, OR HOW TO AVOID THE TEN BIGGEST MAIL ORDER MISTAKES. Every day I get deluged with mail order offers that make me weep for the trees that have died. What rubbish! There are rules to succeed in mail order. Here's what you should avoid — and what you should do. $5

#R43

HOW TO CREATE AND USE OFFERS YOUR PROSPECTS FIND IRRESISTIBLE. The trick to marketing is to create and sell offers — not products and services. Here's

what you need to know about offers, how to create them and use them so that your prospects will buy. $5

#R44

KNOWING WHAT TO DO WHEN PEOPLE OWE YOU MONEY, OR HOW TO GET PAYMENT IN FULL. Don't give way to the rage and frustration of being owed money by deadbeats. Get what you're owed. Here's what you need to do in practical detail. $5

#R45

HOW AUTHORS AND THEIR PUBLISHERS MUST WORK TOGETHER TO SELL MORE BOOKS. Follow these precise steps to construct a profitable author-publisher partnership, so each of you makes money from the book. $5

#R46

YOUR IRA: WHY YOU *STILL* NEED IT, WHAT YOU NEED TO KNOW ABOUT INVESTING IT. If you've lost interest in the IRA, think again. Tax-free compounding of earning's no joke, and millions can still take their contribution off their taxes. Here's the low-down. (By the way, last year IRA contributions were substantially up. This report no doubt helped!) $5

#R47

TELESMARTS: EFFECTIVELY USING TELEMARKETING TO SELL YOUR PRODUCTS AND SERVICES. Most people are hideously ill-equipped to use the phone to sell anything. Here's the basics (and some advanced tips, too) on how you can turn the phone into a profitable business tool. Have I reached out and touched you? $5

#R48

HOW TO OVERCOME SALES OBJECTIONS, INCLUDING THE

BIGGEST ONE OF ALL: "YOUR PRICE IS TOO HIGH!" If you're in sales (and if you're reading this, you are), you've got to learn how to deal with objections. Here's what you need to know so that you can. $5

#R49

HOW TO STOP BEING THE LOWLY ORDER-TAKER, BECOME THE CONSUMMATE MARKETER, AND GET MORE SALES FROM NEW BUYERS. The dumb marketer simply sells a prospect what that prospect wants to buy. The expert marketer learns the prospect's problem and persuades him to take an upgraded solution. Here's how to do that. $5

#R50

TESTIMONIALS FOR YOUR PRODUCT OR SERVICE: WHY YOU NEED THEM, HOW TO GET THEM, HOW TO USE THEM. If you aren't using testimonials now, you are missing a prime marketing device. If you are, make sure you're doing it right! $5

#R51

UNDERSTANDING AND PROFITING FROM THE RULE OF SEVEN: CONNECTING WITH YOUR BUYERS AND CONNECTING WITH THEM AGAIN UNTIL THEY BUY WHAT YOU'RE SELLING. Most marketing gambits don't work. In part this is because you don't hit your prospects sufficiently often to interest them in what you're selling. Now learn how you can. The Rule of Seven is the prime rule of marketing. $5

#R52

MARKETING YOUR BOOK BEFORE IT'S PUBLISHED. Stupid authors and publishers wait to begin marketing and making money from their books until they are physically available. Don't you be one of them.

Follow the detailed guidelines in this report and make money long before your book is even printed. $5

#R53
WHAT TO DO WHEN YOUR PROSPECT SAYS NO. We all get turned down. Now what? Tears? Rage? No! Use Jeffrey's step-by-step guidelines to get the sale after all — or do what it takes to get the next one! $5

#R54
ESSENTIALS OF MONEY MAKING MARKETING. Successful marketing is the key to business success. Now learn precisely what you have to do to improve your marketing. Follow these steps; sell more. $5

#R55
WHY YOU NEED A BUSINESS PLAN, WHY YOU RESIST CREATING ONE. Makes a clear case for why you must have a business plan to succeed, how to overcome your resistance to creating one, and what should go in it. A must, particularly for new and struggling entrepreneurs. $5

#R56
HOW TO GET THE LOWEST CARD-DECK ADVERTISING PRICES AND MAKE THE MOST MONEY FROM CARD-DECK ADVERTISING. Card-decks can get you maximum response for the least price. Now in honor of Jeffrey's new Sales & Marketing SuccessDek, you can learn the secrets of how to get the lowest prices and biggest response. $5

#R57
TEN THINGS YOU CAN DO RIGHT NOW TO GET MORE MONEY FROM YOUR NEXT FUND RAISING LETTER. If you're running a non-profit organization and expect to raise money using fund-raising letters, read this report first. Jeffrey's been writing profit-making

fund-raising letters for non-profits for over a decade. Here's what he's learned to make you more money. $5

#R58
HOW TO GET THE MOST BENEFIT WHEN WORKING WITH CONSULTANTS: THE 10 BIGGEST MISTAKES YOU'RE NOT GOING TO MAKE. All too often organizations hiring consultants don't get their money's worth. This won't happen to you if you follow the guidelines in this sensible report. $5

#R59
WHAT YOU THINK MAY BE A COPY PROBLEM MAY REALLY BE A STRATEGIC MARKETING PROBLEM ... HERE'S WHAT YOU CAN DO TO SOLVE IT. All too often what people think is a copy problem is actually a strategic marketing problem. Your marketing strategy has got to be right before you can create the most effective copy. For just $5 you learn how to create the strategy that gets people to buy what you're selling. (Then you can use CASH COPY to create the copy itself!)

#R60
HOW TO HAVE AN EFFECTIVE MEETING, OR WHAT YOU'VE REALLY GOT TO DO TO STOP WASTING YOUR TIME AT NON-PRODUCTIVE BUSINESS GET-TOGETHERS. Before you waste another senseless minute in a pointless meeting (or, God forbid, chair such a meeting) get this report and learn how to structure meetings so you get what you want — the only reason for having a meeting in the first place. $5

#R61
HOW TO TURN YOUR (PREVIOUSLY UNREAD) ANNUAL REPORT INTO AN ACTION ORIENTED MARKETING DOCUMENT THAT GETS PEOPLE TO DO WHAT YOU WANT THEM TO DO! For most organizations — profit and not-for-profit — annual reports are a complete waste of time and money. Who reads them? But properly created annual reports can become powerful marketing documents that get you new business. Here's what you need to know about creating them. $5

#R62
HOW TO GET YOUR CLIENTS TO GET BUSINESS FOR YOU. There are tricks for getting your existing (and past) customers to get new business for you. Here they are. When you have a customer you get not only current income but future business ... if you use these techniques. $5

#R63
HOW TO SET UP AN INDEPENDENT AGENT REFERRAL SYSTEM AND GET HUNDREDS OF PEOPLE TO REFER YOU TO ORGANIZATIONS NEEDING PAID SPEAKERS. Talk programs remain a superb way to make money — often astonishingly large amounts of money. Problem is: booking agents don't want you until you're a celebrity and cold calling is an agony. The solution? Set up your own Independent Agent Referral System to generate a constant stream of program leads. Here Jeffrey — one of America's best-known speakers — explains just how to do it! $5

#R64
HOW YOU CAN MANAGE YOUR BUSINESS' CASH FLOW EFFECTIVELY. Prosperity in the 'nineties means getting your hands on money earlier and managing that money

more effectively. Here Jeffrey gets tips from Les Masonson, author of a new book intriguingly titled *Cash, Cash, Cash*, about the secrets of better cash management. Details about how to work with your bank you've never seen before. $5

#R66
HOW TO WRITE A BUSINESS PROPOSAL THAT GETS YOU THE BUSINESS. If you have to write proposals to get contracts, learn Jeffrey's secrets for creating proposals that get you the business — instead of wasting your time and money. $5

> *By the way, if your phone isn't ringing like mine and your mail box isn't daily stuffed with checks like mine... you'd do well to follow the advice in my books. I do and so do tens of thousands of other successful people.*

#R68 *New!*
MARKETING IN THE BAD TIMES: HOW TO SELL MORE OF YOUR PRODUCTS AND SERVICES EVEN IN A RECESSION! If you didn't read this in my syndicated column and are still in a part of the country (like I am) where the recession isn't over, here are detailed suggestions to keep selling your product/service — yes *more* of your product/service! — even when times are bad. $5

#R69 *New!*
WHAT YOU'VE GOT TO DO BEFORE YOU WRITE ANY MARKETING COMMUNICATION — FLYER, PROPOSAL, AD, COVER LETTER, ETC., OR DOING THE HOMEWORK THAT PRODUCES THE MARKETING COMMUNICATION THAT GETS YOUR PROSPECT TO BUY WHAT YOU'RE SELLING In honor of the publication of the new Revised Second Edition of his well-known book MONEY MAKING MARKETING: FINDING THE PEOPLE WHO NEED WHAT YOU'RE SELLING AND MAKING SURE

THEY BUY IT, Jeffrey tackles one of the most important marketing problems: showing how lack of client-centered preparation makes it impossible to produce marketing communications that get people to respond. Here are the steps you need to take so you'll regularly produce profit-making marketing documents. $5

#R70
FIVE CRUCIAL THINGS YOU NEED TO KNOW TO MAKE REAL MONEY IN YOUR HOME-BASED BUSINESS. Up to 22,000,000 Americans derive some or all of their income working from home. Yet the vast majority gross only about $15,000 yearly — peanuts! Here Jeffrey, who's run a home-based business for over 12 years and become a millionaire in the process, provides crucial information on how to create a business at home that will produce $100,000 a year — or more. $5

#R71 *New!*
HOW YOU CAN OVERCOME WRITER'S ANXIETY AND PRODUCE EFFECTIVE LETTERS, MEMOS, REPORTS, PROPOSALS, ETC. Virtually everyone in American business is called upon to write something for the job. Yet the vast majority of people hate to write — and do it badly. Here Jeffrey interviews New York writing coach Jim Evers, author of *The Hate To Write But Have To Writer's Guide*, to get specific suggestions on how you can overcome your writer's anxiety and produce effective business writing. $5

#R72 *New!*
HOW TO TALK SO MEN WILL LISTEN. Women regularly report that talking to men (bosses, colleagues, Significant Others) is like talking to a brick wall. They talk, but does anyone really *hear* them? Now Oregon specialist Marian Woodall tackles one of civilization's oldest problems and, as usual, offers detailed suggestions on what women can do to get their points across — and what men should do to hear women. A perfect report for women who want to communicate more effectively with men... and men who really care about women! $5

> *Ordering multiple products? If what you're ordering comes from different producers, it will not be delivered at the same time. So, if you've only received a partial order, don't worry. THE REST IS ON ITS WAY!*

Money-Making Resource For Non-Profit Organizations

#B8
DEVELOPMENT TODAY: A FUND RAISING GUIDE FOR NON-PROFIT ORGANIZATIONS. *Booklist*, the prestigious publication of the American Library Association, has again recommended that every U.S. library get the new Revised 4th Edition of this book — just like they did the last edition. Why? Because it has just the information you need to raise capital, project & operating money for your non-profit organization from individuals, corporations and foundations. This classic book is now used by thousands of non-profits to raise the money they need. It covers everything you need to know to raise money as quickly as possible and, like all Jeffrey's books, is packed with a Samples Section containing ready-to-use documents, letters, log forms, prospect background information, etc. Money tight? Take this write-up to your local library and tell them about the Booklist article... if your library doesn't have the book, they'll get it and you can be the first to check it out! 282 pages $29.95.

Make Money Selling My Products

#F1
Dealers: if you're already a JLA dealer selling my products request camera-ready art with current prices! Call (617) 547-6372 to get yours. Everybody else: if you're not yet a dealer and want to start selling my products, augment your line, get into mail order, develop your own catalog, etc. write #F1 on page 16, and I'll send your Free Dealer Information Kit.

Sell Your Service, Not Your Soul

#B70

CONTRACTING YOUR SERVICES. Attorney Robert Davidson's new 256 page book gives you the crucial information you need for selling your services to others: what/who is an independent contractor; should you become one; the right form for your business; where to get financial backing; the marketing & business plans you need; the right kinds of insurance and how to get them; how to find customers and sell your service; how to create winning proposals; how to find the right lawyer; the IRS versus you; contracts ... and much, much more. Davidson knows becoming an independent contractor isn't the money-making ticket for everyone and knows how you can succeed when you take the plunge. Just $31

#B31

One of the most perplexing problems business people have is how much to charge for their services. Wonder no more. Kate Kelly tells you **HOW TO SET YOUR FEES AND GET THEM**. Her guidebook is filled with information and examples of how to charge the right rates for your services. $21.50

Key Persuasion Resources

#B35

HOW TO WRITE AND GIVE A SPEECH. Joan Detz' book is the best short book I've ever seen on how to give effective speeches ... without falling apart. If you want to know what it really takes to give a good speech, read Detz. She knows. $12.

#B97 *New!*

CAN YOU SAY A FEW WORDS? I've been waiting for years for the sequel to Joan Detz' "How to Write & Give a Speech", a superb book on longer presentations. Here in 180 pages Joan tells you how to prepare and deliver shorter presentations including award presentations, dedications, eulogies & prayers, introductions, retirements and farewell, acceptance speeches, wedding, birthday & anniversary toasts and more. Really, don't put your foot in your mouth. Use Detz — again! $13.95

#B37

THINKING ON YOUR FEET: ANSWERING QUESTIONS WELL WHETHER YOU KNOW THE ANSWER OR NOT. This is exactly what you need if you know someone who can't 'think on their feet', can't answer questions appropriately, and is always embarrassing himself ... or your company. Or perhaps that's you! Either way, you need Marian Woodall's excellent little 100-page book. Stay poised and in control. And answer the question — the way you want it answered. Just $13.95.

Getting The Money You're Owed

#B46

You've got uncollected and uncollectible invoices sitting in your drawer right now. If you used the techniques in **PAYMENT IN FULL: A GUIDE TO SUCCESSFUL BILL COLLECTING**, some of them wouldn't be there. If you'd use it now, you can still collect on some of them. $28.95 is also a pretty fair price to pay to cut the anger you feel about the deadbeats who're ripping you off.

Crucial Desk-Top Publishing Resource

#B20

LOOKING GOOD IN PRINT: A GUIDE TO BASIC DESIGN FOR DESKTOP PUBLISHING. After you've mastered my book CASH COPY (so you've got the right content to attract buyers), you need Roger Parker's ultra-intelligent book on desktop publishing design. Use it to turn your spiffy copy into compelling newsletters, ads, brochures, manuals, letters ... and all the rest of your marketing materials. I love this book ... and your new buyers will be glad you used it! 221 pages $28

Getting Your Merchant MC/VISA Account

#B10 Just Updated!

STRATEGIES FOR GETTING CHARGE CARD MERCHANT STATUS AT YOUR BANK (EVEN IF YOU'RE A MAIL ORDER DEALER). This new 49-page booklet tells you how and where to get a Merchant MC/VISA account and how to handle your credit card sales. Particularly mail order merchants (who know just how difficult it is to get MC/VISA status these days) will want to get this very useful booklet. I referred one friend to it who had had incredible difficulty in getting such an account. By following the steps in this booklet, he had one in just five days. Cheap at $21.95.

Using The Phone To Sell More

#B12

SELLING ON THE PHONE: A SELF-TEACHING GUIDE. James Porterfield's book has always been a good seller for me, and it's no wonder. So many people in this supposed age of telemarketing savvy are downright primative on the phone. Porterfield's is the best beginner's book I've seen and will start you in the right direction to making more sales by phone faster. $20.95

#B45

Millions of people suffer from call reluctance. I got a vivid picture of just how bad this problem was when I ran an article about it and about this book's excellent suggestions on how to overcome it. My telephone rang for days. If you suffer from call reluctance and sometimes just cannot bring yourself to make that next important sales call, suffer no more. Get **EARNING WHAT YOU'RE WORTH:**

OVERCOMING SALES CALL
RELUCTANCE. $23.45

Getting The Money You Need For Your Small Business

#B80

MONEY SOURCES FOR SMALL BUSINESS. If you don't know author William Alarid's books you ought to. He subtitles his latest 222 page book "How you can find private, state, federal and corporate financing", and it's packed with the details you need to find the money you want. Among the many sources covered: loans for businesses in small towns, loans for teenagers, grants for inventions, funds for fishing, fixed rate loans for exports, money for pollution control, physical disaster loans, flood insurance, and much, much, much more. A goldmine. Just $22.95

Just The Facts, Ma'am

#B29

All of us are dependent on information, knowing where to find it and where to find it fast. That's why you need **FINDING FACTS FAST**, the best little book ever written on quick, economical information gathering. $7.45

Developing And Protecting Ideas And Products

#B40

FROM CONCEPT TO MARKET. Gary Lynn's just published book tells you how to protect your idea without submitting a patent, how to license a new idea, market your innovation, start your own company, raise money, build a prototype, write a business plan and price your product. Developing a product is one of the best ways to get really rich there is. Making a small investment in Lynn's extensive research tells you how to develop it right and launch it fast. 243 pages $23.95.

Save the Planet...Get Rich

#B83 *New!*

THE COMPLETE GUIDE TO SMALL BUSINESS OPPORTUNITIES FROM THE ENVIRONMENTAL REVOLUTION. Ecopreneuring is what it's called and in this first-of-its-kind resource by Steven Bennett you get 308 pages packed with business opportunities in recycling, green products, ecotainment, air & water quality, energy conservation, investment advice, safe foods and much more. Ecology not only makes good sense... it's increasingly big business. Here's how you'll profit from it. $22.95

Investment & Insurance Smarts

#B84 *New!*

TAX-DEFERRED INVESTING. Are you using your business to make yourself a fortune. I am. And it works. You don't have to be Bernard Baruch to make it work for you either when you can use "Pre-Tax Dollars for After-Tax Profit." In 232 pages, Michael Thomsett tells you how to profit from IRAs, Keighs, 401ks, trusts & annuities, real estate investments, stocks, bonds, mutual funds, and more. Look at your pension fund. If you're hovering around 40 and don't have at least 1/2 million in it, you're facing a tough old age. Here's the book that'll help you change things. $29.95

#B85 *New!*

INSURANCE SMART: HOW TO BUY THE RIGHT INSURANCE AT THE RIGHT PRICE. Jeff O'Donnell's new 236 page book covers EVERY type of insurance — including homeowners, car, health, business, life, farm & ranch, and medicare supplement. There isn't a single reader of this catalog who wouldn't be better off using what he says to get the best coverage at the lowest cost. Also explains forms & terminology, tells you how to file a claim, provides consumer protection information & more. $17.95

#B96 *New!*

THE NO-LOAD ADVANTAGE: HOW TO BUY MUTUAL FUNDS AND INSURANCE WITHOUT PAYING A COMMISSION. Millions of Americans now invest in mutual funds... the smart ones in no-load funds. Here's where my friend Chris Lowry, CFP and his new book come in. Chris helps you steer your investment dollars into the best no-load funds and away from the expensive load funds. You'll also find out how to save thousands of dollars in unnecessary investment costs and insurance premiums; learn to avoid many of the popular tax shelters and more. You'll profit from this book when you invest in disability income, term insurance, variable life, govt. bond funds, variable annuities, limited partnerships, growth stock funds, universal life and more. $27

#B104 *New!*

THE WEALTHY BARBER: EVERYONE'S COMMON-SENSE GUIDE TO BECOMING FINANCIALLY INDEPENDENT. David Chilton turned this beguiling 200-page book into Canada's best-selling business book thanks to techniques he learned in *The Unabashed Self-Promoter's Guide*. He told me so himself! But I think the book was destined for success anyway. Why? Because few people have any kind of financial plan; most people retire broke. And David's sensible book contains such worldly wisdom in such easy-to-digest fashion; anyone with dreams of retiring with ample means can get the message. I say: walk don't run to your phone and get this book if you 1) have too little money stashed away for your old age or 2) haven't started yet. The president of the International Assoc. of Financial Planners calls this the best book ever written on the subject. He's right! $20.95.

Order Form
Complete 30-Day Money-Back Guarantee!

Photocopy or return this page to: Dr. Jeffrey Lant, Jeffrey Lant Associates
50 Follen St., #507, Cambridge, MA 02138

CLEARLY write down the item number(s) of what you order here. Each number is composed of a letter and a number. Please make sure to give both!

____, ____, ____, ____, ____, ____, ____, ____, ____, ____, ____, ____, ____, ____, ____, ____, ____, ____, ____,

Remember, if you're ordering my Special Reports (#R1 – #R72), you get **any three for $12** Individual Reports are $5 each.

Total your order here $ _____. Are you a Massachusetts resident? ☐ Yes ☐ No

If so, add 5% sales tax here $ _____.   Total enclosed $ _____.

| Your Day Telephone |
| ( )_____ |

Shipping. If you are ordering books, tapes and Special Reports by Dr. Jeffrey Lant, they are sent the day you order (unless you are using a post office box address that is not guaranteed by a MC/VISA). Other books are sent to you direct from their publishers by fourth class/book rate shipping. Allow four-six weeks. If you want them faster, add $3 per item for first class or UPS shipping. Remember: to ship UPS, I must have a street address!

Canada and overseas. If you want your items shipped to Canada, add $1 for *each* item ordered and $1 to the total for our bank's fees, even if you pay in U.S. dollars. If you want shipment to any other country, you must pay by credit card. I'll charge your account surface or air shipping, as you like. Check ☐ surface ☐ air.

Premiums. If your order totals at least $150, you can select any one of my three 60 minute audio cassettes as my gift to you. The three titles are listed on pages 304–305. Write down the one you want here # _____. If your order totals over $225, you get your free audio cassette and any one of my seven "Get Ahead" books (#B1 – #B7). List the item number of the one you want here _____. Remember to get these free premiums, you must order from this catalog by 04/01/93.

Payment & Billing. Unless you are a government agency, college, library or other official public organization (in which case, include your Purchase Order # here _____), COMPLETE PAYMENT MUST ACCOMPANY YOUR ORDER. I cannot invoice individuals and private businesses. If paying by check, make it payable to Jeffrey Lant Associates, Inc. If you are using a post office box number for shipment, I require a Master Card/VISA number and expiration date to guarantee your check, or else I wait for the check to clear. Sadly, several rip-off artists use post office boxes to defraud reputable merchants like me, so I have to inconvenience good people like you.

If paying by credit card (or using a post office box for shipment):

✓☐ MasterCard ☐ Visa. #_____

Expiration date_____   Signature_____

For faster service, place your order by telephone twenty-four hours a day at (617) 547-6372. (Yes, I really do answer my own phone). Before calling make sure your credit card is handy. The order tape doesn't last forever! **Speak clearly!**

Your books and materials will be sent to the address below, unless you indicate otherwise. Please be clear about where you want your items sent.

Send materials to:

Name_____

Organization _____

Street Address _____

City _____ State _____ Zip _____

Telephone ( )_____